CUMBRIA

THE LAKE DISTRICT AND ITS COUNTY

JOHN WYATT

ROBERT HALE · LONDON

First published in Great Britain 2004

ISBN 0 7090 7440 9

Robert Hale Limited
Clerkenwell House
Clerkenwell Green
London EC1R 0HT

A catalogue record for this book is available from the British Library

2 4 6 8 10 9 7 5 3 1

Typeset by e-type, Liverpool
Printed by New Era Printing Co Ltd, Hong Kong

Dedication

To the memory of three good Cumbrian friends to whose encouragement and guidance I owe so much: Captain Charles Michaelson, RN, naturalist; Norman Nicholson, poet; and Dr Bill Rollinson, historian.

CONTENTS

ACKNOWLEDGEMENTS

Thanks are due to: the staffs of Cumbria's Library Service at various branches, but particularly at Kendal and Carlisle for their very substantial help; the Armitt Library at Ambleside; the Cumbria Tourist Board; the staff at the museums at Tullie House, Carlisle, The Dock Museum at Barrow, Kendal Museum, The Pencil Museum at Keswick, The Senhouse Roman Museum at Maryport, The Mining Museum at Threlkeld and The Beacon at Whitehaven; the staff at the BNFL Visitors' Centre at Sellafield; the staff of the Lake District National Park's Information Centres, particularly at Waterhead, Ambleside, also at Coniston and Keswick, and the Yorkshire Dales National Park Information Centre at Sedbergh; Cumbria Wildlife Trust; the Friends of the Lake District; a number of church staff and volunteers, particularly at Cartmel, Whitehaven and Workington; the forbearance of my wife; and lastly to the valuable assistance of Robert Straughton, and my many other friends.

PICTURE CREDITS

Cumbria Tourist Board: p. *x*. Pam Grant, www.pamgrant.com: p. 13.
Ian Brodie: pp. 78 & 79. *North-West Evening Mail*: p. 115.
Andrew Lowe: pp. 137, 383 and 384. Ravenglass & Eskdale Railway: p. 579.

All other images are by the author.

ABBREVIATIONS

ASSI	Area of Special Scientific Interest
BNFL	British Nuclear Fuels Limited
CCC	Cumbria County Council
CNT	Cumbria Naturalists' Trust
CWT	Cumbria Wildlife Trust
EH	English Heritage
EN	English Nature
FC	Forestry Commission
NPA	Lake District National Park Authority
NT	National Trust
RSPB	Royal Society for the Protection of Birds
UU	United Utilities

POPULATION FIGURES

Population figures are based on the Office of National Statistics, 2001. They are included only to indicate the size of towns. Figures for villages and hamlets are not included.

The city of Carlisle has Cumbria's highest population with over 68,830, and Barrow-in-Furness is second highest with over 58,090. Seven other towns have populations into five figures: in diminishing order: Workington, Whitehaven, Kendal, Penrith, Ulverston, Maryport and Dalton. The rest of the 'towns' referred to as such in the following pages have populations into four figures; anything less will be described as a 'village' or 'hamlet'.

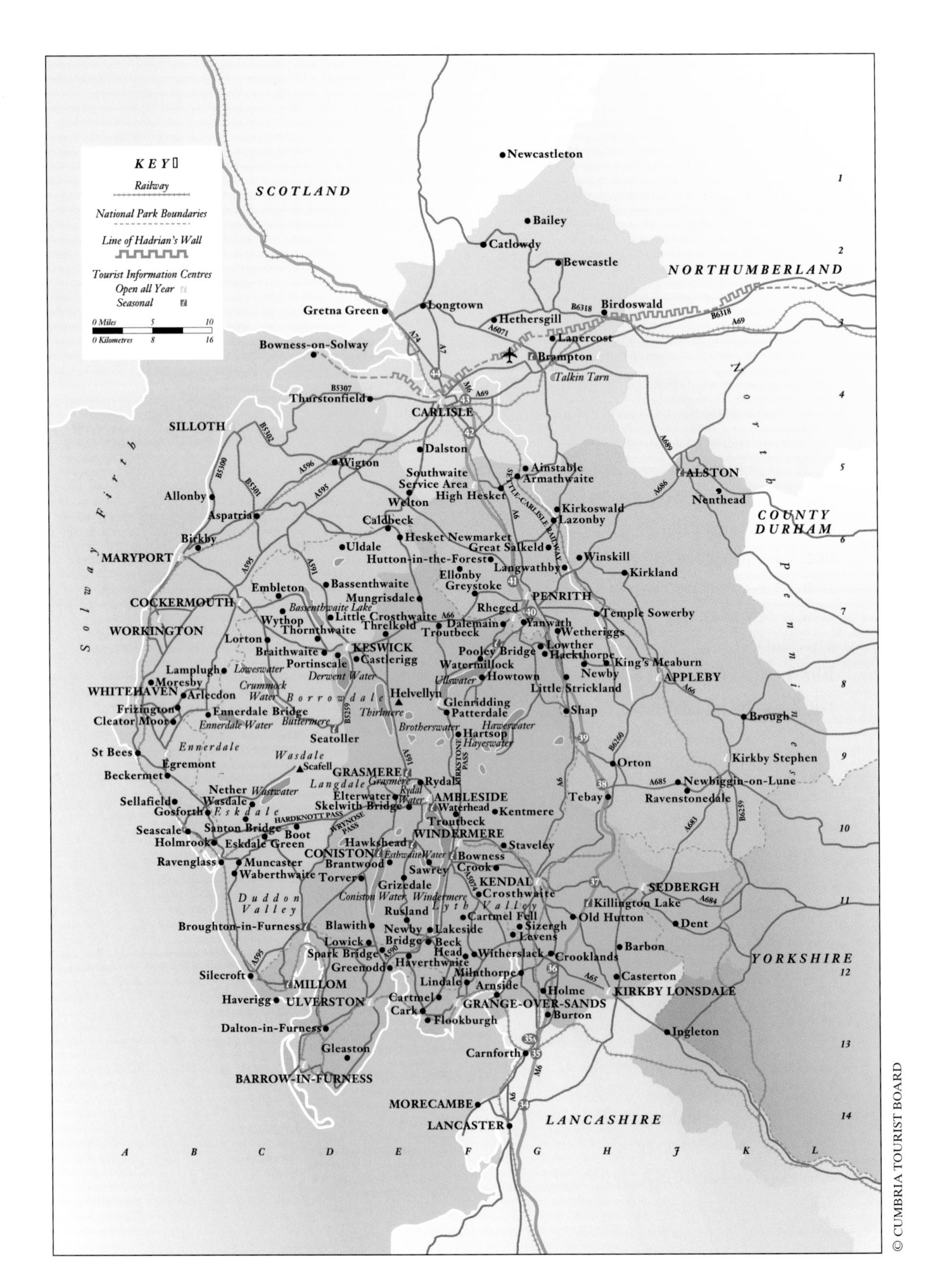
KEY
Railway
National Park Boundaries
Line of Hadrian's Wall
Tourist Information Centres
Open all Year
Seasonal
0 Miles 5 10
0 Kilometres 8 16
SCOTLAND
NORTHUMBERLAND
COUNTY DURHAM
YORKSHIRE
LANCASHIRE
Solway Firth
North Pennines
Newcastleton
Bailey
Catlowdy
Bewcastle
Gretna Green
Longtown
Birdoswald
Hethersgill
Lanercost
Brampton
Talkin Tarn
Bowness-on-Solway
Thurstonfield
CARLISLE
SILLOTH
Dalston
Wigton
Southwaite Service Area
High Hesket
Ainstable
Armathwaite
ALSTON
Nenthead
Allonby
Aspatria
Welton
Caldbeck
Kirkoswald
Lazonby
Birkby
MARYPORT
Uldale
Hesket Newmarket
Great Salkeld
Winskill
Hutton-in-the-Forest
Langwathby
Kirkland
Ellonby
Greystoke
Embleton
Bassenthwaite
Mungrisdale
PENRITH
COCKERMOUTH
Bassenthwaite Lake
Wythop
Little Crosthwaite
Rheged
Temple Sowerby
WORKINGTON
Thornthwaite
Threlkeld
Dalemain
Troutbeck
Yanwath
Wetheriggs
Lorton
Braithwaite
KESWICK
Pooley Bridge
Lowther
Hackthorpe
Lamplugh
Portinscale
Castlerigg
Watermillock
King's Meaburn
Loweswater
Derwent Water
Ullswater
Howtown
Newby
APPLEBY
Moresby
WHITEHAVEN
Arlecdon
Crummock Water
Borrowdale
Helvellyn
Little Strickland
Frizington
Ennerdale Bridge
Thirlmere
Glenridding
Patterdale
Shap
Cleator Moor
Ennerdale Water
Buttermere
Brough
Seatoller
Brotherswater
Haweswater
Hartsop
Hayeswater
Ennerdale
St Bees
Wasdale
Kirkstone Pass
Kirkby Stephen
Egremont
Scafell
GRASMERE
Orton
Beckermet
Langdale
Grasmere
Rydal
Rydal Water
Newbiggin-on-Lune
Nether Wasdale
Wastwater
Elterwater
AMBLESIDE
Tebay
Ravenstonedale
Sellafield
Skelwith Bridge
Waterhead
Kentmere
Gosforth
Eskdale
Hardknott Pass
Wrynose Pass
Troutbeck
Seascale
Santon Bridge
Boot
WINDERMERE
Holmrook
Eskdale Green
Hawkshead
Staveley
CONISTON
Esthwaite Water
Bowness
Ravenglass
Muncaster
Brantwood
Sawrey
Crook
Waberthwaite
Torver
Grizedale
KENDAL
SEDBERGH
Crosthwaite
Duddon Valley
Coniston Water
Windermere
Lyth Valley
Killington Lake
Rusland
Cartmel Fell
Old Hutton
Broughton-in-Furness
Blawith
Newby Bridge
Lakeside
Sizergh
Dent
Levens
Lowick
Beck
Barbon
Spark Bridge
Head
Witherslack
Crooklands
Greenodd
Haverthwaite
Silecroft
Milnthorpe
Casterton
MILLOM
Lindale
Arnside
Haverigg
ULVERSTON
Cartmel
Holme
KIRKBY LONSDALE
Cark
GRANGE-OVER-SANDS
Burton
Dalton-in-Furness
Flookburgh
Ingleton
Gleaston
Carnforth
BARROW-IN-FURNESS
MORECAMBE
LANCASTER
Settle-Carlisle Railway
A
B
C
D
E
F
G
H
J
K
L
1
2
3
4
5
6
7
8
9
10
11
12
13
14

CHAPTER ONE

The County

The county of Cumbria is England's second largest (681,000 ha). Standing outwards in the furthermost north-west of England, encircled by the strong physical boundaries of the sea in the south-west, west and north, and on the east by the Pennines, it is a country on its own. No other region of Britain is quite like it for an extraordinarily wide diversity of wonderful landscapes. An exploration must evoke a response. The lakes and mountains at its heart have inspired poets and painters for over two centuries and it has generated whole libraries of books. Devotees are legion, in Britain and abroad.

The recognition of all its unique qualities is not recent. Camden, the Elizabethan historian, visited Cumberland – the northern part of the area – in 1582. His summary is still apt.

> The country although it be somewhat with the coldest as lying farre North, and seemeth as rough by reason of hills yet for the variety thereof it smileth upon the beholders and giveth contentment to as many as travaile it. For after the rockes bunching out, the mountains standing thicke together, rich of metall mines, and betweene them great meeres stored with all kinds of wildfoule, you come to pretty hills good for pasturage, and well replenished with flocks of sheepe, beneath which againe you meet with goodly plaines, spreading out a great way, yielding corn sufficiently. Besides all this the Ocean driving and dashing upon the shore affourdeth plenty of excellent good fish.

This area, that smiles on beholders, has 189 km of coastline between Morecambe Bay and the Solway. In the north are the Scottish Lowlands, and in the east it is walled by the Pennine borders of the counties of Northumberland, Durham, West Yorkshire and Lancashire. The Lake District National Park occupies one third of the county, and that, of course, is the main irresistible attraction. It is among the most popular tourist destinations of the world. Having all the elements of classical natural beauty its uniqueness is that it is all contained in so little space.

Although it is the largest of the national parks of England and Wales it covers only around 2,292 square km. But gathered into that modest region are sixteen lakes, four mountain summits over 900 m, and eight just below, and over forty above 600 m. The heights and crags are gathered together, shoulder to shoulder, like a congress of giants, with the waters at their feet. The magic effect of assertive mountains contrasting with placid lakes immediately seizes attention and imagination. Further, the teasingly complicated structure of the land can offer a lifetime of exploration. The Lake District is irresistibly addictive and 'Lakers' return year after year.

But if the Lake District's magnificent landscape were non-existent the rest of the county would still be a popular tourist destination. It too contains its special kinds of beauty, and has a very great deal of historical interest. It has green agricultural plains, rolling countryside, high hills, remote austere moors, rivers and long lush valleys, seacoast, ports, unspoilt villages, busy country market towns, and working towns, and the fine historic city of Carlisle. In this land human history has left its marks for all to see. There are prehistoric standing stones and stone circles. There are ruins of Roman forts and defences. The Celtic Christians, and the Angles and Norsemen, left their ancient tombs and crosses, and there are the remarkable remains of Norman castles, and defensive towers, abbeys great and small, old churches and priories. There are stately houses, stone farmhouses and boundary walls netting the hills. All this in a land increasingly enjoyed by tourists, but still eclipsed by the central attraction of the Lakes.

'Cumbria' is a name invented by county boundary changes in 1974. Before that the county of Cumberland, in the north and west, occupied the largest area of what is now the new county. Westmorland was substantially in the south-east and east; and in the south lay a small part of Lancashire. Lancashire, Westmorland and Cumberland once met at the Lakeland road summit of Wrynose Pass, where the Three Shires Stone still marks the spot. Westmorland was swallowed whole. Memories of the old county live on in Kendal, its largest town, and the old county town of Appleby, where there are regrets at its passing. Appleby still gives its full title as 'Appleby in Westmorland'. Two regional newspapers are still called the *Westmorland Gazette* and the *Cumberland and Westmorland Herald,* and many inhabitants still insist on including Westmorland in their addresses. Lancashire lost only a small part of its county that anyway seemed oddly isolated from its main region. It was integral with it in earlier times because Lancashire had claims to Morecambe Bay and the substantial area of land beyond it. The bay sands offered the busy main low-tide route into Cumbria from Lancaster before the development of turnpike roads. At formal occasions in the old Lancashire part of Cumbria you still hear the loyal toast 'The queen!' followed by 'And the duke of Lancaster!' (One and the same person.)

The choice of 'Cumbria' as the new county's name was a good one. At least it has a semantic affinity to the ancient county name of Cumberland. 'Cumberland' has the same root as '*Cymru*' for Wales, which dates back to old British *combrogus* 'compatriot'. Cumberland was Celtic country, 'the land of the Cymry' linked with Wales and south-west Scotland. In Anglo-Saxon times what remained of populations of Celtic-speaking natives, apart from those in Ireland, became forcibly divided and confined by the new settlers into what they probably regarded as unproductive wilderness areas. These were the rugged landscapes of Cornwall, of Wales, the Isle of Man, western Scotland; and included the whole of this wild north-west corner of England, then in the Scottish kingdom of Strathclyde.

This is uncrowded countryside. Indeed the whole of Cumbria has a population averaging only .7 of a person per hectare. (The comparative figure for the whole of England and Wales is 3.2 per hectare.) That doesn't give a true picture, for two thirds of the population live in the larger urban conurbations of Carlisle and Barrow, Workington, Whitehaven and Maryport where they are employed in diverse industries. One fifth live in smaller towns and villages in which occupations are generally centred on agriculture and tourism. For the rest, the county has the highest proportion of its people living in remote rural areas than any other county in England. In its east the density is as low as point .23 of a person per hectare.

Apart from the route across the sands of Morecambe Bay the county's main entry from the south was the A6, from Lancaster, through Kendal, by Penrith to Carlisle and Scotland. It has ancient origins. It was trodden for centuries by armies, latterly those of Bonnie Prince Charlie in 1745. The railway took a line east of it through the Tebay Gorge, and ran by the northern part of its route, and the M6 followed. The main East to West route from Yorkshire is by another ancient way, now the A65 through Settle and Kirkby Lonsdale to Kendal. From the A1 and Durham County the A66 routes through Penrith, to Cumbria's west coast and its towns; which are also linked to Carlisle by the A595. The A69 from Northumberland follows Roman roads alongside Hadrian's Wall to Carlisle. Networks of lesser good roads serve the county, and there are vast wilder areas where the roads are minor, or very minor. The higher fells defied the road builders and are circumvented, so the main ancient mountain passes, once well used by trains of pack ponies, are for walkers only. Cumbria is in fact walkers' country. There are 11,625 km of public footpaths and bridleways, 7,500 km of them in the Lake District National Park, and many hundreds of square km have free-to-roam access.

A busy main through railway line runs from London to Carlisle and Scotland and a link with it connects Lancaster to the south-west along the rim of

Morecambe Bay. There is a rail route from Newcastle to Carlisle and the coastal towns. Two scenic routes, from Penrith through Keswick to Cockermouth, and from Broughton to Coniston, were brutally axed. They could have solved some of today's transport difficulties. Successful campaigning, however, preserved a wonderfully adventurous Pennine line from Yorkshire and Settle across the east of the county to Carlisle. A triumph of Victorian engineering, it offers one of Britain's most picturesque railway journeys, through wild country and the delectable Eden valley. A journey that now could claim, 'giveth contentment to as many as travaile it?'

CHAPTER TWO

The Lie of the Land

Before looking at particular features it helps to know how they fit into the general picture. The complex shapes of the hills and valleys, the beaches, the green hills, the crags, rivers and streams and lakes, the forests, the stone-built villages and towns – they are all part of a long evolving story. What we see from a viewpoint appears as an end of that story. To find a beginning requires some knowledge of the land's earth and rocks, and how the ebb and flow of events over a vast time scale have affected them.

The geologist recognizes that the crust of earth we stand on has been made of material that has grown upwards layer by layer. The oldest rocks, then, are the deepest, and the later, newer ones have been superimposed in layers in an identifiable sequence that can be scientifically dated. That is easy for anyone to grasp. But the picture becomes complicated in Cumbria.

To understand the story, one first has to stretch the imagination beyond thoughts of the mere fractional blink of human lifetime to the many millions of years of the planet's existence. We should then remember that the earth we think of as solid and stationary is nothing of the kind. In fact it moves about. We know that material of lighter weight than water floats on water. In the same way the lighter density of surface earth on the planet floats on the denser fluid material below it. Lands, continents, move around. They sometimes collide, push over or under each other. The forces at work here are almost beyond imagination. The friction of 'plates' of land thrusting against other plates produces such tremendous local heat that it melts rock. The pressures on the surface ruck it up like a squeezed rug.

The structure of the planet is dynamic. Deep in the planet's interior there is intense heat, its elements being in a constant molten state. It is like a gigantic cauldron in which the heat from the depths rises in the process of convection towards the surface, and dips. The earth's 'mantle' floats above this constant turmoil. Not surprisingly it is often pushed and pulled and shaken. Cracks open, and the volcanic magma, that 'soup' of molten minerals from below, breaks through a weakness, blows out under pressure, or oozes out like syrup.

Then there is another stage. Tempests rage. Seas rise and fall, advance and retreat. Rains descend. Temperatures waver between tropical and polar. Ice bites. The earth surface is broken, honed, and scoured and shifted.

UP TO THE ICE AGE: CUMBRIA'S EARLY GEOLOGY

Walk with a team of geologists in Cumbria and one will hear several interpretations of what is observed. But such differences, sometimes strong, are usually in the detail rather than the whole picture. What I hope should be acceptable to geologists here is a very rough sketch of the events that shaped the whole of Cumbria.

To a student of geology the rocks of Cumbria are fascinating. They reveal many interesting problems, and great diversity. So to begin with the apparent contradiction of that layer-by-layer deposition: the newer rocks are generally seen not in Cumbria's higher-level areas, but in the lower. It is the older rocks that thrust themselves at once on our attention in the central hills and peaks of the Lake District. This is because they were thrown upwards by volcanic activity and land movements, and the subsequent rock layers that once covered them were broken up and swept away by weather and glacial erosion.

THE SKIDDAW SLATES

1. Geologists have divided the timescale into identifiable periods. The Cumbrian story begins 450 million years ago in the Ordovician period, when the area was covered by a shallow sea. Pressures of earth movements solidified the huge amounts of accumulated mud and clay on the seabed. They formed the sedimentary 'Skiddaw slates', which were lifted very high later by the upward surge of earth movements. Varying pressures affected the texture and colour of the rock. The deposits built up to a thickness of several thousands of metres, and some areas became affected by the intense heat of later volcanic activity. The material generally resembles shale rather than roofing slate. Under the influence of water and frost most of it breaks down into small thin flakes. The process has continued for millions of years. It yields comparatively easily to pressures of earth movements, and in fact the original height of the mountains exceeded to a huge extent the worn-away, but still impressive-looking, remnants we see today. As this friable material erodes evenly, the mountain profiles are not rough and craggy, but curved or angular. The rocks are exposed now in the north and west of the Lakeland area, seen at their high impressive best behind Keswick. The mountain of Skiddaw (931 m) and its neighbour Blencathra (868 m) are of Skiddaw slates. We see

Skiddaw slate fells around Bassenthwaite Lake, to the north of Buttermere and between Loweswater and Ennerdale. In the south-west the hefty hump of Black Combe (600 m high) is close to the coast – a welcome landmark for seafarers. Further deposits are under the sea and reach upwards again on the Isle of Man. Fossils in the rock are of very primitive sea creatures: graptolites and trilobites.

The friable rock can make deep soils, ideal for tree growth. One of the country's earliest forest plantings by the newly formed Forestry Commission, following the First World War, was at Whinlatter. The forests now extend over both sides of Bassenthwaite Lake and are a great attraction to tourists. Another fine feature of the Skiddaw slate fells is the heather that purples the heights in August.

2. Towards the end of the deposition of the Skiddaw slates, when they were sitting in a shallow sea, catastrophic volcanic activity occurred. Several subterranean vents opened and there were violent explosions. There must have been several volcanoes in the area (whose exact whereabouts exercise the minds of geologists). The explosions scattered a mixture of volcanic material, and the shattered rocks that covered them, widely. This was pressured and cooled into consolidated masses. The resultant rock is known to geologists as agglomerate. Lava outflows also formed hard rock beds as the material cooled. The beds varied according to the speed of cooling and the presence of trapped material.

Skiddaw

Blencathra from Castlerigg stone circle

Massive outpourings of ash and dust also became consolidated. All this material was deposited to a thickness of around 3 km. The varying types of igneous rock that resulted were named 'Borrowdale volcanics'.

THE BORROWDALE VOLCANICS

3. Because the Borrowdale volcanics were hard, they were less affected by subsequent erosion. Upward earth movements tended to break up the mass into blocks. We see the eventual effect, after millions of years of events, in the dramatic, towering craggy pikes and fells of the Lake District's centre: Langdale Pikes, Bowfell, Coniston Old Man, Great Gable, Helvellyn and, England's highest mountain, Scafell Pike (978 m). Even the minor fells have interesting crags and

hollows and peaks. From one of the superlative viewpoints at the foot of Derwent Water, such as the famous Friar's Crag, one can tell the difference between the Skiddaw slate heights and the volcanic. Looking far south into the Jaws of Borrowdale, one sees the craggy fells of the Borrowdale volcanics. The steep volcanic side walls of Borrowdale are generally shaggy with scrub and tree growth – sheep grazing is poor or non-existent. Volcanic rocks are also on the extreme left of the view overhanging the lake. Some have suggested that Castle Crag, immediately on the left, could be a remaining 'plug' of one of the volcanoes. Looking up the lake, the irregular profiles of the distant volcanics contrast with the hump-backs (e.g. Cat Bells) and regular even profiles of the Skiddaw slate fells on the lake's west side and beyond.

Eruptions and the rapid build-up of deposits continued over a very long period. One rock type of the Borrowdale volcanic is a tuff – a rock formed from very fine dust. It is extremely hard and can be worked into sharp edges like flint. This gave Cumbria its early industry in Neolithic/Bronze Age times: the production of stone axes. Several axe 'factories' have been discovered around this vein of rock on several of the high fells, notably Langdale and the Scafells. The axes were roughed out on the fell and then carried to the seacoast sandstone for polishing and sharpening. The resultant tools were very efficient, and so valued that they may have been used as currency. 'Langdale axes' were traded throughout the British Isles and can be seen in a number of the country's museums.

Among the Borrowdale volcanics – Great Gable from the Scafells

Borrowdale volcanic – glacial deposition

Another kind of extremely hard material formed from the volcanic dust, evenly deposited under water, can be broken into slate sheets. It has provided roofing material for centuries. Very hard slate, where the initial bedding of sediments has afterwards been re-aligned under pressure, is especially attractive and can be silver, grey, green or blue. It can show interesting ripple designs, and takes a high polish. This famous 'Lakeland slate' is exported all over the world and much of it faces prestigious modern buildings. Some examples of its fine qualities are exhibited at a quarry's display unit at Skelwith Bridge at the foot of Langdale.

CONISTON LIMESTONE

4. About 440 million years ago the Ordovician period that produced the Skiddaw slates and the Borrowdale volcanics was coming to an end. Much of

Coniston limestone outcrop, Tarn Hows

the area was submerged under a shallow sea and earth movements again uplifted the central fells and produced fracture lines. Storm waters at this time exploited the fracture lines and other structural weaknesses, and brought silt down into the sea. Into this was added the shells of primitive sea creatures: graptolites, trilobites and brachiopods. The resultant rock formed from this silt is known as 'Coniston limestone'. Little of it can be seen, for subsequent erosion and other depositions above it have left only a narrow band observable in the south, which runs from the Duddon estuary through Coniston, Tarn Hows and Ambleside then to the east and north-east to Shap. It has made no impact on the landscape. Fossils are difficult to find. However, the narrow exposure is of interest to botanists. They can follow the line, noting flora typical of limestone soils among the acidic soils around the volcanics.

THE SILURIAN SLATES

5. So far we have referred to the rounded and angular fells of the Skiddaw slates and the craggy masses of the high Borrowdale volcanic. The next series of rocks were formed in Cumbria's Silurian period, and they also make a major contribution to the landscape south of the Lake District and to parts of eastern Cumbria. The Silurian was a time of massive earth movements and storms between 435 and 395 million years ago. Then the sea covered the land in the area of what is now Cumbria. Large deposits of erosion silt and mud were laid down rapidly, forming the sedimentary rocks known as 'Silurian slates'. It is not known how much of this

Silurian-based landscape (foreground), volcanic beyond (Coniston Old Man)

rock was swept away in later periods, but today the thickness is as much as 4 km. The Silurian slates vary greatly in content and hardness. Geologists have identified six layers, the oldest deposit being exposed in the northern parts of the county. The many drystone walls reveal the local variations. Some of the harder stone has been quarried for roofing slate, but it is typically mudstone or gritstone. It breaks down fairly easily and produces in many places a good depth of acidic soil that supports much of the semi-natural woodland in southern Lakeland.

What we see of the rock now, after vast levels of it were swept away, is typically in the softer wooded hilly landscape around the shores of Windermere. One good view is southwards from the rocky Borrowdale volcanic fell of Loughrigg at the lake's head by Ambleside. Another view of the contrasts between the volcanic and the Silurian can be made from the steamer trip from Lakeside at the lake foot, to Waterhead at the head. As the boat enters the lake's northern reaches, the towers of the Langdales, and the sweep of the Fairfield Horseshoe, lift one's eyes from the lake's rather softer wooded Silurian landscape into the more severe amphitheatre of the volcanic.

The Silurian slates extend south-westwards and eastwards. The east side of Coniston Water is on Silurian rock and one can look up from it across the lake to the great volcanic mass of the Coniston Old Man range on the other side. This was the classic view enjoyed by Ruskin from his study window at Brantwood.

The Howgill fells above Sedbergh near the Yorkshire Dales border are of Silurian slates with grits that have been metamorphosed (affected by extreme heat).

THE DEVONIAN PERIOD

6. The catastrophic Devonian period followed the Silurian, between 350 and 400 million years ago. By this time the area was again submerged by the sea at its shallowest over the higher central dome. The collision of a northern continental mass with the European caused enormous earth uplifts. The area was thrust out of the sea levels into a high dome. Under enormous pressure from below, the various rock types reacted according to their nature. Those later Silurian slates were squeezed into folds, splitting and shattering easily along their bedding planes, and their scree fell into and filled the lower levels. The softer yielding Skiddaw slates were thrust upwards to a great height. The tough, resistant Borrowdale volcanic cracked and broke into a complex chaos of troughs and arches.

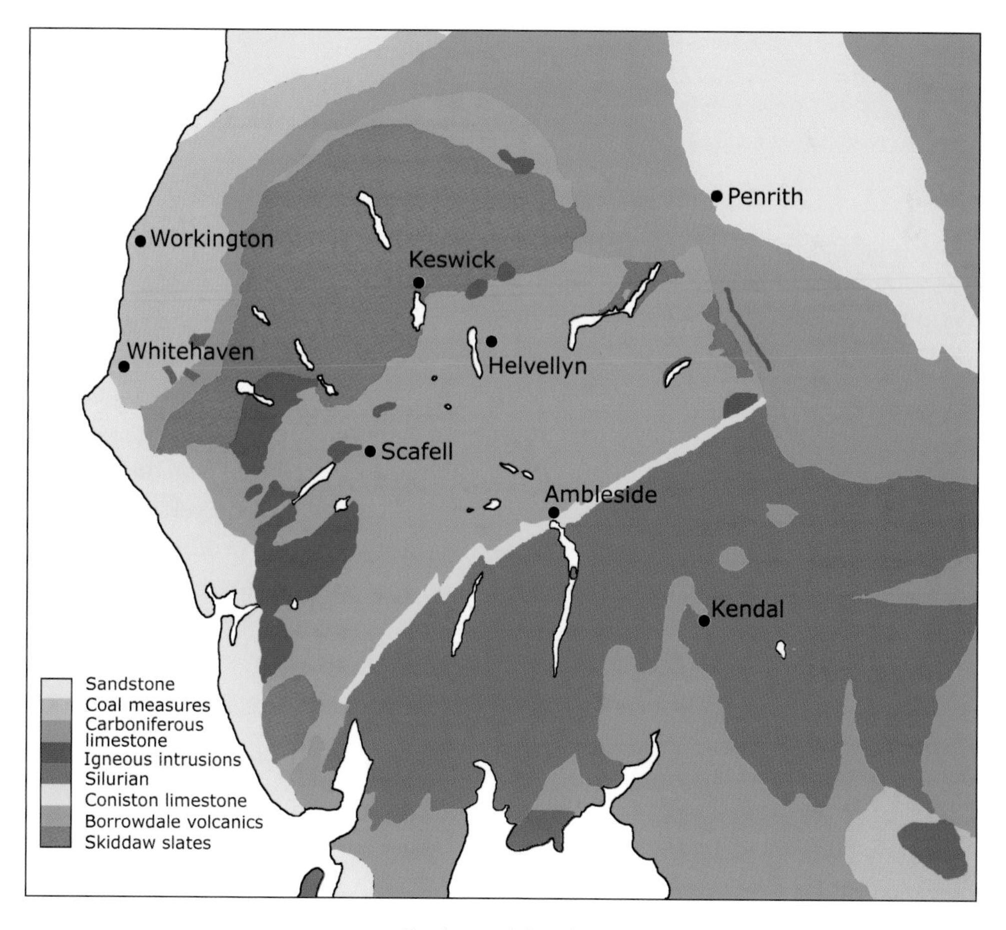

Geology of Cumbria

The earth movements opened up subterranean cavities into which magma from deep below the earth's mantle forced their way into the hollows. The tremendous heat changed the rock within contact chemically and physically. Condensing vapours crystallized into the metal minerals, lead, zinc, copper and iron, the mining of which was to become an important Cumbrian industry. Magma that reached shallow earth and cooled more slowly formed granites. Granite quarrying became another important Cumbrian industry. Granite quarries were located at Threlkeld, Carrock and Caldbeck in the north of the Lake District, but more notably at Shap on the east, and they are still producing into this century. The attractive, high-quality Shap granite has provided material for many important buildings in London and throughout the country. Another type of granite is exposed in the west of the Lake District in Eskdale, Wasdale and Ennerdale. This is pigmented with iron, and local buildings and drystone walls are pink.

In the fifty million years of the Devonian period the rocks were buffeted by extreme climatic conditions – arid periods, strong winds and rasping sandstorms. During storms floods would sweep away material down the faultlines and into the sea to the south. It was a destructive time for the region.

THE CARBONIFEROUS LIMESTONE

7. In the next period, 270 to 350 million years ago, the area was again inundated by the sea. It was shallow, and levels probably never reached the higher land. The sea was very rich with life forms that were developing rapidly by this time, forms such as corals, brachiapods, molluscs and crinoids (sea lilies). The remains of these creatures accumulated in thick beds to form carboniferous limestone. The climate was warm, and as seas receded tropical swamp forests thrived. When the sea again rose these land plants were drowned and became buried under layers of sand and mud. Decaying only slowly because of the wet conditions they produced peat beds. Under pressure from the increasing deposits above them, and with the presence of subterranean heat, the peat beds underwent chemical changes to produce coal. Coal mining became a major industry in the north-west of the county.

Fossil-rich carbon deposits continued to grow, forming the limestone. Much of this was later swept away, but it remains deep to the south of Cumbria and continues in a ring eastwards to a point east of Kirkby Lonsdale, then north-westwards east of Shap and westwards and south-westwards round the northern rim of the Lake District. Another section, separated from this ring by erosion, is exposed to the east, in the Pennine area of the county, northwards through Dufton, Brampton and Alston. The towns and villages in the area are built of limestone. Kendal, for example, has long been known as 'the auld grey town'.

In some areas now one can find 'limestone pavements', fairly level areas of the

Carboniferous limestone pavement, Scout Scar

bare stone eroded into complicated patterns of hollows by rain. Rain is always slightly acid and reacts chemically to break down the limestone. These pavements are increasingly rare throughout Europe as the stone is easily lifted and removed – originally for lime production, but nowadays here regrettably taken for garden rockeries. They are tremendously important ecologically, and of course once gone they are lost forever. They must be preserved in Cumbria.

THE MOUNTAIN BUILDING

8. The Carboniferous period lasted for eighty million years, and near its end, fifty million years ago, came the catastrophic earth movements known as the Hercynian Orogeny (Orogeny = mountain birth), which thrust up great mountain chains across Europe and America. The effect on Cumbria was to lift the area again, further to the south than previously, opening up old faults. Again volcanic material filled the cavities. One effect was a lateral flow of lava under the carboniferous rock. This flowed from Cumbria through Northumberland to the coast and out to the Holy Island. Eventually its covering rock was eroded away along with the softer rock that surrounded it. The exposure we see now is the Whin Sill, the long stream of rock on which Hadrian's Wall was built. The volcanic activity also produced minerals such as lead and copper, later mined on Coniston Old Man, Helvellyn, the

northern part of Cumbria and in the fells west of Derwent Water. It has been suggested too that this period produced the high-quality haematite – the iron veins on which the prosperity of the south-west and west of Cumbria was based. Barrow and its shipyards grew from it. But eventually it declined. The last mine closed in 1980. The remains of the iron mining industry can be seen at Millom on the south-western coast, which has become an attractive nature reserve.

THE SANDSTONE

9. After this mountain uplift a hot dry period followed. At a time when Australia, South America and South Africa were covered in ice, the equator was only 400 km to the south of Britain. Desert conditions prevailed, with abrasive sandstorms. The carboniferous layers over the central dome were stripped away, and the stripped material, together with the debris of older broken rocks, settled round the dome and became consolidated as breccia (from the same root as 'broken'), a rock known locally as Brockram. Desert sand is red because of the iron content and the absence of organic material. The resulting sand-based rock of this period is 'new red sandstone'. It is much in evidence along the west coast of Cumbria, from Barrow to St Bees near Whitehaven, and in the north, and north-east to south-east. The stone is easily dressed into building blocks. We see it in the castles, towers and churches of these areas. It is most impressive at Furness Abbey, near

Red sandstone, St Bees sea cliffs

Barrow, when the ruins seem to glow in the evening sun. Penrith could justifiably be called 'the auld red town', and most buildings in the Eden valley are red. Carlisle castle and cathedral are of red sandstone. But the stone is seen at its raw best by the sea in the red cliffs of St Bees Head.

The many millions of years of the Permo-Triassic were succeeded by the Jurassic period, when land was covered in lush vegetation, and advanced creatures like the dinosaurs thrived. It lasted for 46 million years, but ended. However, the land slowly sank under a sea rich in animal life. This was the time when vast deep areas of chalk were laid down worldwide over a period of 150 million years. It was named the Cretaceous (meaning 'chalky'). But if the chalk covered Cumbria it has left no traces, possibly swept clean away by ice-age glaciation.

THE SECOND MOUNTAIN BUILDING

10. The last sixty-eight million years of geological history is known as the Tertiary period. It heralded a major event. About sixty million years ago, a great mountain-building period occurred, during which the Himalayas, the Alps, the Andes and the Rockies were formed. The effect on Cumbria was less dramatic. The central dome was lifted to not much more than its present height. The largest thrust was under the Scafells. Then storm water falling on the dome channelled itself gradually into the radiating rivers that we now know: the Cocker, the Greta, the Kent, the Rothay, the Brathay, Duddon, Esk, Calder and Liza. In some places, however, the rivers deviated where the running water found geological fault troughs, or broke through less resistant material. Cumbria's longest river, however, the Eden, flows from the Pennines in the east, and down into the sandstone of the Eden valley through Carlisle to the Solway. The River Lune, too, rising in the Pennine hills above Tebay, flows along an eastern boundary of the county, passing through Kirkby Lonsdale into Lancashire.

THE MARKS OF THE ICE AGE

We are now into the last two million years – a very tiny fraction of geological time. About one and a half million years ago, not for the first time, a dramatic change took place in the world's climate. The drastic fall in temperature in the northern hemisphere brought huge falls of snow that did not melt in summer. The polar ice that formed advanced over Scandinavia and Russia, and the North American landmass as far south as what is now Illinois. At its peak an ice sheet covered most of what are now the British Isles, and in the Cumbria region to a depth of around 760 m. We know this because the ice has left scratch marks on the Scafells at that height.

Glacial ice, formed from snow, is granular and flows slowly down from the higher land, or from a higher accumulation of snow to a lower. If the climate becomes milder the flow accelerates. The moving ice follows original drainage channels first, and piles up in the hollows. Then gradually the accumulation increases until only the highest peaks are left uncovered. As glaciers move, their great weight scours away at the rocks beneath, breaking, collecting and carrying them with the flow. The broken harder rocks add cutting edges to the moving mass. So the destructive ice slides and grinds and rasps over the harder bedrock, smoothing and polishing it, and sometimes leaving scratch marks. It takes huge bites out of the valley walls, sometimes undermining them and carrying the resultant rock-falls onwards. Some deep valleys are thus straightened, while other side valleys, left with their heights above the main flow, remain hanging above the crag walls.

While ice was moving with its cargo of rocks down the valleys from the peaks of Lakeland, more ice was advancing from Scotland. The Scottish ice swept down across the plains in the northern area and met the Lakeland flow in the Eden valley. The combined ice, carrying Scottish and Cumbrian rock debris, was pushed east across northern England. Boulders of the very distinct Shap granite can be seen on the Yorkshire coast. Ice from Scotland joined forces too with the Lakeland ice to the west, and swept on down through the Irish Sea separating the Isle of Man from the mainland, and flowed down into Lancashire and beyond. Boulders of Borrowdale volcanic can be found far south in Lancashire and on the Cheshire plain. These 'erratics' can be spotted in unexpected places. For instance, one can meet with boulders from the volcanic areas sitting on carboniferous limestone.

Each advance of ice was followed by milder climatic periods, which then reverted to colder. Three such periods have been identified in Cumbria. The last advance of ice, 8,000 years ago, was the least extensive. All this happened in a blink of geological time. We may still be in the interglacial period of an ice age.

Now we can see various kinds of classical ice age evidence. The bleak high fells were less affected by thaw, particularly on their sides away from the warmth of sunshine, and where winds can pile in the snowfalls. So there, small summit glaciers survived. With added long winter frosts, followed by gentle thaw, they still worked away, breaking into the steep-sided upper faces, thrusting down and grinding at the base. Rock debris was left dumped at the glacier's edge. The result is a hollow. Some still hold tarns, small lakes within them that were originally composed of melt-water. In Scotland these hollows are *corries* (Gaelic for 'cauldron'), in Wales and the South-west they are *cwms* or *coombs*. In Cumbria they can be *coves* (Old English for 'hollow'), as in Nethermost Cove or Brown Cove on Helvellyn. They can also be combs, or combes, as in Ling Combe above Buttermere, and Black Combe in the mountain named after it. Sometimes neighbouring coves cut away at a common wall until the top of it became a thin edge. To a mountaineer these edges are 'aretes'.

Tarns in mountain combs, Coniston Old Man

They offer an obvious, sometime exciting route to a summit. Striding Edge on Helvellyn is Lakeland's best-known, and at the opposite end of the same glaciated cove is Swirral Edge. On Blencathra, Sharp Edge is another.

The cove on Helvellyn between the edges shows a typical example of a post-glacial tarn, Red Tarn. There are others among many of the peaks, and three on Coniston Old Man alone. There is Angle Tarn below Bow Fell; Stickle Tarn below Pavey Ark in Langdale; Codale Tarn and Easedale Tarn above Grasmere; Grisedale Tarn below Dollywaggon Pike; and others can be seen on the maps. Some are deceptively deep. The depth of Blea Water, a tarn below High Street range, is 63 m.

Other glacial features can be recognized in the landscape. Valleys originally carved into V shapes by watercourses have been ground out into distinct U shapes. Dunmail Raise is an example. As larger valleys have been ploughed out to great depths, streams from the minor valleys left 'hanging' high on their walls have become waterfalls. One notable sight is the fall of Sourmilk Gill over the crags in the glaciated valley of Buttermere. Waterfalls used to be high on the list of tourist attractions in Victorian times, the most popular being the Lodore Falls in Borrowdale, Stock Ghyll Force at Ambleside, Dungeon Gill in Langdale, and Aira Force by Ullswater. But there are others, impressive after heavy rain. To view Taylor Gill Force at the head of Borrowdale, or Piers Gill on the Scafells, one needs some stamina and a head for heights. When walking anywhere on Cumbrian hills one is never far from the sound of falling water.

THE LAKES

The sixteen lakes of Cumbria's Lake District were born at last when great areas of melt-water were left behind in the lower valley hollows scooped out by the ice. The longest lake is Windermere. Its deepest end is at its upper basin, where the descending glacier from the north gouged out the lakebed to below sea level. The shapes of the lakes were formed according to the degree of resistance met by the glaciers. Where a glacier encountered softer rock, the circumference widened, or narrowed where there was resistant rock, or was deflected by side-valley glaciers. Ullswater is thus curved like a shallow S.

Long periods of heavy rain followed the milder periods. Flood debris was then swept into the lakes, perhaps filling some and damming others. Accumulating Skiddaw slate debris separated Derwent Water from Bassenthwaite Lake. At times of exceptional rainfall today these two lakes almost become one again. Similarly banks of alluvial material separate Buttermere from Crummock Water. It is possible that the rush of floodwater eventually broke through some of these natural dams. For instance, Langdale probably once held a lake, and after exceptional rainfall it tries to re-form.

Many other signs of glacial activity can be seen. There are the scratch marks on hard bedrock. Sometimes rocks are worn smooth on the side where ice has climbed over it, while the other side is left rough. The effect is known as *'roche moutonnée'*, for the rock can look like a sleeping sheep. The same effect can be seen on some of the debris heaps dumped by thawed ice on low-level areas. Heaps of the finer post-glacial debris are known as moraines. Moraines come in several forms. Some are more or less symmetrical. They are 'drumlins', and exactly how the ice moulded them is debatable. In some places there are whole fields covered by moraines. One example can be seen at the head of Dunmail Raise.

It might be thought that what we see is an end of the story. But of course it isn't. The mountain rocks still crumble and slide down under the effect of weather. Rain washes down the soils, particularly where they are unprotected by tree cover. So the valleys are filling. The lakes are silting. The earth, merely a floating skin on the surface of the planet, shakes and lifts. The great granite dome beneath Cumbria is slowly rising. The climates change, the seas may still rise, the ice may still come. The whole of human time is less than a moment in global time.

CHAPTER THREE

The History

Human activity could not alter the shape of Cumbria; but it gave its scenes colour and texture. The beauty of the high hills and moors remain apparently unspoilt by humans because, for many centuries, the inhabitants have had to learn to compromise, to adapt their productive activity to the sometimes uncompromising environment. Life was easier in the more amenable plains. There the fields are still green that once were worked by ox ploughs. But the scene was not always so placid. Productive land attracts covetous eyes. There is much to see of the history of human life in many particular places as will be revealed. The following general picture is meant to put them into context.

PREHISTORY

How much human activity there was in Cumbria before the ice age can never be known. The ice wiped all traces clean. Stone Age flints have been found in caves near Grange-over-Sands. At that time, maybe 8,000 years ago, the climate was still harsh. Improving temperature after that time meant that the land was gradually covered with forest to the height of the fells, and animal life thrived. Evidence of Middle Stone Age human presence from around 4500 BC has been found at places on Cumbria's west coast. The settlers lived by hunting and fishing. Flint arrowheads, harpoons and knives have been discovered to prove this. The source of the flint, which is found in chalk, has not been convincingly explained, for no chalk exists in the region. But some of the artefacts were made of a volcanic tuff, a local rock.

In the Neolithic (New Stone Age), from around 3000 BC, human activity made its first impact all over Cumbria. Neolithic people had reached a high degree of technical progress. They wore woven cloth, cleared areas of forest, kept domestic animals and farmed the fields. They fired pottery and used very efficient tools. They organized themselves into working communities. As such they could move huge stones for the purpose of ritual. The stones were placed with some precision, no doubt under the direction of a shaman, who observed the stars and planets and

Castlerigg stone circle

could mark the birth and passing of the seasons. Their stone circles, henges, and burial sites can still be seen in Cumbria. Two of them – Castlerigg stone circle and Long Meg and her daughters – are world class. The Druids (to whom they are often mistakenly attributed) may have used them, but in fact they were built long before the settlement of the Celts.

In this New Stone Age, Cumbria's first industry flourished. The veins of very hard volcanic tuff, already mentioned, were exploited to produce stone axes. What is remarkable is not only the skill shown in shaping the axes and hammering and honing them to produce a sharp edge, but the fact that they had the knowledge and skill to trace the run of the special rock through various levels on the high fells. Archaeologists are cautious when dating prehistoric artefacts, but it is generally thought that the industry was at the height of production between

2800 BC and 2000 BC. Production did run on afterwards, and indeed stone axes were still being used in the later Bronze Age. For that matter granite-headed heavy hammers were still being used effectively last century! Probably because of the efficiency of the axes, and with slash-and-burn activity common to produce grazing for domestic animals, the forest cover began a long decline. This is shown by a scientific study of the botanical history of the area, based on pollen samples trapped and preserved in cores extracted from local peat, or from clay deep in the bed of lakes. The levels of the material can be dated. The evidence shows that as the forest cover was depleted in this period, the grass pollens increased, an indication of population expansion and the advance of agriculture.

THE BRONZE AND IRON AGES

Apart from what the Cumbrian stone circles, the henges, the axe finds, pottery, and occasional other artefacts tell us, nothing else is known about the Neolithic people. It is assumed that they lived on, and co-existed with new settlements of people who brought the Bronze Age culture into the region around the second or third century. Finds of their pottery and artefacts show that the new settlers came by several routes. From the east they came from Yorkshire, mainly occupying the fertile land of the Eden valley. From the south they came across the sands of Morecambe Bay to occupy the Furness peninsula. A third group from Ireland settled the western coastal areas, where Bronze Age culture had been nurtured by the presence of copper and tin. The main occupations were the raising of stock, hunting, fishing where possible, and the early cultivation of grain. What we see in Cumbria are the remains of typical Bronze Age burial chambers that contain urns of cremation ashes. On Bannisdale Fell by Coniston, one burial contained the charred remains of woollen cloth, one of the earliest finds in Britain.

In a great number of places in Cumbria can be seen circles of stones. They represent the walls of huts which would have been roofed with wood and thatch. Any settlements built entirely of wood have disappeared, of course. Some of the larger settlements are seen to be enclosed within a series of walls, no doubt to contain stock. There is an impressive example at 'Stone Walls' near Urswick in Furness. Although this is assumed to be Bronze Age, from the finds of typical artefacts in the area, there were also stone axes, and flint arrow heads. In the Crosby Ravensworth area of the Eden valley there are quite a number of settlement remains. The largest is at Ewe Close, with a complex series of enclosure walls and signs of a large round hut and a rectangular one. This was doubtless of importance to the Romans for their straight Roman road from the south to Carlisle deviated to include it.

The Bronze Age culture merged into the Iron Age when the inhabitants at this time are usually referred to as 'Celts' – disparate races of warlike tribes who came from Europe around 600 BC. Roman writers refer to the tribes of northern Britain as 'Brigantes', named from their allegiance to the tutelary Celtic god Brigantia. Little is known about their activity in Cumbria. Agriculture was certainly their main occupation; but evidence of their belligerence can be seen in the remains of hill forts in a number of strategic high places on the fringes of the Lake District fells. There are examples: on Castle Crag in the Borrowdale valley, Castle Crag east of the Thirlmere dam, and at Dunmallard at the foot of Ullswater. Usually all that can now be seen are their ditches and earth walls, but the largest, on the 650 m summit of Carrock Fell, is contained in what were defensive stone walls.

THE ROMANS

The Romans were in Cumbria for three hundred years, but we find no signs of lavish villas, for Cumbria was the serious, no-nonsense, northernmost frontier country of the Roman Empire. What we can see are the remains of roads; and of forts, including one on Hardknott Pass in the most dramatic site in Britain, and another a good second. There are bath house remains, altar stones, tombstones and milestones; and running through Cumbria is a section of Hadrian's Wall, the ultimate line which held back the northern barbarians, and no doubt prevented them from allying themselves with their troublesome cousins in the South. The Celtic tribe that lived on both sides of the wall was the Cervettii, a branch of the Brigantes. Their god was Belatucadrus, a god of war, which suggests that they were never likely to give an amiable welcome to foreign strangers carrying arms.

The Roman army first penetrated Cumbria from the east, from their main northern base at York. This was some time before 74 AD, when a revolt of the Brigantes was put down by Petillus Cerialis. They came by way of Stainmore through Brough, by the Eden valley to Kirkby Thore, and to Brougham. This is a natural east–west route, so the army would have been following existing British roads. They then turned north by Penrith to Carlisle. It was left to Agricola, however, to consolidate the position during his governorship. His army came north from Chester in 79 AD and established marching camps and forts, first walling them with wood and turf, later replacing with stone. The route seems to have been from Lancashire through the River Lune gorge by Low Borrow Bridge to Brougham, and on again to Carlisle. The Brougham crossroads became an important strategic outpost. The two roads were the keys to further consolidation.

There were other roads. One was made from Carlisle through Papcastle near

Cockermouth to the west coast at Moresby. Another road must have come north from Lancashire to Watercrook at Kendal, then to Ambleside. Then it continued an astonishing way. Traces of the road can be seen cutting right across the centre of the fells, zigzagging over Wrynose Pass (393 m) and Hardknott Pass (395 m) to its fort, then down the Esk valley to the Roman port and fort at Ravenglass. Another went north from Ambleside to Brougham along the 609 m-high ridge of High Street Fell. This followed *'brettestrete'*, the road of the Britons. To walkers enjoying such a splendid fell walk now, this might seem a strange route for a Roman road, but in fact it was the easiest, for on either side, below the fell ridge at that time, wetlands, forest and scrub predominated.

The military policy of Rome was to build a road network from which they could quickly enforce authority. Every road had its attendant forts. At intervals some forts would accommodate cavalry as 'rapid response' teams. Stanwix fort, near Carlisle, housed a cavalry unit of around a thousand. The Cervetii doubtless gave them trouble, in the form of guerrilla warfare. But if it came to real battle, the Romans, though vastly outnumbered, had the advantage of sound training and discipline. The Celts, while extremely brave and determined, were divided by clan loyalties, and their battle plan, according to Tacitus, consisted of making a lot of noise whipped up by their druids, leading to a headlong charge. One way in which the Romans tried to pacify the enemy was to bribe them into joining their

Roman fort remains, Hardknott

army, then shrewdly drafting them out of their home territory. Thus the invading Romans in Cumbria were mainly recruits from conquered Europe. For instance, inscriptions show that the legion that built the fort on Hardknott originated in Dalmatia – country east of the Adriatic. The astonishing remains of Hardknott fort are located in surely the most dramatic setting in Britain. It sits high on a ledge overlooking the Esk valley, with the highest peaks in England as neighbours.

Warfare was not constant. The army relied on some local co-operation. They needed to trade for local supplies. It is recorded that each Roman needed 300 to 350 kg of grain per year, supplemented where possible with pork, beef, fish and venison. A 500-man garrison would need a minimum of 163,800 kg of grain (barley and oats) per year. Horses also required fodder. In the Cumbrian fort sites the remains of the grain store buildings show that they were always substantial, probably capable of holding a year's supply. Throughout Cumbria archaeologists have discovered traces of enclosed farms and fields dating from the Roman period. At that time the climate was milder. Oats and barley fields would have been productive and must have been numerous. Traces of many of the farms will have been lost through subsequent agricultural use.

At first the forts were built hastily of wood and turf, then stone later. We see an example at Ambleside's fort at the head of Windermere. Here a turf and timber fort was covered by earth in the second century to lift the site above flood levels, and a substantial stone fort was built on top. Looking at its foundations now, an ideal picnic spot for holidaymakers, one is hard pressed to imagine any hostilities. But a gravestone found here reads: TO THE GOOD GODS OF THE UNDERWORLD/FLAVIUS ROMANUS, RECORD CLERK, LIVED FOR 35 YEARS/KILLED IN THE FORT BY THE ENEMY.

THE WALL

Hadrian's Wall, that magnificent monument to Roman engineering, was begun in 122 AD and was finished before the emperor's death in 138. It was built largely on the natural barrier of the Whin Sill, a long ridge formed by a flow of volcanic lava. The wall was made out of stone and turf, fronted by a deep ditch, and defended by forts. Set into the wall, at intervals of one Roman mile, stood milecastles, and between each, two turrets. The wall stretched for eighty miles from the Tyne and along part of the Solway. It entered Cumbria from the east at the River Irthing at Gilsland, where the remains of a substantial fort command a spectacular view over the Irthing valley. There were six forts along the Cumbrian section of the wall. West of Carlisle, along the Solway coast, the defences continued with a system of forts, watchtowers, ditches and palisades.

Quite naturally some of the forts soon had attendant *vici* – civilian villages. They provided a market for local goods and produce, and for the army's rest and recreation. Roman writing tablets at Vindolanda, by the wall, show that the men were brave enough to drink the local native beer. Some of the *vici* grew larger than the forts, such as one near Old Penrith fort, and at Carlisle.

In 197 Clodius Albinus, the governor of Britain, took away a substantial part of the wall garrison to support his ambitions to become emperor. His adventure failed and the wall fell to the enemy. It was retaken, and again fell when part of the garrison was withdrawn. Later in the fourth century Britain was harassed by invaders, Picts from north of the border, Scots from the north of Ireland and Saxons from the east. In 370 Theodosius took control of the wall, and its defences were repaired and strengthened. However, in 383 things were already getting out of hand when Magnus Maximus again took legions from all over Britain to help him fight in Gaul and Italy for the throne of Rome. The wall was lost and Britain was overrun by invaders. A plea to the Emperor Honorius for defence aid by the Romano-British inhabitants in 410 was answered by the grim news that Rome was powerless to act, and that the populations must fend for themselves.

THE DARK AGES

The Dark Ages have been gaining some illumination in some parts of Britain in which archaeologists continue to turn up relevant evidence. Cumbria remains in gloom. Little archaeological evidence from the period has been found so far, nor contemporary documentation. We rely on Welsh sources for the information that in around the fifth century Cumbria, together with some region north of the Solway, was part of the British kingdom of Rheged under King Urien. He was a heroic figure, according to the Welsh bard Taliesin. However, after Urien's death at the end of the century Cumbria was absorbed by the Scottish kingdom of Strathclyde. It is not known where the southern boundary lay, but certainly the old county of Cumberland was included. It was at this time that the country was known as the land of the Cymri.

We have to rely on old place names for clues. The river names are Celtic. Many place names contain Celtic elements, such as *pen* meaning a hill or a head, which occurs in Penrith and Penruddock. A hill at the southern end of the River Duddon is called simply Penn. The element *glyn*, or glen, occurs in Glenridding and Glenderamakin, while *blaen* for 'top' occurs in Blencathra, Blencow and Blennerhasset. There are many other examples. Astonishingly even today some Cumbrian sheep farmers from old farming stock can (perhaps at the local pub after a pint or two of ale) recite the Celtic way of counting sheep up to fifty used by their forefathers. It varies slightly according to locality, but this is a representative version of one to ten: *yan, tyan, teddera, meddera, pimp, sethera, lethera, hovera, dovera, dick.*

After Roman withdrawal Celtic missionaries from Ireland brought the Christian faith into the region. St Ninian was certainly active around Solway. St Patrick is said to have been present, but it is all tradition with no known facts. Patterdale is thought to be one place where he preached, and there is a 'St Patrick's well'. St Herbert lived on an island on Derwent Water. But St Kentigern, said to be a lowland Scot, and patron saint of Glasgow, was certainly active here in the late sixth century. Eight churches are dedicated to him in the north of the county. His other name was Mungo; Mungrisdale means literally 'Mungo's valley of pigs'.

THE ANGLES AND VIKINGS

In the seventh century Anglian authority expanded in Britain. The Angles defeated Celtic forces at the battle of Chester in 615. The effect was to separate the Welsh Celts from their Cumbrian compatriots. It is not known whether Cumbrian settlement by Angles thereafter took place peacefully, but Anglian place names suggest that they settled in the more fertile plains, where they could use their ox ploughs. Place names ending in *ham* or *ton* are characteristic: Aldingham, Askham, Brigham, Dearham, Whicham, Dalton, Broughton, Eversham, Wigton, Orton, and many more have Anglian elements. They apparently came as Christians. Of two wonderful Anglian crosses, one is a well-preserved example in the churchyard at Irton. The other, without a head, is at Bewcastle. This has a sister cross at Ruthwell, over the Scottish border. According to Pevsner, 'There is nothing as perfect as these two crosses and of a comparable date in the whole of Europe.' An Anglo-Saxon church tower, unspoilt by subsequent building, can be found at Morland.

In the late eighth century Viking raids on the eastern coast of Britain became more frequent, and they began to occupy east and central regions. The few place names of Danish origin in Cumbria suggest that they did not go further west than the Eden valley, but Carlisle, which had impressed St Cuthbert for its beauty, was sacked and remained in ruins, it is said, for two centuries.

The direct Viking raids on Cumbria came from the western seas, and the invaders were Norse rather than Danish. The Norse Vikings had taken over the Orkneys and Shetlands, and occupied parts of western Scotland, Ireland and the Isle of Man. Symean of Durham, writing in the eleventh century, refers to Eardulf, a nobleman, and Tilred, Abbot of Heversham, fleeing across the Pennines from

Viking cross, Gosforth

Viking raids, presumably into Morecambe Bay, in the early tenth century. Later Viking incursions were not necessarily hostile, because of their conversion to Christianity. Norse place names are sometimes close to surviving Anglian names. A wonderfully preserved Norse cross at Gosforth is only 4 km away from the well-preserved Anglian cross at Irton. Some of the Vikings may well have settled as refugees! The Icelandic historian with the splendid name of Snorri Sturluson (1178–1241) tells in the *Heimskringla* saga of the western Vikings being too independent – so much so that they had the audacity to raid Norwegian coasts. The king of Norway, Harald Fairhair, came upon the rebels with a battle fleet. News of the coming retribution reached the Vikings of the Isle of Man, and, according to Snorri, 'then fled all folk into Scotland, and the island was unpeopled of men: all goods that might be shifted – flitted away'. When Sturluson wrote the saga Cumbria was part of Scotland. A good westerly breeze from Man could ship its population quickly to a Cumbrian safe haven.

Linguistic evidence shows that the Norse settled around the north-west, west, and south-west of Cumbria. The mountains are fells (*fjall*), the streams are becks (*bekkr*), a waterfall here is a force (*foss*), the valleys are dales (*dalr*). Norse appears very often in place names. A 'thwait' means a clearing, and is a common suffix; to mention but a few: Rosthwaite, Seathwaite, Haverthwaite, Braithwaite, Satterthwaite. Variants of a Norse–Irish element (from the Isle of Man?), *saetre*, meaning a shieling, or summer pasture, appear in many place names: Seathwaite, Seat Sandal, Seatoller, Arnside, Ambleside (Ama's shieling). There is a scattering of other Norse names – *how* for hill, *blea* for blue, Grizedale (pig dale). Norse buildings being of wood, little clear archaeological evidence of settlements survives so far. What we see is a great many of their sculpted crosses and tombstones.

THE NORMANS AND BORDER TROUBLES

The Norman conquest is perhaps the most significant event in British history. But it made little immediate impact on Cumbria, which was not in England. The Domesday Book, William the Conqueror's huge property survey, mentions only a few places in (the English) southern Cumbria and around the River Kent. In 1092 William Rufus came north and took Carlisle from Dolphin, its Scottish ruler, and Scotland was then effectively pushed north of Solway. A castle was built (probably of wood at first) and garrisoned. William then drafted in loyal English subjects to

Brough Castle

settle and farm the area, and presumably to displace the troublesome natives. He divided Cumbria into several baronies, each of which eventually had its own castle and favoured baron. The Norman way was to build a 'motte and bailey', an artificial mound, surmounted by a tower and strategically placed so the inhabitants had a constant reminder of who was in charge. Towers were later improved and strengthened into castles. There were seventeen in Cumbria, the strongest strategically at Carlisle; and on the main route from the east at Brough, Appleby and Brougham; at Kendal in the south; and Egremont on the west coast. Now they still look impressive, but as ruins.

As things became more settled the barons sought to buy their way to heaven by gifting land to the Church – not the best land of course. The twelfth was *the* century for the building of great abbeys and priories. Furness Abbey in the south of Cumbria became one of the most profitable and powerful in Britain, with farming, mining, forestry, fishing, marketing, and land speculation in other parts of the British Isles helping to generate wealth. Other abbeys were founded at Holme Cultram in the north, Shap in the east and Calder in the west. Priories sprung up at Carlisle, Lanercost, St Bees, Conishead and Cartmel. The establishments did much to civilize and commercialize the region. The Tudor destruction has left us merely with beautiful ruins, especially impressive being those at Furness and Lanercost.

THE BORDER AND THE WARS

North of the border the Scots encouraged some Norman settlement, and Norman religious establishments arose there too. In later events these Normans in Scotland, covetous of what they owned, became extreme Scottish nationalists. Wallace and Bruce were both Normans. The border became a matter of dispute and so it continued through the centuries. David I of Scotland took Cumbria and the northern shires back into Scotland in 1137, but was brought to account at the Battle of the Standard at Northallerton a year later. He kept northern Cumbria though and died in Carlisle castle in 1153. His grandson Malcolm IV succeeded, but he was only twelve and Henry II took advantage of his minority, successfully demanding the surrender of Cumbria and Northumberland along with its castles.

In subsequent years the border remained a matter of dispute, negotiation and warfare. Carlisle castle reverted Scotland twice before Alexander III surrendered the Scottish claim and made peace with Henry III. But Edward I, who succeeded Henry, was not satisfied. In 1291 he saw his chance to take Scotland. He was asked to adjudicate between rival claimants for the Scottish throne. He agreed, but only on condition that the claimants recognize him as direct lord of Scotland. They acquiesced. But John Balliol, the successful candidate, went back on his word, and took his forces into Cumbria. Carlisle was burned, but he couldn't take the castle. Edward returned in a fury, retook Cumbria, pushed into Scotland and appropriated the Stone of Destiny, on which the Scots kings were crowned. Soon Balliol was his prisoner.

Then came William Wallace, acting on behalf of his rightful king, Balliol. He defeated the English at Stirling and his troops crossed the border. He took Carlisle, but again the castle held. But the Scots went on a plundering and burning spree right down the Eden valley and well into the Lake District. Edward, justifiably called 'the hammer of the Scots', retaliated. He pushed into Scotland and razed the border towns. Wallace was defeated at Falkirk, but continued guerrilla warfare until he was betrayed and captured. Charged with invading the counties of Northumberland, Cumberland and Westmorland, burning and killing everyone who used the English tongue – 'sparing neither age nor sex, monk or nun' – he was hung, drawn and quartered.

Edward's troubles were not over. Robert the Bruce recognized no authority from England. Bruce's army was defeated near Perth by Edward, Earl of Pembroke's, force, and he fled to the highlands, but came back (so, it is said, persuaded by a spider) to defeat Pembroke's force near Ayr in 1306. Edward had returned to Cumbria to deal with him, but he was a sick man and died on the Cumbrian bank of the Solway, near Burgh by Sands. A sad lone monument marks the spot.

Edward II, his successor, was no match for Bruce, and the English hold on parts of Scotland were lost. They were defeated at Bannockburn and Bruce's troops flooded into England, plundering cattle and taking prisoners; even abbeys and priories were not spared. Appleby was sacked and burned. They even reached the south of Cumbria and into Lancaster. Furness Abbey almost bankrupted itself to pay for protection. The Scots had won independence. In 1328 its independence was recognized by the Treaty of Northampton.

THE BORDER RAIDERS

Despite independence the border troubles were by no means over. Both sides had been ravaged by pitiless wars. Some of the border inhabitants hardly knew, or cared, whether they were English or Scots. They were borderers. First loyalties were to their families. Most became border 'reivers' – robbers – and cross-border raiding and cattle rustling were rife. By agreement between Scotland and England the unique 'Law of the Marches' was invoked to try to keep a lid on the volatile area and to redress wrongs. As an instance it was lawful to pursue robbers 'on hot trod', using 'sleuth dogs' (tracker dogs) to recover stock soon after the robbery; but later revenge attacks were unlawful. (It is interesting to note that there exists the popular Cumbrian sport of Hound Trails – racing 'sleuth hounds' on hot scent – now an aniseed-soaked rag.) Bishop Leslie of Ross wrote about the reivers' activities. Sir Walter Scott quotes the Elizabethan historian Camden's translation from Latin:

> They sally out of their own borders, in the night, in troops, through unfrequented by-ways, and many intricate windings. All the day time, they refresh themselves and their horses, in lurking holes they had pitched upon before, till they arrive in the dark at those places they have a design upon. As soon as they have seized their booty, they, in like manner, return home in the night, through blind ways, and fetching many a compass. The more skilful any captain is to pass through those wild deserts, crooked turnings, and deep precipices, in the thickest mists and darkness, his reputation is the greater, and he is looked upon as a man of excellent head. And they are so cunning, they seldom have their booty taken from them – unless sometimes, when, by the help of blood hounds following them exactly upon the tract, they may chance to fall into the hands of their adversaries.

Law or not, for the borderers raiding was a normal way of life. From spring to harvest the families on both sides farmed the lean land. On suitable nights in winter they would pull on their leather jackets and steel helmets, mount their sturdy ponies and raid. The border ballads have romanticized their way of life, but the reality was often vicious. Houses were burned, people killed, herds of cattle taken, even household effects and clothing. The raids were not necessarily all cross-border. Sometimes it was family feuds that had to be settled. The reivers introduced a new word into English: 'blackmail' (literally 'black rent'). Although the meaning has changed somewhat since, essentially it referred to a protection racket. A strong family would demand a rent from a weaker, and in return they might be protected. The reivers could become political assets at times of unrest, and were recruited as mercenaries.

The Marches were organized into three sections. The Western March, the most lawless, covered the Cumbrian section and included a 'debatable land' belonging to neither country. It is still shown and named so on maps, but now divided. Wardens of the Marches were appointed for both sides of the Border. Occasionally each would meet his counterpart at a neutral place to settle complaints. One of the notable Western March wardens was Richard of Gloucester, later Richard III, who strengthened Carlisle castle and stayed for periods at Penrith.

James V of Scotland tried to deal with the lawless borders by executing known troublemakers, but the scheme was ineffective. Then he aroused Henry VIII's wrath by marrying Mary of Guise, who was on Henry's prospective list. James agreed to patch up the quarrel by meeting Henry at York, but then failed to turn up. Henry was furious at the slight and sent two expeditions into Scotland to make a reckoning. They accomplished nothing, but the counterattack ordered by James turned out to be the most disastrous defeat ever suffered by Scotland (see p. 235–6) .

The borders remained in intermittent turmoil during the adventurous reign of Mary, Queen of Scots. Her reign came to an end when she aroused the enmity of the Scottish lords, first of all by marrying her cousin, Lord Darnley, whom they denounced for his arrogance and incompetence, then secondly, when he was murdered, marrying the equally unpopular fourth Earl of Bothwell who was thought to be the murderer. Her supporters melted away, Bothwell fled the country, and she was captured by the lords. Forced to abdicate, she was imprisoned in Loch Leven castle, but managed to escape. In 1568 she fled south across the Solway and was received in Cumbria, at Workington, where she found the natives firm but not unfriendly. She was escorted to Cockermouth castle and then on to Carlisle. During her stay in Carlisle, before being taken to Yorkshire, she had freedom to leave the castle and could hunt, and attend church services.

The seventeenth century saw further problems with reiver bands. The border law stated that: 'If any Englishman steal in Scotland, or any Scotsman steal in England, any goods or chattels amounting to 12d he shall be punished by death'. Another Act of Parliament of 1601 made the taking of 'black mail' to be punished by death without benefit of clergy.

However, the border conflicts and robberies virtually ended with the accession of James I/VI of Scotland and the union of the crowns in 1707. His solution was draconian but effective. Some reivers were transported to Ireland. Furthermore, he ordered that the iron gates of the reivers' enclosures were to be made into ploughshares. There should be only working horses, no saddles or riding ponies. Finally, in 1609 a mass hanging of West March reivers at Dumfries brought the troubles to an inglorious end.

We see the legacy of the troubles on the landscape – for example in the many stone 'pele towers' with walls 2 m thick in which a settlement's inhabitants could seek protection. Cattle was secured in a lower storey and upper storeys were entered either by a ladder that could be drawn up afterwards, or by a narrow inner stairway that could be easily defended. Some church towers were specially built to serve a similar purpose. In the eighteenth century, more prosperous times, some of the area's stately homes were built onto their defensive towers.

Fortified border church, Newton Arlosh

Cumbria would see more troubles. During the Civil War the castles of Carlisle and Cockermouth came under siege from one side or the other. Then in the winter of 1745 the young pretender, Charles Edward Stuart, 'Bonnie Prince Charlie', came south from Scotland with his highland army to oust the Hanoverian King George, and claim the throne of England and Scotland for his father, the exiled James Stuart, son of James II. After successful campaigns in Scotland his forces took Carlisle castle and advanced south through Cumbria until they reached Derby. Charles was then persuaded to abandon a further advance until he could get French support, and a retreat began, back through Cumbria, with the English Duke of Cumberland's army in pursuit. The last conflict between armies on English soil was at Clifton, south of Carlisle. Here the Scots were victors, but the retreat continued. The duke took Carlisle and its castle, and so many Scots prisoners were taken that many had to be housed in the cathedral. The remaining Scots army was soon afterwards defeated on Scottish soil at Culloden. The dreadful retribution that followed earned the Duke the name 'Butcher Cumberland'. Carlisle's prisoners were cruelly treated and many were executed.

THE INDUSTRIAL REVOLUTION

The eighteen and ninteenth centuries brought tremendous changes to all parts of Britain, and no less to Cumbria. The countryside landscape began to be dramatically reshaped by the Enclosure Acts. Most of the several thousand miles of dry-stone walls that we see spread like a net over the Cumbrian fells and valleys date from this period. The Acts made some agriculturists wealthy, but ruined many small farmers who could not afford the considerable capital to undertake enclosure. At the same time there began a gradual improvement in farming practices. The use of lime and fertilisers, and new land draining techniques, brought thousands of acres of previously marginal land into profitable production. In the forefront with the agricultural innovators was the landowner, John Christian Curwen of Workington. A national 'Board of Agriculture' was formed in 1793. It had no authority or bureaucratic function, but brought together the influential enthusiasts for the new techniques. One of the most notable members was the owner of extensive Cumbrian estates: Henry Lowther (1736–1802), the 3rd Viscount Lonsdale.

There were also improvements to the roads. During the eighteenth century most of the major roads were rutted and dangerous, and the lesser roads no better than pony tracks. Cumbrian trade depended very much on packhorse trains, even on the long journey to London. Before accompanying their goods it was prudent for businessmen to settle their worldly affairs and make their wills, conditions were so bad. It was the task of each local parish to care for their highways, and this was largely dependent on casual local labour with little or no funding. The improvements came with the passing of the Turnpike Acts in the 1750s. Landowners could undertake the maintenance of roads on their land and to charge for their use. The new roads meant there could be new means of travelling. Post-chaises were introduced from 1754, and carriers' wagons began to be seen in numbers in the following years. In 1763 the first fast coach in the county linked Kendal to Carlisle. It was drawn by six horses, was called 'the Flying Machine', and the journey took six hours. As the road improvements continued, towns on the coaching routes like Kendal, Penrith, Cockermouth and Longtown grew in importance.

The growth of overseas trade brought new wealth into the country, and some prosperity to the ports of Whitehaven and Workington. Manufacturing industries were born of the imports of raw materials: in Cumbria's case cotton and tobacco from the Americas. Poverty however was rife. In rural Cumbria the parish councils had responsibility for the relief of paupers under the Elizabethan Poor Law Act. In 1723 an Act allowed neighbouring parishes to unite to provide workhouses. Workhouses were a source of cheap labour for the mills. The new mills were centred on the growing towns, and their efficient innovative machinery meant the gradual demise of the old cottage industries, and a decrease in rural populations – a trend that accelerated during the nineteenth century as the Industrial Revolution gathered pace.

Mining was hampered by the two problems of flooding and ventilation. Pumps were operated by water wheels until the invention of the steam engine changed everything. The steam pumps meant that mines could exploit areas previously out of reach. As their power and efficiency improved they could also be used to work winding gear. When steam fever increased nationally the need for coal became paramount, and the mines of West Cumbria were rapidly expanded. Coal was exported profitably from the ports and led to the building of a new one at Ellenfoot, which was renamed Maryport.

In the last quarter of the eighteenth century there was need for more efficient and economical means of transport. Canals were being built all over the country to take materials from the ports into the industrial interior – 3,000 miles of them by 1815. A canal was eventually completed from Preston to serve the mills of Kendal. Ulverston grew quickly from a little market town to a busy port with thriving industries as a canal brought shipping in from Morecambe Bay. Carlisle had its canal access to the sea at a new Port Carlisle in the Solway.

The growth in the nation's wealth meant that the middle classes had more money, and leisure time to spend it. The fashionable Grand Tour of Europe brought to the tourists an appreciation of art, architecture and good craftsmanship. This had three effects on Cumbria. First of all, the Cumbrian land-owning gentry were inspired to beautify their houses. Their proud formidable defensive towers could be kept as a wing of an extended, tastefully designed, and more comfortable home where newly acquired treasures could be displayed. Their grounds were laid out into fashionable gardens with exotic trees and shrubs from abroad, with terraces and water features, temples and grottoes. Secondly, the Grand Tour created a new interest in fine landscape, and when political problems in Europe made travel there more uncertain, the Lake District's scenic attractions brought in the first tourists, particularly artists and writers. Thirdly, into the nineteenth century wealthy industrialists were buying property in the attractive county, mainly, but not exclusively, in the Lake District. They built their new homes often in the Italian, Greek or Gothic styles. Some of them were strangely exotic, like the mock castle at Wray by Windermere, with mock romantic ruins, and the great Lowther Castle, now reduced to a façade. The new residents brought wealth into the county and much was spent in buying their way to heaven. New churches were built and old churches refurbished and 'improved'.

In the middle of the eighteenth century, too, and into the nineteenth there was also a growing interest in investigative science. Of the several notable Cumbrians in the field, two were outstanding. The eccentric Henry Cavendish (1730–1800), grandson of the second Duke of Devonshire, at Holker Hall at Cark, near Grange-over-Sands, was able to solve the problem of separating and identifying gases, and made early experiments with electricity. From humble beginnings near Cockermouth, John Dalton (1766–1844) became a leading figure in scientific circles, the first to define the atom as the smallest particle and to calculate atomic weights.

In the early nineteenth century steam engines were powering boats, and in the next two decades the first locomotives were hauling wagons a few miles from mines to harbours. It was the beginning of the railway fever that swept the country and made some villages into towns and towns into villages. In 1847 a new railway-made town was born from Birthwaite, a small hamlet. It became 'Windermere', though it was just short of 2 km from Bowness, the resort on the eponymous lake edge. Through the second half of the century a whole network of railways were being built to serve the mining, quarrying and shipping industries in Cumbria's west and east; and only afterwards were some to become a major contributor to the Lake District tourist industry.

The railways minimized the usefulness of the canals. Ulverston, for instance, lost its harbour status when a line linked the new town and port of Barrow-in-Furness to the main south-to-north line in Lancashire. Barrow had grown from a small fishing village to a major iron, steel and shipbuilding town. Other towns in the west and south-west gained from the discovery of large rich iron ore deposits. This, with new methods of production, resulted in Britain becoming the foremost iron producing country in Europe. This wealth was supplemented by new effective methods of exploitation of the large coal deposits in the north-west. Immigrants from Ireland and the Isle of Man swelled the urban populations. The major figure in the new iron age, and at the vital core of the Industrial Revolution, was the iron-master, John Wilkinson (1728–1808), son of a Cumbrian farmer. Amongst other innovations, he cast the first iron bridge in the world in Coalbrookdale in Shropshire, and floated the first iron boat. He had a home at Castlehead, Lindale, near Grange-over-Sands, and his cast iron obelisk memorial is nearby.

The depression after the First World War and into the 1930s hit the west Cumbrian industries hard and they were slow to recover. After the Second World War, from the 1950s onwards, there was a gradual decline in the heavy industries as they faced foreign competition. New lighter industries had to develop. One saviour in west Cumbria was the expansion of Windscale (later Sellafield) into the nuclear industry. It had grown from a munitions factory that had produced the first British atomic bomb and became a major employer in the area.

The trend in farming after the Second World War was the take-over of small, less viable farms by larger ones. During 2001 Cumbria was to be the worst hit of all British counties by the foot and mouth disease outbreak that took most of its animal stocks.

THE PEOPLE OF CUMBRIA

It used to be said that the true native of Cumbria shows a Viking descent, and even that the more rural communities have a greater number of people with fair hair and blue eyes. Well, it's certainly difficult to spot them at a farmers' market! Romantic fantasies aside, the Viking influence can indeed be found in the place names, and in words and dialect. The Viking settlers must have integrated with the natives; then when William II took the region into England he drafted in a race of more civilized and compliant settlers – Normans and Flemings, and Saxon peasants from the south of England – to take over farms and establish industries. Through the centuries other peoples have migrated there, such as Flemish weavers and miners from Cornwall and Germany. Then during the Industrial Revolution, immigrants from Ireland swelled the work forces in the west coast towns and Furness. Who is a native Cumbrian? The closest one can get is among the old rural families.

The dialect in the south-west of Cumbria, with its Lancashire influence, differs from that of the urban places of the north-west. In the Furness area, for instance, 'I am going home' might sound like, 'Aam gowin wom', while in west Cumbria it could be 'Aas ga-in yam' (literally 'I is going home'). An old joke in Workington concerns a visitor who goes to a rugby match and remarks afterwards that he thought he was standing near two Chinamen, for one said 'We wun yance' and his companion said 'How lang sin' ('We won once' and 'How long since?'). The inflection of Cumbrian speech in the industrial towns has been influenced by the substantial numbers of Irish immigrants they have absorbed. In this it can be compared to Liverpool, which also acquired a large Irish population. There is certainly a difference between Cumbrian urban dialect, and rural, though speakers of each can understand the other.

In the border regions, as one might expect, dialects have something in common with Robbie Burns's Scottish. All this, of course, is changing: many of the old Cumbrian dialects are sadly being lost, because of greater mobility and the influence of the media. It would be a pity if some of the old words with Scandinavian origins are forgotten – like 'dowly' – lonesome; 'brant' – steep; 'clarty' – muddy; 'gey' – very; 'kist' – a chest; 'thrang' – busy; 'sned' – to cut, lop a branch; 'yak' – oak. In *Land of the Lakes,* Melvyn Bragg lists 101 dialect words for 'to beat'. If regional variations were added the number would be even higher.

CHAPTER FOUR

Trades and Industries

FARMING

Kendal's coat of arms contains the motto *'pannus mihi panis'* – 'wool is my bread'. Wool has been the bread of a great part of Cumbria from time immemorial. Shakespeare mentions Kendal Green, a heavy cloth, in *Henry IV, Part 2*: 'Three misbegotten knaves in Kendal Green, came at my back—' The native sheep of Cumbria are Herdwicks, a tough little white-faced breed that can survive the extremes of weather on the fells. It is unique to the area and various stories circulate about its origins. One is that the sheep landed from wrecked ships

Herdwicks – the hardy Lakeland sheep

of the Spanish Armada. Another that they were brought over by the Vikings. Their wool is coarse, and as tough and wiry as the breed. Ideal for durable overcoats and fairly waterproof, it also makes excellent long-lasting carpets. However, the wool is far too scratchy for the long stockings for which the area was once famous. One difficulty is that it resists dyeing. John Peel wore 'a coat so grey', not 'gay'. Wool brought prosperity to the abbeys and priories, and was the basis of cottage industries for centuries. The raw material was carded and spun, sometimes woven, in farmhouses, where it was also often knitted. There were water-powered fulling mills in many villages. The industry declined in the seventeenth century when finer cloths from Spain came into favour. Fulling mills then often converted into sawmills and paper mills. During the rapid growth of the Lancashire cotton industry, mills were often reconverted to turning bobbins, which also helped the woodland coppice industry.

Wool is no longer Cumbria's bread. Hill sheep farming cannot exist without subsidies. The woollen market is almost dead. Herdwick mutton has a high reputation, but the breed is not as productive as others, such as Swaledales and Dalesbred, which Cumbrian sheep farmers have favoured, with cross-breds, for many years now. The National Trust preserves the ancient breed on the farms it owns. Arable farming of barley, wheat and oats, and cattle farming, have prospered on the more favoured lands of the Eden valley and the coastal plains. And in the past there was much trade in fattening up black cattle brought by drovers from Scotland.

The survival of farming in the hills has always depended on close co-operation between farmers. Each farm had its stint (its own grazing area), and trespass of flocks onto a neighbour's land had to be avoided. Sheep carried their owner's marks, called 'smits', and 'lug marks', the cropping of the sheep's ears. The marks were recorded in a shepherd's guide. After the owner's name and farm a description might read: 'cropped near ear, twice slit on far ear, a red pop on each huck, letter T on nearside'. Sometimes a sheep's horn was branded. The fell flocks still require the owners' marks.

There were also shared areas, common land, such as the open fell, which were also subject to disciplined regulation. For instance, a fence of drystone walling, the 'dyke', sometimes called felldyke or headgarth, was necessary to separate the upper fell grazing from the farmland below. Walling was done either by the farmers, or by itinerants. Farming depended on seasonal movement of stock. It was essential to keep stock grazing the fell in spring and summer, and to prevent them from trespassing on crops and hay meadows below. Then at an agreed date they were brought down in winter to the shelter and food of the farmland and barns.

Little has changed. It is difficult for most people to understand the hill sheep-farmer's life for it requires a great leap of imagination in our modern age. He tends a large flock of animals grazing an open fell area that might take the best part of two days to walk round – rough ground rising upwards of 600 m, sometimes to 900 m. Flock management depends upon a regular system of moving sheep upwards to high grazing, and downwards to the better-enclosed 'intake' land and the lusher 'inby' land. He needs to keep good working sheepdogs. He has also to grow a hay crop for winter feeding. He must care for his flock in harsh winter hill conditions, bringing in the unseasoned young stock, and the older ewes that are beginning to lack the strength to face the savage weather, and feed them. In persistent snow he must intensify feeding and bring sheep into shelter. April and May brings lambing time and he must be out from dawn to dusk, making sure that ewes are accepting their maternal duties, and that the lambs are taking feed; bringing 'problem families' in closer into prepared pens, and pushing the successful outwards. All births complete, he has to mark, castrate, watch for health problems and for marauding crows and foxes. Later comes the time for haymaking and clipping, dipping, treating, dosing, injecting against the complaints that sheep are heir to, including flesh parasites, worms, foot-rot, liver fluke, dysentery and scab. In the autumn he must decide what sheep to sell and where, to pick them out, get them to market and achieve the best price he can. Then at mating time, as winter approaches, he must make sure that all the eligible ewes are served. Winter is the time for the other jobs: fence repairs, walling, hedging, draining. He does all this, and this being the twenty-first century, he has to attend to what all regard as the most hateful task of all: the paper work.

By the new millennium, agriculture, while still a significant employer in the county, had declined – a decline of over 50 per cent since the 1970s. A total of 13,082 worked in agriculture, but only 7,706 full time. Then farming in Cumbria suffered the greatest disaster in its modern history. The outbreak of foot and mouth disease in 2001 hit Cumbria harder than any other county in Britain. Help was far too little, far too late; it was also pig-headed and cruelly misguided. Thousands of animals were slaughtered in the valleys and the fells, some bulldozed into funeral pyres. It is difficult to understand the devastation that farmers felt when they saw their animals taken away or destroyed, a mixture of anger and total despair. Compensation was paid, but no compensation can make up for a whole lifetime's work gone within hours. And no part of the county was spared. Moreover, farms free of the disease suffered financial distress, without compensation, from the severe restrictions on animal movement, which in itself involved some animal cruelty. Afterwards, as a result, some farmers decided they had had enough and chose to leave the industry, while younger would-be entrants were discouraged. Farmers increasingly belonged to an ageing population. The industry had to go through a period of reinvention.

Several changes happened after the disease was defeated. Smaller dairy herds were not replaced because of the poor prices paid for milk. On the other hand some of the bigger herds expanded. There were new problems on the hill farms. Fell sheep have always been 'heafed' – that is, generations of sheep for centuries are fed on the same fells; they recognize their home ground from instinct and will seldom stray from it. That means that no fences are needed. But the disease, and slaughter, wiped out many of these fell sheep flocks, and new stock brought in do not have the instinct to stay on home ground, so there arose the need for many kilometres of new fences. Farmers began receiving lots of conflicting advice, and became entangled in red tape. More sheep farmers gave up the struggle, some thought they would hang on as well as they could and hope for the best; but others showed their confidence by building up their flocks. At the end of 2002 a pedigree Swaledale tup (ram) was sold at auction at Kirkby Stephen for a record £100,000. The buyer was obviously confident that eventually he would receive a healthy profit on the investment.

One growing Cumbrian development in 2003 is the growth of farmers' markets in some of the towns. The public are invited to buy direct from the producers. Some farmers are increasing their farms' income by providing tourist attractions. Others are taking the various grants available for environmental schemes.

MINING

Mining goes back to Roman times, when Cumbria's fells and plains were found to be rich in metal ores and coal. Lead was then mined near Alston and probably also on the western side of the Cumbrian Pennines. The earliest form of mining involved digging a shaft down to the ore and then spreading activity outwards so that the workings became bell-shaped. Signs of these many old bell pits can be seen on the fells. In the sixteenth century, when the need for ore brought large profits, new techniques were developed for searching out and reaching the veins. One was by 'hushing'. A small reservoir was made at a water source above the hoped-for vein, and the water was then released as the workers assisted the erosion down to bedrock with pick and shovel, hoping thereby to find a good source of ore.

In 1564 Queen Elizabeth brought German miners to Cumbria to use their famed techniques for discovering ore and their advanced mining techniques, and the Company of Mines Royal began work. The main prospector was Daniel Hechstetter, and he found exposed mineral veins of copper and lead chiefly among the fells around Keswick, behind Skiddaw, on Helvellyn and on Coniston Old Man. The Germans settled in the area and the mines were sunk and produced great profits. At that time the Company of Mines Royal had powers to search for all kinds of metals, the Crown taking one tenth of all gold, silver and copper found. Keswick then became a mining town, and in 1565 housed some fifty German mining experts.

The Germans brought various new techniques. Ore was extracted by digging a shaft to below the vein and digging levels outwards from it, going deeper and repeating the process as far as the ore presented itself. The ore was taken above the miners' heads and dropped into tubs, pushed to the shaft and hauled up in a large bucket – a 'kibble'. But certain problems had to be solved. The mine needed ventilation. Often water had to be pumped away. Sometimes dust became an issue. Various cunning means were employed to keep the mines working. Water wheels provided power, and a fall of water could provide air circulation. Digging out the ore by hand with wedges and hammer was later made easier by the introduction of gunpowder. Drills powered by compressed air came later. Miners laboured hard for long hours, and in the early days young children were also employed underground. Women were often employed at the surface to sort the ore.

A mysterious decline in ore mining occurred during the Civil War, and it is said that Cromwell's followers destroyed the Keswick smelter and some of the Coniston workings, but it is hard to understand why if it's true. Mining continued to varying degrees until a major downturn in the nineteenth century, when cheap imports meant that many mines became unprofitable. One of the last to survive, at Roughton Gill, finally closed in 1960, but gypsum continues to be mined at Kirby Thore. Sometimes when mines closed, the operation changed to quarrying.

Top of the shaft of Brandley Mine by Derwent Water in 1862

Iron has been dug from the ground since time immemorial (and later mined) in west and south-west Cumbria, largely on the fringe of carboniferous limestone. Furness abbey, Holme Cultram abbey and St Bees priory all profited from iron deposits and to the iron-hungry Scots raiders they were priority targets. When pitmen in a mine at Stainton in Furness broke into an ancient working they discovered two stone axes that had been used to hew ore. It was haematite, finest-quality iron, that brought prosperity particularly to the Furness area from the eighteenth century, and built the town of Barrow out of a fishing village to become a major iron and steel producer, and a shipbuilding town. The most productive iron mine was at Millom from 1860 to 1968. Huge quantities of high-class ore were found there, in the 1880s and first one wall, and then another, was built to keep back the sea as the workings extended. Haematite was also found in great quantities along the carboniferous limestone fringe in west Cumbria, and it brought wealth to Whitehaven and Workington. The ore supplied a number of furnaces in the south and west. There is a well-preserved eighteenth-century charcoal furnace by Duddon Bridge. The storage buildings for charcoal there are enormous, which indicates the high demand on local woodlands for charcoal until the furnaces were fired by coke.

COAL MINING

North-west Cumbria was mined for vast quantities of coal from the sixteenth century. It was found at various levels, from deep down to near the surface. Although the mining techniques were similar to those of ore extraction, the difference was that whereas ore is normally found in amorphous depositions, coal is formed from ancient decayed plants lying in near horizontal beds, sometimes less than a metre thick. The miners were forced to work in confined spaces and shovel the coal into tubs. Volatile gasses were an added hazard. Firedamp could not only asphyxiate, it could easily ignite with explosive force if met by a naked flame. Until the invention of the safety lamp it was a killer. Even then there could be problems. Most miners were pipe smokers, and strict regulations were enforced to prevent men taking matches to the workings. However, some accidents were doubtless caused by a breach of the rules. Until the mid nineteenth century children were normally employed in the mines, as were women sometimes, to haul the tubs underground.

In the early twentieth century, twenty-eight Cumbrian pits were in operation, employing over 19,000 miners. Some of the workings extended under the sea for as much as 7 km. There were a number of serious mining accidents, to which I will refer in other pages. Coal mining helped to boost the port of Whitehaven, for coal was its main export. Hard to believe now, but in the eighteenth century Whitehaven was second only to the port of London, and well ahead of Liverpool, in tonnage.

By the 1960s Cumbrian coal mining was practically finished, beaten by competition from more economical pits. The problem in Cumbria was that the most productive seams were under the sea and so far away from the pithead that haulage costs were too great. Eventually mining, like farming, could only continue with subsidies. Unlike farming, however, the mines were left to their own fate, and as a result, all the west Cumbrian mines have gone, along with the mining communities upon whose backs Britain's economic foundations were built.

GUNPOWDER AND QUARRYING

Another offshoot of the mining industry was the manufacture of gunpowder. There were ample supplies of one of its constituents – charcoal – in the coppice woodlands. Saltpetre and sulphur had to be imported, but waterpower for milling was another asset. The powder's potency depended on very fine mixtures, so the materials had to pass through a series of grindstones – suitably spaced along the millrace to limit the damage from possible explosions. Gunpowder works were established from the mid eighteenth century, mostly in the south of the county where supplies of wood for charcoal were plentiful.

The winning of stone by quarrying was also a major industry for centuries, and continues today. It built Hadrian's Wall, the Roman forts, the abbeys, castles and churches and the fine houses of the eighteenth and nineteenth centuries. Granites, in particular, have been chosen for buildings all over Britain, and the fine stone from Shap was used for some of the major historical buildings in London including the Albert Memorial and London Bridge. It can be seen in the Thames Embankment, Holborn Viaduct, and conspicuously as bollards in front of St Paul's. Cumbrian granite was also used for cobbles and setts – even abroad, for Cumbrian cobbles were sometimes carried as ships' ballast across the Atlantic. The hard stone was, and is still, used as aggregate in road surfacing, and in concrete products. Cumbrian slate from the Langdale, Kirkby Moor and Honister quarries produced roofing slates, and the slate is still in demand for its decorative and hard-wearing qualities, and its polished finish can be seen in many modern buildings all over the world.

Limestone quarries provided building materials for many of the towns in the limestone belt, and the material was also employed in agriculture and for use in the blast furnaces. Old limekilns are a feature in some Cumbrian valleys.

Granite quarry, St John's in the Vale

The downside of modern quarrying is that it employs fewer men, since the process is mechanized. When a suitable depth has been undercut it is possible to remove the whole face with suitably placed charges.

SHIPBUILDING

When ships were built of wood shipbuilding was a very major industry during the eighteenth and nineteenth centuries in many of the coastal towns. Then Barrow-in-Furness continued making ships of steel, many for the Royal Navy. Although the industry suffered a decline from the mid twentieth century, Barrow still produces naval vessels.

FORESTRY

Forestry became a Cumbrian industry after the First World War, when the Forestry Commission was born. A first acquisition in Britain was at Whinlatter on the side of Bassenthwaite, then the Commission's plantations expanded into

Conifer forest, Grizedale

Ennerdale, Dunnerdale and Grizedale. 13,000 ha of the Commission's forest is now within the National Park, with over 1,000 ha in other Cumbria areas. From time immemorial, though, the woodlands, particularly in south Cumbria, were important employers, producing charcoal for the furnaces, building material and for the manufacture of gunpowder. The material from coppice woodlands, cut every twelve to fifteen years, was put to scores of uses. Now coppicing hardly pays, but is being revived.

TOURISM

Tourism became a major employer when the Lake District was 'discovered' by the middle classes in the eighteenth century. It grew very significantly with improved roads and maps, and particularly the coming of the railways in the following two centuries. The influx of visitors brought into being the towns of Keswick, Ambleside, Windermere and Bowness. In earlier times visitors stayed in the hotels and guest houses for longer periods than in modern times. Now the motorway systems make day and weekend visits popular now that overseas holidays are a realistic option. The fells remain a major attraction. Indeed, a concern that the hill paths were being unacceptably eroded by walkers and cyclists led to a repair and

Footpath restoration

refurbishment scheme by the National Trust and the National Park that began in the 1980s, some of it part-funded by tourism sponsorship. The volunteer Mountain Rescue Teams attend to between 100 and 200 accidents each year. The lakes are the other draw. Angling, sailing and canoeing remain as popular as ever.

In 1999 tourism contributed £964 million to the county's economy, 55 per cent of it spent in the Lake District National Park. In Cumbria it employed 25,000, 13 per cent of the county's entire workforce. But the industry suffered even more than farming from the effects of foot and mouth disease in 2001 because of needless total restrictions on countryside access. Some isolated tourist establishments endured a year without any income. The Youth Hostels Association's funds were devastated and led to the closure and sale of some hostels. It is astonishing that the calamity was not foreseen when the government put a blanket restriction on all public footpaths. There was no compensation. One, probably modest, estimate is that the crisis lost the industry some £200 million.

CHAPTER FIVE

The Climate and Natural History

Camden described Cumbria's climate as being 'with the coldest as lying farr North'. In this he is less than accurate. But the myth persists. Winter visitors from the south of England still arrive heavily burdened with fleeces and overcoats, then wonder why. Average winter temperatures in Cumbria compare with those of the south and south-east of England, though the summer temperatures are cooler. Keswick's average January temperature (4°C) is similar to that of London and Edinburgh. Grange-over-Sands by Morecambe Bay can compare with England's south coast. The major factors are the prevailing west winds, and especially the nearness to a sea warmed by the gulf stream. This means that there are greater winter temperature contrasts between the west and east of England, than north and south. Also when much of low-lying England is sunk under a blanket of frost and fog, the higher lands of Cumbria can be bathed in winter sunshine. Winter can be a good time to visit the county. However, the scarcity of snow is a constant disappointment to winter sports enthusiasts. Cumbria has far lighter snowfalls than Kent, and when snow does fall it usually thaws quickly, lingering long only on the highest north- and east-facing fells, sometimes into June.

It has been said that Cumbria does not have a climate – it just has weather. Cumbria's weather is definitely something that cannot always be accurately forecast. Wordsworth advised visitors that July and August were not the best months to enjoy the Lakes. The months have that 'rainy weather, setting in at this period with a vigour, and continuing with perseverance, that may remind the disappointed and dejected traveller of those deluges of rain which fall upon the Abyssinian mountains, for the annual supply of the Nile'.

He recommends September and October visits, and he may have had a point. August rainfall averages 9 per cent of the annual fall. May and June are often favoured with better weather and have the advantage of long northern daylight. But it is absolutely impossible to generalize. There can be droughts in August, a source of anxiety to the many remote farms, and holiday establishments, that rely on local

Snow cornice, Coniston Old Man

springs for their water supplies. September can bring cloudbursts. Of course, geography text books state that the wettest place in England is Seathwaite in Lakeland's Borrowdale. More accurately, one might say that high above Seathwaite, on Seathwaite Fell, stands a rain gauge that records the highest average rainfall in England: 330 cm. But higher up the mountains beyond the gauge it might be as high as 450 cm! Moist Atlantic winds lifted by mountain currents are the cause.

But that is typical mountain weather. Away from the hills rainfall is surprisingly lower. Only a few miles down Borrowdale from Seathwaite the amount of rain diminishes, until at Keswick it is much less than half. The decline continues eastwards, away from the hills. Penrith, for example, has only a quarter of Seathwaite's rain. The same can be said of Langdale among its fells, and Windermere: twelve miles separate the two, but the figures are 430 cm for the former and 150 cm the latter. Figures show that the number of wet days in Cumbria, high fells apart, are no greater than in most parts of England. The higher amounts of rainfall are due to the fact that when it does rain it does so seriously – though the contrast, again, is between mountain and valley. Light rain can be a minor inconvenience to walkers perspiring in their waterproofs on the Windermere shore. At the same moment walkers on the Langdale fells can be battling with a deluge. Mountain rescue teams know that gale-driven rain provides more dangerous conditions for the fell walker than snow and ice.

Blea Tarn, Langdale

RIVERS AND STREAMS

It is hardly possible to generalize about the natural history of the rivers and streams, for they offer a very wide variety of habitats, depending on the speed of the moving water, amount of enrichment and the temperature. Salmon can be seen fighting their way upstream in several of the main watercourses, and trout can be seen at any time. Eels are common. They used to be a major export to the London market. Otters, previously scarce, are making a comeback. High mink populations have caused problems to angling interests, but their numbers fluctuate and they are easily controlled by trapping.

The freshwater shrimp, *Gammarus pulex,* is common, and stone-fly larvae of various species proliferate. Turn over a stone and there are invariably *Polycelis,* flatworms, adhering to their bases. These small creatures provide the food source for the ubiquitous dipper, *Cinclus cinclus,* the charming plump black-and-white bird that is able to immerse itself skilfully in swift moving water. The beautifully coloured kingfisher *Alcedo atthis* is seen more rarely, though it is often overlooked. It nests in sand or earth banks and suitable sites are uncommon in stony terrain.

LAKES AND TARNS

The amount of life in a lake depends on the degree to which it is 'eutrophic' (nutriment-rich) or 'oligotrophic' (pure with sparse nutriments). Obviously bird and fish life occupies the former habitat. Wastwater, the deepest lake at 80 m, and Ennerdale Water, are fed by streams directly from the fells and are subsequently pure but poor habitats. By extreme contrast eutrophic, shallow lakes, surrounded by farmland and settlements, such as Esthwaite Water, Rydal Water and Bassenthwaite Lake, sustain a rich community. The amount of life in the other lakes and tarns depends upon the degree to which they range between the extremes.

The amount of plant life varies with the type of bed. The commonest plant of the shallows are quillworts, *Isoetes*, a rosette-formed plant with quill-like leaves. In the deeper shallows grow long-stemmed plants, the pondweeds (*Potamogeton*). Some of them have broad leaves, some linear. An attractive one is Canadian waterweed, *Elodea canadensis*, with whirls of narrow leaves on long stems. Another is the very local Esthwaite waterweed, *Elodea nuttallii*. Many of the vital plant communities in the food chain – the microscopic algae – are not visible to the naked eye.

Much of the animal life of the lakes is also microscopic, but water dipping can reveal a wide variety of species: freshwater shrimp, snails and insect larvae. The

A frozen Derwent Water

fish are high in the food chain. The richer lakes usually hold perch, pike, eels and trout of various sizes. The purer lakes usually hold only trout, and an alpine cousin, the deep-water char, *Salvelinus alpinus willughbii*, a relic of the ice age that can survive only in water temperatures below 15°C. Char are found particularly in Windermere. Potted Windermere char was once a sought-for delicacy on the tables of the gentry in the seventeenth and eighteenth centuries. Perch, identifiable by their stripes and hunched backs, normally thrive in richer lakes where they feed on plankton and lake-bed animals. They grow in size to around 30 cm and can live to a decade. The torpedo-shaped pike is a carnivore that lives on other fish. They are present in many of the lakes, but have a preference for the cover of weeds and reed beds. Esthwaite Water is particularly rich in this species, and specimens up to 13 kg have been landed.

Roach and rudd, the coarse fish, prefer weedy areas in still bays. They may have been introduced by anglers using them as live bait. Among the smaller fish are the minnows, three-spined stickleback, the bull head and, in Esthwaite Lake, the stone loach. There are two rare species of fish found in only one or two of the lakes: the schelly, *Coregonus laveratus*, and its close relative, the vendace (*Coregonus albula*).

Obviously, the lake birds prefer the rich pickings in the reedier, shallower lakes, and the margins of the larger ones. The commonest nesters are coot and moorhens. Mallards are the commonest ducks, and red-breasted mergansers and mute swans are also easily seen. The great-crested grebe nests on Esthwaite Water. The little grebe, or dabchick, nests on small waters including hill tarns. One piece of welcome news came in 2001, when the first pair of ospreys for many years nested successfully in the Lake District. They chose Bassenthwaite Lake, and it is hoped that their numbers will increase. A viewing platform has been erected in the nearby forest. There are great varieties of visitors to the lakes. Cormorants head for rocky islands – they roost on island trees and feed on trout and perch. Herons are often seen standing motionless on the reed beds. Pochards and tufted ducks, teal and the goldeneyes, widgeon, scaup and goosanders enliven the scene further. Winter brings some of the unusual species, such as the great northern diver, *Colymbus immer*, the black-throated diver, *C. arcticus*, and the red-throated, *C. stellatus*. Greylag geese and barnacle geese are often seen. Canada geese have become resident and their great numbers can cause problems. For example, they graze the lakeside fields, which are valuable to the farmers as they give the first flush of spring grass.

At the margins of water, and in the mires, can sometimes be found the haunts of snipe, sedge and grasshopper warblers, as well as reed bunting.

Little grebe (Tachybaptus ruficollis) on nest, Esthwaite

Riverside purple loosestrife (Lythrum salicaria), Cunsey

Grass of Parnassus (Parnassis palustris), Tarn Hows

THE DALES

The largest animal in the lakes is the red deer. The heavier animals mainly occupy the rich feeding grounds of the south woodlands, particularly in the Rusland valley and in Grizedale forest. Their presence there has a long history, predating the arrival of man. They are also resident in Thirlmere forest, and in later years have wandered into the Grasmere area. The herds are very wary, and are easily startled by sound and scents, but can sometimes be seen at the beginning and end of the day in open areas. The quite different fell herds of red deer may have been introduced by landowners long ago. They are lighter animals adapted to life on the mainly treeless heights, and they live in the Martindale deer forest, wandering down onto the banks of Ullswater in winter, and often into Kentmere. The challenging roar of the red deer stag – and its rival's answer – can be heard in the quietness of the late-autumn rutting season, and if the air is still it is sometimes possible to hear the clash of antlers as they fight for mastery.

The other common, smaller deer is the roe. These are beautiful woodland animals, usually seen singly, or in small family groups. They can be anywhere, even in the gardens of Windermere. In Arnside and Grange-over-Sands their increase can create problems for gardeners. Relying on speed rather than caution

Red deer stag with hinds, Grizedale

Roebuck, Rusland Valley

when alarmed, they are often road casualties. Lacking the wolves of old, the deer species have no natural predators and occasionally expand their populations beyond available food supply. They then have to be culled, a task managed by the Forestry Commission and the Deer Society.

The red squirrel still lives in the broad-leaved woodlands. They are scarcer than they were, probably because their ideal habitat, Scots pine with undercover of hazel, is being lost. Although efforts are made to increase their numbers by feeding them, the arrival of the alien grey squirrel in 1876 into Cumbria makes their future precarious. The grey species breeds more prolifically than the red, and is a threat to its food resource. Badgers are common, being less persecuted than in the past. But even protection by law still does not shield them from the activities of the few badger diggers. The fact that bovine tuberculosis has been found in badgers has also led to farmers regarding them as pests, though there is no evidence that the animals spread the disease directly to cattle, rather than vice-versa. Gamekeepers are suspicious of them, although they eat mostly worms and beetles.

Foxes being highly adaptable to habitat and omnivorous are also very common. To what degree the sport of fox hunting controls their populations is debatable. Fox hunting in Cumbria is not for horse-riders. The terrain is too rough, and hunters must follow on foot, though nowadays most try to meet the chase by motoring to strategic positions on country roads, directed with the help of mobile phones. Rabbit populations rise and fall since the introduction of myxomatosis in the mid twentieth century. They are the main prey of stoats and weasels. In winter Cumbrian stoats have been seen to adapt their coat colouring to ermine – white with the tail end black. They are then embarrassingly conspicuous when there is no snow! The hare populations seem stable.

Seven species of bats reside in Cumbria. Adders (or vipers) are very common. This might alarm some, but in fact they are seldom seen as they usually take cover quickly on approach. Risk of bites from the poisonous snake is minimal; the odd incident usually results from one being picked up and handled. They are not more than 60 cm long. Harmless grass snakes can be twice as long as an adder, but are less common. It is sad that so many snakes are killed from ignorance. The attractive bronze coloured slowworm, which looks a little like a snake, but has a very small head, is an insectivorous legless lizard usually between 20 cm to 40 cm long. It is a gardener's friend as it eats slugs. The common lizard is found everywhere, best spotted on hot days when it makes a hasty retreat from basking on stones. The slowworm and the lizard have a trick of discarding their tail ends if caught. Predators are thus left with a snack, rather than a meal.

The big bird often seen soaring and gliding in the upper wind currents is the buzzard. Though often mistaken for the golden eagle, it lacks the size, powerful beak, head profile and the leg feathering.

Hoary rock rose (Helianthemum canum)on Limestone Crag, Scout Scar

THE FELLS

From the naturalist's point of view the fells might be regarded as deserts. Their soil, devoid of tree cover to hold and protect it, can be washed away by heavy rain, leached of nutrients, made unstable by alternate frost and thaw, and conditions of quick drying from wind and sun. Furthermore the fells have been subjected for centuries to the heavy grazing of sheep. That there is any ground flora at all it is surprising. Where soil has collected to any depth it is all too often blanketed by bracken, which is inedible to animals, prevents grass growth, and virtually impossible to eradicate.

The commonest plants on the thin soil are bent grasses and fescue. Nardus, the thin tough wiry grass, is very common on the high fells, as it is hardly touched by sheep. The most frequently seen flower is the small yellow tormentil, *Potentilla erecta,* once a valued herb to deal with 'the torments' – toothache, maybe. The clusters of tiny white flowers of heath bedstraw lie under grass in moist areas. The wetter areas are occupied by various mosses, often sphagnums and hair mosses. At lower levels the sundew obtains nitrogen, absent in the bog soil, by capturing and absorbing small insects on the red sticky hairs on its round leaves. Similarly the common butterwort traps insects in its rosette of tongue-like leaves, which curl round them.

The most common fern among the rocks on the fell is the mountain parsley fern, or mountain polypody, *Cryptogramma crispa*. In spring it is bright green and almost translucent. Often growing alongside is alpine lady's mantle, *Alcchemilla alpina*. These two plants flourish to an extent not found elsewhere in Britain.

The botanist in search of alpines must seek out the 'flushes' among the crags, where running spring water has flushed out the minerals trapped in the rock. Among the rich mosses there are sedums, several species of saxifrage and plants normally associated with wet woodlands.

The characteristic bird of the fells is the raven. Ravens can be seen riding the wind currents on the crag faces and uttering their 'kronk kronk', sometimes the only sound to break the silence of the high fells. Smaller birds include the meadow pipit and the wheatear. Upper moorlands sometimes have skylarks. The falcon of the Cumbrian fells is the crag-nesting peregrene. They are seen more often now that they are protected from persecution. The most exciting sight one can have is the vertical, wing-folded dive of the peregrine as it drops onto its prey. And since the late 1990s one has been able to enjoy the magnificent sight of golden eagles. Near Haweswater is the only eagles' nest left in England – and they were once common.

THE WOODLANDS

Wordsworth's description of the typical Cumbrian semi-natural woodland of his time is still valid today: 'The woods consist chiefly of oak, ash and birch, and here and there wych elm, with underwood of hazel, the white and black thorn, and hollies; in moist places alders and willows abound; and yews among the rocks.' He could have added gean (wild cherry), crab apple and rowan. After the ice ages, and before human settlement, these mixed woodlands once almost completely covered Cumbria to the heights of the mountains, but were almost totally destroyed over the many centuries of human exploitation. Occasionally one can find traces of tree roots in eroded ground on the highest fells. Wordsworth, whose perception of woodland history is remarkable, knew this:

> Formerly the whole country must have been covered with wood to a great height up the mountains; where native Scotch firs must have grown in great profusion, as they do in northern Scotland to this day. But not one of these old inhabitants has existed, perhaps, for some hundreds of years; the beautiful traces yet survive in the native coppice woods that have been protected by enclosures, and also in the forest trees and hollies, which, though disappearing fast, are yet scattered both over the enclosed and unenclosed parts of the mountains.

What he could have observed is that remnants of the old mountain woodland still survive in the gills, the deep ravines inaccessible to grazing animals. Trees continue to live and die there, and the ground flora is typical of woodland. One regrettable change since the poet's day is that the coppice woodlands are not generally maintained, being no longer profitable. Coppicing meant that trees were felled at around every ten to fifteen years, and fenced against animals to allow new growth. In very many places coppice has now been allowed to grow into mature trees, renewed growth is prevented by lack of light because of the dense canopy, and, lacking fence protection, tree seedlings are eaten by animals. The woods have beauty, no doubt. But without new growth they are ultimately in danger of decay. Efforts are being made by the National Trust, the National Park Authority, the Forestry Commission and other landowners to deal with the problem, sometimes returning coppice woodlands to profit.

The many beautiful woodlands in Cumbria are neither ancient nor truly natural, even though, as in some valleys, trees have grown there since prehistory. At some time they have been planted, including trees alien to Cumbria, such as the sycamore and beech.

Masses of bluebells or daffodils are the glory of many woods; their transformations are many, from the new greens of spring to the fires of autumn. The beauty of the Cumbrian woodlands are famous. The woods are typically dominated by sessile oaks – northern oaks – which favour uplands where the soil is mainly

Daffodils, Rydal

The ubiquitous 'Westmorland poppy' (or Welsh) (Meconopsis cambrica)

acid. The ground flora is less prolific and variable than in the open woodlands on limestone. Even so, the least managed woodland on acid soil can hold as many as seventy flowering species. In some of the woodlands, particularly on carboniferous limestone, yews are dominant. Less apparent to the uninitiated are the mosses, lichens and liverworts for which Cumbria woods are notable, some earning the woods protection as Sites of Special Scientific Interest. The woods typical bird communities consist of tits, treecreepers, woodpeckers (mainly greater spotted and the green), jays, goldcrests, chaffinches, nuthatches, wrens, woodpigeons, tawny owls, buzzards and sparrowhawks. Redstarts, pied flycatchers, wood warblers and tree pipits call by in the summer.

CHAPTER SIX

The National Park and the National Trust

The Industrial Revolution transformed not only the towns, it began to have an impact on the countryside. A feeling of alarm grew that some of the country's most beautiful areas could be destroyed for ever, not only by encroaching industrial enterprises, but by the changes made by uncaring rich new landowners, buying into the countryside and building incongruous palatial mansions, clearing woodlands and planting exotic trees. William Wordsworth expressed such a concern in his *Guide to the Lakes* (1835 edition). Under a chapter headed 'Changes, and Rules of Taste for Preventing their Bad Effects' he expressed his hope that control could be exercised to prevent the excesses of Lakeland landowners:

> In this wish the author will be joined by persons of pure taste, who, by their visits (often repeated) to the Lakes in the North of England, testify that they deem the district a sort of National Property, in which every man has a right and interest who has an eye to perceive and a heart to enjoy.

His concern and his hopes were shared by many.

THE NATIONAL TRUST

The first positive reaction came from three idealists in the latter part of the nineteenth century. Robert Hunter was solicitor to the Post Office and an active supporter of public causes, including the Commons Preservation Society. Octavia Hill was a formidable social reformer. Hardwick Rawnsley combined an extraordinary array of talents – as writer, poet, traveller, hill walker, lecturer,

A National Trust property, Tarn Hows

preacher and historian. He also happened to be the incumbent at Crosthwaite church in Keswick. The three concluded that the only way to preserve the beautiful landscape and places of historical importance for the public's benefit was to buy them. After a successful campaign to gain support 'The National Trust for Places of Historic Interest or Natural Beauty' was registered under the Companies Act on 12 January 1895. The first Lake District property, Brandelhow Woods, by the shores of Derwent Water, was subsequently bought by public subscription in 1902.

Further Cumbrian properties were acquired throughout the twentieth century. Thanks to the efforts of Canon Rawnsley, large parts of Borrowdale were taken into trust. Farms were added to the roster, many of them through the generosity of G.M. Trevelyan, the historian; as well as Beatrix Potter, the artist and children's writer, who wanted the Trust to preserve the local breed of sheep. But for this the Herdwick would certainly have died out in favour of more profitable breeds. Other notable acquisitions were the heights of parts of the Scafells, and Great Gable, given to the Trust by the Fell and Rock Climbing Club of the English Lake District as a war memorial after the First World War. The National Trust is now one of Britain's major charities. Trust ownership in Cumbria has grown considerably thanks to the public's financial support, and it is now the largest landowner in the Lake District National Park.

A National Trust farm, Little Langdale

THE LAKE DISTRICT NATIONAL PARK

Although it could be said that Wordsworth, in 1835, was one of the first to suggest that an area of beautiful countryside should have government protection, the National Parks Act was a long time in coming. While the United States acquired its first national park in 1872, Britain had to wait until 1949 – and it was a system far removed from the original concept.

Campaigns for the preservation of the beauty of the Lake District gained early impetus when the incursion of railway lines into the remote valleys was strongly opposed. John Ruskin, one notable objector, deplored the fact that the Lake District could become a 'steam merry-go-round'. Then when Manchester Corporation successfully gained a Bill to flood the Thirlmere Valley for water supplies it spurred a passionate debate involving bishops and statesmen. But campaigns became more focused after the First World War. The newly formed Forestry Commission acquired land at Thornthwaite, near Bassenthwaite Lake, in 1919 and began planting large blocks of alien conifer trees, and that was only the beginning.

In 1929 a government committee under Lord Addison enquired into the feasibility of a system of national parks. They could not follow the American prescription of total land ownership by the state, but nevertheless reached the conclusion that an Act ensuring preservation and access could be achieved. But the country was preoccupied by a severe economic depression and nothing happened.

Ironically it was the Depression in the early 1930s that gave momentum to the public campaign. Popularity in 'hiking' and rambling, away from the smoke of towns, had been growing fast. Special trains, with attractively cheap fares, were run to accommodate the huge parties. The large numbers of unemployed found some consolation from this form of recreation, but found that access to open countryside was often barred. The need for legislation to protect the beauty of open country – but also to make it available to all – became urgent. In 1932 a large organized protest about the lack of progress was staged in the Peak District. Many took part in a mass trespass of a privately owned grouse moor. Six walkers were taken from the crowd and arrested and imprisoned. It became a national scandal. This was followed by outdoor organizations coming together in 1936 to form the 'Standing Joint Committee for National Parks' in order to concentrate pressure. It still exists as 'The Council for National Parks'. The first result was an Access to Mountains Bill of 1939, but it had become so mutilated in its progress through Parliament that it became unworkable. Then the Second World War intervened.

After the war John Dower was authorized by government to make a report on the need for national parks. Dower defined a park as an area in which 'a) The characteristic landscape beauty is preserved; b) access and facilities for open-air enjoyment are amply provided; c) wildlife and buildings and places of architectural and historical interest are suitably protected; d) established farming use is effectively maintained'. Costs of implementation should come from national funds. There followed a Hobhouse Committee commissioned to suggest how to implement the Dower recommendations. The committee expressed the need for national parks thus: '... because this is a highly industrialised and heavily populated country, people need the refreshment that is obtainable from the beauty and quietness of unspoilt countryside'.

The report was accepted. A National Parks Commission would oversee and fund national parks with £50 million from the Land Fund to purchase open country if necessary. The fund would be replenished. The parks would have complete planning control of their areas. But the proposals ran into difficulties immediately. The county councils had been given planning authority under the 1947 Town and Country Planning Act, and they opposed an Act that would hand over the powers to a national park authority two years later. Objections came too from the Ministry of Agriculture and the Forestry Commission, both of which had been given certain exemptions from planning controls and wanted to keep them. A compromise was needed, but what resulted was almost a capitulation. The National Parks Commission would have only an advisory role. There would be no overall central funding, only limited support for defined objectives. (The £50 million pounds did not exist!) Farming and forestry would retain their privileges. The parks would have planning boards with complete control of the park; but the board membership would consist of two thirds county councillors, and one third government appointees. The county councils concerned would finance the administration and provide staffing. Funding would be provided to support projects such as the provision of new footpaths and access areas.

To pessimistic conservationists the arrangement was a recipe for disaster. It seemed to hand over national parks to their opposition. In fact the 1949 National Parks and Access to the Countryside Act had its good points. There were powers to negotiate access agreements with landowners. The widespread public rights of way would be defined on definitive maps and their use enjoy the force of law. Ten national parks were designated in England and Wales. The first national park to be designated was the Peak Park. The Lake District National Park was born second in 1951 and was the largest with 2,292 square km. After that time came gradual improvements. Funding improved, though the entire budget of all the national parks still compares unfavourably with London's parks! In 2003 the Lake District National Park Authority enjoyed the support of a substantial staff of administrators at its Kendal office, planning officers, field officers and maintenance staff, information staff and park rangers, totalling 188, with 307 trained

Wasdale Head, scene on which National Park logo is based

voluntary wardens. It has a National Park Visitor Centre at Brockhole on the shores of Windermere. A National Park Authority has two statutory purposes: 1) to conserve and enhance the natural beauty, wildlife and cultural heritage of the Lake District; 2) to promote opportunities for the understanding and enjoyment of the special qualities of the national park. And it also has a duty to foster the economic and social well-being of local communities within the national park.

As of 2003, the membership of the National Park Authority totals twenty-six, consisting of seven from district councils, seven from Cumbria County Council, five from parish councils, and seven appointed by the secretary of state. The bias towards local representation on a national park is open to question, but it is not really noticeable in policy decisions.

CHAPTER SEVEN

Walking in Cumbria

There are 11,625 km of public footpaths and bridleways in Cumbria, 7,500 km of them in the Lake District National Park, and there are many hundreds of square km of free-to-roam access. No other English county can offer so much. Many believe the Lake District is solely for fell walkers. In fact a walker could spend the best part of a lifetime of exploration without climbing the heights. Nor need the fells be climbed to enjoy the best viewpoints. All a walker needs, apart from stout footwear and sensible clothing, is a large-scale map (1:25 000 scale, or at least 1:50 000) and the know-how to read it, and a compass. The maps show the rights of way and the access areas. There are very many guidebooks for low-level walkers that give advice on where to go and what

Fell walkers on Great Gable

to see: so many that it is impossible to recommend individuals. All that one can say is that purchasing a guidebook needs caution. Most are fine, but it is easy to acquire one that suggests walks beyond the desire or capabilities of most people. Regrettably a few are written by macho walkers who think that anyone who cannot manage the mileages suggested is a wimp. A few guides can even be dangerous. One needs to remember that the typical rate of progress is three miles (5 km) per hour, and to that must be added one hour for every 450m of ascent. One should also add stop times for refreshment and photographs. Ten miles in all is a good starting distance for those who spend a mostly sedentary life indoors. Walking guides should include very clear maps or sketch maps.

To walk the fells requires general fitness, and some serious equipment. Fell guidebooks need careful choosing. Whichever is used it must not preclude the carrying of that large-scale map and compass. Here again, the choice is wide; but, of course, there is nothing to match the eight-volume pocket-size by Alfred Wainwright. However, what is important to remember is that these guides date back to 1955 and have never been revised. Paths and landscapes change. For instance, an ascent to Scafell is recommended via West Wall Traverse, but in 2002 mountain rescuers reported that the gully suffered a rock fall. Since then – and probably for years until the route stabilizes – it has been loose underfoot, and walkers ascending below someone who is advancing above could be hit by falling rock. Second, not all of the Wainwright routes are on public rights of way, and since the books were written some could have been physically obstructed. The prose is vivid, the instructions good and the sketch maps incredibly detailed, but the books should be treated with some caution.

Keep in mind that there is an element of risk in walking the fells. Fell walking should be an adventure, and adventure necessarily entails a modicum of risk – though it would be wrong to exaggerate it. Many thousands enjoy the Lakeland fells every year, summer and winter, without mishap. There are one or two obvious safety rules. Strong footwear is essential. Trainers are dangerous in wet conditions, and can be painful in rough terrain. Windproofs should be worn or carried. Because weather can change rapidly a waterproof jacket and overtrousers, plus spare warm clothing, food and emergency rations, and a torch in winter must all be carried.

In planning the walk reports on the local weather and conditions underfoot should be sought from the Information Service. Details of the route to be taken should be left with someone at 'base'. Though turning back from an ascent might be disappointing, it should always be considered if conditions deteriorate. There is a great difference between walking the fells on a fine summer day, and walking the same fells on the short days and rough weather of winter. Walking on ice is a very bad idea without an ice axe and the ability to use it.

To walk with a party and a guide? Many organizations, such as the Ramblers

Road sign at Cartmel

Association or the Countrywide Holidays Association, offer guided walks graded to suit all capabilities. The tourist information centres should have details of others. The National Park Authority runs mainly low-level walks, from a few hours to a whole day. In winter there are daily courses in the use of ice axes.

Mountain rescue teams of volunteers cover every fell area throughout the county. A team call-out is triggered by a call to the police.

CHAPTER EIGHT

Around Morecambe Bay: Arnside to Barrow

It has been suggested that the name 'Morecambe Bay' derives from the Brythonic Celtic root element *mori* ('sea'), and *cambo* ('curved'): 'a curved arm of the sea'. But this hardly captures it as well as the Gaelic *mor* ('big'), and *cambus* ('bay'): 'Big Bay'. At 17 km wide, from west Lancashire to the long Cumbrian peninsula of Furness, that is exactly what it is.

Bays have their attractions. Morecambe Bay is a particularly fine sight at lowering tide, when still long strands of water glisten between level fingers of wet sand. The bay is then a mirror to the sky and the changing light. If the sky is not too bright there are many reflected colours, either subtle pastel shades or streaks of bronze, changing through tints of orange to pink. Sometimes one can see a surprising pale green, blending to turquoise and blue. The colours are striated, streaked by the movement of the tide, like long brushstrokes. And in the mellow light of sunrise and sunset the bay can be a very special place.

It is of European importance for its wading birds, particularly in winter. The ubiquitous bird of the bay is the oystercatcher, and great columns of them follow the tidal fringe, their piping cry popping up everywhere, sometimes mingling with the bubbling call of the curlews. Great clouds of dunlin and knot sweep and turn about miraculously as one, before dropping in for their feed. Flocks of redshanks and ringed plovers join the winter feast.

It is not always calm. When the high tide is in, westerly gales can do what the seas have always been doing – battering, taking bites out of the shore and destroying property. At the Furness side concrete defences have been lifted and buckled more than once.

From the distant past until the coming of the turnpike roads in the later half of eighteenth century, and even beyond to the middle of the following century, the main way into Cumbria from Lancaster and the south was across these sands of Morecambe Bay at low tide. The route offered an obvious straight, smooth and

Morecambe Bay

level line, far far better than the roads around the bay. Where there were roads, they made wide detours and tortuous courses around swamps and rocks, and they were often potholed, muddy or dusty. But the crossing has always had its perils. From its starting point at Hest Bank, it requires one to cross the channels of the rivers Keer and Kent, and the fordable points are not readily identifiable, especially as the rivers have a habit of changing course. Mists too can easily obscure the route, and patches of quicksand add to the perils. But, above all else, the crossing has to be timed right. The tide tears in 'quicker than a galloping horse'. Over the centuries very many have been caught out by the tide, and memorials stand in Cartmel priory to some of the unfortunates. Parish records show more. But the unrecorded losses on the route over the centuries must be legion. In 1326 the abbot of Furness petitioned the king to allow him to have a

The bay from the south

coroner in Furness, because so many people had drowned crossing the sands to Lancaster to attend coroner's courts there. Many thousands must have chanced their luck on the sands without a guide. It is understandable. At low tide it looks easy and tempting, and there is no sign of the sea. But on the route from the south, the river channels are invisible until their banks are reached. If either crossing is too deep there might be no time for a retreat before the engulfing tide drives in.

The Lord was on the side of George Fox, preacher, religious reformer and founder of the Quakers, when in 1652 he crossed the sands with a companion without knowing the way. Observers on the shore saw them riding 'where no man had ridden before', and swimming their horses. Their survival was put down to witchcraft. John Wesley too, in the following century, was similarly blessed by providence, when, after preaching in Lancashire and arriving at Lancaster with a mission in Cumbria, he was told that it was too late to cross the sands. But he was too impatient to continue his work and off he went, and he made it. Wesley had other adventures in sand crossings and grumbled about the delays caused by the timing of the tides, but especially about unreliable advice –'especially as you have all the way to do with a generation of liars, who detain strangers as long as they can, either for their own gain or their neighbour's'.

Both preachers might have frustrated a gang of observers on the Cumbrian shore who, it was said, on seeing someone riding across the sands at the wrong time for the incoming tide, would cast lots as to which should later collect the saddle, the coat or the pack.

However, the worst tragedy of all occurred in modern times and did not involve travellers crossing on the ancient route. During the winter of 2003 and 2004 a very lucrative export trade in cockles brought many gangs of itinerant workers from other parts of Britain, who began harvesting the extensive cockle beds of the bay. At low tide hundreds of cockle pickers with quad bikes and trailers could be seen far out over the distant sands. Local fishermen who knew the bay well were warning that there could be a disaster. After a number of alarming incidents the worst happened. On the night of the twelfth of February a gang of Chinese immigrant workers was caught by an incoming tide. It was not possible for lifeboats and coast guard vessels to reach them in time, and only one man was saved. Twenty-one bodies were later recovered.

To go further onto the Furness peninsula and onto Cumbria's west coast one could find other crossings, all fraught with danger. One lay over the Ulverston Channel on the Leven Sands to Conishead Priory, then along the coastal sands to Aldingham.

A mid nineteenth-century diary by a William Fisher records:

> a mellancoly los of life 9 persons in attempting to Cros the Sands from Ulverstone to Cartmel on the 4 May got into what the call Black scare hole which is a hole 13 feet deep at Low Water the wear all in one Cart every one with the horse Perrished it was supposed that the weare the wors for licquor.

In 1857 twelve young Furness men seeking work, and on their way together to the hiring fair at Lancaster, never made it. A happier eighteenth-century account reads:

> the mind of the visitor is filled with a mixture of awe and gratitude, when, in a short time after he has traversed this estuary almost dry-shod, he beholds the waters advancing into the bay, and bearing stately vessels towards the harbour of Ulverston, over the very path which he has so recently trodden.

A further route goes over the Duddon Sands to the Irish Sea coast. Originally the monks from Cartmel Priory, Conishead Priory and Furness Abbey would act as guides across their reaches of sands. Then after the dissolution of the monasteries in 1536 and 1537 the responsibility for the main crossing fell upon the crown. The crown's guide is still appointed and lives at

Kents Bank, down the coast from Grange-over-Sands, where the crossing route from the south finishes; he traditionally marks the way with wands of evergreen branches.

In the eighteenth century writers describe the memorable sight of long trains of travellers crossing the sands, including coaches, carriages and carts, horse riders and pack ponies, and lines of pedestrians, children and dogs. J.M.W. Turner came to the Lakes by the same way. He painted two pictures of the remarkable scene. The route is still shown as a public road, but strategically placed notices offer dire warnings about using it without a guide. In spite of that there are still a few casualties from time to time, and not all of them are ignorant of the dangers. People familiar with the sands can make mistakes in mist.

On occasions today there are organized, guide-led walks across the sands at low tides. There are no carriages now, but the distant sight of the long caterpillar of walkers, often sponsoring some charity, could still inspire Turner.

Fishing the bay is recorded as far back as medieval times, when it was an important part of the economy of the religious houses. The main harvest was flat fish: 'flukes' or flounders were easily caught, as were whitebait and plaice. One method of catching all species of fish in past times was to lay hazelwood wicker-

Cedric Robinson, MBE, Queen's Guide to the Bay, marking the safe crossing with laurel wands

A guided walk across the bay for charity

work funnel traps. They were designed to capture fish on the ebb tide, the wide end facing up the bay. Of great importance too was the harvest of shellfish – cockles and mussels. At low tide mussels were prised from the rocks by a 'craam', a three-pronged rake, and collected in a 'tiernal' – basket. Or they were dredged. One method for catching cockles during the wintertime was by using a 'jumbo', a plank with long handles standing upwards at each end. The fisherman stood on the plank which he rocked by treading on alternate feet; by compressing the sand, he would cause the cockles to be squeezed to the surface.

But the shrimp harvest was also critical to the bay's economy. The primitive way of catching brown shrimps was by wading into the bay at ebb tide with hand-held nets. Later came boats, some of which had a boiler on board to cook the shrimps at once. Dredging with a net drawn behind a horse and cart also proved effective. Up until the 1970s it was a surprising sight to see horses working well up to their bellies, with only the cart top visible. Later tractors wholly superseded horses, and nowadays it is quad bikes. Morecambe Bay potted shrimps were once much sought-for by gourmets. The fisherman's household was enlisted to clean the cooked shrimps, then set them in butter with pepper and a touch of nutmeg. Cumbrian fishermen continue working the north of the bay from the Furness coast. Shrimping is not the industry it was, but potted shrimps may still be bought.

THE EAST SIDE OF MORECAMBE BAY

We start at the village of Arnside (pop. 2,410) at the south-eastern corner of Cumbria at the closing northern end of the Morecambe Bay sands. The river Kent channel flows through the sands past the town and it was for centuries navigable at high tide. The Vikings reached here; certainly, one Arn (?) had his *saetre*, or summer pastures, here. In the eighteenth and early nineteenth centuries Arnside's ships traded with Liverpool. They would sail up the channel with cargoes of saltpetre and sulphur for carting to Cumbria's gunpowder industries. They would land their cargo at Sandside and Milnthorpe, up river from Arnside. However after the railway came, in 1857 a 159-m viaduct was built at the northern end of Arnside to take it across the river Kent. Access for vessels beyond it was then cut off, so to compensate, the Ulverston and Lancaster Railway Company erected a pier for Arnside, replacing a wooden one. This was destroyed by a storm in 1934 and was rebuilt, then bought by the parish council for £100. This in turn was destroyed by a great January storm in 1983, and a new stone pier was constructed by public subscription and opened in 1984. It is a very pleasant place to sit on a fine day, and is used by anglers at high tides.

Arnside pier and estuary rail viaduct

Vessels were once built at Arnside. Crossfield's boatyard remained in production until 1938, turning out Morecambe Bay's light fishing boats – the 'nobbies'. With a draught of only four feet the little craft could sail through the shallows and were so sturdy that they could go herring fishing in the Irish Sea. Arthur Ransome had his small boat *Swallow* built at the yard, which inspired the series following *Swallows and Amazons* (1930), the incredibly popular tales of children's boating adventures.

The coming of the canals and railways, and improved road systems, meant that maritime Arnside became side-tracked, and had to be reinvented. Although the railway had done the main damage, it also offered its salvation. Rail access meant that it became a very modest and fashionable tourist resort. The town still attracts many visitors today, even though they don't stay as long as in the old days. It has also become a desirable place to live; it has spread up hill from the shore and has thrived. Housing is tucked away among the pockets of woodland and limestone outcrops.

Above the town with wide views across the bay is the fell of ARNSIDE KNOT (NT) (159 m). 'Knotts' (from the Scandinavian *knutr*, meaning a craggy hill) occur in various parts of Cumbria. Arnside's is a great hump of craggy limestone, offering pleasing broadleaved woodland walks and a wealth of differing viewpoints. Two have been cleared of obstructions and viewing indicator boards have been installed. Across the bay a great sweep of Lakeland hills can be seen, from Eskdale's Harter Fell in the southern prospect, to the other Harter fell above Kentmere in the north. Southwards there is a view over to Lancaster, Fleetwood and Morecambe, and eastwards into Yorkshire's Ingleborough and Whernside. The National Trust has opened up glades in the woodland to encourage butterflies, in particular the scarce Scotch Argus. Beyond the summit the Trust has preserved some fields, maintained in the old way without chemical fertilisers, and botanists can admire the limestone flora, once so common in the countryside fields, now alas so often destroyed by modern agriculture.

Below the knott on the south-east is ARNSIDE TOWER, a dramatic ruin still standing high. It is thought to date from the fifteenth century, when it was owned by the Stanleys, a prominent family in the north-west of England. Before that date the richer families, so far south from the border, probably felt themselves safe from Scottish raiders, and defensive towers were not deemed necessary. Robert the Bruce changed all that. After the English defeat at Bannockburn his armies came south through Cumbria, across Morecambe Bay, devastating, robbing and burning the shoreline settlements, and even entering Lancaster. The tower apparently suffered severe damage in 1602, for an entry in the registers of Lancaster Priory Church states 'That the 27th day of October at night being in the year of

Ruin of Arnside Tower

our Lord God 1602, being a mighty wind was Arnside Tower burned as it pleased the Lord to permit. (signed) Richard Townson, Minister.' A storm in 1884 blew down one of the walls.

There are some enjoyable walks in the area. From Hazelslack, south of STORTH, an intriguing and popular footpath goes over a wooded hill to Beetham. It climbs through two great limestone crags by 'Fairy Steps' and through a fissure in another. A warning to the portly – the fairies that built the steps were obviously quite slender.

The road alongside the bay runs past the grounds of Dallam Tower, a handsome house built around the 1720s that has been occupied by generations of

Wilsons. It is not open to the public, but there are paths run across the park, and from time to time the owners organize public events. The park contains fallow deer, and a classical Tuscan shelter has been built for them on the east side of the hill.

A crossroads with the A6 is met at Milnthorpe village, which, from the thirteenth century on, was a port until the railway viaduct at Arnside cut it off. A branch line from Arnside helped, but it was also eventually lost. Before the opening of the M6 in 1970 it was very heavy with traffic from the A6, which bisects the village. Its Friday market is 800 years old and is still going strong.

Turning back and going south of the old A6, BEETHAM, a small village, is reached. An interesting old church, dedicated to St Michael and All Angels, probably has Saxon origins, but the fabric appears Norman; the tower is twelfth century, as is the arcade of four bays. In the medieval glass in the windows is a portrait of a king, probably Henry IV. A north-west window depicts St Lioba, a British nun who worked as a missionary in Germany; the other shows St Osyth, queen of the East Saxons, who is alleged to have been martyred by Danish pirates. In the Civil War much damage was done by Cromwell's troops, including the defacement of two effigies on a tomb chest. It is said that they used the church to stable their horses, and another story claims that the troops were encouraged in their vandalism by a mob of scholars led by their master from Beetham School.

The now redundant Beetham free grammar school was founded in the seventeenth century, but the existing buildings date from 1827 and enterprising locals (the South Lakeland Stage and Screen Society) have transformed it into the 'Heron Theatre', which has a busy programme of drama and music. A raked auditorium sits eighty, and there is a sophisticated lighting and sound system.

Beetham has a busy paper-making factory by the river. A museum of the industry is housed in the old water mill.

South of Beetham is HALE and by the A6 the Wildlife Oasis, a kind of intelligently organized educational mini-zoo that should fascinate children of all ages.

The old branch railway line served HEVERSHAM, just north of Milnthorpe. The town has ancient origins and is still a thriving community. The twelfth-century church has been Victorianized, but snatches of early structure and ornamentation remain, such as the shaft of a ninth-century cross. The grammar school was founded in 1613, and still has a high reputation. Richard Watson (1737–1816) was born in the village and educated at the school and at Cambridge, where he eventually became Regius professor of divinity, but also the bishop of Llandaff. He established himself at Windermere and lived there in style while delegating all his ecclesiastical duties to a deputy. He was well known to the Lakes poets.

LEVENS HALL is by the crossing of the River Kent on the A6. The hall is to the west of the bridge, the park to the north-east. The park contains a herd of fallow deer, which, in contrast to those of Dallam Tower, are almost black. The delightful Elizabethen house is open to the public. Like many of the big old houses of Cumbria it has its original thirteenth-century defensive pele tower, the rest of the building having been built on to it. Originally owned by the de Redmans family, it was sold in the sixteenth century to the Bellinghams. James Bellingham, during his long life there, extended and improved the hall and installed panelling and plastering in some of the rooms. The grandson of James Bellingham lost the estate through gambling debts and it came into the possession of Colonel James Graham in the seventeenth century. It was during the colonel's ownership that the garden was made. On his death the property passed, through marriage,

Topiary garden at Levens Hall

to Henry Bowes Howard, earl of Suffolk, and again through marriage to the Bagots, who are still there.

The hall contains some fine antiques, portraits and miniatures, and relics of the battle of Waterloo. In the south drawing room the carved oak overmantel, supported by figures of Hercules and Sampson, is a masterpiece, depicting the four elements, the four seasons and the five senses. Some of the wall coverings are made of decorated goatskin, dating from the late seventeenth century. The outbuildings contain a collection of model steam engines.

But it is the amazing garden that has attracted so many thousands of visitors over the years. The design has hardly changed since Monsieur Beaumont, a celebrated gardener, began devising it from 1690. His skills were in demand by many peers and landowners, and his past clients included King James II; but in spite of

Topiary garden at Levens Hall

that he chose to stay working for Colonel Graham at Levens Hall for forty years until his death in 1730. To walk in the garden today is to enjoy a design on what appears to be a grand scale, but which is actually modest in size. Delight can be found in its mixture of formality and curiosity, shifts of perspective, and places of quiet seclusion. But the extraordinary yew topiary is what most come to see. It has a dreamlike Alice-in-Wonderland miscellany of strange forms, spirals and globes, swirls and crowns, cones, blocks, rings and birdlike forms. What does it mean? If the intention is to make one smile and feel good – it works.

The hall once brewed its own notoriously strong beer called 'Morocco', oddly enough, and in recent years it has been resurrected and put on sale.

THE NORTH SIDE OF THE BAY

The A590 for the Furness area leaves the A6 at Levens Bridge and soon crosses the River Gilpin to enter the National Park. This is low-level country and at one time Morecambe Bay must have covered much of it before being blocked by accumulations of river silts. The road is not all that old and had to be built over bunches of hazel rods on boggy land. It is the main road between Furness and Kendal, but the original route, which avoided the wet land, went tortuously over the Cartmel Fells. Some of the land to the south of the road is in a Site of Special Scientific Interest (SSSI). Foulshaw and Meathop mosses are raised bogs in the care of Cumbria Wildlife Trust. Raised peat bogs have become rare as they have been cut into in the past for fuel, or drained for agriculture. The structure of the wet land offers an environment for scarce bog plants and numerous insects.

The road bypasses the village of LINDALE, after passing the house of CASTLEHEAD. John Wilkinson (1728–1808), the son of a Cumbrian farmer turned iron master, made his home here. Father and son developed iron furnaces in Cumbria and then in other parts of the country, and the Industrial Revolution owed a great deal to their enterprise. At Broseley, near Coalbrookdale in Shropshire, John cast the parts for Coalbrookdale bridge, the world's first iron bridge ever to be built. He also cast iron barges and iron boat hulls when most people expected iron boats to sink. He decreed that on his death he should be buried in an iron coffin. A story got abroad that seven years after his death he would rise from his resting-place and visit his blast furnaces. A large crowd assembled to see his resurrection, but apparently his iron box was too comfortable to leave. By the roadside at Lindale is his monument – uniquely of cast iron of course. Castlehead is now a field study centre.

The National Park boundary is left just before GRANGE-OVER-SANDS (pop. 4,160). Its omission from the park is strange as there is nothing about the fine small town that could suggest a reason for exclusion. It is good to arrive by train because the splendid little station, a grade two listed building, is preserved in as colourful a style as it was when it was built in 1863, six years after the railway came to the village.

The 'Ulverstone and Lancaster Railway Company' acquired legal status in 1851. Financial backing came chiefly from Lancashire farmer turned Manchester businessman, John Brogden, and his sons. Its secretary was James Ramsden, an engineer whom we will meet later at Barrow. The railway's chief function was the transport of iron ore from Furness to the ironworks at Staffordshire, and coke from Wigan to the blast furnaces at Barrow.

The line came into the ownership of Furness Railway Company in 1862, of which James Ramsden was managing director. The company acquired much of the land along the sea front, and landscaped the area, as it was deemed possible to develop the town as a first-class holiday resort. Styled the 'Montpelier of Lancashire', the town was no stranger to visitors. A guide of 1847 had stated: 'climate especially beneficial to those suffering from weakness of the lung – a favourable winter and spring asylum for consumptive invalids'.

Grange as a genteel resort, 1890

Advertising was expected to boost its popularity – for instance, the presence of spa water at nearby Humphrey Head. The railway built the very pleasant mile-long promenade still enjoyed by walkers, whether with weakness of the lung or not. Facilities were scarce for holiday visitors, so Ramsden and Brogden founded the Grange Hotel, which featured a therapeutic pool of seawater, pumped by steam engine from the bay, and it was up and open by 1866. Grange also lacked a gas supply – so Ramsden and Brogden set up the Grange and Cartmel Gas &

Water Company, and a gas works was built east of the town at Meathop. The first customer, of course, was the Grange Hotel. The company failed to provide water, and the town had to rely on individually owned water sources until 1879.

Although the resort enjoyed a good start, with visitors staying the whole season, it was never a roaring success. More hotels were built, and in season they filled, but it would never be as popular as the Lancaster coast rivals. It is hard to believe that at one time pleasure boats plied their trade between two piers, and that pleasure boats came regularly to Grange from other places. The sad fact is that Grange's shore has silted up. The 'over sands' has been a misnomer for at least two decades since spartina grass invaded the shallows. What was once an expanse of sand is now pasture for sheep. This has much to do with a change in the pattern of channel currents. The river Kent channel used to sweep round close to the Grange shoreline. Some place part of the blame on the building of a causeway to Holme Island (where the Brogdens chose to live). However, Grange is an attractive place with a line of inviting canopied shops facing a small park with interesting mature exotic trees, and a large pond on which a colourful variety of duck and geese species are cared for. No buildings in Grange are older than nineteenth century, but what remains is classy. The elaborate clocktower at the top of the main street was built in 1912. Grange is an up-and-down place, yet very popular for the retired, and it still

'The Hospice' on Hampsfell

accommodates holidaymakers that use it as a base for exploring the Lakes, but it deserves more.

Above the town is the limestone hill of Hampsfell, and on the summit stands a 'hospice', a small tower built by a 'former pastor of Cartmel parish for the shelter and entertainment of wanderers over the fell'. A line of steps leads up to the excellent viewpoint on its roof, and entertainment comes in the form of verse panels in the interior. The view over Morecambe Bay is fantastic. Over to the west is Black Combe, and a panorama of the fells including the Coniston Old Man range, Scafell Pike, Langdale Pikes and Helvellyn.

CARTMEL is a village that should really have been in the National Park, but this too is strangely excluded. Inland to the west of Grange, this delightful unspoilt village features seventeenth- to nineteenth-century houses clustered round yards, and a peach of an old village square, unfortunately hardly visible as it is constantly used as an informal car park. The place has a warm, friendly feeling about it – and two seductive second-hand bookshops. But the pride of the village, indeed of the whole of south Cumbria, is the ancient priory church. Sometimes called 'the cathedral of the Lakes', it is a gem.

Legend has it that the monk who founded Cartmel Priory was told in a dream to go to the place between two streams that flow in opposite directions. Actually the priory was founded in 1190 by William Marshall (who later became second earl of Pembroke) for the Canons Regular of St Augustine. With it came all the lands in Cartmel district, which included land to the east side of Windermere, and at Kinross in Ireland. Marshall also decreed that an altar should be provided, along with a priest for the local people.

Little is known about the priory except that at one time its buildings lay to the south of the church; then, perhaps in the fourteenth or fifteenth century, the buildings were rebuilt in the north. Were the original buildings burnt by the Scots? What is known is that at the dissolution the earls of Derby and Sussex, acting as Henry VIII's commissioners, confiscated all the lands and did a very thorough job of destroying the priory. Everything of value was removed. Although the lead was removed from its roof, the church itself was saved by the production of documentary evidence showing that the founder had ordained an altar and a priest be provided for the local people. Commissioners were not authorized to destroy parish churches, so a portion of the church, the south aisle, had to be maintained for the purpose. The rest of the priory was subsequently treated as a quarry, and many buildings in the area contain priory stone. All that is left is a gatehouse.

The church, other than the south aisle, was open to the weather and it was not until 1620 that a benefactor, George Preston of Holker, arrived to make repairs. With help from parishioners he had the church roofed, and presented the church

Cartmel Priory church

with its very fine Renaissance screens and stall canopies. The seventh duke of Devonshire undertook further restorative work in 1850.

What we see now is a mixture of architectural styles because the priory was founded in a transitional period. The huge east window dates from the mid fifteenth century. Surviving medieval glass includes the Virgin and Child, and John the Baptist. Some of the glass has been removed to a window at St Martins Church at Bowness-on-Windermere. Work on the nave and tower was done in the fifteenth century but the nave is short and built with irregular stones implying a shortage of funds.

There is a fine example of Norman dog-tooth moulding on the arch of the north door. A pointed arch on the east side of the north transept is typically Gothic, yet the chevron moulding is Norman. Beyond it, before the vestry, is the

Cartmel Street leading to the fourteenth-century Priory Gatehouse (NT)

'piper choir', so called because the pipes of the early seventeenth-century organ, another gift of George Preston, were placed here. Its roof is the only surviving portion of the original structure. The tower has a touch of eccentricity; a first tower raised in height by another tower set diagonally above it.

The misericords in the choir stalls are beautifully carved in oak. There are brackets on the underside of the hinged seats, and when it was necessary to turn the seats up, when the monks had to stand for long periods, they offered support. The woodcarvers' sense of humour is evident from the mermaid with two tails; an ape doctor; a number of grotesque faces; carvings of Alexander's flight; the Trinity; a pelican in piety; an elephant and castle; a unicorn; and intricate foliage.

The oldest tomb intact belongs to the first Lord Harrington, who died in 1347, and his wife. There is an effigy of an unknown priest. Some of the tablets in the floor are interesting, such as the memorial to a young man drowned in the bay, and one to his mother, who not long afterwards was drowned in the same place. Among early treasures owned by the church is a first edition of Spenser's 'The Faerie Queene'. Stolen in 1929 and taken to the United Sates, the book proved 'too hot' to find a buyer and found its way back to the police in Suffolk, oddly enough, who returned it to the church in 1931. Other curiosities include an ancient umbrella, claimed to be one of the first made, and a Vinegar Bible of 1716 (so called for a misprint in the heading of Luke 20: 'Vinegar' should read 'Vineyard'). In the vestry the parish registers date from 1559 and are almost complete.

Buried in the churchyard lies William Taylor, Wordsworth's schoolmaster from his Hawkshead grammar school days. The rather slender headstone, with its inscription from the final stanza of Gray's 'Elegy', is slightly to the western side of the churchyard behind a modern pink granite stone. The teacher's influence on William was enormous, for he encouraged his pupils to try to compose poetry as a means of discovering the craftsmanship of the great poets. William sought out, and found, his old master's grave when he was crossing the sands to visit his sister Dorothy at Rampside in 1794.

> A plain stone, inscribed
> With name, date, office, pointed out the spot,
> To which a slip of verse was subjoined,
> (By his desire, as afterwards I learned).
> A fragment of the Elegy of Gray.

He admitted shedding a few tears, and he remembered

> He loved the poets and if now alive
> Would have loved me as one not destitute
> Of promise nor belying the kind hope
> Which he had form'd, when I at his command
> Began to spin, at first, my toilsome songs.

Cartmel caters for the secular too. At the opposite end of the village from the church is the very popular racecourse, which holds meetings that transform the village twice a year.

South-west of Grange we come to ALLITHWAITE where we turn off west down a narrow lane (signposted 'Humphrey Head' and 'Holy Well') to reach the cliff-sided peninsula of limestone that stretches out into the bay. By the side of the narrow lane is Wraysholme tower, a fifteenth-century pele tower now attached to a farmhouse that was once the seat of the Harringtons. Sir Edgar Harrington, so it is said, killed the last wolf in England hereabouts. The last 'last wolf'? Or one of the earlier 'last wolves'?

Soon one reaches Humphrey Head, one of the only two sea cliffs of Cumbria. This one is of limestone. Famous for a spa spring, the Holy Well, since Elizabethan times, Camden refers to it in his *Britannica*. The water here was 'a certain cure for gout and various skin diseases; and in general debility arising from blood poisoning'. It is said that lead miners made long journeys to the well as it was reckoned to cure lead poisoning. An analysis by a Professor Thorpe in the nineteenth century yielded per gallon: six key chemicals of sodium, lime, magnesium and potash. Thousands sampled the water brought to nearby Grange, and it was even on sale to holidaymakers at Morecambe across the bay at sixpence a glass. So where is it now? The presence of the famous Holy Well, the focus of centuries of pilgrimages from far and near, the cure-all of Victorian times, is revealed by a depressingly tatty notice warning that the water is unfit to drink; and the vandalized remains of a ceramic butt. The spout has gone and a small pipe is all but lost among rock debris.

Further along the cliff side is a memorial stone affixed to the precipice with a warning:

Beware how you these Rocks ascend
Here WILLIAM PEDDER met his end
August 22nd 1857 Aged 10 years
By permission

Humphrey Head itself is now an important nature reserve (CWT) of twenty-three ha. The vegetation on the cliffs includes uncommon species such as hoary rockrose, green-winged orchid and the rare Lancastrian whitebeam tree. It is a good viewpoint over the bay.

Moving west we come to FLOOKBURGH (*Fluke-burra*), for centuries a base for bay fishermen. During the war a Flookburgh man in the Royal Navy was asked by his officer if they were in a good place to drop a depth charge to get some fresh cod. 'Try it', said the Flookburgh man. The charge was dropped, but not a single fish surfaced. 'I thought you were a trawlerman!' complained the officer. 'Aye, sir,' was the reply, 'but I trawl wi' a horse and cart!' Fresh bay shrimps and fish – they could hardly be fresher – can still be bought in the village.

The next village is CARK in the estate of HOLKER HALL, part of which, with its gardens and motor museum, is open to the public in season. A local argument goes on about how it should be pronounced – some say 'Hooker', the majority insist 'Holker'. The hall is not one of those places where visitors feel they are there under sufferance. The lack of ropes or barriers makes one feel refreshingly welcome. Built mainly of imposing red sandstone, the house is now essentially Victorian, though originally owned by the Preston family in the sixteenth century. George Preston, as already mentioned, was the benefactor who saved Cartmel Priory church from ruin. His grandson died without male heir and the estate came to his daughter, who had married Sir William Lowther. Their grandson died unmarried in 1756 having bequeathed the estates to a cousin, Lord Cavendish. The present owner is Mr Hugh Cavendish, who with his wife occupies an old wing that was the original home of the Prestons. The rest of the magnificent hall was built for William Cavendish, seventh duke of Devonshire, early in the nineteenth century. It was the duke who was responsible for the initial design of the gardens and the beginnings of the splendid arboretum.

Holker Hall

In March 1871 a fire destroyed the whole of the west wing, with its priceless works of art. With little waste of time the duke had a new replacement built that was modelled on the Elizabethan style by E.G. Paley and H.I. Austin, the outstanding architects of the North-west. It is this lavishly furnished and decorated wing with its art treasures that is open to the public. There is much to enjoy. The colour harmonies of the room decorations are immediately striking. The fireplaces are exceptional, too. One is framed by fine carvings in Carrara marble and another by oak pillars carved by local craftsmen. The library contains 3,500 volumes, among which are books by the scientist Henry Cavendish (1731–1810), who discovered the properties of hydrogen; the Cavendish Laboratory at Cambridge is named after him. Among many art treasures can be seen a screen embroidered by Mary, Queen of Scots, during her detention. It is strange, and if it was Mary's own design it should interest psychologists.

The motor museum's collection is among the best, a reminder that at one time motoring was an adventure. The beautiful gardens, enclosing an area of woodland, occupy 11 ha and are finest in early summer. A fountain and waterfall is a central feature of the woodland garden, and here is an arboretum with a collection of some rare and old specimens, plus new ones planted for future generations. Old lime trees are amazingly obese. A lofty chile pine, probably planted in 1837, was blown down in a storm in the 1890s, then pulled upright with the help of chains and seven horses, then re-secured to continue thriving.

Herds of fallow and red deer graze in the grounds, and wild roe deer make the occasional visit. Throughout the summer there is often something going on in the grounds: garden festivals, family activities, hot-air balloon events, rallies and competitions.

THE FURNESS PENINSULA

To the west of Cartmel Sands the long Furness peninsula represents the entire west wall of Morecambe Bay. It is a country on its own and traces of its unique dialect can be detected in the conversation of older inhabitants – Lancashire with a touch of Merseyside?

ULVERSTON (*ULVER-st'n* – dialect 'Ooston') (pop. 11,970) is a small friendly country market town immediately across Cartmel Sands, and was once reached by a low-tide highway across it from Cark; it is still a right of way but dangerous without a guide. The route from Kendal crossed the wandering switchback heights of Cartmel Fell to the foot of Windermere, and thence across the flats of Haverthwaite and Greenodd. The busy A590 road to Barrow-in-Furness – what was supposed to be a by-pass – goes right through the town, though at least it avoids the market centre. The town has had its ups and downs, a few scars show and it is not pretty, but it was never meant to be. The alleyways and yards that once had a purpose now seem like oddities, but the fine old cobbled market street still comes to vigorous life on market days, Thursdays and Saturdays. New local industries have brought a shot in the arm for the local community. A pharmaceutical plant has long been an important employer.

Ulverston was once the most important town in south Cumbria. The late eighteenth century and early nineteenth centuries saw a great increase in its industries, and its population grew to 50,000 – over four times greater than today's. The driving force came from local natural resources – iron ore at nearby Newlands; charcoal for the town's furnaces from the woodlands in nearby High Furness; and water power. To this was added a less natural advantage. In 1795 a scheme was launched to make the town a port by linking the town to the bay using a mile-long canal. The famous engineer John Rennie (1761–1821), master dock and bridge builder, directed the work and a year later the canal was opened with a grand procession led by a fiddler and a piper. The canal gave Furness a port, while Barrow on the Irish Sea coast remained a fishing village. In 1847 it was recorded that the port of Ulverston was capable of taking vessels

Ulverston Market Street

with '400 tons burthen which are discharged on the extensive wharfs erected close to the town, where there is a capacious basin'. The average number of vessels cleared was around 600 each year. In 1846 the port cleared 946 ships, and a maritime colony grew around the basin. Shipbuilding became a new industry, and ships' ironmongery – chains, bollards, anchors – were also made locally. The town had many mills and manufactured goods including cotton, linen-check, canvas, sailcloth, sacking, hats and spades. Slate from the quarries of Furness was exported from the port, along with iron ore, local leather, wool, grain, butter and gunpowder. A lively social life sprang up, and a local theatre played to packed houses.

The hugely successful growth of the town had an effect on other towns in Furness. Ulverston took all the trade from the surrounding area, killing permanently the markets of Broughton in Furness, Hawkshead and Cartmel.

The boom ended almost as quickly as it was born. The development of more efficient coke furnaces outstripped the technology of those in Ulverston. But it was the railway, often the engine of commercial expansion, that sealed the town's fate. The railway came in 1856 when the iron financiers were seeking to exploit new-found resources, and it was intended to serve the newly created town of Barrow-in-Furness, with its iron mines, port, new docks and steel industry closer to the sea. All too soon it became apparent that the railway was taking trade away

Remains of lock, Ulverston Canal Head

from the port of Ulverston. The town's fate was sealed once the Furness Railway Company purchased the canal and allowed it to silt up, and big companies bought up the town's small furnaces. They regarded them as inefficient and uneconomic and closed them. Only a few of the small industries survived, and most of the population migrated.

Sir John Barrow (1764–1848), under-secretary to the Admiralty for forty years, was one of Ulverston's more famous inhabitants. Born in a cottage still preserved in the town, he went to sea in a series of epic journeys when nineteen, and later became a teacher of mathematics at Greenwich. One of the books he wrote was the popular *Voyages of discovery and research within the Arctic regions* (1846). His monument (1850), in the form of a 30 m-high imitation of Eddystone Lighthouse, stands on Hoad Hill (132 m) and could hardly be missed. It is easily reached by a winding path and gives good views across the bay.

Another Ulverstonion of note was Norman Birkett, later Lord Birkett, a judge at the Nuremberg trials of the Nazis after the Second Word War. He was a Lakeland enthusiast, a driving force in conservation, successfully modifying the plans to treat Ullswater like a reservoir, and opposing the flooding of Bannisdale. Another famous son was Stan Laurel, born in the town in 1890 and one half of the hugely popular American screen comic duo in the 1930s. A small Laurel and Hardy museum shows some of the vintage films that still raise a laugh. As of 2003 plans are afoot to erect a bronze statue of the two comics somewhere in the town centre.

The Coronation Hall ('the Coro') is the centre of the town's cultural life, and there are concerts, plays, ballet and opera offered by touring companies. They are always well booked.

On The Ellers, near the town centre, is a remarkable modern building, whose design won an award from the Royal Institute of British Architects. It is surmounted by a lattice-work 'lantern'. The 'Lantern House' contains the office of Welfare State International, a company of artists, musicians and poets whose object is to 'pioneer new approaches to the arts of celebration and ceremony in the UK and internationally'. The aim is to involve the public as collaborators in art as well as spectators. With refreshing enthusiasm, they organize community carnivals, shows, theatre, and courses and workshops at home and abroad. One of their spectacular successes is the masterminding of community-made lantern processions, and a grand display occurs in Ulverston every autumn. Indeed Ulverston likes to describe itself as 'the Festival Town'. The town also has a flag festival, in which the town centre is full of banners designed by local children, and the Christmas-themed market is masterly for such a small place.

Walkers head out for the Cumbrian Way from here, and it is on the route of the Cumbria Coastal Way. A hostel, not far from the canal head, serves both routes.

On the west side of Ulverston is SWARTHMORE. Lambert Simnel's forces camped here in 1487 as part of their futile attempt to claim the throne from Henry VII. Swarthmoor Hall is visited by many people at home and abroad, for in the seventeenth century here lived George Fox (1624–1691), founder of the Religious Society of Friends (Quakers from 1675). Fox was a fearless preacher who believed passionately that 'there is that of God in every man'. Priests and churches (he called them 'steeple houses') were unnecessary; anywhere that Christians gathered, he maintained, could be a place of worship. He argued that a prescribed order of worship was an obstacle to worship itself, and that a meeting for worship need only seek for truths in silence. If and when moved by the spirit, anyone present could speak. He was opposed the taking of oaths, for that implied that there were two kinds of truth. Such a man with boundless energy and a strong personality won thousands of converts. But at a time when attendance at the established church was obligatory, it also made him many enemies. Ulverston did not treat him well. At times he was set upon and beaten. But the owner of Swarthmoor Hall, Judge Fell, was a fair man, if not wholly convinced by Fox's philosophy, and the preacher and his friends were given hospitality at the hall, which was later used as a base. Judge Fell died in 1658 and eleven years later Fox married his widow, Margaret, who was wholly convinced and committed to the society. Fox was never at the hall for long, however. He was either on his mission elsewhere, visiting society members or in prison, whether for denouncing the established church, encouraging the non-payment of tithes or refusing to take an oath of allegiance. Margaret, too, had her share of prison at a time when prison conditions were vile and life-threatening. The Swarthmoor Meeting House, the seventeenth-century Quaker place of worship, dated 1688, can be reached down the lane to the east of Swarthmoor Hall. The hall is occasionally open to the public, and it also provides accommodation and convenes courses.

Signs of Ulverston's former shape can be seen. The canal's bank is used as a public footpath to the bay. St Mary's church is the town's oldest building with some evidence of a twelfth-century structure. During the depression of the 1920s and 1930s unemployed Furness men were used to build a coastal road from Ulverston to Barrow, which gives good access to the coastline of the bay.

Kadampa Buddhist Temple, Manjushri Mahayana Buddhist Centre, Conishead Priory

The first place of interest reached from Ulverston on this road is CONISHEAD PRIORY. Though no sign remains of the old priory, on its site in 1823 Col. R.G. Braddyl built a gothic mansion, whose grounds were planted with exotic trees. The owner got into financial difficulties and the building passed through several hands. When it was a hydropathic hotel in 1882, with its own golf course, it had the distinction of being served by a railway line from Ulverston. Actually the plan was to continue the line to Barrow via Roose, but the project was abandoned at the priory, and is, of course, no more. The mansion was later used as a convalescent home for Durham miners. It is now open to the public on some days (enquire at tourist centres), but what will strike a visitor at once is that the welcoming guide will be wearing a saffron robe, for the property is now a Manjushri Mahayana Buddhist centre. The Buddhists have preserved a magnificent house that was fast falling to rack and ruin. The wooded grounds extend to the beach, which is kept as a nature reserve. But near the house a gorgeously colourful Kadampa Buddhist temple was built in 1995 by the 'disciples of the Venerable Geshe Kelsang Gyatso' and opened in 1997, 'Dedicated to the peace and harmony of all living beings in this world'. It is the scene of spring and summer festivals that attract thousands of Buddhists from all over the world.

Opposite Conishead in the bay is CHAPEL ISLAND, a ridge of limestone that holds a fragment of the chapel remains. In his 'Prelude' Wordsworth recalls a crossing of the sands when on his way to Rampside:

> Upon a small
> And rocky island near, a fragment stood
> (Itself like a sea rock) the low remains
> (With shells encrusted, dark with briny weeds)
> Of a dilapidated structure, once
> A Romish chapel, where the vested priest
> Said matins at the hour that suited those
> Who crossed the sands at ebb of morning tide.
> Not far from that still ruin the plain
> Lay spotted with a variegated crowd
> Of vehicles and travellers, horse and foot,
> Wading beneath the conduct of their guide
> In loose procession through the shallow stream
> Of inland waters.

But the reason the incident was etched on his mind for a lifetime was more topical. For it was there that he heard a momentous piece of news that meant a very great deal - almost everything to him. Wordsworth had supported the

French Revolution during his stay in France, but had watched with grief and horror the bloody takeover by radicals that also saw the execution of the moderates he had supported. It troubled his conscience.

> I paused
> Unwilling to proceed, the scene appear'd
> So gay and cheerful, when a Traveller
> Chancing to pass, I carelessly inquired
> If any news were stirring; he replied
> In the familiar language of the day
> That, **Robespierre was dead**. Nor was a doubt,
> On further question, left within my mind
> But that the tidings were substantial truth;
> That he and his supporters had fallen.
> Great was my glee of spirit, great my joy
> In vengeance, and eternal justice, thus
> Made manifest. 'Come now ye golden times'
> Said I, forth-breathing on those open Sands
> A hymn of triumph, 'as the morning comes
> Out of the bosom of the night, come Ye –

Two km along the road one arrives at the village of BARDSEA, once a minor seaside resort, from which one gains a good view of the bay. Father West, author of the Lake District's eighteenth-century guidebook, states, 'the site of Bardsea is romantic, the aspect good, and well sheltered by rocks and woods from every blast, having an easy descent to the south, or a bold shore and pleasant beach'.

A narrow beach road leads to a small headland. Now known locally as Kingfisher Lane, it was once called Red Lane because carts carrying iron ore went along it to one of two shipping jetties, the ends of which can be seen, as faint lines at low tide. Before the area developed more of its own smelters, large quantities of ore from the area was shipped to South Wales.

Bardsea had a pier in the mid nineteenth century, from which steam packets sailed to Fleetwood five times each week, and to Liverpool weekly. The steamer service brought trippers from Fleetwood, to be met by transport to the Lakes. The scene at the time was described by a local: 'steamer at pier, and the multifarious vehicles for conveying the passengers – the unprepossessing "bus", the inelegant tub car, and the much more picturesque donkey shandry-cart'.

The octagon tower by the village is a folly owned by Conishead Priory.

Going inland from Bardsea one crosses BIRKRIGG COMMON, shared by the parishes of Urswick and Aldingham. This high land, consisting of thin soil on limestone, looks sad and overgrown with bracken. Such grass that remains is greatly overgrazed and worn out. Going westwards from the common one is surprised by a sizeable tarn, around whose shores lies GREAT URSWICK. Like many villages in the Furness area it is not the well-groomed picture-postcard place that you might find in, say, the Cotswolds, but the tarn gives it a very special touch. At one time, of course, it was said to be bottomless. Another myth is that beneath lies the drowned village of old Ulverston, swallowed into a watery grave for some dreadful sin. The gem of Great Urswick though is the church of St Mary the Virgin and St Michael. Though originating in the thirteenth century, the church has much earlier Viking connections, including a splendid cross portion that stands in a window. This is the Tunwinni Cross, and it bears a runic inscription, which has been translated to read: 'This cross Tunwinni erected in memory of Torhtred a monument to his Lord. Pray for his soul.' But the real joy of the church stems from more recent times: a series of woodcarvings by the famous Camden Guild of artists, crafted around 1910. Either side of the chancel is a beautifully carved St James of Compostela and a John the Baptist. But more figures can be found on choir stalls, the organ case and the reredos. When you think you have seen them all you find others, all of them delightful. The painting of the Last Supper on the east wall is by James Cranke, eighteenth century, said to be one of the tutors of George Romney.

The Urswick area's historical roots ran very deep. Nearby are the stone walls of a pre-Christian settlement, and there are signs that the inhabitants exploited a surface vein of iron ore.

Three km south of Urswick, GLEASTON CASTLE was built around 1350 by John Harrington. Its limestone walls are nine feet thick, but wrongly built, it is said, of limestone rubble and roughly-dressed rock, with dressed sandstone only round doors and windows. Not really built to last, it is said, but six centuries later the fragments make a romantic ruin, heavily cloaked in creepers. In the sixteenth century it was owned by the earl of Suffolk. When he and his daughter Lady Jane Grey were executed by Mary the property came into the hands of the Crown. But it was recorded as already in decay.

Gleaston Mill is a little below the castle and has been partially restored. The first record of it was in 1608, but there was surely a mill on the site long before that. The present building is dated 1770.

Back on the coast is ALDINGHAM, whose seaside church has an impressive aspect. The manor of Aldingham was granted to Michael Le Fleming in the late eleventh century by William II in acknowledgement of the support he gave to the Norman conquest. In the Norman fashion he built his motte and bailey, an artificial mound on which he planted his first wooden defensive tower. From the churchyard looking south, the mound can be seen by the shore, and it is shown on the map now as Moat Farm. Here lies a problem. The Normans normally built their motte and bailey above the surrounding settlements to display their authority to the inhabitants. But this position is prominent only from the sea. Similarly the church on the shore, also founded by Le Fleming, is not central to the parish. Le Fleming later moved his tower to Gleaston. Does this give credence to the story that the original Aldingham settlement was destroyed by a terrible storm and swept away by waves in the late twelfth century? It seems plausible.

The church of St Cuthbert's at Aldingham was built in the late twelfth century. Traces of the church's early structure can be seen, including the tower and the chancel. Inside, the statue of St Cuthbert with an otter comes from Durham Cathedral. The churchyard is protected from the sea by a wall erected in the mid nineteenth century by the incumbent the Revd John Stonard at his own expense. He was obviously not a poor man for he erected nearby the large Gothic house Aldingham Hall, now a nursing home. Unfortunately he did not live long enough to enjoy the property. On his death he left it to his butler, apparently in gratitude for the servant's saving his life when he got into difficulties on the bay sands. The butler eventually sold the property, moved to Barrow and went into shipbuilding.

After Aldingham the road stays close to the shore until one reaches RAMPSIDE. The late seventeenth-century Rampside Hall is just along on the right. Its strikingly weird peculiarity is its 'twelve apostles' – twelve chimneys in a row along the roof's peak. The unlikely story behind it is that a local man of substance would only allow his daughter to wed her suitor on condition that he built a house with twelve chimneys. From then on every wedding anniversary day, each chimney had to smoke. Why? Was the man a coal merchant?

In the late eighteenth century Rampside was a place visited by the gentry of Furness for its excellent sea bathing. The Concle Inn had a therapeutic sea-water bath. Dorothy Wordsworth stayed here in June 1794 with her cousin Elizabeth Barker, eldest daughter of uncle Richard Wordsworth of Whitehaven. In August of the same year William stayed there for a whole month, a holiday recalled in his poem about Piel Island.

In Victorian times Rampside attracted steamer trips from Morecambe and Fleetwood, and the trippers would then go on to Furness Abbey and the Lakes.

The Victorian parish church is away from the village on the road to Barrow. In the graveyard, apart from maritime headstones, an elaborate monument stands to a John Dickinson who was killed in 1878 by overwork. A verse around its four sides ends with a terse note: 'It was 232 hours labour in 12 days That brought poor John to his grave.' How was he employed? There is no clue.

It was the custom until the mid nineteenth century to bury drowned sailors here. Early in that century a ship put into Peel harbour with fever on board. The cook, a black man, died, and because of the assumed risk of infection was buried here at once in his sea chest.

Passing through Rampside a causeway is reached, leading to ROE ISLAND, which is not an island. The causeway was built in 1847 by John Abel Smith to carry a railway line. On the end it had a pier and it served as an active steamer port with connections to the Lancashire coast, the Isle of Man, and Ireland. The enterprise failed when the opening of a new Ramsden dock in 1882, 4 km up the channel at Barrow, proved a better option for vessels. The line was removed, and a road now leads on to the settlement, which consists of an hotel and a hotch-potch of buildings, and very many small boats, stored on land and moored in the water on the lee side of the causeway. The large modern structure is the lifeboat station. It houses an impressive Tyne-class high-tech boat, 14.3 m long, capable of a speed of 18 knots, as well as an inflatable capable of higher speeds. A lifeboat has been stationed here since 1864 and since then there have been very many rescues. They are now concerned less with commercial shipping activity and more with recreational.

A ferry leaves here for PIEL ISLAND (originally called the Isle of Foudrey, and sometimes spelt 'Peel') one km away. It is small, but large enough to have an inn, a row of cottages, and the famous ruin of Piel Castle (EH) (originally 'the pile of Foudrey'). A castle was built here in the twelfth century, but rebuilt by Furness Abbey in 1327 as a secure warehouse, and to guard its harbour, which was further along the Piel channel. The port was the abbey's important asset, for its wealth was based very much on wool exports. Inevitably rumours spread of smuggling activities centred on the castle – the monks were suspected of avoiding paying duties. In 1423 parliamentary records show that a petition was written by the merchants of Calais, complaining that the abbot of Furness (Robert) had been smuggling wool out of the kingdom without paying custom or subsidy, and mentioning a ship of 200 tons which sailed out from the 'Peele de Foddry' to Zeeland.

The castle was really a three-storey square piel tower, and substantial parts of it still stand. Although it never really faced an attack, a bizarre incident occurred there. In 1487 Lambert Simnel, a teenager who had been persuaded to claim to be Edward VI, landed here from Ireland with a force of 8,000 mercenaries. After parading around the North of England the invaders were defeated at Stoke, only twelve days after landing. The castle fell into disrepair at the dissolution of the abbey, but the port was busy. In the sixteenth century Queen Elizabeth, concerned about security, commissioned a report on 'all ports, creeks, and landing places in Britain'. The report stated, 'Between Mylford Haven and Carlisle – there is not one good haven for great shyppes to londe or ryde in but one whiche is in the furthest part of Lancashire called Pylle of Fodder.'

During the Civil War it offered a safe anchorage for the Parliamentarians' fleet. The island seemed to have continued as a base for smugglers, and it was targeted by revenue officers with some success. As the island and harbour grew in importance it had its own custom house – necessary as there could be as many as 200 ships anchored at the same time. The row of cottages on the island was built to house the Barrow harbour pilots. At the popular Ship Inn, the landlord could for many years bestow on a person the 'knighthood of Piel'. Applicants had to sit in an ancient chair and promise always to be of good behaviour, be an ardent lover, smoke only in moderation and, of course, buy drinks all round.

Wordsworth's memory of the castle, and his feelings about the sea, were recalled in 1806 when he saw a painting of it in a storm, with a shipwreck, by Sir George Beaumont. It revived painful memories of the grief he felt when his brother John, captain of the *Abergavenny*, was lost with his ship in a storm off Portland Bill. The grief he felt made him question his belief in a compassionate God and his early feelings about the benevolence of the natural world. His poem 'Stanzas Suggested by a Picture of Peel Castle, in a Storm, Painted by Sir George Beaumont' expresses it movingly.

I was thy Neighbour once, thou rugged Pile!
Four summer weeks I dwelt in sight of thee;
I saw thee every day; and all the while
Thy form was sleeping on a glassy sea.

And:

How perfect was the calm! It seemed no sleep;
No mood, which seasons take away, or brings;
I could have fancied that the mighty Deep
Was even the gentlest of all gentle Things

And a further verse:

So once it would have been, – 'tis so no more;
I have submitted to a new control:
A power is gone, which nothing can restore;
A deep distress has humanised my Soul.

Piel Island was long used as a port for shipping ore well into the nineteenth century.

From a small car park on the Roe Island causeway, another causeway leads from it to FOULNEY ISLAND. Foulney is within an area of Special Scientific Interest and is an important bird reserve managed by CWT. It supports colonies of nesting Arctic, common, little, and sandwich terns, as well as eider ducks, ringed plover and other species. The island also attracts winter bird visitors. A spit, bending northwards from the island, contains the main nesting area, and the law forbids all access to it during the season from 1 April to 15 August. The flora on the shingle is also of interest to botanists.

The road continues past Rampside church and the bay's gas terminal and power station and passes Roose, with a row of terraced cottages on the right. The cottages were built for Cornish miners brought here to work the iron mine at Stank, two km north-east, and a railway line once ran alongside.

We reach BARROW-IN-FURNESS (pop. 58,090), Cumbria's largest town, second only to the city of Carlisle. The rocketing rise of this supreme product of the Industrial Revolution is an extraordinary story. In the eighteenth century it was a fishing village; by the nineteenth century's end it was growing rapidly as rich iron-ore deposits were being exploited, iron works built, and it was expanding as a port. The demand for workers brought immigrants from other parts of the country, and from Ireland. A desperately overcrowded shanty town of crude huts, sometimes housing up to eighteen, including women and children, developed on Barrow Island (not to be confused with Walney Island), with few privies and no running water. Inevitably disease spread – smallpox took lives, and a makeshift 'hospital' cared only for the workers, not their families. Hard drinking, fighting and general lawlessness were common. Imagine Dawson City in the Klondike's gold rush. The steamer trippers' itinerary from Fleetwood and Morecambe took in Barrow Island, and the excursionists must have been entertained by this curiosity, a kind of human zoo. By the 1880s, the building of the new town by James Ramsden (later Sir James) was well underway and the shanty town slid into history.

Burgeoning industry is synonymous with dirt, smoke and unplanned development. The difference here is that much of the murk was blown away by offshore breezes (towards Coniston to John Ruskin's disgust). Large pleasant sandy beaches that would be the envy of many holiday resorts are to hand at Walney Island. And the town was built to a plan by James Ramsden, whose thinking can be seen at once on the main approach from the north to the centre, down Abbey Road. Good and wide and straight and tree-lined, it ends in Ramsden Square, a focal point named after the man who designed the grid system of streets, became the town's first mayor and much more.

In 1835 the rich iron ore found in deposits in the Furness area was already being exported from jetties along Morecambe Bay and at Barrow. But the iron sources were thought to be so rich and promising that developers moved in. Among them was Henry W. Schneider, a young speculator with a talent for developing new industries. Prior to the advent of modern-day technology, mining was a risky business. If ore was found, permission had to be sought from the landowner. In the Furness area this meant two main landowners: the Duke of

Buccleugh was Lord of the Liberty of Furness, and the Duke of Devonshire (of the Cavendish family) had inherited the land once belonging to Furness Abbey. Then the prospector had to sink capital into extracting the ore. The result could be a bonanza, or the ore could be limited to a small pocket and result in a financial loss. Schneider came to the Lake District on holiday in 1839, but he belonged to a city business family interested and financially involved in mineral exploration, so the holiday was combined with a visit to the iron-ore producers in the Furness area, and to make an assessment of its potential investment.

Later Schneider received permission from the landowners to make exploratory soundings, but the first few years were disappointing. Then he was luckier discovering promising finds north of Dalton, and the ore from there was exported from Barrow. However, the mines made a disappointing return and Schneider was tempted to expand his business elsewhere. But just as he was about to abandon hope he was persuaded to make one more effort to find a rich source. What happened is part of Furness's history. The miners in his workings near Park, north of Barrow and east of Dalton, tried to convince Schneider that the area showed potential. In fact they were so sure of it that they offered to work without pay for a week to reach the ore. By the end of the week they had run into a huge deposit of the finest quality. It made Schneider a fortune, and rapidly brought employment and prosperity to the region. Soon the mine's average production was equal to 1,000 tons every day.

To develop the mining at Park Schneider needed more capital and it was fortunate that a wealthy Scottish landowner – Robert Hannay – was seeking a profitable activity. He went into partnership with Schneider, and the firm of Schneider, Hannay and Company was formed. It made both men wealthy.

Problems of carting the ore from the mines, and slate from the quarries, to be shipped from Barrow were eased when 30 km of railway line was built by the new Furness Railway Company. The first two engines were shipped in from Fleetwood across Morecambe Bay. The earl of Burlington and the duke of Buccleuch (who owned mining land in the Dalton area) provided much of the capital. The Railway Company also began the task of dredging the channel, and building a stone pier, so that ships could more easily use what had been only a small port. Then James Ramsden, a remarkably energetic and far-seeing man, became manager of the railway's engineering department in 1845. He was a very practical but innovative operator, later a driving force at directors' meetings, but never afraid to get his hands dirty. Once on a train journey, when the driver was found to be the worst for drink, Ramsden climbed into the cab and drove the train himself.

In 1857 the railway was connected to the main north–south railway line at Lancaster, and great quantities of Furness iron ore could then be transported to other industrial areas in England. But why export ore when it could produce iron in Barrow? The line also allowed the importation of coal and coke, and Schneider and Hannay, then Ramsden, took on the lease of land at Hindpool, north of the town centre, from the railway company, to establish first two blast furnaces producing pig iron, then five. Skilled workers were brought in from Staffordshire to start the venture.

Mines were producing haematite – the finest rich ore – from all over this Furness peninsula. An account of the time by John Bolton in *Geological Fragments of Furness and Cartmel* in 1869 gives an idea of the hugely productive and frenetic mining scene as he looks out from the High Haulme hill, north of Dalton:

> Before us is the real California of Britain – the great haematite iron ore district of Furness – some of the principal mines forming a semi-circle at the base of the hill. Commencing our review at the north-west, we have first, the new mines of Messrs Kennedy Brothers, on the Askam estate; almost adjoining these the splendid mines of Messrs. Schneider, Hannay and Co. (this firm has now become the Barrow Haematite Iron and Steel Mining Co.), at Park; close to which are the Ronhead mines of Kennedy Brothers. Glancing round the foot of the hill we find Elliscacles, Messrs. Ashburner and Son; Butts Beck, Ricket Hills, Cross Gates, J. Rawlinson Esq. The Ure Pits, Ulverston Mining Company; Mousell Mines, Messrs Schneider, Hannay and Co; all skirting the vase of High Haulme, and constituting a circle arc of 180 degrees, with a radius of half a mile. – Besides the above, there are the mines of Schneider, Hannay, and Co. at Old Hills, Whitriggs, and Marton, all within half a mile at the base of Haverslack Hill – There are also mines at Carrkettle, of J. Rawlinson, and the splendid mines of Lindal Moor, Whinfield, Gillbrow, and Whitriggs Bottom, of Messrs Harrison, Ainslie and Co; and at Lindall Cote, those of the Ulverston Mining Co; also at Dalton, those of J. Denny and Co. and J. Rawlinson, and near Highfield House, those of J. Clegg Esq. All these mining works are within a mile and a half of High Haulme; besides, about a mile further, we have the Ulverston Mining Co's works at Stainton, Bolton Heads, Stone Close, and California; also at Wadham's at Crooklands, and Messrs Schneider, Hannay and Co. at Newton. We have omitted some ...

So vast quantities of fine haematite were pouring into Barrow, ideal for use in the Bessemer process (see p. 173), and to add an extensive steel works. In 1859 the first two Bessemer furnaces were in production, and five years later, the new company, the Barrow Haematite Steel Company, which had bought the Park mine from Schneider and Hannay, took over the Hindpool business. The site was developed to provide no less than fourteen blast furnaces, and extensive steel works, and the project became the largest in the country. Schneider and Hannay became directors. In J.T. Smith the company was fortunate in having an efficient and very experienced technician in overall charge. The speciality was the production of steel rails for the country's expanding railway system, and for railways all over the world. It was Schneider who convinced the railway companies that steel rails were far superior to the wrought-iron rails commonly in use.

During this time Barrow had grown phenomenally. The town was totally in the grip of the Furness Railway Company, the Barrow Haematite Steel Company and its major investors and directors. The town's all-powerful men were Ramsden, Schneider, Hannay, the Duke of Devonshire, and a builder and anti-trades unionist, William Gradwell; and they wanted to see effective local government. They wanted to break away from reliance on the towns of Dalton and Ulverston for some services. A petition was sent to Queen Victoria, asking her to grant a charter of incorporation to the town. After a royal commission of enquiry a charter was granted in July 1867.

The first council was appointed, without direct elections, by the duke of Devonshire, and not surprisingly the four aldermen appointed were James Ramsden, Myles Kennedy (mine owner), H.W. Schneider and Robert Hannay. They were safely ensconced, because aldermen were appointed by the council and not dependent on the town's voters. Among the councillors were a steelworks manager, a landowner, ore merchant, coal agent, shipping agent, iron founder, shipbuilder, Furness Railway surgeon, and William Gradwell, builder and contractor. Predictably, at the first council meeting in July 1867, James Ramsden was appointed mayor, and Alderman Kennedy his deputy.

The export business had been hindered by the overcrowding of the loading berths at Barrow, and Ramsden devised a scheme for the building of docks and shipbuilding yards, and for better loading wharves. In 1863 an Act was passed allowing the Furness Railway Company to raise capital for the building of docks and a harbour. The first of the large docks, the Devonshire dock, covering 30 acres, was opened by the eponymous duke in September 1867, followed by celebrations, a salute of guns, a sports day and a banquet.

The satirical magazine *Punch* had its say.

> Never did Barrow on furnace make such a blaze as did Barrow in Furness the other day, when its docks were opened by Dukes, Lords, Honourable and Right Honourable, M.P.s, J.P.s, Mayors, Magistrates, Magnates, Local and Municipal in short by such an assemblage of big and little wigs as it was a triumph to have got together in the dead season.
>
> But the occasion was certainly worth a crowd and a crow! A Barrow that has grown, one may say, from a barrow into a coach-and-four in ten years. A Barrow that has swelled almost within the memory of the youngest inhabitant

> from the quiet coast-nest of some five-score fishermen, into the busy, bustling, blazing, money-making, money-spending, roaring, tearing, swearing, steaming, sweltering, seat of twenty thousand iron workers, and the crime and culture, dirt and disease, the hard-working and hard-drinking, the death and life, the money and misery they bring along with them! A Barrow out of which they are tipping 600,000 tons of iron every year! A Barrow big enough to hold a Monster Iron-Mining-and-Smelting Company, with two Dukes among its directors, to say nothing of Lord knows who in the way of Lords, and Lord knows how many millionaires!!!

After the Buccleuch dock was completed, a year later, the steel trade suffered a setback and reduced production. The Furness Railway hoped in vain for a shipbuilding company to occupy land that it owned on Barrow Island. Then James Fisher, town councillor and a shipping agent, took a site near the iron works to repair his fleet of eighty ships and to build new ones. Then economic conditions improved, the steel company got new orders and there were even expansion plans. The company also set up a jute mill to employ women and children. Within three years the boom times were back, with great demand for steel. The town's industries became more diverse, and one enterprise was the formation of the Barrow Shipbuilding Company, in which both Schneider and Ramsden were involved.

Ramsden's grid-pattern plans for the town came to fruition. In 1871 the town's population was 18,911, and two years later it had grown to 32,000. By 1881 it had swollen to 42,259. Most of the newcomers were young males seeking work and inevitably outbreaks of rowdiness, drunkenness and fighting were common. Houses were being bought as soon as the foundations were laid. Steamer services ran from the port, with regular services to Glasgow and Belfast. James Fisher's ships were going as far as Montreal.

With other towns and villages in Furness Barrow had been building wooden ships for a century. Ashburner's sawmill and shipbuilding yard continued as the most productive, with schooners a speciality. Earlier the yard was asked to design and built a passenger boat for Windermere, and they produced a beautiful paddle-steamer, 49 tons, powered by two steam engines and launched in May 1845. The saloon of the *Lady of the Lake* was a picture of pink and white luxury. The yard produced a second one, *Lord of the Isles*, in 1846.

The railway company decided to exploit the tour potential of the area with passengers from the Lancashire and Yorkshire areas, and in the 1870s it devised a series of tours with discount fares. The choices were attractive. A 'Five Lakes' tour took passengers to Windermere, then by coach past Rydal Water, Grasmere and Thirlmere, to Keswick and Derwent Water, then by return on the Keswick to Penrith line, changing at Penrith and back on the London and North Western line.

In 1872 Ramsden was knighted by Queen Victoria for services to the country and its industry. And ten years later Barrow had an impressive Gothic town hall. Whose idea was it to have eight rams on the pinnacles of the octagonal tower? A rams' den! Was Ramsden amused?

Barrow, with the docks, and the steel works, could take advantage of the demand for iron ships. The Barrow Shipbuilding Company, under Ramsden's influence, began to receive orders. Most of the ships built before 1859 were relatively small, then the 62,000-ton liner *City of Rome* was constructed for the Inman Company. It was one of the first passenger liners to be launched at Barrow. In 1877 the yard received its first orders from the Royal Navy. Ramsden was encouraged to believe that the best prospects for the yard was to specialize in naval ships, and the company merged with Nordonfelt's Gun and Ammunition Company. From then on orders for warships began to come from many countries.

By this time Barrow already had the largest steel works in the world. James Ramsden died and the shipyard was taken over by the Vickers family. The company became known as Vickers, Sons and Maxim Ltd and boasted that it could not only build warships, but could design them, equip them with engines and arm them. The iron and steel industry gradually declined as it became cheaper to import ores for steel making; thereafter shipbuilding became Barrow's main industry. In 1901 the yard built the first of five submarines for the Royal Navy. Submarines were to become the yard's speciality. It began making more ships for the British and foreign navies, among which Japan was a good customer. The Barrow built *Mikasa* (15,150 tons) in 1900, which became the flagship in Japan's naval war with Russia. It is now preserved in Japan as a national monument.

By the beginning of the twentieth century Vickers was the town's major employer and the population grew steadily to 60,000; by 1920 it was reaching its peak of 72,000. A new model town, 'Vickerstown', was built on Walney Island to accommodate shipbuilding workers. As the new century dawned warships were getting larger. The Cunard White Star line ordered two 20,000-ton ships, the *Scythia* and the *Antonia*, launched in 1910/11. Another large naval ship, the *Princess Royal*, of 26,000 tons, was launched in April 1911. Then during the First World War the yard built thirty-five warships, 132 submarines and twelve merchant ships.

The yard launched the battleship *Vanguard* (19,250 tons) in 1908 and orders continued to roll in from other countries. It was always an emotional event when a really big 'boat' hit the water. The men who had worked on her for months stood gazing, looking upwards, as the great ship they had created towered high above them. The townspeople turned out in strength for the occasion, one that was to happen many times over the coming years. A contemporary press report of the launch of *Vanguard* described how the great crowd watched in silence:

> Inch by inch it went at first, to a slow, solemn rumbling of props falling away from under sides, and the silky squealing of a heavy iron mass moving on greased wood. Then fast and further, till the falling props had almost the rhythm of a boy's stick on a pailing. With this came the clamorous uncoiling of great chains, which, with their ends fastened to the ships bows and sides lay in heaps by the 'ways' nicely 'ranged' so as not to foul. They rattled and jumped, and then grovelled unwilling along after the ship, throwing up a cloud of dust in their writhings.
>
> The suspense of the launch was over. A breathless suspense it is in the case of so big and heavy a ship. There was shouting and hat waving from the crowds on either side of the slipways, on the roofs to the left hand on the raised platform at the top of the ways, on Walney Island beyond and on Walney Bridge away to their right, and even from out at sea, where a shoal of craft – sail, steamer, and oars – were lying, anxious to see the warship dip her head. The people stood up in their boats and waved, notwithstanding that their craft were bobbing about like corks on the waves the Vanguard had sent rolling along. The day had been made a general holiday, nearly all the schools had shut.

Sadly the *Vanguard* was lost in 1917 at Scapa Flow, with 800 of her crew.

But to return to happier times: Alfred Aslett, a new secretary and general manager of the Furness Railway Company, with ample experience, was appointed in 1895. His ideas for expanding tourism included improving passenger coaches, which now had corridors, toilets and electric light. In particular he had an eye on the masses of holidaymakers at Blackpool and Morecambe. Steamboats could bring them to Barrow. The Barrow Steam Navigation Company already had a landing stage with a railway station, to accommodate its service to Belfast, and it could be used. A paddle steamer was ordered from John Scott Company of Glasgow, and was launched in 1900. Named *Lady Evelyn* after the wife of director Victor Cavendish, in her first season of 1901 she carried 29,165 passengers. In 1902 it could not cope with demand and was supplemented by the company's tug, *Furness*. So another larger steamer, the *Lady Margaret*, was bought from the Lady Margaret Steamship Company of Bristol ready for the 1903 season. With two steamers Aslett could widen the tour options, with regular services bringing passengers from Morecambe and Fleetwood. The *Lady Evelyn* had proved to be too small, but rather than sell her she was enlarged to accommodate a further eighty passengers. In 1907, for undisclosed reasons, the Admiralty bought *Lady Margaret*. A new steamer was acquired – the *Philomel* –which proved to be a bad buy. Passengers called her 'Full o' Smell', and she needed a new boiler in only two years. After failing to attract a buyer, she was scrapped. The replacement was the *Gwalia*, from the Barry Railway Company. It could carry 1,014 passengers and was renamed *Lady Moyra* after the wife of Lord Richard Cavendish. Mr Aslett acquired a large model of the steamer, and had it mounted on wheels to advertise the tours on the streets of Blackpool.

One popular tour organized from Blackpool took passengers on a short train journey to Fleetwood, where they boarded the steamer for the crossing of Morecambe Bay. A four-piece band entertained them on board and a photographer took pictures. They disembarked at Barrow and the train took the holidaymakers to Lakeside station on Windermere, where they could dine in the refreshment room to musical accompaniment. The steamers then took them along the lake to Ambleside where they were picked up by horse-drawn 'charabanc' and carried to Coniston. Tea could then be taken at Coniston station if required, before training back to Barrow and steaming back to Fleetwood. On the return crossing the photographer sold the pictures taken on the outward journey. The tour took eleven hours, and cost twelve shillings first class, eight shillings third class. An exhausting but happy day for all.

In 1914 both steamers were requisitioned by the navy to serve as minesweepers. After the war they were acquired by P. and A. Campbell, renamed the *Brighton Belle* and *Brighton Queen*, and they served as pleasure steamers until 1939. They were then minesweepers once more but were sunk at the Dunkirk evacuations.

Barrow's ironworks kept up production into the early 1920s. W.G. Collingwood, in *The Lake Counties*, paints the Barrow scene:

> Coming fresh from the mountains and abbeys with Wordsworth in one's pocket, one might feel that Barrow had little to show, with its streets of poor-looking houses and tall chimneys, dominating the scene as persistently as the Pikes in Langdale. There is abundant poetry and picturesqueness, for anyone who does not travel in blinkers, at the shipyards and steelworks, and even in the streets of Barrow. I remember one December night, wet and gloomy, when the working folk, rough coated men and lasses hooded in their shawls, were shopping after the day's work, under the gas-lamps that streamed their reflections down the pavement; and suddenly aloft from enormous towers, bulking on the darkness like some Babylonian architecture in a picture, there flared out great banners of fire, lighting up the cloud into a brown glow against interspaces of deep violet. It blazed and flickered and faded again, and the people in the streets were like ghosts hurrying to and fro.

Civilian ships continued to be built, the *Corinthia*, for Cunard White Star, being launched in 1925. The Orient Line, famous for the sumptuous interiors of its passenger ships, had three built in the yard, and the P & O line another three.

The depression of the later 1920s hit the town hard, and nothing could stop the decline. Whereas the shipyards had employed 15,000 men, the numbers plummeted to 3,800. The steelworks suffered too, and the workers there faced a long Christmas holiday. Business picked up towards the 1930s, but shipyards, so dependent on naval spending, were bound to suffer when the 1930 Treaty of London required a reduction.

However, the Orient Line had two more ships of over 20,000 tons built, and the P & O two. The launching of the 23,371-ton *Orion* for the Orient Line, was officiated in December 1934 by the Duke of Gloucester – who was in Brisbane, Australia! The speech was transmitted by radio. After he had named the ship he pressed a button that transmitted a pulse that triggered a switch at the Barrow slipway.

But how to lessen the town's dependency of shipbuilding? Tourism. Make Walney Island a seaside holiday resort. Why should Blackpool have it all? Plans were prepared: a pier, bathing pool, miniature golf course and an airfield to provide pleasure flights over the Lakes. But it came to nothing through lack of enthusiasm as well as funds. In 1939 a private firm was encouraged to provide an amusement park, with sideshows, dodgem cars, the 'Demon Whirl' and special rides for children. It could not last. War loomed again.

The yard launched HMS *Illustrious* (23,000) in April 1939, and during the war produced two aircraft carriers, two cruisers, twelve destroyers, thirty-five transport vessels and no less than 112 submarines. The joiners also produced fuselages for Wellington bombers. The Germans appreciated what was going on and bombed Barrow severely for a week in April/May 1941. The railway station was destroyed and very many houses demolished or damaged. There were civilian casualties; but Vickers suffered only slightly and production continued.

In July 1944 work had started on a 22,000-ton aircraft carrier HMS *Elephant*, but at the war's end, work ground to a halt. She stayed, partly built, on the stocks until her place was wanted for a passenger ship. At last she was renamed HMS *Hermes* and launched in an incomplete state in 1953. She then remained at Barrow until the Admiralty decided that she should be finished. After being part of the town's scene for more than a decade she eventually left Barrow in November 1959. It seemed to leave protesting – there was great difficulty, hampered by a wind and a series of mishaps, in a 'shoehorn' exit. The ship had two refits, then, in March 1982, the *Hermes* was required for active duty – as flagship in the Falklands campaign. Four years later the ship was sold to the Indian navy and renamed *Viraat*.

The P & O line had three ships of over 28,000 tons built in the late 1940s, at the same time as the Argentine navy had three ships on the stocks of over 12,000 tons: The *Peron, Eva Peron* and *17 de Octobre*. Orders for large oil tankers in the 1950s brought more work, and big tankers were produced in the following twenty years.

The launch of the luxury liner 'Oriana' from Barrow shipyard in 1959

But on 3 November 1959 the darling of the shipyard was launched for the Orient line – the 41,923-ton *Oriana*. Tears were shed as the beautiful liner dipped into the water. On the day of her first visit to San Francisco, on 5 February 1961, the city council named it Oriana Day. The ship was withdrawn from service after twenty-five years, and became a Japanese floating hotel.

In 1959 history was made as Queen Elizabeth launched the *Dreadnought*, Britain's first nuclear-powered submarine, made of special alloy steel, and the first of several more. In the 1980s HMS *Invincible*, and HMS *Manchester* were launched. In 1984 the Campaign for Nuclear Disarmament, several thousand strong, descended on Barrow to stage a protest against the Trident submarine programme. And in 1986 the huge building block that towers over the town – the Devonshire Dock Hall – was constructed to allow submarines, and other ships, to be built under cover, thereby improving security. According to the workers it was 'Barrow's answer to the Wembley Stadium'. Then the awesome giant, *Vanguard*, a 16,000-tonne ballistic-missile submarine, nosed out of the newly built great hall in 1986 to be launched by the Princess of Wales; it was the first of four of the same class. Who would have guessed in the nineteenth century when submarines were being developed, that a battleship of this size would be navigated underwater, and that it could carry on board the ultimate weapon, capable of wiping out cities? 'The Royal Navy is out there,' someone said during the First World War. 'We can sleep safely in our beds.'

GEC had bought the shipyard in 1985 and four years later their Marconi Electric Systems merged with British Aerospace to form BAE Systems. The company then began concentrating its Barrow workforce on submarines. No other yard has built so many. It was a pioneer. As early as 1886 the yard was building experimental submarines for the Swedish firm Nordenfelt, and in 1901 the first Royal Navy submarine was built under licence from the American Electric Boat Company. Since then 309 submarines have been constructed at Barrow for the Royal Navy, and twenty-six for other navies. Other naval ships will doubtless be built. The problem with building warships in the present age is that technology progresses more quickly than a ship can be designed and completed. Each design thus has to factor adaptability into its construction.

Now submarine building remains as practically the yard's sole activity. Only one tall crane is left out of the six that used to dominate the skyline. In 1990, 800 job losses were announced, and by 1996 something like a thousand jobs had gone at the yards. No longer are you overwhelmed by a human avalanche of cyclists and pedestrians pouring out of the dock gates after five o'clock. Barrow still has its shipyard, but it is a mere shadow of what it used to be. The decline of the yards was not the only blow to employment that Barrow has had to face. Iron and steel factories were closing or under threat all over Britain, and eventually Barrow Haematite Steel Company went into liquidation and closed in 1983. The site was bulldozed to provide land for new businesses.

The future of Barrow is open to question. It is sad to see shop fronts boarded up as businesses fail, although yet another supermarket opened in 2003. Parts of the town centre look neglected and dirty. Once again there is serious talk of the tourism industry as an answer, and the developing of tourist attractions. At the same time the council hopes that more light industries might be persuaded to base themselves in the area. The main drawback, often stated, is that Barrow is too isolated – 'at the end of the longest cul-de-sac in England'. The main road route to Barrow, the A590, is criticized as being woefully inadequate, at one point, at Low Newton, actually passing through what was once a farmyard. Residents lobby for a relief road, in spite of the environmental impact on prime surrounding countryside, but even that would not wholly solve the problem – a problem that all other Cumbrian coastal towns share to a lesser extent. But Barrow, in a sense, is more isolated than it was. For now commercial traffic arrives mostly by road and via a tortuous route. Lorries must turn off the M6, then on the A590 road, meandering north of the Milnthorpe Sands, then veer south-west and sharply north-west to avoid the fells, before going south-west through Ulverston. People felt less isolated when most commercial traffic, and passenger traffic, came by rail more quickly and directly over the viaducts of the river Kent and the Levens. Even now a slow stopping train on our run-down railway system can link Barrow to Manchester in 2½ hours while carrying considerable loads. Several lorries carrying the same load along the motorways are pushed to match that time, particularly if they meet with congestion.

And once again (2003) there is discussion of building a bridge or barrier across Morecambe Bay to carry the road traffic and at the same time generate power from tidal flows. The cost would be even more astronomical than it was when first mooted in the 1960s, and ecologically the construction would still be open to serious question.

The council's commendable DOCK MUSEUM, on a waterside site, tells the story of Barrow's development from a village to a major industrial town, of the iron industry and shipbuilding, the Furness Railway, and life in wartime. The shipbuilding section displays some incredibly detailed models of some of the ships launched here and recounts the design and construction process. A wooden shipbuilder's shed has been reconstructed, complete with artefacts and pictures. It is well worth a visit. A popular walkway from the museum building goes along the channel side.

One of the fine scale models of Barrow's ships in the Dock Museum

WALNEY ISLAND, 15.5 km long, curves around Barrow like a shield, sheltering it from direct contact with the Irish Sea. It can be reached by a bridge over the Walney Channel. This connects with Vickerstown, a housing estate built for the shipyard workers. Along its coast, long sandy beaches are a great attraction, Biggar Bank in the centre being the base for those in holiday mood. If this was a holiday resort, as the Barrow burghers like to suggest it should be, it would be given care and attention – and it would need it. Some beaches collect seaweed, some shells, but Walney, like other beaches on the Cumbrian west coast, attracts litter, presumably much of it from passing ships in the Irish Sea. Occasionally, but not often enough, it is cleared by volunteers, but the task is great. Sadly visitors, who already see the wind-blown litter, feel less inclined to deal with their own sensibly, and contribute to the problem.

The island holds two very important nature reserves, both within areas of Special Scientific Interest. South Walney Nature Reserve covers 93 ha on the hook that curves round to the east at the island's southern end. Access is by permit only (with a charge) from the warden at Coastguard Cottages. During the sea birds' breeding season, between 1 April and 31 August, visitors are advised to wear old clothes and a hat for obvious reasons. No dogs are allowed. Twenty-five species of birds nest here, including the largest mixed colony of lesser black-backed and herring gulls in Europe; and there are great black-backed gulls, eider duck, terns, mallard, shelduck, oystercatcher, ringed plover, lapwing, skylark and meadow pipit. Huge numbers of ducks and waders come to spend the winter here. During migration periods the reserve becomes a staging-post for a great number of species from various habitats, and often there are a few surprises. The reserve is managed by the Cumbria Wildlife Trust.

No permit for access is required at North Walney National Nature Reserve,

Walney's deserted beach

which occupies 146 ha, but visitors are warned that the sandbanks can be dangerous because of quicksands and incoming tides. Swimming is not advisable either. Dogs have to be under close control. The reserve is important for its variety of habitats, including sand dunes, dune heath, saltmarsh, shingle and gravel ponds with islands. Neolithic settlers occupied the site, and Furness Abbey farmed it during its ownership. Over twenty species of breeding birds and 300 species of flora have been identified, including several orchids and one unique species: the Walney geranium, or bloody cranesbill (*G. sanguineum var lancastriense*). In the ponds a colony of the very rare natterjack toad has made its home. The reserve is managed by English Nature and Cumbria Wildlife Trust.

SANDSCALE HAWS (NT), a bulky promontory of the mainland opposite the northern tip of Walney Island, is an area of sand dunes with access to a wide bay of the Duddon Sands in front of what was once the profitable Roanhead (Ronhead) iron mine. Now a nature reserve, its flowers are typical coastal and dune varieties: sea holly, bloody cranesbill, heartsease and burnet rose, as well as orchids.

The expansive sands could be the envy of many a seaside resort, with the added bonus of good mountain views – particularly Black Combe. The sands extend northwards to the villages of IRELETH and ASKAM IN FURNESS, which profited from the mining of high-quality iron ore. To ship the ore from Askam a pier was constructed from mining waste. The sandy shore here is also of great interest to botanists, and it is a very pleasant place to be on a fine day.

Bloody cranesbill (Geranium sanguineum), seashore, Millom

North, and still with the estuary, lies Kirkby in Furness. Above it to the north-east is the huge working Burlington slate quarry, the largest in England, and 300 ft (91 m) deep from the top of the floor. The quarry site has been worked for centuries. In the nineteenth, under the ownership of the earl of Burlington, it was the main incentive for the building of the Furness Railway. The economics of quarrying depend absolutely on the means of transport.

The several lakes by Sandscale Haws were formed from relics of Roanhead mines; some are very deep indeed, and are popular among anglers, whom the Furness Fishing Association controls. The lakes hold bream, carp, eels, perch, pike, roach, tench and trout. Carp can reach over 20 lb (9 kg) and bream 6 lb (2.7 kg). The area is within the ASSI, and is very notable for the number of maritime and dune plant species. Views sweep across the bay to Black Combe, and part of the Lakeland's central fells.

FURNESS ABBEY AND WESTERN FURNESS

Furness Abbey (EH), to the north of Barrow, used to be on every Lake District tour, and it ought to be today, for although it is out of the Lakes country and into an urban area, it is undoubtedly one of the finest abbey remains in Britain. Built of striking red sandstone, the complex is secluded in a hidden ravine all to itself. In spite of the plunder of its fabric since the dissolution, which saw most of the nave destroyed, the first impression one gets on the approach down the hill of Manor Road is its astonishing size and beautiful colour. Although the west tower has lost a great deal of its once great structure, the walls of the transepts and the choir stand to within a stone or two of their original height. The great east window, missing the top of its arch, is 15.4 m high and 7.5 m wide, and was no doubt designed to uplift the soul as it uplifts the eye. Its effect has hardly diminished.

The building of this Abbey of St Mary started in 1127 under the Savigny Order, after the count of Bologne, later to become King Stephen, transferred the abbey from Tulkeith, near Preston, to this site, called 'the dale of the deadly nightshade'. The Savigny monks settled here for twenty years, before beginning the building. They had a problem; because level space was restricted within the narrow valley, the abbey's orientation had to be unusual, and it was set north-east to south-west. Nor was it possible to follow the typical plan of having the outer court on the western side; it had to be on the north. The building followed the Savigny plan and design, but in 1147 the order merged with the Cistercians, and the work took a different direction on a grander scale. Parts of the original design, blended with the new, can be seen on the site.

The Cistercians lived simply and would accept no gift except land – and they did very well. Furness Abbey gained a great deal of land in Lancashire and Yorkshire, the south and central Lake District, Lincolnshire, and from its harbour on Peel Island, it acquired land on the Isle of Man, and in Ireland. The order believed in hard work, and had gathered a strong workforce of lay brothers. They established sheep farms, and developed a lucrative trade in wool, much of it exported from their harbour. They had arable farmland to produce cereals, exploited the iron deposits where they were found near the surface and fished the bay and the sea, the rivers and lakes. The woodlands were managed to supply coppice wood for fuel, timber for construction, wood to make utensils and bark for tanneries. They prospered. Sister houses were established at Calder, Swineshead in Lincolnshire, at Rushen on the Isle of Man, in Ireland at Iniscourcy in County Down, and Abingdon in County Limerick. They constructed granges

Ruins of Furness Abbey

Ruins of Furness Abbey

from which the estates were managed. They also managed corn mills, tanneries, forges, bakeries and breweries. Furness Abbey was second only to Fountains Abbey in wealth.

The abbot had the status of an independent feudal baron, and he could throw his weight about when necessary, capable of leaning hard on the lesser gentry. He was the law on his own territory, and held law courts, and the abbey had a prison at Dalton castle, and he had another castle built on Peel Island. There were good abbots and bad. On 16 December 1516 Abbot Alexander Bankes, along with twenty-two monks, turned out all the inhabitants of the nearby village of Sellergarth and razed the buildings to make way for a sheep farm.

The serious problem was the raids from north of the border. Scottish incursions into England in 1316 led to plundering of the abbey's wealth; and in 1322 Robert the Bruce himself came well into Cumbria. Fearing disastrous damage to the abbey and its estates, the abbot rode out to meet him and offered ransom in return for a pledge to avoid the burning or looting of the Furness property. It is thought that Bruce stayed overnight as 'guest' in the abbot's guest room. Nevertheless, pledge or not, it would seem that the estates suffered a crippling disaster. No doubt Bruce would have had problems controlling his scattered forces.

The abbey steadily recovered its lost fortunes, and the lands and populations under its control benefited economically. Markets were established in strategic villages, and tenants were normally treated well. For example, every tenant with a plough could send two people to dine in the abbey once each week from Martinmas to Whitsuntide. Labourers and their children could go to the abbey for meat and drink. Children studied at an abbey-founded school and were given meals as they learned. When the dissolution came it had a serious impact on the region's economy.

The advent of the dissolution found the abbot, then Robert Peel, in danger when he had persuaded his monks to incite local people to protest at the closure of the lesser monasteries. When he saw that this was in vain, he kept his head well down. On 9 April 1537 the Abbey of Furness surrendered all its assets to the king, the deed being signed by the abbot and twenty-nine monks. Two of the monks were incarcerated in Lancaster prison on suspicion of being involved in inciting revolt. Directly after this the abbey was made uninhabitable. Lead was stripped from the roofs, and the timbers removed. Two years later the abbey and some of its lands were granted to Thomas Cromwell, the king's minister; and two years after that to Sir Thomas Curwen, and then to his son-in-law John Preston, who lived in a manor house on the site. From the Prestons the abbey passed in time to the Lowther family, and then to the Cavendishes. In 1923 Lord Richard Cavendish placed the ruins in the care of the then government's Office of Works, which became the Ministry of Public Buildings and Works, and thereafter it came to English Heritage.

During the growth of the tourist industry from the eighteenth century the abbey was very popular. It became even more so with the coming of the railways in the next century. Indeed the railway came too close. In his guide Wordsworth said that he was told that the intention was to drive the railway through part of the abbey site: 'an outrage which was prevented by some one pointing out how easily a deviation might be made; and the hint produced its due effect on the engineer'. But even so it came too close. There was a bit of exaggeration when he was told that the railway trains came 'so near the East window that from it Persons might shake hands with the Passengers!'. He was, however, moved by the respect shown to the ruins by the navvies laying the track nearby, and wrote the very good sonnet 'At Furness Abbey'.

> Well have yon Railway Labourers to THIS ground
> Withdrawn for noontide rest. They sit, they walk
> Among the Ruins, but no idle talk
> Is heard; to grave demeanour all are bound;
> And from one voice a Hymn with tuneful sound
> Hallows once more the long-deserted Choir
> And thrills the old sepulchral earth, around.
> Others look up, and with fixed eyes admire
> The wide-spanned arch, wondering how it was raised,
> To keep, so high in air, its strength and grace:
> All seem to feel the spirit of the place,
> And by the general reverence God is praised;
> Profane Despoilers, stand ye not reproved,
> While thus these simple-hearted men are moved?

A railway station was duly opened in 1847 close by the abbey; and the railway company built the Furness Abbey Hotel on the site of what was the nearby manor house. They promoted its facilities widely. This put the abbey ruins very firmly in the forefront of tourist attractions in Furness and the Lakes, and many thousands visited the site – very many more than visit it today.

In a lecture in Oxford in 1884 Ruskin, too, expressed his disgust at the too close intrusion of the railway station:

> It is continually alleged in Parliament by the railroad, or building companies, that they propose to render beautiful places more accessible or habitable and that their 'works' will be, if anything, decorative rather than destructive to better civilised scene ... Let me take, for instance, for the most beautiful and picturesque subjects once existing in Europe – Furness Abbey – A railroad station has been set up within a hundred yards of the abbey.

And in a letter in 1875 Ruskin mentioned his fears that his 'own sweet Furness Abbey' would be shaken down by the vibrations from the nearby railway. Later people complained that the heavy mineral traffic on the railway was causing some collapse.

The hotel shut in 1938, and during the war the army requisitioned it. Then in the air raids on Barrow in 1941 a bomb hit it, and part of the station was also destroyed. The hotel was largely demolished in 1953, leaving only the section that is now the Abbey Tavern; the rest of the site is a car park for the abbey. The station has gone, but the line is still used.

One should really start the tour outside the complex, because north of the abbey – and the inn – is the *Capella extra portas*, the outer chapel, built in the early fourteenth century, without its roof but still comparatively undamaged. Approaching the abbey from this north side entrance, one would once have passed by the great gatehouse, which has now gone.

Entrance is now gained through the English Heritage's reception area. The staff, on request, can loan a hand-held audio device that explains what one can see on a walk around the ruins. Sometimes these gadgets can be an irritation and even a hindrance; but in this case they are excellent; the talk is easy enough for the complete novice to understand, while not insulting the intelligence of the better informed. But such a recommendation should not rule out a free, easy and leisurely exploration of the site, which is also rewarding; for it is not just a visible episode in history that is here, but a scene of beauty.

As you leave the reception area the whole north side of the church is in view. The eastern end is still high, most of the nave has gone and the greater portion of the tower at the western end has collapsed, though it still stands over 18 m high. It is thought that originally it could have stood at about 49 m, a stunning sight, and its bells would have been heard on the plains and far-off hills for miles around. This tower was added to the complex around 1500, and because there was not enough room for it on the site restricted by the ravine, it had to be partially built into the church nave. This meant that the west door had to be sacrificed, and a new entrance was provided at the north-west corner by stairs.

The approach now is past the cemetery gate and into the north transept. In part this stands at almost its original height, with three bays, still with their altar platforms. Beyond, at the crossing, the authorities built a central tower, being a usual feature of abbey-churches. However, some disaster occurred and the structure collapsed – and a similar fate befell Fountains Abbey, it is thought. The fault rested with the central piers, which could not take the added weight. Following this crisis the east end had to be rebuilt, and three of the piers buttressed. Thereafter the abbot decided to build the belfry tower at the western end.

The eastern end, the presbytery containing the high altar, dates almost entirely from the fifteenth century, and has the frame of the colossal east window. It has lost the top of its arch, but what an awesome sight it must have been when it was intact with its stained glass! It was the work of Sir John Petty, the York glass painter. If one steps outside and looks up at the external hood moulding, two heads can be seen at their termination. These are thought to represent Queen Matilda and King Stephen. The next striking feature in the presbytery is the sedilia group, with the canopied heads in good condition, the finest in the country. Here sat four priests. In a left-hand recess is the piscine, where hands were washed; towels were kept in recesses on each side. In the north transept one can see the stairs connecting it to the dormitory.

In the nave little remains beyond the foundations. The base of the screen that separated the lay brothers from the choir can be seen. Near the end of the south wall was the doorway from the first-floor lay brothers' dormitory, from which a stairway led down into the nave.

Now step outside into the cloister area and look east towards the chapter house, for this is the stirring sight that lingers in the memories of all visitors. The five round-headed arches are magnificent. Their mouldings have been weathered over the centuries, but this seems to add to, rather than detract from, their beauty. From left (north) to right they are, first, a book cupboard; then the entry into the chapter house; another recess, probably also a book cupboard; then entry into the parlour; and then a door leading to the slype – a covered passageway. Go then into the thirteenth-century chapter house, which makes an immediate impression. Only portions of the slender columns remain, but one is struck by the beauties of the arched windows, with the leaves of the trees beyond, and the sky visible through what was the upper floor. At the head of all the twin-lancets nestle delicately carved medallions.

To the south of the cloister on the eastern side are the remains of the undercroft; above this would have run the dormitory, the largest in England, which indicates the large number of brothers the abbey required. The ruins of the guesthouse lie at the south-east and beyond is the circular foundations of a

Furness Abbey chapter house

kitchen; but the standing building, still with its vaulted roof, is the chapel, which served the long building that stood at its western end: the infirmary. The original infirmary stood hard by the natural eastern wall of the complex, and the ruin can be seen. This became the abbot's house. Only some of the foundations of the long buildings west of the cloister remain. This was the home of the lay brothers, with kitchen, dining area and accommodation on an upper floor.

This only sketches what can be seen. The rewards of a visit here depend upon the feelings and interests that are brought to it. Botanists, for example, can spend hours of enjoyable exploration. The ivy that once covered the walls was causing damage and had to be removed. Now the ubiquitous little purple flower that grows out of the cracks and crannies in the summer is the ivy-leafed toadflax, which seems to revel in ruined buildings. And there are the pale blue flowers of harebell (Scottish bluebell) clinging to walls; the yellows of hawkbit and St John's wort, and the delicate little spleenwort fern. Children can find faces carved into the stonework in places. Otherwise it is very pleasant to find a quiet seat and let worldly thoughts float away.

A display area in the reception building contains several tomb monuments: among them are two knights from the mid thirteenth century, with crossed legs and closed helmets, quite rare, and a statue of a deacon with a book, about the same age. Panels display the history of the abbey.

Two km north of the abbey is the small town of DALTON IN FURNESS (pop. 12,060), the one-time capital of Furness. The castle (NT) is a grim square ugly tower, built in the fourteenth century by the abbot of Furness Abbey to serve as a stronghold and prison. The old marketplace fronts the castle, and behind it is the splendid church of St Mary. Large and Victorian but unlike some grim examples of the age, it is inviting both inside and out thanks to its architects, Paley and Austin. In the churchyard, but not under this stone, lies George Romney (1734–1802), son of a local builder, who became the celebrated portrait painter of the rich and famous. At first, when he settled in London in 1762, Sir Joshua Reynolds was his only rival; but then ambition and volume of work marred his talent, and like his other brilliant contemporary, Thomas Gainsborough (1727–88), his work fell just a little short of the pure genius of Reynolds. A frequent sitter was the great beauty, Emma Hart, later Lady Hamilton and Nelson's mistress. He painted her many times in different guises. One group portrait, considered one of his best, is *The Gower Family*, now owned by Abbot Hall Art Gallery in Kendal (see p. 343).

In the churchyard, too, is a flower border memorial to 360 unknown parishioners, more than half the population of the time, who died in the plague of 1631–2.

Iron was doubtless mined hereabouts by Furness Abbey brothers. In 1396 William de Merton bequeathed land in the area to 'The Abbot and Covenant of the Blessed Mary of Furness', so the monks could 'throw and raise all manner of mineral ore here found out of the mines'. Where they mined cannot be traced, having been dug away by the mining activity in the centuries that followed. Dalton lay at the heart of the iron mining boom in the eighteenth and nineteenth centuries, and had several very rich mining operations in the area. Reference was made to them in the Barrow entry.

Cumbria's zoo, South Lakes Wild Animal Park, is here at Dalton. It is sited on earth red with iron, and the rhinos, which doubtless roll in it, are red too. The zoo is also home to giraffes, tigers and the largest collection of kangaroos outside Australia. In all some 500 species of animals live here.

North-east of Dalton is the village of LINDAL IN FURNESS, prettily arranged round a green. To the north of here was a very rich mine.

CHAPTER NINE

West Coast: Millom to Whitehaven

The long stretch of coastline in its west meant that for many centuries Cumbria was a maritime country. As early as the Stone Age, fisher-hunters lived on the shore. In the Roman invasion the army's supplies came through its sheltered ports. Early Christianity was brought to northern England by missionaries landing here from Ireland. The Vikings came in from their longships first as raiders, then as settlers, and Angles bought their ox ploughs and farmed the rich land. Through history its ports were a main channel of Cumbria's commerce and shipbuilding was a major industry. Then shipping became even more important when iron and coal mining brought wealth and growth to the coastal towns. The subsequent decline of the heavy industries have brought many changes. Some of the industrial towns are not pretty – but then they were not meant to be. Their outstanding feature, however, is the fierce loyalty of the inhabitants to their home ground, and a friendship often born of hardship. Some of its seascape, swept by winds from the Irish Sea, can be rather bleak, but on clear days the views across to the Isle of Man are very fine and the sunsets magnificent.

MILLOM (pop. 7,110) sits on the west side of the Duddon estuary at the foot of the long coastline, and is the quintessence of a Victorian industrial town, but it has much older origins. Approaching the town from the east the road takes a sharp turn and here is Millom castle's remains, around, and integrated into, farm buildings. Most prominent is its tower, with massive walls, that has stood for 700 years. This was the seat of the Hudlestons. East of the castle is the 'hanging stone' – 'On this spot stood a Gallows, the ancient lords of Millom having exercised Jura Regalia within their Seigniory.'

The old Norman red sandstone church of Holy Trinity is hard by, much altered, and only the south aisle shows its early thirteenth-century origins. Alabaster effigies of Sir John Hudleston and his wife, 1494, lie on top of the tomb chest, which has figures of sons and daughters. Another sixteenth-century tomb chest, and the tomb of Sir Joseph Huddleston, died 1700, and his wife, died 1714.

Suitably red – sculpture of iron miner, Millom

Millom started as a village and became a mining town, and like all of them, it has suffered from the industry's decline. Here the material was iron – rich haematite ore was mined here in the mid nineteenth century. Millom's story is like any other of the mining towns of Furness and west Cumbria – a discovery of potential that led to a rush of immigration, including that of redundant miners from Cornwall. A grid plan of a new town was planned, but although rows of terraced houses were quickly built they could not cope with demand, and slum conditions led to outbreaks of typhus and smallpox. Mining prospects proved even better in 1868 after deposits of 17 fathoms in thickness were discovered, and the Cumberland and Iron Mining and Smelting Company, and the Hodbarrow Mining Company, invested in an expanding town with more and better housing, and churches and chapels, schools, shops and a market. The large red sandstone parish church was built in 1874 to a design by those supreme church architects of the period, Paley and Austin.

At the peak of mining activity no fewer than seven shafts were sunk, which produced around 340,000 tons per annum. Production was eventually hampered by the ingress of seawater. Although a Cornish beam engine was employed to pump it out, by 1885 it was found necessary to erect a protective barrier around the workings. However, further rich veins of ore were discovered to seaward, and when seawater again broke into the workings a further outer defence was needed. In 1900 a mile-long arc barrier was built from mine rubble, with a heart of clay, and steel and timber pilings. Concrete blocks were placed to break the sea waves. The barrier became the town's seaside promenade, and so it is enjoyed today. By this time some thirteen million tons of ore had been won from the mines. It could not last and the town's prosperity declined in the 1920s, but some mining continued until closure in 1968. In the town square is a splendid monument to the miners – suitably ore red in colours, just as all the workers were, from head to foot, as they emerged from the pits.

What can be seen now to seaward of the town are the two barriers; the hollows left behind and between are filled with water. The area is not only of interest to industrial archaeologists, it is now a rich nature reserve. An RSPB hide near the old lighthouse is available for birdwatchers, and the enclosed water is a great attraction to many bird species. The surrounding banks and hedges are rich in flora.

Norman Nicholson (1914–87), the Lakeland poet and a keen naturalist, would have approved. He was a genius: in his time one of England's most talented poets. Millom was his birthplace and his lifetime home, and although the town is hardly handsome, and hardly poetically inspiring, he loved it. His home was above his father's men's outfitter's shop in St George's terrace. (It now sells health food.) Norman suffered from tuberculosis in his teens, and after a stay at a far away sanatorium, must have spent hours at the window of his attic room – a window turned into a casement for his benefit, for he lived there for the rest of his life.

> Lying in the dark, I hear the bray
> Of the furnace hooter rasping the slates, and say:
> 'The wind will be in the east, and frost on the nose, today.'
> Or when, in the still small, conscience hours, I hear
> The market clock-bell clacking close to my ear:
> 'A north-west wind from the fell, and the sky-light swilled and clear'
>
> But now when the roofs are sulky as the dead,
> With a snuffle and sniff in the gullies, a drip on the lead;
> 'No wind at all, and the street stone-deaf with a cold in the head.'

Apart from his books of poetry Nicholson also wrote about the Lakes. *The Lakers* (1995) tells of the notable discoverers of the region. Other books include *Cumberland and Westmorland* (1949), *Greater Lakeland* (1969) and *Portrait of the Lakes* (1963).

It has been said that Nicholson did not receive the recognition he deserved, because he was too parochial, anchored to his home territory. He answered the criticism in a radio broadcast 'On Being a Provincial'. He certainly stands with Wordsworth as a pre-eminent Lakeland poet. It is because he is less well known nationally that many still discover his poetry with delight. The poet's grave is in the churchyard. Its inscription is from his poem 'Sea to the West', where he weaves a sublime picture of the evening's bright glow of sunshine on the western sea.

> Let my eyes at the last be blinded
> Not by the dark
> But by dazzle.

The great mass of fell above Millom is BLACK COMBE (600 m), which, being separated from the central fells by a large area of comparatively uninteresting moorland, is generally neglected by fell walkers. It is of Skiddaw slate, lacking the spectacle of many crags, and sharp edges, but there are a few; yet its views on good days, westwards over the sea to the Isle of Man and Ireland, and towards the hills of Scotland and Wales, as well as inland to the high fells, are extraordinary. In 1813 Wordsworth climbed the height and wrote a poem of praise, 'View from the Top of Black Combe'.

> This Height a ministering Angel might select:
> For from the summit of Black Combe (dread name
> Derived from clouds and storms!) the amplest range
> Of unobstructed prospect may be seen
> That British ground commands:–

He also wrote 'Written with a Slate Pencil on a Stone' on Black Combe, in praise of Colonel Mudge, a distinguished surveyor whom the poet met on the fell.

West of Millom are the extensive sand dunes of Haverigg. Travelling 3 km west one enters the National Park, at which point a turn-off leads to SILECROFT and a popular beach. This west coast gets a hammering from winds and high tides, doubly bad when they come together, so the beach's profile changes over the years. The approach is over rocks and pebbles. When the tide is out there is a great deal of sand, but broken here and there by shingle banks. Unfortunately Silecroft has one of those beaches that receive a lot of rubbish, most of it from traffic in the Irish Sea. Volunteers, organized by the area's National Park ranger, do litter sweeps at intervals.

Travelling north from Silecroft one can get an idea of the great mass of Black Combe, which is above the road for 5 km until one reaches BOOTLE village. Bootle church has old origins but is now obviously Victorian. Unusually for Cumbria it contains a brass-plate monument, this to Sir Hugh Askew (d. 1562). A road from the village crosses the west coast railway line and leads to a pleasant section of beach, marred by broken brick walls; here again sand stretches are broken by shingle banks. It used to be claimed that in Selker Bay, just south of the beach access, '... in calm weather may be seen the sunken remains of small vessels or galleys which ... were left by the imperial legionaries of Rome in one of their invasions'. There's little chance of seeing such sights now, if ever there was, and a feeling of freedom is limited by some ugly modern intrusions. BNFL Sellafield is in sight, and just north of the beach is a Ministry of Defence gun testing range with an observation tower. A red flag flies when firing is imminent.

Passing by the range, though, ESKMEAL DUNES undulate on a peninsula round which the River Esk bends, running north then turning abruptly south-west, separating it from the Drigg peninsula on the opposite bank. The way into the port of Ravenglass lies between the two. The sand dunes here occupy a nature reserve in the care of Cumbria Wildlife Trust under an agreement with the MoD. Visitors are required to report to the gun-range gatehouse before entering – the reserve is closed when a yellow flag is flying. The dunes are relatively undisturbed and for that reason their typical flora is a happy exploration ground for botanists. The species include the uncommon moonwort fern, centaury, carline thistle, sea holly, Portland spurge and smooth catsear. The shore and the Esk estuary have saltmarshes and drift zones that are also rich in interest. The resident birds here include shelduck, red-breasted merganser, ringed plover, curlew, redshank and partridge, and in summer skylarks can be seen and heard – a rarer sound in England nowadays. Foxes, stoats, hedgehogs and roe deer also frequent the reserve, and sometimes otters and grey seals.

A main task of the reserve, though, is to preserve the breeding ponds of the rare natterjack toad, the rarest of Britain's amphibians, which occurs in large numbers only on this west Cumbrian coast. The toad is smaller than the common species, and has a yellow stripe. Nor does the natterjack hop or crawl; it uses its shorter rear legs to run at its prey. Ominous notices warn visitors not to touch what is hoped to be another rarity: 'shell, bomb, missile or strange object found on the sands or beach'. The request is to note the position and report it at the first opportunity.

The road continues along the Esk bank to the small settlement of WABERTHWAITE. Cumberland sausage, which come in one long length instead of links, can be had at all the county's butchers. Some are excellent, and some do not deserve the name, but Waberthwaite is reputed to produce the very best. Its unique recipe is a secret.

Waberthwaite's little church is hard by the estuary, a good example of a dale church left alone by Victorian meddling; just one long barn-like nave and chancel, with box pews, dating largely from the sixteenth and seventeenth centuries. In the churchyard – with views east to the high fells – stands part of an Anglian cross shaft.

Continuing north the road crosses the Esk, and MUNCASTER CASTLE is reached. The castle has been home of the Penningtons and Lords of Muncaster since 1208; and the gardens are famed for rhododendrons and azaleas. It is away from the central tourist areas, but to all who love fine houses, art and gardens, it is a treasure that must not be missed.

Like many of our northern houses Muncaster Castle is built onto a fourteenth-century defensive pele tower. In the mid nineteenth century Anthony Salvin, well known for his skilful work in adapting castles and old buildings into elegant, comfortable and tasteful modern dwellings, was commissioned by the fourth Lord Muncaster to rebuild (1862–6). The present building is a very happy result. Salvin gave the house an uncluttered symmetry, balancing the pele tower at one end with a second tower at the other.

The house has an immense variety of classical furniture, paintings by Kneller, Reynolds and Gainsborough, wood carvings, tapestry and *objets d'art*. There is a full-length portrait of the famous fool Thomas Skelton, employed by the Penningtons, who brought 'Tomfoolery' into the language. Here he is in solemn mood, holding his last will and testament, which is written in doggerel. The best rooms are the octagonal library and the drawing room with a white marble chimney-piece. But there is more to see.

Each old castle has its legend. Muncaster's is unlikely, but just possible. The

Muncaster Castle

story tells that Henry VI, on the run after his defeat at Towton in March 1461, fled through Cumberland and arrived near Muncaster, exhausted. He was brought to the castle by shepherds and was given hospitality for nine days while he recovered enough to flee to Scotland. As a token of his gratitude the king gave his host a green glass bowl, bearing gold and enamel decoration, that became known as 'The Luck of Muncaster'; with it came the blessing that so long as the bowl was unbroken the family would prosper. How come that when he was on the run he just happened to be carrying a glass bowl? From 'the king's bedroom' at the castle one can see an eighteenth-century 'pepperpot' monument on the nearby hill, which is supposed to mark the spot where the king was found. The castle, of course, has a ghost.

At rhododendron time the gardens are especially magnificent, making an exotic contrast to the wild landscape of England's highest land, seen in the background and often capped with snow at this time. The terrace walk round the contours of the castle hill brings one to a sudden view up Eskdale. Given the right conditions this is a classic, absolutely fabulous, and lacks only the heraldic sound of silver trumpets and choirs of angels.

The grounds contain the World Owl Centre with a large collection of birds, ranging from huge to tiny. Among the rescued birds are other birds of prey as well as herons. There are regular organized bird flights, as well as walks, trails and a playground. A friendly welcome is given by the Penningtons (the Lords Muncaster are part of the family), who own the castle. This is a happy place.

Nearby is the little church of St Michael, dating from the twelfth century but standing on an earlier site, for there is an Anglo-Norse cross shaft in the churchyard, and a wheelhead cross. Memorial stones in the floor include one to John Pennington, who 'led his soldiers at Flodden'. The Angel windows in the chancel were given by Josslyn, Lord Muncaster, in memory of friends of his, killed in Greece by brigands in 1870. It is a sad story. He and his friends were held as hostages and Josslyn was released to arrange payment of a ransom, but in his absence the bandits panicked and killed their prisoners.

RAVENGLASS is a hamlet by the shore just beyond the castle. Before silting, centuries ago, it served as an important port for the earliest inhabitants of the region – Romans, and then Saxon and Norse settlers. The Romans built a fort here, Glannaventa, 'The Town on the Bank', but although the settlement must have been extensive, little now remains; those parts of the site that are not covered by a plantation are crossed by the west coast railway. One remnant, though, and a remarkable one at that, is the bath house, strangely known as Walls Castle, with walls that still stand to a height of 3.5 m. This is on woodland to the east of the fort. Close vegetation must have protected it over the centuries. It is also very probable that it was lived in long after the Romans left. One

'Walls Castle' Roman bath house, Ravenglass

suggestion is that the Penningtons lived here before the move to Muncaster; another that it served as a leper hospital.

The delightful hamlet lies alongside the estuary of the Rivers Esk and Mite, and consists of a wide street flanked by cottages and buildings of various ages from the eighteenth century. The street was once a market – a charter was granted in the thirteenth century – and it ends in a launching ramp, only usable at high tide. A solid gate protects the street from the extra-high tides, open normally, closed when necessary. A small 'millennium garden' on the estuary side of the street contains a mosaic designed by local children and adapted by an artist. National Park staff tackled the work in 2001 when their movements were restricted elsewhere by foot and mouth disease. The metal seats along the estuary side were also designed by schoolchildren – a great idea – and they represent features of local history: a Roman head, a Viking ship, a ship's wheel and anchors. Another long-term project is to replace the cobbles that were once a feature of the street. The hamlet, cared for by a local inhabitants' forum working with the NPA, should be the model for many more elsewhere.

Ravenglass once had a reputation as a base for smugglers, and before that a place to find pearls. Camden reported: '… the shell-fish having by a kind of irregular motion taken in the dew, which they are extremely fond of, are impregnated, and produce – shell berries, which the inhabitants, when the tide is out, search for, and our jewellers buy of the poor for a trifle, and sell again at a very high price'.

Ravenglass (low tide)

Ravenglass is the starting station for the Ravenglass and Eskdale narrow-gauge railway (see p. 578–9). A little railway museum is housed here. Muncaster Castle is within walking distance by public footpaths.

Across the river estuary is a stretch of sands, as a future nature reserve, which contains the largest black-headed gull colony in England. Inexplicably, the population fluctuates. There are also terns – sandwich, arctic, common and little – and ringed plovers, shelduck and mergansers.

Going back to the main road and heading north there is a turning to the hamlet of DRIGG and a road past the station to the seashore. There can be found a very extensive sand dune system, with saltmarsh, mudflats, dune grassland and heath. This is an absolute gem of a reserve for nature lovers, with over 250 species of flowering plants, many birds resident and visiting, three reptiles, six amphibians, ten species of dragonflies and twenty butterflies. Some of the species are rare. A naturalist could spend hours exploring here. The area offers another habitat – the largest colony in the country – for the rare natterjack toad. The reserve is overseen by a committee formed by English Nature, Cumbria County Council, Cumbria Wildlife Trust, the Ministry of Defence, the Lake District National Park Authority, and Muncaster Estates. Part of the area away from the reserve is used by BNFL as a store for nuclear waste, suitably fenced, hidden and patrolled.

Further north along the shore the road passes through WHITRIGGS, where iron ore was mined in the eighteenth century, and reaches the village of SEASCALE. It grew around the railway, and most of it is little more than a century old. A very attractive seaside town, it is far enough away from BNFL at Sellafield to hold the modern industry at bay, but close enough to give some of its inhabitants employment at the works. As a quiet unassuming holiday resort, and despite its small size, it is hard to fault, though the nearness of the nuclear power station is off-putting to some. The sands are really excellent, the beach fine and uncrowded, the shopkeepers helpful, and there is access to some of the best country in the Lake District; indeed the Scafells and Great Gable can be seen from some points in the village.

Early railway poster advertising Seascale

The railway came to the west coast in 1849, and in 1866 it was acquired by the Furness Railway Company. The company had already developed Grange-over-Sands as a genteel seaside resort, and they could see potential at Seascale, which was then only a small settlement, but already attracting sea-bathing visitors. A great plan was drawn up. Seascale was to become a major resort with a large luxurious hotel overlooking the sea, and the town would grow as a result; there would be villas, promenades, a parade equal to Bath, and the railway would bring in visitors by the thousands. It did not happen. The 1870s brought financial and industrial depression and the scheme never went beyond a dream.

A little northwards of the town is Grey Croft Neolithic/Bronze Age stone circle. The circle, 24 m in diameter, was buried by a farmer in the nineteenth century, and located and re-erected in 1949. Ten of the original twelve standing stones remain.

THE NUCLEAR INDUSTRY

During the war British scientists were working in the United States to help produce the world's first atom bomb. In 1946 the UK government deemed it necessary to have its own nuclear bomb as a deterrent to other countries that might consider starting wars in the future. Where to build the ultimate weapon? During the war a Cumberland ordnance factory was producing ammunition on windswept fields beside the River Calder, 2 km up the coastline from Seascale. The factory site was thought to be a good place to begin the necessary production of plutonium. It was isolated in case of accidents, had access to a constant supply of pure water, and a workforce was readily available. The site was renamed WINDSCALE, and construction began on the country's first reactors, in twin piles. By the 1950s the reactors were producing weapons-grade material, and in 1954 the first nuclear weapons were deployed on Britain's submarines. At the same time the United Kingdom Atomic Energy Authority was set up to produce nuclear energy for peaceful purposes, and it wasted no time. In 1956, on part of the site named Calder Hall, the first reactor to produce electricity on an industrial site was opened by the queen.

Then in 1957 a fateful accident occurred that became a national disaster. Because of a human error, a fire started in Windscale's number one reactor at 11.05 a.m. on 8 October; but unbelievably it was not detected until two days later, 05.40 a.m. on the 10th, when instruments recorded radioactivity reaching the top of the stack that was only supposed to be discharging cooling air. By this time molten uranium, its cladding and graphite were ablaze, beyond control and spreading, fanned by the rush of air in the stack. Soon eleven tons of uranium were affected and the question was what to do about it. Water could trigger an explosion and a disaster on an international scale. A tanker load of liquid carbon dioxide was poured onto the fire. This made matters worse, and on the following day Tom Tuohy, the general manager, decided he had to try using water. Having cleared the site, only he, a colleague and a fire officer were present when they poured water through the fuel ports. This terrible risky ruse gradually worked, but that was only the start of troubles of which, at this stage, the general public was blissfully unaware.

How much radioactive contamination had passed through the filters at the top of the stack and spread throughout Cumberland, Westmorland and North Lancashire? The most dangerous radioisotope was iodine-131, which is absorbed easily by the human thyroid and could be in milk produced by dairy cattle grazing on polluted grass. A decision was reached between the Atomic Energy Authority, the police, the Ministry of Agriculture and the Milk Marketing Board to pour away all the milk being produced by farms in an area covering 500 square kms. Nothing could be done about the milk that might have been contaminated before the emergency measures. Luckily iodine-131 has a short life, but the panic measures, combined with confusing messages of assurance, caution and warning, had an adverse effect on Cumbrian public reaction. Confidence in the site was further undermined when it was revealed that nuclear particles had been leaking from the site for some time, and contamination was found on the beaches. For many years later the majority of Cumbrians came to distrust official pronouncements coming from the site and the relevant government departments. Indeed it is thought that only part of the story has been told. Windscale was considered a very bad and dangerous neighbour. Norman Nicholson wrote

> The toadstool towers infest the shore:
> Stink-horns that propagate and spore
> Wherever the wind blows....

After the fire both piles were immediately closed down and sealed off. Luckily the Calder Hall reactor operated at lower temperatures and was not at risk, and continued producing power. In 1963 a new gas-cooled reactor in a huge 'golfball' became operational, and the following year Windscale began reprocessing spent fuel from other nuclear power stations.

In 1971 British Nuclear Fuels (BNFL) was born to take over the reprocessing and disposing of spent fuel. Ten years later the whole extended site reverted to the old name of the area: Sellafield. Cynics concluded that this move aimed to wipe out the bad memories of the Windscale disaster.

It was not only many Cumbrians that regarded the Sellafield complex as a bad neighbour, Ireland has been critical of its contaminated discharges into the sea. And fisheries as far away as Scandinavia have recorded radiation from the site. Gradually in the 1990s the amount of discharge into the sea was eventually reduced to only 1 per cent of that in the 1970s.

In 1994 after eleven years in construction 'Thorp', the Thermal Oxide Reprocessing Plant, began operation, and three years later the 'Mox' – mixed oxide – plant was completed. The work is now wholly reprocessing and waste management. Generation of electricity finished at the end of March 2003. Calder Hall was closed, and its site will be unusable for many years. Ironically, given that the industry had been extolling the green benefits of nuclear-powered electricity, the plant now finds itself relying on a generator fired by fossil fuels.

As of 2003 about 7,000 workers are employed at the site, and if account is also taken of agencies and contractors the total workforce could amount to 11,000. So Sellafield is tremendously important to the economy of west Cumbria, not only for employment, but also for other economic and cultural investments in the region.

In the 1980s BNFL became more open about information, and a visitor centre was provided on the site in a bid to sell to the public the advantages of nuclear power. It is approached from Calder Bridge. In 2002 the presentation became much more unbiased when London's Science Museum took over half the exhibition space to air 'Sparking Reaction', a stimulating, sophisticated display offering arguments for and against nuclear expansion. It is an extraordinary presentation and very well worth a visit.

GOSFORTH TO ST BEES

GOSFORTH is a Cumbrian village 3 km east of Sellafield, given some new life in the last half century by an influx of residents working in the complex. Gosforth's claim to fame is the cross in the churchyard. Historians who gaze on this amazingly slender tenth-century Norse cross standing 4.5 m high, must anxiously wonder why it is not tucked away in some museum, shielded from the elements. The carvings on the cross shaft are remarkable. On three sides they tell the Norse story of the triumph of good over evil, and on the one other side there is the crucifixion of Christ. The side facing south shows Odin on horseback with a wolf and a stag. On the west side Loki, the evil one, is bound with a poisonous snake above him, but his wife Sigga is catching its venom in a cup. Above that is Odin and Heimdal, with his staff and horn, who guards the bridge and entrance to Asgard. Both are fighting off invading dragons. On the north side Odin is fending off – who? And on the east side at the top Vidar, son of Odin and sole survivor of the gods, is killing Fenrir, the monster wolf son of Loki, by prising open its jaw, and thus becoming born anew as a god of the world. Then below, Christ on the cross is the symbol of the saviour of a new world. The whole is topped by a richly decorated cross head. The supporting shaft is carved to represent the bark of an ash tree, Yggdrasil (literally 'world ash') that supports the universe. See it and wonder.

Inside the church are two magnificent carved Viking hogback tombstones that were revealed in 1896 when the north wall was being demolished prior to building extensions. They must have been used in the foundations when the Norman church was being built in the twelfth century to replace a former chapel. One has a battle scene, with two armies facing each other. One cross fragment has two men fishing from a boat. This has been set in a wall and has push-button illumination. On a window sill sits a large Chinese bell, captured by a local naval commander at Canton in 1841. It is cracked because an iron clapper was inserted to convert it into a church bell. It failed – Chinese bells are supposed to be struck by padded hammers. The church has been altered many times in its long history, the only obvious evidence of Norman origin being a doorway in the south wall.

Tenth-century Norse cross, Gosforth churchyard

Norse cross, detail

In the churchyard is a rather picturesque cork tree (*Quercus suber*), incorrectly reckoned to be the most northerly specimen. In Spain and Portugal the bark is regularly used to provide corks for wine bottles, but the tendency to use other cheaper materials is putting the conservation of the trees there at risk. This tree, at least, is protected and may still be in its prime.

Continuing northwards one arrives at the River Calder at CALDER BRIDGE, where stand two red sandstone Victorian churches. By the road is the imposing St Bridget's, the parish church of Beckermet, and just south, in Ponsonby parish, is the other, with its thirteenth-century flavour. William Morris designed the superb east window, and the west's is by Henry Holiday. The 1653 memorial to Thomas Curwen features a 'very rustic' (Pevsner) relief of two men, one with an axe, the other with a skull, but the message is obscure. There are also two coffin lids with cross, sword and sheep shears.

Only 3 km away from the Gosforth Norse cross – ninth-century Anglian cross, Irton churchyard

Going up the riverside, in 1 km CALDER ABBEY is found. The privately owned ruins are very picturesque, tranquil and solitary, but the walls too unsafe to allow public access, and one must be content to observe it from the nearby right of way. The abbey, a sister to Furness Abbey, was built in 1134 for William de Meschines, for the order of Savigny, which was later united with the Cistercians in 1148. A west doorway, the oldest surviving detail, remains, with five high bays of the north aisle, the tower, now standing at 19.5 m, around half of its original height. The north and south transept arches, and part of the chancel, survive. Of the monastic ranges, only part of the east range is evident. A Georgian house occupies part of the site.

The abbey suffered from the Scottish raids, and its existence at times was precarious. The Scots drove out the monks in 1138, and they walked to Furness

Calder Abbey ruins

Abbey, but meeting with an oddly uncharitable reception, they left, and eventually found their way to Byland in Yorkshire, where they founded another, safer, abbey. Calder was repossessed by Furness Abbey monks, until it was dissolved in 1536.

BECKERMET (*bek-ER-met*) is 2 km on. Here is the old parish church of St Bridget, built like a barn and very simple (the new St. Bridget's we saw at Calder Bridge). In the churchyard are two Saxon (?) cross shafts, one holding a runic inscription that has exercised the minds of the experts and prompted several guesses. 'Edih ginel miec' has been interpreted as 'Edith little maid'. St John's church is Victorian, but here again there are Anglo-Saxon cross fragments.

Beckermet also had its castle, not far from the main road. The only evidence now is the motte, oddly named 'Carnarvon Castle'.

A minor road from Beckermet follows the coast to Nethertown. To the south-east of this settlement a major archaeological discovery took place here in the 1870s when Ehenside Tarn was being drained for agriculture. The peaty soil revealed evidence of early human occupation. Here it was that the stone axes, roughed out on the 'factory' sites in the central fells, were polished and sharpened, for sandstone grinders and polishers were found among axes, one with its shaft (beech has been suggested, but surely not). Wooden objects included a canoe and spears. Radiocarbon dating suggests a period between 3314 and 2714 BC.

Nearby EGREMONT (pop. 7,550), like some other Cumbrian villages, has an impressively wide main street, a feature that sometimes deludes the unfamiliar traveller into believing that a large town lies behind. The place has seen good days, and then bad. In the past iron ore of good quality was Egremont's strength. The industry dates back centuries: the earliest extant record shows that a gift of an Egremont iron mine was made to Holme Cultram Abbey by the third earl of Albermarle (d. 1179). The mines were at their most productive in the early twentieth century. Some 146,000 tons of excellent ore were lifted from three mines in 1907. A small single mine, 'Florence', is still continuing small-scale production.

In 1913 there was an accident at Townhead iron mine and the rescue was difficult and long. To the two surviving miners it was the stuff of nightmares. On 13 March, twelve men had descended into the 90 m-deep pit, and made their various ways to their workings. Two miners were walking down to their work station when they were hit by a blast of air that extinguished their candles. They knew that something was wrong, and in the pitch darkness struggled to get back to the shaft. A rush of water from nearby old workings had broken in. The two men with two others reached the cage through the rising water. Five others made their way out by a manway. The cage came back to the pit bottom and one miner got in, who called to his mates but it lifted before any answer came back. The cage was sent down again, but was jammed in the rising water. A head count on the surface revealed that three men were unaccounted for: John Cairns, James Bewley and James Ward.

Down in the darkness of the pit, John Cairns, a miner with long experience, led James Ward upwards through the rising water to a drift connecting to old workings, that he knew had been penetrated by a bore hole a few weeks earlier. They reached it safely with water still rising, and they could look up to the bore hole – a mere 15 cm in diameter. It was five hours before they heard, to their great relief, a call down the hole.

Divers from Barrow and Liverpool were called to the scene to descend the shaft and release the cage, but failed. Meanwhile down the borehole candles, hot soup, Oxo and some food were lowered to the two men – and a watch.

Days passed. On the 18th the water levels had lowered sufficiently to allow the divers to release the cage. They found the body of Bewley. A rescue team entered the mine in an attempt to reach the other two men, but they were hindered by roof falls and debris, and it took time before they could unblock the obstructions and go on in dangerous conditions. The survivors had been staring up at the bore hole for five days, but at last the rescue team reached them. Their release was a matter of celebration, but after a check by a doctor, Cairns opted to walk home – two miles to Cleator Moor.

The mining company struck gold medals for all involved in the high-risk rescue. John Cairns was awarded the Edward Medal, the 'miner's VC'. James Ward was awarded a medal and a purse of gold in recognition of his ordeal.

The local quarries of fine red sandstone also employed many. Solid blocks of the stone built the Norman castle, although Egremont's buildings are largely of limestone. The castle's remains are on the hill south of the town. It is presumed to have been the work of William de Meschines in 1135. The best part of the ruin is the gatehouse, where typical Norman herringbone stonework and rib-vaulting in the roof can be seen. The front wall of the great hall, dating from the first half of the thirteenth century, still stands with doorways and windows. There are also remnants of the massive defensive walls, the domestic buildings and the postern gate. Like other castles it was built to withstand raids by the Scots, and must have endured several serious attacks. The castle is wide open to the public.

Of course, the castle has to have a legend. The improbable one associated with the place concerns 'The Horn of Egremont'. This horn, supposed to have been hung over the castle's gate, could only be sounded by the true lord of Egremont. That true lord, Sir Eustace de Lucy, went on crusade with his younger brother Hubert. Hubert saw his chance to gain the family's fortunes for himself and hired assassins to drown Sir Eustace in the River Jordan. He then promptly returned to claim the estate; but, naturally, try as he might he could not get a decent sound out of the horn. One day, years later, as Hubert was feasting with his retinue, the true lord of Egremont returned unscathed. When he blew the horn, Hubert suddenly remembered a pressing appointment and left by a side gate.

Egremont Castle

Egremont Castle, 'herringbone' masonry

It was the sort of story loved by the early tourists, and Wordsworth exploited it in his poem 'The Horn of Egremont Castle'. On the sounding of the horn:

> 'Tis the breath of good Sir Eustace!
> He is come to claim his right:
> Ancient castle, woods, and mountains
> Hear the challenge with delight ...
> Hubert! though the blast be blown
> He is helpless and alone:
> Thou hast a dungeon, speak the word!
> And there he may be lodged, and thou be Lord!

Egremont's church of St Mary was restored in 1880. It has four original lancet windows and some carved stonework of the thirteenth century, plus a medieval sedilia. The striking font is held by a kneeling angel.

Egremont is the scene of the famous annual Egremont Crab Fair. This dates back to the days when the local landowner would shower the local children with crab apples. The tradition continues, with more usual fruits being thrown from lorries and trailers. The fair, like any other, has its side-shows and commercial activity, but a key event is the gurning competition: 'Gurning through a baffin', or grimacing through a horse collar. The man who is judged to have pulled the most hideous face wins the prize.

St Bees is on the coast west of Egremont. It is mainly Cumbrian folk who enjoy the exceptionally fine sands and the airy cliff walks with views across to the Isle of Man and the hills of Galloway. One of the beach's features is the variety of coloured pebbles – a mixture of geological samples from the area. Being outside the National Park, planning is more relaxed and inevitably there is a caravan park, but it is not too intrusive. This is where the Wainwright's cross-country coast-to-coast walk starts. Tradition has it that walkers must first dip their feet in the sea.

St Bees is assumed to have got its name from the nunnery of St Bega. The story goes that St Bega was an Irish noblewoman who fled to Cumbria to escape an undesirable marriage, asked the local lord for some land for a nunnery and got the dusty reply that she could have as much land as could be covered by snow on midsummer's day. Snow duly arrived on midsummer's day, miracles being more common in those times. The Benedictine nunnery, founded around 650, was later destroyed by sea raiders, but the Normans founded a priory on the same spot in the twelfth century.

Wordsworth tells St Bega's story in a long poem, 'Stanzas suggested in a Steamboat off Saint Bees Head, on the Coast of Cumberland', part of which runs as follows:

> When Bega sought of yore the Cumbrian coast,
> Tempestuous winds her holy errand crossed:
> She knelt in prayer – the waves their wrath appease;
> And, from her vow well weighed in Heaven's decrees,
> Rose, where she touched the strand, the Chantry of St Bees.
>
> 'Cruel of heart were they, bloody of hand,'
> Who in these Wilds then struggled for command;
> The strong were merciless, without hope the weak;
> Till this bright Stranger came, fair as day-break,
> And as a cresset true that darts its length
> Of beamy lustre from a tower of strength;
> Guiding the mariner through troubled seas,
> And cheering oft his peaceful reveries,
> Like the fixed Light that crowns yon Headland of St Bees.
>
> To aid the Votaress, miracles believed
> Wrought in men's minds, like miracles achieved;
> So piety took root; and Song might tell

What humanizing virtues near her cell
Sprang up, and spread their fragrance wide around;
How savage bosoms melted at the sound
Of gospel-truth enchained in harmonies
Wafted o'er waves, or creeping through close trees,
From her religious Mansion of St Bees.

When her sweet Voice, that instrument of love,
Was glorified, and took its place, above
The silent stars, among the angelic choir,
Her chantry blazed with sacrilegious fire,
And perished utterly; but her good deeds
Had sown the spot, that witnessed them, with seeds
Which lay in earth expectant, till a breeze
With quickening impulse answered their mute pleas
And lo! a statelier pile, the Abbey of St Bees.

The priory (sometimes called abbey) grew wealthy, owning land and rights in Eskdale, Ennerdale and the western dales, as well as salt pans, iron and coalmines and quarries, and the port of Whitehaven. St Bees sandstone was shipped from Whitehaven in the twelfth century for the building of St George's Chapel, Windsor. Needless to say the priory was ravaged by the Scots in 1314 after Bannockburn; but it survived until dissolution in 1538. The parish church of St Mary is a remaining portion of the priory. Beyond the superb Norman doorway, the rest of the church is the usual mixture of original and not so original details. There are stone fragments and inscriptions dating back to the twelfth century, and one stone between the churchyard and the vicarage, thought to be eighth century, may have come from the nunnery.

St Bees School, alongside the church, was founded by Archbishop Grindal in 1583. The north side of the courtyard has the original schoolhouse of 1587.

The village itself is colourful, but not pretty, except in summer when the villagers fill the place with flowers.

The cliffs of St Bees Head to the north, 90 m high, are the area's crowning glory. The head is topped by a lighthouse dating from 1867. The cliffs offer nesting sites for kittiwakes, fulmars, guillemots and razorbills. The walk to the lighthouse alongside the cliffs is invigorating, and part way along, a path leads down to Fleswick Bay. It collects nasty plastic litter from the sea, unfortunately, but beyond it the red cliffs contrast with the general blue-greyness of the pebbles below; and some of the rock slabs that have dropped to the cliff foots are smoothed into unusual shapes by pounding and grinding pebbles. It is a

Sandstone cliffs, St Bees

sort of artist's surreal dream of colours and forms. Semi-precious stones have been picked up on the beach, but to the uninitiated all the wet pebbles can seem precious.

THE PORT AND TOWN OF WHITEHAVEN

Beyond St Bees Head, WHITEHAVEN (pop. 24,890) is Cumbria's third largest town, struggling, very successfully since the new millennium, to heal some of the scars of industry. It is a harbour town and its harbour is largely what it should be – well planned and well used by commercial interests and by weekend sailors. It is a treat to walk around it, but a pity that a supermarket has an obtrusive claim to the north end.

It began as a fishing port. Jonathan Swift (1667–1745), author of *Gulliver's Travels*, spent some of his childhood here in the town's early days, in mysterious circumstances. He was born in Dublin, son of the steward of the king's inns, who died leaving his wife poorly provided for. Swift wrote (of himself) in an autobiography:

Entrance to Whitehaven harbour

> His nurse, who was a woman of Whitehaven, being under an absolute necessity of seeing one of her relations, who was then extremely sick, and from whom she expected a legacy, and being at the same time extremely fond of the infant, she stole him on shipboard unknown to his mother and uncle, and carried him with her to Whitehaven, where he continued for almost three years. For when the matter was discovered, his mother sent orders by all means not to hazard a second voyage, till he could be better able to bear it.
>
> The nurse was so careful of him that, before he returned, he had learned to spell, and by the time he was three years old he could read any chapter of the bible.

He admitted that for the rest of his life he loved Whitehaven as if he had been born there. Local opinion is that Swift was staying at the Red Flag public house, above the town to the east. (It would fly a red flag when the militia recruits were at firing practice, and was certainly there in the early eighteenth century.) From here, it is suggested, he would view the distant inhabitants of the town as tiny people – the inspiration for Lilliput, perhaps?

The Wordsworths had an early fondness for the town. William remembered visits he made in the 1770s when they were staying there with their uncle Richard Wordsworth, controller of customs:

> I remember being struck for the first time by the town and port of Whitehaven and the white waves breaking against its quays and piers, as the whole scene came into view from the top of the high ground down which the road ... then descended abruptly. My sister, when she first heard the voice of the sea from this point, and beheld the scene before her, burst into tears. Our family then lived at Cockermouth, and this fact was often mentioned among us as indicating the sensibility for which she was so remarkable.

Getting lost in Whitehaven is difficult, for it was the first town in Britain to be planned, with streets laid out in grid fashion by Sir John Lowther (1642–1705) from around 1680. Sir John decreed that the houses on the main street should be three storeys high, spaced out with gracious gardens. The church had to be in the centre. He built a mansion for himself called 'The Flatt'. The scheme was completed by his son James. Sir John could not have predicted how the town would have to adjust to an economic revolution, for afterwards, sadly, many of the fine houses were demolished to build basic accommodation for workers.

The Lowthers became the major landowners of the area, after inheriting the land, and its coalmines, previously owned by St Bees Priory before the dissolution. Coal from the Lowther mines was Whitehaven's making. Earlier than Whitehaven, up the coast at Workington, coal was already being exported from the mines owned by the Curwen family, and at Ellenborough (Maryport) from those owned by Humphrey Senhouse. Rivalry flared between the three families, and that between the Lowthers and the Curwens became bitter.

It is difficult now to believe that in the mid 1800s the port of Whitehaven was second only to London, handling twice the tonnage of the ports of Liverpool and Bristol. Prosperity came mainly from the export trade in coal to Ireland from the town's own mines; but the slave trade, and the importation of tobacco, sugar and rum from Virginia, also generated wealth. Records show that in 1740 the importation of tobacco amounted to over 2 million kg, but trade later declined during the American War of Independence (1775–83).

The harbour that we see now has evolved from 1634. The quay that enclosed the inner harbour to the seaward side of the 'Beacon' museum was the first construction, though it was added to and lengthened later. Then between 1709 and 1711 the Bulwark Quay, or Mr Lowther's Bulwark, was built – this is now the barrier that separates the marina at its north end from Queen's Dock beyond, although it was not a dock at that point but a harbour. The next structure was the 'Sugar Tongue', the enclosure wall of the south harbour in front of the Beacon. A wet dock enclosed by gates was constructed in 1876 and then named the Queen's Dock in honour of Queen Victoria. Unfortunately the dock gates soon broke, and were not fixed until 1882. Now the greater docks area is enclosed by gates at the end of the old quay and the end of an arm enclosing what is now the north harbour.

In the nineteenth century the harbour kept very busy. In 1862, 4,787 ships with a total tonnage of 412,073 docked there. The town grew from a tide of immigrants seeking work, and in 1816 the town was the third largest in northern England, after Newcastle and York.

A bizarre episode in English history occurred in 1778: an American invasion; and it happened at Whitehaven. It was led by John Paul Jones, a well-known figure in the American War of Independence and a naval hero. John Paul was born in 1747 in Kirkbean across the Solway in Kirkudbrightshire. Jones was added to his name later. At the age of twelve he was sent to serve an apprenticeship as a seaman at Whitehaven. While still a mere boy he was promoted to third mate on Whitehaven's slave ship, the *King George*. It was built in 1763 specifically to carry slaves, atrociously closely packed, from Africa to the plantations. Then at the age of nineteen he was made chief mate of *The Two Friends*, a Jamaican-owned ship also in the slave trade. He was paid very well, but was sickened by the business. He joined a Kirkudbright brigantine, and when its captain and first mate died of fever, he sailed it home. The owners duly confirmed him as captain of the ship, but on a voyage to Tobago he gained a reputation for cruelty from his crew. The death of one of them after a flogging gave him a bad name at Whitehaven and at his home. A second command of a London ship bound for the West Indies led to a mutiny and the ringleader was killed. His reputation plummeted further and he was persuaded to flee to the American mainland, where he added Jones to his name. During the Revolution, he applied for a commission in the Congressional Navy. In 1777 he obtained the command of a privateer, the *Ranger*, and after a series of adventures, in April 1778 he sailed with this ship across the Irish Sea and attempted a night raid on Whitehaven.

His intention was to set fire to the ships in the harbour. However, the winds were too light for the *Ranger* to come close to shore, and the raiders, in two ship's boats, had a long journey to make against an unexpectedly strong tide. By the time they reached harbour dawn was beginning to break. Jones's boat party stormed the fort and because of the complete surprise, met no resistance; they spiked thirty-six cannon of the fort and battery. At this point the second boat inexplicably returned to the *Ranger* without accomplishing anything; their excuse was that their candles had burnt out during the unexpectedly long trip to shore. Jones pressed on with his plan to burn the ships – there were about 150 in the harbour – but the candles he had brought had also burnt out, and a light had to be acquired from a watchhouse on the quay! Then the ships would not ignite and only three of these sustained damage. Jones retreated at 8 a.m. under the fire of three guns from ships in the harbour. The attack, understandably, caused consternation in the town, and a public subscription raised £857 in only four days to repair and improve the defences. Within ten years the town's fire power was increased to ninety-eight cannon in four batteries.

Whitehaven has further links with the American Revolution – though less traumatic than the John Paul Jones incident. In the graveyard of the St Nicholas parish church the grandmother of George Washington lies buried, together with a daughter and a servant. In 1699 Mildred Washington, as a widow living in Virginia with three children – two boys, John and Augustine, and a girl, Mildred – married George Gale, a merchant trading from Whitehaven with the colonies of Virginia and Maryland. Gale brought the family to his home port, and the boys were sent to Appleby for their education. The widow died in 1700 and the boys were sent back to Virginia. Augustine married and eventually became the father of George Washington, first president of the United States.

Whitehaven's coalfields were in two areas: a large area between St Bees valley and the sea (and under the sea); and another to the valley's north-east. The seams dipped to seaward. In addition to this Charles II granted to Sir John Lowther (1642–1705) stretches of nearby coastal land between high and low water. New pits were being sunk as the town grew. In Daniel Defoe's guidebook, *Tour through the Whole Island of Britain* (1724–6), he wrote of Whitehaven, that it has

> grown up from a small place to be very considerable by the coal trade, which has increased so considerably of late, that it is now the most eminent part of England for the shipment of coals, except Newcastle and Sunderland, and even beyond the last, for they wholly supply the city of Dublin, and all the towns of Ireland on that coast.

Over twenty pits were sunk in the Whitehaven area, and as early as 1715 Sir James Lowther (1674–1755) introduced the first steam engine to pump out water. In 1781 his successor, another James, the first earl of Lonsdale, sent his chief steward, Carlisle Spedding, to Newcastle to see what could be learned from mining there. Spedding gained work in the Northumberland mine, and came back, not only with new ideas, but having recruited a few of the Newcastle men. Pockets of gas, sometimes the cause of explosions, were a major problem in the mines. To replace naked flames Spedding invented a 'steel mill'. A steel disc, mounted in a frame, was turned by a handle and spun at high speed against a piece of flint – which produced an arc of sparks. This means of illumination became established in mines all over the country, until the advent of the safe miners' lamp. It was, however, tiresome to operate. Spedding also introduced new systems of ventilation and proposed that undersea mining should continue, since pump engines were seen to be successful. The first level was sunk at Saltom just south of the town, in 1729, and in the process inflammable gas rose under pressure to the surface. Spedding offered to give the town and harbour trustees their own supply of gas to light the town if they would care to provide the piping. The offer was turned down, but gas was piped to the laboratory of Dr William Brownrigg, a scientist working in Whitehaven. He used it to heat furnaces.

In 1782 a massive engine was introduced at the Saltom pithead. It had a beam over 24 ft (7 m) long, and three boilers 13 ft 6 in (4 m) in diameter and 9 ft 4 in (3 m) high. It continued to work until 1866. In 1755, ironically, Carlisle Spedding was killed in a pit explosion. His son James Spedding (1720–88) succeeded him as engineer and caused more pits to be sunk.

The mines were sources of wonder to the gentlefolk of the eighteenth century, particularly when they learned that some of the levels went under the sea. They featured in the travellers' itineraries. Thomas Pennant (1726–98), the travel writer praised by Dr Johnson, paid a visit to Whitehaven on the way to Scotland in 1772. He was escorted down a mine and remarked: 'The immense caverns that lay between the pillars exhibited a most gloomy appearance. I could not help enquiring here after that imaginary inhabitant, the creation of the labourer's fancy, "the swart fairy of the mine".' Fairies? The miner to whom the query was addressed could not resist a true Cumbrian reaction. 'I was seriously answered by a black fellow at my elbow, that he really had never met with any; but that his grandfather had found the little implements and tools belonging to this diminutive race of subterranean spirits.'

And the miner also informed him, doubtless with a straight face, about the subterranean gases.

> Formerly the damp of fiery vapour was conveyed through pipes to the open air, and formed a terrible illumination during the night like the eruptions of a volcano; and by its heat water could be boiled; the men who worked in it inhaled inflammable air, and, if they breathed against a candle, puffed out a fiery stream.

Like many of the middle-class tourists of the time he lacked imagination, and regarded the lower classes with some hardness. At Whitehaven workhouse he could 'look with pleasure' at the sight of old and mentally ill people, and 'even infants of three years of age, contributing to their own support, by the pulling of oakum'.

In 1791 an incident occurred that soured relations between the inhabitants of Whitehaven and the then Lowther, the earl of Lonsdale, and that led to great hardships. A main band of workings lay at a shallow level under the town. Under Duke Street a rush of water drowned two men, a woman and five horses in the working. The ground subsided and houses in three streets were cracked and damaged. The inhabitants left their homes in alarm, and had to be reassured that there was no further great danger. A Mr Henry Littledale, a mercer of Somerset House, was also affected by the subsidence, sued the earl of Lonsdale at Carlisle Assizes and won. In a fit of temper the earl closed down his mines, making all his workers unemployed. They were only reopened after a petition, signed by 2,560 people, was delivered, begging him to reopen the mines and promising to indemnify him against future claims.

Steam engines for pumping water from the pits eventually increased production, but surprisingly it was not until 1791 that they were used to work winding gear. (Workington introduced them two years earlier.) In the nineteenth century more and more pits were sunk. Under the direction of John Bateman, William pit, to the north of the town at Bransty, was reckoned to be the most advanced in the country, with efficient pumps and winding equipment. Bateman was succeeded by another brilliant engineer, John Piele. He sank the profitable Wellington pit, also driven seaward. During Piele's term the mines were producing 250,000 tons per year and employing 900 miners. He retired in 1847.

The Lowthers kept control of the industry until 1888, when the mines were leased to the Whitehaven Colliery Company, and by this time all the workings were under the sea. Production continued well into the twentieth century, but not without incident. The history of mining here, as elsewhere, is one of bad working conditions, starvation strikes and accidents. Men were regularly killed and injured by explosions and roof falls, in this, most dangerous of industries. From 25 June to 1 October 1904 miners went on strike for better pay and conditions.

On the evening of 11 May 1910, there was an explosion and fire in Wellington pit, where 136 men and boys were working 3.5 miles down the mine's 'main road'. Rescue teams were soon at the mine but were beaten back by the heat, and the next morning they were joined down the shaft by two inspectors of mines. The heat was so intense that they gave their opinion that the rescue attempts should be abandoned; but some of the team members refused to leave and had to be dragged into the shaft cages. By that evening further rescue teams had arrived with breathing apparatus, and descended the shaft, but they too had to withdraw. But two of the rescuers from Sheffield, named Thorn and Littlewood, struggled on to within a mile of the trapped men, but by this time they were suffering from burns, some to arms and legs severe. They too had to surface. They were then told by the chief inspector of mines that they had not been warned of the risk of further explosions. 'We knew the danger,' said Littlewood; 'it made no difference.'

The final decision was heartbreaking. They would have to seal off the fire, building a brick wall to starve it of oxygen. Wives, parents and other relatives of the trapped men and boys had assembled at the pit head in dire need of a glimmer of hope. When they heard about the final decision, a wave of grief and utter despair washed over the crowd. On 14 May, Lord Lonsdale, the chief constable and the assistant manager descended into the pit and stayed for half an hour. They concluded that there could be no survivors.

Rescue teams made two more attempts to reach the affected area by way of a return airway that ran parallel to the main road, but they could not get anywhere near because of the heat and roof falls. The return airway had also to be blocked off with a brick wall. This was really the final blow, and the death count of 137 shocked the country. Alexandra, the Queen Mother, had been widowed only a short time before by the death of Edward VII, but she wrote to the mayor of Whitehaven on 14 May:

> Even in my crushing grief I am not insensible to that of others. Please therefore let all bereaved widows and members of the families of these poor men who have lost their lives in the terrible colliery disaster at Whitehaven know at once that in my own sorrow my heart bleeds for them.

The king sent another message of condolence.

That was not the end of the tragedy, for 600 men who were not on the fatal shift were put out of work. The disaster happened on 10 May, and the pit did not reopen for work until 15 August the following year.

The Whitehaven disaster prompted the introduction of an Act of parliament introducing enforceable safety measures and establishing trained emergency rescue teams. But it was not the end of disasters: on July 1922 an explosion at Haig pit, that had been opened eight years previously, killed 39 people.

In 1926 the long national strike of miners came to an end. In 1927 the Whitehaven mines employed 3,800 men, but a depression was looming. Then in 1928 at Haig pit, there was a series of explosions in which three men were killed, and while recovering the bodies and discovering the cause of the explosions, a rescue and inspection team was three miles underground when another huge explosion occurred. The death toll rose to thirteen, and included the works manager and under-manager, as well as two mines inspectors. In 1931 another accident at Haig pit claimed 27 lives.

That was not the end. In 1947 the last really major disaster happened. One hundred and eighteen men were working in the William pit, most on a seam under the sea 2½ miles from the shaft, when a shot-firing operation ignited a pocket of gas, which exploded and started a rapid fire. Some 110 men, dead or alive, were trapped by falls. The rescue team was quickly on the scene, but failed to reach the men, while hundreds of people assembled at the pit head. Some were volunteers preparing timber and blocking boards, but mostly they were relatives aching for good news. Twenty hours later, as rescuers cleared a fall, they came across three survivors, one of whom cried out of the darkness 'Thank God! There is a God in heaven!' But they were the only three. One hundred and seven men had died by burns, asphyxiation and roof falls.

Now, though mining is finished at Whitehaven, the memory of an industry that affected almost every family lives on. A group of mining enthusiasts who will not let the past die have opened a museum on the site of the Haig pit, which they bought for £1 in 1993. Some restoration work continues. A reminder of the old Wellington pit, which finally closed in 1933, is its 'candlestick chimney', a landmark on the east side of the harbour.

Another industry that contributed to the prosperity of the town was shipbuilding. Here again it was Sir John Lowther, at the end of the seventeenth century, who set it in motion when he needed more ships to carry his coal. Between then and 1889 over a thousand ships were built in the Whitehaven yards, and this was during a period when practically every coastal village along the Solway, where launching was achievable, was producing ships. But at this time a great proportion of goods traffic was being carried by coastal ships, and more ships were needed to serve the country's overseas commercial interests. Moreover the loss of ships was high. Sailing ships were vulnerable. Riding out a storm when close to shore was dangerous. Records show that great numbers of vessels ended their lives at the bottom of the sea. During the American War of Independence 100 Whitehaven-owned vessels were lost. On one exceptionally stormy night on the Solway in 1820, twenty vessels were lost. Seamen came second only to miners in having the most dangerous occupation.

In the eighteenth century the Woods family were prominent shipbuilders for sixty years, over which time they built 157 vessels. Other yards came and went. The speciality was mainly brigantines of 100 to 200 tons, and ships and barques of 200 to 300 tons. The 'most valuable ship ever built in Cumberland' in its time was the *Neptune*, 363 tons, with twenty guns. A nineteenth-century demand for larger ships was met by the construction of vessels of 500 tons, the largest being the *Princess Charlotte*, of 514 tons, in 1815. Forty years later *John O'Gaunt*, a vessel of 871 tons, was built and there were more of between 500 and 600 tons.

The demand for iron ships forced a decline in the town's shipbuilding in the latter half of the nineteenth century, and shipyards began to close. A new company, the Whitehaven Shipbuilders, took over one of the redundant yards in 1869 and began building clippers. In ten years the company produced forty-two vessels, mastering the art of making steel hulls; then, in financial difficulty, it was forced to close. Struggling to make a comeback, the company at last found new capital, which helped them to reopen in 1880. Thirty-four vessels were constructed, but in 1891 it had to accept the inevitable and finally stop building to concentrate on repairing ships.

One of the last ships to be built has an interesting story. It was a large three-masted steel-hulled full-rigged ship, and it had to be sold at a time when the market was cold. But Whitehaven traded regularly with Ireland, and as luck would have it, an Irish shipping firm, Martin of Dublin, expressed an interest in investing in the ship and a deal was done. It was named *Dunboyne* and her first cargo was of iron rails for Portland, Oregon. This was the first of several voyages round Cape Horn, and in twenty years she sailed all over the world. Then in 1905 she was sold to the Norwegians, then purchased again by the Swedes as a training ship and renamed *G.D. Kennedy*, a tribute to a Swede of Scottish descent. In 1923 she was taken over by the Swedish navy and renamed *Af Chapman*, after a famous admiral, and she was again sailing away across the world on diplomatic missions. She retired in 1934. After the Second World War she was up for sale again. Stockholm wanted to keep the ship as a decorative feature of the waterfront. The solution was a happy one – turn it into a youth hostel. There it is today providing 136 bunks, one of the best-loved youth hostels in the world. She is the *Af Chapman*, but one can still see, etched into the iron under the paint, the old name, the *Dunboyne*.*

An economic downturn in the early nineteenth century also meant a decline of the port, just as Liverpool was being developed to serve Lancashire's growing cotton industry, and the railways were extending. In 1845 Workington gained an advantage on Whitehaven when a new railway connected it to Carlisle. William Lowther, second earl of Lonsdale, wanted a link and got it two years later, but in addition he wanted the line to extend southwards down the coast to Furness. The Whitehaven and Furness Junction railway was incorporated in April 1847. In 1950 the new line was constructed to Broughton where it met with the Furness railway. In 1854 branch lines were established, and the Whitehaven, Cleator and Egremont railway linked the important mining towns.

The town had had very successful times. Employment prospects for males was offered by the mines, the iron works, ships' crews, shipbuilding and sail-making. Working conditions were often harsh, and more and more men flooded into the town in the hope of work. Overcrowding led to slum conditions. In 1858 a visitor viewed the area around the harbour and wrote:

> There is only one street in England that we have seen to beat Quay Street, Whitehaven, for squalor and filth; and that was Lace Street, Liverpool, before the sanitary act came into operation. From what we noticed there is some

* I am indebted to Robert Straughton for the above information.

> analogy between the two. The sprinkling of Manx people, whose wide mouths, high cheeked bones, and broad speech there is no mistaking, will not tend much to promote the cleanliness or purity of Quay Street. Houses, shops, jerry shops, courts, public houses, everything you come on speaks plainly of over-crowding. Sallow looking women, covered with rags, thrust their heads and half their bodies through the windows to look after you, and as they do this, they appear to gasp for fresh air.

Shelley was no more complimentary when he stayed in Whitehaven in 1812, waiting for a ship to Ireland.

> We are now at Whitehaven, which is a miserable manufacturing seaport Town.... We may be detained some days in the Island (of Man), if the weather is fine we shall not regret it. At all events we shall escape this filthy town and horrible inn.

The town is now at the other extreme, clean and colourful. It has some lovely Georgian houses, many of them restored, and it is a pleasure to walk around and admire them. The seventeenth-century St Nicholas church was almost totally damaged by fire in 1971, and never rebuilt, its function being taken over by St James' church. The old church's surviving tower is surrounded by an appealing

One of Whitehaven's fine eighteenth- and early nineteenth-century buildings

open space with a beautifully maintained garden. A mosaic in it states 'In memory of the 1,200 men, women, and children, who lost their lives in the Whitehaven coalmines 1597–1987.'

The church of St James crowns a hill near the town centre. It was designed by local mining engineer Carlisle Spedding, who was in charge of the Lowther mines in the mid eighteenth century. The Georgian façade belies what is beyond – an absolutely superb interior of white and gold, all carefully preserved. Unusually, the entry is through automatic glass doors engraved with two national symbols of Sri Lanka. It is a memorial to the much loved Sri Lankan vicar who served the church for ten years and died in 1995. Inside, galleries on three sides are supported by Tuscan columns. But it is the altarpiece that makes an unforgettable impact: a vast *Tranfiguration* by the Italian Giutio Cesare Procaccini (1548–1626), presented to the church by the third earl of Lonsdale in 1869. It was carefully restored in 2002. There are other gems: two stucco roundels in the ceiling thought to be the works of Italians Arturo and Baggiotti and depicting the Annunciation and the Ascension. The pulpit is an eighteenth-century 'wine-glass' shape, alas no longer the high three-decker admired in the past; and there is an excellently carved memorial to Thomas Spedding, first minister, who died in 1783.

The shopping streets are like any other, but Lowther Street has the famous antiquarian booksellers, Michael Moon. It is worth a special visit to the town just to browse and browse the shelves of glorious treasures.

There are three museums. The Beacon, on the harbour side, has an upper floor explaining how the weather is forecast, and other floors feature well-thought-out exhibits on the town's history. Though designed mainly for children, adults will also find things of interest, if they can endure the repetitive recorded voices. 'The Rum Story' on Lowther Street explains how rum was made and its dependence on the slave trade. The Haig Colliery Mining Museum is another, at the south-east end of the town.

Reminders remain of the three major Whitehaven imports: tobacco at Kendal snuff works; rum butter (a mix of rum, butter, brown sugar, and spices) which can be enjoyed in most good cafes and restaurants; and sugar, in the form of Kendal Mint Cake, part of the essential kit of mountaineers and eaten on Everest (the brown bars are authentic).

The hinterland east of Whitehaven is a strange mixture of fine rural landscape and urban drabness. In north-west Cumbria's countryside generally, many settlements did not evolve naturally and blend into the rural scene as agricultural settlements have done. They grew quickly around workers' cottages at a mine head. The result is sometimes bizarre; in a place of exceptional landscape you might come across rows of terraced houses looking as if they have been lifted and dropped directly from Manchester's Coronation Street. In the V of land between the A595 and the A5086 several of these iron mining settlements can be found.

THE INLAND INDUSTRIAL TOWNS

The rich iron deposits that became a major contributor to the economy of west Cumbria were found mainly in the beds of carboniferous limestone between the coal fields of the coast and the Lake District fells. From Egremont the limestone outcrops producing the ore run in an arc, up to 1.5 km wide on the west side of the River Ehen, north-eastwards through the foot of Ennerdale to Lamplugh on the edge of the National Park. Unlike coal the ore occurs in 'sops', or irregular masses.

CLEATOR began life as a rural settlement, and off its village street is a church of Norman origins. But it was on the edge of the rich and excellent mass of haematite, iron ore in its purest form. In 1800 there was a flax mill in the village, by the River Ehen, and a forge producing spades. The mill fell on hard times, then was rescued from dereliction by Thomas Ainsworth. It was Ainsworth who then made the investment that expanded the iron and coalmining activity in the area and created the new town of CLEATOR MOOR (pop. 6,760). One mine here had ore quite near the surface that may have been exploited long before the major workings in the eighteenth and nineteenth centuries. A near-surface rich deposit of iron was north of the village at Todholes, with first-class ore 5 to 10 m deep.

The potential Ainsworth saw in more efficient exploitation of the mines was directly linked to the coming of the railways, and he had the means to increase the labour force. His flax came from Ireland, and with it the nucleus of an Irish community. Irish immigrants would soon outnumber the indigenous population.

Two blast furnaces, owned by the Whitehaven Haematite Iron Company, were operating to the west of Cleator Moor in 1842. There were four main mines here, and the ore produced was of the best. Henry Bessemer, inventor of the method of producing cheaper steel from pig iron, said that he 'relied entirely upon haematite iron made at Cleator Moor and Workington'. The Cleator Moor mines began to produce one third of the total production of west Cumbrian haematite. The Montreal pit was extraordinary in that it not only produced iron from deep rich deposits, the largest mass of ore in west Cumbria, but also coal. In 1854 the railway duly reached Cleator, and extended eight years later through Cleator Moor to Rowrah, and not surprisingly the ore output was boosted. Between 1860 and 1870 the Montreal pit alone produced half a million tons of ore. East of Cleator Moor at Parkside another rich mass was mined in an area of 14 ha.

Unfortunately, as in other Cumbrian towns racial and religious bigotry divided communities. The population was a combustible mixture, including Scots (the Todholes mine was Scottish-owned) and a large Irish element. Significantly the first church to be built – after the old parish church of St Leonard's at Cleator – was the handsome Roman Catholic Church of Our Lady of the Sacred Heart (1853). Anti-Irish Catholic feeling rose to a pitch in 1884 after an Orange demonstration at Cleator Moor, and there were running fights.

Nowadays one can generally say this of the small west Cumbrian towns like Cleator Moor, spawned by the Industrial boom times – while it is true that the populations come from several racial backgrounds, they are united in being fiercely Cumbrian.

John Stirling, the Scottish mine owner, had a concern for the well-being of the local population – Catholics and all – and provided schools, a library, a reading room and a billiards room. When the new parish church of St John was built at Cleator Moor, in 1872, Stirling provided school premises. He also donated a hospital. Other benefactors were the Lindows of nearby Ehen Hall.

In 1871 Cleator Moor lacked a visible centre; there were just rows of houses. Something needed to be done. A board meeting decided that a market square should be built, and so it was. The market place was constructed on top of waste slag to give it a solid base, and in 1877 a local (Irish) contractor was commissioned to build a market hall and public offices. On the south side appeared the Cooperative Society's shop with an ironwork verandah. The town was one of the first to embrace the cooperative movement, which had thirteen branches in the area and from its base it became a dominant retail establishment in Cumberland. Each branch had its appointed committee that organized the purchase of food supplies in bulk at wholesale prices. The workers could then buy their essentials at the cooperative shop only a little above cost, and periodically the net profits were shared.

By the end of the nineteenth century the ore was being worked out and mining began to fizzle out. The railway lines have gone and all that remain are the spoil heaps. Yet Cleator and Cleator Moor live on. No small town could be more urban than modern Cleator Moor. Its own slag heap was flattened to give a base for a trading estate, yet it is in the attractive valley of the River Ehen, with delectable Ennerdale only 6 km away. In its heyday the red ore dust must have been everywhere; now the town has been face-lifted and is hardly depressing.

Nearby Moor Row was built to provide for workers at two pits. Bigrigg had three. Further north Frizington, Arlecdon and Rowrah had mines near the side of the National Park boundary and a short distance from Ennerdale. Rowrah's quarry produced limestone, necessary for use in the furnaces.

The Lowthers did not quite succeed in getting a monopoly of the coal stocks in the Whitehaven area. Just north of the town is PARTON. The land and the coal seams in that area were owned by the Fletchers of Moresby Hall. The Moresby estate decided to build a harbour at Parton, but Sir John Lowther did not want the competition and claimed that no harbour could be built there without his permission, since he had been given the land between high and low water marks from the Crown in 1678. So the Moresby estate had to pay for the use of a Whitehaven pier. However, the Lowther claim subsequently proved to have no legal status and the Parton pier was built in 1705.

LOWCA, a short way up the coast, had its own iron works and produced railway engines. Prior to the First World War a chemical works here, supported by German investment, produced ingredients for explosives. In 1914 when war broke out, the Germans did not forget. The works were shelled by a U-boat, an act of destruction apparently watched by townspeople from a high viewpoint! It is said that smoke was released by workers at the plant to give the U-boat commander the impression that the attack was a total success. The problem now seems to be unstable waste tips.

DISTINGTON (*DIZZ-ing-ton*) (pop. 2,300), alongside the Cockermouth road, had its mine and an iron works, and an industrial complex has grown around the town.

Along the coast the old port of HARRINGTON (once Haverington) was based on the coal export trade, and shipbuilding, the yards linked to those of Workington. The town was the seat of the Haveringtons, but came to the Curwen family in the mid sixteenth century. Henry Curwen built a quay in 1760 for the shipment of coal from his local pits. A timber yard was established near the quay and the production of ships began in 1788. By 1879 the yards had built something like a hundred ships. As always shipbuilding brought ancillary industries, anchor, chain, rope and sail making.

At one time there were nine coal pits in the area. In 1901 the mines employed 446 men, and 100,000 tons of coal were raised from three pits. There was an iron works here and in 1856 four blast furnaces operated, and in 1911 forty coke ovens were established.

The port is now used as a marina.

CHAPTER TEN

The Solway Coast: Workington to Port Carlisle

THE SOLWAY FIRTH

Several theories have been advanced for the origin of the name 'Solway'. The most plausible is the old Norse *sul* (pillar) and *vath* or *wath* (ford): the ford of the pillar, with the old Norse *fiord* (firth, estuary). The 'pillar' refers to the Lochmaben Stone, south of Gretna, that marks the ford crossing from the Scottish side of the Solway's rivers Sark and Esk. So the Solway was named after one of its fords. The Lochmaben Stone played an important part in the history of the area as it was the point where the Scottish warden of the West March met the English warden to settle differences and breaches of the border law. It has been speculated that the stone was placed by humans, and might have been part of a prehistoric stone circle.

The Solway marks the northern boundary of Cumbria, and part of the English border. The views from the coastal road that runs 60 km, from Workington to the outskirts of Carlisle, look across the water to Scotland. If the conditions are right the views in some places are stunning, and sunsets can be awesome. Inland from the coast the scene appears to be largely flat and uninteresting agricultural terrain – though it holds a few surprisingly attractive villages and settlements.

Solway is a haven for wildfowl. Over 130 species have been recorded, but the main interest is in the wintering birds. As many as 30,000 can fly in on a single day. The sight of flocks of geese in riotous conversation is memorable. The whole population of barnacle geese from Spitzbergen arrives here in October, though most of them congregate on the Scottish side until they come over to Cumbria's Rockcliffe in March. There are also hosts of pink-footed geese and greylags. Thousands of oystercatchers follow the retreating tides, and regimented clouds of dunlin, knot and golden plover fill the sky, as well as thousands of widgeon, teal and pintails.

Visitors to the nature reserve at Rockcliffe Marsh, in the care of the Cumbria Wildlife Trust, at Rockcliffe Marsh can also see goosander, goldeneye, red-breasted merganser and most of the common waders. The summer breeding birds include colonies of lesser black-backed gulls, herring and black-headed gulls, arctic and common terns; with lapwings, oystercatchers, common sand-pipers and sand martins.

Solway has long been famous for its salmon. Fishermen on both sides of the firth have netted and hooked them for centuries, and some fishing is still done in the ancient way by 'haaf net', which may date from Viking times. The 'haaf net' fisherman must wade out into the bay, sometimes to chest-high. His net is held onto a rectangular frame, wooden on three sides, with a billowing net fixed tight to form the fourth side. The frame is quite large – 5 m wide by 1.5 m deep – and a handle is fixed to the middle of the long, top side, at right angles. The frame is carried out into the channel and the long tail of the net, arranged so that it is divided to splay out on both sides of the handler, opens out with the tide. Handling the net, landing the salmon, and knowing the ways of the tides and currents require both strength and very special skills, which have been passed down through generations.

Solway Firth has also been a highway since time immemorial. We forget that before the gradual improvements of the roads from the eighteenth century, and the coming of the railways in the century following, the waterways were the main conduits for the transport of goods. We can imagine the Solway busy with sailing crafts of all kinds: full-rigged schooners, barques, barquentine, brigs, ketches, smacks, brigantines and, at the coming of the Industrial Revolution and the development of Cumbria's iron and coal mines, actual traffic congestion with ships packed in every harbour. Meanwhile the ports Whitehaven, Harrington, Workington, Flimby and Maryport were not only importing and exporting, but building ships by the hundreds, from small coasters to the transoceanic clippers.

WORKINGTON

WORKINGTON (pop. 25,310) is the port at the end of the Solway proper, and Cumbria's second largest town. It is where the River Derwent enters the sea, after its long journey from Borrowdale and Derwent Water. There must have been early human settlements in this area but signs of them have been lost as silting and storms reshaped the land around the estuary many times. The existing town must certainly stand upon the site of others. Nowadays it is the west coast's shopping centre, and in 2003 more developments are planned, and included in the debate is a vacant site caused by the total destruction of a supermarket by fire. The town is an awful jumble, with no street plan like Whitehaven's. One could not call it a handsome town, and could even sympathize with Dorothy Wordsworth, who was frightened by it. However, it is like many Cumbrian towns, where friendly folk are all too ready to help lost visitors (but confusing if advice comes from more than one person at the same time, and even more so if a former miner is giving help in miners' dialect which is like no other). Its bustle belies the fact that the town's economy has suffered much from the contraction of traditional industries.

The earliest signs of occupation are Roman, and the place was clearly of strategic importance. Just north of the town at Burrow Walls, by the side of Siddick Pond (Siddick = sea dyke) stood a Roman fort, which, without certainty, may have been called 'Gabrosentum', but there is nothing much left to see. Encroaching seas probably took part of it, and the railway slices through a third of it. Hadrian's Wall effectively finished at Bowness-on-Solway, and from then on, as protection from sea raiders along the Cumbrian Solway coast, there were a system of fortlets or mile stations, supported by substantial forts at Beckfoot to the north; then moving south to Maryport, then here at Burrow Walls, and south at Moresby. They were surely linked by a road. Then inland back-up forts were located at Carlisle itself, Old Carlisle near Wigton, Caermote and Papcastle near Cockermouth. During archaeological digs on the fort site, Roman pottery was found in what had been a defensive ditch, dating to the fourth century AD. The Romans would certainly have used Workington as a port.

As the Romans were abandoning Britain, Irish missionaries were bringing Celtic Christianity to the area, probably from around the fifth century. It is thought that the earliest, St Ninian, who founded a stone church at Whithorn directly across the Solway, was born hereabouts. St Kentigern (or 'Mungo'), bishop of Glasgow, was also an active missionary in north Cumbria, which was then in the Scottish kingdom of Strathclyde. Quite a few churches in the area are dedicated to him (for example Crosthwaite and Keswick). Although the Welsh may dispute it, St Patrick is also thought to be a Romano/British Cumbrian, for in his *Confessio* (autobiography) he states that he was the son of Calpurnius, a Roman tax collector, at Banavem Tabernia, a Roman settlement thought to be close to Hadrian's Wall, but has not been identified. At the age of sixteen he was captured by Irish coastal raiders and sold as a slave. Pirate raids from Ireland and the Isle of Man became more frequent on the Solway when Romans began abandoning this northern frontier. St Cuthbert also visited Cumberland. According to the Venerable Bede in *The History of the English Church* he would set out from Lindisfarne to preach.

> He used mainly to visit and preach in the villages that lay far distant among high and inaccessible mountains, which others feared to visit and whose barbarity and squalor daunted other teachers. Cuthbert, however, gladly undertook this pious task, and taught with such patience and skill that when he left the monastery it would sometimes be a week, sometimes two or three, and occasionally an entire month before he returned home, after staying in the mountains to guide the peasants heavenward by his teachings and virtuous example.

The town's name (the estate of Weork) confirms that the area was settled by Angles, probably after the Battle of Chester, when the Celtic tribes were subdued, though it is probable that the Celts remained as part of the population. The coast must have again been subject to attacks, this time not by Irish but by Viking raiders. Cuthbert died in 687 and was buried at Lindisfarne. However, the Scandinavian raiders forced an evacuation of Lindisfarne in 875, and the monks took up the saint's relics and fled with them through the north of England to try to find a safe place for them. They decided at last to sail for Ireland and arrived at 'the mouth of the river which is called "Dyrwenta" '. The voyage from Workington, however, was foiled by a violent storm and they turned back. The legend has it that the book containing the Lindisfarne Gospels was washed overboard, but St Cuthbert told the leader of the party in a dream where it could be found – on the other side of the Solway, at Candida Casa – Whithorn in Galloway. When recovered, the book was found to be quite unspoiled by the sea.

The Vikings came also as settlers, and Christians. Carved stone fragments of Celtic, Anglian and Viking origins have all been discovered in the town, notably by St Michael's Church.

Workington was too insignificant to have a reference in the Domesday Book, and it was within Scotland anyway. As the Normans increased their influence north, it fell under the barony granted to William de Meschines by Henry I. Its castle, on the site of the Roman fort at Burrow Walls, was probably built by Orm in the late eleventh century. Nothing remains of it. Sir Gilbert de Curwen obtained a licence from Richard II to crenellate it in 1379, but the castle's site was later moved across the river. Was it because it was damaged by coastal erosion? It was moved to the present site of the ruined Workington Hall, and occupied by the Curwen family, lords of the manor of Workington, from then until the twentieth century. The hall consisted of a pele tower, and later other buildings, including a great hall, were added. In the seventeenth century, like so many other castles in the period, the buildings were transformed into a mansion.

The first reference made to Workington as a port was during Edward II's campaigns in Scotland, when the port was used to bring his army's supplies.

Leland, writing in the reign of Henry VIII, described Workington as 'a pretty fysher town'; the estuary and the River Derwent have always been famed for their salmon. In the sixteenth century Queen Elizabeth, concerned about security, commissioned a report on 'all ports, creeks, and landing places in Cumberland'. The reference to Workington states 'Workington Creek having a town – 30 households of the inheritance of Henry Curwen - There are three vessels here called pickerdes, of seven or eight tons – their trade is to go to Chester and Liverpool with herrings, and they bring back salt. The mariners are hired fishermen.' Later the depths of the Solway coastal seas were tested and Lord Scrope, warden of the Western Marches, reported that Workington could be more than a pretty fishing town – it, and the other ports, could take ships of 60 or 90 tons 'on the spring tide'.

On the evening of 16 May 1567 Mary, Queen of Scots, with three lords and sixteen servants, landed here after fleeing from her enemies in Scotland. The lord of the manor, Sir Henry Curwen, and his wife, were away from Workington Hall, but their senior household servant gave hospitality to her party. While there Mary wrote the famous long letter (in French) to Elizabeth telling of her escape and ending with this passage:

> I entreat you to send to fetch me as soon as you possibly can, for I am in a pitiable condition not only for a queen, but for a gentlewoman; for I have nothing in the world but what I had on my person when I made my escape, travelling sixty miles across the country the first day, and not having since ventured to proceed except at night, as I hope to declare to you if it pleases you to have pity, as I trust you will, upon my extreme misfortune, of which I will forbear complaining, in order not to importune you, and to pray God that he may give to you a happy state of health and long life, and to me patience, and that consolation which I expect to receive from You, to whom I present my humble commendations.
>
> From Workington, the 17th of May. Your most faithful and affectionate good sister and cousin, and escaped prisoner. Marie R.

The next day Richard Lowther, deputy warden of the March, arrived with a troop of 400 horsemen and hustled the queen away to Cockermouth, and on to Carlisle Castle.

William Wordsworth's sonnet on the episode is not of his best, and historically incorrect:

> Dear to the Loves, and to the Graces vowed,
> The Queen drew back the wimple that she wore;
> And to the throng, that on the Cumbrian shore

Her landing hailed, how touchingly she bowed!
And like a Star (that from a heavy cloud
Of pine tree foliage poised in air, forth darts,
When a soft summer gale at evening parts
The gloom that did its loveliness enshroud)
She smiled; but Time, the old Saturnian seer,
Sighed on the wing as her foot pressed the strand,
With step prelusive to a long array
Of woes and degredations hand in hand-
Weeping captivity, and shuddering fear
Stilled by ensanguined block of Fotheringay!

When Keswick was enjoying the mining boom, the Company of Mines Royal in 1569 rented a parcel of land near the port from Henry Curwen to use as a wharf, and it became a supply base. The harbour had to carry a human cargo when England and Scotland were united under James I, and he came down hard, once and for all, on the reivers who had robbed and pillaged the borders for centuries. The harbour's ships were then used to transport deportees, including almost the complete Graham clan, to Ireland. (Some of them changed their names and returned.)

The harbour came into its own, but had to be improved, when coal production began to increase in the eighteenth century, and an export trade developed with Ireland. By 1730 it was recorded that 208 ships served the port, carrying coal and returning in ballast. Before this the harbour was not impressive. An exchequer return of 1682 states that there were no 'wharves or quay'. Goods were loaded and offloaded onto the river bank, in 'that open place at Workington, a creek under the collection of Whitehaven, from the house of late Jno. Miller, near the church, 500 yards down the River Derwent, on the south side thereof'. As coal exports increased it was found necessary to improve the situation, and a group of harbour trustees was formed to do it. There was one small quay, and a second one was constructed on the north side of the estuary. Records show that in 1727, 187 ships were serviced at the harbour, and 208 in 1730.

In later years wooden railways were built to bring coal to the ships. The trucks carrying the coal approached the quay on 'hurries', wooden platforms erected over the quay that enabled the trucks to tip and drop their loads directly into the holds of the ships. They were constructed by the Curwens for their own mines, and rented to the independent mine owners. Ideally the movement of the trucks would depend on gravity from the pit head. Otherwise they were horse-drawn.

Problems arose regarding the ownership of the harbour. Previously all the land, with some exceptions, belonged to the Curwens, but at the death of Henry Curwen in 1725 a family quarrel led to the manor of Seaton, including the north quay, being bequeathed to Charles Pelham, a cousin. In 1768 Henry Curwen defeated Sir James Lowther (1736–1802) in parliamentary elections, and Sir James saw his chance to get even with a hated rival. (This Lowther was the 'Wicked Jimmy', who omitted to pay what he owed his agent, the father of William and Dorothy Wordsworth. It was a debt not paid by the Lowthers until his death.) The Lowthers owned mines to the north of Workington, and at Henry Curwen's death Sir James attempted to dominate the whole of the harbour's activities. He not only claimed the anchorage duties on the north quay, but also the tonnage duty on his side, sums that formerly went to the harbour trustees for maintenance. To claim even more of the harbour for himself, he even threatened to restore the old course of the river by taking down a breakwater, which interrupted the old manor of Seaton boundary. Even when the Lowther pits north of the town were closed, Sir James continued to be vindictive. A Bill to parliament to improve the harbour was submitted in 1777 and immediately opposed by Sir James. He appointed the engineer John Smeaton to examine the proposals, and his criticism led to the dropping of the Bill.

When the raid by John Paul Jones on Whitehaven harbour was made in 1778 a small fort with cannon defended the entrance to the harbour. It was reported to be threatened once, three days after the raid when an unidentified cutter had launched a boat 'full of men'. On the mustering of the cannon crews the ship and boat retreated.

In 1794 John Christian Curwen (1756–1828) caused the dock quay to be built, using church land got in an exchange of lands agreed by the bishop of Chester. This was a useful basin, though not strictly a dock as it could not be closed, but after expansion this south quay could hold eighty-eight vessels.

John Christian Curwen opened up several pits in the area at the close of the eighteenth century, and in the first five years of the next, an annual average of 45,000 wagons of coal were shipped out. In 1856 there were twenty-eight collieries throughout Cumberland producing 913,900 tons of coal, and 13 per cent of that coal was exported from Workington.

The next substantial improvement to the harbour did not happen until 1860. This was the Lonsdale dock, a gated dock, which unfortunately could not accommodate the increased trade when the iron industry expanded. The Prince of Wales dock now occupies the site.

The Curwen mines of Workington were in seams that dipped towards the coast, and workings continued under the Irish Sea – it was reckoned that there were some twenty miles of tunnels. Up to around forty mines were sunk in the area. The invention of steam engines, with air and water pumps, made deeper mining possible. Adam Heslop, a Workington man and son of a Scottish blacksmith, had worked for a time at Coalbrookdale, seat of the Industrial Revolution.

He invented a patent steam engine, renowned for its efficiency, which served at the Curwen pits from 1792 and elsewhere in the country. Later, in 1798, with his two brothers he manufactured them at Lowca, on the coast south of Harrington. The engines served, not only to remove water, but supply fresh air.

The roofs leaked often in the mines under the sea, and water had to be pumped out continually by day and night. In July 1837 after a major collapse, three connecting pits were inundated. Of the fifty-seven men and boys in the mine, thirty managed to escape. The tragedy stemmed not only from the loss of life, but from the fact that the mines were lost and several hundred miners became unemployed, and the harbour also lost trade heavily. Blame fell on Ralph Coxon, mine manager, for increasing production without regard for the miners' safety. He evaded a lynch mob and disappeared. Henry Curwen was also blamed 'for his love of gain, having counselled the destruction of his own mines'. There was relief for a time when further seams were found and worked, but the mines became unprofitable by the end of the nineteenth century. Now nothing is left of the once prosperous industry.

Shipbuilding in Workington probably dates back centuries, but it became a major employer in the town from the middle of the eighteenth century to the nineteenth. In 1767 ships were being built on land leased from the church. On construction of the dock quay the first yard was moved and a second one opened. The yard owned by William Wallace was known to have built fifty ships averaging 175 tons. The first yard's lease was renewed and K.Wood Peile and Company (which had yards elsewhere) launched their first ship in 1809, and by 1821 had built forty-four ships at Workington averaging 186 tons. When John Christian Curwen obtained the church lands after the Workington Enclosure Act, the shipyards were extended to make the building of larger vessels possible. Up to 1869 forty-nine ships were built, averaging 316 tons.

When a visitation committee for Lloyd's Register visited a shipbuilding yard they reported 'It seems scarcely possible to produce a finer standard of naval architecture'. One notable designer and builder was Jonathan Fell (1800–70), who had the reputation of building the largest ships in the country. In 1851 he completed *Sea Horse* – 900 tons and 180 ft long. It is interesting to note that even merchant ships were fitted with cannon, not only to protect them from French and American fleets, but also the Solway pirates. For instance, three Workington vessels were taken in 1781 by pirates and not returned to their owners until ransom money was paid – water-borne reivers?

In 1860 Charles Lamport's shipyard launched the impressive *Sebastian Cabot*, 180 ft long by 32 ft wide with a depth of hull of 21 ft and capable of carrying 1,009 tons, and at its stern was carved a lion supporting the globe. In the same year the yard produced a man of war of almost the same size, the *Speedy*. Its launch was a spectacle, attended by forty members of the Cumberland Rifle Corps which fired a salute over its bows. The *Speedy* remained in service for almost thirty years.

Many fast clippers that raced each other on the tea trade to and from Shanghai were built here. Four featured regularly in the races: Lamport's *Whinfell*, Jonathan Fell's yard's *Corea* (581 tons), *Belted Will* (773 tons) and *Melbreak*.

Although records are incomplete it seems that during all this time at least 330 ships were launched from Workington's yards. But from 1870 the industry dwindled as the demand for steel vessels grew.

At the same time that wooden ships were being built, Workington had a growing iron industry from 1763. Some ore was brought in by sea from Furness, and some overland from Cumbrian mines in the south. The works, established by James Spedding of Whitehaven, were on the north side of the river at a place called Barepot and usually referred to as Seaton Ironworks, or later the Quarry Ironworks. Charcoal for the furnaces was shipped in from Scotland, but coke was also used later, presumably by processing local coal. There were two blast furnaces, a forge for refining pig iron and making bar iron, a foundry, a boring mill and a turning house. One speciality was the making of cannons, which were in great demand for almost every ship that was built carried them. They also produced tools and equipment – everything that the mines required, but also a wide range of household effects, such as grates, stoves, pans and kettles.

By 1791 they were producing engine parts, particularly for the patent Heslop engine. Heslop himself worked at the mill before moving to expand production at Lowca. The plant was sold and bought a number of times, until 1852, when the owners, Henderson and Davies, also founded another ironworks called Quayside Ironworks, or the Derwent Tinplate Works. Fortunes varied, and works were sold and let a number of times.

In 1858, again north of the river at Oldside, the Workington Haematite Iron Company's works launched production with two blast furnaces and six coke ovens. A massive steam engine, with a beam 11 m long, and a flywheel with a diameter of 6.7 m and weighing 15 tons produced the blast. Two more blast furnaces were added and another engine employed. Then onto the scene came Henry Bessemer. Before Bessemer discovered the cheaper way of making steel he recorded in his autobiography, 'there was no steel suitable for structural purposes, ships, bridges, railway rails, tyres and axles were constructed of wrought iron.' Removing the impurities of pig iron produced steel, but the process was costly. He had discovered that steel could be produced more cheaply by blasting air through molten pig iron, which oxidized away the impurities. He came to Workington, for he knew that the Cumbrian mines produced the purest ore. At first he was puzzled why the smelted iron at the works contained a large amount of phosphorus, until he discovered that this came from the flux mixed with the iron to promote fusion. The flux, or rock material, was furnace waste from the Midlands, which came as ballast in ships. Switching to another flux was the simple answer.

Soon Workington was the only source of the pure Bessemer pig iron, and its demand grew. Four new-type blast furnaces were constructed of steel plate, the hot gases from them being recirculated to pre-heat the air blast. The works were extended to produce 2,000 tons of Bessemer pig iron each week. Then in 1872 they began producing steel ingots from four Bessemer converters.

Booms are so often followed by depressions, but the industry continued to flourish after the last war, and then declined, until recently it has become only a shadow of what it was. A chemical industry also brought much work to the town from the 1950s, but that too has succumbed to cheaper processing abroad.

John Christian Curwen pioneered enlightened agricultural practices, and was one of the first of the landowners to plant forest. Notable among his work was the mass of trees on Claife Heights (now mainly National Trust) that add so much to the beauty of Windermere. But his innovative approach to agriculture made a huge difference to the rural health of Cumbria. The opportunity came with the Enclosure Act of 1801, when huge areas of relatively unproductive land could be fenced and cultivated. Whereas the Act benefited the farmers who could afford to pay for the fencing, the poorer farmers lost out. John Christian Curwen acquired large areas, and after cleansing the land, and fertilizing it, began producing arable crops on land that was once only good for rough grazing. He began to experiment with various types of seed, and new breeds of cattle and sheep. He produced turnips and linseed-oil cake for animal feed. The success of his experiments was widely disseminated and eventually adopted nationally. He received two gold medals from the Society of Arts and Sciences, for 'achievements in agriculture'. One success dear to his heart was to persuade dairies to follow his methods. They thereby produced greater supplies of milk, much needed by children in urban areas. Without a doubt John Christian Curwen was one of the fathers of modern agriculture.

The Whitehaven Junction railway's line reached Workington from Whitehaven in 1846, to run on to Maryport and link to the Maryport and Carlisle railway. Railways were opening up the whole country, and Workington prospered from it. Bessemer iron and steel could be acquired widely. Another line connected Workington to Cockermouth, which in turn linked Keswick, Penrith and Carlisle. Best-quality coke could be imported from the north-east. The Cockermouth line, and the Keswick to Penrith line, were eventually axed by Beeching, but the west coast line still survives, largely perhaps because it serves the BNFL works at Sellafield.

The parish church of St Michael has some eleventh-century features in its structure, though it was rebuilt in 1770–2. But in 1887 it was almost completely destroyed by fire. The clock in the tower escaped damage, however, and the story goes that it kept on chiming the hours as the firemen fought the fire. The church was rebuilt, but it was again struck by fire in 1994 and again restored, this time in a very modern style, with pews of ash and oak, airy well-equipped conference rooms and cheerful lighting – none of which spoils the church's ambience. A healthy congregation of all ages attends services, and volunteers welcome visitors at the door. Maybe the fire did the place a good turn. The tomb effigies of Lord and Lady Curwen, dated about 1450, survived the two fires but are the worse for wear. The lady has two angels by her pillow, while two puppies bite her skirt. The fifteenth-century stone font also survived. The eight bells have been recast, and their ringers now have computer assistance in learning and timing the changes.

The Norman tower of the church has doubtless survived because of its thick walls, built as a defence against Scottish raids. Incidentally, it should be remembered that similar defensive tower churches were being built on the other side of the Solway, for the reiver raids were not all one way. In fact members of the Curwen family were raiders. 'Black Tom' Curwen dwelt at Camerton, east of Workington (his effigy is in the church there, though he was buried at Shap Abbey). He, with some of his Workington family, mounted raids into Scotland and pirate raids on the Solway. Until the accession of James I robbery was the border way of life.

Records show that the chancel was rebuilt around 1543, for Sir Thomas Curwen wanted his body 'to be buried within the new chantry of my Parish Church of Workington'. In 1595 Henry Curwen makes another such reference in his will – 'to cause the chantry to be rebuilded and builded with one lean-to roof covered with lead, with two windows of four lights'.

In 1762 the church was obviously too small for the growing population and permission was sought to enlarge it. Some curious obstacles got in the way, however. One objection came from Sir James Lowther ('Wicked Jimmy') of Whitehaven, who, as we have seen, had bitter feelings against the Curwen family, seeing them as business rivals, and nasty Whigs to boot. Permission for the enlargement was granted in 1766 but reversed after James Lowther won an appeal. The grounds of objection – the rules concerning ownership of pews – were solved at parishioners' meetings, and an application was resubmitted in 1767. Sir James again lodged objection and litigation dragged on until 1769, though eventually the appeal was dismissed in 1770. The Ecclesiastical Court granted permission and work started on the handsome Georgian interior. One of the treasures lost in the subsequent fire of 1887 was the finely carved Curwen pew, made of oak. Wicked Jimmy's revenge?

Why is it that west Cumbrian churches are so combustible? The Methodist church in South William Street was destroyed by fire in 1889. The replacement has a flamboyant Italianate front, quite decorative when you expect chapels to be stern and uncompromising.

In 1814 the first Roman Catholic chapel was established in the town and it led to disgraceful riots. John Christian Curwen had encouraged an influx of Irish workers into the area, mainly to work on his farms, and most were Catholics. Some of the townspeople thought that their livelihoods would be threatened by the immigrants, and religious differences, as so often in history, were the trigger for fights. It started with pub brawls and got worse. On 13 April an Irish tailor drew a musket during a fracas; whether or not he fired it, his dead body was found shortly afterwards with a fractured skull. The murder remained unsolved. Then matters got worse when a staunchly Protestant collier distributed copies of the anti-Catholic 'Orange Lodge Warrant'. Running fights broke out on a September Saturday night, and things got worse on the Sunday, as larger crowds armed themselves with weapons. So much so that John Christian Curwen rode out from Workington Hall, and with difficulty persuaded the crowds to disperse.

Then matters deteriorated even further. A Methodist minister, along with a relative, armed with drawn swords, led an Orange march in the town, preceded by fife and drum. The mob ransacked Irish homes and many occupants fled into the fields. Unfounded rumours of an influx of more immigrants fuelled the fires and the Catholic chapel and school were severely damaged. The militia from Whitehaven at last arrived to restore order, later replaced by the Third King's Own Dragoons. They stayed for nine months until further threats of mob violence had abated. The ringleaders were well known, but there seem to be no record of their being brought to justice.

In 1678 Workington Hall had fallow deer in its park and the house was described as one of the fairest in the country; but it ceased to be a Curwen home. John Christian Curwen had bought the island on Windermere in 1780, and named it 'Belle Isle' after his wife. The Curwens left Workington in 1929 in favour of their island home. The hall eventually came into the possession of the town, which shamefully allowed it to fall into ruin. The decimated remains are now at last cared for and open to the public.

Workington's pride is the lovely surprise of Portland Square, long and narrow, with two rows of trees, and surrounded by streets laid out around 1780, with the assembly rooms in the south-east corner. This is where the professional townsmen and the nineteenth-century equivalent of modern-day executives lived.

The huge Tuscan portico of St John's church is impressive. Built in 1823 by Thomas Hardwick, it was modelled on the Inigo Jones portico at London's St Paul Covent Garden (which Hardwick had rebuilt after a fire). A tower was added in

1846. Some of the town's history is displayed in the admirable Helena Thompson Museum.

Every Easter the town becomes the scene of mass civil disorder. It is a sort of game that begins with a ball being thrown into the centre of a huge crowd, consisting of two teams: the 'uppies' and the 'downies'. The uppies must try to battle their way with the ball to Workington Hall, while the downies must try to get it to Quayside. The only one rule is that ... there isn't one. If there ever was one it has been lost to history. In the resulting mêlée, people get bruised and dirty and clothes get torn. Whoever wins or loses hardly matters, for they all earn welcome refreshment after the event. The origin of the strange game is lost in time.

THE SOLWAY TOWNS

SEATON, to the north-east of Workington, is very much an industrial town that has seen good times and bad, and a history very much part of Workington's. It had an ironworks in 1760. Inland, GREAT CLIFTON and LITTLE CLIFTON had working mines, and Little Clifton a small ironworks from 1750, linked with a railway line to Workington. Little Clifton's church dates from 1858, but it has a Norman doorway.

Going up the coast, one reaches FLIMBY, not a pretty town. It was once Flemingby, then Flemby, which suggests that it was first settled by Flemings, brought into the area by William Rufus when he was seeking to tame the area by introducing more submissive inhabitants with rural skills. The place was owned by Holm Cultram Abbey, whose monks had salt pans on the seashore, but after the dissolution it passed eventually by sale to Sir James Lowther in 1772. He was onto a good thing, for here were rich coal seams. The town grew as more and more miners were needed. Collieries continued production into the mid twentieth century, the coastal railway giving the town a boost when it came in 1844. There are a paper works and a wind farm here now.

Driving 6 km along the coast, one comes to the town of MARYPORT (pop. 11,300). The River Ellen meets the sea here after its 21km journey from the north-west corner of the Skiddaw range, meandering via the fields and hamlets of west Cumbria. Originally here was a fishing village called Ellenfoot. In 1748 landowner Humphrey Senhouse saw it as a potential harbour from which to ship his coal from his expanding coalfields. He began to extend the town following Sir John Lowther's grid-pattern example at Whitehaven, and he renamed it after his wife Mary – hence the current name.

Senhouse Dock, Maryport harbour

The town prospered and the population grew as immigrants from Ireland, Scotland and the Isle of Man swelled the workforce. As well as coal, iron mines were opened and there was a blast furnace working in 1752. In 1777 the port owned between seventy and eighty vessels, mainly transporting coal. In the next century the sharp rise in shipping brought problems, as the *Maryport Advertiser* reported in 1864, the year when the harbour exported 460,000 tons:

> There have been upwards of two hundred sail of vessels in Maryport harbour at one time during the last week, and many of very large tonnage. These vessels, be it known, have not been driven hither by stress of weather as to a harbour of refuge, but they are all here for the legitimate objects of trade. The dock is crammed, and the old harbour, even above the bridge, is crowded with vessels; yet owing to the want of room all trade is at a stand-still – there being no possibility of moving the vessels to and from the loading berths.
>
> We last week inserted an article from a correspondent on the subject of harbour extension, and we have since been informed that the article has the entire approval of the maritime community; and the prevailing wish is to have a new dock on the north side. This is a growing opinion, and should not be any longer disregarded by the trustees.

It is said that it was often possible to walk from the south quay to the north across the decks of vessels. One can imagine the scene if several ships were making for the harbour at the same time, racing to get in first to claim the best berth. To make a profit every ship's master wanted a quick turn-around to make as many trips as possible. Waiting to get loaded, then waiting to make a way out, was very frustrating.

A report on the projected harbour on the north side was made in 1874, but in the traditional way that decisions were made in west Cumberland, a dock was instead made on the south side, and Mrs Elizabeth Senhouse cut the first sod of the Senhouse Dock in 1880.

Ships were built here too. Between 1780 and 1914 five yards were working and several hundred ships were launched, mostly wooden, but latterly of iron and steel. Records are incomplete but it is known that shipbuilder William Wood launched the brig *Sally* (106 tons) in 1765. In 1780 a second shipyard was established by John Peat that produced ships for sixty years. Peat launched his big ships broadside-on because of the restricted channel. The four-master, 1,994-ton *Peter Iredale* and the 1,925-ton *Auchencairn* were launched in this manner. In 1830 Ritson's yard began shipbuilding, and the *Maryport Advertiser* carried an account of a night broadside launch of the 1,000-ton *John Currey*. The reporter was clearly a man with frustrated literary ambitions:

> Every workman of the establishment was at his post at 12 at night. The novelty of a night launch attracted large numbers who thronged the surrounding embankments ... The two senior partners silently paced the deck of the ship, filled with hopes and fears of the issue, while the junior (William Ritson) hurried with torch in hand and encouraged this man and rallied the other, amid the incessant rattling of a hundred hammers. When the rattling ceased at one o'clock a solemn silence reigned and, with the last dread stroke, and fall of the spurs, the boldest held his breath for a time.
>
> The huge mass began to creep on her cradle, slowly, as if reluctant; the ways too were creaking under the ponderous weight and a breathless silence pervaded the multitude in the grandeur of the quiet moonlight. On the ship's first kissing her destined bridegroom Neptune, on this her nuptial night, one universal applause rang from the heights to the ship and again re-echoed from the occupants of Moat Hill. As the vessel increased her speed down the ways, and the massive chain was dragged after her the links in collision sparkled like a train of gunpowder, while the bursting wedges were flying in all directions.
>
> She adds another laurel to the chaplet of fame long since won by the justly celebrated firm which built her.

Charles Dickens visited a busy Maryport in 1837, and in *The Lazy Tour of Two Idle Apprentices*, he writes as Francis Goodchild:

> I go to a region which is a bit of water-side Bristol, with a slice of Wapping, a seasoning of Wolverhampton, and a garnish of Portsmouth, and I say `Will you come and be idle with me?' And it answers, `No, for I am great deal too vaporous and a great deal too rusty, and a great deal too muddy, and a great deal too dirty altogether; and I have ships to load, and pitch and tar to boil, and iron to hammer, and steam to get up, and smoke to make, and stone to quarry, and fifty other disagreeable things to do, and I can't be idle with you.

The oddest boat launch was of the *Lord Ellenborough*, a sloop of 28 tons built in a yard a mile distant from the water, which had to be carted through the fields and along a high road. Ritson's yard built over eighty ships, the last being launched in 1903.

Humphrey Senhouse was attracted to the idea of a railway line from Maryport to Carlisle. The city also thought it a good idea since their canal and Port Carlisle were not the hoped-for success. Maryport could well serve as Carlisle's port. A scheme was drawn up by George Stephenson, taking a line up the Ellen valley to make a necessary link with the coalmines, then by Aspatria and Wigton. Permission for the construction of a Maryport and Carlisle railway came with an Act of 1837 and work started on the section from Maryport to Aspatria in May 1838, reaching Aspatria in April 1841.

Not long afterwards the line was met by the Whitehaven Junction railway (WJR) from Whitehaven through Workington, then to Maryport and connecting it to the MCR. The iron industry flourished, grew and diversified, and in the latter half of the nineteenth century Maryport was making railway engines and rolling stock, and did so for forty years.

By 1923 the region was hit by a devastating fall in the demand for iron and steel. Coalmining in the area was in decline as the pits became worked out. Workington had a new dock and it stole the traffic in rails and ore from Maryport. The economy of the town did not improve and the railway stations on the MCR were closing down. The final insult came with the demolition of Maryport station in 1972. Though hardly a spectacular piece of architecture, it deserved better than to be replaced with a miserable little shelter.

Now like so many of west Cumbria's towns that depended so much on heavy industry, it has passed through hard times. Although struggling to improve its image, it has a long way to go. It is very sad to see dereliction, property crying out to be occupied and, worse still, boarded-up shop windows. As of 2003 the whole area is being redeveloped, and new flood and sea defences built, and a spirit of optimism is in the air. It is trying to remodel itself as a holiday town, and in this it has potential. The harbour is the most attractive draw, being very scenic, with large green spaces in between. Elizabeth dock contains fishing vessels, and a small fleet working for the Solway and Maryport Cooperative bring in their catches. The harbour floors are spread with colourful nets and floats of the fishing industry. One can wander around and see written up on a board the 'catch of the day', and buy a choice of fish fresh from the sea. Two steamers belonging to the Steamboat Museum are moored in the dock. They are owned by a charity that obviously failed to obtain the funds needed to repair and maintain them. Every steamship had character, and seeing one corroding away is like witnessing cruelty. Rumour has it that one of them is to be scrapped and the other, the tug, acquired by a south-coast buyer. Senhouse dock beyond is now a very busy and prosperous marina.

Two attractions by the harbour can occupy an interesting hour or two: the Maritime Museum and the Aquarium.

A pleasing promenade leads from the harbour, and behind it lies an attractive green, made as a picnic and children's play area to celebrate the millennium. The seashore is mainly shelving slabs of red sandstone, with shingle and sand at low tide; the carboniferous limestone, with its coal seams, is behind the town. On the horizon one can see Scotland and its lowland hills, Criffell being the most

Maryport fishermen, sculpture in the harbour

prominent. As this is written, the Scots have made a proposal to erect a series of high windmills that will dominate the scene, and Maryport inhabitants are almost unanimous in shocked opposition. Some businessmen in the town, however, have made the incredible suggestion that the windmills would attract more tourists.

The town has some eighteenth-century buildings, and a unique square ringed by trees. Fleming's Square is quite a sight, containing one of the largest cobbled areas left in Britain, and an admirable rival to Workington's Portland Square. Some of the streets would be ideal industrial scenes for L.S. Lowry (1887–1976) paintings – and so they were. Lowry visited here.

Thomas Henry Ismay was born in Maryport 'in humble circumstances', served most of his working life in Liverpool, and founded the famous White Star line, dying a millionaire in 1899. His son became executive director of the line when it built the *Titanic*. He sailed on the fateful maiden voyage, and survived, but he was a broken man.

During the Roman occupation Maryport was of strategic importance in defence against raids from across the Solway, and it was a supply port. Alauna, the Roman fort, lay north of the river and the present town centre. Traces of its foundations, facing the sea, can barely be seen as the entire site was robbed of its stone in Victorian times. At first the fort may have been built of turf and wood during Agricola's north-west campaigns, then later rebuilt of stone. A sequence of altars found in the nineteenth century record some of the fort's garrisons, and there is evidence that occupation continued well into the fifth century AD. A coastal road must have left the fort on both sides, but only a few traces are apparent. A road also left the castle south-eastwards to the fort at Papcastle (Derventio) near Cockermouth, a little over 10 km away. A straight section of the A594 uses the route, and the last 1.5 km to Derventio is a public path.

The SENHOUSE MUSEUM is neighbour to the fort and can be reached from the promenade by steps, or more easily from the town. The observation tower is a great idea. From there, one can look down on the fort's site and see how it was well chosen. Anyone with an interest in the Roman occupation of Britain should come to this museum, for it contains some seventeen Roman altars in superb condition, found buried in pits on the site, together with inscribed stones and sculptures also collected by several generations of the Senhouse family. Of two very early stones, a building stone inscribed 'LEG XX' (twentieth legion) shows its early age because it omits the title '*Valeria Victrix*' that was awarded to the legion in AD 86. A tombstone is also thought to date from the first century. Most of the material reflects the importance of this fort as an outer defence of Hadrian's Wall.

The stones show that the first recorded commander of the garrison was Tribune Marcus Maenius Agrippa, an Italian, with a first cohort of Spaniards, a thousand men, of whom a quarter were cavalry. Later in Agrippa's career he became the second most important Roman in Britain. The command of the

Spanish garrison fell next to Caius Caballius Priscus, also Italian and a tribune, and after this the fort was assigned to prefects, from France, Austria and Tunisia, and then an Italian. The garrison was replaced by Dalmatians (modern Croatia) after 137, then by Baetasians, from Holland.

The altars are dedicated to several gods, most to Jupiter 'best and greatest', but also to Mars, Vulcan, Victory, Sol, Hercules and Minerva. The remarkable 'Serpent Stone' is thought to have been erected to ward off spirits of the dead; and there are stones dedicated to local Celtic gods adopted by the Romans – Epona, the horse-goddess, is one, and the goddess Setlocenia. Among the tombstones found is one recording the burial of a man who died in Galatia (Turkey) but wished to be brought here to be buried in the tomb of his father.

Apart from the Roman artefacts, the museum contains an on-loan copy of the 1695 edition of Camden's *Britannia*. The Elizabethan historian's book is open at the pages recording his visit and research at Maryport, when he stayed with John Senhouse.

The observation tower has a display suggesting how the Solway would have been patrolled by ships of the Roman navy. The supply ships could move at four to six knots, and it was quicker to go to Roman Chester by sea – two or three days – than the week's journey on land.

Up the coast again and to one side of the coastal road is the hamlet of CROSSCANONBY. The little Norman church of St John the Evangelist rewards a

Old saltpans by Solway shore, Crosscanonby

visit. It is one of those little churches that have a special quiet ambience that comes from 800 years of worship. Almost certainly the chancel arch is a Roman entrance arch – possibly won from the fort at Maryport. The Norman font is a relative newcomer compared to the sixth-century stone, found while digging a drain. On the shore side are saltpans, made about 1650 by the Senhouses; salt was extracted from sea water with the help of coal fires. They were profitable for a time, and workers were housed in nearby cottages to tend them. They closed in 1736.

Further north, ALLONBY lying within an area of Outstanding Natural Beauty, is an attractive village straggled alongside the coast road. After a period of neglect it is hoped that the Solway Rural Initiative and the borough council can continue to make improvements, as it has fallen into rack and ruin. Some of it, such as a burnt-out building, has been crying out for demolition for a long time. The village has long green areas and sand dunes between the colourful seaside houses and the extensive beach, here with exceptional views across to Scotland.

Allonby made an early bid for the tourist trade, being developed with that object in mind from 1748. At that time it had a good reputation for its sea-bathing. For some years it became very popular, at holiday times quite crowded. Although there was no railway, a good bus service brought people from Maryport, and charabanc trips came from Carlisle. Nowadays Allonby is patronized by nearby caravan sites. A stroll on the cobbles behind the front buildings from the village hall brings one into another world. Here are the splendid tall porticoes of the sea water baths, opened in 1835, but now no longer functional.

Dickensian Allonby (and still little changed)

Among the holidaymakers in September 1837 were Charles Dickens and Wilkie Collins. They stayed in 'a clean little bulk-headed room' at the Ship Inn. Collins had sprained his ankle and was confined to the inn while Dickens took strenuous walks. While there they collaborated on *The Lazy Tour of Two Idle Apprentices*. Collins described what he saw:

> ... a watering place can't be five gentlemen in straw hats on a form on one side of a door and four ladies in hats – on a form on another side of a door, and three geese in a dirty little brook before them, and a boy's legs hanging over a bridge (with a boy's body I suppose on the other side of the parapet) and a donkey running away.

Dickens, meanwhile, walked to Maryport to collect the mail.

Joseph Huddart (1741–1816), the hydrographer and innovator of ship's safety measures, was born in Allonby, and buried at St Martin-in-the-Fields in London.

Now a long stretch of coastal road brings one to SILLOTH (pop. 2,910), an absolute gem of a Victorian seaside holiday town. Please let it stay so! This is one of the best villages in Cumbria. Some places have an immediate attraction beyond what one can see, and it is often hard to define. Silloth is just one of those places that make you feel good.

Silloth, late nineteenth century

Silloth 2000 – unchanged

Silloth was linked by railway to Carlisle in 1856, and the Silloth Bay railway company built a dock in 1859 to serve as Carlisle's port. It had a lifeboat station in 1860. In 1862 the town was taken over by North British railway and publicized as a holiday resort. Within seven years it became one of the most popular resorts in the north. Then the railway company got into difficulties and could not maintain services. Silloth was in danger of decline when it was taken over by a Holm Cultram Board, a committee elected to promote the resort, improvements were made, and the tourists began to return. But the clientele changed: the gentility were replaced by largely working-class holidaymakers. The attractions included donkey rides, putting greens, Pierrot shows, band concerts, bathing machines and public baths. Day trips were offered across the Solway to Galloway, and out to the Isle of Man. At the height of the season 117 boarding houses were filled, and as many as 2,000 day-trippers came on some days.

Between the wars Silloth remained a popular tourist destination, but its railway line, which once brought visitors in their thousands, has gone. But the resort still retains its excellent wide tree-lined streets. They lack the comfortable convenience of tarmac, paved as they are with stone setts and cobbles, and vehicles judder as they pass through. It did not really succeed as a port for Carlisle. That plan was abandoned, though the small harbour still serves a flour mill and is haven for a few fishing boats. Between the long wide promenade and the town lies a very large area of green, behind a shelterbelt of pine trees. On this level green in Silloth's heyday stood most of the holiday attractions.

Portico of Silloth's old bath house

The fine houses are all colourful and elegant, and it is all clean and neat, striking one at once as being special. For those who don't crave sophisticated entertainment and want nothing particular to do it is still good for a lazy holiday break. The views across to Scotland are absolutely sublime and they are often complemented by the famous sunsets.

A once popular walk from Silloth led from the lighthouse to SKINBURNESS, further along the coast. The harbour once here was owned by Holm Cultram Abbey and used by Edward I in his Scottish campaigns. Around thirty vessels, from as far away as the Cinque Ports, supplied his army. There is hardly anything to see now, for harbour and village were lost to the sea in a calamitous storm in the fourteenth century.

From this point, on the northern Solway plain, the older buildings, apart from the fortified towers and churches, are rather different to the rest of Cumbria. The Romans could find no wealth of local stone for extending their frontier wall, and house builders had the same problem. One solution was to construct the walls using the available rounded cobbles. Cobbles could not lock neatly together, so the spaces between them had to be filled with clay, or later lime mortar.

The other solution was to build walls using clay mixed with small pebbles. This was once a community operation, it was probably accomplished very quickly by an assembly line of clay cutters, puddlers and kneaders, and shapers. Clay could be pressed flat like dough, formed into rolls, then unrolled for each course. A thin layer of straw was sandwiched between the layers of clay. In both cases, as slate was unavailable, the roofs would be thatched with straw, or possibly heather. The surviving clay-walled buildings may not now be apparent, as they were often later rendered, and, later still, some faced with stone. The coming of the railways changed everything. It meant that roofs, at first thatched, could be covered in inexpensive Welsh slate, and thus only a handful of thatched cottages remain.

To the east of Skinburness the land is swallowed by Morecambe Bay. The road must go inland and round it to ABBEY TOWN, the home of HOLM CULTRAM ABBEY. The older buildings of the hamlet are largely constructed of stone 'quarried' from the ruins of the abbey after the dissolution. Its sad remains represent a mere fragment of its former glory and are used as the parish church (that is, the major part of the abbey church's nave, without the aisles). From the outside it looks dull and unimpressive and bears the marks of restorations. But some features are worth a closer look.

Holm Cultram Abbey was founded in 1150, by Cistercians from Melrose Abbey, when this part of Cumbria was in Scotland. King David I donated the land. During its construction, of Scottish red sandstone brought over the Solway, the area was taken into England by Henry II, and the grant to the abbey was confirmed. The abbey's lands were extensive; iron and salt were produced, but wool was the main source of wealth, and the abbey enjoyed an export trade through its then port of Skinburness.

From the outset, however, the abbey suffered from border raids, time after time. Its proximity, vulnerability and, above all, its wealth made it attractive to the Scots. No doubt Edward I's use of the place as a military base during his successful Scottish campaigns – the abbot was seconded as a member of the king's council – increased its appeal, later on, as a target for revenge. After Bannockburn Robert the Bruce pillaged all the Cumbrian church establishments, and even though Robert's father was buried in the abbey, Holm Cultram fared no better.

The abbey was dissolved in 1538, but the surviving church remained as the parish church and received an endowment from Queen Mary's benefaction to the University of Oxford, one of the conditions being that the university supply a parish priest. The church fell on hard times. It suffered from a fire, and later the tower fell, bringing down much of the chancel and part of the roof of the nave. Special efforts were made to restore it in the early eighteenth century. The building's size was then reduced by removing the aisles and the east end, and walls were built up between the twelfth-century piers. Further work was done in the late nineteenth and early twentieth centuries.

Of particular interest in the church are the old pulpit, a fine Norman west doorway, and a porch, with dog-tooth moulding from 1507. Monuments include one to the earl of Carrick, the father of Robert the Bruce, and another to Abbot Rydekar (d. 1434). Carvings include a carved niche, probably of the fourteenth century, and a carving of Henry VII.

Going north round the bay the road brings one to NEWTON ARLOSH. Newton's name derives from 'new town'. The new town in question was built in 1304 to replace the Holm Cultram Abbey's loss of Skinburness. The church of St John the Baptist was founded by the abbot. In granting the licence for its construction the bishop of Carlisle remarked that the church should be built 'with the safety of souls' in mind, in view of the depredations of border raiders. So the church was built as a fortification, and it is one of the best examples of its kind in the country. In the nineteenth-century restorations the north wall of the church was breached and an extension built, but the remaining massive walls of the nave and tower remain from the fourteenth century.

The nave walls are 1.1 m thick and the narrowness of the old entrance door, only 0.79 m, indicates its defensive function. But it is the tower that impresses. These walls are 1.2 m thick, built with more care than the nave, and the two storeys have only narrow openings. Internally the ground floor is tunnel-vaulted. Access to the upper floors was from a narrow first-floor doorway above the nave.

Fortified church, Newton Arlosh

A wooden ladder to the door could be removed after the 'souls' had entered. The second storey and the upper part of the tower have been restored.

After Newton Arlosh the coast road must pass by KIRKBRIDE village, which has a mainly Norman church; then it crosses the River Wampool. There is a nature reserve at DRUMBURGH MOSS (CWT), part of an area of Special Scientific Interest, at this side of the river to the north-east. In the mossy area here no less than thirteen species of sphagnum moss have been identified. Adders are common (though make a hasty retreat on approach), as are lizards, newts, toads and frogs. As well as the more common birds, there are red grouse, partridge and curlew, redshank and whinchat, twite and reedbunting. It is a haven, too, for dragonflies and damsel flies; and the magnificent emperor moth and drinker, large heath and northern eggar moths can be seen.

The coastal road turns west around the promontory by settlements of Anthorn and Cardurnock, and by a sinister and unlovely complex of communication aerials, then follows the coast north-eastwards as it approaches Scotland. In the days of railway expansion this part of the Solway was an obvious place to build a line on a causeway and viaduct across to Scotland at Annan. The Solway Junction railway made it, opening for traffic in 1869. The remaining piece of causeway can be seen, with its Scottish equivalent less than 2 km across the firth. The line was doing very well until damaged by a severe winter in 1875, when water in the viaduct's iron pillars froze and cracked them. But worse was to come in another bad winter of 1881, when the viaduct was battered by large ice floes that pierced holes. The structure was repaired and the railway continued to use it until it was considered unsafe and closed in 1921. After that and until it was demolished in 1934 it was sometimes used illegally as a dangerous footway. It is said that Scots sneaked across on Sundays when their pubs were closed. The return must have been hazardous in the dark, especially with a strong wind, and particularly after a binge.

BOWNESS ON SOLWAY (*BOW-ness*) is a small village at the narrowest point of the firth. At exceptionally low tides, with the River Eden flow diminished by drought, it was easy in the past to ford it by Bowness Wath (*wath* = ford). A Roman fort, Maia, stood here on what was thought to be the western end of Hadrian's Wall, but subsequent researches have found evidence of further defences further along the coast. No sign remains of the fort. The village is built upon it, and the church is built from its stones. Needless to say, the place suffered badly from Scottish raids, even apparently after the borders became settled following the Act of Union, for the church bells were stolen in a raid in 1626. The thieves were chased and dropped the bells in the Solway. Not to be slighted the locals organized a raid on Scotland and stole the bells from the churches at Middlebie and Dornock. The bells are still in the church, and if the Scots want them back they will need to return the Bowness bells – after dredging them up from the sea bed.

PORT CARLISLE is a short distance on, the remnant of another failed scheme. The businessmen of Carlisle financed the construction of a canal, 18 km long, from the city to this place, then called Fishers' Cross. Work began in 1819 and the canal, containing eight locks, was opened in 1823. It meant that passengers and small cargo from Carlisle could reach Liverpool by sea in one day. The journey down the canal took an hour and forty minutes and was made in small barges. The project was acclaimed a success, but as such it was short-lived. Within six years the canal was beginning to run into financial difficulty and the expansion of the railways sealed its fate.

BURGH (*BRUFF*) BY SANDS is where Edward I, weary and ill and facing yet another campaign against the Scots, died at the age of sixty-eight on 7 July 1307, before he could engage with his enemy. Anticipating his death, he asked his son to have his body boiled and the bones removed, so that he could carry them with him on campaigns into Scotland until the country was defeated. His heart should go to the Holy Land. His son (Edward II to be) might have agreed, but as it turned out, took his father's body to Waltham Abbey to await a conventional burial. A monumental pillar of 1803 by the Solway, replacing one of 1685, supposedly marks the spot on which the tent of the dying Hammer of the Scots was pitched.

Edward I monument on the Solway site on which he died

Burgh is on the line of Hadrian's Wall, only sketchy in this area now. A fort, Abalava, lay astride the wall and is now obscured by the siting of the village. The road running through the village follows, roughly, the via principalis, the fort's main thoroughfare.

The stones of the fort were incorporated into the church walls, and this church is remarkable for being another fine example of a fortified church, into which sanctuary for the inhabitants of the village could be secured from Scottish raiders crossing the fords. The church has Norman origins, but it is the fourteenth-century west tower that is impressive if not very handsome – built like a keep with massively thick, 2 m walls. At ground floor the windows are high up the wall and small. The only way into the tower is from inside the church, and this is protected by a heavy iron gate (a 'yat' in Cumbria) with wall staples for a drawbar and bolts. A gun slit defends its approach from the north doorway of the nave. A spiral staircase within the tower wall gives access to the upper levels. At the east end of the building stood a second tower of which only the ground floor remains. This was also built for defence. Why two? It is assumed that one tower accommodated the clergy; the other the laity.

ROCKCLIFFE MARSH is at the head of Solway with the Eden on its south side, the Esk and the Sark on the north, each river contributing its silt over the ages and altering its profile in times of flood. Rockcliffe's point is only a very short distance from Scotland's Gretna, and it was on either side of the water in centuries before the seventeenth that the border wardens, English and Scottish, declared a truce and met to discuss complaints, and administer such justice to miscreants that the ancient border laws demanded. This would take place at the Lochmaben Stone on the Scottish side. With an air of formality, the parties would assemble on either side in some numbers, comprising accused and accusers. Then a leading English rider would cross the ford and ask the Scots for an assurance of peace until the next sunrise. Having been assured, he would be accompanied back by a Scottish rider who would seek the same pledge from the English. Then both wardens would hold up their hands and demand of their followers that they honour the truce. Then the English party would follow tradition and cross to the stone. Twelve men would then be appointed – the Scots would choose six English, and the English six Scots. Fines would be levied on the accused, usually for stealing stock, or he would be required to return the property to the rightful owner. It was rough justice, a sort of tit-for-tat balancing act, that wiped the slate clean. It helped to keep an uneasy peace.

ROCKCLIFFE village, on the banks of the Eden, has suffered in the past from flooding. The worst recorded instance was in 1796, when several houses were washed away. The church, with spire, is 1848. The interest is in the churchyard stones, a cross with a solid wheel head with interlace work and dragons, and old gravestones with flowered crosses.

Rockcliffe Marsh nature reserve was mentioned at the beginning of the chapter, on p. 165.

CHAPTER ELEVEN

North-east Cumbria and the Border

The border between England and Scotland has known 1500 years of conflict since the Roman Emperor Hadrian built his wall to keep back the barbarians and serve as a base for military operations. Through the centuries that followed the course of the borderline was disputed time and time again. When armies of Scotland and England were not in conflict, cross-border tribal thieving and violence was still the normal way of life. The robber gangs – the 'reivers' – were a law unto themselves. English and Scottish wardens of the Marches, with their small forces, struggled to keep some sort of control, but until the dreadful reckoning of the seventeenth century the towns and settlements of Cumbria's border land, and those below it, were constantly burned and pillaged. The history of the area is one of repeated destruction and restoration.

This is a very fine area of countryside largely yet unexplored by tourists from Brampton and the River Irthing to the south, to the River Esk in the north.

BRAMPTON

BRAMPTON is a lively and very attractive rural market town with strange twists and turns and cobbles. The marketplace, a hive of activity on Wednesdays especially, has a Moot Hall where the town's business was conducted. Built in 1817, it is in this case octagonal, and rather engaging, with two storeys, outer staircases and a turret. The church of St Martin was built in 1874–8 for George Howard, ninth Earl of Carlisle, of Naworth Castle, replacing a much earlier church. The architect was Philip Webb. Pevsner, the sage of British architecture, was impressed by the structure, but found it lacking in beauty, though he conceded that Webb was a man of character and imagination. But inside, its great glory is the astonishing and enchanting windows by William Morris and the Pre-Raphaelite Edward Burne-Jones. They are worth travelling miles to see. The glowing colours in the east window show the Good

Shepherd with angels to left and right above, and below, the Saints with a central pelican. The three-light south windows feature Faith, Hope and Charity. The north aisle windows have figures; in the south aisle small panels tell stories; and its west window has angels. In all, fourteen figures in mauve, red, gold and blue.

The abandoned old church, which the new church replaces, is out in the west of the town. Its beginnings are very old indeed, perhaps Cumbria's earliest Christian place of worship. It occupies the site of a Roman fort, whose stones form part of the ruined church. The region was in Scotland, and when it fell under Norman control in the twelfth century, the church came under the wing of Lanercost Priory. The parish was razed in the border wars of the fourteenth century and the church was repaired 200 years later. However, its inconvenient distance from the town centre lay behind the buildings of the new church.

Brampton was twice occupied by Jacobite armies from Scotland – in 1715, and again by Bonny Prince Charlie's forces in 1745. The prince stayed in a house in High Cross Street above the marketplace, now a shop bearing a plaque, while some of his officers stayed in the Half Moon Inn in the main street, now also a shop. The prince received a delegation of Carlisle citizens offering surrender, but the prince would not accept it until he had word that the castle had also yielded. When the castle fell, Carlisle's mayor and corporation returned and offered the keys to the city, then the prince left Brampton to march through Carlisle on 18 November. Of course, it all ended in tragedy, and south of Brampton in woodland is the CAPON TREE monument, recording that here after Culloden, from tree branches, were hanged six men – English as well as Scots - who fought in the belief that the Stuarts were the rightful heirs to the throne.

The building of the military road from Newcastle to Carlisle in 1758 made a big difference to the small rural town of Brampton. A Newcastle textile company moved into the town, allowing it to play its part in the Industrial Revolution. A factory started from small beginnings, producing ginghams and checked and striped cotton fabrics. Some of the weaving was done in sheds, but also in the weavers' homes. Weavers' cottages were built; one row of eight houses with eight four-loom weaving shops was named 'Shuttle Row'. Weavers, working from fourteen to sixteen hours a day, could earn from ten to twenty-one shillings per week, and that was good. The town grew and there were dye houses, a brewery, tailors, tanneries, hatters, a shoemaker, saddlers, coopers and a clockmaker, and the town had eighteen inns. Farms in the vicinity cultivated oats and barley, and kept sheep and black cattle. So in the eighteenth and into early nineteenth century Brampton was doing better than other Cumbrian towns. There were poor people in the town too of course, and Lord Carlisle had coal delivered to each indigent household. The coming of the railway offered even brighter prospects, but alas it passed the town by.

Like many Cumbrian towns it had its unusual characters. Rosalind, wife of the ninth earl of Carlisle, devoted her life to politics – votes for women, home rule for Ireland – and dressed herself entirely in blue, the colour of the Liberals in Cumberland. She was a fanatical teetotaller and had all the public houses on the Howard estates closed. She became president of the National British Women's Temperance Association and in 1883 she somehow persuaded 1,300 inhabitants of Brampton to sign a pledge of total abstinence. How did the breweries survive? Or the inhabitants for that matter?

East of the town is a motte – an unusually large constructed mound on which the first Norman castle was built. The summit gives a good view of the town, and the area is popular for picnics. A path leads on to woodland walks at Ridgewood (CWT). Some 2 km south of the town, by Low Gaitbridge, other first-rate woodland walks follow the banks of the River Gelt. Stone was quarried around here for the building of Hadrian's Wall. Here is the 'written rock' with inscriptions carved on a rockface by a Roman soldier while working in the quarry in the early third century. The River Irthing flows to the north and west of the town and is well stocked with trout. Permits to fish this river, and the River Gelt, can be got at the White Lion hotel, agent for the Brampton Angling Club.

Where the river takes a turn south, Hell Beck joins it; and here was fought a grim skirmish between sizeable forces in 1570. It was a time of serious insurrection. Leonard 'Crookback' Dacre, a former deputy warden of the West March, felt he had been cheated of the ownership of Naworth Castle by an Elizabethan edict. On the death of Thomas Dacre the estate should have gone to Leonard's nephew, but he was killed in an accident. Leonard believed he then had a major claim to the property – but it was given instead to the Howards, related to Dacres by marriage. Leonard, bitter and furious, occupied Naworth castle anyway. As one of the leaders of a powerful group of rebels on both sides of the border, he favoured Mary, Queen of Scots, as the rightful queen; though he was more anti-Elizabeth than a supporter of Mary. He supported a first botched insurrection in 1569, backing off to evade the punishment that included many executions. The earl of Moray was an active champion of Elizabeth who had dealt with the rebels on the Scottish side, but when he was assassinated in 1570 the grip on the border loosened and Mary's supporters again rallied to the cause. Leonard Dacre was more confident of its success and he raised an army of 3,000 men, riders recruited from the rough, lawless reivers of the border.

Lord Henry Carey Hunsdon, warden of the Eastern March and captain of Berwick garrison, was ordered to leave Berwick and obtain Dacre's arrest. But even with the support of Sir John Forster, warden of the Middle March, and his riders, he knew that he had a force only half that of Dacre's. He decided to make for Carlisle to gain reinforcements. But Dacre's scouts made him aware of the plan. He saw his chance; he would meet Hunsdon's force at its most vulnerable point: at Gelt ford. He waited. Hunsdon arrived, and seeing Dacre's formidable opposition on the river bank, he immediately placed Forster in his rear with 500 riders and prepared to meet Dacre's attack. Not only did he withstand it, he retaliated with a cavalry charge. Vicious hand-to-hand skirmishes broke out in and around and up and down the river. Then suddenly Dacre's force was broken. Dacre himself was almost taken, but fled to Scotland, leaving 400 dead and 200 prisoners. How could it happen? Perhaps it was because Dacre's force consisted of rough and ready border folk, not amenable to discipline; and Dacre was not a born leader. Fierce fighters though his forces were, they were not a match for a unified force under the professional control of Hunsdon.

A little over a km away to the east from the scene of this bloody episode TALKIN TARN can be found in a country park now owned by the county council,

Talkin Tarn

but currently (2004) up for sale. Whatever happens, public access is surely secure. This is a really lovely tarn, clean to its depths, occupying some 26 ha and surrounded by woodland and fields. The tarn was formed naturally as a 'kettle hole'. Here in the last ice age a moving mass of ice was halted by a build-up of rock debris, and covered by it. It then melted to form a small lake, now maintained by natural springs and populated by perch and pike. It has become a very popular recreational space. Here a rowing club, dating back to 1859, holds regular, deadly serious, races. There are scenic walks around the tarn, some possible with wheelchairs, and the banks are accessible for anglers, with permits available on site at the shop.

Running south from Talkin the B6413 crosses the River Gelt and takes a sharp bend at the village of CASTLE CARROCK. No sign of a castle can be seen here now but there surely once was one. The church of St Peter was built in 1823, and altered sixty years later; but it stands on the site of an earlier church. From the village one gains access to the river and to Geltsdale, and the seldom-walked fells of what was once a part of the great royal forest that Henry II 'put in regard' to add to Inglewood. The addition included a great part of the Solway region, and land east of the Pennine slopes, making the forest the largest in England. The highest point in this area is due west at Cold Fell (621 m).

The A689 leaves Brampton to the east and after 8 km reaches TINDALE. There is nothing much to see here now, but in 1845 it became the site of an industrial spelter (or zinc) works. A lease of the land was obtained from the earl of Carlisle by Lord Morpeth for the smelting of spelter. The lessee, James Henry Attwood, a shrewd member of a family of industrialists, had seen that zinc was a growing market, and on this site was everything that he required for its production. There were coal mines too – not on the scale of west Cumbria; but productive enough for Lord Carlisle to invest in a branch railway from his mines, 2 km further on at Midgeholme to Brampton. (It no longer exists.) Conveniently, this line passed Tindale; zinc was mined locally, and coal and limestone was available for the smelter. On Attwood's death in 1865 the industry fell under the ownership of the Tindale Smelter Company, run by a Newcastle mineral merchant, John Cameron Swan. In 1882 Swan founded the Nenthead and Tynedale Lead and Zinc Company. This was a shrewd move, as one product could be balanced by the other in a fluctuating market.

The production of zinc from the ore was complicated. First, it passed through a furnace to produce zinc oxide. Second, the zinc oxide was mixed with coal in fire-clay cylinders, or retorts, which were heated in coal-fired furnaces. This produced gaseous zinc that had to be cooled in condensers and collected as liquid. Eventually the works had a range of 912 retorts and fourteen furnaces. Workers were housed in a village, and in common with other mining enterprises the management provided a chapel, a school, a reading room and a cooperative store.

In 1895 the markets slumped at the same time as the 50-year lease on the land expired. It has been estimated that during its lifetime the works had produced 40,000 tonnes of zinc. Although closure would have spelled disaster for the workers, not everyone was unhappy. The fumes and smoke were a constant source of complaint. Large areas of farmland had become contaminated and unusable. Lord Carlisle placed strong conditions on a new lease, including the adequate housing of workers, who till now had been, according to him, living in 'kennels'. It was also pointed out that the land used had spread beyond the boundaries by the dumping of waste. In the end the lease was not renewed, the workers had to find employment elsewhere, and the site was demolished and abandoned.

NAWORTH AND LANERCOST

The A69 also leaves Brampton from the east and goes, straight as a ruler, along the Roman road into Northumberland, but we must leave it at the crossroads 6 km from town and take the minor road left to pass NAWORTH CASTLE. The castle is owned by the twelfth earl of Carlisle, and open to the public on some days during the summer, details of which can be discovered at tourist information centres.

Naworth Castle

The castle dates back to 1335 when Ranulph de Dacre received the licence to crenellate, permission from the crown to put it into a defensive state. He had come into possession of the estate of Gillesland by marriage to its heiress Margaret de Multon, having eloped with her from Warwick Castle. He was sheriff of Cumberland and the governor of Carlisle. Thomas Lord Dacre, who distinguished himself at the battle of Flodden, improved and added to the castle around 1520. The dispute by Leonard Dacre over ownership of the estate has been already mentioned. The 1604 legacy brought the castle into the possession of Lord William Howard ('Belted Will') who had married a Dacre.

Sir Walter Scott records his theory of how he became known as 'Belted':

Costly his garb – his Flemish ruff
Fell o'er his doublet, shaped of buff,
With satin slash'd and lined;
Tawny his boot, and gold his spur,
His cloak was all of Poland fur,
His hose with silver twined;
His Bilboa blade, by Marchmen felt,
Hung in a broad and studded belt,
Hence, in a rude phrase, the Borderers' still
Call'd noble Howard, BELTED WILL.

The estates the earl inherited included Henderskelf, which became Castle Howard. Lord William became enthusiastically involved in the ending of border lawlessness after the accession of James I. Just as the troublesome reivers were being hounded and punished, he was involved in a successful all-night pursuit from Naworth into Yorkshire of three notorious malefactors, Tom Armstrong, Jock 'Stowlugs' Armstrong and Chris Irvine. They were duly hanged. A list made by Lord William of 'Fellons taken and prosecuted by me for felonies in Gillsland and elsewhere, since my abode there' contained the names of sixty-eight persons, and nearly all of them were executed. Once word was brought to him while he was busy with his books that a 'moss-trooper' had been taken prisoner. Asked what should be done with him, he impatiently replied 'Hang him in the devil's name!' Then some time later when he ordered the prisoner to be brought before him, he was told it was too late, the man was no longer alive.

Lord William converted the castle into a comfortable mansion, which is how it stayed until a disastrous fire in 1844. Fire engines had to be summoned from Carlisle, and they came by train, 2½ hours after the first flames were seen! Then the water was in short supply. Over this time all that the staff and local volunteers could do was rescue as much of the castle's treasures as they could. Thereafter renovations fell under the care of the architect Anthony Salvin, who restored everything to their original designs.

The view of the castle from the minor road is impressive. Entrance is gained through a gatehouse. Two towers stand on either side of the range, the left being Dacre Tower, the right Lord William's. When the castle is open to the public, what impresses is the huge size of the great hall (23 m by 7.3 m) and the line of large heraldic beasts carved in oak. On the left side of the fireplace is the red bull of Dacre on his hind legs and supporting a heraldic flag, on the other side a griffon ditto, that appears in the supporters of Baroness Dacre, twenty-seventh in the title. At the end of the room are two more creatures: a dolphin of the Greystokes, and a puzzling sheep that may allude to the de Multons, sometimes de Muttons. It has been suggested that these animals inspired the artist John Tenniel in his illustrations for *Alice's Adventures in Wonderland* and *Through the Looking Glass*. In the library (which was the private chapel of the Dacres before the fire) is a memorable overmantel with a representation of the battle of Flodden in plaster of paris. It was designed by Pre-Raphaelite Edward Burne-Jones, modelled by Sir E. Boehm, then painted by Burne-Jones. The Pre-Raphaelites held meetings here.

Going north across the River Irthing, LANERCOST PRIORY (EH) is a spectacular substantial ruin, whose nave had been preserved as a parish church. The priory was dedicated to St Mary Magdelene and founded as an Augustinian house by

Lanercost Priory ruin, south transept

Robert de Vaux in 1166. Inevitably, being so near the border, the building was used and misused by armies and plundered by thieves from both sides. During Scottish incursions in 1296, the cloister was burned. Peter Langcroft, canon of Hexham and a local poet, wrote:

> Corbrigge is a toun, thei brent it whan thei cam;
> Tuo hous of religioun, Laynercoste and Hexham,
> Thei chaced the chanons out, their goodes bare away,
> And robbed all about, the bestis tok to prey.

The canons returned and began repairs, but they were undone a year later by William Wallace's forces. In 1300 Edward I, Hammer of the Scots, stayed here on his way to a hammering, and again in 1306 on his way to Carlisle, but on that occasion he was taken sick and stayed for seven months with his entourage of 200. Five years later it was Robert the Bruce's turn to lodge at the priory, after imprisoning some of the canons. Yet again in 1346 King David II of Scotland came here and wrecked the buildings. The repairs over those years cost the priory dearly and it had to sell properties to meet its debts.

Then in 1536 came the dissolution. Some of the canons had taken part in the pilgrimage of grace, and King Henry ordered the duke of Norfolk to go to Lanercost and hang the canons 'without further delaye or ceremony'. It is not known whether the order was carried out. The priory was granted to Sir Thomas Dacre, who converted some of the buildings as a residence. The north aisle was retained first as a parish church, and later the nave was restored to enlarge the space. The rest of the buildings were allowed to deteriorate. When the branch of the Dacre family living at Lanercost died out, the property became the Crown's. The earl of Carlisle bought it in 1869, and later it was transferred to the Department of the Environment, and then to English Heritage.

Before going into the priory precincts it is worthwhile looking at the beautiful medieval bridge over the Irthing. The way into the priory precincts was through the nearby two-storey gatehouse, the remains of which can be seen. The vicarage is the first building beyond, most of it having been constructed during the sixteenth century, but the eastern end is the thirteenth-century guest house of the canons.

The west front of what is now the parish church is an impressive example of Early English architecture, built in King John's reign. At its top is a figure of Saint Mary Magdalene, thought to have been carved about 1270. The west door leads into the nave, with only one aisle to the north. This was because a second aisle to the south could not be accommodated because of the presence of the cloister. The east wall and window were constructed in 1740, and some of the glass fragments are sixteenth century. Thomas Dacre's arms in the central window show the 'bar sinister' indicating that he was an illegitimate child. The wall of the north aisle is enlivened by several recent memorial stained-glass windows, three of them by the masters William Morris and Edward Burne-Jones. In the north aisle there is a cross shaft, whose cross originally stood outside in the precincts. It was apparently used as a gravestone for the top part of the original inscription has been used as a memorial: '— who was buried here ye 20 July 1657 2nd yere of his age.' And below (translated): 'In the 1214th year from the incarnation and the 7th year of the Interdict, Innocent III holding the Apostolic See, Otto being Emperor in Germany, Phillip King of France, John King of England and William King of Scotland, this cross was made.'

Originally two doors in the south wall of the church led into the cloister. The four side passages around the open square were originally covered. On the south side are the remains of the lavatorium where the canons washed before going to the refectory for meals. In the south-west corner lies a stone with the Roman inscription 'C CASSI PRISCI' ('the century of Cassius Priscus'), which proves that some of the stone for the building was lifted from nearby Hadrian's Wall. The eastern end of the cloister would have held the chapter house. It appears from the remains that an old one was superseded by another beyond it and considerably larger one beyond it. Then to the south of the east range was the accommodation building for the canons.

At the southern end of the cloister, the refectory, where the canons ate their meals, would have been on the first floor but this has now gone. What remains is the impressive cellarium at ground level, with its surviving nine bays and octagonal piers. The large fireplace at the end of the cellarium means that at one time an intervening wall stood here, for this is where the canons warmed themselves.

On the south side of the west range is the pele tower, where the Prior lived. This block was altered after the dissolution when it was made into a residence for the Dacres.

A door from the east end of the cloister leads into the south transept of the old church. Here is the tomb of Sir Thomas Dacre (d. 1525), who fought at Flodden and was rewarded by being created a knight of the garter. An effigy of another Dacre has been defaced. The ruins of the choir and sanctuary lie beyond. The high altar stood on a raised step. A chapel in the north transept contains the graves of some of the Howard family, including the ninth earl of Carlisle, and his wife Rosalind, the Victorian campaigner for social reforms. Here too is a tomb of Sir Humphrey Dacre, lord warden of the Western March (d. 1485), and his wife Mabel Parr, aunt of Catherine Parr, the surviving wife of Henry VIII. On the north wall of the north transept is the tomb of Sir Rowland de Vaux, nephew of the founder of the priory.

Two yew trees in the ground have been estimated to be 700 years old. A general plan of the area can be acquired from the custodian's shop.

THE WALL AND BIRDOSWALD ROMAN FORT

Leaving Lanercost northwards one reaches Hadrian's Wall, and the road follows it, sometimes on top of it, eastwards. The wall was guarded by turrets, and the remaining ruins of one, east banks turret, can be seen. A stop here gives a grand view over the Irthing valley. On the left of the wall as we continue, one can make out traces of sections of the great defensive ditch along the northern side.

Birdoswald Roman fort remains, east gateway

The remains of BIRDOSWALD Roman fort (*Banna*) (CCC), among the best on Hadrian's Wall, are revealing. Part of the site is occupied by a farm and farm buildings. The wall was built around AD 122, originally of timber and turf, and the fort at Birdoswald was built on top of it, on a strategically important spur of land in a bend of the River Irthing. The fort had walls rising to 4.2 m high, with crenellations that took it to about 6 m, and there were double-arched gates in each, with two-storey towers at each side, and the ruins of these can be seen. The east main gate (*principalis dextra*) is the best preserved, with guard chambers each side that occupied the ground floor of the two towers. The double wooden doors in the gateways opened inwards, and at the south gate the sills against which the doors closed are still evident. The gates were pivoted on wooden posts, which were fixed by iron bars at top and bottom that turned into holes in the stonework in the floor and roof. (Interestingly, some Cumbrian farm and estate gates turn on pivots in the same way today.) The corner towers and interval towers, at the same height as the gateway towers, all added to the highly formidable appearance. The buildings in the fort followed the standard pattern, with large grain stores, here probably originally two stories high, and a headquarters building.

Excavations in 1989 produced a great surprise. They revealed the base of a large building, 42.7 m long and 16 m wide, now partly under the modern farmhouse. The plan shows a central nave flanked by two aisles, with the roof supported by eleven piers, in construction similar to that of medieval churches. Daylight would have been provided by high windows in the arcade, above the lower walls and roof of the aisles. The function of such a large building is open to question, for the headquarters building was treated in the fort's centre, and the bath house lay outside the perimeter. Archaeologists have concluded that the building was a *basilica exercitatoria*, or drill hall. The great strength of the Roman army derived from its disciplined use of tactics and arms, and regular drill sessions were crucial. Such drill basilicas were built to stage training sessions in bad weather. This building stayed unaltered throughout the life of the fort, which proves its importance.

The fort was built astride the turf wall, and when this was replaced with the stone wall it did not follow the same line. The wall bridged the River Irthing on the east side of the fort at Willowford, and ran alongside the fort's northern end. Several different garrisons occupied the fort for 300 years. Modern-day army personnel mark their name on their personal belongings, and the same applied in Roman times. A fragment of a drinking cup found in an earth rampart was scratched with the owner's rank and name: 'MARTINI DIIC' –Martinus, with the rank of Decurian, a cavalry officer. Cavalry would have an important role here as a rapid-response force, and there is little doubt that Banna was either a cavalry fort, or more likely, a mix of cavalry and infantry – *cohors equitata*. The only other evidence from inscriptions shows that in the third century the fort was held by *cohors I Aelia Dacorum milliaria*. As Aelius was Hadrian's family name, this was Hadrian's own, the first cohort of Dacians – a 1,000-strong unit that was initially formed in what is now Romania, but that would have collected other nationals, including Britons, in its progress through Europe. There are building stones and altars marked with the names of some seventeen tribunes, and sometimes centurians – the different fort commanders. One puzzle is the occupation by *venatores Bannienses* ('the hunters of Birdoswald'). Was this a hunting club? Or was their quarry the barbarians? One sad stone marks the death of Aurelius Concordius – 'he lived 1 year and 5 days, son of Aurelius Julianus, the tribune'.

Even after the withdrawal of the Roman forces in 409 there is evidence that the fort continued to be occupied by unpaid former army personnel. Most of them by this time were recruits from the north country anyway, and gradually the fort would have become a base for a Romano-British clan. The ruined parts were gradually re-roofed and occupied as farm buildings. However, in the lawless times of the borders, some kind of defence would be needed. Archaeological investigation at this site shows that a bastle house replaced the crude earlier building. The oblong bastle houses, or fortified farmhouses, were features of this north-east Cumbrian border area. Like the pele towers the walls were massive, and the main living quarters were located on an upper floor, while the ground floor, guarded by a heavy door, housed the most valuable breeding animals. In the event of a raid the animals would be rushed in and the door bolted with heavy bars. Then the human occupants would ascend by a ladder to the upper floor and draw it up after them. It could be assumed that that was all that was required; the reivers would take the unprotected stock and go. But if they were more determined they could attack the house, and the weak point was the ground-floor door, which could be burnt. That would be enough to take the precious animals; but if the raid was particularly nasty the occupants on the wooden upper floor could be burnt out too.

The farm was occupied in the sixteenth century by the Tweddle family (Tweeddale?), who complained to Lord Scrope, the warden of the West March, about reivers of the Elliot family taking all their stock and household goods. It was not the last time. The notorious Elliots, who lived in Scotland's Liddesdale, were a constant source of trouble.

In the less troubled seventeenth century the bastle house was replaced by a more comfortable farmhouse. Then in the eighteenth it was extended. A datestone records that it was built in 1745 by Anthony and Margaret Bowman. Thomas Crawhill, to whom the farmhouse was sold in 1830, was the first man to excavate the Roman site. Then in 1840 Henry Norman, another enthusiast of Roman Britain, purchased the property and did further digs to reveal several of the features seen today. He also discovered a seated statue of the goddess Fortuna, now in Tullie

House Museum in Carlisle. Norman decided that an ordinary-looking house was unworthy of the historical site, so he added a tower and battlements.

After Norman's death it passed through the Wright family, and during their occupation further excavation work was done by Durham University and Cumberland Excavation Committee. In the 1930s the property was sold to Lord Henley, who placed it under the guardianship of the Ministry of Works; and in the forties and fifties the ministry consolidated the stonework for public display. After Lord Henley's death the site was passed to Cumbria county council in 1984 in lieu of death duties. The county council has managed the site since then, and developed visitor facilities and displays, while the central archaeological service of English Heritage undertook further excavations. It is visited by many as a major feature of Hadrian's Wall.

The Irthing valley, view from Birdoswald Fort

Leaving by the gateway on the south, in a short distance from the edge of the spur, one sees another striking prospect across the River Irthing to the north Pennines. A wealth of Roman remains have been found in the area, some of them associated with the original turf wall. If the river is crossed at Gilsland (see below) and the minor road south-west taken, we come to Upper Denton, where stands a small Norman church built with Roman stone. Its chancel arch, for instance, is all Roman and does not fit the piers on which it stands. Archaeologists found that on the hill to the south, Mains Rigg, there once stood a substantial Roman signal tower, 6.4 m square, surrounded by a ditch and causeway. Further down the road at Nether Denton, the church has been built on what was an early Roman fort, and below the south wall of the churchyard the rampart has been identified – over 9 m thick. When the vicarage was built in 1868, the bath house was discovered. Coins found here show that the fort was erected in the time of Agricola to control the east–west road, the 'Stanegate', before the wall was built.

Taking the road back from the fort, alongside the wall on the road to Brampton, by Wall Bowers (limited car parking but reached by the Hadrian's Wall bus), a path leads through woods down to the Irthing that contain some of the quarries used for the building of the wall; some are inscribed. The woods are managed by the RSPB.

GILSLAND AND BEWCASTLE

Starting back again at Birdoswald the minor road leaves the fort northwards to a road junction. A right turn here brings one to the village of GILSLAND on the edge of the county; in fact part of the village is in Northumberland. The most probable source of its name is that it was the home of Gill, or Gilbert, the son of Beuth, whose land was to the north, in what is now Bewcastle. After the Norman conquest Ranulph le Meschyne, earl of Carlisle, granted it to his son, William, but it seems that it was still occupied by Beuth. After Gill's death Henry II granted the land of Gilsland to Hubert de Vallibus. The barony of Gilsland included Brampton, Castle Carrock and Lanercost. In 1250 it came by marriage to the family of de Multon, and again by marriage in 1317 to the Dacres.

Gilsland was much bothered by Scottish reivers and was also the centre of family feuds. A branch of the Bell family occupied the area and they were at deadly odds with the Armstrongs. Border politics were always complicated, but it was in Gilsland that one old score was settled. Thomas Carleton was the land sergeant of Gilsland, and in July 1598 he allowed David Elliot, a notorious reiver, to hide out in a local house. Elliot had killed a member of the Ogle family and the Ogles were bent on revenge. Thirteen of them rode into Gilsland, found out where the man was living, broke in and killed him, then rode away. An alarm was raised and Carleton took off after the Ogles with a posse of six riders. When he overtook them he vowed to take the lives of some of them for killing a man who was in his charge. There was an argument. The Ogles pointed out that they were only settling a local score with an evil man. But Carleton lost his temper and charged with his lance, knocking off one rider and firing his pistol at another. The response was swift. Carleton was shot dead. The Ogles were later held at Carlisle Castle, but no record exists of what happened to them. They could have been let off, for the warden of the West March was Lord Thomas Scrope, who had no love for Carleton and would not have been sorry to see him dead.

It was the Victorians, not the reivers, who descended in numbers on Gilsland when the railway could bring them from the smoke of the Industrial Revolution to the peace and cleanliness of the Irthing valley countryside. Houses were built to accommodate visitors in a minor resort. It was particularly attractive, too, for 2.5 km up the valley lies GILSLAND SPA, which became a fashionable place to stay even before the Shaws Hotel opened there in 1840.

Gilsland Spa, the well

The spa well was famous. Every year the canons of Lanercost made a procession to the well on St John the Baptist Day (June 24), and blessed its water.

The spring is down on the river bank, and to get to it you descend from the hotel into a ravine through a grand mixed woodland of coppice and mature trees, native and exotic – some very large, right to the river's edge. This is away from everywhere and the only sounds are running water, the wind in the trees, and bird song (unless, that is, military exercises are in progress on the War Office land to the north). The path bridges the river, and the spring is on the right before it, possibly easily located by the smell of sulphur. The approach is nothing like it was. In the fashionable days, a paved path led beside the bank next to several outbuildings. The spring, as of old, is housed in a stone-built alcove, though this one was nicely restored in 1964. The water emerges from a pipe and all are free to sample it – there are no nasty warning notices, but one should remember to take a cup. The taste is devastatingly awful – the drinking-water of Hades! In the old times it was only the foul-tasting medicine that was thought to be any good. The water was credited with a diuretic effect 'unrivalled among mineral waters' and it was said to be good for the kidneys. Would-be imbibers were advised to start with half a pint, then to augment the daily amount when the stomach had acclimatized!

An analysis of one imperial gallon of the water revealed the following:

> Carbonate of Soda 21.48; Chloride of Sodium 5.07; Sulphate of Soda 2.62; Carbonate of Lime 2.39; Protocarbonate of Iron 0.66; Carbonate of Magnesia 0.73; Sulphate of Potash 0.11; Sulphide of Sodium 1.78; Organic matter (?) 1.92; Silica 0.81. Total 37.99; Combined Carbonic Gas 22,56 cubic inches; Free Carbonic Acid Gas 0.44. Oxygen Gas 2.2 cubic inches; Nitrogen Gas 5.8 cubic inches; Sulphurated Hydrogen Gas 21.0

The invalid was invited to visit the spa for 'pure air and pleasant company' and 'every convenience which his enfeebled conditions may require'. We could find there 'balmy mountain breeze ... animating with freshness his languid frame, and as sympathy from a brother-sufferer is, in many cases, the most consolatory medicine to the afflicted ... condoling with him on their mutual sufferings and privations' was a good idea. What a happy conversation could be had by all! If they got too enthusiastic about their mutual privations, half a pint of the spa water might halt all talk for quite a while.

On 27 August, 1859 the Shaws Hotel caught fire. Fire engines were rushed to the scene – from Carlisle by train. Water was pumped on the flames for two hours, but in vain. The hotel was a dead loss, and a new hotel was erected on the site by a George Mounsey of Carlisle (who also had the church built in the village). It cost him £12,000. This created a resurgence of interest in the spa and it was included in guidebooks alongside Bath, Buxton and Harrogate.

When spas went out of fashion the hotel was acquired by the North of England Cooperative Societies and became a convalescent home. Now it is back to being a first-class hotel, a good base particularly for Hadrian's Wall enthusiasts.

The young Walter Scott was fond of this country, and stayed at Wardrew House (now a ruin) on the Northumberland side of the Irthing when he was twenty-five years old. While there, he fell in love with another resident, a Mlle Charlotte Margaret Charpentier, daughter of a French businessman from Lyons. John Gibson Lockhart (1794–1854), critic, biographer, novelist and son-in-law of Scott, tells the story:

> [Scott] riding one day with Ferguson, they met, some miles from Gilsland, a young lady taking the air on horseback, whom neither of them had previously remarked, and whose appearance instantly struck both so much, that they kept her in view until they had satisfied themselves that she also was one of the party at Gilsland. The same evening there was a ball, at which Captain Scott produced himself in his regimentals, and Ferguson also thought proper to be equipped in the uniform of the Edinburgh Volunteers. There was no little rivalry among the young travellers as to who should first get presented to the unknown beauty of the morning's ride; but though both the gentlemen in scarlet had the advantage of being dancing partners, their friend succeeded in handing the fair stranger to supper – and such was his first introduction to Charlotte Margaret Carpenter [sic].
>
> Without the features of a regular beauty, she was rich in personal attractions; 'a form that was fashioned as light as a fay's;' a complexion of the clearest and brightest olive; eyes large, deep-set and dazzling, of the finest Italian brown; and a profusion of silken tresses, black as the raven's wing; her address hovering between the reserve of a pretty young Englishwoman who has not mingled largely in general society, and a certain natural archness and gaiety that suited well the accompaniment of a French accent. A lovelier vision, as all who remember her in the bloom of her days have assured me, could hardly have been imagined; and from that hour the fate of the young poet was fixed.

On that occasion at Gilsland, Scott must have written the little poem, 'To a Lady with Flowers from a Roman Wall' (not published until 1808 in *Edinburgh Review*):

Take these flowers, which, purple waving,
 On the ruined ramparts grew,
Where the sons of freedom braving
 Rome's imperial standards flew.

Warriors from the breach of danger
 Pluck no longer laurels there:
They but yield the passing stranger
 Wild-flower wreaths for Beauty's hair.

So Scott and Charlotte walked in the woods. They forded the river, strolled along the woodland banks of the Irthing past the well (it is not known if they sampled the water) and some way beyond it upstream where they came to a boulder. This was a suitable place for the young lady to sit and rest, and when she was sitting comfortably Scott popped the question. He was probably not a good catch at the time, but his prospects were promising. Anyhow she said yes and they were married at Carlisle on Christmas Eve, 1797. And surely Scott remembered with affection the woodland and the river in his introduction to *The Bridal of Triermain*, taking the usual line of inventing the poetic names Lucy and Arthur. Arthur tells the tale to Lucy when she is sitting on the stone:

Come, Lucy! while 'tis morning hour,
 The woodland brook we needs must pass;
So ere the sun assume his power,
We shelter in our poplar bower
Where dew lies long upon the flower
 Though vanished from the velvet grass.
Curbing the stream, this stony ridge
May serve us for a sylvan bridge;
 For here, compelled to disunite,
 Round petty isles the runnels glide,
And chafing off their puny spite,
The shallow murmurers waste their might,
 Yielding to footsteps free and light
 A dry-shod pass from side to side.

Arthur helps his nervous Lucy across stepping stones, along the rough and slippery pathway:

And now we reach the favourite glade,
 Paled in by copsewood, cliff, and stone,

Where never harsher sounds invade,
To break Affections whispering tone,
Than the deep breeze that waves the shade,
Than the small brooklet's feeble moan:
Come! Rest thee on thy wonted seat;
Mossed is the stone, the turf is green.
A place where lovers best may meet,
Who would not that their loves be seen.
The boughs, that dim the summer sky,
Shall hide us from each lurking spy,
That fain would spread the invidious tale,
How Lucy of the lofty eye,
Noble in birth, in fortunes high,
She for whom lords and barons sigh,
Meets her poor Arthur in the dale.

After telling Lucy the story of the bridal of Triermain, Arthur leads her back :

The evening breeze, as now, comes chill;
My love shall wrap her warm,
And fearless of the slippery way,
While safe she trips the heathy brae,
Shall hang on Arthur's arm.

Now the 'Popping Stone' where Scott asked for Charlotte's hand in marriage is still visited by many. It is said that when Scott became famous, young ladies would go and chip a piece off the stone to place under their pillows in the hope of conjuring up a similar romantic situation. Really? Doubtless they were carrying a hammer and chisel in their reticules ...

The Gilsland area features in Scott's *Guy Mannering*; and 4 km east is the ruin of the castle of Triermain, and in the *Bridal of Triermain* the hero is Roland de Vaux – who existed in fact as lord of Gilsland, and had carried lance against the Scots. In the fictional poem:

Sir Roland de Vaux he had laid him to sleep,
His blood it was fevered, his breathing was deep:
He had been pricking against the Scot,
The foray was long and the skirmish hot;
His dinted helm and his buckler's plight
Bore token of a stubborn fight.

North of Gilsland a large area of countryside, called Spadeadam, is used by the military for training. So we must take the road east and the fragment that is left of Triermain castle can soon be seen. Four km on from Triermain a minor road leaves to the right for Bewcastle, passing Mollen Wood, made a site of Special Scientific Interest to preserve its ancient woodland. Then marshy grassland supports a bird community of lapwing, snipe and curlew, and then we are in the heart of what was, until the seventeenth century, a bleak lawless terrain.

BEWCASTLE (or Shopford) has a medieval castle, church, rectory and farm, all within what were once the boundary walls of a substantial Roman fort, built to serve as an outpost of Hadrian's Wall. A straight Roman road connected it directly to the fort at Birdoswald. To fit on to the plateau on which it stood it was built, unusually, with six sides. From its Roman name, *'Fanum Cocidii'*, it has been deduced that the fort was built upon a temple of Cocidius, a native god whom the Romans seemed to have adopted and equated with Mars. The first building was of wood and turf, but later built of stone to coincide with the wall. It held a thousand men, probably a mixture of cavalry and foot soldiers.

If Hadrian's Wall was built solely for defence, an outpost like this, 19 km away, would be highly vulnerable. However, the wall not only served to prevent the barbarians from the north infiltrating and allying with the barbarians in the south; it marked a frontier base line from which forces could be launched to deal with any trouble from the north. As well as the road, Bewcastle had a direct line of communication with Birdoswald. At a high point on the road between them, at Gillalees Beacon, stood a signal tower. Bewcastle itself had a very extensive view of the north and west from Barrons Pike, 6 km to the east; signs have been found there of a Roman presence. The function of the fort was thus to signal to Birdoswald any impending trouble, and also to ride out and meet it head on.

Though evacuated when the Roman frontier moved north to the Antonine Wall in AD 142, the fort was reoccupied when that wall was abandoned in 163. It is assumed that the fort was finally deserted around 370, as no Roman coins or pottery dating from after that period have been found.

The area around Bewcastle became known as Bewcastle Waste, implying that it had no value. But archaeological evidence shows that there were populated settlements in the Bronze Age, at which time the climate was warmer. When the Romans left the fort, Saxons later occupied it. The precious attraction at Bewcastle is the stunning evidence of the Christian settlement here during the Dark Ages – an amazing 4.4 m-high late seventh-century stone cross shaft standing in the churchyard. The west face has four panels. Facing the prevailing winds for 1,300 years it has been much weathered. The top panel shows John the Baptist carrying the Agnus Dei; below is one of the earliest carvings of Christ, with the figure standing on two creatures – possibly a lion and a snake; below this is a runic inscription – unfortunately untranslatable, particularly as it appears to have been interfered with by over-zealous scholars. At the foot is a man with a stick in the right hand and a bird on the left wrist. This could be a figure of St John the Evangelist with his symbol of an eagle.

The north face has a band at the top containing a runic inscription – 'Jesus'. Below this a vine scroll curls down to another interlaced design, and further below is a complicated chequered and interlaced knotwork. A runic inscription – 'Kyniburg' – lies below that. Cyniburgh was the sister of Ine, king of the West Saxons, and wife of King Alcfrith. Below that twists another vine.

The east side is more light-hearted. Decorated with a tree or a vine scroll spreading from a single stem, it holds two squirrels, two birds, two other unidentifiable animals and a single one on its hind legs, perhaps a dog. The south face contains five panels of intricate designs and what was a sundial.

Bewcastle Cross, east side

Bewcastle Cross, south side

Sadly, the cross is missing. It had been separately made and fitted into a socket at the shaft's top. It is thought to have been lost when it was removed before 1615 for study by an antiquarian, but nothing is certain. Remarkably, the cross was almost certainly one of a pair, for a cross of the same age and quality, surely by the same sculptor, can be found at Ruthwell church, on the Scottish side of the Solway. That cross is contained within the church. Pevsner maintains that there is 'nothing as perfect as these two crosses and of comparable date in the whole of Europe'. It is thought that the cross and shaft were originally coloured. In an outbuilding by the churchyard an exhibition room has been organized, and an illustration depicts how the cross probably looked. It would have attracted a great deal of attention. Who was the craftsman? And why here, and nowhere else?

The exhibition also tells something of the history of the area, as does the little church dedicated to St Cuthbert. The original church must have been built of stone taken from the ruins of the Roman fort. Obviously it had mixed fortunes over the centuries, being right in the forefront of the contentious border wars and raids. It was rebuilt in 1792, and restored in 1901, but even so, some of its twelfth-century construction remains in the east wall. The stained glass in the east windows, put in at Christmas 2000, is modern and appealing, and was designed and made by Alex Haynes of Albion Glass at Brampton, and paid for largely by well-wishers. The designs are copies of those on the stone cross, with the figure of Christ at the centre.

In the early part of the Norman occupation Bueth, the father of Gilles, who gave his name to Gilsland, built his fortlet here. The first mention of a castle – 'Bothecastell' – occurred in 1379, but it remained only sporadically intact, as it was in a sort of no-man's-land of conflict. It is known that King Edward IV granted it to his brother Richard of Gloucester (later Richard III) in 1470. After Flodden it became a stronghold held by a captain – Jack a-Musgrave. During the 'rising of the earls' – against Elizabeth and in support of Mary, Queen of Scots – the borders were in turmoil and Bewcastle was put to flames; but later Musgrave and his tenants had their revenge in successful campaigns against the Scots.

Bewcastle, castle remains

Tenants of the lord of the manor were given special privileges because they were required to defend the border – to arm themselves, mount horse and assemble at the lord's command, at the firing of a beacon or the peal of church bells. This gave the border families what they regarded as special status; they felt themselves a cut above the ordinary, even though they might have been living at subsistence level. In the periods when not required to defend their country they might use their arms and armour for nefarious purposes.

The border families were nearly all reivers, and robbery was a normal way of life. When the wars with Scotland were over Bewcastle Waste had a reputation for being a nest of thieves. There were Armstrongs – with branches in Scotland – and Routledges, whose names are still to be seen in the churchyard tombstones. But there were also the Bells, Crosers, Musgraves and Nixons, with the powerful Grahams, specializing in extortion and murder over their shoulder to the south-west. Many families had branches on both sides of the border. Across the border was Liddesdale, the turf of the notorious Elliot family, the most troublesome area along the entire border. While just to the west lay the Debatable Land, belonging for centuries neither to the Scots or the English and recognizing the laws of neither. Bewcastle Waste lay along one of the favourite direct routes for the Scots to come down from Liddlesdale to raid in England and return. In the words of Lord Dacre, warden of the Western March in 1528, 'theye come thorow Bucastledale, and retirnes, for the moste parte, the same waye aganye.'

The settlements in the Bewcastle and Gilsland region suffered continually from raiders; but the counter-raids were just as bad. It used to be said that no men of Bewcastle were buried there, only the women, for the men were all taken away and hanged for their misdeeds.

It was difficult for a farmer to make a living when his cattle were vulnerable to thieves. Not only that, for as well as paying rent to his landowner he might also be paying 'black rent' or 'black mail' for protection by a stronger neighbour. If he defaulted on the latter the consequences could be violent.

Sir Walter Scott in *The Black Dwarf* has his character romanticize reiver robbery:

> Hout, there's nae great skill needed; just put a lighted peat on the end of a spear or a hayfork, or siclike, and blaw a horn, and cry the gathering-word, and then it's lawful to follow gear [loot] into England, and recover it by the strong hand, or to take gear frae some other Englishman, provided ye lift nae mair than's been lifted frae you. That's the auld Border Law, made at Dundrennan in the days of the Black Douglas. Deil ane need doubt it. It's as clear as the sun.

That is a travesty of what was happening. The 'Border Law' did not count for a great deal. In reality the reivers were answerable only to themselves and their families. Not infrequently, people were wantonly killed for simply defending their own. Sometimes, no one was spared. In 1581 Isabell Routledge, a widow, who owned a small herd, was raided by thirty Elliots who took everything – her oxen, her cows, her only horse – and they ransacked her house. Margaret Foster of Bewcastle suffered a similar fate – a gang led by the notorious raider and murderer Dick of Dryhope made off with her entire small herd of eighteen cattle, and looted her home. Every home was vulnerable; even churches and chapels were rifled on occasions.

If their stock was stolen the victims could lawfully call on neighbours to make haste to steal some back, but revenge attacks were illegal. To follow the trail of raiders on a 'hot trod', 'sleuth dogs' were employed to follow the scent, and the hounds changed hands for high prices. It was a strange system of tit for tat. So numerous were the raids that there could be activity on both sides of the border on the same night. One chronicle recounts the time when a successful Scots raiding party of Elliots were returning home to Liddesdale through Bewcastle Waste with eighty head of English cattle, when they met an English raiding party coming south from Scotland, which instantly stole back the cattle.

Occasionally the wardens of the Marches caught the persistent troublemakers and had them hanged; but it made little difference. Sometimes the reivers, ever vengeful, might seek to attack the wardens' forces if they could be sure of success. On one notorious occasion, Lord William Dacre, warden of the Western March, and his men followed a group of about thirty Scottish Nixons and Crosers who had taken cattle from an English family and were hastening home across Bewcastle Waste. They had also kidnapped one of Dacre's tenants, which particularly infuriated the warden. He should have been suspicious when he sought support from the Bewcastle garrison, and it was not forthcoming. They knew something of which Dacre was unaware and was soon to find out. The warden continued in pursuit, for he still had a far superior force. Just short of the River Liddel, and the Scottish border, Dacre and his men overtook the miscreants, and were about to deal with them when they realized that they had been drawn into an ambush. A great force of mixed Scottish families from Liddesdale descended upon the warden's force, and in the resulting fight forty lawmen were taken prisoner. Thirty of these were Dacre's personal followers. Eleven were immediately executed, and the rest were taken into Liddesdale.

The result of this outrage was an extraordinary agreement from James, king of Scotland, giving the right of the representatives of the king of England to enter Liddesdale to take revenge on offenders.

Cross-border hostilities were sometimes shelved. Rival families could meet quite amicably on Carlisle's neutral ground, and even greet their enemies of yesterday in the marketplace. Oddly enough, there were even cross-border sports challenges, such as horse races and football matches. In 1599 six Armstrongs from Scotland came down to challenge six Bewcastle men to football. The rules of this specific game are not known but it was probably more like rugby than soccer. After the game, the teams and spectators took to some hard drinking at a Bewcastle house. Englishman William Ridley then took it into his fuddled head to muster a crew to lay in wait and capture the Scottish reivers, preventing their return to Scotland. The Scottish Armstrongs, though, were warned and the would-be kidnappers were set upon by 200 Scottish riders. Ridley and his friend were killed, many were hurt and thirty taken prisoner, presumably later freed for a ransom.

One notorious Bewcastle man was 'Hobbie Noble', whose exploits are told in Border Ballads. They describe him as being outlawed by the English for his crimes, betrayed by Armstrongs and as living and raiding with Scotland's Liddlesdale reivers.

Until the accession of James I the castle must have suffered from attacks and neglect, and Cromwell's troops made their later contribution. Moreover in 2003 English Heritage had to defend it against the wild weather that the place is subject to, and began the long task of consolidating the ruin.

The main industry of Bewcastle Waste has always been farming. Black cattle were the main breed of beasts in the past. A warning on the churchyard gate still asks for it to be closed to keep cattle out. Poverty must have been prevalent here before the passing of the Enclosure Acts and the improvement in farming methods. Sporadic attempts at coalmining were made, but the seams were found to be quite slim.

The area has a varied landscape, much of which occupied by Kershope and Kershopefoot Forest. To the north-west, moorland borders on Northumberland at Christianbury Crags, a remarkable away-from-it-all area with a sandstone high-point weathered into contorted shapes. It is in a large clearing within dense forest but the views are magnificent. (Access is gained from a forest car park at Cuddy's Hall.) Much of the land of the Waste comprises of blanket bog, with typical bog plant communities.

The Waste is drained by several watercourses. The White Lyne from Bewcastle is joined in the west by the Black Lyne, and both run into the River Lyne. Where the tortuous roads from Bewcastle bridge the Black Lyne just before the confluence of the two Lynes, scenic footpaths run along the western bank by woodlands on the organic Whiteholme Farm. The walk can be combined with a visit to the organic resource centre. On the west side of the River Lyne from Whiteclose (car park), an exciting walk leads to the popular beauty spot in Shank Wood with its natural rock formations the 'fairy castles' and a 'fairy table'.

Historical interest is not the only reason for a visit to Bewcastle. Its tranquillity, and the feeling of being off the beaten track – increasingly rare qualities – make it worthwhile too.

THE BORDER TO LONGTOWN

Going west from Bewcastle, one reaches the Scottish border at the River Liddel. A minor road then goes south, on the Cumbrian side to Longtown; but at least one feature of the Cumbrian border country may be best seen 3.5 km along the road south from Canonbie on the Scottish side. The first lay-by (on right side) offers a fine view to the defensive tower of Liddel Strength, one of many towers in this Graham (Graem) family country. They had fifteen in all.

On joining the main A7, one goes back into England and Cumbria once more. At this point over to the right the Scots Dyke runs westward, giving a permanent boundary through what was once the Debatable Land. That was all the land seen on the right – belonging to neither Scotland nor England, and the most lawless area of all, about 124 sq. km. Both the Scots and the English were sorely troubled by the Debatable Land reivers – mainly the Grahams and the Armstrongs, who were loyal to neither country, unless there was profit in it. Frequently the land was devastated by English or Scots forces, anxious to get rid of the troublesome families, and the area made uninhabitable. One such 'solution' was a foray into the area by the Scots warden, Lord Maxwell, in 1551 that left no building standing. But on this and other occasions, no sooner had the families left than they returned again to continue their thieving. In 1552 Scots and English decided to fix a border across the Debatable Land, and a meeting was arranged, with a French ambassador in charge, to adjudicate the line's position. On the English side was Lord Wharton, and on the Scottish side Douglas of Drumlanrig. As a result a treaty was signed, giving the Scots the greater share, and a bank thrown up on an east-west line represented the physical border. It became known as the Scots Dyke, although even to this day the region is still known as the Debatable Land. With the border determined, the wardens on both sides could now enforce the law – at least in theory.

A little way further on the left is another sixteenth-century defensive tower at Kirkandrews (not accessible). A track leads past it to the interesting 1776 church of St Andrew. The screen and reredos in green and gold are its most elegant features. Across the river one can see (but not visit) the great park of the eighteenth-century

Kirkandrews church

Netherby Hall. Sir Walter Scott wrote of it in 'Young Lochinvar'. His fair Ellen is being forced to marry an aristocrat against her will, but the hero arrives at the wedding feast. He has ridden hard, and only just makes it:

> He staid not for brake, and he stopped not for stone,
> He swam the Eske river where ford there was none;
> But ere he alighted at Netherby gate,
> The bride had consented, the gallant came late:
> For a laggard in love, and a dastard in war
> Was to wed the fair Ellen of brave Lochinvar.

He arrives among the guests and says that he had come to 'lead but one measure, drink one cup of wine'. While the bridegroom stands dumb, and the bride's mother fumes, he takes Ellen's hand for a dance.

> One touch to her hand, and one word in her ear,
> When they reached the hall-door, and the charger stood near;

Kirkandrews Tower

So light to the croupe the fair lady he swung,
So light to the saddle before her he sprung!
'She is won! We are gone, over bank, bush and scaur;
They'll have fleet steeds to follow,' quoth young Lochinvar.

There was mounting 'mong Graems of the Netherby Clan;
Forsters, Fenwicks, and Musgraves, they rode and they ran:
There was racing, and chasing, on Cannobie Lee,
But the lost bride of Netherby ne'er did they see.
So daring in love, and so dauntless in war,
Have ye e'er heard of gallant like young Lochinvar?

Netherby was a Graham house, built on the site of a Roman fort, and many of the defensive towers and houses in this part of northern Cumbria belonged to Grahams. The Grahams of Esk were one of the most notorious families; for many generations they had caused trouble on both sides of the border. When, on the accession of James I in the early seventeenth century, the border commission was given the task of hanging and transporting the reivers, the Grahams were among those on the top of the list. One hundred and fifty were sent to serve in the British garrisons in the Low Countries. Twenty-eight were jailed in Carlisle, then escaped; and the commission responded by ordering the houses of the fugitives to be burned down and the families expelled. Those Grahams who were shipped out, sneaked back. Henry Leigh of the commission complained that while no Grahams were left in England, they were all hiding in Scotland. Some were found and hanged, but the Grahams were quite slippery. They even hit back. When Leigh was riding with a companion from Dumfries they were ambushed by a band led by the wanted man Fergie Graham, and were lucky to get away alive – they lost a horse and had to ride two up. The commission's next plan was to round up all the Grahams they could and offer them cash inducements to settle in Northern Ireland. That failed too. The land was poor and nothing like as fertile as the land they had been forced to leave. The Grahams were shipping back home. Their comeback is indeed a puzzle. By the eighteenth century Netherby Hall was back in Graham hands and being expensively rebuilt. Land and property elsewhere around the Esk were owned by Grahams again, and they played a big part creating nearby Longtown.

In October 1885 a robbery at the hall led to a hunt for the armed burglars. The three criminals, a Lancastrian, an Irishman and a Londoner, had been lodging at Longtown. They gained entry to Lady Graham's room by a ladder when the family was at dinner, and escaped with some of her jewels.

In three encounters with police that followed, two officers were shot and wounded, one was beaten and laid out on a railway line (but staggered to safety) and one killed. After a nationwide alert the three men were arrested, convicted of murder and hanged at Carlisle. The jewels were returned.

A little further down the A7 from Netherby, at a bend, a right-hand turn leads off to OAKBANK LAKES COUNTRY PARK. This is really an anglers' park, with three lakes and some pools, offering great scope, as well as brilliant access for disabled. Children are also catered for, and tuition is available. There is fly-fishing for brown and rainbow trout on the well-stocked lakes, as well as carp, bream and tench. But the park also has the right to fish salmon on the Longtown Bridge water on the River Esk.

LONGTOWN, until the later part of the eighteenth century, was a village at a ford crossing of the River Esk. When Bonnie Prince Charlie and his army came

The River Esk on the Scottish border

through Longtown in 1745 on retreat, they had to ford the winter-cold waters of the Esk shoulder high. Having crossed, they apparently contrived to get warm and a bit drier by dancing to the prince's pipers.

The town now makes an instant impression with its straight, very wide thoroughfares and sturdy buildings. It was planned thus in the late 1700s by local landowner Dr Robert Graham, a clergyman of Netherby Hall, who at the same time made improvements to the local agriculture. Many of the town's inhabitants at the time were home weavers for the Carlisle industry. A ford was acceptable for highlanders, but Dr Graham, with others, built the very fine bridge, opened in 1756, and it made a difference to the town's economy.

So despite being a scion of the notorious clan, was this Graham benevolent? William Gilpin, the travel writer, who wrote the book with the fine crisp title,

Observations Relative Chiefly to Picturesque Beauty Made in the year 1772 On Several Parts of England, Particularly the Mountains and Lakes of Cumberland and Westmorland, met the man. After commenting on the natural indolence of the area's rural population, he writes:

> Mr. Graham immediately set himself to alter the state of things. He built a noble mansion for himself; which makes a grand appearance, rising on the ruins of a Roman station ... He divided his lands into moderate farms; and built commodious farm-houses. As his lands improved, he raised his rents: and his tenants in proportion found it necessary to increase their labour. Thus he had doubled his own income, and introduced a spirit of industry into the country. These indolent inhabitants of the borders begin now to work like labourers; and notwith-standing they pay higher rents, live more comfortably: for idleness can never be attended with the comforts of industry.
>
> To bring about this great change, Mr. Graham thinks it necessary to rule his subjects with a rod of iron. While he makes them labourers, he keeps them slaves. Perhaps indeed the rough manners of the people in those parts, could not easily be moulded by the hand of tenderness.
>
> The feudal idea of vassalage, which has long disappeared in all the internal parts of England, remains here in great force; and throws a large share of power into the hands of the landholder. Mr. Graham's estates, which are very extensive, contain about six hundred tenants; all of whom, with their families, lie in a manner at his mercy for their subsistence. Their time and labour he commands, by their mode of tenure, whenever he pleases. Under the denomination of boon-days, he expects, at any time, their personal service; and can, in a few hours, muster the strength of five or six hundred men and horses.

The last sentence is remarkable. Why should Graham need to muster such a force by whatever alarm, nearly two centuries after the borders were tamed? Gilpin records that Graham actually had cause to raise his force when he was confronted by a Scottish mob furious that he had been interfering with the salmon fishing. Sir Walter Scott describes what happened in his notes to *Redgauntlet*:

> Shortly after the close of the American war, Sir James Graham at Netherby constructed a dam-dike, or cauld, across the Esk, at a place where it flowed through his estate, though it has its origin, and the principal part of its course, in Scotland. The new barrier at Netherby was considered as an encroachment calculated to prevent the salmon from ascending into Scotland; and the right of erecting it being an international question of law betwixt the sister kingdoms, there was no court in either competent to its decision. In this dilemma,

> the Scots people assembled in numbers by signal of rocket-lights, and, rudely armed with fowling-pieces, fish spears, and such rustic weapons, marched to the banks of the river for the purpose of pulling down the dam-dike objected to. Sir James Graham armed many of his people to protect his property, and had some military from Carlisle for the same purpose. A renewal of the Border wars had nearly taken place in the eighteenth century, when prudence and moderation on both sides saved much tumult, and perhaps some bloodshed. The English proprietor consented that a breach should be made in his dam-dike sufficient for the passage of the fish, and thus removed the Scottish grievance. I believe the river has since that time taken the matter into its own disposal, and entirely swept away the dam-dike in question.

The Esk and the Liddel have long been, and still are, great salmon rivers.

Longtown's bridge made the place more attractive as a coach route to Scotland, and the Graham Arms, a coaching inn, helped travellers to appreciate the impressive little town. Tourism boomed, but coaching declined when the railways came by the town. The Waverley line, from Carlisle to Edinburgh, named after Scott's novels, was one of the most scenic in Britain. It was axed, and many grieve at its passing.

The A7, the so-called scenic route to Edinburgh, passes through the main street, but the pavements are generally wide and the traffic is not dangerously close. A nice feeling of freedom is in the air, and visitors are made welcome. There are pleasant green areas for picnics and recreation alongside the Esk.

During the foot and mouth epidemic in 2001 the Longtown's large livestock market was hit early on, and was forced to close for thorough disinfection. No farms in the area escaped the calamity, and the inhabitants are unlikely to forget the traumatic sight and smell of the incinerations. Some bitterness remains about the government's prevarication and its early insistence, with the National Farmers' Union, on burning; not to mention its chaotic attempts at organization. The farming community here proved its resilience, however, and was soon striving to get back to normal. Longtown has the largest sheep market in the country.

ARTHURET CHURCH is at Longtown, signposted at the south end of the main street. St Michael's church must have been savaged during Scots raids as it is so close to the border, but a rebuilding of the ruin was started in 1609 by permission of James I. Its immediate impression is of its great size, and the style is perpendicular. The common names on the gravestones prove that the Graham, Bell and Armstrong families – though notorious border thieves in their families' earlier days – earned respectability by the nineteenth century. 'Archie' Armstrong was born in Arthuret, a sheep stealer in his youth but strangely later a member of King

James VI of Scotland's household. When James became king of England too he brought Archie with him as court jester. He remained in the post on Charles I's accession, but was expelled when he insulted an archbishop. He is buried here.

Now, Arthuret? Myth or reality, there is much of King Arthur in north Cumbria. Near the church is the hill called Arthur Knowes, and below, it is said, is located the battlefield of Ardderyd, where the pagan forces of Gwenddoleu, king of Strathclyde, was defeated by Rhydderch, king of Cumbria, in AD 573. It is said that 80,000 were slain.

Although England's west country insists on proclaiming itself King Arthur's territory, the Cumbrian Arthur theories will not go away. In the last decade Professor Norma Goodrich's research of manuscripts dating from the Dark Ages and the medieval era, in various languages, leads her to the conclusion that Arthur's territory was in the borders in a square bounded by Carlisle, Glasgow, Stirling and Berwick. The activities of Arthur, spelled with a U, are centred on Scotland, while references to other 'Arthors' (spelled with an O) point elsewhere. She suggests that Arthur fought his last battle near Gilsland, and is buried somewhere in this area, north of Hadrian's Wall. She points out that in Pictish and Gaelic the suffixes '-et' and '-pet' or '-pent' refer to tribal territories. Arthur-et pointed her to Longtown.

St Michael's well is behind the church. Solway Moss, where the Scottish force was defeated with great loss in 1542, is to the right of the road from Longtown to Gretna, but since the land has been drained, the scene is not one of pastoral peace.

CHAPTER TWELVE

Carlisle: Cumbria's City

CARLISLE (*CAR-lile* – dialect *CAR-il*) is Cumbria's cathedral city, a busy industrial, administrative and market centre with a population of 68,830. Though an old border ballad has it as 'Merry Carlisle', it has had a long and troubled history; no other English city has endured so many assaults and conflicts. Carlisle was, and still is, of the borders – Scottish accents and names are much in evidence, and Scotland is only 15 km away. But in the modern city little visible evidence remains of the struggles of the past – so bad at one time that the city's defenders were compelled to tear down the cathedral walls to make hasty repairs to the castle. There were many occasions in Carlisle's history when 'border' meant 'frontier'.

Carlisle acquired the status of a town and major administrative centre as early as the Roman occupation, because of its strategic position. The Roman fort was at Stanwix, on the northern outskirts of the present city, on the north side of the River Eden and within a bend. It was large, housing a thousand men and cavalry. It protected the Roman town but it was also an essential part of the defensive command system of Hadrian's Wall, which continued its route westwards through the city. Just south of Stanwix the wall bridged the river, though the precise point is not known, but in the process of dredging, stone blocks were recovered, one with Roman inscriptions. The wall then followed the bank of the Eden, using the river as a natural barrier, then went west through Burgh by Sands (see pp. 191–3) to join the Solway coastal defences.

Carlisle was the civilized frontier Roman town of Luguvalium, a large and important settlement laid out in a grid pattern centred on what is now the cathedral site. There were other Roman forts on the site now occupied by the castle; recent archaeological digs have uncovered three, predating Hadrian's Wall. Indeed Roman history is buried under the city. Excavations have uncovered a good deal, and recent digs in a city centre development area have revealed evidence of substantial Roman buildings, including one with under-floor central heating. The town apparently continued as an important commercial centre long after the Roman occupation of Britain ended. Some of its Roman relics can be seen in Tullie House museum.

When the Romans left, the area fell under the kingdom of Rheged, which extended across the Solway into Scotland's lowlands; and south, probably as far as the Ribble. In any event Carlisle was almost certainly its capital. However, during the sixth and seventh centuries the area was gradually absorbed into the Anglian kingdom of Northumbria. Around 680 Ecgfrith, the Anglian king of the region, gave the town to St Cuthbert. The Venerable Bede records a visit by the saint in 685 who was much impressed with his town, being particularly entranced with a fountain at its centre. However, the Scandinavian raiders put an end to its elegance two centuries later. They reduced all to ruins. The ensuing power

Town hall and market cross, Carlisle Square

Carlisle's old Guildhall

vacuum was filled when the region became absorbed into the kingdom of Strathclyde. In 1018 Malcolm II held Cumbria in Scotland until it passed back fourteen years later into Anglian control. Then, however, in 1061 Malcolm III brought back Cumbria into Scottish power.

It appears that Dolfin, son of the earl of Northumbria, held Carlisle (for the Scottish king?) and the surrounding area while William the Conqueror was busy subjugating England. It was not until 1092 that a son of the conqueror, William Rufus, advanced 'with a great army', drove out Dolfin, and built the castle, probably first of wood, then stone from the Roman forts. He enclosed the town within a defensive wall. He then drafted in an army of compliant civilians, Normans, Flemings and Saxon peasants from Kent, Essex and Middlesex, to till the fields and set up the town's industries and commerce. Henry I, William's successor, recognized the strategic importance of Carlisle and in 1122 founded a priory and appointed the first bishop of a new see.

On Henry's death Stephen took the throne, but the succession was disputed. David, king of the Scots, supported the rival claimant, Matilda, and to prove his point sent his troops into Carlisle and Cumbria, reclaiming it once again for Scotland. He died in Carlisle castle in 1153. David's successor, Malcolm, was no match for Henry II who took Carlisle and all its territory back into England. When William the Lion acceded, he demanded the return of the northern regions to Scotland and made two attempts to take Carlisle castle, on the second occasion unsuccessfully laying siege for three months with a force of 80,000 men. He eventually abandoned further attempts and suffered defeat by Henry at Alnwick.

During John's reign Scotland's Alexander II was more successful, taking Carlisle castle at the second attempt, and bringing it back to Scotland's domination. But a greater reckoning was to come when Edward I came to the throne, he who for good reason was to be called 'the hammer of the Scots'. In 1292 Edward took Carlisle, but four years later, when the Scots tried to reassert their independence, he took his army into Scotland for a decisive final reckoning. He successfully routed the Scots and took away the Stone of Scone on which the kings of Scotland had long been crowned, then left the country under the control of his governors. The regime was cruel and oppressive and William Wallace, the son of a Norman/Scottish knight, gathered strong popular support and led an unexpected revolt against it. After defeating an English army at Stirling, his followers swept through Carlisle, looting and pillaging through and beyond Cumbria. Edward came north again with a powerful army and took ruthless revenge, and Wallace was defeated at Falkirk in 1298. Thereafter the king made Carlisle castle his base. It became a royal palace and was substantially improved. Two parliaments were held there in 1300, and again in 1307.

Wallace had got away, but a price was put on his head. He had not enjoyed the full support of Scotland's aristocracy and in 1305 he was betrayed by his own countryman, John de Menteith, governor of Dunbarton castle, who captured him by surprise when he was unarmed. He was brought to Carlisle in chains, then taken on to London, where he was executed after a mock trial.

Wallace was gone, but Edward's presence on the border was necessary to deal with the threat from the new Scottish leader, Robert the Bruce. The Bruce family owned land on both sides of the border, and its members were more involved in English than Scottish politics in the thirteenth century. In fact Robert the Bruce's father had fought on the English side against Wallace. Not surprisingly Bruce himself had previously sworn loyalty to the English king, and had actually served under him in bloody Scottish campaigns.

Robert the Bruce had different motives from Wallace. Wallace's fight for independence was in support of his king, Balliol. Bruce had given no notable support to Wallace, for Bruce's fight for independence was underpinned by the claim that he himself was the rightful king. He had defiantly claimed the Scottish crown after killing a prominent opponent, John Comyn, the most powerful man in Scotland, at a meeting in Greyfriars church in Dumfries. Some powerful Scottish barons, particularly the Comyns, and others linked by family loyalties to the English king, did not support Bruce's subsequent coronation at Scone. They backed an attack on his army by English forces, at Methven Park, near Perth, in 1306. Bruce was defeated and fled, possibly to Ireland. When Bruce returned a year later, Edward planned another campaign against him, but died an old and sick man on the banks of the Solway.

Edward II had none of the strength of his father and Robert the Bruce, this time gathering more popular support, was on the march. His forces ravaged Lanercost Priory in 1311 and entered Carlisle, but the castle held. Bruce made another, more determined, attempt after his successful routing of an English army at Bannockburn. He brought with him 'siege engines' – huge catapults that hurled boulders at the walls. But the castle was in the command of Andrew D'Harcla, who knew his business. He responded with better engines. The Scots brought a 'sow', a device to undermine the walls, protected from missiles dropped overhead by a canopy, and ladders to scale the walls. But the defenders threw down the ladders and sent such a fury of darts that the Scots had to retire. The Scots then unfolded the ultimate siege weapon, a 'berefray', or 'belfry', a large protected wooden tower on wheels that could be brought under fire to the castle walls after a section of moat was infilled. This would enable a strong close-range arrow attack from the top of the tower on to the wall defenders, and a drawbridge could be dropped on to the top of the wall to enable access. Unfortunately, however, the contraption got stuck in the mud of the moat and had to be abandoned. Bruce contented himself by leaving the castle alone, and pillaging and burning Cumbria and beyond into Lancashire with the help of the notoriously savage 'Black Douglas'.

In 1322 Bruce's forces invaded Cumberland again, plundering Holm Cultram Abbey (even though Bruce's father was buried there). On their way back from raids deep into Lancashire they stayed outside Carlisle city for five days, 'trampling and destroying as much of the crops as they could by themselves and their beasts'. Not long afterwards, while the English king was attacking Scottish forces in north-east England, Bruce's men took advantage by crossing the Solway, and burning and pillaging around Carlisle and into north Yorkshire.

Sir Andrew de Harcla, who had been made the earl of Carlisle after commanding a force that defeated the rebel baron Thomas de Lancaster's forces at Boroughbridge in 1322, successfully held Carlisle castle against repeated Scottish attacks. He also made successful counterattacks, and was well known to Bruce. The respect was no doubt mutual. But de Harcla could find no end to the continual warfare. He met the king at York, and according to the *Lanercost Chronicle*:

> he found the king all in confusion and no army mustered ... Wherefore, when the said Earl of Carlisle perceived that the king of England neither knew how to rule his realm nor was able to defend it against the Scots, who year by year laid it more and more waste, he feared lest at last [the king] should lose the entire kingdom, so he chose the less of two evils, and considered how much better it

> would be for the community of each realm if each king should possess his own kingdom freely and peacefully without homage, instead of so many homicides and arsons, captivities, plunderings and raidings taking place every year.

The king approved of peace talks, but considering what followed, he proved himself untrustworthy. Bruce was only too willing to talk peace. His motives for advancing into England were not only robbery, but also to press home his need for recognition as king of an independent Scotland. De Harcla met Bruce at Bruce's castle over the border at Lochmaben on 3 January 1323, in order to discuss a peace agreement. But he had enemies in the English court who reported his meeting to the king. His negotiations could not be tolerated and he was summoned to the king's presence at York to answer for himself. He declined. To the king this amounted to treason, and he ordered the sheriff of Cumberland, Sir Anthony de Lucy, who was at Cockermouth, to go and arrest him. Lucy approached Carlisle with three knights and attendants. He pretended that he was making a private visit, but he and his men had weapons hidden in their cloaks. They were allowed in at the main gate, and Lucy had men stay behind to hold it. He then was allowed into de Harcla's apartment, where he made an arrest and spirited the earl away from the castle before an alarm could be raised.

The treatment meted out to De Harcla was scandalous. The sword, given to him by the king, was 'broken across his head', and he was stripped of his furred tabard, coat of arms and girdle. He was then taken away and hung, drawn and quartered. His head was spiked on London Bridge, and his quarters put on exhibition at York, Newcastle, Carlisle and Shrewsbury. What had he done to arouse such vicious enmity?

A peaceful solution with Scotland was not achieved until Edward II's successor, the young Edward III, after unsuccessful attempts to best Bruce's forces, came to sign the Treaty of Edinburgh, when English sovereignty over Scotland was relinquished, and Bruce agreed to pay Edward £20,000.

The quarrels with Scotland were not over, however, and during the reign of Richard II the borders were again stirred into warfare and Carlisle was twice besieged. The castle held; but on one of the attacks the city was taken. Inevitably the castle had been severely battered, and during Edward IV's reign Richard of Gloucester (later Richard III) was sent to repair the border's stronghold. Extensive improvements were made under Richard, and the Scots must have been suitably impressed, giving it a wide berth in later struggles. The city's defences were also overhauled. At this time the city was enclosed by roughly lozenge-shaped walls, enclosing some 18 ha. It had the natural protection of the River Eden in the north, with its tributaries Petterill and Caldew on the flanks. It had three gates, one east and one west, with the main gate to the south. The land rose to the north, and the castle was on its highest point. The grounds of the abbey, on which the cathedral stood, took up a quarter of the city's space. The strengthening of the castle and the city walls were undertaken by the German expert, Stephen von Haschenperg, who brought with him 800 German mercenaries.

In 1542 James of Scotland invaded with a large force directed towards Carlisle. It came about after Henry VIII was furious with James for giving refuge to those who had rebelled against his dissolution of the monasteries. Matters deteriorated when Marie of Lorraine declined Henry's advances and instead married James, then a widower. Henry arranged to meet James at York to settle differences, but insult followed injury: James agreed to the meeting then did not turn up. James apologized later, but there were a number of other provocative incidents that made Henry want to teach the Scottish upstart a lesson. An army under the duke of Norfolk advanced into Scotland and spent a week burning and destroying before returning for provisions to the Eastern March at Berwick.

Now James saw his chance for retaliation in Carlisle and the Western Marches while Norfolk's force was resting in the east. James spread misinformation that he was to attack in the east, but then his forces (he himself was laid up with illness) advanced on Carlisle with 18,000 men under the formidable Lord Maxwell, warden of the Scottish Western March. Sir Thomas Wharton, warden of the English Western March and governor of Carlisle castle, was limited by the finances available for his office, and his personal force was small. He could use his own 300 Cumbrians at once, and could muster additional riders from those tenants who by the terms of their tenancy were obliged to arm themselves and be ready to ride to Carlisle at the firing of beacons. In total that would mean a force of only 3,000 men. Without waiting for the arrival of the general muster, he set off with his men to scout the Scottish disposition.

Having observed how the Scots were deployed, he soon had his full complement of men, on horseback and armed with their 'prickers' – long lances – ready at dawn on 24 November. Instead of standing and defending Carlisle, he had his force ride forward to meet the large Scottish force on Solway Moss, on the far side of the Esk. As the Scots began to cross the ford Wharton ordered his 'prickers' to attack their flanks, and this they did with good effect, for the Scottish army was hampered by the ford, and the bogs of Solway Moss behind. The Cumbrian tactics were to harass – breaking in, using their lances, and running back; re-forming and attacking. Although outnumbered six to one, that made no difference. They repeated the attacks time and time again. The Scots had no answer to the tactics, and they began to crumble; their morale was broken. Many, it was reported, were drowned. By contrast, only seven of the 3,000 Cumbrians were lost. Some 1,200

Scots were taken prisoner, among them earls, barons and lords, including Lord Maxwell, along with all their cannons and hand guns. It was the most humiliating defeat in Scottish history. To add insult to injury the Scots who had fled the field back to Scotland were robbed of their arms, and their horses, by the waiting Scottish reivers.

One theory among others is that the Scottish defeat was compounded by a disagreement as to who was in command. Whatever the cause it was a severe blow to the already sick James, and he died shortly afterwards.

ELIZABETH, MARY AND THE BORDER INCIDENT

When Elizabeth I acceded she encouraged a policy of reconciliation with Scotland – but at the same time prudently ordered more extensive improvements and repairs to Carlisle castle. The city itself had to maintain security. The three city gates, incorporating inner and outer doors bound with iron, were locked at sunset. The main gate was defended by a citadel, designed and built by Stefan von Haschenperg, that consisted of a defensive tower with embrasures for guns on each side, a battery on the roof, and a courtyard between with two guardhouses. He planned similar arrangements at the other two gates, but they were never built. After the ringing of a curfew bell a curfew was enforced on the streets. No Scot was allowed to live in the city nor be seen walking in the city after the watch bell unless accompanied with a freeman. No apprentices from Scotland were allowed. Watchmen patrolled the wall day and night. The cattle grazing outside the city in daytime had also to be brought in at evening to be protected from raiders. As there was no sewerage system the result must have been unpleasant on hot summer evenings.

The castle soon had a distinguished guest. Mary, Queen of Scots, out of favour, fled to Cumbria with her retinue in 1568, and was a prisoner in Carlisle castle, though she had her own apartment and was free to wander out under escort, to worship in the cathedral and to hunt. From all accounts she was a good horsewoman and would ride at the gallop, to the concern of her captors. She took daily exercise on the green sward below the castle's southern wall, and it became known as 'Lady's Walk', while twenty of her retinue played football on the castle green – strongly and skilfully according to reports.

During Mary's incarceration she received an assurance from Queen Elizabeth that she would be as careful of Mary's 'life and honour' as Mary herself could be, and that it would be one of 'her highest worldly pleasures' to receive her as soon as she was acquitted of the murder of Darnley.

Sir Francis Knollys, the vice-chamberlain, was at Carlisle castle with Lord Scrope, warden of the March, and needed to know what to do with their guest. He wrote a report to William Cecil – Elizabeth's secretary of state – on Mary's disposition. The following is a part:

> This ladie and prynces is a notable woman; she semethe to regard no ceremonious honor besyde the acknolegying of hyr estate regalle: she shoethe a disposition to speak motche, to be bold, to be plesant, and to be very famylyare. She shoethe a great desyer to be avenged of hyr enymyes, she shoethe a redines to expose hyr selffe to all perylls in hoope off victorie, she delytethe motche to here of hardiness and valiancye, commendying by name all approved hardye men of hyr countrye, althoe they be hyr enemyes, and she concealithe no cowardnes even in hyr frendes. The thynge that moste she thirstethe after is victory, and it semeth to be indifferent to hyr to have hyr enemyes demynyshed eyther by the sword of hyr frendes, or by the liberall promyses and rewardes of hyr purse, or by devysyon and qwarylls raised amongst theym selffes: so that for victories sake payne and parylle semethe plesant unto hyr: and in respect off victorie, welthe and all things semethe to hyr contemptible and vyle. Nowe what is to be done with sotche a ladie and pryncesse, or whether sotche a pryncesse and ladie to be norysshed in one's bosome? or whether it be good to halte and dismbyll with such a lady, I referr to your judgement.

After two months at the castle she was taken to Bolton castle in Yorkshire.

For many years no serious conflict reached Carlisle, although tiresome incidents of lawless raiding and feuding continued among the border reivers. But in 1596 there was a major incident. William Armstrong, 'Kinmont Willie', was a notorious Scots raider, murderer and protection racketeer who lived across the border in his tower at Morton Rigg, 16 km from Carlisle, and he was caught and imprisoned in Carlisle castle. How the imprisonment came about was a matter of serious contention. On 17 March a day of truce had been declared, and an officer of the Scottish Western March, Deputy Warden Scott of Haining, had met his counterpart from the English March, Deputy Thomas Salkeld, at Kershopefoot on the border. It was a routine meeting to consider grievances, to make amends and to deal with offences. There were around 200 riders from the English side, while the Scottish contingent included the middle-aged Kinmont Willie. The truce, according to ancient border law, assured peace sworn between the two sides until sunrise on the following day. However, when the meeting finished, and was dispersing, an incident occurred that prompted the English riders to ride down the hated Armstrong and take him to Carlisle castle. This grave and unforgivable breach of the truce caused fury.

The matter could have ended if Deputy Salkeld had immediately released the captive, or if English warden Lord Thomas Scrope had done so when he returned to the castle after an absence. But Scrope decided to hold the prisoner until receiving assurance that he would mend his ways and make recompense for the grave damage done to English borderers; but there was more to it. Since the post of Scottish warden was vacant, the cause had been taken up at once by the unofficial deputy warden, the keeper of Liddesdale, Scott of Buccleuch, a man whom Scrope loathed. He regarded Buccleuch as a murdering reiver: and of course he was probably no better or no worse than any other. The incident caused a flurry of cross-border diplomatic activity that got nowhere.

Buccleuch, a proud young man, resented the slight to his authority, and thought that his honour had been impeached. The border ballad tells its version of the story. (Note that 'Hairibee' – is Harraby, Carlisle's place of execution.)

O have ye na heard o' the fause Sakelde?
O have ye na heard o' the keen Lord Scroope?
How they hae ta'en bauld Kinmont Willie,
On Hairibee to hang him up?

Had Willie had but twenty men,
But twenty men as stout as he,
Fause Sakelde had never the Kinmont ta'en
Wi' eight score in his companie.

They band his legs beneath the steed,
They tied his hands behind his back;
They guarded him fivesome on each side,
And they brought him o'er the Liddel-rack

They led him thro' the Liddel-rack
And also thro' the Carlisle sands;
They brought him to Carlisle castell
To be at my Lord Scroope's commands.

'My hands are tied but my tongue is free,
And wha will dare this deed avow?
Or answer by the border law?
Or answer to the bauld Buccleugh?'

When word of Willie's capture reaches Buccleuch, he says:

'O were there war between the lands,
As well I wot that there is none,
I would slight Carlisle castle high,
Tho' it were builded of marble stone.

'I would set that castle in a low,
And sloken it with English blood!
There's never a man in Cumberland,
Should ken where Carlisle castle stood.

'But since nae war's between the lands,
And there is peace, and peace should be;
I'll neither harm English lad or lass,
And yet the Kinmont freed shall be!'

He calls together his followers:

He has called him forty marchmen bauld,
Were kinsmen to the bauld Buccleuch
With spur on heel, and splent on spauld,
And gleuves of green, and feathers blue.

There were five and five before them a'
Wi hunting horns an bugles bright;
And five and five came wi' Buccleugh,
Like warden's men, array'd for fight:

The party, led by Dickie of Dryhope, cross the border and meet the 'false Salkeld', who challenges them:

'Why trespass ye on the English side,
Row-footed outlaws, stand!' qho' he;
The never a word had Dickie to say,
Sae he thrust the lance through his fause body.

They ford the river and arrive at the castle in bad weather:

And when we left the Staneshaw-bank,
The wind began full loud to blaw;
But 'twas wind and weet, and fire and sleet,
When we came beneath the castle wa'.

We crept on knees, and held our breath,
  Till we placed the ladders against the wa'
And sae ready was Buccleugh himsell
  To mount them the first before us a'.

They get inside:

'Now sound our trumpets!' quo Buccleuch;
  'Let's waken Lord Scroope right merrily!'
Then loud the warden's trumpet blew –
  'O wha dare meddle wi' me?'.

The garrison was terrified, so the ballad says, believing it to be a full-scale Scots invasion:

Wi' coulters and wi' fore-hammers,
  We garred the bars bang merrily,
Until we cam to the inner prison,
  Where Willie o' Kinmont he did lie.

On being set free, Willie calls:

'Farewell, farewell, my gude Lord Scroope!
  My gude Lord Scroope, farewell!' he cried –
'I'll pay you for my lodging maill,
  When first we meet on the Borders side'.

They ride away:

We scarce had won the Staneshaw-bank
  When a' the Carlisle bells were rung,
And a thousand men, in horse and foot,
  Cam wi' the keen Lord Scroope along.

Buccleuch has turned to Eden water,
  Even where it flowed frae bank to brim,
And he has plunged in wi' a' his band,
  And safely swam them thro' the stream.

He turned him on the other side,
And at Lord Scroope his glove flung he –
'If ye like na my visit in merry England,
In fair Scotland come visit me!'

All sore astonished stood Lord Scroope,
He stood as still as rock of stane;
He scarcely dared to trew his eyes,
When thro' the water they had gane.

'He is either himself a devil frae hell,
Or else his mother a witch maun be;
I wadna have ridden than wan water,
For a' the gowd in Christentie'.

The ballad, of course, had it all wrong. There was no prospect of Kinmont Willie being hanged. It is true that Buccleuch did resolve to raid the castle and release the prisoner. But whereas Scottish myth had it that this was a brave swashbuckling Commando-style raid, the truth was very different. Buccleuch did it with eighty followers in a rainstorm on the night of 13 April. Salkeld was not killed. The Scots gained entry into the castle, not by ladders, but through a postern gate. They freed the prisoner and got away. In fact the deed was almost achieved certainly with inside knowledge and help, for the raiders seemed to know that their passage to the castle would be unimpeded, that they would be able to gain access, and be able to find the prisoner, once inside the castle. In fact the castle's layout had been previously revealed to Buccleuch by English March officers who hated Scrope. And there would have been no shortage of helpers, for the Armstrongs had strong cross-border alliances; indeed Willie's daughter had married an Englishman.

Scrope was humiliated and made his excuses to the Privy Council. According to him there were 500 men in the raid making full use of the cover of terrible weather, while the watch were sheltering. He had also accepted surety from the prisoner that he would not attempt escape, and because of that he was not shackled. Queen Elizabeth was angry. Ambassador Bowes in Edinburgh visited King James and asked for Buccleuch to be handed over to England for violating the English castle, since the two nations were supposed to be at peace. James may have been amused by the incident, but was keen to keep the peace, and assured the queen that the raid had not been done with his authority. The incident also led to reprisal raids on both sides of the border that were not to James's liking and he was moved to end the matter. Buccleuch was persuaded to hand himself over to the English in late 1597. Apparently he did so willingly and proved a model prisoner. He was released in the following February in exchange for his young son as hostage.

THE END OF THE REIVERS BUT NOT THE END OF STRIFE

On the death of Elizabeth a fresh flurry of cross-border raiding broke out, since it was traditional among the border reivers to believe that while there was no ruler, there was no law of the land! When the Scottish king James VI acceded to the English throne as James I, he resolved to unite England and Scotland, and that meant settling the border problem once and for all. The border had to be disarmed, and the old order had to go, along with its March wardens and tit-for-tat raids. Lord Hume for Scotland and George Clifford, earl of Cumberland, for England, then carried out the pacification ruthlessly, using a mixture of hangings and banishment. In 1605 Carlisle became the headquarters of a commission of five Scots and five English to police the borders, arresting known offenders, and enforcing the new laws that prohibited the carrying of arms, allowed only work-horses without saddles to be owned and insisted that iron gates on towers be turned into ploughshares. The enforcement was arbitrary and cruel. Families were broken, and many were shipped off to Ireland. There were hangings at Carlisle. The brave Buccleuch, the great Scottish hero of the Carlisle castle Kinmont Willie raid, was one officer acting with authority of the king. He was involved in finding and dealing with many who were once his fellow reivers. He oversaw many hangings, and burned some reivers out of their towers and houses.

The end of the reivers meant that trade between Scotland and England could improve. Scottish cattle, mainly from Galloway, had always been sold in Carlisle – the city had been granted a market charter in the twelfth century, and fairs were held north of the River Eden on several days between late summer and midwinter. Now the Scottish drovers could bring their cattle south freely. The drovers were tough cattlemen, hardened to the worst that the weather could bring. If there were no inn to accommodate them on the way, they would wrap their plaid around themselves and sleep outdoors with their animals. Food, between times, was raw oatmeal, moistened with water and mixed in a shoe. But the drove roads, many of which were destined to Carlisle, had inns at strategic points, with enclosed grazing for the animals. Evidence of them has been fragmented, superseded by modern roads or lost in field enclosures – for they were mainly unsurfaced. The recognisable feature of drove roads are that they are enclosed between walls and have wide verges, where animals can graze.

One road to the city, directly from the north, forded the Esk at Longtown. Another from Gretna also forded the Esk, probably at a place near the present Metal Bridge. Another was the Solway low-tide crossing by the 'Sandwath' (wath = ford), between a point east of Dornock on the Galloway coast, and the Cumbrian coast somewhere near Drumburgh. A second Solway crossing was by the 'Stonewath', from south-east of Annan to Bowness. These were the ways well known in the borders and previously used by the reivers, and the armies of both sides. And they all converged on the city.

It was the English Civil War of 1644 that once again brought military strife to the city. Sir Thomas Glenham, commander-in-chief of the king's forces in the north, fled to Carlisle after the surrender of York and took charge of the castle. General Lesley, a Scot, laid close siege for parliament with 4,000 troops, but the castle held, although the inhabitants were reduced to a diet of rats, dogs and linseed meal. It seemed that it could hold out indefinitely, but when the royalists heard of the defeat at Naseby they lost hope and surrendered. The castle and the city walls had taken a battering and repairs were needed. The parliamentarians – Presbyterian Scots – cared little for the sanctity of the established church. They quickly began to tear down the walls of the abbey buildings and the canons' residences for stone for the defences; and when this supply proved insufficient, they began to dismantle the cathedral, which admittedly had been in poor shape for some time. Six bays of the nave were taken.

A castle is only as strong as its defenders. Even in its strengthened state it fell to the king's troops under Sir Phillip Musgrave three years after the repairs, but in the same year he had to surrender it to Cromwell's forces fresh from their victory at Preston. The parliamentarians garrisoned the castle with 800 infantry and 1,200 cavalry and used it as a base for the forays that followed. Then for seventy years, Carlisle was left in peace.

In 1653 the castle had an unusual visitor when George Fox, founder of the Quakers, came to preach. He records in his journal:

> I went to the castle among the soldiers, who beat a drum, and called the garrison together. I preached the truth amongst them ... by which they might be turned from darkness into light, and from the power of Satan unto God. I warned them all that they should do no violence to any man, but should show forth a Christian life; telling them that He who was to be their Teacher should be their condemner, if they were disobedient to Him. So I left them, having no opposition from any of them, except the sergeants, who afterwards came to be convinced.

After preaching pacifism to the army Fox could have expected some opposition, but in fact when a crowd threatened the preacher later, the army protected him. It did not prevent him eventually being thrown into Carlisle gaol, under threat of hanging, where he had to endure the atrocious conditions alongside 'moss troopers', the name then given to the remnants of the reivers. But hanging people for their religious beliefs was out of favour with the new parliament, and magistrates eventually ordered his release.

At the beginning of the seventeenth century Carlisle was no better than other cities of England, but perhaps in some respects worse. It was still walled and entered via three gates, nicknamed, according to their disposition, English gate, Scots gate and Irish gate. The main street, English Street, ran from the English Gate to the market cross where two other streets were joined: Scots Street, leading to Scots Gate, and Castle Street, which ran past the cathedral to the castle. The peaceful interlude, and the promise of more peace by the Act of Union in 1707, meant that improvements could more safely be made to the city, and new buildings were erected. But apart from the castle, the cathedral, the town hall (1717) and Tullie House (1689), little from this time survives.

The intrepid traveller Celia Fiennes visited Carlisle in 1698 and recorded her mostly negative impressions:

> ... there remaines only some of the walls and ruines of the Castle which does shew it to have been a very strong town formerly; the walls are of a prodigious thickness and vast great stones, its moated round and with draw bridges; there is a Market place with a good Cross and Hall and is well supply'd as I am inform'd with provision at easye rates, but my Landlady notwithstanding ran me up the largest reckoning for allmost nothing; it was the dearest lodging I met with and she pretended she could get me nothing else, so for 2 joynts of mutton and a pinte of wine and bread and beer I had a 12 shilling reckoning; but since, I find tho' I was in the biggest house in town I was the worst in accommodation, and so found it, and a young giddy Landlady that could only dress fine and entertain the soldiers.

But in 1715 Carlisle was yet again under threat from across the border, this time from an advancing army of supporters of the exiled Stuart dynasty. Jacobite sympathizers, including many Roman Catholics, were living in Cumbria. But there were many who were simply dissatisfied by the government's being under the control of an alien Protestant king who spent nearly all of his time in Hanover and could not even speak English. The government took the precaution of imprisoning in the castle known prominent supporters of the Stuart cause: Curwen of Workington, Howard of Corby and Warwick of Warwick Hall. But in any event the Cumbrian sympathizers had little enthusiasm for an armed uprising.

The advancing Jacobites lacked artillery, so an attack on the city was impractical. They resolved to pass by, but the lord lieutenant of Cumberland and the bishop of Carlisle were determined to halt the advance. However, the days were gone when suitably armed and ever-ready Cumbrian horsemen would take up arms at the call of beacons and church bells. The militia they raised to face the rebels was armed with pitchforks, scythes and obsolete muskets, and when they assembled on Penrith Fell and saw the advancing opposition, they decided that they would much rather go home. The lord lieutenant galloped away to Appleby, and the humiliated bishop, who had arrived in a coach and six, raced back to his home at Rose castle. While shouting to his coachman through an open window he lost his wig. Local poet of the time, Thomas Sanderson, reported the incident:

> The bishop gained his snug retreat
> Thanked Heaven he breathed the air;
> And all his bliss had been complete,
> Had not his head been bare.
> For, ah! When on a length of road
> His troubles waxed great,
> The thatch, which hat and wig bestowed,
> Unkindly left his pate!

After the Jacobites' defeat at Preston, seventy-four were imprisoned in Carlisle castle. The garrison was so poorly manned that the prisoners had to be kept crowded into three rooms. In November 1716 half were released and half tried in the town hall – it was quite an occasion, and seats for spectators were on sale at sixpence each. They were all found guilty, but subsequently released under the Act of Grace of 1717.

THE 1745 REBELLION

Having failed in the 1715 rising, the Jacobites were on the march from Scotland again in 1745. This time their leader was Prince Charles Stuart, the 'bonnie prince'. Fresh from exile in France, this grandson of James II was also the son of one who he was convinced should be James III. He led a motley army of highland rebels, mixed with some Irish, English, French and other supporters, and they were bound for London. A successful advance was made through the Scottish lowlands. He took Edinburgh. Charles then had the choice of advancing down the east side of England and taking Newcastle from General Wade's army – an army in poor condition. Instead he decided to move west, take Carlisle and advance south through Cumbria. In November Carlisle was within reach of the main part of his followers under the duke of Perth.

Before this Dr Waugh, the Chancellor of the Carlisle Diocese, had drawn the attention of the government to the poor condition of the castle, and the vulnerability of the city. Its answer was to dispatch Lieutenant-Colonel Durand, of the Coldstream Guards (who was recovering from gout), to review the situation. He saw that the castle was poorly garrisoned, to say the least – with only two regular officers, eighty more or less elderly and semi-retired soldiers, and four gunners. He immediately asked for 500 regular infantry. He was told that his requirement could not be met, so he was forced to obtain the services of 700 men of the Cumberland and Westmorland Militia, who were in training at Whitehaven. All were poorly armed countrymen without uniforms. He arranged for sandbags to be placed at vulnerable points on the walls, and obtained some townspeople as auxiliaries. He then posted two clergymen on the top of the cathedral tower with a telescope to look for the approach of the enemy.

On 9 November the alarm was raised, as Scottish cavalry was sighted north of the town. Soon afterwards a farmer's lad arrived with a letter from the prince's quartermasters demanding quarters for 13,000 infantry and 3,000 cavalry. The castle answered with gunfire and the highlanders withdrew. Durand sent a message to Marshal Wade at Newcastle, informing him of the threat to Carlisle and asking for help. Next morning three highland columns were observed approaching the town, and soon afterwards another messenger arrived with a letter from the prince, calling for the city gates to be opened in order to avoid bloodshed, and warning of the dreadful consequences that could attend a city taken by force:

> Charles Prince of Wales, Regent of the Kingdoms of England, Scotland, France, and Ireland, and the Dominions thereunto belonging.
>
> Being come to recover the King our Father's just Rights, for which we are arrived with all his Authority, we are sorry to find that you should prepare to obstruct our Passage: We therefore, to avoid the Effusion of English Blood, hereby require you to open your Gates, and let us enter, as we desire, in a peaceable Manner; which if you do, we shall take Care to preserve you from any Insult, and set an Example to all England of the Exactness with which we intend to fulfil the King our Father's Declarations and our own: But if you shall refuse us Entrance, we are fully resolved to force it by such Means as Providence has put into our Hands, and then it will not perhaps be in our Power to prevent the dreadful Consequences which usually attend a Town's being taken by Assault. Consider seriously of this, and let me have your answer within the space of two Hours, for we shall take any farther Delay as a peremptory Refusal and take our Measures accordingly.
>
> November the 10th, 1745
> Two in the afternoon
> For the Mayor of Carlisle

The answer was another burst of cannon fire, and the messenger was detained.

Then the city was relieved for a time. The prince had been told that Marshal Wade was coming to the assistance of Carlisle from Newcastle, and he withdrew all his forces to Brampton determined to meet him there. No highlanders could then be spied from the cathedral tower. The mayor of Carlisle, Henry Aglionby, lived out of the city and only rarely visited it. The mayoral duties were carried out by the deputy mayor, Alderman Pattinson, landlord of the Bush Inn, even when Aglionby's term of office finished in September 1745, and Joseph Backhouse became mayor. Pattinson thought it was all over, thanks to the cannonade, and wrote gleefully to the lord lieutenant of the county, Lord Lonsdale.

> Last Saturday night our city was surrounded with about nine thousand Highlanders. At three o'clock that afternoon I received a message from them for billets for thirteen thousand men to be ready that night. I refused. On Sunday I received the enclosed message [the demand of the prince].The answer returned was only by firing our cannon. Then Charles and the Duke of Perth, with several other gentlemen, lay within a mile or two of us, but have now all marched for Brampton, seven miles on the high road for Newcastle. – I told your Lordship that we would defend this city; its proving true gives me pleasure, and more so since we have outdone Edinburgh, nay, all Scotland. We are bringing in men and arms, and covered wagons frequently. I shall in a little time fully set forth everything for your Lordship. If you think proper I would have you mention our success to the Duke of Newcastle and to General Wade.

In due course the alderman received an acknowledgement from the duke of Newcastle, to say that his report had been seen by the king:

> … his Majesty was so sensible of the loyalty and courage which the magistrates and officers have showed – his Majesty commanded me to take the first opportunity of returning his thanks to them – I most heartily congratulate you upon the great honour the town of Carlisle has gained by setting this example of firmness and resolution, which it is to be hoped will be followed in other places should the rebels attempt to advance further.

The congratulations were, of course, premature. On 13 November Durand was disappointed in his appeal for help from Marshal Wade. Wade's army, unused to winter warfare, was half-starved and demoralized after an abortive attempt, in appalling weather, to make contact with the highlanders in the east. He had found that the road from Newcastle was impossible for the transport of artillery. He said that he did not think that the rebels intended to take Carlisle, but added that he wished the garrison success. It was his intention to move south with his forces and engage with Charles in Lancashire.

The day before Wade's answer the prince received intelligence that Wade was not leaving Newcastle. He would therefore take Carlisle, after all.

Lord George Murray, the best of the prince's commanders, moved close to the city and began making plans to lay siege to the castle, such as felling trees to make scaling ladders, without knowing that it was pitifully garrisoned then with eighty elderly and infirm men, 220 militia and eighty 'townsmen'. Even that force was depleted when some of the militia had begun to drift back to their farms and homes because of the lack of money to pay them. When the nervous militia's officers heard that no help could be expected from Marshal Wade they too opted for capitulation, feeling that they had already done what they could. They handed the following document to Colonel Durand:

> The Militia of the countys of Cumberland and Westmoreland [sic] having come voluntarily into the city of Carlisle for the defence of the said city, and having for six days and six nights successively been upon duty, in expectation of relief from his Majesty's forces, but it appearing that no such relief is now to be had, and ourselves not able to do duty or hold out any longer, are determined to capitulate, and so certify that Col Durand, Capt. Gilpin and the rest of the officers have well and faithfully done their duty.
> Given under our hands this 14th Nov., 1745

It was signed by thirteen officers. Durand tried hard to persuade them that they could hold the fort, but they dispersed to their homes.

A force under the duke of Perth and the duke of Athol began to throw up earthworks to the east of the city, both noblemen digging alongside their men to encourage them, as highlanders were renowned for not descending to such menial tasks. Lord George Murray prepared to surround the city. The townspeople became alarmed when they saw the militia deserting, and a meeting was held at the town hall. Quickly they reached a decision to send a delegation to the prince at Brampton under a white flag to offer the city's surrender, and they did so without delay. Durand then could do nothing except abandon the city, spike the guns on the city walls and hasten to defend the castle with his few remaining supporters. At Brampton the prince told the townspeople delegates that he could not accept the surrender of the city without the castle's capitulation. This caused even more alarm, and a deputation of militia officers and townspeople called on Colonel Durand and begged him to surrender the castle. He then saw that he had little choice. Much to the surprise of Lord George and the duke of Perth, the castle was theirs within the week.

On 15 November the duke of Perth entered the city by the southernmost, English Gate, and with his regiment and the city dignitaries in attendance, James was at once proclaimed king at the market cross. The next day the mayor and corporation in their ceremonial robes went to Brampton, and on their knees presented the keys of the city to the prince. Then the day after that the man himself entered on his white horse in a triumphal procession led by his pipers – a hundred of them, it was said.

He stayed for four days at the house of a Mr Highmore, attorney-at-law, in English Street near the city centre. The owner was pleased to receive the prince's generous payment of twenty guineas for the mere use of a room; and the prince even treated his landlord and his wife to 'two dishes of meat at dinner, and as many at supper'. It was the prince's order that his force's accommodation should all be paid for, and that his highlanders should behave decently and show respect to women. This they apparently did, though there was some anxiety about the rough appearance of some.

Suitably refreshed the prince left a small garrison in the castle, and followed the main advance a day behind, marching at the head of a column. But the expected strong support from Jacobite sympathizers en route failed to match his hopes. Before the end of the same year, unaware that he had been near to victory at Derby, when the English opposition was in disarray, his army retreated in the hope of regrouping in Scotland, reinforced by an army from France. On reaching Carlisle, and just before falling back across the border, Charles chose, against advice, to leave 400 men from his Manchester regiment at the castle with orders to make a stand. It was a futile gesture. The pursuing army under the duke of Cumberland, third son of George II, reached the city. The duke, a seasoned military commander, saw he would have no difficulty in taking either the city, or the castle, which he called 'a hen coop'. He sent to Whitehaven for ships' cannon, and six eighteen-pounders were trained on the castle walls. Francis Townley, holding the castle with the Manchester regiment, saw how desperate the situation was, but thought that it was better to die rather than surrender to Cumberland. But Colonel John Hamilton, in command, sent a messenger with an offer to surrender the castle as long as the garrison was allowed the privileges of prisoners of war. The messenger never returned. On 30 December a white flag was hung from the battlements and a message sent to Cumberland asking what terms his Highness would grant to the garrison. His reply was that they would not be put to the sword, but be kept at the King's pleasure.

So Cumberland took the city that he despised so much for yielding to the rebels so quickly, and the prisoners taken from the castle were treated cruelly; there was no Geneva Convention. Writing to the duke of Newcastle, Cumberland showed what a vicious man he was. He said that he would have preferred to put the garrison to the sword, 'but it would have cost us many a brave man, and it comes to the same thing in the end, as they have no sort of claim to the King's mercy, and I sincerely hope will meet with none'. After using the accommodation earlier used by the prince – even sleeping in the same bed as the prince – (there is no record to show if he was as generous as his predecessor) the duke returned to London to inform the king.

According to reports the king's army was not so inclined to behave decently to the citizens as the highlanders had been. On the contrary the forces treated the city as occupied enemy territory, as the incident of the cathedral bells shows. A Major Balfour demanded of the cathedral's prebendary Wilson that they be handed over to him 'as a perquisite to the train of artillery'. The protest that the bells were the property of the dean and chapter, who were 'dutiful and loyal subjects', was to no avail. They appealed to the duke, who said that he would not interfere. The major threatened to take the bells down, but seems to have dropped his demand.

Robert Wardale, Dr Waugh's curate, who was looking after the chancellor's quarters while he took refuge in Durham, wrote to his wife:

> One thing happened since our people got possession of the town which gave me much uneasiness and still does. A dragoon, who lodged in the servts. Rooms, had forced open the closet door over the pantry and stole all the china out of a small box, which was corded up there ... I found out the fellow, and had him severely whipped and drumm'd out of the regiment. But what satisfaction is that? ... The town is still very unsettled and uneasy.

The duke's army also left unpaid bills.

The prince's army was pursued into Scotland, and the rebellion, denied the hoped-for French support, finally perished on the battlefield of Culloden. This time no Act of Grace awaited the prisoners. In fact, the duke unleashed a dreadful retribution that earned him the title of 'Butcher Cumberland', in England as well as Scotland. Carlisle became a place of great misery for many of the captured. The castle, and even the cathedral, were filled with prisoners, many of whom died in appalling conditions. Some were marched out to other prisons to face trial. Some were moved to London where they were put on display before execution. The heads of some were returned to Carlisle and placed on spikes at the city gates. The trials of some of the prisoners at Carlisle – 119 of them – lasted fourteen days. They were a very mixed group of clerks and artisans, craftsmen and farmers, and by no means all Scotsmen. Notables among them was Thomas Coppoch, a cleric who had been promised the bishopric of Carlisle. He called to his fellow prisoners, 'Never mind, boys, for if our Saviour were here these fellows would condemn him!' and when one of the prisoners began to weep he cried, 'What the devil are you afraid of? We shan't be tried by a Cumberland jury in the other world!' On the scaffold he spoke for half an hour, quoting texts in Latin, and asking God to bless his enemies, 'especially that corrupted judge, Baron Clarke'.

The hangman, William Stout of Hexham, was paid twenty guineas, plus all the clothing of the hanged. Nineteen were hanged in October at Harraby on the south-east side of the city, and their bodies mutilated in ways that sickened the Carlisle citizens; no protests were recorded. They were hanged within an hour's journey of Scotland, and from the death of one of them, on the low road by the grave, came the sad song of 'Loch Lomond'. An old Scottish belief had it that when a man dies in foreign parts, his spirit returns home 'by the low road'. So when one was condemned and a companion freed, as the song goes, 'Ye'll tak the high road, and I'll tak the low road,/ and I'll be in Scotland afore ye/ But me and my true love will never meet again/ On the bonnie, bonnie banks o' Loch Lomond'. Some of the more fortunate were transported, and others pardoned on condition they joined the king's army.

The decision to house prisoners in the cathedral could well have been on the orders of the duke, as a gesture of contempt for the city. Wilson, the prebendary, reported to Dr Waugh that the floor of the cathedral was 'corrupted', with most of the pews broken in pieces, and until the mess was removed it would not be possible to hold services. After the removal of prisoners, services resumed after the 'burning of sulphur and tar' within the building.

PEACE AT LAST AND NEW INDUSTRIES

After all that the city was left in comparative peace, and commerce began to flourish. A company of Hamburg merchants made investments in the woollen and textile industry and it thrived. The city had always had tanneries fed by the cattle trade from Scotland, and they too began to prosper. The roads and bridges communicating with Carlisle also improved. The road from Newcastle was ameliorated quickly, as it was found lacking by Marshal Wade during the rebellions, when it was necessary to move troops to defend Carlisle. From 1752 turnpike roads began to be constructed. Acts of Parliament were passed in 1772 and 1779, allowing improvements to the roads from Wigton and Penrith. In 1763 a coach named 'The Flying Machine', pulled by six horses, could make the journey from Kendal to Carlisle in six hours. Improvements to sections of the London road made it possible for a fast post coach to reach the capital from Carlisle in three days, and by 1788 it could make it in two days. Some of the larger houses were converted into coaching inns.

However, a description by R. Longrigg, writing in *History and Topography of Cumberland* in 1794, showed what a sorry state the city was in towards the beginning of the nineteenth century:

> [there are] no marks of modern convenience and elegance. The buildings, mostly of wood, clay and laths, bespoke the poverty and bad taste of the inhabitants – houses were not then painted either within or without; this being only a modern improvement. The streets, though spacious, were paved with large stones, and the centre part or causeway rose to a considerable height. The fronts of the houses were paved in the same manner, the consequence of which was that the kennels or gutters were deep trenches, and stone bridges were placed in many different parts, for the convenience of passing from one side of the street to the other. The gutters were the reservoirs of all kinds of filth, which, when a sudden heavy rain happened, by stopping the conduit of the bridges, inundated the streets, so as to render them impassable on foot.

In the middle of the eighteenth century Carlisle had a weekly market for wool and an expanding textile industry. Linen cloth was woven and further expansion began with the import of American cotton. One product of the Carlisle mills was a cheap striped and checked calico to clothe the American slaves. Better communications stimulated trade, so in 1758 it meant that a Newcastle textile firm, Scot Lam, specializing in printing calico, could establish itself in the city and employ hundreds of men, women and children. Much land around the city was then occupied by 'print fields', for one stage of the printing process meant that the cloth needed to be put out into the sun and rain. By 1794 textile works employed about a thousand people, and other small-scale industries, such as iron works, tanneries and breweries, were in operation.

Even with better roads, most of the commercial goods were more easily carried by coastal shipping, and overland canals were fast being developed. In 1795 there was a great plan to join Newcastle to Carlisle by a canal with a hundred locks, and on to the port of Maryport. Although it turned out to be just a dream, a canal from Carlisle to a new port – Port Carlisle near Bowness on Solway – would greatly assist the city's trade. The first sod was cut in 1819. When it was finished its opening ceremony was, according to the *Carlisle Journal*, a great occasion with upward of 18-20,000 people lining the banks.

> About nine o'clock the Committee of the Canal Company proceeded in coaches to Burgh, where the vessels (fourteen in number) were waiting orders to advance, and having taken their places on board the 'Robert Burns' the whole moved forward ... [Boats were] decorated with a profusion of flags and

> streamers, and some of them were provided with small cannon which were frequently fired during their progress.

A ship entered:

> with a general cargo from Liverpool, preceded by an excellent band of music in a boat, entered the basin amidst loud cheering, and at the moment of her entry a salute of 21 guns were fired from two 6-pound field pieces which had been procured from the castle and placed at the entrance of the canal, and the signal was promptly answered by 21 guns from the batteries of the castle.

The canal enjoyed success for some time, servicing many vessels. A Carlisle and Liverpool Steam Navigation Company had a wharf for its exclusive use, built by the canal company, and employed a second-hand ship, the *Bailie Nicol Jarvis*.

A popular passenger service was offered by the *Arrow*, a 20 m-long boat (with a public bar) towed by two horses, which made the journey to Port Carlisle in an hour and forty minutes. From there, steamers could take trippers on to Liverpool all in the same day, a speedy journey impossible by road. In 1829 the canal carried a cargo that could be said to be the seed of its own destruction. George Stephenson, the innovative engineer who made the famous *Rocket* locomotive, had it transported to Carlisle from Stockton-on-Tees, then by the canal to Port Carlisle and on by ship to Liverpool. There it won the Rainhill trials to choose a locomotive for the Liverpool – Manchester railway.

The city's expanding population increased pressure to build, and by now the walls were redundant. Dorothy Wordsworth referred to them while visiting Carlisle with her brother and Samuel Taylor Coleridge: 'Walked upon the city walls which are broken down in places and crumbling away and most disgusting from filth ...'

Filth was indeed everywhere. The Industrial Revolution was growing too fast for the city. An influx of men from Ireland and Scotland seeking work added to the desperate problems. The conditions in common lodging houses were atrocious. There was no sewerage system, and no fresh water to households until 1896. Building in and around the city increased. The main gate's citadel obstructed expansion and was actually robbed of its stone for new housing. A new twin citadel with twin round towers was designed by Sir Robert Smirke with a suggestion of the original, and accommodated the law courts. Sir Walter Scott was critical of the City's developers: 'I have not forgiven them for destroying their quiet old walls, and building two lumpy things like mad houses.'

Even though the mills were employing many people, in 1819 it was reckoned that half the population was suffering in extreme poverty, and another quarter were struggling to make a living. The population was too high for the industry to support. And because of the free availability of workers, men, women and children, wages were low and the working hours long. By 1840 it was estimated that 1,963 looms were in production.

The canal was doing well during the first half of the nineteenth century. In 1837, for example, 1,186 vessels used the port. But in the end it was the railway that killed it off. In 1845 a railway linked Carlisle to Maryport, and two years later a line from Lancaster reached the city. So, to join them rather than be beaten, the canal was filled in, a railway line was built in its place, and later it ran from beyond Port Carlisle to Carlisle's new projected port at Silloth.

By 1860 the textile industry was in decline. Ironically it had been supported by the export of material used to clothe the American slaves, and when the slaves were liberated after the American civil war, they naturally wanted nothing to do with the striped and checked material from Carlisle that was a symbol of their oppression. They wanted gaudier cloth, and the city seemed unable to adapt. However, towards the end of the nineteenth century more industries grew. One notable company, remembered well with affection, was the biscuit firm, Carrs, established by Jonathon Dodgson Carr (1806–84), a Quaker and a baker. In Quaker tradition he took a keen interest in the welfare of his workers. The factory is below the castle, over on the other side of the bridge that crosses the railway and the River Caldew. (Biscuits are still produced, but now by McVitie.) Nearby is the old brewery, now a student residence of the University of Northumbria. In 1916 the brewery was taken over by the government, with all the other public houses in the city. This was because there were too many drunks in the city, and many were employed in the ammunition factory at nearby Gretna. Prime Minister Lloyd George is reputed to have said, 'Their drunkenness is causing more damage to the war effort than the German submarine fleet.' The beer from the state brewery, served in the state pubs, was reckoned to be very good, but ownership was relinquished in 1971.

There were engineering firms, and the city had a reputation for printing. The growth of the town as an administrative centre eventually meant that something like 62 per cent of the workforce were employed in administrative and service industries. One reminder of the industrial past survives in the form of a tall mill chimney. A forest of mill chimneys belching out smoke is an abomination, but a single sleeping chimney has appeal. When it was proposed to demolish the Dixon chimney the citizens protested. They wanted to keep the city landmark, and they got it, receiving grants for its maintenance. There it stands straight, pointing to the sky, looking almost elegant. It is, after all a masterpiece of workmanship. It was built to a height of over 92 m in 1836 to complement the seven-storeyed textile mill, which was designed by architect Richard Tattersall of Manchester. Not far from the chimney, textiles are still produced by Linton Weaving Mill, making fine fabrics for fashion designers such as Dior and Yves St Laurent.

THE CASTLE

Carlisle castle

Though the CASTLE had withstood assault after assault over the centuries it could not withstand the onslaught of the Victorian 'improvers'. The outer ward was razed to make a barracks square, and buildings were erected round it. The great hall that once housed Edward I's parliament, and was used as a fashionable assembly room in the eighteenth century, became a military store. Queen Mary's tower, where the queen once lodged, was almost completely levelled, and to the disgust of the citizens the renowned ancient ash trees at the entrance to Lady's Walk were cut down. The walls of the city also fell victim to developers.

What one now sees of the castle from the city is less than inspiring – a large squat ugly red beast of a building – and the impression is reinforced on entering it. Perhaps it depends on whether one sees it as a symbol of oppression or a bulwark against aggression. The castle (EH) occupies an area of around 1.2 ha, enclosed by high walls. At the foot of the southern wall lies the first defence – a deep ditch – though originally there was another ditch in front of this, backed by a stockade. Built by the curtain wall remaining on the east side is the Tile Tower, attributed to Richard of Gloucester when he was governor of the castle and warden of the Western March. The outer ditch we see now was much deeper and contained water in the thirteenth century, and was stocked with fish. The approach over it to the castle gatehouse was originally by a drawbridge, which, when shut, covered the doorway. A stone bridge now crosses the ditch. The barbican, which is entered under a drop-arch, is defended by arrow-slits that can be seen in the parapets; further hostile progress could be thwarted by the iron-shod portcullis.

If an enemy force managed to break through the gateway to get into the outer bailey (courtyard or ward), which seems very unlikely, they would come under fire from defenders on the walls. The next obstacle is the inner ditch, which was also full of water. They might manage to cross the ditch from a narrow point where the defenders' wooden bridge had been, now taken away. They could throw their own bridge across, but the bridging position was chosen where it could come under heavy fire from a number of angles. At the tower's side of the ditch there is a half-moon battery dating to Henry VIII's reign. The position of the embrasures shows that the part of the bailey opposite must have been lower than it is now, and the ditch was much deeper.

The next formidable obstacle would be the gate and barbican leading on to the inner bailey, the three-storey captain's tower, originally fourteenth century. This has been altered several times over the centuries. The inner bailey, as might be expected, contains the earliest part of the castle, the great, heavy twelfth-century tower or keep, which shows few obvious signs of the many alterations that had to be made over the years. As well as the keep, the inner ward, on the north-east side, contained the palace built by Edward I, to accommodate him on his Scottish campaigns. A gatehouse once stood on the south-east corner but it was later closed off. Here also was the Lady's Tower, where Mary, Queen of Scots, had her apartment. The queen could leave by a postern gate (presumably under guard) and exercise on the raised ground outside the wall, ever afterwards called Lady's Walk.

If the inner bailey was reached by enemy forces, the Norman tower would present another fearsome obstacle. The present gateway entrance is not original, but made in the thirteenth century, and just as defendable as the outer two, though earlier the entrance was on the first floor at the south-east corner, and reached by a stairway.

Having entered, one descends steps to a lower floor. This was originally the store, once all one room, but later divided into compartments. Similarly, the first floor was later divided and now contains a display showing the history of the castle and the city. The second storey has an exhibit telling the story of the Jacobite rebellions. Rooms on the south side were once used as prison cells. Within an embrasure some carvings on the walls have been attributed to prisoners, but another suggestion is that bored militia did them during siege. The latter seems more plausible as the carvings include shields of arms of noble families – and aristocratic prisoners were few and far between. One can also see dragons and other mythical creatures, fifteenth-century armoured knights, a Virgin and Child, a wheel of fortune, a George and the Dragon and well-favoured women. The inner bailey contains a military museum. The outer barracks buildings were built in the nineteenth century.

THE CATHEDRAL

After the castle the CATHEDRAL, once the Augustinian abbey church, is the most imposing building. Its unusually short length stems from the fact that six bays of the nave were removed for the repair of the castle's walls during the Civil War. The siting of the cathedral on what was once a Roman fort was chosen after Henry I's grant was received in the early twelfth century. The king, being a patron of Augustinian canons (black canons), wished the cathedral to be a house of that order. When he founded the see of Carlisle in 1133 he appointed Aethelwold, his confessor, as the first bishop. The early years were hard, for the see was poor and vacant for some time, though little affected by secular politics. Little remains of the early building except what can be seen in the south transept. The walls of the cathedral are mainly of red sandstone, like the castle, but partly of dark grey stone. This dark stone was probably cannibalized from the Roman buildings on and around the site. Later local quarries supplied the red sandstone.

The cathedral underwent extension in 1225, but a serious fire in 1292, whipped by gales, did great damage to cathedral and the city as a whole. The rebuilding gave the cathedral much of its Decorated Gothic features, of which the fantastic tracery of the east window is the prime example. Little of the original

A miraculous survival? The fine tracery of Carlisle cathedral's east window

glass survived. But the survival of the tracery is an extremely happy miracle. After the end of the fourteenth century the cathedral changed little from what is seen today, with the exception of the reduced nave. When William Strickland became bishop in 1400 further work was done. The tower was built then, though it originally had a lead-covered spire, as were the north transept and the forty-six stalls – with their delightfully carved misericords that are worth inspection. There are mythical creatures, dragons, birds, human faces, a mermaid, lions, storks and eagles. In the chancel the carvings on the capitals represent each month of the year. On the back of the choir stalls are bizarre comic-strip stories, restored in 1936, of the lives of St Augustine, St Cuthbert, St Anthony and the twelve apostles.

Like many others, the cathedral's low point followed the Reformation. The Salkeld screen was erected by Lancelot Salkeld, the last prior, after 1541 and made its point about the new order, showing the secular emblems of the heralidic Tudor rose and beast. During the Civil War, when the nave and chapter house were being demolished by Scottish Presbyterians for castle repairs, the cathedral was already in a poor condition. Charles I had earlier warned that 'if there be not present care taken for the repair thereof it cannot be long upheld'.

The cathedral was luckier than many in its Victorian 'restorers'. Ewen Christian began work in 1850, and the west end of the building (1870) is his. In that year St Mary's church, where Sir Walter Scott had married his bride on Christmas Eve 1797, ceased to occupy the nave. The south door was modelled on the chapter house door at Southwell. Owen Jones restored the semi-circular ceiling of oak in the chancel, adding a delightful blue background studded with stars. He replaced many of the original coats of arms of local families originally on the medieval roof. One cannot leave the cathedral without an image of that wonderfully large east window being etched in the mind.

The precincts of the former abbey were originally protected by a wall. Only three buildings survive. The tunnel-vaulted gatehouse was built in 1527, and an inscription on the arch attributes it to Prior Slee. This was defensive originally, with massive doors and drawbars; the entrance is divided into two parts, both tunnel-vaulted, one for pedestrians and one for carriages. Second comes the fourteenth-century fratery building, or refectory, which is still in remarkable shape, despite only minimal later remodelling and some understated late Victorian restoration. The rib-vaulted undercroft is superb. Thirdly, there is the former prior's lodging. This was originally a defensive tower, with storage in the basement and access to the upper floor via a defendable spiral staircase.

The cathedral played another part in the defence system. As already stated, its tower served as an observation post for watching the border. In the case of threats, the bells would be rung as a warning, and a beacon on the turret summoned those Cumbrians who were obliged by the terms of their tenancies to be ready to muster at a moment's notice, with horse, body armour and arms.

Nearby the cathedral the parish church is dedicated to St Cuthbert. From the outside the church looks grim, like a barracks block, but inside it is all white, pale green and gold. There was a structural problem here. How to enable the congregation in the galleries to see the pulpit – a very large and heavy nineteenth-century piece hidden in the church wing. The answer was to haul it on rails to the centre at sermon time, in front of the chancel, and it was cranked into position using ropes from the vestry. It must have been a welcome break for the congregation, rather like a scene change at the theatre. The lines are still there, but like many other railways, it seems no longer to be used. The oldest glass is in a north window. One window shows St Cuthbert on his holy island, with an otter and eider ducks. Another is a gift from Latvians, 'who found refuge in Great Britain after the Second World War'. The tithe barn, which served the priory as well as the church, is on the side of the churchyard.

THE CITY FROM THE EIGHTEENTH CENTURY TO TODAY

If the castle and the cathedral took some punishment from the troubles, the city took even more. Little remains of the pre-eighteenth-century buildings, as one would expect considering the violent times. And the city walls survive only in fragments but here developers from the nineteenth century are to blame. Visitors strolling through the city today are not seized by the historical past, as they would be in many of our ancient cities in more settled areas of the country. The oldest parts are around the cathedral, where in fact the old walled city was built between the three rivers, the Caldew, the Petteril and the Eden. Within this core area there are some fine Georgian and Victorian buildings, some inevitably desecrated at ground floor level by commercial façades. The town hall, standing before the market, is seventeenth century but with nineteenth-century additions. The column of the market cross, surmounted by a sundial and a lion, dates from 1682, but has been replaced by a replica. Smirke designed the round towers of the assize courts, still known locally as 'the citadel', which they replaced. The large Tudor-style railway station of 1847 is a classic of its kind, designed by William Tite who was also responsible for the London Stock Exchange. The trains make a nice theatrical entrance round a curve. In its early years the station had seven railway companies operating in it; and no doubt the trains all ran to time.

Tullie House, built in 1689 but since much altered, contains a very good museum and art galleries with some Pre-Raphaelite gems. The museum tells the history of the town, from earliest to modern times, especially those dreadful reivers, in a sensible not too gimmicky way. In the railway section one can sit in reproductions of early railway carriages – a clever thought. One happy hands-on feature is a cast of the carvings on parts of the Bewcastle cross shaft, on which rubbings can be made using the paper and crayons provided. The castle can be enjoyed from an outside viewing platform.

The museum spills into a tunnel under a busy road, giving safe access to the castle. Here a granite boulder has written on it the terrible curse of the archbishop of Glasgow, Gavin Dunbar, in the sixteenth century, who excommunicated all the thieving murdering reivers of north and south, and demanded that the curse be read out in all the churches of the diocese. It is such a classic that a very small extract from the massive original gives the appropriate flavour. The archbishop was not a happy man.

> I curse thair heid and all the haris of thair heid; I curse thair face, thair ene thair mouth, thair neise, thair toung, thair teeth, thair crag, thair schulderis, thair breist, thair hert, thair stomok, thair bak, thair wame, thair armes, thair leggis, thair handis, thair feit, and averilk part of thair body, frae the top of thair heid to the soill of thair feit, befoir and behind, within and without.

And so on!

Another improvement, funded by millennium money, is a handsome footbridge (with lifts) from the city centre to the castle area. A plan to build a large glass pyramid nearby, with no apparent function, was thankfully dropped after popular protests.

In the nineteenth century Carlisle began to prosper and expand. There were no more threats and alarms except in the first few decades when the city was the target of 'body-snatchers', with graves being raided to provide corpses for the Edinburgh medical schools. Because fresh bodies were required, the thieves needed to know of burials in advance. The discovery of thefts caused some panic, and at one stage frantic relatives of the deceased were descending on graveyards at Stanwix, St Cuthbert's and St Mark's, and digging up graves to make sure their loved ones were still there. This led to iron gates and fences being put up around burial sites, and watches were organized. On more than one occasion suspicious boxes being transported by coach to Edinburgh were opened to reveal corpses, and coroners' inquests followed. An Act of 1832 allowed bodies to be donated legally, and the grave-robbers lost their market.

Carlisle was the county of Cumberland's capital, and here were its law courts. Through history, it must be second only to London for the number of executions. The old county jail was on the site now occupied by 'the citadel' buildings, and a sign on the wall recalls the last public hanging, which took place there as late as 1862. But that date was not the end of judicial hangings. Twenty-six men were hanged at Carlisle jail between 1800 and 1893, not all of them murderers. There was John Hatfield for one, who had the bigamous marriage with the Maid of Buttermere (see pp. 425–6), and was executed for forgery. If anyone wanted to see the condemned men through the bars, they could slip the warder a few coins. It is hard to believe that Wordsworth and Coleridge came to gawp at Hatfield on their way to Scotland.

Between 15,000 and 20,000 people attended the last public hanging in Carlisle. The prisoner was convicted of murdering a woman railway-crossing keeper. For a fee it was possible to watch the ceremony from a high window or a rooftop. But the crowds were puzzled by a hitch over the time. The railway station clock struck the appropriate hour and nothing happened, the crowd began murmuring, wondering if the prisoner had been reprieved. But there was no delay – railway time was ahead of Carlisle city time. At last the solemn act of hanging began. It followed a ritual that you could see puppets enact in Victorian seaside penny-in-the-slot peep-show machines. After the tolling of the prison bell the chaplain, the prisoner and the executioner arrived on the ramparts in full view. The hangman placed a white cap over the prisoner's face, followed by a noose, then left the platform. The chaplain then said a few words and stepped back; soon after, the trapdoor opened and the prisoner dropped and was hanged. A strange noise filled the air as crowds sighed or exclaimed or applauded. Nowadays we have television.

The three counties were united into the new county of Cumbria in 1974, and Carlisle became the capital and the main administrative centre, though departments are scattered among other towns. The city is still an important main-line railway centre. Although the days are long gone when all the road traffic to Scotland rumbled through the city centre, the coming of the M6 motorway did not solve its traffic problem. The market square is mercifully given over to pedestrians, and this is the city's finest feature. The shopping mall is much like any other shopping mall, but, alas, for the indoor market, a vestige of how it once was. Traditional indoor markets are not superstores. They are places where the regular stallholders are trusty friends known by name, some stalls having been held by generations of the same family. All too often the city fathers intervene, believing that the market should be dragged into the new century. The place is modernized, and inevitably stall rents rise. The old firms, which existed on low profit margins, cannot afford the rents and leave. The place becomes a sort of mini-mall, and 'stalls' are rented by businesses that seem to come and go. Carlisle is not the worst example of this, and something of the original friendly service persists in a few stalls, but those who remember how the market was, must feel saddened.

Carlisle is the home of the *Cumberland News*, and *Evening News*, and the newspaper group also publishes the popular magazine *Cumbria Life*.

Pleasant parks and green areas surround the city and the city council has made efforts to maintain the footpaths and encourage public use. Most areas are along the banks of the Eden and north of the city, where there are three nature reserves. Kingsmoor Sidings occupies the old railway sidings; nature likes to reclaim these places and here are now oaks and birches and orchids, and prospects of more discoveries. The names of Kingsmoor South and Kingsmoor North derive from Edward III who gifted the area to the city. They were designated as reserves as early as 1913 and offer a nice mixture of habitats: woodland, grasslands, ponds and wetlands, served by a network of paths, some of which are suitable for wheelchairs.

The city centre is kept clean, but like most cities the side streets and back alleys are neglected. The railway embankments are a disgrace. Industries here are diverse, a fact that has perhaps buffered the city from the depression that has hit other northern centres. Though it no longer stands at the troubled frontier of old, a stretch of imagination would be necessary to describe it as the 'Merry Carlisle' of the old ballads. But in spite of its turbulent history it is not glum and glowering and unfriendly, like some cities. Remember, though, that friendly shop assistant could well be a descendant of those dreadful reivers.

CHAPTER THIRTEEN

The Settlements and Countryside of North Cumbria

North-east of Carlisle, by the side of the road to Brampton, lies the pretty hamlet of SCALEBY. Its church is as old as the Magna Carta, as can be seen in spite of restorations in the eighteenth and nineteenth centuries, mainly affecting the nave. The tower, with narrow windows and entry through a lone narrow door, was built as a means of defence against Scottish raiders. A strange sculpture has puzzled antiquarians. It is a slab fragment with two robed headless figures in relief. Some say Roman; Pevsner guesses they're as old as the church. South of the hamlet is the gaunt ruin of Scaleby Castle, which is approached by a public path. Home of the Gilpin family, it was built after the church and was twice besieged in the Civil War.

East again and south of the Brampton road, IRTHINGTON is within sight of the Eden and sits astride the Roman road of Stanegate. There was a Norman castle here but it has gone, except for the motte on which it sat. King John stayed here in 1201, it is said. The church is another one dedicated to St Kentigern, bishop of Glasgow, and has Norman signs, but it has been wholly restored. A chapel probably stood here long ago centred on a holy well, and tradition has it that the saint came here to preach.

South-east of Carlisle, the attractive village of WETHERAL, well known to river fishermen, serves largely as a dormitory for Carlisle, and stands around a green. Recommended are the celebrated walks through surrounding woods, owned by the National Trust. A Benedictine priory, founded around 1100 by Ranulph de Meschines, stood near the river at the south side of the village, but only an echo – the fifteenth-century gatehouse remains. It is quite impressive. A tunnel-vaulted entrance below lies beneath two storeys, entered by a spiral staircase. The crenellated top shows that the priory originally had a defensive wall.

The church of the Holy Trinity was restored in Victorian times but the exterior is still essentially early sixteenth century, and there are thirteenth-century piers and fifteenth-century glass. A sculpture by Joseph Nollekens of the dying Lady Maria Howard (d. 1789 at the age of twenty-three), with her dead baby in her lap, greatly affected Wordsworth; the sculpture is one of Nollekens' major works and is definitely world-class. There are two alabaster effigies, of Sir Richard Salkeld and his wife Jane.

Nearby are caves cut into the sandstone of the Eden gorge: they are known as St Constantine's cells, or, alternatively, the Wetheral Safeguards. Their purpose is not really known, but one suggestion is that they were safe hiding places for the priory's treasures during Scots raids. The beautiful Wetheral viaduct, north of the village and across the Eden, was one of the first major railway viaducts in the country. Built in the 1830s it has five arches, and stands about 30 m high.

Just south of Wetheral lies the hamlet of CUMWHITTON, whose church of St Mary has Norman portions – the north arcade is thirteenth century, but a window in the north wall could be Anglo-Saxon.

CORBY CASTLE, on the opposite side of the Eden from Wetheral, is a seat of the Howards. It began life as a fourteenth-century pele tower, now a ruin, but a range was added by the Howards in the seventeenth century. This was further extended in the early nineteenth century. The grounds were landscaped in 1740. The castle and estate are not open to the public.

Continuing east of Wetheral, one reaches the village of WARWICK on the west side of the river, by a very handsome bridge, built in 1837, with the village of WARWICK BRIDGE on the other side. Near the bridge, on the same side, is the remarkable little church of St Leonard, much restored but still showing very early Norman features. Pevsner calls it 'the most memorable Norman village church in Cumberland'. The apse is most unusual on the outside, having no less than twelve pilasters with small arches, and recesses only 32 cm apart. This seems a genuine eccentricity; Pevsner noted that this motif is exceptional in England though it occurs here and there in France. This emphasizes its early Norman origins, and inside the arch mouldings are similar in style to those found in Carlisle cathedral, which could date it as early as 1130. The arch is impressive, with quite massive capitals, leading one to wonder whether the church was once much larger.

In ancient times INGLEWOOD FOREST lay south of Carlisle. One hated institution that the Normans brought with them was the royal forest with its harsh forest courts. As much as a third of the new Norman kingdom's land was appropriated so that the royal court could enjoy hunting. According to the *Anglo-Saxon Chronicle*, a collection of historical records written by clerics, from the period of the early Christian church to 1154, William the Conqueror

> made large forests for deer and enacted laws therewith, so that whoever killed a hart or a hind should be blinded. As he forbade killing the deer, so also the

> boars. And he loved the tall stags as if he were their father. He also appointed concerning the hares that they should go free. The rich complained and the poor murmured, but he was so sturdy that he reckoned nought of them.

A great area of Cumbria south of Carlisle became royal forest. The forest of Inglewood ('or Engelwood, the wood of the English') stretched from Cross Fell in the east to roughly Bowness-on-Solway in the west, and southwards as far as Penrith. This was serious for the inhabitants of the villages who needed the forest to supply some of their food; so out of necessity, poaching was common in spite of the risks. The laws included a prohibition on the carrying of bows. Farmers were not allowed to erect fences, so that deer could move about freely – and feed on their crops. No tree could be felled, or bush cut down or undergrowth removed that might give cover to game. Farm stock could graze, but only on payment of a rent.

The harsh laws brought bitter resentment, and like the forest of Nottingham, Inglewood had its famous outlaw heroes, skilled with their bows, that predated Robin Hood. Here it was Adam Bell, Clym of the Clough and William of Cloudesly. The story of Adam Bell must have been well known in Elizabethan times, for Shakespeare in *Much Ado About Nothing* has Benedick denying that he will fall in love: 'If I do, hang me in a bottle like a cat, and shoot at me, and he that hits me, let him be clapt on the shoulder and called Adam.'

The old border ballad recounts the tale (the spelling has been modernized here):

Merry it was in the green forest
  Among the leaves green,
Where that men hunt east and west
  With bows and arrows keen;

To raise the deer out of their den;
  Such sights hath oft been seen,
And by three yeomen of the north countrie,
  By them it is I mean.

The one of them hight Adam Bell,
  The other Clym of the Clough,
The third was William of Cloudesly
  An archer good enough.

They were outlawed for venison,
  These yeomen everyone,
They swore them brethren upon a day,
  To English-wood for to gone.

Now lith and listen, gentlemen,
That of mirthes loveth to hear,
Two of them were single men,
The third had a wedded fere.

The married man was William of Cloudesly, and the ballad continues with a story worthy of a Hollywood classic. William, against the advice of his two comrades, decides he must go to his Carlisle home to see his wife and children. He sneaks into the town and taps on the window of his house. His wife welcomes him and gives him food and drink. An old woman, helping round the house, has some grudge against William and leaves to inform on him and claim a reward. The justices rush in to arrest him.

They raised the town of merry Carlisle
In all haste that they can,
And came thronging to William's house,
As fast as they might gone.

William sees them coming and barricades the house. He then let fly with arrows until he has none left.

Set fire on the house, said the Sheriff,
Sith it will no better be,
And burn we therein William, he said,
His wife and his children three.

They fired the house in many a place,
The fire flew up on high,
Alas, then cried fair Alice,
I see we here shall die.

But they get away, William lashing out with his sword and scything down 'many a man'. Eventually, outnumbered and overpowered, he's bound and thrown into a cell. Carlisle's gates are closed so that no one can enter, and gallows are erected. A small boy who witnessed William's capture runs off to tell Adam Bell and Clym of the Clough. They make haste but are stopped by a porter at the locked city gate.

Then cometh none in said the porter,
By his that died on a tree,
Till a false thief be hanged,
Called William of Cloudesly.

Using trickery, however, they sneak in, just in time to find William of Cloudesly bound hand and foot on a cart with a rope around his neck. William then witnesses his two friends loosing their arrows, killing the justice and the sheriff. The spectators flee. The Mayor of Carlisle and his men try to capture the outlaws but they escape.

The three later go to London to ask the king's pardon for killing the justice, the sheriff, and, er, 300 men ... In the end they are pardoned after William shows off his skill with a bow by splitting a hazel rod, and shooting an apple off his son's head. The ballad ends the story thus:

> Thus endeth the lives of these good yeomen;
> God send them eternal bliss:
> And all, that with a hand-bow shooteth;
> That of heaven they may never miss!

Clym of the Clough is mentioned in Ben Johnson's *The Alchemist*.

Two main roads ran from Carlisle through Inglewood. One divides at Thursby, the fork heading through Wigton to Maryport, and the other to Cockermouth. The second road from the city goes to Dalston, and on south, then peters out among a maze of minor roads. This is agricultural country, and all the minor roads turn this way and that, following field boundaries, and it is a notorious area for strangers to get lost in. It is hardly possible to aim in one direction without going round sharp corners, as though one were a rook moving round a chessboard. It was not always so. Many old tracks have been lost. The straight-line patterns follow field boundaries, and came as a result of the Enclosure Acts.

To get to DALSTON (pop. 2,760) is easy enough, however. Now it is a pleasant enough village with medieval features in its church and some eighteenth-century houses that face the square. It once had four cotton mills and a flax mill, and still has a textile business. The village has grown over the years, with modern housing providing for the city commuters. Some 3.5 km south of Dalston a side road passes ROSE CASTLE, the seat of the bishops of Carlisle since the thirteenth century (not normally open to the public), in the lovely green valley of the River Caldew. The Wordsworths and Coleridge visited here in 1803. Coleridge wrote that they were delighted with the place, and enthuses about the ivied gateway springing from 'one great root', the swallows casting their shadows on the walls and the whole offering 'Cottage Comfort and ancestral Dignity'. Wordsworth, drawing on Dorothy's journal, wrote:

> Rose Castle being an Episcopal residence has in consequence fortunately escaped those alterations in the Buildings and gardens to which under the

> name of improvement it would have been liable, had it been private property. The castle stands pleasantly upon ground that slopes gently to the River Caldew and commands an interesting view of the opposite woody bank of the river & the stoney summit of Carrock Fell beyond. But the peculiar recommendation here is the House itself – an ancient Building of red stone with hanging gardens, an ivied Gateway, velvet lawns, old garden walls, trim flower-borders with stately and luxuriant flowers.

The castle did not escape improvements, in the end, but they are not tasteless, and the bard may even have approved.

The road crosses the river and climbs to the agricultural hamlet of RAUGHTON HEAD (*RAFT*-on-head) with its eighteenth-century church. Stopping here, one can look back for a good view of Rose Castle. One hardly need say that the church's basic structure is that of a defensive pele tower. Originally ranges were built around a courtyard, but when the castle was severely damaged by fire around 1646 the east and south ranges were demolished, leaving the tower remains at the north end. The grounds have been landscaped and planted with fine trees.

Going north from Raughton Head to the hamlet of Gaitsgill, one takes narrow roads east as far as they go, across the motorway and under the railway, to arrive at the hamlet of WREAY (*REE-ah*). Why here? WREAY CHURCH is not ancient, being built in 1842, and its setting now is hardly serene, as it is too near the noise of the M6 and jammed in between the road and the railway; but it is well worth seeking out, for there is no church anything like it in Britain. The outside gives a clue to what is inside. The gargoyles under the roof are sculpted in the form of snakes, crocodiles and tortoises. Around the western doorway and windows are carved beetles and moths, flowers and ears of corn. Inside is even more extraordinary, a fantastic mixture of styles. In the chancel the arcade, with thirteen stone seats, is divided by pillars all carved differently. At one end there is a bat and a pelican, at the other an eagle and a serpent, and there are many small windows of multicoloured glass, the grilles before them in the shape of leaves. The altar is a green marble slab supported by two great brass eagles. An eagle and a pelican support two lecterns. The font is alabaster, carved with lily, vine, pomegranate and butterfly. An owl and a cock perch on a bracket. The pulpit is an irregular-shaped hollow bog oak stump, and a palm tree holds its light. It is delightfully bewildering. The church was designed by Sara Losh, daughter of the owner of an iron works in the north-east, and local builder was employed to realize her design; his son and a gardener did much of the carving. Sara was an exceptionally talented and learned woman, skilled in the arts, and an original architect, and she was devoted to her sister Katherine who died young in 1835. Sara designed the church as a memorial to her sister. But that is only half the story. Among the decorations, often repeated, are pine-cones and arrows. Sara Losh was in love with a Major William Thane, who was killed by an arrow in the Khyber Pass. Before he died he had sent Sara a pine-cone. To Sara the arrow was a symbol of death, and the pine-cone one of life after death. Inside Katherine's mausoleum in the churchyard one can see, through a peephole, the marble statue of a girl reading.

Return to THURSBY, a pleasant enough town of modern buildings around a green. The church is nineteenth century, but the first church here was built in the seventeenth century and possible stood on an old temple of Thor. Sir Thomas Bouch was a Thursby boy. He became a great civil engineer, responsible for building the tramway systems in many English cities. Alas he is remembered not for his achievements, but for one monumental failure: the first great Tay railway bridge. Scotland's Tay is its longest river, gathering other large rivers in its progress to the sea, and it carries a greater volume of water than any other river in the British Isles. To cross the estuary from Fifeshire to Forfarshire required a bridge 3 km long, a colossal undertaking. Bouch achieved the crossing with eighty-four spans of girder cages, and the bridge opened in May 1878. On 28 December of the following year a train was crossing in an exceptionally severe gale, when thirteen of the spans were blown down. The train plummeted into the river and not one passenger was saved.

A government report concluded that the bridge was badly designed, badly constructed, and badly maintained, and that defects in the structure would sooner or later have brought it down. To be fair to Bouch, such a project was unprecedented – nothing like this undertaking had been done before. But the calamity broke him. He died at Moffat a year after the disaster.

From Thursby it is not very far to Wigton. But we must take the slow way directly south of the village and go by West Curthwaite, then south on a dead-straight road to ROSLEY. Why Rosley, when there is hardly anything in the place? This was a major meeting of drove roads from Scotland: directly from the Stonewath ford south, avoiding Carlisle, with branches from it to west Cumbria and southwards for Penrith, Eaumont Bridge, Shap and the road south into Lancashire and Yorkshire; and east to Durham. It is possible to see the Galloway hills from its highest point. Rosley held the market for cattle and buyers from all the surrounding country. Rosley Hill fairground was in the now enclosed fields on the west side, and the building there was its centre – the Camp House, later the Hope and Anchor Inn. Now the land is farmed, and it is hard to understand how important it was before the railway network and the turnpike roads destroyed some ancient fairs and markets, and opened others. It is commemorated in a song by Mark Lonsdale (1758–1815):

I'e ne'er forget the time,
  I went to Rosley fair,
Wi' a pair of new soled pumps,
  To dance when I got there;
How I o' th' aild grey nag,
  Was mounted like a king,
And Dick ran on before
  Wi' Hawkie in a string.

Then soon as I'd selt my cow,
  And drunk till I was fou.
Wi' 'Neighbour, how's a' wi'-
  And 'Neighbour, how's wi' you?'
Tee iddle tee dmp tee dee;
  Wi' a whoop, lads, whoop,
And hey for bonnie Cumberland!

In 1799 Ewen Clark wrote the whoopless 'Description of Rosley Hill Fair', in which he describes some of the wares on sale:

Here the white labours of the loom proclaim
The weaver's skill, and thrifty house-wife fame.
There heaps of ginger-bread their charms display,
And shine refulgent in the face of day.

Gauze, ribbon, lace, in gay profusion lie,
Hats, caps and cloaks to catch the female eye.
Brooms, baskets, beehives, and bright Burslem-ware
Shall not remain unsung in Rosley-fair.

The nights got a little rough and there were fights:

Potations powerful then inflame the brain,
And oaths, and uproar fill the reeling plain,
– Not but a glass I've ta'en – the truth confest –
Jack Todd still keeps a bottle of the best!

Rosley hamlet is growing to serve commuters, but still has a lively indigenous community.

WIGTON AND ASPATRIA

The road west goes to WIGTON (pop. 5,380) or 'The Throstle's Nest' as it is affectionately called. Wigton is a busy little market town with a charter dating back to 1262. Though it contains some very pleasing Georgian buildings, it is one of those towns that has just evolved from a medieval plan, and the yards, alleys and backstreets just happened. A startling feature is the big square fountain in the market square, made of polished Shap granite and topped by a spire decorated with leaves against a gold background. On its four sides are four bronze reliefs of Acts of Mercy by Pre-Raphaelite Thomas Woolner, who also designed the Wordsworth memorial in Grasmere church. George Moore, a local man who made good, commissioned the structure in memory of his wife. Another feature, which should surely raise a smile, is the eccentric 40 m-high bell tower, crowned with an open lantern turret, that was built by William Banks in 1887 at his Highmoor House – and why not! It once played tunes three times each day, but now the tower has been converted into flats.

The church of St Mary of 1788 looks rather heavy and grim from the outside, but inside it is a delight, with three galleries on columns in a colour scheme of

Wigton market

grey, pink and gold. John Betjeman called it 'a triumph'. The lectern is very special – an astonishing piece of wood carving from the eighteenth century.

Wigton has always been an agricultural centre, as evidenced today by its livestock market on two days a week and twice-yearly horse sales. Two centuries ago at least, on the outskirts of Wigton, 'potters', travellers, tinkers or gypsies used to congregate. Did the horse sales originate with them, or were they attracted to the area to trade at existing fairs? Dorothy Wordsworth mentions a 'traveller' woman calling at Dove Cottage:

> On Tuesday, May 27th, a very tall woman, tall much beyond the measure of tall women, called at the door. She had on a very long brown cloak, and a very white cap, without bonnet; her face was excessively brown, but had plainly once been fair. She led a little bare-footed child about 2 years old by the hand, and said her husband, who was a tinker, was gone before with the other children. I gave her a piece of bread ...
>
> On my return through Ambleside I met in the street the mother driving her asses; in the panniers of one of which were the two little children, whom she was chiding and threatening with a wand which she used to drive her asses, while the little things hung in wantonness over the pannier's edge. The woman had told me in the morning that she was from Scotland, which her accent fully proved, but that she had lived (I think) at Wigton, that they could not keep a house and so they travelled.

As so often, Dorothy's diary was a source of William's inspiration:

> She had a tall man's height or more;
> Her face from summer's noontide heat
> No bonnet shaded, but she wore
> A mantle to her very feet
> Descending with a graceful flow,
> And on her head a cap as white as new-fallen snow.

Wigton had, at one time, two water mills, and four windmills for grinding corn. At the town's Whitsun fair would-be hired hands would wait and hope for an offer of work from a farmer. A visitor might find farmers' language rather strange, rural Cumbrian, being quite different to west Cumbrian. Here's one loud and hearty greeting heard at the market: 'Well noo Wully! oow-ista, y' auld booger?' (Hello, William! How are you, old friend?)

But if the town has strong farming connections, it also has a textile industry, whose employer enjoyed a post-war revival when it began manufacturing artificial silk or rayon and in 1936 became British Rayophane. In 1963 Rayophane merged with British Sidac, and in a joint venture with ICI began making biaxially orientated polypropylene (BOPP) in a purpose-built factory. Now named Surface Specialities, the factory is one of Cumbria's major enterprises, producing a wide range of films, including a biodegradable and compostable wrap for foodstuffs that is made from wood pulp, a sustainable resource. One hopes this means that eventually all those wrappers littering Cumbria's towns and countryside and beaches will actually melt away.

Wigton's notable sons include the artist Robert Smirke RA (1752–1845), an illustrator, especially of Shakespeare's plays; his son Sir Robert Smirke (1781–1867) became a much sought-after architect who designed the British Museum. His Cumbrian works include Lowther castle (now reduced to a shell), the 'citadel' (law courts) at Carlisle, and the screen at the foot of Boroughgate in Appleby.

Dr John Brown (1715–66) was brought up in a Wigton vicarage and went on to be appointed a canon of Carlisle cathedral in 1737. Arguably it was he who created the initial interest in the Lake District, following which artists and poets flocked to the Lakes. His *Description of the Lake and Vale of Keswick* (1767), eulogizing Derwent Water vale, was quoted in Father Thomas West's hugely popular guidebook of 1778.

Another Wigton man, Melvyn Bragg, is the author of fifteen novels and biographies, and a playwright; but he is perhaps best known as a television and radio presenter and editor, particularly of arts programmes. For his outstanding contributions to art and literature he was honoured by being created Baron of Wigton in the county of Cumbria in 1998.

Why is Wigton called 'The Throstle's Nest'? The thriving Wigton Choral Society might be a clue. And why was Wigton referred to as the gateway to the Lakes? Wordsworth's Guide says: 'Travellers from the North would do well to go from Carlisle by Wigton, and proceed along the Lake of Bassenthwaite to Keswick.'

The Roman fort at Wigton, 'Old Carlisle', is by the A595 to the south, though only the foundations can still to be seen. Aerial photography has revealed that an extensive civilian town clustered around the fort.

Following the road to Maryport, one comes upon ASPATRIA (*SPAT-tri-a*, with an a in 'pat') (pop. 2,560), a settlement near enough to the coast to catch a view of Scotland. Mining took over from agriculture, but reverted when the pits closed down. Although the land around the town was ringed with mines there is little sign left, though one give-away is the clump of miners' cottages to the east at Harriston. A look at the tombstones in the churchyard suggests that its most prosperous period dates from the early nineteenth century. Its chances were boosted by the railway from Carlisle to the coast, which came through the town in the middle of that century. An old local joke recalls that in the past when a train pulled into the station the guard would shout, 'A' they wi' clogs on, lowp oot!' ('All you with clogs on, jump out!'), or otherwise, ''Spattri, lowp oot!'

The church is another dedicated to St Kentigern; one wonders why when the town's name suggests St Patrick (*Askr* = old Norse for 'ash tree', 'Place of St Patrick's ash tree'. A record of 1230 reads 'Ascpatric'). Norman and Early English parts can be spotted in the church, but all has been rearranged, particularly in 1846–8, and old features moulded into the new. There are many Anglo-Norse stone fragments, and a strange Norman font on five pillars, its bowl carved with large leaves and a root, which a grotesque creature is biting.

In the churchyard is a copy of the Gosforth Cross as a memorial to vicar and archaeologist W.S. Calverley. West of the church a round barrow was excavated in the eighteenth century and found to contain a stone cist in which was buried a Viking with sword, dagger, axe, shield and a gold brooch.

The main industry in the town now is the manufacture of beds, developed to a fine art with the help of orthopaedic surgeons. Sealy, the company in question, has made a universally respected name for itself and supplies hotel chains and retail stores.

Taking the Penrith road from Wigton we reach the hamlet of SEBERGHAM (*SEB*-er-am) with its bridge over the Caldew. Six mills once clustered here by the river. Five buildings can still be identified. St Mary's church is of 1825, but with fourteenth-century lancet windows preserved, and a pleasant welcoming interior. Its notable feature is a memorial to Thomas Watson by his son, Musgrave Lewthwaite Watson, a sculptor 'of Rome'. The stunning white oval features three women in profile, modelled on *The Three Witches* from *Macbeth* by Johann Heinrich Füssli (1741–1825). A tablet also celebrates the life of Josiah Relph, who died at thirty-one years old, but had already made his mark in educating the local children and writing a volume of dialect verses.

HUTTON IN THE FOREST AND INGLEWOOD

Continuing towards Penrith we reach HUTTON IN THE FOREST (Inglewood), which finds us back in King Arthur's territory. Indeed, again the castle here is reminiscent of the one featured in the tale of *Sir Gawain and the Green Knight*, from the fourteenth century. Here live Lord and Lady Inglewood, and their house and gardens are open to the public on some days in seasonal weeks. A visit has to be recommended.

Hutton in the Forest

The house again originating from a defensive pele tower, is mentioned in the border ballad of 'Dick o' the Cow'.

> Then they are come to Hutton Ha'
> They rade that proper place about.
> But the laird he was the wiser man
> For he had left nae gear [loot] about.

The tower was owned by the De Huttons (or Hotons), but it was sold to a Cockermouth merchant, Sir Richard Fletcher, in 1605, and he set about the task of making the place a comfortable home. It was his son, Sir Henry Fletcher, who filled in the moat and built the long gallery. The pele tower's front door and window were inserted in the nineteenth century. The old door was to the left and there was a spiral staircase to the two upper floors. A five-bay wing adjoins the pele tower and another added in the nineteenth century.

The long gallery was built around 1635 but restored in the Victorian era when the panelling, probably taken from a seventeenth-century hall, was added. The library interior was designed by the brilliant Anthony Salvin, with the curtain material by William Morris, and the furniture is mainly Georgian. From the library one enters the ante-room, with decoration by the talented Lady Diana Beauclerk;

a copy of Sir Joshua Reynolds' portrait of her hangs above one of the doors. The drawing room is in the Victorian tower, designed again by Salvin for Henry and Lady Vane in 1871, and largely left as a Victorian room. Salvin also designed the cantilevered staircase, at the head of which is a tapestry showing Atlanta and the Caledonian bear hunt. The lovely dining room is by Salvin and George Webster, again with wallpaper by William Morris, and there is furniture by master craftsmen from Gillow in Lancaster. The hall is a Victorian renovation that nevertheless keeps its seventeenth-century looks. The Cupid staircase, with its cherubs and foliage, is a delight. The garden features the topiary yew hedges typical of the seventeenth century, and the woodland gardens below the house feature some magnificent tree specimens.

West of Hutton in the Forest, and still in Inglewood, the landscape is dotted with a few villages and hamlets. SKELTON's church of St Michael has a fourteenth-century tower. CASTLE SOWERBY is easily missed because one can only approach by a very minor road or by footpaths, and it is marked simply as Sowerby on maps. Indeed no sign of a castle remains, but there is a peaceful little gem of a chapel dedicated, like so many in north Cumbria, to St Kentigern, bishop of Glasgow. It is Norman, twelfth and thirteenth century, possibly built over Saxon foundations. The manor of Castle Sowerby was given to Queen Margaret of Scotland, to bring it into cultivation or preserve it for deer. Later John de Balliol inherited it, but Edward I took it into English hands after his contretemps with Scotland, and gave it to the prior and convent of St Mary at Carlisle. The manor seems to have prospered into the beginnings of the fourteenth century, then suffered severely from the Scottish raids, so much so that the population scattered. If there was a castle here, where?

The road south from Hutton brings one to GREYSTOKE, with houses nestling round a green. The church of St Andrew here is very special, large and with many thirteenth-century features. Three east windows light the chancel, with some old glass assembled in 1848, depicting the story of St Andrew. It was once a collegiate church, a centre for learning, and was richly endowed. In the stalls are the canon's seats and some entertaining misericord carvings: St Michael and a dragon, a pelican, a unicorn, two youths and a donkey, a man and a horse and faces. The church contains two alabaster effigies of knights, one of them being John, Lord Greystoke (d. 1436).

Greystoke castle is not open to the public. Here again, the first part of it is a pele tower, but the castle was burned down twice, and the building is now largely nineteenth century – designed by Salvin. The families who owned it were respectively the Greystokes, the Dacres and, to date, the Howards. It sits in 2,428 ha. of parkland. The Greystoke farmhouses are built like follies and named after America's Jefferson, Bunker Hill and Fort Putnam.

Greystoke is the home of the famous Gordon W. Richards racing stable, which has trained some 700 winners, including some in the Grand National.

From Thursby the road to Cockermouth is built on the line of a Roman road. To the east of this, before it reaches Bothel, lie two villages. One of them is TORPENHOW (*tre-PENN-aw*), a village with a view to Solway and Scotland, containing a remarkable Norman church. It is entered through a Norman doorway, the nave has Norman arches and the chancel has a Norman arch and windows on the north, and a blocked one to the south. The slightly later east window is emphatically Norman. The nave ceiling, however, is modern by the standards here – it was donated to the church in 1689 by T. Addison, brother of Joseph the essayist. It is said to have come from a London livery hall and is crawling with cherubs. There is little to see of the Roman fort that stood nearby on Caermote Hill.

IREBY, east of Torpenhow, is a scenic spot, with Skiddaw range to the north. Given the moot hall and a market cross, why is there no market? Is Heskett Newmarket to the east a clue? It has a ruined Norman church just outside the village, and a new one of 1847 to compensate. It is a strange fact that two centuries ago it seems that there was hardly a Cumbrian village without its dancing master, along with its parson, schoolmaster, blacksmith and cobbler. Ireby was no exception. Keats and his friend Charles Brown had walked on Skiddaw and, on arriving at Ireby, called at the Sun Inn:

> We were greatly amused by a country dancing school, holden at the [Sun] it was indeed `no new cotillon fresh from France'. No they kickit & jumpit with mettle extraordinary, & whiskit, & fleckit, & toed it, & go'd it, tatooing the floor like mad; The differenc [e] between our country dances & these scotch figures, is about the same as leisurely stirring a cup o' Tea & [b]eating up a batter pudding. I was extremely gratified to think, that if I had pleasures they knew nothing of they has also some into which I could not possibly enter – there was as fine a row of boys & girls as you ever saw, some beautiful faces, & one exquisite mouth. I never felt so near the glory of Patriotism, the glory of making by any means a country happier. This is what I like better than scenery.

COCKERMOUTH

Ireby is built on a Roman road that linked Roman Carlisle with the Roman fort of Derventio at present-day PAPCASTLE. It now lies buried in the fields by the village, which is on the edge of Cockermouth. The stones were long ago taken to construct Cockermouth castle. The fort was a strategic cavalry base, able to dispatch reinforcements to the Solway defences, to the west coast or to the western part of Hadrian's Wall. The area of the fort is 3 ha, and seems to have been occupied until the end of the fourth century, and evidence has been found of a large civilian *vicus* (village) standing outside it. The manor at Papcastle belonged to the lords of Egremont. 'The boy of Egremont', who fell into the Strid near Bolton Abbey and drowned (see Wordsworth's poem 'The White Doe of Rylstone'), was the son of Ochtreda of Papcastle, heiress of the lord of Egremont.

COCKERMOUTH (pop. 8,250) is a very appealing small town of character and deserves to be better known as a holiday base for exploring the northern fells and county. As Keswick is in the National Park, Cockermouth should surely be in it too. It stands at the confluence of the Rivers Derwent and the Cocker and has a very fine wide tree-lined main street, at the far end of which is its finest house. The house was built for Joshua Lucock, sheriff of Cumberland, in 1745, and later came into the possession of Sir James Lowther, later earl of Lonsdale. His steward, John Wordsworth came to live in it with his new bride Ann Cookson. Son William Wordsworth was born in it in 1770, along with his brothers Richard, the eldest, and sister Dorothy (1771), and John, and Christopher the youngest.

The Wordsworths were comfortably off, living in a large house with servants. William's loving parents gave him the perfect start. His father, though distant, encouraged him to learn poetry by heart, especially Milton and Spencer, and gave him free access to his large library. The family was more or less isolated, and made few friends. John Wordsworth appeared to keep himself to himself. This may partly have been because Sir James Lowther, his wealthy employer, was an unpopular, even hated, man. He did not pay his debts. John Wordsworth spent four thousand pounds of his own money in serving his employer, and subsequent legal battles to gain repayment of the debt would trouble the young Wordsworths for years.

In the 'Prelude' the poet reflects on his childhood home near the river at Cockermouth.

> When, having left his mountains, to the towers
> Of Cockermouth that beauteous river came,
> Behind my father's house he passed, close by,
> Along the margin of our terrace walk.
> He was a playmate whom we dearly loved.
> Oh, many a time have I, a five year's child,
> A naked boy, in one delightful rill,
> A little mill-race severed from his stream,
> Made one long bathing of a summer's day;
> Basked in the sun, and plunged and basked again,

> Alternative, all a summer's day, or scoured
> The sandy fields, leaping through flowery groves
> Of yellow ragwort; or when rock and hill,
> The woods, and distant Skiddaw's lofty heights,
> Were bronzed with deepest radiance, stood alone
> Beneath the sky, as if I had been born
> On Indian plains, and from my mother's hut
> Had run abroad in wantonness, to sport,
> A naked savage, in the thunder shower.

Wordsworth briefly attended the same local grammar school (now demolished) where Fletcher Christian, the mutineer of the *Bounty*, was also a pupil, albeit six years earlier. However, the Wordsworth children had to move to relatives when their mother died in 1778. When their father died five years later, the house fell into neglect.

In the poet's early days Cockermouth was rather different to today's town. Like other Cumbrian market towns it had a moot hall, this one standing on pillars in the main street. The church stood at the end of a sidestreet, Kirkgate. The moot hall has been demolished, the church rebuilt, and new houses and streets have sprung up. The Wordsworth house was in danger of demolition when a bus company bought it before the Second World War – they needed the site for a station. In face of public protest the company relinquished its contract, and the house came into the possession of the National Trust, and was opened to the public. The large and impressive drawing room is sometimes the setting of concerts. A terrace behind the house overlooks the River Derwent.

Cockermouth castle (not open to the public) lies on the east side of the town and dates from the twelfth century. The original structure was built by Waltheof, son of Gospatrick, earl of Dunbar, in 1134, making use of stones taken from the ruins of the Roman fort at nearby Papcastle. The castle was the administrative centre of regional justice in late medieval times. The castle is mentioned in 1221, when the sheriff of Westmorland was ordered by Henry III to besiege and destroy it, after its owner William de Fortibus, earl of Albermarle, proved himself a rebellious baron. It was then that the castle was reduced, but shortly afterwards the earl returned to the king's favour, and he was allowed to reinforce it again. It was inherited through marriage by Edmund Crouchback, earl of Lancaster and brother of Edward I. Later its constable was Andrew de Harcla – he who held Carlisle castle against Robert the Bruce, and was later hung, drawn and quartered for treason. Anthony de Luci, who captured de Harcla by stealth, received Cockermouth castle as a reward. It later came by marriage to Henry Percy, earl of Northumberland, then it was burned by the Scots in 1387, and rebuilt with stones quarried again from the local ruins of the Roman fort. It came into the hands of the Wyndham family when the Percy line died out.

During the Wars of the Roses it was a disputed strongpoint. The Lancastrians held it until the battle of Towtown Moor, after which it passed to the Yorkists. In the Civil War in 1648 it was again in dispute, finally becoming ruinous. General Wyndham restored it in the nineteenth century. It is now a home of Lord Egremont.

A walkabout reveals that the town has some elegant Georgian and Victorian houses, with Kirkgate and Castlegate looking particularly dignified. The now ruined old hall, off the market place, received Mary, Queen of Scots, here in 1568 on her escorted way to Carlisle after she had fled from the defeat of her followers at Langside near Glasgow, and escaped across the Solway. The hall was owned by wealthy merchant Henry Fletcher, who took pity on the queen when he saw that she had arrived with hardly any possessions. He gave her 16 ells of rich crimson velvet to augment her wardrobe.

The statue in the main street is of the earl of Mayo, who was ten years an MP for Cockermouth and became the viceroy of India, but was assassinated on a visit to the Andaman Islands.

All Saints church (1852–4) seems far too large and grand for a modest town like Cockermouth. It is a replacement of the earlier church, where Wordsworth was confirmed. Father John Wordsworth (d. 1783) is buried here, by a path at the south-east corner of the church.

John Dalton, the first proponent of modern atomic theory, was born of Quaker stock in the nearby village of Eaglesfield in 1766. He showed an early genius and was appointed a schoolmaster at Pardshaw Hall at the age of thirteen, and afterwards taught at a private school in Kendal. He published papers on his atomic theory in 1802, 1803 and 1804.

Fletcher Christian was born in 1753, also at Eaglesfield, and went on to lead the mutiny on the Royal Navy ship *Bounty* in 1789, against the allegedly cruel regime of Captain Bligh. The captain was cast adrift with other officers, and Fletcher Christian took the ship to the Pitcairn Islands, where the crew founded a colony. He most probably died there, though stories abound of his secret return into the community.

There is one art gallery and three museums in the town: a mineral and fossil museum, a working museum of printing, and a toy and model museum. There are two other reasons for visiting Cockermouth. One of Cumbria's favourite beers, Jennings, is brewed here, and the company arranges tours around its Castle Brewery. Just outside town is the Lakeland Sheep and Wool Visitors' Centre where various breeds of sheep are paraded for close inspection on an indoor stage. It is surprisingly entertaining as well as educational.

A minor road goes north-east from Cockermouth to follow the wandering River Derwent. Just short of 4 km along here, one reaches ISEL, just inside the National Park, an insignificant settlement with a lovely church in a perfect setting, among fields and by the river. John Betjeman was in raptures about it, and Norman Nicholson was entranced. The church is essentially Norman, dating from the 1130, with its doorway and chancel arch, its thick walls and small windows being fairly typical.

Nearby Isel Hall (though closed to the public) can be admired from the road-side. The oldest part is the pele tower, and the rest is Elizabethan. It was the seat of the Lawsons.

CHAPTER FOURTEEN

The Eden Valley

The River Eden rises above Mallerstang Common on Black Fell Moss, 688 m above sea level at the south-east of the county, and flows north-westwards for 105 km to Carlisle and the Solway. It flows through a different kind of country to that found in the rest of Cumbria. The area has only half the rainfall of the county's centre and west, and it is generally rich, green agricultural land suited to cultivation, stock rearing and dairy farming, for which purposes it has been profitably used since the first Neolithic settlements.

The Eden valley is a country of its own – enclosed by the hills of the Pennines to the east, the Lakeland fells to the west and to the south by the Howgills. It was, however, open to the north when the glaciers of the Lake District met those from Scotland and thrust outwards to the east. The River Eden is a sublime river in an Elysian landscape. Wordsworth wanders by it on a tour in 1833 and regrets that he had not sought it out before:

> Eden! Till now thy beauty had I viewed
> By glimpses only, and confess with shame
> That verse of mine, whate'er its varying mood,
> Repeats but once the sound of thy sweet name:
> Yet fetched from Paradise that honour came,
> Rightfully borne; for Nature gives thee flowers
> That have no rivals among British bowers;
> And thy bold rocks are worthy of their fame.
> Measuring thy course, fair Stream! at length I pay
> To my life's neighbour dues of neighbourhood;
> But I have traced thee on thy winding way
> With pleasure sometimes by this thought restrained:
> For things far off we toil, while many a good
> Not sought, because too near, is never gained.

In its early history the Eden valley suffered from its fertile land, a land that offered easy pickings for Scottish reivers. It was also open to pillaging from English armies moving against the Scots. The Romans, and later the Normans, fortified the route through the valley at the strategic centres of Brough, Appleby, Brougham and Penrith, and in later centuries the wealthiest built defensive towers to shelter family and breeding stock from the raiders.

The settlements are largely built of local red sandstone, more durable than the sandstone of the west. And the roofs are often 'slated' with slabs of sandstone or millstone grit, giving the buildings a heavy, sturdy look. The Eden is an anglers' river, providing good fishing for trout, greyling and salmon.

KENDAL TO APPLEBY

The first village on the road from Kendal to Appleby is ORTON (once Overton). Edward I granted the place a market charter for a Wednesday market, and a licence to hold fairs came from Oliver Cromwell, persuaded, so it is said, by Lady Anne, Countess of Pembroke, though as she was staunchly loyal to the Crown, this seems unlikely. Orton still holds its market – a regular local farmers' market is a great attraction.

The church of All Saints dates back to the early thirteenth century, but much has changed. Original features include the arch to the south transept, and within it a piscina. Orton Old Hall, in the village centre, is dated 1604.

George Whitehead (1636–1723), an Orton son, was second only to George Fox as a campaigner for the Quaker movement. He travelled and preached extensively about the country, challenging the need for Christians to conform to established church rituals, and the need to employ paid priests; and like his fellows in these intolerant times, spent years in and out of prison. A writer of pamphlets, he was well able to hold his own in disputes with his peers. His personal presence was such that he even got an audience with King Charles II, who was so impressed that he ordered that all Quakers be freed. However, there followed subsequently a period of bitter persecution that saw even the followers having their properties confiscated, and many were imprisoned again. Even then Whitehead was accepted to the royal presence and he successfully persuaded James II to free Quakers under the Toleration Act of 1689 that aimed to legalize Roman Catholicism. Thereafter Meeting Houses could be built . Even then Quakers, as well as other nonconformists, were excluded from public office. On the accession of William and Mary he campaigned successfully for the recognition of the Quaker faith.

The limestone pavement of Orton Fell

From Orton the road climbs Orton Scar, mounting the splendidly wide-open moorland. There are areas of limestone pavement here, in which level areas of the rock, uneven and pitted from the action of rain over eons, have been broken into a pattern of grykes. In these fissures grow a rich fern flora, including hart's tongue, hard shield, limestone polypody, rigid buckler and a variety of flowering plants. Limestone pavements, along with their rare habitats, have been disappearing all over Europe as the limestone is easily removed. Here it used to be more extensive, but much has been taken away for the garden rockery market. It is now protected by law.

The road eventually sweeps down to APPLEBY IN WESTMORLAND (pop. 2,820), which once was the county town of Westmorland. The county courts and the county prison were once located here, but it gradually lost its importance as administration focused on Kendal. Then, in 1974, the county disappeared altogether in local government reorganization. Appleby is nearer to the Pennines than the Lake District fells and has the feel of a hill town, though it is only 122 m above sea level. The town is a great treasure, refreshingly neat and unspoiled, and has many devotees.

It was in Scottish hands until William Rufus took Carlisle in 1092, and then he settled it with farmers from the south whose loyalty could be depended upon. The town was then part of the possessions of Ranulph de Meschines and he commissioned the building of a castle, firstly of wood. He passed property to the crown in 1120. At the death of King Henry I the succession to the throne was disputed between Stephen of Blois and the Empress Matilda. King David of Scotland favoured Matilda, and fourteen years of war ensued. During this time Appleby, with a great part of northern Cumbria, was again in Scottish hands. The Scots were finally defeated at the Battle of the Standard near Northallerton in August 1138, but in the terms of peace Henry, son of King David, retained the area as part of Scotland. And so it remained until 1157, when Malcolm, king of Scotland, returned it to King Henry II.

Henry then granted the land to the de Morvilles. However, Hugh de Morville, as one of the knights who took part in the murder of Thomas à Becket at Canterbury cathedral, fled and his land was forfeited to the crown. In 1174 the eldest son of Henry II, Prince Henry, rebelled against his father and sided with William the Lion, king of Scotland, who was intent on winning back the part of Scotland that had been lost. His invasion failed to take Carlisle but he left it under siege and his forces took the Eden valley, with Appleby once more reverting to Scotland. The castle was readily surrendered it seems. Could it be because the stronghold's constable, Gospatrick, was the grandson of the earl of Dunbar, and related to the Scottish king?

Yet again the Scots were forced to abandon the town after Henry II captured King William the Lion at Alnwick, but before leaving they wasted the area. In 1179 Henry gave Appleby its charter as an independent borough, making it one of the oldest boroughs in the kingdom and one of the first to have a mayor. As it was owned by the crown, its mayor was the king's resident representative, and it gave him a very high rank, even over the king's judge of assize. The charter was confirmed by King John in 1200 and three years later he granted Appleby and Brough, with the rent of the county of Westmorland, to Robert de Vipont and his wife. Because of the town's royal charter of independence, the Appleby of the grant was not the town proper but the castle and the ward of Bongate on the east side of the river.

Robert de Vipont's two daughters married Roger de Clifford and Roger de Leybourne, and the two men tried to impose their authority on the rest of the town, but the burgesses brought a writ against them, declaring that they were the king's tenants, and not those of the de Viponts or their heirs. They won their case. So the town's coat-of-arms proudly displayed the three leopards of the royal arms of England. Later this was thought to be an error, and that the leopards should be crowned to distinguish them from those of royalty; but the original was quite correct.

The town had not finished with Scottish raids; it was sacked in 1388 when it 'lay dismembered and scattered one street from another, like so many scattered villages; and one could not know but by records that they belonged to the same body.' However, placed as it was in a protective loop of the River Eden with a formidable castle on the hill, it was less vulnerable than other towns within reach of the border. The protective loop of the river has occasionally betrayed its defensive function. Throughout history it has flooded the land many times. Possibly the worst recorded flood occurred in February 1822, when many buildings in the town were up to a metre deep in water, and five of the Eden bridges to the east were swept away and four others severely damaged. The restoration cost Westmorland County £7000, a tidy sum in those days. Modern protective measures should, one hopes, be more successful at dealing with the worst threats of floods to come.

So Appleby comprises two parishes on opposite sides of the Eden. The older part of the town, St Michael's parish, has Bongate ('street of the bondsmen') and is on the east side of the river, while on the west is St Lawrence's, with the market, the main street of Boroughgate (street of the burghers) and a grammar school.

St Michael's church in Bongate is probably older than St Lawrence's. A Saxon hogbacked gravestone, used as a lintel in a blocked doorway in the north wall, dates from the tenth or eleventh century, which suggests that a church has been on this site since that time. Otherwise the oldest fabric is of twelfth century. The church was damaged several times in raids and much restoration was done by Lady Anne Clifford, but further work was done in 1885.

Here something must be said about Lady Anne Clifford, for her influence in Appleby and throughout the region was extensive. She was the owner of the Cumbrian (old Westmorland) castles at Appleby, Pendragon, Brough and Brougham. She was born in Skipton Castle, Yorkshire, in 1590, the daughter and sole heir of the third earl of Cumberland, George Clifford, a champion and favourite of Queen Elizabeth, a sea captain, explorer and scourge of Spanish shipping and commander of the *Elizabeth Bonaventure* against the Armada. The young Anne was one of Elizabeth's favourites at court.

The Appleby and Craven estates in Yorkshire (including Skipton Castle) came to be owned by the earl. To make sure that they were left to the family's males on his death, he made his will in favour of his younger brother Francis (who would inherit the title) and to his male heirs, with a proviso that failing such heirs, the property should come to his daughter Anne. He was in error, for a deed during the reign of Edward II stipulated that the northern estates were to be handed down from parent to child, irrespective of sex.

On the earl's death in 1605 the extensive estates in Yorkshire were duly inherited by brother Francis, but the Westmorland estates were passed to the earl's widow, the dowager Lady Cumberland, to be held in her lifetime by Act of Parliament of 1593. Her estates had problems. The castles were in poor condition.

Appleby had been partially dismantled, making it no longer defensible, Brough had been seriously damaged by fire and Pendragon had been wasted by the Scots. Brougham, the birthplace of George Clifford, was at least habitable. Lady Cumberland, and seventeen-year-old daughter Anne, came north in 1607 and made their home at Appleby castle. Because the earl had seldom been with his wife and child, Anne and her mother were very close.

The countess was aware that although the Westmorland estates were hers in her lifetime, by the terms of the will they would not pass to Anne on her death. She was sure that this was wrong in law and employed a researcher to confirm her belief. In Anne's later words:

> She shewed herself so wise and industrious that she caused diligent search to be made amongst the records of this kingdom touching those ancient lands, and caused copies to be taken out of them of such records as concerned her said daughter's inheritance.

Anne continued to be a favourite at court, and in 1609 she married Richard Sackville, who would inherit the title of earl of Dorset. It was a love match, but it was also encouraged by Richard's grandfather, very probably Anne's mother and previously by her father. Although the bridegroom was only nineteen, the marriage had to be hastened because his father was on his deathbed, and if he had inherited the title as a bachelor before his majority, he would become a ward of court and a marriage would be arranged for him by the sovereign. His father died shortly afterwards.

The new earl of Dorset and his wife had their seat at Knole, in Kent. Because the earl spent much of his time at the royal court, he needed a fortune to sustain his lifestyle. He tried to persuade Anne to make legal arrangements for her to renounce her rights to her inheritance of the Westmorland part of the Clifford estates, in lieu of a cash settlement from the Cliffords. She refused, and when her mother died she was all the more determined to hold on to what her mother had won for her. The earl then tried to persuade her to make the estates over to him and their young daughter. She again refused and this became a long bone of contention between her husband and herself. The Cliffords also contested the matter of her ownership of the estates, and the matter became so serious that it was talked about at court, and the king decided to intervene. He summoned Anne and Lord Dorset to his presence. They knelt before him and the king asked them to place the matter in his hands. Then Lady Anne shocked the king. She records, 'I beseech'd His Majesty to pardon me for that I would never part from Westmorland while I lived upon any condition whatsoever.' The king did his best to change her position, but she would not be moved. Lord Dorset was astonished, for the king was quite aggrieved, but he could not help admiring the firmness of his wife's stand.

The problem would not go away and the king duly convened another meeting. This time it was attended by the other contestants: Anne's uncle Cumberland; a cousin Clifford, Lord Arundel (a Howard, and also a claimant), the earls of Pembroke and Montgomery, and vice-chamberlain Sir John Digby. The lord chief justice, and the attorney general, represented the law; and Sir Randal Crewe attended as counsel for Lord and Lady Dorset. In this Lord Dorset was defending his wife's claim against the Cliffords. The arguments were listened to, and the king said that he would consider the deliberations and make a judgement. The Cliffords agreed, but Anne stipulated again that she would never agree to any judgement that left her without Westmorland. As Lord Dorset had stood by his wife the affair meant that he was no longer among the king's favourites and he had to do what he could to get on better terms. In the event the king favoured the Cliffords' claims and they took possession of the Westmorland estates.

Two children, both girls, survived the marriage of the Dorsets. In 1624 Lord Dorset died. In 1628 Anne entered a formal claim to her right of succession to the Clifford estates in the absence of male issue. Two years later Anne married the widower, Philip Herbert, the earl of Pembroke, which proved unhappy as the earl had a bad reputation and was unfaithful. In 1642 came the Civil War while Anne was staying at the earl's seat at Baynard's Castle. Then a year later saw Lady Anne's fortunes change irrevocably: her cousin of Cumberland died, leaving no male issue, and the Clifford estates were in her possession.

After the execution of King Charles in January 1649, life at the royal court ended for Anne, and she went north to visit her property. She stayed at Skipton castle that had held out for the king and had been 'slighted' – made indefensible – on surrender. Then she inspected her Westmorland properties at Brough, Brougham and Pendragon, before staying at her castle at Appleby. The castle had been a royalist stronghold, but was surrendered in 1648 and occupied by parliamentarians. Here in January 1650 she learned of her husband's death. Without delay she set in train the repairs of her Westmorland castles. She also had the hospital of St Anne built to accommodate thirteen Appleby women who were too infirm to work. Immediate work at Appleby castle was hindered by the fact that Lady Anne had to share it with those parliamentary troops. They were there because Charles II had been crowned at Scone in Scotland and a possible invasion of the Scots had to be met with a strong parliamentary border presence. Anne, as a keen royalist, was locked in dispute with General Harrison, the garrison's commander, but she stayed on until the threat from the north evaporated with the king's defeat at Worcester. Thereafter Anne was able to concentrate her energies on restoring her properties.

During the Civil War the town had remained stalwart royalists, naturally as they owed their town as a royal gift, and the resistance came in spite of the castle's garrison of Roundheads. The Revd Thomas Machell tells us what happened (he was a teenager then), when the Roundheads attempted to make an official proclamation to the gathered townspeople declaring Charles, the son of Charles I, a traitor. It could not be done.

> The mayor withdrew himself, and the bailiffs (whose office it was) threw up their commissions, though but poor men, inasmuch that the soldiers were glad to have recourse to a fellow in the market, an unclean bird, hatched at Kirkby Stephen, the nest of all traytours, who proclaimed it aloud, whilst the people stopped their ears and hearts ... And the townsmen were not far behind this gallant example of their noble leaders; who when captain Atkinson came down from the castle with his musketeers to chase Roundhead mayor, and clapped his hand on his sword, saying, 'I'll do it by this', yet made resistance, for they then conferred the office (to prevent bloodshed) on a moderate man, who had acted on neither side, except in bearing that office before, and so he was mayor two years together.

At the restoration there was great rejoicing on Coronation Day. Machell continues:

> There was almost as many bonefires as houses, and two stately high scaffolds at each end of the town, hung with cloth of arras and gold; whither, after service done at the church, the countess of Pembroke [Lady Anne] with the mayor, aldermen and all the other gentry of the county ascended, with I know not how many trumpets, and an imperial crown carried before them, where they proclaimed, prayed for, and drank the health of the king upon their knees; the aged countess seeming young again to grace the solemnity. The expenses of that day were very considerable. For throughout the town was kept open house, after the example of that noble countess, who thought not her gates then wide enough to receive her guests, which before had been too wide for receiving armies of soldiers.

When Anne set to work in earnest to repair her properties, she not only undertook work on her castles; she had the churches and chapels at Brougham, Ninekirks and Mallerstang put in good order too. At the spot where she made the last parting with her mother she erected a pillar. The countess's pillar is a column carrying the arms of Clifford and Russel. From a flat stone nearby she ensured that an annual bequest of bread and money for the poor of Brougham would be dispersed on each anniversary of the parting. The pillar can be seen by the side of the busy A66 road, east of Brougham.

Appleby's old castle, then above the town, owes its recovery to Lady Anne Clifford's enthusiasm. The large earthwork motte-and-bailey defences were built by Ranulph de Meschines in the eleventh century. The typical but splendid keep was built in the twelfth century, and still stands, surrounded by moats. It is open to the public in season, but the castle is privately owned. This east range is seventeenth century, rebuilt by the earl of Thanet, the son-in-law of Lady Anne Clifford. Stone from Brougham and Brough castles is said to have been used in its construction; if that is so Lady Anne would surely be turning in her grave.

The castle stands above the memorable broad street of Boroughgate that contains the marketplace, sloping down by the moot hall, with the church of St Lawrence at its foot. It was so even in Elizabethen times, according to Camden: '... all the beauty of it lieth in one broad street, which from North to South riseth with an easie ascent of the hill: in the upper part whereof standeth the castle aloft, environed wholy almost with the river. In the nether end of it is the church ...'

It has changed a little since Camden's day, for it is now lined with some very decent substantial buildings of the eighteenth and nineteenth centuries, fronted with greens and trees. At its head stands the high cross, which carries the legend that served Lady Anne well, as well as the town's burghers: 'Retain your Loyalty.

The courtyard, St Anne's Hospital, Appleby

Preserve your Rights.' Part way down on the right is St Anne's Hospital. It is approached through an archway on to a secluded courtyard surrounded by the almshouses, built by Lady Anne Clifford to house the 'thirteen poor widows of the estate'. There is also a little chapel. The hospital is still maintained by a Trust established by Lady Anne Clifford, and occupied by widows. One of them serves as 'mother', as overseer. Visitors are welcome in the courtyard but are asked to observe quietness.

The moot hall is where the burghers assembled for a 'mote' – a meeting to transact the town's business. The plaque at the door gives the date as 1596, but the windows are eighteenth century, and it was altered and improved in 1811. It now houses an information centre. At this end of the street is the low cross.

St Lawrence's church, like its sister on the other bank, suffered badly in the border raids. The oldest fabric is of twelfth century, but the church was burned and repaired more than once. Externally the style is Perpendicular, internally it is predominantly Decorated. The main part of the tower is probably unscathed, and the 2.5 m thickness of the walls suggests that it was originally built as a refuge against raiders, and opened up later with arches when raids declined. An archway at the entrance to the fourteenth-century porch shows dog-tooth moulding on reused twelfth-century masonry. The church organ is rather special. Originally in Carlisle cathedral, it was donated to the church by Dean Smith in 1684; portions of it date back to Elizabethan times. The church contains the tomb of Margaret Clifford, countess of Cumberland (d.1616) and widow of George Clifford, the third earl, and champion of Queen Elizabeth I; and Lady Anne's mother. The effigy is carved in alabaster. Lady Anne had it made and had to ask for permission from the burghers of Appleby for it to be placed there. Nearby is her own: the equally fine black marble tomb of the indefatigable daughter, the countess dowager of Pembroke herself. The tomb emphasizes her position as a Clifford, the extensive heraldry on display illustrating the noble descent.

In the seventeenth century the market prospered. The town's income was gained from tolls on the market users and sellers of goods in other parts of the town. Tolls were also charged for traffic passing through the town, in cash or in kind. Cattle and sheep were sold in the street, and were slaughtered in the shambles in the lower part of Boroughgate, while the meat was sold in the upper part above the moot hall. It is not hard to imagine what a mess the market was. Improvements were demanded in 1748 when it was ordered that 'no butcher shall empty the baggs of any beast cattle that they kill, or lay garbage, in any part of the street'. And there was a fine of six shillings and eightpence on anyone 'who do not lead their dung hills clean away four times in the year'. This was a time when it was not illegal, rather it was customary, to dump refuse in the street or the river. As well as horses and dogs kept on the street, pigs roamed freely, though swine lookers were appointed to make sure that they caused no excessive nuisance.

In the eighteenth century Appleby began receiving its first tourists. Among them was Gilpin, making his northern tour in 1792, and writing his observations on the scenic qualities of the countryside. All are recorded in his best-selling book, which stimulated tourism among the landscape painters and the educated middle class. Though he liked the situation of the castle, he cast a critical eye over its appearance:

> The castle is still in good repair; and is a noble pile. But, in a picturesque light, it loses its beauty, from its being broken into two parts. A smaller break from a grand pile removes heaviness; and is a source of beauty. We have seen the principle exemplified in mountains and other objects. But here the whole is divided into two parts, of such equal dimensions, that each aspires to pre-eminence. Each therefore becomes a separate whole, and both together distract the eye ... But what is said of these two detached parts of the castle, is meant only with regard to that view of it, which appears from the road. If you go round it, you are presented with other views, in which it is seen more advantageously; particularly where you see the bridge, and the first opening into the vale of Eden. There the castle takes a very grand situation on a hanging rock over the river; and the detached part makes but an inconsiderable appearance.

In the late nineteenth century a sewerage scheme and a mains water system were installed. The last of the shambles were demolished. The county gaol was still in use and in 1844 its governor, Thomas Thwaites, in a quarterly report states: 'Since my last report 11 prisoners have been committed, viz. 2 for larceny, 4 for poaching, 1 for vagrancy, 1 for want of Sureties, and 3 debtors. Unfortunately one of the youths for poaching has been killed on the tread wheel.' The 1865 Prisons Act required higher standards, and two years later a dispute broke out with Kendal. Kendal wanted one gaol for the whole county, on grounds of economy, and their authorities wanted it in Kendal to replace their 'House of Correction'. But the Appleby magistrates would have none of it, fearing the loss of the assizes and the revenue that came with it. The prison was reconstructed, but four years later it had fallen out of use and become the police headquarters.

The railway came to Appleby in 1862 with the opening of the Eden Valley Railway, and in 1876 the Settle to Carlisle line brought London within reach of a day's journey. The town had two stations then, and new street systems were laid out below them. It made a huge difference to the town's development.

The town completely loses its relatively quiet character in June during the annual horse fair, when 'travellers' from all over the country congregate to meet each other, and sell horses, among a riot of activity. Horses are put through their paces, washed in the river, assessed and haggled over, and it is all very lively and colourful. Actually, though, the growing popularity of the event produces crowd problems. Although the traditional horse-drawn caravans still exist, many travellers nowadays arrive with motor vehicles and large trailers. In 2002 it was reckoned that 13,000 visitors descended on the little town, which raised ongoing concerns about law and order, safety and the welfare of the animals.

The scenic Settle and Carlisle railway line serves Appleby, and arriving by this route could put one in the right mood to enjoy this delightful little town. The information centre provides a plan for pedestrians.

THE VILLAGES OF THE EDEN VALLEY

Keeping to the south side of the River Eden, a minor road leave Appleby northwest to Bolton, passing, on the left, the ruins of Bewley castle, once the fortified refuge of the bishops of Carlisle. BOLTON has a captivating Norman church, restored but not spoiled, with two typical Norman doorways, north and south. Above the north doorway is an exceptionally rare relief of two knights jousting, still crisp for its age, that could be from the eleventh century. Outside there is a figure of a lady, once on a tomb, but now by a wall. A west tower has gone, and a bell turret was added in the seventeenth century.

Further on is KIRKBY THORE. Bravoniacum ('The place of querns – or stone handmills) was a Roman cavalry fort guarding the Stainmore Pass, which was probably the earliest route of a road made by the Romans, branching from their main road from York to Brougham and Carlisle. The site now lies partly buried under the houses, and the stones were looted long long ago for building. The fort is also thought to have been a checkpoint and depot for the lead coming south from the mines around Whitley castle (Alston) for transport to the Roman base at York. The lead would be carried by the Maiden Way, a Roman road that came south from Alston across the flank of Cross Fell at heights above 600 m.

The village offers fine views. There is a busy gypsum mine and plant at Kirkby Thore, owned by British Gypsum. Gypsum is formed from deposits after shallow lakes are dried out by evaporation in arid times. It was the base material for ornate plaster work, and is now much used to make plasterboard for buildings.

St Michael's red sandstone church has parts dating back to King Stephen's reign in the mid twelfth century, and it boasts that it has the county's largest bell, said to come from Shap abbey after the dissolution. Much was added in the seventeenth century.

Eleventh-century relief of knights at tournament, All Saints' church, Bolton

Nearby TEMPLE SOWERBY, a neat and attractive village, is regrettably cleft into two by the A66, which makes it an accident blackspot. The village hopes for, and deserves, a bypass. The village gained its odd name from early owners of the manor of Sowerby, the Knights Templars. After their suppression in 1308 the manor was transferred to the Knights Hospitallers. The village contains some seventeenth- and eighteenth-century buildings around a large green.

At nearby ACORN BANK is a handsome house (NT) dating from the seventeenth century. The house is not open to the public, but the woodlands, the water-mill and the gardens are, and reward a visit to this friendly place. The celebrated herb garden contains specimens of numerous plants used in the treatment of most known illnesses.

The River Eden goes north from Temple Sowerby, and a minor road follows it to its junction with the road from Penrith to Alston at LANGWATHBY (*lang-WATH-by* or *LANG-anby*) – 'the village by the long ford', an agricultural village. The 'wath' has been replaced by a bridge; this is a replacement, for the original was washed away. It still has a railway station.

Crossing the bridge a minor road goes left to EDENHALL. Little remains of the village that once stood here, except a good church and an old story. Eden Hall itself was demolished in 1934. The church is approached past an ancient Celtic cross, and has a lovely setting. It is dedicated to St Cuthbert, and what is seen dates from the fourteenth century, including the stained glass, although Norman features can be found. There is a monumental brass (1458) to William Stapildon and his wife.

The story concerns 'the luck of Edenhall', a thirteenth-century Syrian glass goblet that was probably brought home from the Crusades by a member of Edenhall's Musgrave family. One day a butler, it is said, saw fairies drinking and dancing on the lawn round St Cuthbert's well. When he approached the fairies fled, one of them dropping the goblet. He picked it up, and one of the fleeing fairies called out a warning:

> Whene'r this cup shall break or fall
> Farewell the luck of Edenhall.

St Cuthbert's church with its fourteenth-century defensive tower, Great Salkeld

Longfellow translated a dramatic poem by Johann Uhland that used the legend and tells of its breaking:

> As the goblet ringing flies apart
> Suddenly cracks the vaulted hall;
> And through the rift the wild flames start
> The guests in dust are scattered all
> With the breaking luck of Edenhall!

It never broke. The yellowish goblet, enamelled in red, blue, green and gold, is kept in the Victoria & Albert Museum, London.

THE SALKELDS AND LONG MEG AND HER DAUGHTERS

Going back across the river, then turning north on a minor road, we come to the hamlet of LITTLE SALKELD (dialect: *laal saffel*). The village watermill here has been restored by enterprising hands, and is producing organic wholemeal flour. The process can be watched as it is open to the public on some days, and real stone-ground flour can be bought, and its fresh-baked products consumed on the premises. The smell is irresistible.

Continuing along the road, going right at the fork and then left on a narrow way there is a stone circle: LONG MEG AND HER DAUGHTERS.

> A weight of awe, not easy to be borne,
> Fell suddenly upon my spirit – cast
> From the dread bosom of the unknown past,
> When first I saw that family forlorn.

Such was Wordsworth's reaction to the remarkable sight. The early Bronze Age people who built the circle must certainly have groaned under a 'weight of awe' when they were moving and placing the heavy stones. Twenty-seven massive stones, less than half the total number, are still standing, and they represent a good geological mix. The ring is quite large, oval in plan, with dimensions of 110 m by 91 m. A farm track passes through the circle and trees have been planted. Long Meg, the tallest stone, is about 3 m high and carries the mysterious 'cup and ring' markings sometimes found in stones of this era. A porch or gateway breaks the circle with exterior standing stones. Was there once an avenue? It has been

Long Meg and one or two of her daughters

observed that if one stands in the dead centre of the circle, which is very difficult to determine, Long Meg is in line with the setting midwinter sun.

The circle comes with the usual romantic tales. It is said that the farmer started to remove the stones, but after a nighttime storm with a violence that the area had never known, he put them back. Another tale is that a group of maidens, sinfully dancing in the ring on the sabbath day, were instantly turned to stone. A third story is that the ring was once a coven of witches, turned by magic to stone, and if you count them twice and get the same number, best to start running, for they will all be returned to life. For the record there are almost certainly sixty-nine. Celia Fiennes tells another tale in 1698, but has the location wrong:

> A mile from Peroth in a low bottom a moorish place stands Great Mag and her Sisters, the story is that these soliciting her to an unlawfull love by an enchantment are turned with her into stone; the stone in the middle which is called Mag is much bigger and have some form like a statue or figure of a body but the rest are but soe many craggy stones, but they affirme they cannot be counted twice alike as is the story of Stonidge.

One can only guess at the significance of the circle, or the motive that lay behind its construction. One thing is certain: if Long Meg and her Daughters were not so remotely situated they would be much better known, and the lush green grass on which they stand would probably be trodden bare, or alternatively carefully mown and tended by the staff of the appropriate ministerial department. As it is, the family broods in silence.

Going back to the road and then north one reaches GLASSONBY. The church here is known as Addingham church, but there is no such place as Addingham, as it was washed away, church and all, in an Eden flood. Some of the stones in this church are from the lost one. The simple building has features dating back to the fourteenth century. Some stone fragments in the porch include two heavy pieces of a ninth-century cross. In the churchyard is a large wheel-head cross, and part of a shaft.

Going back to Little Salkeld and taking the left fork, a footpath follows the side of the railway and reaches the river side, and in the sandstone cliff here are the remarkable LACY'S CAVES. Though naturally made, they were then carved out further by hand – by whom nobody knows. Perhaps it was Colonel Lacy's estate workmen from nearby Salkeld Hall, who were not allowed to be idle when the weather was wet.

GREAT SALKELD (dialect: *gurt saffel*) is on the other side of the River Eden, and to get to it one must go back and cross the bridge at Langwathby. This is among the most attractive villages in Cumbria: it is neat, clean and airy, with red sandstone buildings set among greens. A special feature of the village is its fortified church, with an impregnable fourteenth-century tower. The nave is entered by a distinctly Norman doorway, carved with zigzags and human heads. But the defensive tower can be entered only from the nave through a doorway defended by a heavy iron and wood 'yat' (gate). The gate can be locked from the inside by two massive bolts, the slots protected by an iron bar. Inside there is a tunnel-vaulted storage chamber below the ground floor. The upper floors are reached by a staircase built into the south-eastern turret. Light is obtainable from small inaccessible window-slits, heat from fireplaces. The tower could hold the entire village in the event of a raid. The parapet probably served as a place for a beacon. The nave has a Norman doorway to the south with three orders of columns, and capitals with strangely carved heads and beasts.

On northwards, the road passes through the hamlet of LAZONBY. The church is 1863, by Anthony Salvin, but there is a cross shaft of greater antiquity. An auction market near the railway station has weekly sales of sheep, the autumn sales being reckoned to be the largest in the north. Apart from serving the farming community, a large bakery here manages to make supermarket bread that is not only edible, but very good indeed.

Here an eighteenth-century bridge, replacing a sometimes dangerous ford across the Eden, brings one to KIRKOSWALD, a neat picture-book village with a small market square and clusters of old, well-kept buildings. The village has possessed a market charter from the thirteenth century, allowing it a fair day and, on Easter Monday, a sports day. It is said that at one time a market was held in the churchyard. The church of St Oswald is built in a hollow, and the bell tower – perhaps for acoustic reasons – is sited separately on a hill. The reason for the odd location of the church dates back to the seventh century, when it was said that St Aidan, observing that the local pagans worshipped a well there, built a Christian church on top of it. St Oswald's well is at the west end of the church. The early wooden church was replaced with a stone one in 1130. All that can be seen of that Norman stone church is the base of the chancel arch and a portion of the square piers in the arcades. In the fourteenth century the Scots burned the village but the church seems to have been spared. Alterations in the sixteenth century brought

The oaken porch of twelfth-century St Oswald's church

the church to its present shape. Chancel aisles were pulled down and windows added, and the wooden porch, still surviving, was erected. When the church's foundations were strengthened in 1970 it was found that the original foundation was constructed on oak piles.

The college, with its very beautiful late seventeenth-century entrance, stands opposite the church. It was founded in 1523 by Thomas de Dacre and Isabel de Greystoke. In 1590, after the dissolution, the state sold college and lands to Henry Featherstonehaugh of Southwaite, near Dacre. A very appealing path, flanked by an avenue of limes, starts opposite the college and leads down to the church. There are some interesting stones in the churchyard, including Saxon grave covers. The present bell-tower dates from 1897, replacing an earlier wooden structure of 1747.

Kirkoswald Castle, built by Ralph Engayne in 1200, was wrecked in the seventeenth century and is a complete ruin. A tower survives, with the remains of a spiral staircase; but other fragments are buried in undergrowth.

From Kirkoswald a minor road goes north, then west to cross Croglin Water to what was a nunnery. The present house was built by Henry Aglionby in 1718, but it stands on a Benedictine nunnery, and a doorway with dog-tooth moulding in a back wall probably dates from the thirteenth century. It is now a secluded guest house, from which lead the famous NUNNERY WALKS that follow the Croglin Beck falls down to the River Eden, sometimes on paths engineered from the

The River Eden from the Nunnery Walks

sandstone. It is a delight all the way – but slippery after wet weather. The walks were created by Christopher Aglionby and improved on his death by his sister Elizabeth (d. 1822). The property was sold to the Denman family in 1919, but by then the walks were already famous, following their mention in the best-selling *Excursion to the Lakes* (1774) by William Hutchinson. Wordsworth visited the walks in 1833, and was unduly pessimistic about its future in his sonnet:

> The floods are roused, and will not soon be weary;
> Down from the Pennine Alps how fiercely sweeps
> Croglin, the stately Eden's tributary!
> Her raves, or through some moody passage creeps
> Plotting new mischief – out again he leaps
> Into broad light, and sends, through regions airy,
> That voice which soothed the Nuns while on the steeps
> They knelt in prayer, or sang to blissful Mary.
> That union ceased: then, cleaving easy walks
> Through crags, and smoothing paths beset with danger,
> Come studious Taste; and many a pensive stranger
> Dreams on the banks, and to the river talks.
> What change shall happen next to Nunnery Dell?
> Canal, and Viaduct, and Railway, tell!

The minor road continues north-west to join the Eden at ARMATHWAITE, where a stop at the bridge might indeed inspire a pensive stranger. Or if he stays at the Duke's Head hotel here he or she might try casting a fly for a trout. A castle, standing by the river, began life as a pele tower but was added to in the eighteenth century.

THE SETTLE TO CARLISLE RAILWAY LINE

One Eden valley landscape cannot be seen from its highways and byways. The Settle to Carlisle railway line offers England's most scenic route, and it runs through the Eden valley, having its beginnings in Yorkshire and ending at Carlisle. The journey is an adventure. Having come through the Yorkshire Dales it enters Cumbria at the source of the River Eden, at Aisgill (357 m), the highest point reached by any railway in England. It then follows the Eden valley high above the river at Mallerstang with a view over to Pendragon castle, and descends to Kirkby Stephen station, south-west of that town. It then goes west of the Eden, over a magnificent high twelve-arched viaduct above Scandale Beck, then after two more bridges it rejoins the Eden, crossing it at Great Ormside over a ten-arched viaduct, and runs into Appleby. It then follows the Eden to the north, and runs by the British Gypsum works at Kirkby Thore, which supplies much of its freight traffic. The view east is dominated by the great bulk of Cross Fell. Then it runs north-west to Langwathby – a forty-minutes' walk from Long Meg and her Daughters; past Little Salkeld over a seven-arched viaduct, crossing the Eden south of Lacy's Caves via another seven-arched viaduct; then through Lazonby and Kirkoswald, past the nunnery walks, and close by the Eden through woodland; over a nine-arched viaduct to Armathwaite, following the curves of the river, before taking a short cut to its west through Cumwhinton and under the motorway to join the line from Newcastle to Carlisle. In all, from Settle, the line required some twenty-two viaducts, fourteen tunnels, many small bridges and many cuttings and embankments.

It was built using thousands of navvies with picks and shovels, and teams of horses, taking seven years to complete. The workforce had to contend with very wild and exposed countryside, and through harsh winter conditions, and they lived in shanty towns along the route. The graveyards of churches on the route contain the tombs of those who died from accidents or disease.

The line opened for goods traffic in August 1875, and for passengers in May of the following year. It was a success. Passenger comfort improved – the Midland was ahead of its rivals in this – and there were dining cars, and through coaches to Stranraer for Northern Ireland, and Aberdeen and Inverness. Advertised as the tourist route to Scotland, it was brought under temporary government control during the First World War, and then, in 1923 absorbed into the London Midland and Scottish railway (LMS) when all the railways were grouped into four main companies. Then the LMS concentrated its principal services on the west coast route and the Settle and Carlisle's importance diminished. The Eden valley route was, however, heavily used in the Second World War when government again took control. Then in 1948 the lines were nationalized and the route fell once again into a serious decline as traffic focused again on the west coast line. Then along came Dr Beeching's report on 'The Reshaping of British Railways' in 1963. The line survived – but only just. It was run down, and all the stations were closed except Appleby.

In the 1980s British Rail seemed intent on closing the line in view of increased maintenance costs. Public support for its continuance coalesced around the Friends of the Settle–Carlisle line in 1981. Two years later, when the line indeed faced its end, objections were lodged by 22,265 people (and one dog). British Rail responded by experimenting with an increased service, and this resulted in improved use. Eight of the closed stations were reopened. In 1986 the line was still under threat and a hearing considered objections to closure. Passenger levels reached half a million in 1988, when the government minister was 'mindful' to consent to closure, but wanted more evidence of public support, and queried whether a buyer for the line could be found. Some 32,000 would-be passengers registered their objections to closure, but no buyer came forward. On 11 April, amid great rejoicing, the minister announced his refusal of closure, and British Rail had to get on with the job of line repairs and improvements. It was no surprise when they discovered that the major expense – the repair of the great viaduct over the River Ribble – would not be as large as formerly estimated. In 1991 the local authorities on the route declared the line a conservation area, offering protection to buildings and structures and making it available for grant aid. Freight services increased from 1994, and in 1997 privatization brought it under the eventual umbrella of Northern Spirit.

The line offers a unique experience and is well used, particularly by walkers in the summer. It deserves much more.

CHAPTER FIFTEEN

The Cumbrian Pennines

KENDAL TO PENRITH

Running northwards from Kendal is the A6 over Shap Fell, 245 m high, a road to Scotland steeped in history. Packhorses, carts, stagecoaches, drovers, travellers of all ages and columns of heavy trucks in the pre-motorways days have gone this way, sometimes exposed to the bleakest winter conditions. Armies too; the last one was the highland infantry and cavalry of the Jacobite rebellion. They came south over the fell on 20 November 1745, and after reaching Derby, retreated north on 15 December. Lord George Murray, the most competent of Prince Charlie's officers, had the task of bringing up the rear. With the duke of Cumberland's cavalry in hot pursuit, and in drenching winter rain, he was commanded with safeguarding the baggage and artillery that the prince insisted he should retain.

The new road does not strictly follow the old, which can be traced in places. Murray's main problem was that the baggage carts were too wide for the narrow packhorse road, and one sharp bend over a stream has such little turning space for the horses that the carts had to be manhandled by men waist deep in cold water. They were struggling in the rain, pushing cannon and freeing stuck wagons. Even light carts 'borrowed' from nearby farms were too wide. Baggage had to be abandoned. The party that had gone before had also abandoned carts and baggage and cannon was lost in a stream. The men were soaked, tired and hungry. To add to Murray's problems a message came down from the prince that cannonballs, left by the party who had gone before them, must be brought forward. Murray was unperturbed. He offered sixpence of his own money on top of the soldier's pay to every one of his MacDonalds who would carry a cannon-ball wrapped in his plaid.

They reached Shap village in the dark, to find it stripped of provisions by the previous passage of the main army. English General Oglethorpe's horsemen arrived soon afterwards, and took a position east of the village with orders to attack if the highlanders amounted to less than 500. But he learned from local people that the number was closer to a thousand. His men were soaked too, the gunpowder was wet, and to rough it out in the foul weather until daylight without food and fodder was unthinkable. He opted to take his men to Orton, which turned out to be a nasty rough journey 8 km away to the south-east.

In daylight Murray moved on with extra carts from Shap, picking up the artillery left behind at the town by the main army, and he sent a messenger on to Penrith to ask the prince for reinforcements. Four km on, near the hamlet of Thrimby, a body of horsemen appeared before them, part of the duke of Cumberland's cavalry forces, with instructions to cut off the rearguard. They were face to face with the duke of Perth's party that had been sent south to help with the baggage. Murray was out of contact in the rear, so without waiting for his orders, Perth's commanding officer called 'claymores' and his men charged; Glengarry's men, further in the rear, charged with them. The horsemen turned and fled. One luckless cavalryman who fell from his horse was cut to pieces.

A half-hour later the highlanders were again faced by Cumberland's horsemen at their rear. At this point the road was closed in by walls and hedges and the pursuers could only attack a few abreast, and were held back. When Murray reached Clifton, 5 km on, he decided to make a stand.

CLIFTON is a little over 2 km south-east of Penrith, and to the east of the A6, and nearby was the site of the last skirmish ever fought by armies on English soil. The village has been altered quite a lot since. The M6 passes close to the site on the west, and the railway to the east.

South of Clifton, government horsemen met the Scottish cavalrymen of Lord Pitsligo, sent down from Penrith to assist the highlanders' rearguard with their baggage. There was an inconclusive exchange of fire and the horsemen dispersed.

And here, south of Clifton, was an area of small fields, hedges and drystone walls where Murray decided to make good his position and to check the disposition of his pursuers. His request for reinforcements had been met by Cluny's Macphersons, and with Ardshield's Stewarts of Appin, he had a total of about a thousand men. It was late afternoon when a strong force of government cavalry came into sight to the south, and drew up in two lines. They did not seem to want to make an immediate attack and opened ineffective fire.

As Murray made ready to engage with the government troops he was surprised to receive a message from Charles to withdraw, and make all haste to Carlisle. He was appalled by the order. The obvious dangers of a retreat at that time, hindered with baggage, with a superior, more mobile force in close pursuit, were absolutely unthinkable. And not when he had an opportunity to slow them down. He consulted with his officers, John Roy Stewart and MacPherson of Cluny, and they agreed to ignore the order. Murray wrote later:

> It was now about an hour after sunsett, pretty cloudie, but the moon, which was in its second quarter, from time to time broke out and gave good light but this did not continue above two minutes at a time. We had the advantage of seeing their disposition, but they could not see ours.

In closing light, Murray had his men line the hedges and walls. At the east end of the line were the MacPhersons, the Stewarts of Appin were central and the Glengarry men lined the enclosures in the west.

On his side, Cumberland gave orders for detachments from his three dragoon regiments to dismount and close with the highlanders. It was now dark, but even so the highlanders had glimpses of the dragoons' yellow belts, and a contingent could be seen crawling beside a wall towards the enclosures on the east side. Murray ordered the MacPhersons, nearest to them, to clear the first hedge and take a position behind the second. He told Cluny that they were likely to engage with the enemy, and he would support them on their right. As the MacPhersons took up their new position they were subjected to gunfire too accurate for comfort. The Scots answered in the normal highland way: Murray shouted 'Claymore!' and the men bore down on the dragoons with their swords. The dragoons broke and ran, but their retreat was hindered by a deep ditch where many fell and were cut down under the highlanders' blades. Those who got away fled over the moor under fire from MacDonalds.

Cluny had difficulty halting the charge of the MacPhersons at the ditch. One large clansman, though, Angus of Knappach, was deaf and did not hear the order, and charged on after the fleeing dragoons; then finding that he was alone, he looked back and called, 'Why the divvil do you turn back? I see a great many more further on!' Lord George wrote: 'We had now done what we had propos'd, and being sure of no more trouble from the enemy, I ordered the retreat.'

Cumberland, an army general with skill and experience in combat, must have been humiliated at the news of the dragoons' poor showing, but had to make his excuses. He wrote in his dispatch to the duke of Newcastle: 'Our men drove them out of Clifton in an hour's time, with very small loss [but] dared not follow them because it was so dark.' And besides this, of course, he said that his horses and men were exhausted by forced marches. And he turned on General Oglethorpe for not engaging with the enemy earlier. Oglethorpe was court-martialled, but acquitted.

Two monuments preserve the memory of the skirmish. In the churchyard, to the right of the entrance, a small monument stands to the dragoons who died in the action. The dead highlanders were buried where they fell. At Town End, at the southern end of the village, a lane leaves the A6 and tunnels under the railway. Just beyond the tunnel, behind a farmyard, on the south side of the lane, the highlanders are thought to be buried by an oak tree, known as The Rebels' Oak. A small memorial stone marks the place. Clifton church dates from the thirteenth century but has been much altered. Nearby is a pele tower which is all that remains of Clifton Hall.

SHAP FELL

Going back to SHAP – Shap is the high fell unavoidably climbed by the A6, the main line railway, and more recently the M6 motorway. The summit is a bleak wild area given to winter gales and snow, and Shap village, before the advent of the M6, occasionally resembled a refugee camp as stranded truck drivers waited for the road to be ploughed. Shap could tell many a tale about the travellers who have been this way. Some visitors have been daunted by the open scenery. Others like it. When John Ruskin wrote about a wild alpine scene that he had admired he stated: 'Ever since I passed Shap Fells, when a child, I have had an excessive love for this kind of desolation.' Shap village is at 245 m, though the highest point that the railway climbs is at 279 m. Shap is now a touring base for holidaymakers, who presumably can be guaranteed better treatment than Bonny Prince Charlie received when he lodged here. He always insisted on paying for accommodation during his campaign; but here he complained that he was overcharged.

In the days when every township had to be self-sufficient Shap had a postmaster, two shoemakers, a tailor, a station master, a schoolmaster, a surgeon, a registrar of births and deaths, a joiner, three blacksmiths, a wheelwright, a painter and glazier, a saddler, a brewer, a stonemason, as well as shopkeepers, seven public house landlords, a railway inspector and, of course, the vicar.

Shap was extensively settled in Neolithic times when the climate was more temperate. A stone circle near the village, approached by an avenue of stones, was of that period, though the assembly was destroyed by the railway. There are still a number of standing stones and cairns in the area. The village itself boasts little of great historical interest beyond the market house on the main street, which was built around 1690. The church of St Michael has twelfth-century remnants.

West of the village, though, reached by a narrow road, is the ruin of SHAP ABBEY. The site, low down on the banks of the River Lowther, seems oddly chosen, though the sudden appearance of the tower as one approaches is a pleasing surprise. Little is left standing apart from the heavy tower, but it is possible to

Sole remnant of Shap abbey, the tower

follow the layout in the foundations. The abbey, dedicated to God and St Mary Magdalene, was founded in 1199 by Thomas, son of Gospatrick, for The Premonstratentians, or White Canons, having coming from their site at Preston-in-Kentdale to this more favourable position. They had rights and privileges in the surrounding and over time were granted more land in Scotland and in Yorkshire.

After the dissolution the abbey was used as a quarry, and many of the stones were used in the building of Lowther Castle.

South-east of the abbey is the hamlet of Keld, which has a small surviving sixteenth-century chapel (NT) of a type that must once have been common.

The Shap quarries that produce the granite for which the place is famed are located 5 km south of the village. The most important one, which produced the beautiful polished stone for buildings in London and all over the country, is the pink quarry. The rock structure consists of white felspar grains and crystalline quartz, with grains and crystals of black mica; but characteristically has the large oblong crystals of pink felspar. The granite structure changes when it comes into contact with other rocks, or when the cooling process of the magma is slower. The 'blue quarry' holds blue-grey rock and contains garnets. Other quarries provide stone that has been much used for road building and cement products. The granite is unusually on the fringe of a junction between Coniston limestone and carboniferous limestone. The latter is also quarried and processed in a nearby cement works.

The well, Shap Wells

One approaches Shap Wells 6 km south-east of Shap, by a very uninviting stretch of bleak road through farm fields, and suddenly the happy surprise of a green oasis is revealed in a dip. The medicinal waters were 'discovered' in the early nineteenth century, but were known well before that. In the 1780s a Dr Burn wrote:

> ... by the side of the River Berbeck, was discovered some few years ago a spa water, known by the name of Shap Well, to which in the summer season is a considerable resort. It is impregnated with sulphur, and smells like rotten eggs, or the barrel of a musket just fired, and hath been found serviceable in scorbutic disorders.

When improved roads made access much easier, the popularity of the spa grew, and the earl of Lonsdale had a hotel built by the well that has since been modernized and improved. The well itself lies under an ornate Victorian canopy (restored by the hotel), and its sulphurous waters can be smelled for some distance. In 1828 Dr Alderson, a Yorkshireman, stated that the water was milder than that of Harrogate and much more active than Gilsland's. His analysis concluded:

> ... there is not a medicated spring in the kingdom more efficacious than the Shap Spa, in rousing the energies of the debilitated stomach, and inspiring the whole frame with a new animation, giving to the blanched and cadaverous cheek, the glow of health, and to the turgid and spiritless eye, the sparkle of life and energy.

Who could resist drinking the foul-tasting elixir?

In *The Spas of England* Dr Granville remarks on the presence of sulphurated hydrogen gas in the water, 'made manifest by its taste and smell, its deposition, its action upon lead and iron, and – on the oil paint in the bath room.'

Nearby, the extraordinary Queen Victoria monument of 1842 consists of a column surmounted by Britannia, in all 9 m high. 'To commemorate the accession of Queen Victoria to the throne of these realms, June 20th 1837.' On the north panel there is a wreath of palm and olive, surmounted by the Lowther arms. On the west panel is a bas-relief of the British lion, its paw resting upon a globe. And on the east panel an invalid holds up a shell while the goddess Hygeia pours water into it from a goblet. The design was by Mr Mawson of Lowther, and the sculpture by the self-taught Thomas Bland, of Reagill.

THE VALLEY OF THE LYVENNET

CROSBY RAVENWORTH is a neat and attractive village east of Shap. The church of St Lawrence dates from the twelfth century, but repairs and rebuilding inevitably followed Scottish raids, and continued with improvements over the centuries. The main old feature obvious now is the Old English doorway. The church site, however, has a much earlier history, and the first Christian congregations might have gathered in the open around a stone cross. Part of an old cross stands in the churchyard near the church doorway, but even that might not have been the beginning. For the stone cross may have replaced a wooden one, just as in Saxon times a wooden church would have occupied the site.

The Revd Sydney Swan, an eccentric clergyman, lived here, and after experimenting with bicycles and cars, went on to build aircraft in the vicarage stable. He even made flights from the nearby fields and gained a place in the 1909 *Daily Mail* challenge at Aintree racecourse. He made the 500 km journey to London in less than twenty-three hours.

Many signs of early Bronze Age settlements linger in the area. South-west of the village are the remains of a later one – a large pre-Roman settlement, and one of the most important in the north of England. (Seven others have been identified in the area.) This settlement, Ewe Close, is a complex system of walls and hut circles measuring about 213 m by 167 m. In the main, more regularly shaped, enclosure is a large hut base (possibly a chief's hut or an assembly hall) 15 m in diameter. The suggestion that the site is pre-Roman carries conviction, for the Roman road from Lancaster to Carlisle, which passes 18 m to the west, has unusually made a detour to visit it.

North of Crosby Ravensworth we come to the hamlets of MAULDS MEABURN and, further north, KINGS MEABURN. The land was in the barony of Sir Hugh Morville, but after he was involved in the assassination of Becket his land was forfeited, one half of Meaburn going to the crown, and the other to Morville's sister Maud, who was married to William de Veteripont. Hence the names. The hamlets, running alongside the River Lyvennet are pleasant enough, but the nearby village of MORLAND is exceptionally charming, not least for its special church: St Lawrence's the only church building in Cumbria with an Anglo-Saxon tower. An extra storey was added in the seventeenth century. The Normans did not demolish the church, but added to it in the twelfth century, but much has happened since, and the twelfth-century evidence is somewhat fragmented – after all it is over a thousand years old. Other notable features include a fifteenth-century oak screen with very odd carved heads and an impressive thirteenth-century coffin lid with a foliated cross in the south transept.

It is good to see commercial premises in a village that do no harm to its rural character.

THE OLD TOWN OF PENRITH

Moving north, one crosses a bridge over the River Leith to reach CLIBURN. The Elizabethan hall, notably unspoilt, was built by Richard Cliburn. The church of St Cuthbert is Norman, as shown by the stonework in the nave and chancel. At the south doorway the stonemason has carved two odd figures.

The A6 road passes Lowther Park to PENRITH (*PEN-rith;* dialect: *PEE-rith*) (pop. 15,190), the northern gateway to the Lakes. Since the Bronze Age the old red sandstone town has always welcomed weary travellers going north or south. This was a staging post. Romans, Angles and Normans, armies and traders, have visited and stayed. In the 1960s the constant stream of heavy traffic on the A6 through the town centre sometimes made life here intolerable, and it was hoped that the building of the M6 would give back to Penrith something of its old identity. Most of the heavy commercial traffic has thankfully gone; but on market days care is still needed to cross Penrith's busy streets.

The Romans built their fort at Old Penrith some 6.5 km to the north of the present town and called it Veroda; it was roughly halfway between the important forts at Brougham and Carlisle. There are signs that a vicus, a civilian settlement, was close by.

In medieval times marauding Scots had a quick and easy journey to Penrith. After Bannockburn in 1314 the town was burned and it suffered the same fate in 1345 at the hands of 'Black Douglas', and again a few years later. So in 1382 licence to crenellate a defensive tower was given either to Bishop William Strickland, or to Ralph Neville, later the first earl of Westmorland. It was originally a simple tower, but when Neville received the town and manor of Penrith from Richard II he made improvements and extensions. A later Neville to occupy the castle was Richard, earl of Warwick and Salisbury, 'Warwick the King Maker' (1428–71). Then when Richard, duke of Gloucester, was made lord of the Western Marches, necessarily spending some time in the borders, he also made improvements to the castle. He

Penrith castle ruin

married Anne Neville, the earl of Warwick's daughter. Later as Richard III he made further improvements, including the addition of a large banqueting hall and comfortable apartments.

The castle deteriorated after Richard's death at Bosworth Field, and in the sixteenth century it became a free 'quarry' for local builders. A survey of the ruins in 1572 recorded three stables, a great chamber, great hall, two kitchens, bake-house and brewhouse, a chapel and offices. Today the south wall still stands to some height, together with the east tower and remains of the south-east tower. The land is now a public park.

Churches suffered no less than the rest of the town at the hands of Scottish raiders. A chapel probably stood on the site of the present St Andrew's church in Saxon times. An Augustinian priory was founded in the town in 1291, and provided lodging for Edward I on his Scotland campaigns, but there is now no trace of it apart from the street name of Friargate. A church served by the friars was in use in 1133. Dedicated to St Andrew, it was extensively rebuilt in the eighteenth century, and all that was retained was the tower – little wonder as it was a defensive tower with very heavy walls. Indeed, they had difficulty in cutting an entrance through it. Much repair work has been done since, including the happy redecoration of grey and gold pillars leading to the galleries; gallery pillars peppermint green and gold; and ceiling panels in red edges with gold. The atmosphere is dignified.

A plaque in the church, at the head of the tower stairs, commemorates the 2,260 people who died of the plague brought in by travellers in 1597. On the north-west corner of the tower are the arms of the earl of Warwick – the Neville family's bear and ragged staff. Old glass in a window of the south aisle repeats the badge alongside figures thought to represent Ralph Neville and his wife Joan Beaufort, daughter of John of Gaunt. In the sanctuary on either side of the east window are two large murals of 1845 by a local artist, Jacob Thompson. On one side an angel announces the birth of Christ to shepherds, and on the other an angel appears to Jesus in the garden of Gethsemane. One charming feature in the south wall is a window of stained-glass art produced by six-year-old school pupils.

The clock in the tower is a 1712 wooden-framed masterpiece by local clock-maker Aaron Cheeseman. In the churchyard is the peculiarity known as 'the Giant's Grave'. A popular tradition, maintained until recent generations, has it that this large mound, with two high stones at each end, is the grave of Owen Caeserius, king of Cumbria from c. 920 to c. 937. Actually the stone grouping consists of two tall Angle or Norse cross shafts at each end, with hogback grave-stones of the same period at the sides. On the cross on the east side the theme is repeated of the wicked god Loki, bound under a snake, and his wife attempting to protect him from its venom. Another standing stone in the churchyard, known as 'the Giant's Thumb', is a headless pre-Norman cross.

'The Giant's Grave', Penrith churchyard

The town houses overlooking the churchyard are of considerable interest. Queen Elizabeth grammar school is one, founded in 1564 and continuing as a school until 1915. On the west side of the churchyard stands a building's gable end with a date stone of 1563. This was where Dame Birkett kept a school, and where the infants William and Dorothy Wordsworth started their learning at the ages of seven and six respectively when living with their grandparents in Devonshire Street.

The town hall might look like any other town hall, but in fact is a 1906 adaptation of two houses attributed to Robert Adam; sadly, only two chimneypieces survive as Adamish features. There are two old inns of note. The Two Lions dates from the sixteenth century and the Gloucester Arms has stood from at least the fifteenth century, although the earliest feature now seen is Elizabethan; Richard of Gloucester is said to have occupied the inn on occasions. Other town buildings of interest include the mansion house of 1750, behind the parish church, and the George Hotel, where Bonny Prince Charlie took rest and refreshment during the '45 rebellion. Next door to the George Hotel is Arnison's shop front, where the maternal grandparents of the Wordsworths lived and had a draper's shop. Both William and Dorothy had to spend time here as children, and, resented and unloved, they hated the place. William even contemplated suicide to escape the misery of staying here. In 1787–8 Dorothy had to return as a teenager and only the nearness of her friends Mary and Peggy Hutchinson made her stay tolerable.

The town's information centre has an adjacent small museum, containing pictures by the local but nationally acclaimed artist Jacob Thompson (1806–1879), who owed much to the patronage of William, earl of Lonsdale. He exhibited regularly at the Royal Academy and the British Institution and was on friendly terms with major artists of the day, some of whom stayed as guests at his home at the Hermitage on Lord Lonsdale's estate. He painted the altarpiece in St Andrew's church in 1845.

PENRITH BEACON, once a link in the country's communication chain, now serves as a great local viewpoint with superb vistas over the Lake District hills. When Dorothy Wordsworth and Mary Hutchinson walked here as teenagers, William sometimes joined them during the summer holidays. His attachment to Mary was probably formed in this period, and later she became his wife. In 'The Prelude' Wordsworth records an infant haunting episode that was to become a lifetime's memory. He had lost his adult guide in a mist on the Beacon hill, and was suddenly afraid.

Down the rough and stony moor

> I led my horse, and, stumbling on, at length
> Came to a bottom, where in former times
> A murderer had hung in iron chains.
> The gibbet-mast had mouldered down, the bones
> And iron case were gone; but on the turf,
> Hard by, soon after that fell deed was wrought,
> Some unknown hand had carved the murderer's name.

He was terrified and sought his guide.

> Faltering and faint, and ignorant of the road
> Then, reascending the bare common, saw
> A naked pool that lay beneath the hills,
> The beacon on the summit, and, more near,
> A girl, who bore a pitcher on her head,
> And seemed with difficult steps to force her way
> Against the blowing wind. It was, in truth,
> An ordinary sight; but I should need
> Colours and words that are unknown to man,
> To paint the visionary dreariness
> Which, while I looked all round for my lost guide,
> Invested moorland waste, and naked pool,
> The beacon crowning the lone eminence,

The female and her garments vexed and tossed
By the strong wind.

RHEGED, a visitor centre west of Penrith off the A66, is named after the ancient British tribe that occupied this area. It has been designed to blend in with its environment, and with its roof of grass, does so reasonably well. The centre promotes Cumbrian arts and crafts and attempts to persuade tourists to expand their travels beyond the National Park to the Cumbrian fringes. A cinema with a screen 'the size of six double-decker buses' draws viewers impressively into the picture. In 2003 the centre was showing Rheged, the Lost Kingdom, a film on Everest, and Shackleton's Antarctic adventure. There is also a permanent mountaineering exhibition that can occupy a visitor for a couple of hours. Using some rare film footage, it tells the story of mountaineering and rock climbing from its birth, pioneered – largely in the Lake District – by an elite. It continues with the popular growth of climbing after the last war, to the modern-day athletic approach. Most moving, though, is the story of the conquest of Everest and the death of George Mallory in the 1924 expedition. The display shows some of the equipment found on his body when it was discovered seventy-seven years later.

South from Penrith roundabout, along the A6, are two ancient henges. MAYBURGH and KING ARTHUR'S ROUND TABLE are situated in an 'island' formed by the M6, the A6, the B5320 and the River Eamont. Mayburgh is a henge monument, thought to date from late Neolithic times. It is unusual in that the stone circle consists, not of a ditch and bank of soil, but of a bank of water-worn cobbles rising to a height of about 4.5 m, enclosing about half a hectare of land. It has been estimated that the banks contain some 20,000 tons of stone, and every one was carried to the site from the river. There is one larger stone standing within the circle, but in the eighteenth century three others stood near this one, with two others standing at what was assumed to be the entrance. A broken remnant was found in the latter place in 1879.

Nearby and downriver is another henge thought to belong to the same period. Known as King Arthur's Round Table, this is a circular earth mound area surrounded by a ditch with two entrances, both about 18 m in diameter. This mound has been greatly damaged.

The purpose of these constructions can only be guessed at. Why, for example, are two so very close together? Were they two denominations of one religion? They are positioned in what has always been a key area: the important natural crossroads in which ancient tracks comprising the north–south route from England to Scotland met pathways coming east–west from Northumberland and Yorkshire into Cumbria. The Roman roads followed the same obvious routes, and nowadays the modern road system, the M6, only misses the village to bypass nearby Penrith.

THE CASTLES OF BROUGHAM

The busy A66, eastwards from Penrith, soon passes another important historical site. BROUGHAM (*BROOM*) also sits at the strategic crossroads, explaining why the Romans built a fort here. The Roman roads came from their main bases at York, Carlisle and Chester. From Brougham a road went northwards through Old Penrith to Carlisle; southwards by Low Borrow Bridge, through Lancaster to Chester; eastwards to York; and westwards through the Lakeland Fells over High Street, to the fort at Ambleside; and on westwards to their port at Ravenglass. The fort at this strategic point was named Brocavum, inside a bend of the River Eamont, and alongside grew a thriving village. The remaining lines of the fort can be seen in a field south of Brougham castle. The fort was probably built, or rebuilt, in the second century and occupied through to the end of the fourth by up to a thousand infantry and cavalry. A large civil settlement lay outside the fort's walls.

Long after it was abandoned the Normans saw its obvious strategic importance and BROUGHAM CASTLE was built near the same site with stones from the Roman fort. Henry II had brought the area into English hands after the death of David I of Scotland. Gospatric, son of Orm, was granted the land and built a keep. Lordship passed to the Vipont family in the late twelfth century and thence to the

Part of Brougham castle ruin, the keep

Cliffords, through marriage, a century later. It remained with the Cliffords until the death of Lady Anne Clifford, last of the line, in 1676. The remains (EH) are substantial enough to stir the imagination.

Entrance to the ruins is by the outer gatehouse, which carries above it the inscription 'thys made Roger'. Roger was the fifth Lord Clifford. In the gate-hall beyond, an inscription records the repair of the structure in 1652 by the elderly Lady Anne Clifford, who characteristically quotes her titles.

> Countess Dowager of Pembrook, Dorsett and Montgomery, Baronesse Clifford, Westmerland and Veseie, Ladie of the Honour of Skipton in Craven, and High Sheriffesse, by inheritance, of the countie of Westmerland, in 1652 after it had layen ruinous ever since about August 1617 when King James lay in it for a time on his journie out of Skotland towards London until this time.

She ends with a quote from Isaiah lviii: 12: 'And they that shall be of thee shall build the old waste places; thou shalt raise up the foundations of many generations; and thou shalt be called, The repairer of the breach, The restorer of paths to dwell in.'

The slab bearing this inscription is now held for safekeeping in the reception centre. Lady Anne's story of her acquisition of Brougham Castle and the other Clifford properties is told in the section on Appleby (see p.287).

Passing through a small courtyard one reaches the late thirteenth-century inner gatehouse. The second storey above this contains the chamber in which Lady Anne passed her late years, and died in 1676. Beyond lies the keep. The original castle would have consisted of a keep, with outer wooden buildings, and a stockade and ditch. Accommodation quarters, with protective curtain walls, were progressively added from about the thirteenth century on. In later building programmes the keep was heightened, a south-west tower built, and the external defences improved, the keep being brought into the inner defences with the building of inner and outer gates.

This twelfth-century keep is still impressive in its ruined state. It is possible to climb up to the third storey, which offers a wide prospect over the river and the countryside, and makes one ponder on the men who raised such a heavy structure, and how they did it.

Wordsworth and sister Dorothy climbed here with the Hutchinson sisters in 1788, and the poet notes in his 'Prelude':

> ... those mouldering towers
> Have seen us side by side, when, having clomb
> The darksome windings of a broken stair,
> And crept along a ridge of fractured wall,

> Not without trembling, we in safety looked
> Forth, through some Gothic window's open space,
> And gathered with one mind a rich reward
> From the far-stretching landscape, by the light
> Of morning beautified, or purple eve

The first floor comprises the hall. Approaching the second floor from the stair passage, one can see a Roman memorial slab in the ceiling that reads in translation. 'To the spirits of the departed Titus M— lived 32 years more or less. M— his brother set up this inscription.'

On the second floor one finds another large chamber, into which a door was inserted later to gain access to the inner gatehouse and Lady Anne's chamber. Above, on the third, is the addition built by Robert Clifford in the late thirteenth century. In the south-east angle is a small private chapel.

At ground level again, beyond the east side of the keep, the great chamber is now completely ruined, and south of this lie the foundations of the fourteenth-century great hall. The hall lay above on the first floor, while ground floor would have been used for storage. Beyond this are the ruins of the kitchen – again the working area would have been on the first floor above. Then west of this stood the chapel, again on an upper floor; the lower part of the east window is there, and in the south wall are two trefoil-headed windows, a piscina and a sedilia of three bays. The three-storey building west of the chapel, of around 1300, probably housed the retainers. Just beyond this was the all-important well. Then at the south-west corner is the tower of league, again built by Robert Clifford, which still extends to its top, third floor. This was a defensive tower, but also served as a guest house.

Along the west wall lay a range of buildings, most likely ovens and bake-houses, but they were demolished by Lady Anne. The moat and banks are well preserved.

The castle's first historical significance emerged when Henry II took this region into England from the Scots. It was held by the Clifford family for centuries, and figured strongly in campaigns against the Scots, and at one time Edward I stayed here. Roger Clifford was killed in the Barons' War of the thirteenth century. The Cliffords were active men and great soldiers of their time, and the family history records the casualties. Roger Clifford II was killed in the Barons' War against King John in the first quarter of the thirteenth century. In 1282 Roger Clifford II was drowned while crossing the Menai Straits in action against the Welsh. His son, Roger, was killed when leading a cavalry charge at Bannockburn in 1314. His eldest son Roger Clifford IV was severely wounded at the Battle of Boroughbridge in 1322 and died five years later. Other Cliffords fought and fell in the Wars of the Roses.

Lady Anne's successors, the earls of Thanet, neglected the castle, and in 1714 the final insult came when the lead and the timber were stripped and taken away. The estate later came into the possession of the Tufton family, and in 1928 Lord Hothfield passed the guardianship to the then commissioners of Her Majesty's Works; it is now in the hands of English Heritage.

The chapel of St Wilfred's, easily overlooked, is south-west of the castle, near Brougham Hall. Its origins are uncertain, though documentary evidence suggests late fourteenth century; but it certainly fell into disrepair until it became another of the many buildings restored by Lady Anne in the seventeenth century. She wrote in her diary:

> This Summer I caused the Chapell at Brougham to be pulled down and new built up again larger and stronger than before at my own charge and it was wholly finished about the latter end of April 1659 for which God be praised. During the time of my lying at Brougham Castle I received the Sacrament thrice, once at Christmas in the Chapell at Brougham Castle, once at Ninekirks on Easter Day and once at Brougham Chapell on 27 of Julie which Chappell I have lately built and this was the first time that I ever received the Blessed Sacrament at this Brougham Chappell and I seldom else went out of my chamber or upon the lands of the Castle as I used to doe but only into the painted chamber to have prayers.

In the 1840s William, brother of Lord Brougham and Vaux, was mainly responsible for alterations; and he filled the chapel with an amazing collection of carved woodwork belonging mainly to the sixteenth and seventeenth centuries. The sixteenth-century Flemish triptych that used to be a feature, was removed, first to the Victoria & Albert Museum for restoration, and can now be seen at Carlisle cathedral. John Betjeman was ecstatic about the chapel's interior, but one needs luck to find the place open. Some old yews stand majestically in the churchyard and a fine lime tree, in middle age, spreads its canopy over the graves.

Brougham Hall is a remnant. From the outer walls one expects to find something substantial behind, but it is like a hollow tooth. The hall was more or less demolished in the 1930s and suffered a fire in 1956. A band of hopeful enthusiasts are working on restoration while opening it to the public and selling crafts there.

The original hall was bought by John Brougham of Scales in 1726, from James Bird, a steward, who had bought it from John Tufton, grandson of Lady Anne. This meant that the Brougham family was coming home to an estate previously in their ownership. The hall became the home of John Brougham's grandson, the famous politician the first baron Lord Brougham and Vaux (1778–1868), who pulled down the original Tudor hall and medieval buildings and built a mansion. He is immortalized by the brougham – a horse-drawn carriage, with the driver perched outside, that he favoured. As a character he was much criticized, but he spearheaded important judicial reforms. Through him slave-trading became a felony, and while lord chancellor between 1830 and 1834 he helped the Reform Bill to pass through the House of Lords. He was also responsible for the establishment of London's Old Bailey.

The ornate octagonal Countess Pillar is 1 km east of the castle, by the side of the A66. It was erected by Lady Anne in 1656 to commemorate the place where she bade farewell to her mother forty years before.

Just over 2 km east of the castle, and reached by a track alongside the River Eamont, is St Ninian's chapel (Ninekirk). A Saxon church here was replaced by a Norman version, then completely rebuilt by Lady Anne in 1660. It is an interesting piece of Gothic survival, strangely remote from habitation. This is because the original village of Brougham used to be close to the Roman road nearby, but was moved, families, lock stock and barrel, by the landowner, Robert de Veteripont, who wanted the land for his Whinfell Park.

KENDAL TO KIRKBY STEPHEN AND THE PENNINES

North-east from the town one can choose between the M6 motorway or the old road, the A685; both of them enter the valley of the River Lune. Some 13.5 km from Kendal the roads and rail pass at Low Burrow Bridge, the site of a Roman fort that the railway took a bite out of. Then northwards the routes go through the Tebay gorge where the river has bitten deep into the Silurian rock. Here is TEBAY, a village most of whose inhabitants worked for the railway in the days when locomotive transport was the key to the country's prosperity. The railway came in 1846, and Tebay grew as a junction in 1861. Those were the days when the Royal Scot speeded through the gorge, and the Mallard locomotive broke the speed record. The village is marked by terraces of typical railway cottages, and the church with its prominent spire was paid for by the railway companies and its workers. The track ran north past the quarries of Shap granite, so what better stone to build a church with, since it was chosen for its strength and beauty to grace so many London and city buildings. But Tebay goes much further back than the railway, as its one-time Norman motte and bailey castle proved. Now it is a favourite haunt of anglers.

The A685 runs East from Tebay towards Kirkby Stephen, and passes RAVENSTONEDALE (*RUSS-en-dale*) village, in an enclave off the main road. Here was a monastic settlement of Gilbertines at a time when the manor of Ravenstonedale belonged to the Gilbertine priory at Watton in Yorkshire. The order was founded by Gilbert of Sempringham in 1131, the only specifically English religious order, with no connections with establishments founded abroad, following the Augustinian rule that spread rapidly mainly in the east of England, and held leper colonies and orphanages. Gilbert was later canonised. The order broke up at the dissolution. The foundations of the settlement can be seen on the north side of the church of St Oswald, whose front is dominated by huge cypress trees. The church is largely eighteenth century, though some stones in the structure are 500 years older. One is instantly struck by the unusual interior, for the lines of pews face each other across the nave in collegiate style. Next one notices the size of the pulpit – a three-decker with a sounding board, and – an unusual feature – the top landing has a door and a seat, to accommodate, so it is said, the minister's wife. Does it still?

KIRKBY STEPHEN is a busy agricultural market town and a holiday centre. Interesting buildings, some Georgian, surround the market square. But the surprising sight is the peculiar cloisters, consisting of a red sandstone screen between the churchyard and the square, and featuring eight Tuscan columns, with a pediment and bellcote. It was built in 1810 with money left by John Waller, a local man who became a Royal Navy purser. We must assume that he came by the money honestly – though pursers were renowned for having ill-gotten gains. The cloister once served as a butter market – its cool shade would have its uses in summer. Another interesting building is the temperance hall of 1856, with a statue of Temperance and strange lettering.

The impressively large church dates back to the thirteenth century, though it is very much restored after 1897. It is shared with Roman Catholics. The original arcade makes the really big impression, and the pulpit is a gem too – made of polished granite and Italian marble. In the Musgrave and Hartley chapel lies a knight's effigy, probably that of Sir Richard Musgrave. It is he who is supposed to have killed the last boar on English soil at nearby Wild Boar Fell. Andrew D'Harcla (Hartley) of these parts was the warden of the English Western March during the border wars. He defended Carlisle castle successfully during Robert the Bruce's advance into England, even though the city fell. He was made earl of Carlisle, but had enemies – accused of treachery when trying to negotiate a peace with Bruce, he was arrested by the sheriff of Cumberland and subsequently executed. There are effigies too of Thomas, first Lord Wharton, with his two wives. Cornelius Nicholson, the nineteenth-century historian, translated the Latin inscription thus:

The cloisters, St Stephen's church, Kirkby Stephen

Here I Thomas Wharton do lye
With Lucy under my head,
And Nelly, my wife, hard by,
And Nancy as cold as lead.
Oh! How can I speak without dread?
Who could my fortune abide?
With one plague under my head,
And another on either side.

A fragment of a tenth-century cross shaft shows a horned figure in chains – this is surely Loki, the evil one of Scandinavian mythology, bound by the gods to a rock.

The Temperance Hall, Kirkby Stephen

Kirkby Stephen was once described as 'that nest of traitors'. The effect of Henry VIII's dissolution and the end of the abbeys was to destroy the social infrastructure of country life. It meant the loss of hospitals, law courts, schools and poor-law institutions, as well as hostelries for travellers. An insurrection against the harsh treatment of abbeys and clergy, known as 'The Pilgrimage of Grace', took off in the north of England and its followers were mercilessly punished. Local man Nicholas Musgrave led 8,000 men in the cause and defeated a force of the king's men near Kirkby Stephen, then marched on Carlisle; but there they met their match. All the leaders, except Musgrave, were taken prisoner, 6,000 men. Seventy-four were hanged from the city walls, and around forty were taken and hanged at Kirkby Stephen to deter others.

Taking the switch-back Hawes road from the town towards Yorkshire, along the side of the Eden, one is immediately engulfed by another country – the Pennine hills under Mallerstang Edge, and in 6 km one passes the ruin of PENDRAGON CASTLE. It was named Pendragon by its fourteenth-century builder, who had heard the story that Uther Pendragon, father of King Arthur, had a castle in the valley in more ancient times. It was probably built (on a previous structure?) by Sir Hugh de Morville, sheriff of Northumberland and Cumberland, who was

The remains of Pendragon

one of the four knights involved in the murder of Thomas à Becket. For the crime he forfeited his titles and possessions. His sister Maud was married to William de Veteripont, so the castle came into possession of the Veteriponts around 1204. It later came to the Clifford family, the last one of whom was Lady Anne Clifford, the widow of the earl of Pembroke. The Pembroke memoirs record that Idonea de Veteripont, widow of Sir Robert, in the reign of Henry III (1216–72) lived at Pendragon 'which was her chief and beloved habitation'. It was set ablaze twice in Scottish incursions and last restored in the seventeenth century by Lady Anne Clifford, but it fell to neglect and is now very ruinous. There is another ruined castle in the valley, on the other side of the River Eden, 4 km from Kirkby Stephen: Lammerside castle, a Norman pele tower.

BROUGH

BROUGH (*bruff*) (Brough-under-Stainmore) is a village close to where the A66 makes its ascent over Stainmore, a notoriously bleak spot in winter storms. It was a route used by the Romans. The Romans built a fort here on the brow of a steep escarpment and named it Verterae, a fort which they occupied for three centuries. Little remains. A memorial to a sixteen-year-old soldier is found here in a Cambridge museum.

The imposing ruins of the Norman castle (EH) were built on the site of the Roman fort, and in fact some of the original stones tower above the landscape.

Brough castle ruins – the tower

The great keep is on the western end and the walled bailey extends eastwards. The foundations of the keep and sizeable portions of the walls come from the original eleventh-century structure. On the north side of the gatehouse some herring-bone masonry of that period can also be seen. The castle was probably built shortly after 1092, the date when William Rufus won back the area from Scotland. In 1174, however, the castle was retaken by Scotland's William the Lion. The castle was probably repaired in the early thirteenth century when it was granted by King John to Robert de Vipont, ancestor of the Cliffords. During the Scottish wars the castle was in the thick of it, but although the forces of Robert the Bruce, after their victory at Bannockburn, set fire to the town of Brough in 1314, and again in 1319, the castle sustained no damage, and throughout the fourteenth century its defences were improved.

The ninth Lord Clifford, who held the castle during the War of the Roses, was a Lancastrian, and because of his persecution of the Yorkists he acquired the nick-name 'Bloody Clifford' and 'The Butcher'. Shakespeare places him as an outspoken supporter of Henry VI (*Henry VI*, Part III). He was killed in action, reputedly by an arrow in his throat, in 1461, and the castle came into the possession of Warwick the King Maker. The Tudors restored the castle to the Cliffords, and Henry, the son of the ninth Lord Clifford, came back to Brough.

The castle was accidentally set alight in 1521, and remained in ruins until 1659, when Anne Clifford, countess dowager of Pembroke, Dorset and Montgomery, restorer of the Clifford castles and of many village churches, undertook repairs. Much extra work was done, including the rebuilding, on existing fourteenth-century base courses, of the Clifford tower in the south-east corner. In 1666 another fire finished of the castle. By the end of the century masonry was being 'quarried' for buildings elsewhere and the fabric slowly turned to ruins. In 1923 its owner, Lord Hothfield, handed it over to the commissioners of Her Majesty's Works, for its conservation.

St Michael's church stands in the half of Brough known as Church Brough; the other half being known as Market Brough. The original church was built in the twelfth century but like most other buildings of that age in the area, was much damaged by raiding Scots. The church was under royal patronage between 1200 and 1350, the Lionheart and that of Edward III; it then came under the patronage of Queen's College, Oxford. The sloping floor of the nave, to allow worshippers at the rear of the church a greater degree of participation, is a medieval feature. There is a typical Norman main doorway arch. The roof of the nave is Tudor, the Norman original having doubtless been burnt by the Scots. The stone pulpit's age is debatable: although dated 1624 it could be fifteenth-century work.

The church tower is a sixteenth-century addition and its bells, given to the church by John Brunskill, a yeoman of Stainmore, were the subject of a poem by

Robert Southey. Brunskill, with two priests, also founded a chantry in Market Brough: one of the priests taught grammar and the other singing; the chantry included a hospital with two beds for travellers. Following reports of miracles, the chantry became a place of pilgrimage.

The charter giving Brough a market and fair day two days before St Matthew's day was obtained by Lord Clifford in 1330.

Just over 7 km east of Brough, past North Stainmore, is Maiden Castle, the remains of a Roman fortlet, occupied from the second to the fourth centuries. It is well sited with a long view down the Eden valley.

WEST AND NORTH OF KIRKBY STEPHEN TO THE PENNINES

A narrow road running westwards from Kirkby Stephen crosses the Scandal Beck and reaches the prime hamlet of CROSBY GARRETT, at one time 'Crosby Gerard'. The church on the hill has one of the best viewpoints for miles around; over to the fells of the west and eastwards into Yorkshire. And the church is rather special too, with a narrow arch, blocked off by a later one, almost certainly Anglo-Saxon. Like Morland church near Penrith, it looks as if an Anglo-Saxon church has been moulded into a new twelfth-century Norman structure. The north arcade is distinctly Norman, with its heavy columns, and capitals carved with leaves and heads, and there is a thirteenth-century bell turret.

A northern road from Kirkby Stephen runs by the Eden to the peaceful little village of WARCOP, with its small Norman church restored in 1855. This is one of the churches that holds an annual rush-bearing ceremony, dating back to the time when the floor of the church was earthen and strewn with rushes, which were renewed annually. On the special day a procession of children carries rushes and flowers.

Beyond Warcop is the busy A66; cross it and take the minor road through the military training area to Hilton, and Murton and on to Dufton. Here is country very much dominated by the Pennine hills, which were extensively mined for lead. The fells here are nothing like the Lake District's. They have a lean austerity. While the fells of the Lakes are challenging – 'Try me. See what you're made of' – here they seem to be indifferent: 'Take me, or leave me.' Their offer to the hill walker is one of wide-open freedom – great in fine weather, but grim, shelterless and uncompromising in poor weather. It is where the sandstones meet carboniferous limestone, and on the summit a bed of intrusive volcanic dolerite (the 'Whin Sill'). The steep slopes of the curve of High Cup Nick, on the Pennine Way, added drama to the scene. High Cup Nick is interesting geologically. The rim is composed of erosion-resistant dolerite, a bed of volcanic larva, 24 m thick, that has spread its way through the limestone. Glaciation and water erosion through the ages has left a cove, whose scree is a mix of dolerite and limestone.

DUFTON is a lovely fell village. To stalwarts pounding the Pennine Way and the Pennine Bridleway that pass through, it is a staging-post and a haven. Once it owed its existence to the lead mining, at its most prosperous in the eighteenth and nineteenth centuries; now, apart from hill farming's contribution, it is almost wholly given over to the tourist trade. The village has a large green with trees and a peculiar stone drinking fountain, now dry. Otherwise a blend of pubs, cafés and shops supply everything walkers need. Indeed they might be reluctant to leave.

Dufton village

Running north through Knock village minor roads lead on to MILBURN, another handsome typically English village with eighteenth- and nineteenth-century houses set round the village green, with a very tall maypole in the centre. In effect it is possible to enclose the green by shutting off the several entrances, which is handy if you are selling or buying stock.

Minor roads lead northwards to MELMERBY (*MELL-er-by*), another village around greens and trees, but famous for its innovative award-winning organic wholemeal bakery which makes bread in the old way – in pre-heated brick ovens fired by wood. Baking courses are run here too. Two limestone scars (cliffs) overhang Melmerby Fell, which is crossed by the Roman road of Maiden Way.

The long, climbing road from Melmerby to Alston winds and weaves up the fell to a height of 580 m at Hartside Cross. In winter it can be bleak here when all below is cosy. When nowhere else avails sometimes good snow for skiing can be found here. The route must once have been rough and even more treacherous in earlier times, for the present road was constructed only in the 1820s. This and other roads around Alston follow the old tracks used by pack ponies and drovers, and some were rebuilt by John Loudon McAdam, the Scottish inventor of roads surfaced by hard-packed small stones, who would give cost estimates to the Alston mine owners: fifty-six miles of old road repairs at £80 per mile; sixty-six miles of new road at £203 per mile.

The Hartside road drops down to 274 m to the highest market town in England. ALSTON (ancient: Aldeneston) village is at the junction of the North Tyne and Nent rivers, and it is superb among the hills. High it may be, bleak it is not. It has the distinctively clear air of an alpine village, and when the valleys are shrouded in wet mist, Alston can be bathed in sunshine. The town is built upon a hillside and the up-and-down angles take some getting used to. The streets are of cobbles or setts, and from the Gothic town hall past the church the cobbled main street climbs to the market place and the market cross, and continues to rise beyond. The eighteenth- and nineteenth-century buildings are of creamy-grey sandstone, some rendered, and some have outside staircases. Because of the lack of slate in the area, they are roofed with heavy slabs of local stone. There are odd corners, lanes and yards, and the whole effect is strikingly 'old world'. Not surprisingly it has been used for film locations; in 1999 for *Oliver Twist*. Alston is a village one can easily grow to love, not just for the physical quality of the place, but the friendliness of the locals. Alston, like other comparatively isolated Pennine villages, has its own singular character, and the same can be said of some of the individuals who choose to live here.

Alston goes back to Roman times. The Maiden Way, the Roman road from Brough (Bavoniacum) to Hadrian's Wall, runs west of the town; and Whitley castle, the remains of a Roman fort, can be seen to the north-west of the town.

Its vulnerable north and west sides were protected by no less than seven mounds and ditches. The fort doubtless defended the important supply road, but there are also traces of a further road going north-east, with bridge abutments over the South Tyne river, and one strong possibility is that this was a route to mine workings. (Signs of old mine workings are often obliterated by later workings.) The direction of the route also points to a road leading to the important supply base of Corstopitum, near Corbridge, where ore from Alston has been identified.

Not surprisingly Alston gets no mention in the Domesday Book, for in the earlier years of Norman occupation it lay in Scotland. In the twelfth century William the Lion of Scotland gave the manor of Alston to William de Veteripont, and Alston's first church dates from that period. The church is dedicated to St Augustine, who according to local legend, was credited with the exorcizing the demons of nearby Cross Fell, then called 'Fiends Fell'. It is also interesting to note that the prior of Hexham, in extreme poverty, petitioned King Edward III to be granted the revenues of Alston church:

> To our Lord the King, pray his poor chaplains, the prior and the convent of Hexham, who are burned out and distressed by their enemies of Scotland ... that he will, in aid of the said house, of his grace grant them leave to appropriate a poor church of Alston, which is of their patronage.

The king refused their plea, but in 1378 the bishop of Durham granted the revenues of 'Aldeneston' church to Hexham because Hexham abbey's 'belfrey, bells, houses and books and ornaments have been destroyed by fire in hostile incursions of the Scots'. In 1420 Bishop Langley of Durham defined what the vicar of Aldeneston should have: 10 silver marks per year, and every kind of oblation belonging to the church; also the small tithes, namely the pennies arising for holy bread; all mortuaries, and tithes of geese, foals, kids, hens and ale from the whole parish.

In 1769 the old church of St Augustine was demolished and a new church built to a plan by John Smeaton (1724–92), the man who conceived the revolutionary design for Eddystone lighthouse after the first two timber structures were destroyed by storm and fire. He also designed the navigable tunnel canal to nearby Nenthead. The archdeacon of Northumberland did not like the new church, however, and wrote to the bishop of Durham:

> The new church is a large and handsome building and tolerably well executed, but the chancel is too small, but that cannot be remedied now. I found the inhabitants much at variance, and some of them very clamorous.

In 1869 it was decided to pull down the church and rebuild from scratch: the pleasing result is what one sees now. Interestingly the church has ten bells that cannot be pealed because the tower is unable to sustain their moving weight. Instead they are struck by clappers controlled by a keyboard. The old one-hand clock, together with the first bell, came into the ownership of the commissioners of Greenwich hospital from the earl of Derwentwater's estate and were presented to the church in 1767. The clock was restored in 1978 and placed in the church as a working exhibit.

John Wesley visited the village in 1748 and did not find the inhabitants 'clamorous'; on the contrary, 'At noon I preached at the Cross, to a quiet staring people, who seemed to be little concerned one way or the other.'

From medieval times at least, the area of Alston moor was farmed, and evidence of this can be seen among the field boundaries, where lynchets (cultivated terraces) can be seen on the fell sides. In the keeping of livestock co-operation was needed between the farming communities, because grazing was on common land. Peat was also cut on the moor, and when the population grew with an influx of miners in the seventeenth century the demand for fuel meant that some regulations were required on cutting. A court order ruled:

> We order that noe landlord shall tollerate or suffer any cottager about of adjoyning the village of Aldston to cutt or grave any turbary (peat area) upon the comon without the leave of adjacent neighbours & that none of them or for them shall cast or cutt any turbary which properly any cottager shall use within the compass of a mile distant from their cottage house & shall ask leave for doeing the same —- upon the penalty for either default of the sum of £1.19s.11d to be levied upon the landlord that letts to farme the said houses.

The Romans were lured to Alston for its lead, of course, when the ore was found near the earth surface; and it continued to be mined, interrupted only by the border raids, until set in decline in the seventeenth century. In its true beginning the Alston manor came under the ownership of the Radcliffes, but it was short-lived. James Radcliffe, the last (third) earl of Derwentwater, lost everything, including his life, after supporting the 1715 Jacobite rebellion, so in 1734 the estates were granted by the Crown to the commissioners of the Royal Hospital for Seamen, at Greenwich, and mining activities increased. A peak was reached in the nineteenth century when not only lead, but silver, iron, zinc and copper were mined, with the minerals of fluorspar and barytes. In 1821 total mine revenues climbed to over £100,000. Some of the principal mine owners – the London Lead Company – were Quakers, who launched experiments in workers' welfare: education, disablement funds and sick relief – measures that served as models for other reforming Victorians. The seventeenth-century Quaker meeting house is on the main street. Cheaper foreign sources of metals brought the industry to its knees in the late Victorian era. Today employment comes from farming with some tourism and light engineering.

Walkers on the Pennine Way pass through Alston, and are no doubt impressed. The riverside walk to Garrigill is one of its most popular sections. The area has a network of public footpaths, all of which make good exploring. As botanists might expect in a limestone alpine area, there are some uncommon species, including spring gentian. Several routes can be taken to Cross Fell summit (893 m), which is on the Pennine Way.

From the old railway station a narrow-gauge South Tynedale railway is an attraction for steam buffs, giving a half-hour scenic journey.

The A689, going east from the town, brings one from the highest market town to the highest village (over 457 m). NENTHEAD, lying close to the borders of Durham and Northumberland, is a past centre of mining activity. The village is relatively new for the Quaker mine owners planned it as a model village in 1753, rebuilding in 1825. Each cottage had a small garden, and the rent was £4 to £6 per year. As in Alston they pioneered an enlightened relationship between employers and workers. For the community there was a wash-house, reading room and library (reputed to be the first public library in Britain), shops, a bath-house, a market hall, a doctor's surgery and a village school with a staff for over 300 pupils. The miners were encouraged to form their own 'corn association', where they could buy cheaply in bulk and pass on the benefit to the shoppers – an early co-operative venture. The Quakers made no effort to convert the villagers to their faith. Methodism was strong in the area since John Wesley visited and preached at Nenthead in 1748. The Quakers gave land and assistance for the building of a Methodist chapel in 1826. They also assisted in the building of a new Anglican church and vicarage in 1845, and gave endowments to both establishments. They were also aware of the villagers' secular needs and helped to provide a public house – the Miners' Arms, now the Nenthead Hotel. In 1850 a public water supply was provided and older cottages rebuilt. The company offered prizes for the best cultivated gardens and acquired land so that workers, if they wished, could have allotments. The company also improved land for farming, and 263 ha of land were planted with Scots pine and larch to supply the mines with timber. Later some of the waste dumps were planted with trees.

The company offered several other novel benefits, and emergency measures came into force during tough times. In the 'hungry forties', when the price of bread was so high it was causing great hardship, the company bought corn in bulk from Newcastle, ground it in one of its own mills and sold the flour without profit.

The economy of mining fluctuated and in 1882 the Weardale Lead Company bought the leases, then sold to a Belgian company that also had a tradition of caring about workers' welfare. Twenty-two mines were exploited in the area and foreign miners were brought in. After the First World War the price of minerals dropped and mining declined. Nenthead is now the site of a mining museum, where the techniques are explained, and visitors are invited to go underground on guided tours.

GARRIGILL village sits in a hollow on the south side of the Alston to Nenthead road. This very pleasant little village is memorable for its church built deep within the ravine. It is on the site of an early church but was heavily restored in the nineteenth century.

From Garrigill the Pennine Way runs southwards and on to CROSS FELL. In 1747 George Smith, a geographer, described Cross Fell as 'a mountain that is generally ten months bury'd in snow, and eleven in clouds'. Hardly correct! Cross Fell, however, is the highest point in the Pennine chain at 893 m, and the highest in England outside the Lakes. When volcanic magma breaks through the earth's crust it sometimes forces its way horizontally along the bedding plain of sedimentary rocks. In subsequent erosions this hard table rock protects the softer rock below while all around may crumble away. The result is a steep-faced hill capped with a large summit plateau. Such is Cross Fell, the volcanic rock being the long Whin Sill, which supports Hadrian's Wall to the north-east. Every aspect of the fell seems austere; but there is evidence to indicate that at one time the now treeless slopes had forest growing to within 150 m of the top. The summit itself is a mess of aerials, discs and ugly buildings, but on a fine clear day the views to points around are tremendous: across to the Durham coast, the Cheviots, into Scotland, the Solway, round to Morecambe Bay. The Lakeland fells are arranged in spectacular fashion. South-east of Cross Fell the Pennine Way runs over the neighbouring summits of Little Dun Fell (842 m), and Great Dun Fell National Nature Reserve (848 m).

Cross Fell has long been well known for generating the 'helm wind', a violent wind formed from strong north-easterlies scouring over the peculiar configuration of the mountain mass; the air stream behaves rather like a torrent of water pouring over a weir. While further west might be calm, furious gusts can be damaging the roofs of houses below the western escarpment.

Returning to Melmerby a minor road leads through GAMBLESBY village with a church that looks like thirteenth century, but was built in 1868. Cross the Ravensbeck then enter RENWICK, with its small church of All Saints, built in 1845, but replacing an earlier church. The village huddles under Renwick Fell whose highest point is Thack moor, at 609 m.

North again across Croglin Water, that Wordsworth praises as it reaches the

Eden at Nunnery Walks, q.v. is Croglin village. The church replaces one that had Norman origins, but successfully retains its Norman appearance; and the interior is impressive. There is the effigy of a lady in the churchyard, but sadly defaced, a scythe sharpening stone? There is a pele tower opposite. Croglin Fell is an easy walk to 591 m.

CHAPTER SIXTEEN

Kendal and the South-east

Although some towns, with the exception of Penrith, may claim to be back doors, side doors or alleyways into the Lakes, only KENDAL (pop. 27,830) can claim to be 'the gateway'. As Wordsworth's guide acknowledges, 'much the greatest number of Lake Tourists begin by passing from Kendal to Bowness upon Windermere'. But right through the town the main street is the A6, which for centuries was the main road, west of the Pennines, connecting England to Scotland. Kendal was a travellers' town, a coaching stop, then, more recently a rest and refreshment stop for the drivers of heavy lorries. An old milestone on the main street shows 'London 258 miles. Edinburgh 135 miles.' The A6 route running

Kendal, 'the auld grey toon'

north from Kendal to Penrith goes back for many centuries. A charter granted to Shap Abbey describing the abbey's boundaries refers to *'Magna strata que venit de Kendale'* – the great road that comes from Kendal.

It is hard to imagine now that all the motor traffic to and from north and south, meaning traffic to and from Windermere and the Lakes, passed through the town. The problem has now eased by the construction of the M6 to the south and a Lakes bypass to the west. Why then has it still got a nagging traffic problem? Traffic management schemes have been permanent items on the town's agenda for years; suggested solutions have been dogged by controversy. As of 2002 experiments are being made to divert traffic from the town centre and eventually make the busy commercial section of the main street pedestrian-friendly. Meanwhile the just-out-of-town supermarkets, with their large car parks, prosper.

The town stands on the River Kent which takes water run-off from a wide area of fells around Kentmere, Longsleddale and Shap. The Kent is joined by the River Mint from Bannisdale and the north, and the Sprint, which in turn are fed from side becks along 10 km of fells above Longsleddale. It is not surprising, therefore, that until mills began to be steam-driven, there were very many water mills – corn mills, saw mills, wool-fulling mills. Mills' functions varied according to economic circumstances, so one could also find tobacco snuff mills, brewing mills, gunpowder mills, bobbin mills, rope mills, paper mills and mill wheels supplying drive for weaving sheds.

The large gathering ground for water has also caused the town to suffer from serious flooding. Judicious engineering, including the deepening of the river in 1970, may now have solved the problems. Six bridges span the river, whose banks offer very pleasant walks.

Kendal was the largest town in the old county of Westmorland, and remains an important administrative centre for Cumbria. In early days it was 'Kirkby Candale', and has long been called 'the auld grey toon', because its buildings are of the local grey limestone. The main thoroughfare – the old A6 – is in three sections. From the south and the parish church there is Kirkgate; a bend then takes it into Highgate past the town hall; and lastly into Stricklandgate. From Highgate a street runs down towards the river through Stramongate, and a bridge takes the road north to Penrith and east to Appleby. ('Gate' = street from old Norse *gata*.) Some of the oldest, mainly Georgian, buildings have survived. Some changes have been made, notably in the last century, and sadly, some vandalism has occurred. And there are still original yards – some named, some numbered – to be found down alleyways near the town centre. The yard system, with houses and workshops packed around an open communal area, was common in many of the old northern towns. Originally Kendal had no less than

150 of them. Many were demolished because the workers' cottages around the yards were very sub-standard; others because they stood in the way of more modern development. One suggestion is that the yard system developed as defensive units against Scottish raiders, the gates to the yards being locked when necessary. But this is nonsense, as the raids were no longer a problem in the eighteenth century when the yards were built. Each yard housed its local community and the workshops in which most were employed. A mid nineteenth-century census revealed that a yard could house some seventy adults. One cottage could accommodate as many as eleven people. On a walk along Highgate – the main central street – one can see alleyways that once led to yards, and as I say, some yards still exist.

One of Kendal's alleyways

Some of the town's older buildings are timber-framed, though the wood is often concealed behind rendering and roughcast; but one can see typical jettied upper storeys, for example on the Fleece Inn on the main street. Some of the fine buildings can only be recognized by casting eyes upwards, above the shop fronts. In the words of Norman Nicholson: 'Once-elegant, eighteenth-century houses have had shop fronts shoved into them like ill-fitting false teeth, and one or two of the larger stores flaunt facades that hit you in the eye like a slap with a wet fish.' Traffic apart, the streets and buildings up, down, around and criss-crossing the town centre are interesting, and town walks with a guide booklet from the information centre can be engaging. The poet Thomas Gray visited Kendal in 1769 and what he wrote about it still seems true: '... houses seem as if they had been dancing a country-dance, and were out: there they stand back to back, corner to corner, some up hill, some down, without intent or meaning'.

A Kendal yard

The church of the Holy Trinity is in Kirkland, at the south end of the town. The earliest part is thirteenth century. There may have been a Saxon church on this site, for a ninth-century cross shaft is built into a window sill in the south aisle. Initially Ivo Taillebois gifted the church to St Mary's abbey at York, but after the dissolution the rectory of Kendal was granted to Trinity College, Cambridge. The exterior, which suffered Victorian 'improvement' in the 1840s, is not impressive, and only hints at the surprise one gets when entering and finding the house interior. One of the widest parish churches in the country, it is spaced over 43 m by 31 m in four arcades of thirty-two columns; one feels as though one is wandering through an open petrified forest. There is much of historical interest too. Chapels commemorate the Parr family, the Stricklands of Sizergh and the Bellinghams of Levens. In the latter is a thirteenth-century coffin lid, and a tomb-chest (1533) with brasses of Sir Roger Bellingham and his wife, as well as one of Alan Bellingham. Included in the tablets on the wall is a memorial to George Romney, the portrait painter, a resident of Kendal, but buried at Dalton. Over the altar is a corona in memory of Bernard Gilpin, an itinerant Protestant preacher from Kentmere, known as the 'the Apostle of the North' in Elizabeth's reign. The black marble font dates from the fifteenth century.

Hanging on the wall by the Bellingham chapel is a sword and helmet. The story goes that these belonged to 'Robin the Devil' of Belle Isle on Windermere, a Royalist during the Civil War, who rode into the church in a fit of anger to seek out his Cromwellian enemy, Colonel Briggs. There are several versions of what happened afterwards. One has it that failing to find Briggs, Robin rode out, but the doorway was too low and he was struck down from his horse and so humiliated that he left his sword and helmet behind. Another version of the story has an angry congregation dragging him from his horse. It is well reported that he entered the church in the hope of finding Colonel Briggs, which certainly fits the character of the man; how much of the rest is true is unknown. The tale was used by Sir Walter Scott in his poem 'Rokeby'. Bertram Risingham rides into the church at Rokeby, shoots his rival Oswald, but fails to get away and is himself killed.

In the old chancel there is a memorial brass to the Revd Ralph Tirer, vicar between 1592 to 1627. He composed the inscription:

> London bredd me, Westminster fedd me.
> Cambridge sped me, my Sister wed me.
> Study taught me, Living sought me,
> Labour pressed me, sickness distressed me,
> Death oppressed me, & grave possessed me,
> God first gave me, Christ did save me,
> Earth did crave me, & heaven would have me.

'My sister wed me?' In what sense? Did she persuade him into a marriage?

The church hosts a number of concerts each year and the spaciousness makes for great acoustics.

The Society of Friends (Quakers) was founded by George Fox in 1652, and they were strong in Kendal from 1660. A meeting house in Stramongate still serves a Quaker community, and houses a tapestry, open to the public, featuring the history of the Society in fifty panels. It was made in the 1980s by 4,000 people from fifteen countries. Much of the town's industries were established by Quakers in the eighteenth and nineteenth centuries. They also ran a school. John Gough, the blind botanist, mentioned by Wordsworth in 'The Excursion', Book VII, was a Kendal man, born into a Quaker family in 1757. He attended the school and later taught at it. Considering his handicap, he was a genius. In the 1835 edition of Wordsworth's *Guide to the Lakes*, Gough was asked to contribute a botanical list. He was an authority on the nature and classification of plants, and he wrote papers on many subjects including gases, geology, plant physiology and seed germination.

In 'The Excursion':

> ... No floweret blooms
> Throughought the lofty range of these rough hills,
> Nor in the woods, that could from him conceal
> Its birthplace: none whose figure did not live
> Upon his touch. The bowels of the earth
> Enriched with knowledge his industrious mind:
> The ocean paid him tribute from the stores
> Lodged in her bosom: and, by Science led,
> His genius mounted to the plains of heaven.

Gough had a hunger for natural history, classical poetry and mathematics. Indeed one of his pupils in maths was the undoubted genius John Dalton (1766–1844), the father of modern atomic theory, who also taught at the school as a young man.

The notable building near the church is ABBOT HALL, built in 1757 as a private house for Colonel Wilson of Dallam Tower. The approach is through an archway by the house's stables. An outside staircase fronts the main door. This is a very fine building converted to an excellent art gallery, one of Cumbria's treasures and a credit to the independent Lakeland Arts Trust that manage it. Care has been taken to decorate the rooms in keeping with the hall's period, with some period furniture by Gillows. The art collection is very extensive for a small gallery, ranging from Elizabethan to modern. Watercolours include a dramatic Turner painting of *The Passage of St Gothard*. Local scenes feature heavily and there is one of a Coniston dawn by John Ruskin, another of Windermere by Turner and Constable is represented by an oil painting of clouds, and a sketch of Rydal Falls.

But, of course, Kendal was the home, when he was at home, of George Romney (1734–1802) the portrait painter, and Abbot Hall often has eight or nine Romneys on display, depending on the gallery's current theme; they can be seen among pictures by his contemporaries, such as Reynolds and Hogarth. Romney was born in Dalton, son of a wheelwright, carpenter and cabinetmaker, and showed promise as a good craftsman himself. He made fiddles and flutes, but also showed that he was rather good at drawing and became apprenticed to a Kendal artist. During an illness at the age of nineteen he was nursed by his landlady's daughter, and he married her. He was not able to set up house until the end of his apprenticeship when he made a modest living in Kendal, painting portraits. Because photographs of people are so taken for granted, we forget that before the 1850s an artist who could paint a person's likeness was in great demand. But Romney was more ambitious, and leaving his wife and two children at home, he went to London to seek more profitable assignments. (Fellow artists advised him that married life spoiled artistic talents.) His exceptional skills were soon recognized by the wealthy and thereafter he was never without work. Although ill-educated, and doubtless uncultured in speech, he was so popular that at his peak he rivalled Gainsborough and Reynolds. His finest pictures were of single figures, though there are exceptional groups, such as *The Beaumont Family*, and here at Abbot Hall, the immediately striking *The Gower Family*. In 1773 he went to Italy for two years, and the classical themes he found there influenced his future path. He painted many portraits (around thirty) of Emma Hart, Lord Nelson's beautiful Lady Hamilton, as any number of allegorical subjects. He returned to Kendal and his wife only occasionally and briefly over the years he was away, but when in 1789 he began to suffer from ill-health he returned for the last time. In his declining three years his wife performed the role of nurse that began their relationship. Tennyson wrote 'Romney's Remorse', a sad poem about his return to his wife in his last days. As he returns to a fitful consciousness,

> Wild babble. I have stumbled back again
> Into the common day, the sounder self.
> God stay me there, if only for your sake,
> The truest, kindliest, noble-hearted wife
> That ever wore a Christian marriage-ring.
> My curse upon the master's apothegm,
> That wife and children drag an artist down!

Abbot Hall's old stable block is an award-winning 'Museum of Lakeland Life' that contains, among other imaginative displays, re-creations of farmhouse rooms, shops and workshops. There are special displays and activities for children. Every trip to Kendal should include a visit.

The Lakeland Arts Trust also run an excellent museum, on behalf of the district council, near the station. Older people may have nostalgic memories of the type of museum founded by the Victorians, with motley and sometimes bizarre collections jostling for space; nowadays they are usually condemned as dull and unimaginative. But many were treasure chests of discovery. The old museum here was like that. Founded in 1796 – one of the country's oldest museums – it has retained that atmosphere of cluttered wonder, with its stuffed birds and Egyptian artefacts. Stuffed animals could never be sanctioned nowadays. But this is not dusty old tat; some very skilful taxidermy is on display here, beautifully mounted in representations of the creatures' habitats. The advantage is that they can be seen up-close, much nearer than a zoo, and one is impressed by the size of, for instance, the polar bear rearing on hind legs (one of the most popular exhibits), the lion, tiger and the albatross. Some history of the Kendal area is told imaginatively.

Along Kirkland from the church some attractive buildings lead one into

Highgate, where handsome late Georgian buildings congregate. The eighteenth-century Old Brewery is brewing art now, not ale. A thriving arts centre has a theatre, films, live music and a national reputation. It is deservedly very popular and an example to other towns of like size.

A clock preserved here and standing in the grounds was once a familiar landmark to lorry drivers on the bleak Shap Fell road from Scotland, long before motorways.

The nineteenth-century town hall has a carillon ringing seven daytime tunes: a heartwarming sound to servicemen returning home from the war. A steep street opposite leads to Castle Howe. When the Normans arrived around 1090 they built their motte and bailey on the high ground here, on the western side of the town. The mound was built on a ridge out of soil thrown up from the surrounding ditch. The tower would be built of wood by, most probably, the first baron of Kendal, Ivo de Taillebois. Later this tower was replaced with a more substantial castle across the river on the town's east side. Castle Howe now is a public green, and on the top of the motte is an obelisk from 1788 – 'Sacred to Liberty' – that commemorates the 'Glorious Revolution' of a century earlier, when William and Mary mounted the throne. The motte is a good viewpoint over the town.

From the Fleece Inn on Highgate a way under an arch leads into the Old Shambles. Butchers slaughtered their beasts and sold their meat here. This must have been a foul place, with gutters running with blood and offal, and it was decided later to move to a New Shambles near the marketplace. The classical-fronted building at the top is an old dye works.

The market place is not as spacious as in other Cumbrian towns. The narrow cobbled corridor of a street leading from it is the New Shambles, quite unspoilt and thankfully without blood. Leading from the market, cobbled Branthwaite Brow is a nice period piece and should stay so.

Kendal began life in Roman times. The Romans used a bow of the river as a defence when they build their fort south of the town at Watercrook. Now only its platform is evident. It used to be assumed that the fort was Alauna, but historians now assert that it was probably Mediobogdum, 'the fort in the middle of a bow', a name originally thought to belong to the fort at Hardknott. Archaeologists have found evidence of occupation from between c.AD 80 to the fourth century. It was large enough to accommodate around 500 men. Even then Kendal was the gateway to the Lakes, for it is assumed that a road must have connected the fort to the one at Waterhead, Ambleside – and indeed it can still be traced over the passes of Wrynose and Hardknott to the Roman port at Ravenglass. There are signs that a civilian settlement stood outside the fort area.

It was in the twelfth century that the inadequate Norman motte and bailey on Castle Howe was replaced by a castle on a hill to the east of the town. This can be

The remains of Kendal's Norman castle

seen from several vantage points. Much of its masonry had been filched over the centuries, and what we see looks rather like a decayed tooth. All that is left are the remains of a curtain wall and three stunted towers. In the early part of the sixteenth century the castle was owned by Thomas Parr, father of Katherine Parr, the only surviving wife of Henry VIII. Was Katherine born here? So it has long been claimed since the seventeenth century. But in any event after Henry's reign the castle was abandoned to ruin. It is owned by the town and thankfully in recent years has been receiving care.

Richard I gave Kendal a market charter, but the town fell victim to the border lawlessness, and in 1210 the earl of Fife sacked, then burned, the town, allegedly putting all to the sword, and 'sparing neither age nor sex', including those who had sought refuge in the church. Whether the story was an exaggeration or not, raiders certainly did not respect religious establishments and the first church was probably destroyed, for charred timber was found in restored parts of the present parish church, which stands on the site of an earlier incarnation.

Kendal was targeted by Scottish raiders for centuries. The last Scottish incursion, though the town escaped hostilities, happened during the Jacobite rebellions. The rain-sodden, bedraggled highlanders marched with the earl of Derwentwater and Tom Forster, MP for Northumberland, into Kendal on 5 November 1715, preceded by six pipers. King James was proclaimed king at the market cross, then the party procured overnight quarters before moving on to Kirkby Lonsdale. Forster, the main instigator of the rising, called on his grandmother, Mrs Bellingham, who lived in a house in Stramongate, to pay his respects. He was far from welcome. His grandmother, it is said, boxed his ears and called him a popish tool! The northerners were not generally as hostile as the grandmother; the rebellion had a lot of northern sympathy, but petered out through lack of practical support. Mrs Bellingham's house is now a bookshop.

On a late November day, thirty years later, Bonnie Prince Charlie was marching through the town in the second rising of the Jacobites, on their advance to Derby. They came in two divisions, one led by the prince himself on foot, preceded by his hundred pipers. Everyone enjoys a musical parade and the townsfolk turned out to enjoy it. The Scots reported that the townspeople were civil; though many of them were no doubt wondering quite what the pageant was all about.

Later in the same year the Scots were back in retreat and the townspeople had turned against them. Why the change of mood? There was no parade this time. Tales must have been circulating about fighting and retreat. Rumours were circulating that highlanders ate babies, propaganda reminiscent of the First World War. (But note that a large haggis looks rather like a baby's torso!) And weren't all these rebels Roman Catholics out to displace the Protestant king? The duke of Perth arrived ill and in a carriage with two ladies, escorted by 120 horsemen with a mission to link up with reinforcements in Scotland. Rumours had it that one of the ladies was really the prince in disguise. They were attacked by cudgels and stones, and the horsemen were compelled to open fire, killing four. This enraged the crowd more, and four cavalrymen were pulled off their mounts and taken prisoner. The party pushed on to Penrith, but finding their passage to Scotland frustrated, they turned back to meet the prince's forces, which reached the town on 15 December. Hostility seems to have been muted when the Scottish rearguard came through Kendal, led by Lord George Murray with a baggage train. An epic journey over Shap Fell ensued. The prince and his officer, O'Sullivan, at least had something to cheer them – they had found a bottle of cherry brandy in Kendal which helped them on their wintry way to Penrith. Later the duke of Cumberland came through the town in pursuit.

Kendal's past prosperity was built on its being centre of the woollen cloth trade. The town motto sums it up: 'Pannus mihi panis' ('Wool (or woollen cloth) is my bread'). In the sixteenth century bread was in good supply. 'Kendal Cottons' (a combed woollen cloth – nothing to do with the fibre of a Gossypium plant) made blankets and 'Kendal Green' clothing. It was well-known in Shakespeare's time. 'As the devil would have it,' said Falstaff, lying about being mugged: 'three misbegotten knaves, in Kendal green, came at my back, and let drive at me – for it was so dark that thou could'st not see thy hand'. Prince Henry was sceptical. 'Why, how could'st thou know these men in Kendal green, when it was so dark thou could'st not see thy hand?'

Cumbrian wool had long been an important export to Europe and had made its abbeys rich. But gradually more of it was finding its way into Kendal to feed the cloth-making industry. The town specialized in every aspect of the processing of raw wool into various grades of cloth. The fleece was first sorted, then washed. Then it was carded – combed by leather pads set with wire teeth – to clean the wool further and to draw it out for the next process – spinning. Spinning was done in many farmhouses for centuries using a distaff, a stick which held raw wool at its tip and which was pulled down and spun round a weighted spindle. Spinning-wheels of various kinds, and each one required a particular skill, speeded up the process. Then some of the wool, already spun, would have been brought from the surrounding villages and farms. The wool was woven largely by independent craftsmen, either working at home or in rented weaving sheds. The cloth they produced was then washed, dyed and fulled. Fulling involved treading the cloth in a tub of hot water to compress and tighten the fibres. Fulling, however, was also best done in bulk in water-powered fulling mills. Kendal's mill wheels were never short of a head of water, but fulling mills in the surrounding countryside were also used in the production of Kendal cottons. The final process was tenting. The cloth was hung outdoors on tenter-hooks on wooden fences. This was finally to stretch and dry the cloth after washing. The lines of parallel fences, hung with coloured cloth, were a feature of Kendal. Captain Budworth, a hero of the siege of Gibraltar, while travelling in the area in 1792, said, 'The tenter grounds on the side of the hills resemble the vineyards in Spain, and from having much cloth upon them, I should hope trade flourishes.' The poet Gray also remarked, 'I entered Kendal almost in the dark, and could distinguish only a shadow of the castle on a hill, and tenter-grounds spread far and wide round the town, which I mistook for houses.'

Kendal's famed colour was green – made by mixing a dyer's green weed, which produced a yellow, with woad that produced blue. But other colours were also available. The wool that comes from the backs of the fell-hardy Lakeland breed of sheep, the herdwicks, is coarse and wiry and does not readily take dye, so it must have been mixed with other wool – such as swaledale. In fact mixtures were common, and some woollen cloth contained threads of linen, itself a product of several Cumbrian villages. Wool dyed prior to weaving could be used to make patterned cloth. Celia Fiennes, the intrepid lady traveller, stated in 1698 that 'Kendal cotton is used for blankets and the Scots use them for plodds' (plaids). Was Kendal then weaving tartan?

Most of the country folk wore undyed clothing, most probably of the tough herdwick wool. John Peel wore his 'coat so grey'. The Quaker communities, too, thought it vanity to wear dyed clothing. Coats of herdwick grey would last forever, and were fairly waterproof.

Kendal had a reputation for producing rough, cheap clothing. The town's early produce was exempt from the tax on textiles because it was of rough quality and produced in widths much less than the common ell. Later the speciality became blankets for people and for horses. Cloth for army uniforms was also made, and in times of war the trade was very profitable. However, demand grew for finer clothes, and 'Linsey' – wool woven on a cotton warp – was popular, Kendal exporting it to Europe.

One would think that most, if not all, Kendal Cottons came from Kendal, but in fact it just described a sort of cloth; just as tweed may once have been manufactured near the eponymous river, but later became generic.

Kendal stockings were also well known nationally, and large orders came from the military. Knitters were employed in the surrounding area, those from Dent being the best known. Everyone knitted there – men, women and children. Kendal had constant trains of packhorses bringing material in and trade out – at least twenty long trains every week. They linked Kendal with Whitehaven and the west coast, Hawkshead market, Cartmel and Ulverston, Sedbergh, Appleby, Penrith and Carlisle; and covered the long routes to and from Glasgow, York, Hull, Manchester, Liverpool and London.

Until the mid eighteenth century the roads to and from Kendal were very poor, and for miles unusable by carts. Yet Kendal was an important centre in a communications network. The '45 rebellion focused minds on the need for improvements. The Turnpike Act meant that the building and maintenance of roads could be taken away from parochial responsibility and funded by tolls. By the end of the eighteenth century no fewer than nine turnpike roads were connected to the town. The commercial prospects improved as a result.

It could do better. A network of canals were being developed in Britain, and a Kendal to Lancaster canal was planned in 1791, to hook up with Lancashire industry, importing coal and exporting limestone. It ran into problems when finance to construct locks north of Carnforth dried up, and the canal did not ultimately reach Kendal until 1819. It was well used in its heyday, even as a passenger service on a packet boat – 57 miles to Preston and 57 miles back. Each journey took fourteen hours, but this was later improved upon by an express boat, the *Waterwitch*, which moved briskly, changing horses every four miles. That took a mere seven hours – snail's progress by today's standards – but such restful smooth comfort in heated cabins! In 1846 the rail link from Lancaster meant that the canal was no longer viable. The Lancashire end is still in use, however, mainly for recreation, but its link with Cumbria near the boundary was effectively broken by the M6 motorway. Bridging was asked for but the canal was shamefully culverted. Of the 9 km of canal that remain in Cumbria there are plans afoot to clean out and open the 5 km, filled-in section to Kendal, but a submarine would be needed to connect it to Lancaster.

There was another late product of the woollen industry. A carpet weaving mill, an offshoot of the woollen industry, was in production in 1822 and one continues to the present day. The National Trust, some of whose farm tenants still keep herdwick sheep, have been promoting the wool for carpet making. Nothing better could be used. Otherwise, the market for this tough wool has largely disappeared.

Kendal weavers continued to be employed into the mid nineteenth century, with increasing mechanization, and produced some very fine cloth. The American Civil War boosted production, since the cotton famine resulting from it brought new demands for alternative threads. Then towards the end of the century the demand for finer imported materials led to the industry's gradual decline, but not extinction.

Wool was not the sole source of Kendal's bread. There had always been a trade with Scotland for cattle and the town made good use of hide and horns. Tanneries flourished, providing leather for saddlers and glovers, and for shoe- and clog-makers. Cattle horns were made into combs, shoe horns and cutlery handles. There were blacksmiths and metal workers, brewers and barrel makers, wheelwrights and cart makers, rope makers, potters and stonemasons. There were makers of furniture, watches and brushes. Local limestone quarries were worked and produced lime for mortar as well as building blocks. One industry that Kendal became famous for, thanks to trade links with Whitehaven, Lancaster and beyond, was the production of pipe tobacco and, using secret recipes, snuff. As better communications gave access to coal and coke, foundries went into production, engineering farm machinery, laundry machinery and turbines.

The leather industry gave birth to shoe-making in a big way. Two brothers, Robert and John Somervell, opened a factory in the 1840s, not far from the site of the Roman fort, making leather uppers for shoe and boot makers. In the 1860s the firm began to make the whole shoe and became so successful that the factory expanded, eventually spawning the famous 'K' trademark. K shoes were eventually famed for their top-class workmanship and comfort, and as the business thrived new plants opened at Askham and Shap. The firm specialized in producing many fittings and their customers were nationwide. Then the firm was subjected to a take-over in the 1990s, and eventually, probably caused by the import of cheaper footwear, it closed, a horrible bitter loss to the town.

One of the town's most famous products is Kendal mint cake, which developed after the import of West Indian cane sugar. The sweet-making firm of Wiper's claim to have 'invented' the famous energy-provider for athletes, explorers and mountaineers. Two other firms, Quiggin's and Romney's, began production later.

Shackleton took mint cake with him on his Antarctic expedition, but most famously it was consumed by Tensing and Hilary on the top of Everest in 1953. A quotation from Hilary is printed on the wrappers: 'We sat on the snow, looked at the country far below, nibbled Kendal Mint Cake – it was easily the most popular item on our high altitude rations – our only criticism was that we didn't have enough of it'.

Roads and canals were insufficient during the Industrial Revolution. There were discussions about a western railway route to Scotland from the existing line at Preston. Kendal needed to be included in any scheme. The final proposal was a line from Lancaster through Carnforth, up the Lune Gorge and over Shap by Penrith to Carlisle. It would pass through Oxenholme, missing Kendal by two miles. The Bill was given assent in summer 1844, the first sod cut in November and the work completed in two years by the hard work of several thousand navvies, masons and horses. The opening was a grand affair. A decorated train carried the directors and 200 guests from Lancaster to Carlisle at 20 m.p.h. In anticipation, a line had already been completed from Oxenholme to Kendal, and was set to run on to Birthwaite near Windermere. There were great celebrations in Kendal, though, when the main line was completed.

The line was too important to suffer Beeching's axe. Somehow the line from Oxenholme to Windermere was spared. But what happened to Kendal station? The walk up the once busy station approach brings one to the 'quite picturesque' (Pevsner), half-hipped, gabled station building – but it is now let for commercial uses. The way to the station platform is hidden to one side of the approach, as if the railway were ashamed of itself, and it ought to be. The station is reduced to a mere shelter now, and everything looks tawdry and uncared for. According to the railway announcements Oxenholme station is 'Oxenholme, the Lake District', and 'customers' change for Windermere.

The *Westmorland Gazette*, once edited briefly by Thomas de Quincey from 1818, is published in the town. The 'Kendal Gathering' is a great annual festival event in August, when the main streets are graced by a grand torchlight procession and entertainers perform.

Within a modest distance from Kendal is one of the finest viewpoints in the whole of the county. Beginning from All Hallows Lane opposite the town hall the road climbs over the limestone escarpment of Scout Scar in 2 km. A short walk from the car park to the ridge opens up a superb panorama of the Lake District fells.

Five km south of Kendal SIZERGH CASTLE (NT), in hiding west of the A6, has been the home of the Strickland family for 700 years and twenty-seven generations. The land was granted to Gervase Deincourt by Henry II in the twelfth century, passing by marriage to the Stricklands in 1239. Like other land-owning gentry in fourteenth-century Cumbria, the Stricklands had to replace the original house by a pele tower to withstand Scots raids. The tower still stands, 18 m high, with walls 3 m thick.

The Stricklands were long involved in fighting the Scots. In 1297 Walter Strickland recruited 1,000 men to assist Edward I with an invasion of Scotland. He evidently served the cause well for several years, for he was made a Knight of the Bath and granted a Charter of Free Warren, which gave him the exclusive right of killing game on his land, a prerogative normally reserved for the king. A Strickland later fought at Agincourt. But the losing cause was served by the family in the Wars of the Roses and they had to seek a pardon from Edward VI for any 'illegalities and excesses'. The family was not treated so leniently, however, after supporting the Royalists in the Civil War: for their Stuart sympathies they were exiled for eleven years. One of the Stricklands, Francis, was a friend of Prince Charles Stuart (a subversive friend, it was said) and was the only Englishman among his close 'seven men' raising the standard at Glenfinnan at the start of the '45 rebellion. However, he never got further in the advance than Edinburgh, where he died of influenza.

The great hall of the castle was built on to the north-east wall of the pele tower in 1450. There were later Elizabethan additions and alterations. Oak panelling in some rooms dates from this period, as do some exceptionally fine benches and five remarkable chimney pieces. Pevsner comments: 'No other house in England has such a wealth of Early Elizabethan woodwork of high quality. Moreover, it was one carver or one group of carvers that must have been at work over twenty years.' The castle is worth a visit for this display alone.

Also worthy of note are the adze-hewn oak beams in the second floor of the pele tower. The museum on the top floor has much of interest. In season the gardens are magnificent.

South of Sizergh, and east of the roundabout giving access to the M6, some late eighteenth-century gunpowder mills once stood at SEDGWICK by the River Kent, and further east at GATEBECK on Peasey Beck. Why here? Water power was essential, and remoteness an advantage; an abundance of woodland was key too, particularly alder woodland, to provide charcoal, one of the powder's ingredients – 15 per cent. A second ingredient, unrefined saltpetre (75 per cent), was imported first from India, later from Chile; and the third, sulphur (10 per cent), was imported from Italy and Sicily. All of these commodities came through the port of Milnthorpe.

The process involved a series of mills strung along the water source, with space between each for safety, and with blast screens. The ingredients had to be very finely ground and thoroughly mixed. Strict measures were enforced to prevent accidental explosions, including the wearing of leather clothing, ponies having copper shoes, hot flues from the fires being channelled away to a distant chimney. Even so there were always accidents. The powder found a ready local market in the county's mines and quarries. There is little to see now, for on closing their gates, the buildings, and working areas, had to be carefully destroyed, with all metals taken away for scrap, to ensure that no dangerous materials could be left in corners and crannies.

KIRKBY LONSDALE

KIRKBY LONSDALE (*Kirby LONS-dale*) lies south-east of Kendal on the A65, on the road to Skipton. It is one of those delightful, slightly off-track country towns, with a market charter dating back to 1227, and built of the local limestone; which has

Old Kirkby Lonsdale

'Devil's bridge', Kirkby Lonsdale

not had its Georgian character too assiduously 'developed', though a supermarket has appeared on the fringe. The town has two distinct personalities. On Thursday, market day, it bustles with activity as farmers and families from scattered communities converge for business and a 'crack' to catch up on local news. Stalls sit cheek by jowl in the market square and folk jostle in the narrow street. But walking through the churchyard to an alley on the south-east side of the town, you are walking on cobbles into the eighteenth century, into the quiet square of the horsemarket among oddly named streets of neat old houses.

The town sits on a high bank overlooking a bend in the River Lune. The views over this area of the Lune valley are much admired: Ruskin was particularly enthusiastic about them (it was 'one of the loveliest scenes in England – therefore in the world'), and Turner painted a prospect looking towards Howgill and Casterton Fell from the churchyard. The old bridge over the river, now closed to traffic, probably dates from the thirteen century; a bridge was certainly mentioned in documents at that time, and repairs were documented in 1365. Like many old bridges that survived despite the depredations of time, it is known locally as 'Devil's bridge'. The story is that a poor Yorkshire woman (why Yorkshire?) had her cow and horse swept down the Lune in a flood and they finished up on the opposite bank from where she stood. She cursed her misfortune, for they seemed lost forever, and the devil heard her and offered to help. He would build a bridge on condition that eventually he would have possession of the first to cross it. The woman agreed, for her survival depended upon her two beasts. The bridge was quite splendid and she arrived at it with her mongrel dog. The devil was sure that she would cross to collect her animals; but she then took a bun out of her bag and threw it across the bridge. The dog ran after it, and the furious devil disappeared in a puff of smoke.

A new bridge, built by the highway authority, functional and not as beautiful as the devil's, replaces it on the main road. The old bridge end has become a meeting place for motorcyclists who congregate in great numbers on Sundays. At one time the riders were mainly wild young men, but nowadays most are civilized, mature and even elderly – 'born again' motorcyclists, acquiring wonderfully expensive machinery, presumably out of reach of the less affluent young.

The run of the River Lune here is a gorgeous sight and has long been a favoured spot for anglers. Large salmon have been caught in the deep pool in the gorge. The run has declined from what it used to be; heavies are scarce, but some ten-pounders are not unusual. To get five-day permits anglers need to be staying in the village, and why not? Night fishing used to be practised here but was quite dangerous. Canon Rawnsley had his say about it:

He who goes fishing in the Lune
Without the aid of sun or moon,
Needs not a rod, but wants a stick
About his back, the lunatic!

The church of St Mary the Virgin stands near the site of a Saxon church. That church with its lands was given to the abbey of St Mary at York around the end of the eleventh century by the baron of Kendal, Ivo de Taillebois. The land, and the subsequent Norman church built on it, was held by the abbey until the dissolution, when it came through the Crown to Trinity College, Cambridge.

The interior is a surprise. Even though damage was inflicted by the nineteenth-century 'restorers', this church's interior still presents one of the most impressive early Norman displays in Cumbria. Immediately striking are the sturdy columns and the arches on the north side of the nave, the diamond ornamentation on the columns being a fine example of the style current between 1096 and 1130. This dating is assumed because of the identical carving seen on the massive pillars at Durham cathedral, and at Lindisfarne, built during the same period. Church scholars speculate about how the design came to be repeated here – whether because the same masons were used, or a group of itinerants from the same school. They raise another question. Why did such impressive columns feature on the north of the naves when, the rest of the nave's arcading is so much simpler?

It is assumed that, having built the north arcade columns, the cost of continuing in the same style and scale proved too much. Restorers in 1866 discovered that the Norman arcading had once extended beyond the present structure, and past damage by fire was evident. This burning could date to the period of Scottish raids in the fourteenth century. An explanatory plan fixed to a pillar outlines the main additions and alterations to the structure.

The tower has been altered several times: the lower part is Norman, and the tower foot has a late Norman portal. The church was extended eastwards in the thirteenth century. The pulpit is elaborately carved oak, originally three-tier, but the Victorian improvers disliked it and cut it down to its present size. The chancel suffered too, and an iron screen was added around the choir. The fourteenth-century font has a strange history. It was 'rescued' by a neighbouring farmer from a disused chapel which stood at Killington within Kirkby Lonsdale parish. He used it as a feed trough for his animals. It was presented to the church in the 1930s and has been used in baptisms since. One wonders why it had to be reconsecrated though? Didn't a rather important child once lay in just such an unconsecrated thing?

An octagonal gazebo in the churchyard, moved from the vicarage grounds, is depicted in one of Turner's pictures of the Lune. Beneath the yard winds a scenic riverside path. Country market towns sometimes give the impression that they cannot make up their minds whether they are town or village: 'God made the country; man the town; but the devil made the country town.' Here the devil only made the bridge.

Just north of Kirkby Lonsdale on the east side of the River Lune is the hamlet of CASTERTON, the former site of a girls' school for the daughters of clergy that were moved here from Cowan Bridge in Lancashire, 3.5 km away. This was the infamous school featured in *Jane Eyre*, in which girls faced a harsh regime. Charlotte Brontë stayed there for an unhappy year. There is still a girls' school here, but of course nothing like its predecessors; the only suffering there now is over exams. The neighbouring church of Holy Trinity was built at this time. Inside, if the church by chance is open, look out for the wall paintings by James Clarke featuring bible stories, and in the chancel superior ones by Henry Holiday.

A little further north, on the opposite side of the river, is Underley Hall, now a college. Built in 1825 in the Jacobean style for Alexander Nowell, it was purchased fifteen years later, together with the estate, by William Thompson, who was a director of the Bank of England, a wealthy ironmaster, alderman of London and later MP for the county.

BARBON is the next hamlet to the north, with an 1898 church admirably superior to most built around that time. The road from here climbs through Barbondale between Barbon Fell and Middleton Fell, in delightfully remote moorland, dropping down to Gawthrop a short distance from Dent village. A truly great route.

SEDBERGH

The road from Kirkby Lonsdale by the Lune reaches the village of SEDBERGH (*SED-bra* or *SEB-ra*), while the busier road from Kendal to Sedbergh is a drunken, twisting switchback of a journey through farming country, and before it crosses the M6 it passes below the gyrating monsters of Lambrigg Wind Farm. Wind farms can seem hideously intrusive on the landscape but this one does not seem too out of place. After bridging the M6 the road continues contorting its way upwards to what feels like an alpine village, but Sedbergh ('Setberg' = old Norse for flat-topped hill) is but 113 m above sea-level. It stands below the shapely Howgills and Brant Fell, which climb to above 609 m and overlook the village streets. These fells are of the Silurian slates and shales similar to the rocks south of Windermere; yet Sedbergh is properly Yorkshire, and noted for its carboniferous limestone. Indeed the village is in the Yorkshire Dales National Park; but it was annexed by Cumbria county during the boundary revisions in the seventies. The Howgills offer some exhilarating hill walks. The fells have few crags and cliffs – the exception is Cautley Crag on the fells' eastern side. Here is Cautley Spout, a 200 m cascade. The falls can be reached at lower levels from a footpath from the Cross Keys Hotel, 6 km from Sedbergh on the Kirkby Stephen road.

Only earthworks can now be seen of Sedbergh's Norman motte and bailey castle to the east, that once dominated the market town. The village has some handsome seventeenth- and eighteenth-century buildings. The narrow main street has a character that is typical Yorkshire Dales. Until recent years it was cobbled, which was a major part of the town's attraction. Now, sadly, it is buried in tarmac. There are features typical of the modern country town – the ubiquitous estate agents, a Chinese takeaway, a chippy, and some very decent cafés and shops, as well as a helpful and friendly Yorkshire Dales National Park information centre.

The church of St Andrew exhibits its twelfth-century origins but has gone through many alterations and additions. The east window is striking, less than a century old, but it shows a whole picture of St Andrew and his brother Simon Peter as fishermen being called by Jesus to become 'fishers of men'. One great feature worthy of appreciation is an 1866 restoration of the woodwork on the pews, stalls and pulpit undertaken by the famous Lancaster carpentry and cabinet-making firm of Waring and Gillow.

The main street, Sedbergh

Sedbergh is the home of the very famous boys' public school founded in 1525, in fact it is the town's major feature. Horrors! Can it be true that it is now co-ed? The school building of 1716 is now the village library, and the modern school lies to the south of the town.

At nearby Briggflatts to the west a Quaker meeting house dates from 1674, a time when the area had a strong Quaker following. The interior has seen little change, and includes a pen where the Quakers' dogs were kept, for members attending for worship were shepherds. George Fox, founder of the movement, records a meeting of followers at Brigflatts in 1677: '... a great concourse of other people came; it was thought that there were five or six hundred people. A good meeting it was, wherein truth was largely declared.' It was not George Fox's first visit to the area. The building is one of the first in the area to be roofed with stone flags. Most of the other houses, including Sedbergh's church, were originally thatched.

North-west of Sedbergh, Firbank Fell has more Quaker connections. In a natural amphitheatre on this fell in 1652 the charismatic George Fox addressed a crowd of over a thousand people, most of whom had been at Sedbergh Fair. A memorial tablet marks the spot. Asked why he preached on a mountain and not in the church, he replied, 'The steeple-house, and the ground wherein it stands, is no more holy than this mountain.'

By Ingmire Hall, near the River Lune, sits a small, sadly redundant church – hardly a 'steeple house', more of a barn. This is St Gregory's, not at all old, but worth a visit for its special ambience. It was built by Miss Frances Upton (d. 1876) of the hall, and designed to be 'a plain building of studied ugliness'. Not true; the furnishings, in local oak by estate carpenters, are excellent; the stained glass exceptional. There is a local natural history window by George Smith, and a window depicting Justice and Fortitude by William Morris, and two more figures of peace by the same artist. A small window in the north wall depicts the arms of Upton and Ingmire. It is a very pleasant place to sit in quietly and enjoy.

DENT

DENT, or 'Dent town', is a small village at the head of the dale, south of Sedbergh. The road to it is 8 km of delight, though the driver of a vehicle may disagree as he must cope with very narrow stretches with passing places, as well as blind bends. This is prime dales country, enclosed by high green fell sides netted with walls, and scattered with very typical stone barns and farmhouses.

Cobbled village street, Dent, with Sedgwick memorial stone

Clog dancers, Dent

Dent is sought out as a very distinctive dales village, still with narrow cobbled streets – Yorkshire Dales that is; confusingly, we are still in Cumbria, but within the Yorkshire Dales National Park. Perhaps because it is somewhat off the beaten track it has escaped being vulgarized by too much commercialism. This is unique – please let it never be defiled! Cars are a boon in seeking out the countryside, but also a curse when they cause jams. An alternative approach to the village for walkers is to travel by rail, on the Settle to Carlisle line, but because of the hilly terrain, the station is 3 km away. But the dale makes for great walking.

One of Dent's greatest sons was Adam Sedgwick (1785–1873), the son of the local church vicar who went on to become a pioneering geologist. After being educated at Dent and Sedbergh school, then Trinity College, Cambridge, he was appointed Woodwardian professor of geology, a post that he transformed from a mere sinecure and held until shortly before his death. He was a friend of Wordsworth, and changed the poet's views about the origins of the landscape; indeed in the 1842 edition of his guide Wordsworth included three letters on geology from the professor. A memorial to Sedgwick in Shap granite stands by the church.

Dent produced the best millstones for gunpowder works, as they contained no iron pyrites likely to cause sparks. But it was wool that made Dent. Southey referred to the 'terrible knitters of Dent', and everyone knitted – young old and both sexes – and they were terribly good at it. They even clicked away in church – the minister had to ask them to put down their needles before saying 'Let us pray'. The church looks rather large for the village, and there are also substantial-looking non-conformist chapels. The explanation is that the pre-nineteenth-century parish population was much larger than today. Early in that century poverty drove many into the mill towns of Yorkshire and Lancashire, and others emigrated. The church has Norman features in the pillars and the arched doorway, now blocked off in the north wall, but the whole structure has become much altered after a long cycle of dilapidation and restoration. The original tower was damaged by an earth tremor and replaced; Adam Sedgwick had recognized the occasional shudder as the 'Dent fault' that created the dale's landscape.

A Quaker in the seventeenth century remarked that Dent had fourteen alehouses, and that the church priest was familiar with them all. Now only three pubs survive, but they are all of good quality.

South of the road from Kendal to Sedbergh, next to the award-winning motorway service area, is Killington reservoir. This was made to supply a reserve of water for the Kendal canal and now offers quiet recreation and a habitat for water birds.

West of the motorway and still south of the Kendal road is NEW HUTTON. The 1828 church has little to remark on except the two grand lifelike stone hounds on the pillars of the churchyard gates. Where did they come from?

OLD HUTTON is to the south. Its church was rebuilt in 1873, its only remnant of the fourteenth century being the window in the organ chamber. But the church treasures a beautiful silver chalice made c. 1500, patterned with foliage and with an engraved crucifix.

HUTTON ROOF was mentioned in the Domesday Book as 'Hotun' and 'ruf' may have been added in later medieval times when it came into the possession of Rudolph. It is west of Kirkby Lonsdale. The village church is neat and nineteenth century, and lies on the site of a fourteenth-century chapel. In the chancel two memorial tablets from 1913 commemorate the village's vicar, who earned the Victoria Cross in the First World War. The Revd Theodore Hardy spent a great part of the conflict in the trenches. In the autumn of 1917 he was awarded the DSO for bringing in wounded under fire, and a month later he was awarded the MC for helping stretcher-bearers bring in wounded, also under fire. It was the next year that, with no regard for his safety, he helped to dig out men buried by shell fire, extricating one man who was completely buried, and organizing and helping a stretcher team carry back a wounded man from an abandoned area. More valour went unrecorded, but he was awarded the VC 'for most conspicuous bravery and devotion to duty'. A little before the end of the war he was killed.

The village hall is worth a mention for it was built by the local volunteers in the 1980s, when grants were obtained for the materials. This is the sort of cooperative venture that happened in centuries past, and is a great thing for bonding a community. Towering over the hamlet to the west is Hutton Roof's hill. It is protected as a Site of Special Scientific Interest because of its exposed limestone pavement, with its water-worn 'grykes', or fissures, holding specialized flora, including some rare species. The woodland areas have the characteristic flora that flourishes in lime-rich soils: herb paris, primrose, cowslip, false oxlip, orchids, wood anemones and bluebells. As well as the common trees there are buckthorn and spindle. The area is particularly special for its butterflies, such as the scarce high brown, and the pearl-bordered fritillaries, the brimstone, green hairstreak and grayling. Part of the area is a reserve managed by Cumbria Wildlife Trust.

Hutton Roof Crags, scheduled as a Site of Special Scientific Interest, rise 245 m above the village to the west. Some 99 ha of it is a nature reserve in the care of CWT and has a section of limestone pavement, some ancient and some new woodland, again with typical limestone flora, including uncommon species. The fauna includes roe deer, red squirrels, butterflies, slow worms, lizards and newts.

BURTON-IN-KENDAL is at the southern end of the Cumbrian boundary with Lancashire. Burton was a staging-post in coaching days, a place where horses were changed and refreshments taken in two inns. Now the motorway (M6) passes close by, and since there is a service area for travellers on it at this point, it would appear that the tradition continues. Burton-in-Kendal (not to be confused with Lancashire's Burton-in-Lonsdale not all that far away) is an attractive place of long standing, mentioned in the Domesday Book. Few of the present buildings are very old but those with projecting storeys show how a building technique has lasted long beyond the period of its general usage. As in so many old villages, the street and yard names are intriguingly resonant: Neddy Hill, Tanpits Lane, Cocking Yard, Boon Walks.

Burton was once noted for its busy corn market, established in 1661, but this declined when communication with the larger towns improved in the nineteenth century. The neat marketplace surrounded by attractive buildings contains an eighteenth-century cross, and the recesses in the steps were for leg irons. The

Norman church, mentioned in the twelfth century, was another given by Ivo de Taillebois to St Mary's Abbey at York, and was finally heavily restored in 1844 and 1872.

North-west of Kendal and touching the National Park boundary is the village of BURNESIDE (*BUR-ny-side*) with busy James Cropper's paper works that have been in production for over a century. Their speciality is coloured paper and card, and craft and art workers will find the shop an Aladdin's cave. The church of St Oswald is nineteenth century, in the Decorated style. On a nearby hill is an obelisk erected in 1814 by James Bateman of nearby Tolson Hall, to celebrate 'William Pitt – the Pilot who weathered the storm' – the storm being Napoleon's defeat. Burneside Hall is part fourteenth century with a partly ruined pele tower, walls and gatehouse (not open to the public).

CHAPTER SEVENTEEN

The National Park: Keswick and the North-west

The north-west quarter of the National Park is where the Lake District's popularity began. Derwent Water, ringed by its hills and mountains, and the dramatic scenery of Borrowdale, seized the imagination of the first tourists: the artists and writers of the eighteenth century. The views over Derwent Water are sublime, and there are five other lakes all with their own unique character. For walkers there is a wealth of exhilarating options unrivalled anywhere, among the many hundreds of footpaths in the placid valleys, or up among the free access of the high fells. We start at its south-east corner.

The old border line between Cumberland and Westmorland crosses the pass of Dunmail Raise, on the main road from Keswick to Grasmere and Ambleside. An old saying, south of the Raise, states that, 'Nowt good comes o'er t Raise,' an undoubted reference to Scottish raiders coming this way. On the other hand Keswick folk have been known to quote the same saying.

After one crosses Dunmail Raise from the south, a descent opens up a glimpse of Thirlmere. On the way down, let into the wall end on the right is a memorial to a faithful horse, easier to read a few decades ago; now, in seeking it, one risks being knocked down by traffic. It reads:

30th 9mo 1843
Fall'n from his fellow's side,
  The steed beneath is lying:
In harness here he died;
  His only fault was dying.
WB

It was William Ball of Rydal who mourned the passing of his horse.

The descent northward into old Cumberland enters the Scandinavian landscape surrounding THIRLMERE. Thirlmere is a lake made into a reservoir, fringed by conifer forest; it is not a true Lake District scene, but an alien imposition. Having said that, the valley has its beauty. The lighter greens of larches break up the darker greens of spring; and the larches again glow gold in the autumn. And if the lake is at its normal level, and not drawn down to produce the sight of wide dead shorelines, it has elegance. The dam is not a glaring intrusion, hardly visible until a close encounter. Some might object to the areas of dark conifers, but gradually, native hardwoods are replacing the introduced species around the lake.

In 1867 an amazing suggestion was floated that Ullswater could supply London with water. Impossible? The Victorians could do anything. That London scheme did not happen, but Manchester had designs on the Lake District, and after looking at Ullswater and Windermere they thought seriously about Thirlmere.

At that time Thirlmere was 5 km long, with a narrow waist in the centre crossed by a bridge on stone piers. Thirlmere is a late name; previously it was Laythes Water, then Leathes Water. It occupied about two thirds of the valley, now wholly taken up by the new lake.

High fells surround the valley: Helvellyn's long massif covers the whole of the east side, while to the west Wythburn (*WYE-burn*) Fell, Armboth, High Seat and Castlerigg Fells wall in the west. There were once several settlements in the valley, one at the south end being strangely named The City. The inhabitants were fairly self-sufficient. Sheep farming was the main activity, and one could find the usual blacksmith and clogger, a mill and a miller, all probably also having a few sheep; someone would likely produce ale – probably one or more of the three inns, the Nag's Head and the Cherry Tree at Wythburn at the southern end, and the King's Head at Thirlspot at the northern end. The fells provided peat for the fires, and the lake supplied fish – mainly trout and pike.

A well-trodden trading route passed through the valley, and the three inns served the many travellers. The Lakes' poets, in their journeys between Grasmere and Keswick, knew the road very well. A rivalry sprung up between the inn owners. The story is told of the landlord at the King's Head answering a knock at the door in the early hours. Having got out of bed, he hears a voice calling, 'Where is the Nag's Head?' Angrily, he answers, 'On your shoulders!' and slams the door. Over the door, early in the nineteenth century, was the legend:

John Stanley lives here and sells good ale,
Come in and drink before it goes stale,
John succeedeth his father Peter,
In't ould man's time it was never better.

The intrepid Captain Budworth, the one-armed veteran of the siege of Gibraltar and the Lake District's first recreational fell walker, was happy to record the hospitality he and his guide received from 'chatty old women' at the Cherry Tree, in his 1792 *A Fortnight's Ramble to the Lakes*. Coming down from Helvellyn:

> ... between ten and eleven we found ourselves in the high road, and tript lightly to the Cherry Tree ... they gave us breakfast fit for labouring men; we had mutton, ham, eggs, buttermilk, whey, tea, bread and butter, and they asked us if we chose to have any cheese, all for seven pence a piece. Don't imagine, good reader, that we gluttonised, we did not forget our repast upon Helvellyn – however we did our duty at this second breakfast. Two grandmothers were in the kitchen, one was employed in nursing, the other in toasting bread and butter, and the landlady in spreading the table. ... I mention these to make known how healthful and cheery they live under the Cherry Tree.

The style of Wordsworth's poem 'The Waggoner' reminds one of Robbie Burns. A man takes shelter on a stormy night, at the Cherry Tree, and finds that a Cumberland 'Merry Neet' is already in full swing. He joins the throng:

> `Blithe souls and lightsome hearts have we,
> Feasting at the CHERRY TREE!'
> This was the outside proclamation,
> This was the inside salutation;
> What bustling-jostling-high and low!
> A universal overflow!
> What tankards foaming from the tap!
> What stores of cakes in every lap!
>
> `Tis who can dance with greatest vigour–
> `Tis what can be most prompt and eager;
> As if it heard the fiddle's call,
> The pewter clatters on the wall;
> The very bacon shows its feeling,
> Swinging from the smoky ceiling!

Wordsworth must have remembered 'Merry Neets' from his youth. He was far too serious to attend one in adulthood.

The poet John Keats stayed at the Nag's Head in 1818 while on a walking tour.

There were two large houses in the valley. Dale Head Hall was originally a fortified tower, then altered into an elegant house by the owner, Adam Laythes.

George Fox, founder of the Quakers, records in his journal that he dropped in here on fellow Quaker Thomas Laythes in 1663 and 'we had a fine opportunity to be refreshed together'. The other large house was Armboth House on the west side of the lake. The only church was at Wythburn, Wordsworth's 'Wythburn's modest house of prayer/ As lowly as the lowliest dwelling' in 'The Waggoner'. Standing high, with a new school building nearby, the church managed to survive the flood.

Thirlmere was lauded for its beauty. Coleridge wrote in his notebook in October 1803: 'O Thirlmere! – let me somehow or other celebrate the world in thy mirror,' and he goes on to describe the variety of scenery and the reflected colours of fields and trees:

> Conceive all possible varieties of Form, Fields, & Trees, naked or ferny Crags – ravines, behaired with Birches – Cottages, smoking chimneys, dazzling wet places of small rock-precipices – dazzling castle windows in the reflection – all these within a divine outline in a mirror of 3 miles distinct vision! ... All this in bright lightest yellow, yellow-green, green, crimson, and orange! The single Birch Trees hung like trestles of SeaWeed – the Cliffs like organ pipes! – and when a little Breath of Air spread a delicious Network over the Lake, all these colours seemed then to float on, like the reflections of the rising or setting Sun.

Coleridge's son, Hartley, was also a talented young man and wrote of Wythburn church:

> Humble it is and very meek and low
> And speaks its purpose with a single bell,
> But God himself and He alone can know
> If spiry temples please Him half so well.

Although the main occupation of the valley residents was farming there were also one or two small mines seeking ores of lead, iron and copper, and quarries where building stone and roofing slates were produced. The most productive mine was high above Wythburn, dug into the side of Helvellyn. Wythburn lead mine was worked for forty-seven years before the coming of the Manchester Corporation scheme. During its time it employed miners from Cornwall, as well as Cumbrians. It was a difficult mine to work, having levels above 600 m on the fiendishly steep, inhospitable mountainside. In bad winter weather the ore could be frozen solid, and some of the miners would find it difficult to get to work, as some lived in Grasmere, and others beyond the foot of Thirlmere. Transport of the ore was a herculean task. It had to be lowered down the mountainside on mules, pack by pack, to waiting carts that were driven to the smelting mills: round Helvellyn to the Greenside Mine complex, or over to Alston, or even to the Solway to be shipped to North Wales. In 1863 matters were improved by the building of a 550 m-long incline: the roped tubs of ore, controlled at a winding house, ran down this on rails. A water-powered crushing mill had been constructed at the foot of the incline. Several mining companies were involved in the mine over the years as the profits waxed and waned. Then the final blow came with the passing of the Manchester Corporation's bill, and the land and mines came under Manchester's possession. Lead mining had to cease, as it would pollute the reservoir. One estimate of the lead and silver produced over the years is 1,500 tons – not that great. The mining companies had always been aware of the great profitability of the Greenside mines on the other side of Helvellyn, and hoped to reach the same source of ore.

Manchester Corporation promoted its bill to flood the valley in 1876. The project had been well researched, the engineering works detailed, and costs carefully estimated. The lake could be raised by 50 ft (15.24 m), increasing its size to around 800 acres (324 ha). The embankment (dam) would be 286 yards (261.5 m) in length, and 61 ft (18.6 m) high. The catchment area from the surrounding fells amounted to 11,000 acres (4,453.46 ha) and the council would need to purchase the whole. Two new roads would have to be built above the waterline, the main one on the east under Helvellyn, and another on the western side. The water would be drawn from a straining well on the east shore, and the first part of its route to Manchester would be through a tunnel bored through Dunmail Raise. The water's journey to Manchester would then continue along tunnels, pipes and 'cut and cover'. The height of the valley meant that the water could flow all the way by gravity.

The investigations of the catchment area by Manchester Council members a year earlier amounted to a farce. Five members, including John Harwood, who was later to become Manchester's chairman, set out first to look at Ullswater; then on foot, clad in city clothes and footwear, they planned to walk over the flank of Helvellyn by Sticks Pass to Legburthwaite at Thirlmere's foot. All might have been well, but incredibly they lost the way and ended up on Helvellyn's summit! Councillor George Booth was in trouble and had to ride the horse they had brought with them to carry equipment. At one stage the horse, and Councillor Booth, had to be rescued from a bog. Having reached the summit they decided to descend to Wythburn, rather than Legburthwaite. This was a questionable decision, since though it is somewhat shorter, the descent is very steep, and not surprisingly two of the members fell on the way down, receiving cuts and bruises, while George Booth and the horse took a wider route. The party, minus Booth, arrived at the Nag's Head at 10 p.m. nursing their wounds, and had to wait for three hours while transport was arranged to take them on to their Keswick hotel. They were lucky that none was more seriously hurt.

A second visit was just as foolhardy. The party of councillors had arranged to ascend Seat Sandal on the east side of Dunmail Raise, where, they were assured, they would have a good view of the catchment area. They set off at 3 p.m., but on reaching the summit they were hit by a snowstorm and freezing wind. Again they were clad in city clothes, and carried no food. The guide, usually, it was said, quite competent, made the extraordinary decision to take the party down to Ullswater – a very much longer walk. Was it because it was more sheltered from the worst of the weather than on the descent to Wythburn? In any event he got lost on the way. They arrived at last at Ullswater at 9 p.m., again lucky to be alive. Here they managed to hire transport to get them to Portinscale, where they arrived at two o'clock in the morning.

The scheme aroused some heated controversy, with bishops lining up on both sides – the 'vandals' and the 'sentimentalists'. According to the bishop of Manchester: '... if it had been made by the Almighty expressly to supply the densely populated district of Manchester with pure water, it could not have been more exquisitely designed for the purpose'. By contrast the bishop of Carlisle objected to:

> the substitution of engineering contrivance and utilitarianism for nature in her most primitive and untouched beauty ... May Cottonopolis be sent nearer home for its water supply and not interfere with the public pleasure in things on which it has itself never set any value; the solemnity of solitude, the unruffled aspect of nature, the glories of mountain, and the peacefulness of the mere.

Manchester's chairman had his say, too:

> Nature has been at work for ages destroying her most primitive and untouched beauty. Perhaps [the bishop of Carlisle] prefers the swamps and bogs which nature always tends to make whenever she has the chance (and never removes again except with great convulsions) to the artificial conversion of them into dry land.

It should be explained that the Victorian's had an abhorrence of undrained land, thinking the dampness unhealthy and the source of fevers. 'Sinks of putrefaction', as Gilpin had remarked earlier.

The scheme was opposed by many through a Thirlmere Defence Association, eventually including many of the literary personalities of the time: John Ruskin, Thomas Carlyle, Matthew Arnold, William Morris and a founder member of the National Trust, Canon Rawnsley, the incumbent at Crosthwaite, Keswick.

Manchester was not getting a good press. In fact it could be said that the controversy sparked the beginning of conservation movements – the Thirlmere Defence Association led indirectly to the National Trust, and the campaign for National Parks. The *Spectator* wrote in September 1877:

> For our parts, we have always held that one of the most precious inheritances of the people of England is the mountain scenery of England, and we believe that even very great sacrifices should be made to keep its beauty intact, more even for the sake of the toiling millions of our great cities than for the benefit of the countryside specially threatened. England, with its lake scenery placed at the cruel mercy of such improvers as these, would be a country with its heart of rest and peace cut out of it. Parliament, we hope, may see this as clearly as it will see the sanitary side of the question. Indeed what is more truly sanitary to a busy people than the solitude and loveliness of the few natural gardens in which they can forget the thick atmosphere and the incessant noise of city life?

But the council was already making approaches to local landowners with hopes of purchase. One of these was Sir Harry Vane, lord of the manor of Wythburn. He eventually agreed a sale price, after bargaining, of £52,000, more than twice the original offer. It was then a matter of persuading the other landowners to sell. The parliamentary Bill received royal assent in May 1879 while negotiations continued.

Dale Head Hall and its estate, on the east side of the lake, was owned by an absentee, George Stanger Leathes, who was living in Australia. He agreed to sell. The owner of the other large house and estate, Armboth House, on the lake's west side, was not so easy to persuade. Countess Ossalinksy, an English heiress with roots in the Thirlmere valley, was the widow of a Polish aristocrat. She held out for a good price, to be settled by independent arbitration. She eventually got £70,447, and the corporation would have to buy the sheep on her tenants' farms. Then her tenants were given notice to leave. Her sale resulted in a collapse of opposition from the more minor landowners. The last large owner who held out for a good price was Lord Lonsdale, who owned land at Dunmail Raise. The Bill went through its readings and became law. Hundreds of labourers, some with families in tow, arrived in the area and most had to be accommodated in temporary huts. White Moss Common, by Rydal Water, now a popular picnic area, was the site of one encampment; another was set up on the bleakness of Dunmail Raise; and on the side of the Thirlmere itself at Armboth, which scattered beyond the valley foot. Some dormitory huts for unmarried men accommodated up to thirty. Others obtained lodgings in the valley and in Grasmere.

The dam construction would not present as big a problem as the tunnelling and digging-out of the Straining Well. Even using drills powered by the new air-compressor system, and dynamiting, the work in the Lake District's hard volcanic rock proved slow and difficult. An added hazard was the faults in the rock, which meant that the workers had to be aware of the danger of rock falls. The tunnels had to be large enough to receive a lining of bricks and a cement floor to secure smooth flow. The work continued over twenty-four hours a day, in eight-hour shifts.

The dam was built with two walls, the one at the lake face of millstone grit blocks from Lancashire, and the outer one of sandstone from across the Solway at Dumfries. The filling in-between was of huge granite boulders lodged with a cement mix. The dimensions are 17.7 m high, 261 m long, 15 m thick at the base, and 5.6 m at the top. The road on the dam parapet was 5 m wide, 2 m above the high-water mark. A valve house, designed to look like medieval architecture (or Manchester's odd idea of medieval), was constructed to ensure that an agreed amount of water would be fed to maintain a supply in St John's Beck. The Straining Well building was also designed to look like a kind of medieval tower.

When the dam was completed the settlements of Armboth, what was called 'the city' and others around the lake were evacuated as the water levels rose by 15 m. Only Wythburn church, the school, and the nearby pub, the Nag's Head, were left as they were above water level. (The Nag's Head and the school were later demolished.) The new lake was to hold 9,000 million gallons of water, of which 50 million gallons per day could be released.

The survivor – Wythburn church

The corporation had realigned the main road on the Helvellyn side, and engineered another on the opposite side of the lake. The lake was 167.6 m above sea-level, and the 154.5-km line of the tunnelling and piping to Manchester was finely calculated and a great engineering feat – a feat achieved wholly by gravity, with a fall of 20.4 cm in every km. But the valley was transformed, and Chairman Harwood was proud of it.

> Is there anything hideous in the handsome embankment we have formed? Is there one of you who thinks that jaded men and women, who seek restoration to health and strength in the quiet contemplation of the unspeakable beauties of nature, will be deterred from seeking all they need in this sequestered region? – No a thousand times no!

'Trespassers will be Prosecuted' notices were then erected round the lake!

The official opening on Friday, 12 October 1894 was a grand affair. The reservoir should have been opened by the Prince of Wales, but he had to decline, so the ceremony was instead officiated by the man who had been one of the main instigators – Alderman Sir John James Harwood. The dignitaries came by special train to Windermere, and from there were paraded in horse-drawn conveyances in front of cheering spectators at Ambleside and Grasmere. The reception committee at the Straining Well greeted them at 2 p.m.

One great puzzle is why the great champion of opposition to the scheme and a stout defender of natural scenery, and later founder of the National Trust, Revd Hardwicke Rawnsley, changed sides. So great was his conversion that he was among the officials at the ceremony, and opened it by offering a prayer: 'We bless Thee, O Heavenly Father, for the love that inspired this vast design, the wisdom that planned and oversaw, the patience that endured to its completeness.' Speeches followed, one by the lord mayor, and another a long one, by Alderman Harwood.

At last the hydraulic machinery was operated, to release water into the Straining Well. Then the party left for a celebration lunch and more speeches. Canon Rawnsley, again, praised Harwood – once his enemy – in rather sickening terms:

> For you had gauged the future,
> Felt the stress
> Of that great city's toil and thirst
> And strife.
> And when men's tongues were
> Clamorous and loud [including Rawnsley's?],

> You held high commune with
>   The silent cloud.
> You trusted the wild Atlantic waves
>   To bless.
> And claimed from Cumbrian hills
>   Their gift of life.

The next day Sir John Harwood stood in Albert Square, Manchester, in front of a crowd, to officially receive Thirlmere's water. He was presented with an illuminated address and a golden key with which he opened a valve. The crowd cheered as good pure water rose up in a fountain. The police band struck up the national anthem and the church bells pealed. Two days later it was Monday, wash day, and some Lancashire houses, at least, had their linen washed in water from Helvellyn.

The objections continued afterwards, but to no avail. Thirlmere valley for a time resembled a landscape on the moon. It was necessary to use trees to stabilize the slopes, and some 2,000 acres (810 ha) of conifers were planted from 1908. Footpaths were left open to Helvellyn summit, and on the west shore to Armboth Fells and by Launchy Gill, but access to the lake was strictly barred. It took twelve years for the lake to fill to capacity.

Those who remembered the old lake could not accept what had happened. W.G. Collingwood, writing bitterly in his *The Lakes Counties* guidebook from the early twentieth century, said it all:

> Thirlmere has no expanse, but it once was the richest in story and scenery of all the Lakes. The old charm of its shores has quite vanished, and the sites of its legends are hopelessly altered, so that the walk along either side is a mere sorrow to any one who cared for it before; the sham castles are an outrage, and the formality of the roads, beloved of car-drivers and cyclists, deforms the hill-sides like a scar on a face.

For a century nobody thought of challenging the council's right to grow any trees they liked. In fact an agreement had been breached to plant only native trees around the lake shores. Then a private individual took up the challenge in 1985. Mrs Susan Johnson, an active conservationist, was also daughter of the Revd H.H. Symonds, the author of a 1920s classic *Walking in the Lake District* and founder of the Friends of the Lake District. She took the authority to court and won. As a result the council had to agree to increase the planting of indigenous trees, and to soften the hard lines of the plantation boundaries.

In the 1970s, after more efficient methods of filtration and purification had been installed, the shore of the lake could be opened to the public, and even the launching of non-powered craft permitted. This was announced in a ceremony in the presence of the media, nowhere near as grand as the official opening. Were there red faces when it was pointed out that, although the lake shores were officially open, the nasty 'Trespassers will be Prosecuted' signs remained still in place? Over the long time of their presence they had blended into the scenery.

Access to the shore is on the west side and part of the east (most of the east side is too near the road), and new footpaths offer pleasant walks. The position of Armboth House, the valley's largest to be demolished, can be identified near a car park by the remaining monkey puzzle tree (or Chile pine) that stands in what was the garden. What then happened to its ghosts? Armboth farm was said to be haunted. Tales abounded of a nocturnal marriage and a murder, of strange lights appearing at windows and shadowy figures roaming the night. Certainly people talk of the black dog of Thirlmere. Whenever it is seen swimming the lake it is a portent of something awful. The surviving Dale Head Hall, opposite, also had a reputation, before Manchester Corporation smartened it up for the junketing of councillors and holidays for the mayor. A murder occurred there too, and a strange fire in the night sometimes blazed above the trees, but no sign of scars or ashes were found afterwards in the light of day.

There is a herd of red deer on the estate. To avoid the deer's expanding population in an area of limited food resource, there has to be a culling policy. Even so, in 2002, to the surprise of residents and visitors, part of the herd descended into Grasmere. Commendable efforts are being made by the authority to aid the population of red squirrels and to keep out the greys.

HELVELLYN'S WEST FACE

The great west flank of HELVELLYN (*Hel-VELL-in*) looms over the side of the valley. Helvellyn attracts more walkers than any other mountain in the Lakes, and deservedly so. Nearly every Lakeland enthusiast feels a need to climb the mountain. Many who struggle to its summit at 950 m are not habitual high fell walkers, and afterwards will regard the climb as their great adventure, for they may never climb a mountain again. Perhaps it is the intriguing name that fires people's imaginations. It has a barbaric ring to it, and is undoubtedly Celtic. But possibly the main attraction is its easy accessibility from the A591 on this west side of Thirlmere, and from the Ullswater road on the east. Helvellyn has two distinct characters. From Thirlmere, with no peaks visible, the impression is a huge heap of featureless fell above the forestry plantations – like a great sleeping monster; but from the craggy Ullswater side the monster shows its claws.

The Helvellyn range is a substantial sprawl of high fell, extending to 14.5 km from Grisedale Tarn in the south to Threlkeld common in the north, and as wide as 7 km. It has several peaks, some neglected by most walkers. To name them: there is Dollywagon Pike at 858 m at the southern end ('Dollywagon' – a name without a hint of an origin), and on its west flank is 'Willie Wife Moor', also a puzzle. Moving north, just less than a km from the summit, is Nethermost Pike (890 m). Northwards after the summit comes Helvellyn Lower Man (925 m), White Side (863 m), Raise (881 m); then beyond Sticks Pass, which crosses the range from Thirspot to Glenridding, comes Watson's Dodd (789 m) and Great Dodd (856 m), the lesser peak of Calfhow Pike, then Clough Head (726 m).

Four lines of ascent are possible from the A591. From Grasmere a bridleway runs by the Great Tongue to Grisedale Tarn, then zigzags its way up Dollywagon Pike; or one can cheat by walking from a higher point at Dunmail Raise, then by Grisedale Tarn and Dollywagon. A popular route runs from Wythburn church at the head of Thirlmere; or from the northern end of the forest at Station Coppice and by the path to Lower Man. All these demand stamina, and the Wythburn route is steep, dull, relentless and leg-straining on the descent. All are less interesting than the approach from the east, which are described in the Ullswater chapter (see pp. 457–60).

A few metres from the summit is a cruciform wind shelter, and if there is a cool wind the lee quarter is bound to be occupied by picnicking adventurers. The ruined Victorian shelter was rebuilt by the National Park Warden Service and volunteers in 1968.

On a clear day the summit views are exceptionally fine. All the Lake District's major fells can be seen, the highest peaks being at south-west and west. Morecambe Bay is visible to the south; and Solway Firth, with the fells of southern Scotland to the north-west.

A little way down to the west of the summit is a spring, Brownrigg Well. In the early days when everyone ascended the mountain with a guide (mainly from Grasmere), a draught from the cold clear water of the well used to be part of the itinerary. The ebullient early Laker, Captain Joseph Budworth, in his 1792 book *A Fortnight's Ramble to the Lakes,* records in verse his joy at sampling the water:

> Eager I drew the cooling stream,
> And all fatigue was gone – a dream!
>
> The bubbling was the sweetest sound
> That ever tinkled o'er the ground.

Wythburn shore, autumn

He was a better fell walker than poet.

Coleridge walked the entire ridge of Helvellyn in 1800, a feat unknown – at least for the sake of pleasure. He set off from Mungrisdale, so before he even reached the mountain he had walked nearly 9 km. He then climbed White Pike, proceeding as he said he habitually did, in a series of leaps and bounds. Clough Head, the Dodds; 'O Joy for me,' he exclaimed on seeing Ullswater from Stybarrow Dodd. Raise excited more enthusiasm – and notes. He was absolutely enthralled, gazing about him in wonder. But by now night was falling. He wandered around, delighted with all he saw, and lingered on the summit until the moon rose. Then he made a dangerous descent in poor light down the steep slopes of Nethermost Pike to Grisedale; then along the side of Seat Sandal to Dunmail, continuing on down to Dove Cottage, arriving at eleven o'clock. Dorothy Wordsworth was in the garden enjoying the moonlight; the Wordsworths did that sort of thing. She broiled Coleridge a chop and William, left his bed and joined them in his dressing-gown. They sat and talked about mountains, and Coleridge read them a draft of the second part of the poem 'Christabel', which he happened to have in his pocket. His ridge walk would have been at least 26 km, plus the nine – 35 km, then not to mention in all around 4,000 m of climbs.

Apart from the lakeshore paths on the eastern side of Thirlmere, there is, at the top end by Dob Gill, a bridletrack that goes through the forest by Harrop Tarn, and on to the fell, by one of the Blea Tarns and Long Moss – a wet boggy place at times – to Watendlath and Borrowdale. Strollers just make for Harrop Tarn and a round walk through the forest and back. A forest trail offers a walk by the waterfalls of Launchy Gill and the large Cop Stone, and the apparently finely balanced Rocking Stone. On Armboth Fell, above Launchy Gill, tradition has it that trading was done by a large stone during the plague of 1665, because all the usual markets were closed for fear of spreading the disease. Goods were exchanged and coins placed in a rock hollow filled with vinegar before collection. Above the foot of the lake a forest path leads to Castle Crag, where earthworks of an ancient British hill fort can be seen.

AROUND THIRLMERE

At the northern end of Thirlmere a road leaves the A591 and enters St Johns-in-the-Vale. On the right as one enters the dale, a crag towers over the side of the fell, offering a challenge to experienced rock climbers. This is the Castle Rock of Triermaine, which inspired Sir Walter Scott's poem, 'The Bridal of Triermaine'. The story was dreamt up from a fanciful impression in William Hutchinson's *Excursion to the Lakes* in 1774. He described the towering crag appearing to a

The enchanted Castle Rock of Triermaine

traveller as an ancient ruined castle at one moment, with turrets, battlements and buttresses, then melting magically into little more than a 'massive pile of rocks'. Scott has King Arthur approaching the deserted castle, blowing a trumpet hanging outside and bringing the castle alight with life. He is met by a band of hospitable fair damsels, and its beautiful owner, Gwendolen, who is actually a witch. Eventually, fearing that he's neglecting his duties, he tries to get away. To prevent him leaving, Gwendolen offers him a drink to pledge their parting:

The courteous Monarch bent him low,
And, stooping down from saddlebow,
Lifted the cup, in act to drink.
A drop escaped the goblet's brink –
Intense as liquid fire from hell,
Upon the charger's neck it fell.
Screaming with agony and fright,
He bolted twenty feet upright!
The peasant still can show the dint
Where his hoofs lighted on the flint.
From Arthur's hand the goblet flew,
Scattering a shower of fiery dew,
That burn'd and blighted where it fell!
The frantic steed rush'd up the dell,
As whistles from the bow the reed;
Nor bit nor rein could check his speed
  Until he gain'd the hill;
Then breath and sinew fail'd a pace,
And reeling from the desperate race,
  He stood, exhausted, still.
The Monarch, breathless and amazed,
Back on the fatal castle gazed:
Nor tower nor donjon could he spy;
Darkening against the morning sky;
But, on the spot where once they frown'd,
The lonely streamlet brawl'd around
A tufted knoll, where dimly shone.
Fragments of rock and rifted stone.

Know, too, that when a pilgrim strays,
In morning mist or evening maze,
  Along the mountain lone,

That fairy fortress often mocks
His gaze upon the castled rocks
Of the valley of St. John;
But never man since brave De Vaux
The charmed portal won.
'Tis now a vain illusive show,
That melts whene'er the sunbeams glow
Or the fresh breeze had blown.

The little dale is quite delightful, seen on foot on the west side of St John's Beck, rather than being worried by traffic on the narrow carriage road. The little chapel of St John is worth a visit for its charming situation. At the school here John Richardson (1817–86) was master for thirty years. He was not well educated, being a stone mason by trade; his work is seen on this chapel, and many buildings nearby, and at Keswick. In different circumstances this brilliant man probably would have made a name for himself. He published tales and poems in dialect. One light little poem about a robin redbreast that visits in winter and is not seen in spring and summer ends with this reflection:

Noo, burds an' fwok ur mickle t'seamm
If they be i' hard need;
An' yan hes owt to give, they'll come,
An' be girt frinds indeed.
But when theer nowt they want to hev,
It's nut sa lang they'll stay,
Bit just as Robin does it spring,
They'll seun aw flee away.

He is buried in the churchyard.

Naddle Fell, on the west side of the dale, makes for one of the most pleasant minor fell walks, with delightful views.

On the east side one can see the remains of mining activity. At Fornside, north of Castle Rock, a mine that originated in Elizabethan times was reopened in the nineteenth century but proved to be unproductive. Another, under Wanthwaite Crags on the side of Clough Head, the northern arm of Helvellyn, is also of ancient origin. This was also reopened to produce iron pyrites and lead, but no production figures are available. At the very head of the valley, on the site of Threlkeld granite quarries, a mining museum holds a large number of old artefacts related to the industry, and mine enthusiasts lead visitors on an underground experience.

THRELKELD, BLENCATHRA AND THE NORTHERN FELLS

Across the A66 at the foot of St John's is the village of THRELKELD, which has thrived in the past on its granite quarries and mines, and was settled as far back as Neolithic times. The church of St Mary is eighteenth century. The remains of Threlkeld Hall, the seat of Sir Launcelot Threlkeld, is now incorporated into a farmhouse. In the fifteenth century he was wont to boast that he had 'three noble houses; one for pleasure at Crosby in Westmorland, where he had a park full of deer; one for profit and warmth at Yanwath "nigh Penrith"; and one at Threlkeld, well stocked with tenants to go with him to the wars'. His tomb is at Crosby Ravensworth. He married into the Clifford family. At the Roses' battle of Towton, Lord Clifford was killed. His son's life was in danger and he came on to the Threlkeld estate and was hidden as a shepherd lad. The tale is touched on in Wordsworth's 'Song at the Feast of Brougham Castle'.

> Now Who is he that bounds with joy
> On Carrock's side, a Shepherd-boy?
> No thoughts hath he but thoughts that pass
> Light as the wind along the grass.
> Can this be He who hither came
> In Secret, like a smothered flame?
>
> – he wanders forth at will,
> And tends a flock from hill to hill,
> His garb is humble; ne'er was seen
> Such garb with such a noble mien;
>
> Love had he found in huts where poor men lie;
> His daily teachers had been woods and rills,
> The silence that is in the starry sky,
> The sleep that is among the lonely hills.
>
> In him the savage virtue of the Race,
> Revenge, and all ferocious thoughts were dead:
> Nor did he change; but kept in lofty place
> The wisdom which adversity had bred.
>
> Glad were the vales, and every cottage-hearth;
> The Shepherd-lord was honoured more and more;
> And ages after he was laid in earth,
> 'The good Lord Clifford' was the name he bore.

Why have the middle classes throughout the ages thought that shepherd lads and lasses lived an idyllic life? It might have been so in Arcadia – it was hard labour in Cumbria!

Five Threlkeld mines produced lead, copper, blende (zinc sulphide), iron pyrites, and zinc blende (sphalerite). Gategill mine was the oldest, and nearby Woodend mine the most productive. The work of pumping and drawing was done by steam engine, and a water wheel powered the dressing plant, but as early as 1908 electric power was supplied by generator. Mining has now finished, but in its day it thrived.

On the fell road going west from Threlkeld is the Blencathra centre (NPA). Once a hospital for tuberculosis patients, it is now an educational centre run by the Field Studies Council. A steep path from it leads to the summit of BLENCATHRA

Blencathra from the stone circle

(*blen-CATH-ra*) , or 'Saddleback' , the great bulky neighbour of Skiddaw. Seen from the foot of St Johns in the Vale, with its peaks spiked against the horizon, it looks every inch a mountain, and far higher than it is. It is the great backcloth to the north when seen from Castlerigg stone circle. 'Blencathra' is a name with Celtic origins; 'Saddleback' describes its outline shape, particularly when seen from the south-east.

The mountain is not a top priority for fell walkers, but it deserves all the praise it gets from those who make the summits. Wainwright called it 'a mountaineer's mountain'; 'one of the grandest objects in Lakeland'. The highest point is 868 m. One approach, Sharp Edge, rivals the popular Striding Edge on Helvellyn for excitement, but many lines of ascent are possible. The fell is composed of Skiddaw slate, usually a rock of uniform consistency – but not on Blencathra. Unlike neighbouring Skiddaw, the glacial grinding and plucking action of the ice ages met resistance in some parts of the fell, and scooped out two corries (or cirques) containing the lonely and lovely tarns of Scales and Bowscale. The steepest sides, which were undercut by moving glaciers, are to the south and east. The interruption in the radiating glacial pattern that one would expect is accounted for by the fact that ice pushing southwards from Scotland met the Cumbrian ice, which was deflected east and west. The visual result is that the fierce-looking steep cliffs and screes tower over that view from St Johns in the Vale and the A66 road, dwarfing Threlkeld.

Rivers circle the mountain. The Celtic-named Glenderamackin (*glen-de-ra-MACK-in*) flows eastwards from Scales Tarn, northwards round Souther Fell, then back southwards and westwards along Blencathra's southern boundary. When it is joined by St John's Beck it becomes the River Greta. Glenderaterra (*glen-der-AT-er-ra*), another name to wonder at, is on the western boundary, dividing the fell from Skiddaw, and its valley was mined for lead. On the north-western and northern boundaries the River Caldew takes its water from the fell, including a flow from Bowscale Tarn (*BOscl*), before turning northwards to join the Eden near Carlisle.

From the airy summit ridge five arms reach out to the southern valley and each is named as a separate fell. The two outer fells fall away steeply but fairly tamely in grassy slopes. The central fells are fairly loose and craggy, and in season are purple with heather bloom. To the east and north, and partly detached, are Bowscale and Souther Fells. Bowscale Tarn is a gem cut deep into the side of Bowscale Fell. Its water evoked the often repeated myth in Victorian times that the sun never reached it; and it was possible, at midday, to see reflected in it the moon and the stars. Even Sir Walter Scott was impressed by the tale. Souther Fell is also linked to an unusual haunting on the fell: a phantom army with cavalry has been seen marching back and forth, on more than one occasion. The first sighting was on midsummer's eve in 1735. A farm servant saw it and was ridiculed. Two years later the whole farm family saw it and they too were thought mad. At midsummer's eve in 1745 they invited a large party of respectable and sober local people to watch. They observed a large army manoeuvring, with horses and carriages, for over an hour. So real did the vision seem to them that in the morning they ascended the fell to look for hoof-prints – but not a thing. Several theories were advanced. One incredible opinion was that it was a mirage; by some 'transparent vapour' the reflection of a Jacobite army floated into view parading and marching far in the north. The view southwards from Blencathra's summit takes in, most notably, the High Street and Helvellyn ranges, and the view over the abyss into the valley is impressive. Northwards one can see into Scotland. The cross in quartz on the ground north of the summit is said to be a memorial to a walker, long past, who died here. There are several old mine workings at various places on the fell sides.

One of the earliest fell walkers was Coleridge, who explored the area when he and his family rented Greta Hall in Keswick. In August 1800 he climbed Blencathra from the Blease Fell side, walking along the ridge, then dropped down to Scales Tarn. His descriptions are always excellent.

> ... a round basin of vast depth, the west arc an almost perpendicular precipice of naked shelving crags (each crag a precipice with a small shelf) – no noise but that of loose stones rolling away from the feet of the Sheep, that move slowly along these perilous ledges.

He made a further exploration later in the month.

The main road from Thirlmere to Keswick has been widened and improved from its narrower predecessor from the coaching days. Accidents were not uncommon in those days. One famous accident involved the mail coach from Keswick, which was making a descent from Nest Brow when the 'off-wheeler' horse tossed its head and got its bit entangled in a shaft. The coachman lost control and the vehicle collided with a pony-chaise that was knocked through a wall. The chaise contained two middle-aged men, and to the relief of the coachman neither was hurt. One of them picked himself up and said solemnly, 'I shall have this matter thoroughly investigated.' It was William Wordsworth. 'Thank heaven!' said the coachman David Johnson afterwards, 'I thowt we'd kilt the poit.'

KESWICK

KESWICK (*KEZ-ick*) (pop. 4,960) has transformed itself from a small mining town into a tourist's town, and in season it is crowded with jostling holidaymakers. But there are no bingo halls and amusement arcades. The tourists come for the

Keswick from the Keswick Hotel

magnetic and magnificent setting in this, the best of the Lake District's holiday towns. It is not beautiful or picturesque, but crags and high fells crowd the little town on three sides, and at its open end one surveys the wide magnificent expanse of Derwent Water with its lakeside walks, backed by the most picturesque valley in England; and beyond, its highest mountains. Superb viewpoints, including Friar's Crag over Derwent Water, Castle Head, Latrigg and Walla Crag, surround the town. Keswick serves as a superb base for a great variety of enjoyable walks, low-level and fell, and for anyone with an adventurous turn of mind it crackles with promise. In short it does not come better than this.

Some would say it has its downside: too mobbed with crowds at bank holidays ... an all-pervading smell of fish and chips ... too commercialized ... too many outdoor gear shops. The latter might be true, but they are probably the best in the country. Improvements have been made too. The town centre around the distinctive Moot Hall has been pedestrianized, and the days are long gone when only chip shops ruled; good pubs and cafés now provide varieties of good meals. The Saturday open-air market was established in 1276 and is still a lively affair with many bargains to be snapped up.

The buildings in Keswick grew out of the local stone. There is hardly anything glaringly out of place, nor can there be now, as it is in the National Park. Almost the whole of it is Victorian, built as it was with the coming of the railway from Penrith.

The earliest known history of Keswick starts with the famous Castlerigg stone circle (NT), 2 km east of Keswick and reached by a minor road south of the A66. The early guidebooks and maps call it the 'Druid's circle', whereas, of course, it dates from Late Neolithic to Early Bronze Age, between 3,000 and 4,000 years ago, long before the druids appeared. The uniqueness of this circle consists in its placing. Others are on the county's fringes, where those early communities were supported by good agricultural land: the coast, the Cumbrian plain and the Eden valley. But Keswick's stone circle is placed stupendously in the centre of a ring of fells. It is calculated that the view from the circle takes in all the high peaks in a circle of about 160 km in circumference, Blencathra and the Helvellyn range being prominent. Why is it here? The site must have been carefully chosen. Professor Thom and others have theories about its astronomical meaning, with stones aligned to the stars and sun. Other stones that were once outside the circle have been lost. Thousand of years ago the stars undoubtedly held a religious meaning to many communities worldwide. The first holy writ was before clay or parchment, and was built of stone. The Neolithic shaman who had this stone circle designed and made, had no doubt learned from his forebears, and was as familiar with the stars as he was his earthly landscape.

Keswick Town Square and Moot Hall

Castlerigg stone circle from the entrance

Maybe too, as with the early Christian stone crosses, this was a meeting place, a tribal forum, a market. Now it captures the moods of the fells around it, the light and shadow. It is best seen at the beginning and end of the day when it is less likely to be thronged with visitors – whatever the weather. Keats saw it brooding on a bad day:

> … a dismal cirque
> Of Druid stones, upon a forlorn moor,
> When the chill rain begins at shut of eve,
> In dull November, and their chancel vault,
> The Heaven itself, is blinded throughout night.

The circle, roughly 30 by 33 m, is very slightly oval. There remain forty-eight stones, some of them bulky if not massive, and on the east side is an unexplained oblong 'chamber' within the circle. An entrance is at due north.

The presence of earthworks of 'hill forts' around the area suggests an occupation by Celtic tribes, but their age is the subject of debate: before, during, or after the Roman occupation? The Celts were certainly here, as witness the large number of Celtic placenames. The Roman period poses another question. Was there a Roman presence in Keswick? It seems not only possible but likely, for a Roman road ran from Old Penrith, Voreda, to Troutbeck, east of Keswick. Traces of Roman encampments dot the route, and there are signs of an agger, the raised base on which Roman roads were built, from Troutbeck to the edge of Keswick. Further, a possible section of Roman road has been discovered west of Keswick, and logically this would continue over Whinlatter Pass to Papcastle's (Cockermouth's) Roman fort, Derventio. So it is very possible that the road passed through, or close to, Keswick.

Angle settlers occupied the western half of Cumbria in the Dark Ages. 'Keswick', as a placename, has been interpreted as Old English for 'cheese farm'. This seems specious. 'Wick' could mean a dwelling, but 'Kes' is more likely to allude to the owner's name. Would Keswick really have specialized in making cheese? Cheese making requires rich pastures and Keswick of old would have had rough grazing on a lot of rocky marsh land.

Keswick's visible history in buildings is concentrated in the north-west at Crosthwaite ('the clearing of the cross'). Here is the parish church dedicated to St Kentigern, otherwise St Mungo, the patron saint of Glasgow who was an active missionary in Cumbria – then in Scotland – in the seventh century. He may have preached here next to a cross that preceded any building. The oldest fabric can be found in the foundations of the north-aisle wall and is assumed to date from 1181, but, with this exception, and that of the fourteenth-century north chapel, St Kentigern is a late Perpendicular church. Additions and alterations were made in the fourteenth, seventeenth and nineteenth centuries. The sixteenth-century tower is exceptionally strong, and was almost certainly built to provide a refuge from border raiders. There are ancient relics: fifteenth-century alabaster effigies thought to be of Thomas and Margaret Radcliffe, and brasses 60 cm long of Sir John Radcliffe (d.1527) and his Lady Alice. One notable feature is the number of consecration crosses cut into the stone, inside and outside, where the bishop has anointed the church fabric with holy water after a rebuilding.

The marble figure of Robert Southey, poet laureate and once presiding genius of Keswick, lies recumbent, with one hand on heart, the other appropriately on a book. (When he died it is reckoned that he had 18,000 books in his library.) His friend Wordsworth composed the epitaph on the plinth. Striving for perfection,

Wordsworth often had a habit of re-editing his work. In this case he consulted others and comments in a letter to his nephew Christopher:

> It is creditable to Mr. Southey, and perhaps in some small degree to myself, that the Inscription has given birth to so much minute criticism ...
> I question whether there is a couplet in the whole that has not been objected to, by some one or other.

It can be seen that when the stonemason finished his job, the last couplet of the epitaph was changed and had to be recut.

This is not the laureate's tomb, he being buried in the northern part of the churchyard with his wife Edith. Apparently, and rather touchingly, a servant is interred here too. An inscription reads:

> Also of Elizabeth Thompson, for 50 years the faithful servant and attached friend of Robert Southey and of his children, who died Feb 5th 1862 aged 85 years.

Another stone plaque records that the tomb was restored by the president of the Brazilian government in 1963. Why? Because amongst Southey's prodigious literary output was a three-volume *History of Brazil*, written between 1810 and 1819.

By the ringing chamber under the tower is an 1826 list of rules for the bell-ringers, composed by 86-year-old Thomas Martin, a master of Crosthwaite school:

> You ringers all observe these Orders well,
> He eight pence pays who overturns a Bell;
> He who presumes to ring without consent,
> Shall pay one Shilling and it shall be spent;
> And he who rings with either Spur or Hat,
> Shall pay his eight pence, certainly for that;
> He who in ringing interrupts a Peal,
> For such offence shall pay a quart of Ale;
> In falling Bells, one penny must be paid,
> By him who stops before the signal's made,
> And he who takes God's Holy Name in vain,
> Shall pay one shilling and this Place refrain,
> You Ringers all take care, you must not fail,
> To have your forfeitures all spent in Ale.
> With Heart upright let each true Subject ring
> For Health and Peace, to Country, Church and King.

One of the church's incumbents was the conservationist, campaigner, fell walker and founder member of the National Trust Canon Hardwicke Rawnsley (1851–1920). During his long stint here he made many improvements to the church. A memorial in the church reads:

> In Memoriam. Who battled for the True the Just. H.D. Rawnsley Vicar of this parish for 34 years. Canon of Carlisle. Chaplain to the King. And Edith his wife.

He is buried in the churchyard. No one did more to bring about the preservation of so much of the Lakeland landscape, and his memorial is fittingly at the lake's viewpoint of Friar's Crag.

Apart from St Kentigern's there are only a few buildings of note in the town. Nearby the Catholic church is modern and simple. The handsome St John's church near the town centre is nineteenth century. The Moot Hall eccentric and jocular, presides over the marketplace, and it is the town's really special feature. This one, dating from 1812, replaces other moot halls. In the tower the clock has just one hand, but it serves its purpose. The bell has confusing inscriptions: '1001' should read 1601, the correct date. The ground floor is now an excellent National Park and tourist information centre whose upper floor is used for functions, coffee mornings, meetings and lectures.

Of the town's two parks, Fitz Park is close to the town centre; the land was acquired largely through the efforts of local businessmen. Hope Park, on the way to the lake, was donated by Percy Mirehouse Hope (1888–1972), a local businessman who spent much of his life in service to the town.

Up by the old railway station is what was supposed to be a swimming pool, but a common pool was not good enough for the district councillors. So it is a 'leisure pool', with plastic landscaping, a wave-maker and a flume, all in sub-tropical temperatures. Supposed to be financed by a council-owned timeshare development by the Greta, the enterprise failed and has led to no end of headaches.

The *Keswick Reminder* is a local institution, having started out as a free advertisement sheet, and in 1897 becoming a newspaper with a fine reputation. The owner and editor was George Watson McKane, and it has been in the family ever since. It's two principles are: no court cases, and no scandals. It is taken by practically every house in Keswick and beyond.

Keswick grew in importance from the sixteenth century as ore from rich copper mines in the surrounding hills, and from Coniston, was carted and packhorsed in to the Keswick smelters. The search for copper ore came at a time when demand for it was high. Queen Elizabeth needed copper for the production of arms and in the building of warships; but she also needed mining expertise, which at that time was all in Germany. So German mining experts Daniel Hechstetter and Hans Loner, along with twelve workers, were brought to the area, began an exploration and found promising signs around Keswick. The Queen gave them permission to 'search, dig, try, roast and melt all manner of mines and ores for Gold, silver, copper, and quicksilver'. She could claim nine-tenths of all gold and silver at a favourable rate, and royalties on the copper.

To finance the operation, the Company of Mines Royal was incorporated in 1568. The shareholders make interesting reading: the queen's secretary, Lord Burghley; the lord mayor of London; the earls of Pembroke and of Leicester; and the lord lieutenant of Dorset. Letters patent were granted to Daniel Hechstetter; and to Thomas Thurland, who had German mining contacts. One of the first discoveries was at Scope End in Newlands; a rich mine that came to be known as 'Goldscope', thought to be a corruption of the German *gottesgab*, or 'God's gift'.

When the mines began producing, assay chambers, smelting works, smithies and ancillary workshops were needed; and these were built by the River Greta, east of the town, an area that is now under the modern, horribly alien flyover of the A66. A huge demand arose for timber, too, for the manufacture of charcoal for the furnaces, and for props, water troughs and water wheels at the mines. Borrowdale woodlands were stripped, and whole areas of woodlands all over the Lake District were taken. Wood was even imported from Ireland. It is not known what factors contributed to the industry's decline from the Civil War on. Parliamentarians have been blamed for the smelters' destruction, but was this likely?

Although copper and lead were the chief minerals mined in the neighbourhood, Keswick was famed for its 'wad', or black lead, mined at the head of Borrowdale (see pp. 414–16). From this the town's pencil factory was born, and still survives from those times, although the black lead is now imported. The fascinating Pencil Museum tells the story of the birth of the factory, and the variety of pencils it produced – including the pencils that contained hidden maps, sent in Red Cross parcels to prisoners of war. It also shows how modern artists' coloured pencils are made. This is really a must for all visitors.

The town's other small Victorian museum and art gallery is on Station Street, between the greenery of Lower and Upper Fitzpark, dating from 1898, with fixtures and fittings unchanged. It contains manuscripts and letters of Lakeland writers and poets. There are also geological and mineral exhibits, a model of the Lake District by Joseph Flintoft (1827–43), landscape painter, with all its mountains, hills, valleys and roads of scale three inches to the mile and covering 1,200 square miles. It is still good, though it looks as if it were made from dark-green jelly. Don't miss the famous 'Richards' Rock and Bell and Steel Musical Instrument', made from carefully tuned pieces of volcanic rock with steel bars and bells. The musical stones were played by royal command at Buckingham Palace in

1848. This is a hands-on museum and, if you have any musical talent, you must play it. A natural history section is full of stuffed birds and archaeological artefacts found locally. It is interesting to see the comments of visitors to the museum in 2002. Without exception they want the museum to stay just as it is, without modern electronic sophistication, in the face of the local council's improvement plans. Modern museums are fine if done well – like the Science Museum's at Sellafield – but there should still be a place for the old kind, with their caves of discovery, where the exhibits do not shriek for attention. This is one of a threatened species that should be kept, and advertised as such.

Keswick had earlier museums, opened to profit from the growing tourist trade in the late eighteenth century. One was owned by a remarkably energetic Thirlmere man, Peter Crosthwaite, who had seen service at sea with the East India Company and had also worked as a customs officer in Northumberland. He was eccentric, but talented in his way – producing fairly accurate maps of Derwent Water and Windermere, Coniston Water and Bassenthwaite Lake, with verses extolling their beauties, and small vignettes of building and features. The maps were also marked with 'stations', or viewpoints, and headed thus: 'P. Crosthwaite, Admiral at Keswick Regatta, Keeper of the Museum at Keswick, Guide, Pilot, Geographer, and Hydrographer to TOURISTS .'

He kept weather records; engineered, with his son, a zigzag tourist path up Latrigg and surveyed routes for canals. His exhibits were remarkable to say the least: fossils, shells, stuffed birds, that first 'stone dulcimer' using musical stones; the straw hat of a sailor who was with Bligh on the *Bounty*; two barnacles from the bottom of Captain Cook's ship; a piece of bamboo brought back from India by John Wordsworth, brother of William; a stuffed lamb with claws instead of hoofs (explained by the story that a pet racoon, belonging to Mrs Bradyle of Conishead priory, had escaped and copulated with a sheep); the hand of an Egyptian mummy; a chicken with two heads, and more.

His advertisement bill read:

> PETER CROSTHWAITE Formerly Naval Commander in India, Surveyor and Seller of the Maps of the Lakes, MASTER of the Celebrated MUSEUM, of eleven years standing, and the Quadrant, Telescope, and Weathercock, A little below the Middle of Keswick.
>
> Returns his most grateful Thanks to the Nobility, Gentry, and Others for crowning his labours with Success. His house is the loftiest in Keswick, and has the Advantage of most delightful prospects quite around the Vale.
>
> In 1784, Sir Ashton Lever, and several other able Virtuosos, declared his Museum the most capital one North of Trent. Since which time it is improved as Three to One. It consists of many Hundred Natural and Artificial Curiosities,

> from every Quarter of the World; the Fossils, Spontaneous Plants, and Antiquities of Cumberland; Coins, Medals, Arms, Quadrupeds, Birds, Insects, Shells, Landscapes, Pictures, Grottos, and his much admired Organ; together with many Models and useful Inventions of his own; and if it were not for the low Cunning, and mischievous Falsehoods continually circulated against him by an ungrateful JUNTO of Impostors in the Place, it is thought few of the Gentry would pass him; but, being covetous to an Extreme, and much hurt by Envy, they all Advantages of misleading the Gentry to this Day; and all this after he has laid out several Hundred Pounds in the Museum and spent near Thirteen Years of his time in collecting Curiosities, making and repairing Roads, Surveying the Lakes, &c &c all of which has been done for the better Entertainment of the Gentry, and an honest Livelihood for his Family.
>
> Admittance to LADIES and GENTLEMEN, One Shilling each; COUNTRY PEOPLE, Sixpence Each.
>
> Open from 7 A.M. till 10 P.M.

He had two instruments to bring the museum to the attention of tourists. One was a very loud 6.5 kg Chinese gong with a sound like a cathedral bell that, when struck, could be heard four miles away. The other was a very loud, but tuneful, barrel organ reputed to be capable of playing seventy-seven tunes. He sat in a chair at the museum door, and used a set of variously angled mirrors so that he could spot the arrival of coaches and possible customers. When he did, a drum was thumped, the gong hit, and the barrel organ struck up a tune. How could anyone resist?

Thomas Hutton ran the rival museum, which had a less bizarre collection of fossils, mineral specimens and stuffed birds. He was a knowledgeable man with an interest in mineralogy and botany and he had accompanied Father West in his explorations of the district for his famous guidebook, suggesting the location of some of the viewing stations. He offered himself as a tourist guide and was in his spare time a weaver. Crosthwaite confronted his competitor with a hate that amounted to obsession. He poured vitriolic scorn on his rival, accusing him of being the greatest liar in England, and being prepared to do anything for gain. No record exists of Hutton's response to the constant invective; but the battle for supremacy must have entertained the tourists.

Keswick played a great part in the fortunes of the Wordsworths. In 1794 William and his sister Dorothy stayed at Windy Brow, under Skiddaw, to the north of the town, in the home of William's schoolfriend William Calvert. They stayed for six weeks, going on walks around the area. In the autumn of that year Wordsworth was to accompany Raisley, the sickly younger brother of William Calvert, on a trip to Lisbon. They got no further than Penrith when Raisley was taken ill. Wordsworth stayed with him for three months, but he died in January 1795. In gratitude Raisley had left £900 to Wordsworth in his will to enable him to make a start in writing for a living – 'enough to secure me from want,' recorded the poet, 'if not to render me independent'. He expresses his gratitude in a sonnet:

Calvert! it must not be unheard by them
Who may respect my name that I to thee
Owed many years of early liberty.
This care was thine when sickness did condemn
Thy youth to hopeless wasting, root and stem –
That I, if frugal and severe, might stray
Where'er I liked; and finally array
My temples with the Muse's diadem.
Hence, if in freedom I have loved the truth;
If there be ought of pure, or good, or great,
In my past verse; or shall be, in the lays
Of higher mood, which now I meditate;-
It gladdens me, O worthy, short-lived Youth!
To think how much of this will be thy praise.

Not far from the pencil factory is Greta Hall. When William and Dorothy Wordsworth moved to Grasmere in late 1799, Wordsworth's great friend and collaborator Samuel Taylor Coleridge, with his wife Sara and family, followed them to the Lakes in the next year, and rented part of the hall. It was then on the outskirts of Keswick and commanded fine views. Coleridge boasted to William Godwin, the philosopher: 'I question if there be a room in England which commands a view of Mountains and Lakes and Woods and Vales superior to that in which I am now sitting ... a great camp of mountains – Giants seem to have pitched their tents there.' He wrote to Francis Wrangham: '... my glass being opposite the window, I seldom shave without cutting myself. Some Mountain or Peak is rising out of the Mist, or some slanting Column of misty Sunlight is sailing across to me – so that I offer up soap and blood daily, as an Eye-servant of the Goddess of Nature.'

The hall became a base for his extensive walks in the area. Then, unfortunately, Coleridge's circumstances worsened. His relationship with his wife deteriorated. Almost certainly Wordsworth's rejection of 'Christabel' for a second edition of *The Lyrical Ballads* and his obvious reservations about 'The Ancient Mariner' hurt him deeply. He took solace in laudanum, an addiction that was later his undoing. He made several sudden disapperances from Keswick and in 1803 left permanently after his quarrel with the Wordsworths.

Earlier, at Coleridge's invitation, Robert Southey, the husband of Sara's sister, had visited Greta Hall, and although it was not at first his intention, he stayed there for the rest of his life, taking care of the abandoned Sara and the three children as well as his own family. In 1807 he was awarded a government pension, but he sustained his own and his sister-in-law's household as a long-standing contributor of essays for the *Quarterly Review*. His literary output was great and in 1813 he was appointed poet laureate.

Southey received many literary visitors to Greta Hall, including Percy Bysshe Shelley, who was staying with his new bride for three months in the town when he visited in 1811. At the age of nineteen his views were radical and at odds with Southey's, whose politics had veered more comfortably to the right. William Hazlitt stayed several times and painted portraits of Coleridge and his son Hartley, and Southey. He finally left hurriedly with paintings unfinished, and in mysterious circumstances, chased out of town by some angry inhabitants to seek asylum in Grasmere with the Wordsworths. What happened? It is rumoured that a woman or women were involved.

In 1830 the eleven-year-old John Ruskin attended Crosthwaite church and records his sight of Southey in remarkable verse for his age:

Now hurried we home, and while taking our tea
We thought – Mr Southey at church we might see.
And then unto sleep we our bodies resigned,
And sunk in oblivion and silence our mind.
Next morning the church, how we wished for the reaching!
I'm afraid 'twas as much for the poet as preaching!
And oh what a shame! – were shown into a seat
With everything, save what was wanted, replete;
And so dirty, and greasy, though many times dusted,
The ladies all thought it could never be trusted.
Howe'er I forgave – 'deed, I scarcely did know it, -
For really we were 'cheek by jowel' with the poet!
His hair was no colour at all by the way,
But half of't was black, slightly scattered with grey;
His eyes were as black as coal, but in turning
They flashed, – ay, as much as that coal does in burning!
His nose in the midst took a small outward bend,
Rather hooked like an eagle's, and sharp at the end;
But his dark lightning-eye made him seem half-inspired,

Or like his own Thalaba, vengefully fired.
We looked and we gazed, and we stared at his face;
Marched out at a slow, stopping, lingering pace;
And as towards Keswick delighted we walked,
Of his face, and his form, and his features we talked,
With various chatter beguiling the day
Till the sun disappeared and the light fled away.

Keswick was already a holiday town before the coming of the railway. As well as the regular coach services and the mail coach local entrepreneurs organized tours. There were runs to Windermere, the Royal Oak Hotel offering seven four-in-hands per day. There were trips into Borrowdale; and over to Buttermere; five shillings return with a three-hour stop at Buttermere, a shilling more for a boat to see Scale Force waterfall. On steep hills the passengers were required to get out and walk. The competition between operators was fierce.

But when the railway came, it triggered a spurt of building and the town was transformed. The coach hire businesses were not happy, of course, and the recorded comment of one coachman is worth quoting: 'Don't yer travel by those new-fangled steam engines. Suppose you travel by my coach, and you meets with an accident? There you are! But suppose you travel by rail and you meets with an accident? Where are ye?'

The route of the Cockermouth, Keswick and Penrith railway line was surveyed by Thomas Bouch, the Thursby man who designed the ill-fated Tay Bridge. In 1862 the first sod was cut at Keswick, a day celebrated with a great procession of soldiers and clergy, dignitaries and children, accompanied by three bands. The celebrations ended with an official dinner at the Derwent Water Hotel. The chairman, Thomas Hoskins, made a speech forecasting that the line would bring an upturn in the flagging economy. In total some twenty-five speeches and toasts were made, though how many guests were fully aware of the proceedings after the tenth toast is anyone's guess.

The building of the Cockermouth, Keswick and Penrith railway began at once, winding its way through the gorge of the River Greta, and offering one of the most scenic routes in England. It was completed and open to traffic within two and a half years; and all thirty-one miles of it, including 135 bridges, made with navvies using pick, shovel, wheelbarrow and blasting powder. Beat that today? Their fuel was 2 lb (.9 kg) of beef and a gallon (4.5 l) of beer per man per day. Because of the riots that arose during the construction of the main Lancaster to Carlisle line, precautions were taken to prevent a repetition here. The Revd W. Whitelegg of Threlkeld, and the Revd G. Truman of Wythop, were appointed chaplains, and their presence, it was thought, would encourage good behaviour.

In Keswick the workmen were entertained in a civilized manner with a mind for their social and moral welfare. Incredibly 150 navvies were given tea at a school, served by a group of local ladies, where they listened to several addresses 'on various topics suited to the capacities of men in their station of life'. Which topics, one wonders.

The line's important purpose was to carry that Cumbrian coal not suitable for use in smelting to the north-east of England, and to bring back coke for west Cumbrian furnaces. Passenger traffic increased as freight declined. The next cause for celebration in Keswick was the arrival of the first locomotive in July 1863, pulled through town by fourteen horses. Then it was taken in procession to be transferred on to the rails.

At its best, in 1913, the railway brought nearly half a million holidaymakers to Keswick, and it continued to be well used between the wars. But the magnificent railway was wickedly murdered in the 1960s. One reason for its demise was too few ticket sales at Keswick station. But Keswick was a destination! This was the most unkindest cut of all. What residents have instead is an unlovely fast highway, the A66, a spur of the M6, violating the Greta Gorge, despite a recommendation at the public inquiry that a less damaging route should be taken. At least one small scenic part of the old railway line, from Threlkeld to Keswick, with five bridges over the river, was rescued by the National Park Authority and is now a popular level walk. From this stretch one can begin to appreciate the achievement in building the line. It is regrettable that the NPA did not acquire all the line to Penrith.

The railway station buildings have been preserved, and one can see how easy it was for passengers to stroll from the platform into the railway-owned Keswick Hotel through the palm trees and ferns of the conservatory, with a porter trundling their baggage behind them. The hotel was the town's largest and most splendid, and it still is.

Although access on the many public footpaths and bridleways is taken for granted, some of it had to be fought for. Once again we have to thank the assiduous Canon Rawnsley for leading the way. Long-used footpaths were being closed by landowners in other parts, and to secure the rights he revived a Keswick and District Footpath Preservation Society. The spur was the 1887 closure of an old packhorse track at Fawe Park, on the north-east shore of Derwent Water, that was enjoyed by walkers. When the owner, Mrs Spencer Bell, erected barriers across the path a party of protesters marched in and removed them all. The barriers were replaced but repeatedly torn down until Mrs Bell was forced to relent. Meanwhile by Latrigg, the hill overlooking the town in front of Skiddaw, the terrace walk was being disputed by Mr Anthony Spedding, who locked gates, planted trees on the path and built wire fences. The climax of the long dispute came to a head when five youths were taken to court for a shilling's worth of

Skiddaw from Derwent Water, east shore

damage. Spedding then, surprisingly, invited protesters for a face-to-face confrontation, where the legal case could be tested and settled. The challenge was accepted – no fewer than 2,000 people assembled, tore down the barriers and marched up Latrigg singing 'Rule Britannia'. Among them was the local MP, Samuel Plimsoll. The ringleaders (Rawnsley was absent for some reason) were taken to court and charged with trespass. Judge Grantham brought the two sides together and they thrashed out a compromise route to Latrigg summit.

For a fortnight in July, Keswick becomes home to the Keswick Convention, when evangelists from home and abroad gather for meetings and services. Its beginnings came in 1875 when Canon Battersby of St John's church saw the value of bringing together Christians of all denominations to meet and worship.

Robert Wilson, a Cockermouth businessman and Quaker, supported him. It started as a three-day event in a tent in the vicarage garden. But such was its success that in subsequent years special trains had to be booked to bring in the hundreds of attendees. Though the trains are no longer required it still pulls in the crowds.

Keswick Mountain Rescue Team, one of the first to be formed in the Lake District, has its headquarters by the car park on the road to the lake. It was formed in 1946 after an incident in which Wilfred Noyce, who was to join John Hunt's team on the successful ascent of Everest, broke a leg when he was blown off a rock climb on Great Gable. A scratch team of mountaineers brought him down in the dark with very great difficulty, and it was quickly realized that the rescue could itself have been a disaster. What was necessary was a trained and equipped team of volunteers, ready day or night, and the group was formed without delay. Nowadays they have very sophisticated equipment and can turn out more than forty times each year.

Keswick's Theatre by the Lake lies on the approach to the lakeshore boat landings. The development aroused controversy, because sites were available in town. Being so close to the prime attraction of the lakeshore would entail some restriction of access and some tree felling. The company won the development on appeal with the argument that a well-designed theatre would replace the tatty, mobile Century Theatre – an eyesore – that existed there since 1952 (pre-National Park). It is now an accepted feature and one of the north of England's prime art centres.

There are a variety of short walks around the town, apart from the lakeshore walks by Derwent Water (see pp. 404–5). The level path along the old railway line to Threlkeld is maintained by the National Park Authority. A good proportion of the path is suitable for wheelchair users. Castlehead, on the south-east side of the town, is thought to be a volcanic 'plug' and is a good viewpoint. Another popular viewpoint is from Latrigg (367 m), the hill overlooking the town, which can be approached by footbridges over the A66.

SKIDDAW

Every walker who stays in Keswick has to climb SKIDDAW (*SKID-aw*), which looms large in the northern landscape of the Lake District and towers over Keswick. Its great sprawling bulk is best seen as Bassenthwaite is approached from the A66 from Cockermouth. At 931 m it is the fourth highest fell in Cumbria. Its great angular outline, lacking the dramatic crags and shattered aspects of its brothers in Borrowdale and Thirlmere, is explained by its

Skiddaw from Derwent Water

geology. Skiddaw slate is sedimentary and the oldest type of rock in the Lakes. Unlike the hard volcanic, it breaks easily into fragments, hence the uninterrupted outlines, and the comparatively even terrain.

Skiddaw looks larger than it is, and was once thought to be one of the highest mountains in England. Joseph Nicolson and Richard Burn wrote in their 1777 *The History of the Antiquities of Westmorland and Cumberland*:

> The mountain Skiddaw is about eleven hundred yards perpendicular from the Broadwater [Bassenthwaite Lake]. It rises with two heads, like unto Parnassus; and with a kind of emulation beholds Scruffel [Criffe] hill before it in Annandale in Scotland. By these two mountains, according as the misty clouds rise or fall, the people dwelling thereabouts make their prognostication of the change of the weather, and have a common expression,
>
> If Skiddaw hath a cap
> Scruffel wots well of that
>
> Like as there goes also another saying concerning the height of this hill with two others in the kingdom,
>
> Skiddaw, Lanvellin [Helvellyn] and Casticand [Catstye Cam]
> Are the highest hills in all England.

It's not true of course – and indeed the saying has variants that includes Yorkshire's Pen-y-ghent.

The main route up the mountain offers a good introduction to hill walking – the path is clear and if the weather is good one is hardly likely to go astray. The average walker should reach the summit in under three hours. This common approach is by the track beside Latrigg, a short walk by a field side (the view from Latrigg's summit can be remembered for another, half-day), then a straight-up, unrelenting climb. The first peak to be reached is Little Man (865 m). This sometimes deceives walkers into thinking that they have made the peak and turn aside to it, but the true summit, High Man, is still some distance on. The views are absolutely tremendous, and apart from the Lake District hills, include the Pennines, the Isle of Man and across the Solway into Scotland. One can see why the summit was a crucial point for beacon signals. The other peaks in the vicinity also offer fine views; the heather-covered Ullock Pike, on a spur west of the summit, arguably offers the best prospects of all.

Being so near Keswick Skiddaw was the mountain climbed by the first intrepid tourists. The early accounts of their adventures are nearly all delightfully exaggerated. Mrs Radcliffe, the writer of Gothic novels, ascended Skiddaw on horseback in 1794, apparently edging her way along narrow paths above precipices. She recoiled in horror at the view – 'the breaking up of the world' – and the air was 'intensely cold and difficult to inspire'.

Skiddaw's waterfall is in the Dash Beck valley at the north end of Skiddaw, and reached by footpaths from Bassenthwaite village.

THE LAKE

But Keswick's charms are by no means all perpendicular. There is the supreme lake. A short, level walk from Keswick, past the boat landings at the head of DERWENT WATER, and a short distance further on by the lake shore, is FRIAR'S CRAG, one of the most famous viewpoints in Britain. The view across the levels of the lake, enclosed by its fells, with the rugged backcloth of Borrowdale encased by a framework of trees, offers the complete balance of form. John Ruskin himself, first Slade Professor of Art at Oxford, the supreme arbiter on beauty, described the view as 'one of the three most beautiful scenes in Europe'. He recalls a visit here as a child:

> The first thing which I remember, as an event in life, was being taken by my nurse to the brow of Friar's Crag on Derwent Water; the intense joy mingled

Friar's Crag

> with awe, that I had in looking through the hollows in the mossy roots, over the crag into the dark lake, has ever associated itself more or less with all twining of roots of trees ever since.

An inscribed stone by a crag records his words. The views, good at any time, are best seen in the mellow lights of morning and evening, or in any season but high summer. Winter is an excellent time, with the snow on the hills. In a more romantic period, the walk was deemed particularly special in moonlight.

Keswick was the birthplace of tourism in the Lake District. It all began with a letter from a Dr Brown of Wigton, to Lord Littleton, that was later included in the Lake District's first and hugely popular guidebook (1778) by Father West, a Jesuit priest living in Furness.

> ... at Keswick, you will on one side of the lake, see a rich and beautiful landskip of cultivated fields, rising to the eye in fine inequalities, with noble groves of oak, happily dispersed, and climbing the adjacent hills, shade above shade, in the most various and picturesque forms. On the opposite shore, you will find rocks and cliffs of stupendous height, hanging broken over the lake in horrible grandeur, some of them a thousand feet high, the woods climbing up their steep and shaggy sides, where mortal foot never yet approached. On these

> dreadful heights the eagles build their nests; a variety of water-falls are seen pouring from their summits, and tumbling in vast sheets from rock to rock in rude and terrible magnificence: while on all sides of this immense amphitheatre the lofty mountains rise round, piercing the clouds in shapes spiry and fantastic ...
>
> To this I must add the frequent and bold projection of cliffs into the lake, forming noble bays and promontories: in other parts they finely retire from it, and often open in abrupt chasms or cliffs, thro' which at hand, you see rich and cultivated vales, and beyond these at various distances, mountains rising over mountain, among which, new prospects present themselves in mist, till the eye is lost in an agreeable perplexity.

'... the full perfection of Keswick consists of three circumstances, beauty, horror, and immensity united.' Dr Brown compares the scenery to pictures painted by the three most popular classical painters:

> But to give you a complete idea of these three perfections, as they are joined in Keswick, would require the united powers of Claude, Salvator, and Poussin. The first should throw his delicate sunshine over the cultivated vales, the scattered cots, the groves, the lake, and the wooded islands. The second would dash out the horror of the rugged cliffs, the steeps, the hanging woods, and foaming water-falls; while the grand pencil of Poussin should crown the whole with the majesty of the impending mountains.

Another oft-quoted phrase was by Charles Avison, composer and organist at Newcastle, who stood at Friar's Crag and described Derwent Water as 'beauty lying in the lap of horror'. Having read such exciting descriptions how could one resist a visit? Particularly after reading Father West's introduction to his best-selling guidebook written in the same period:

> Such as wish to unbend the mind from anxious cares, or fatiguing studies, will meet with agreeable relaxation in making the tour of the lakes. Something new will open itself at the turn of every mountain, and a succession of ideas will be supported by a perpetual change of objects, and a display of scenes behind scenes, in endless perspective. The contemplative traveller will be charmed with sight of the sweet retreats, that he will observe in these enchanting regions of calm repose, and the fanciful may figuratively review the hurry and bustle of busy life (in all its gradations) in the variety of unshaded rills that hang on the mountain sides, the hasty brooks that warble through the dell, or the mighty torrents precipitating themselves at once with thundering noise from

> tremendous rocky heights; all pursuing one general end, their increase in the vale and their union with the ocean …
>
> Such as spend their lives in cities, and their time in crowds will here meet with objects that will enlarge the mind, by contemplation, and raise it from nature to nature's first cause. Whoever takes a walk into these scenes must return penetrated with sense of the creator's power in heaping mountains upon mountains, and enthroning rocks upon rocks. And such exhibitions of sublime and beautiful objects, cannot but excite at once both rapture and reverence.

This was enough to excite artists and writers; and the leisurely middle class, bent on unbending their minds, who were thwarted from taking their Grand Tour of Europe because of political unrest. Moreover West's guidebook contained a tolerable map of the Lakes where previously they had been ridiculously, even dangerously, poor.

West details eight stations, or viewpoints, around Derwent Water, with descriptions of the views from each. His book was the essential one for the first tourists, who would stand at the station, turn their backs to the view and hold up their Claude glass, a slightly convex mirror in a handsome frame, and observe its reflection.

Station 1 was from 'Cockshut-hill', or Cockshot wood, above Friar's Crag, now obscured by trees. Station 2 was Crow Park, describing what is now the field (NT) opposite the theatre. Three lay above the shore line of Stable Hills, a little below Lord's Island, and still reachable by public footpaths. Four was from the top of Castle Crag in Borrowdale, still excellent. ('From the summit of this rock the views are so singularly great and pleasing, that they ought never to be omitted.') Swinside, on the west side of the lake, is the location of station 5, but is difficult to pinpoint. Six is from the shore at 'Foe-park', 'a sweet evening walk'. This is on the north-west side of the lake, still offering sweet woodland walks on public footpaths, but the views are largely obscured. Station 7 is from Latrigg, above Keswick, previously described, and 8 is the vicarage garden. The poet Thomas Gray discovered this and his record is repeated in West's guide. He fixes it in his Claude glass:

> I got to the parsonage a little before sun-set, and saw in my glass a picture, that if I could transmit to you and fix it in all the softness of its living colours, would fairly sell for a thousand pounds. This is the sweetest scene I can yet discover in point of pastoral beauty …

When the artists began hurrying to the Lakes, it was Derwent Water and Borrowdale that were the first attractions. Many of their pictures grossly exaggerated the 'horror and immensity'. Indeed artistic licence was encouraged by Gilpin, who argued that nature hardly ever produced the best image, so that some views in the early pictures are hardly recognizable. But there were serious artists who painted what they saw. Joseph Farrington (1747–1821) produced many prints, while Sir George Beaumont (1753–1827) was a Lakeland enthusiast and friend of the Wordsworths. His first picture accepted by the Royal Academy was *A View of Keswick 1779*. J.M.W Turner (1775–1851) visited the Lakes in 1797 and produced many pictures, while John Constable (1776–1837) toured in 1806 and painted over seventy watercolours. There were many other professionals, as well as numerous amateurs, who were producing fine works in those early years.

Derwent Water is about 4.8 km long and 1.8 km wide. It is a shallow lake, reaching a maximum depth of 22 m, and shallowest at its foot; for this reason it is one of the first lakes to freeze in a cold spell in winter, when it attracts skaters. The lake's fish include trout, pike, perch and roach but also shoals of the rare vendace, *Coregonus albula* – a white fish, found only here and in Bassenthwaite Lake. The Keswick Angling Association sells fishing permits for the National Trust. In the last decade one plant has invaded the lake – the New Zealand pygmy weed, *Crassula helmsii*, which doubtless originated from garden centres that cater for aquariums. The weed is spreading and threatening to displace native species. The lake's bird visitors include tufted duck, pochard and goosanders.

To many regular visitors to the Lake District, Derwent Water was their first love. The lake probably has a more faithful following than any other and deserves it. It is fed from many sources, the main body coming from the high fells at Styhead Tarn,

Derwent Water, winter

Sprinkling Tarn, Langstrath and Honister, joining into the main River Derwent in Borrowdale. More water flows from Watendlath and down the falls of Lodore. The lake has four islands: Derwent Isle, nearest to Friar's Crag; Lord's Island (NT), south of Friar's Crag, and towards the lake centre, St Herbert's Island (NT).

St Herbert's Island held the hermitage of St Herbert, disciple and friend of St Cuthbert of Holy Island. It is said that they were so attached to each other that, in accordance with the prayer of St Herbert, they died on the same day in 687. The island became a place of pilgrimage. It is said that Friar's Crag gets its name from the point where friars would wait to embark to visit the saint, or perhaps where the pilgrims would wait to receive his blessing.

Derwent Isle was bought by the mining company to house its German miners. The immigrants made themselves at home there with a brewery, bakehouse, a pigsty and a windmill, and planted an orchard. In the eighteenth century, after mining's decline, the island showed no sign of the earlier German occupation, but some Germans remained and married local girls. Then a wealthy eccentric, Joseph Pocklington, bought the island (for £300) and built his house in its centre. He chose to erect a number of odd buildings around it, including a 'mock-Gothic' wooden church (James Clarke, writing in *Survey of the Lakes* in 1789, states that the more substantial church tower was 'not furnished by bells, but with good roast beef and claret'); a boathouse like a non-conformist chapel; a battery ('Fort Joseph') with cannons – five four-pounders, and a nine-pounder that were fired to produce amazing echoes; and even a 'Druids' Circle'. Visitors were amused, amazed and, sometimes, appalled.

From the island he organized regattas on the lake between 1781 and 1790, installing himself as the island 'governor'. His partner, Peter Crosthwaite, the eccentric who owned and furnished one of the Keswick museums, was 'admiral of the fleet'. On special days marquees were put up on the lakeshore to accommodate the large numbers of spectators, and there were boat races, entertainments and side shows. But the main excitement was the stupendous mock battle. A naval force under an admiral's command assembled behind Friar's Crag and a flag of truce was taken to the island. The governor naturally rejected the request for surrender and the assault began. Cannonades roared; marines landed with muskets and swords; guns and cannons were fired; bodies lay on the ground. So noisy was the cannonades, it was said, that the sound could be heard at Appleby – 27 km away. The days ended with fireworks, a dance and food.

Pocklington was condemned for his excesses, but he was a generous supporter of local charities.

One of the great pleasures of Derwent Water is that it is so wonderfully accessible. There are narrow roads with good viewpoints on both sides of the lake, but it is easily possible to get a closer involvement in the lake by walking round it, which one can do in almost its entirety; and further help is at hand with the excellent scheduled boat service, which has request stops at points round the lake. The boats operate from the Keswick landings, and you can get on and off the boat from the various landing-stages as you please. Rowing boats can also be hired from the Keswick landings, or from Nichol End Marine on the north-east shore. From a boat the landscape of the lake shores can be best appreciated. On the east side of the lake are the crags of Borrowdale volcanic rocks, with Walla Crag at its summit, and by contrast on the west there is the oddly named Catbells, a sweep of fell with a curved outline shaped like an impatient sweep of an artist's brush. This side of the lake is on the more malleable Skiddaw slate. The finest shore walking area is through the woods below Catbells, by Brandelhow, but one of the best views, if not the best, with Skiddaw behind, is from the tip of Barrow Bay on the lake's east side.

It is hard to believe that at one time, on the west shore near the lake head at Manesty, there was a busy lead mine, the Brandlehow, one of the most extensive in the area, with a long history. At its peak around 1848 it employed eighty men and boys. A 9 m-high water wheel pumped water from the mine, but this was replaced by steam engines. It produced around 300 tons of galena (lead) every year. Apart from lead, the mine produced silver – nine ounces per ton of lead, and even traces of gold were found. Eventually the amount of water that the mine had to pump out proved too much and it closed for a time until 1884, now equipped with a fifty-horsepower steam-engine pump, while a water wheel still worked the machinery to crush and dress the ore. Four years later the engine was replaced by a 350 horse-power beam-engine. The mine finally became uneconomic in 1891. Nature took over, so much so that the traces of it are not obvious. The site is now in the care of the National Trust, and is near one of the lake's landing-stages, at Brandelhow Point.

The one great problem of the mine, eventually making it unprofitable, was the need to pump out so much water – which was salty. At Manesty also this saltwater became a tourist attraction. Many believed strongly in the healing qualities of spa waters in the eighteenth and nineteenth centuries, and here, away from mining activity, was a spring with suitably nasty-tasting ingredients that offered 'a rough, severe purge' with 'Chloride of Sodium, and of Calcium and Magnesium, and Sulphate of Magnesia'. Monks were very good at finding this sort of thing, and the spring was very likely one of Furness Abbey's main sources of salt. It was claimed in 1740 that the spring could cure 'Dropsical, cacochymic, cathetic disorders, foulness of the stomach, slipperyness of the Bowels from Relaxations, or much Mucus, some icteritious disorders'. And if one did not suffer from any of these strange and alarming afflictions, might it not be best to take the drink just in case? The landowner, Sir John Woodford, KCB, dug out the well and covered it with a small building. Bathing in it was the thing, and two baths were made, both with a depth of around 1 m. Oddly there were too few takers of this therapeutic amenity and it died of neglect. The site, now a ring of stones, can be found east of the road, just south of the woodland caravan park.

Manesty was not the only mine. At the head of the lake is Great Bay, where the German miners were active. Manesty copper mine was north-east of the salt well. Another one was by the road north of Manesty, and trial excavations can be found in several places. The eastern face of Catbells is pock-marked by mining activity, perhaps only noticeable by mine and mineral enthusiasts.

Above Manesty Park by the roadside is the former home of Hugh Walpole (1884–1941), best-selling novelist and author of the *Herries Chronicles*, who set his fiction amid the Cumbrian landscape around the lake.

The fells on both sides of the lake are loved by many, so many so that Catbells (451 m) in particular shows signs of boot erosion. It is a hard push for the summit, usually taken from its northern end, but the views are worth it. There is no need to be a rock climber to reach the summit of Walla Crag (379 m) on the eastern side, and enjoy a stupendous view. It can be reached from a path in Great Wood (NT) or from Castlehead at Keswick. An ascent by Lady's Rake is not recommended. A story behind this spot thrilled the early tourists. The Jacobite rising in 1715 was supported by the third earl of Derwentwater. Following the defeat of the rebel army at Preston on 9 November the earl, with other noblemen, was taken prisoner, and he was subsequently beheaded, being spared the usual hanging, drawing and quartering because of his rank. His defence at his trial was that he had been persuaded to join his fellow peers and had not taken part in any plotting. Most probably his Roman Catholic wife was one of the inciters. Where truth is fogged by fiction is in what happened to Lady Derwentwater. Did she have to flee to avoid arrest, and was she on Lord's Island at the time, evidently the Derwentwaters' main estates were in the north-east. Anyway the story goes that she fled the island and escaped with her jewels by climbing up Walla Crag via a ravine. This became known as Lady's Rake, and is shown as such on today's maps. In scrambling up the crag she dropped a white handkerchief, which could be seen by tourists two centuries later! Actually, a dab of white paint on a prominent rock did the trick.

On the higher east side of the lake one of the best viewpoints is from the lakeshore path at Barrow Bay. Barrow House, nearby, is a youth hostel. In the grounds is one of Cumbria's oldest trees – a yew reckoned to be 900 years old. Long before the house became one of the most popular hostelries, it was one of the properties of Joseph Pocklington, the eccentric of Derwent Isle. He had the waterfall behind the house enlarged by diverting a stream. It is still impressive, but too unstable for a close approach. Pocklington set up a small hermitage in the grounds and tried to find a resident hermit who would live there for a wage of 2s 6d per day. The job description meant that the candidate would have to agree never to leave his cell or speak to anyone for seven years, and never wash or cut his hair or nails. Oddly enough there were no takers.

Opposite and to the south there occasionally appears a floating island, a phenomenon that fascinated the early tourists, and its origins led to much conjecture. It appears for a few weeks, and then submerges. The most probable explanation is that in hot weather the submerged mass of peat and decaying vegetation produces methane gas, causing the undergrowth to balloon out, and rise to the surface. George Bott (*Keswick: The Story of a Lake District Town*) recalls the report that in 1930 Keswick girl guides planted a union flag on the island and claimed it for England.

WATENDLATH AND BORROWDALE

Just north of the youth hostel, opposite the Ashness Gate boat landing-stage, a narrow road leaves for Watendlath. This is a captivating diversion. It is better walked, although it is a tarmac highway open to traffic. (The last section of the settlement is narrow, and many a car has received scratches from the drystone walls, which are often streaked with multi-coloured paint.) Two very famous viewpoints are on this route. The first is at the arched ASHNESS BRIDGE. The view

Ashness Bridge

Surprise View, Ashness

from a little above this takes in the elegant bridge, part of Derwent Water and the northern fells beyond. It is probably the most photographed and painted of all the Lakeland prospects, and has appeared on many thousands of postcards since photography was invented (1839), and on greetings cards, chocolate boxes and calendars. Though a cliché, it is still a photographer's dream, combining the foreground interest of the arched bridge, and the drama behind. The really dedicated are known to stand in the cold water to line up the best composition.

Further on, as the road ascends through woodland (NT), it passes close to the edge of a crag (car parks opposite). Here is SURPRISE VIEW, a sensational airy cliff-head perch overlooking Lodore Wood, though the surprise hits one better on the downward journey from Watendlath. Derwent Water is seen below almost entire and one looks beyond to the western fells and the foot of Bassenthwaite Lake. Coleridge discovered it in 1803 when he was walking from Watendlath and wrote in his notes:

> There should be some mark, some Cross or Heap of Stones to direct the Traveller to turn off on his left, 15 or 20 yards thro' the Coppice, about a 100 yards or so before he comes to the road-view of the Lake of Keswick [Ashness Bridge]. 20 yards thro' this open Coppice brings him suddenly to the Edge of a finely wooded Precipice, with Lodore beneath him at a small Distance on his Left, & on the Right the Promontory of Birches on the Lake/ the House at the Foot of Lodore, the Bridge, the Road seen in 3 different distances, so very beautiful – the Lake of Keswick – & of Bassenthwaite/ – the Height from the extreme steepness & direct plumb-down Look on the Lake seems vast – the breezes rush in pencil brushed over it –/ you look down on every thing, & every thing spreads in consequence, broad & long and vast! / This is/ I have no hesitation in saying it – the best, every way the best & most impressive View in all the Lake Country – why not in all the Island?

For walkers to Watendlath the nuisance of having to dodge traffic is avoided by parallel footpaths in the wood. WATENDLATH (*wa-TEND-lath*) sits comfortably behind Watendlath Tarn. Victorians loved this place. It became popular again between the wars when Hugh Walpole (1884–1941) wrote his best-selling novels set in the area. His *Judith Paris* lived at Fold Head Farm. The farm also appears in two other of his novels, *Bright Pavilions* and *Katherine Christian*. The tarn has been stocked with trout from Seathwaite Trout Farm.

Back down to the valley and from the head of the lake one enters BORROWDALE (*BOR-RA-dil*), for many the National Park's greatest gem. The first view of it is usually that distant one south from Friar's Crag, across the levels of Derwent Water and through the steep tree-clad walls at the dales' approach: 'the jaws of Borrowdale'. Then one continues into a widening floor drained by the River Derwent, and upwards to the river's source, among the highest land in England.

The dale's great beauty defies description. A mass of colour in spring or in autumn, the dale lies engulfed in steep woodlands, mainly hardwoods of oak, birch, ash and hazel, from the river to the heights. Everywhere there is a richness of ferns, moss and ground flora, and you are always aware that half-hidden soaring crags wall everything in. Then there is the river, clear to its deep, smooth rock and cobbled bed. Borrowdale stirs the soul.

Sadly at holiday times the narrow road is burdened with cars driving too fast. The modern car seems designed to be comfortable at fifty miles per hour, and the public has become more impatient. A driver moving at fifteen or twenty miles per hour so that his passengers can enjoy the view would be deemed a nuisance. Borrowdale is a place to linger in – which means it is a walkers' valley.

The road enters Borrowdale at Lodore Wood, whose waterfalls was another major attraction on the Victorian tourists' itinerary. And after rain, for sheer volume and sound, it is the district's most impressive. Its source is Watendlath Tarn. The poet laureate, Robert Southey, enhanced the fall's reputation in his poem for children, *The Cataract of Lodore*, a tongue-twisting description, in five verses, of the course of the falls from source to foot.

> From its sources which well
> In the tarn on the fell,
> From its fountains
> In the mountains,
> Its rills and its gills;
> Through moss and through brake,
> It runs and it creeps

Until finally in the last verse:

> And flapping and rapping and clapping and slapping,
> And curling and whirling and purling and twirling,
> And thumping and plumping and bumping and jumping,
> And dashing and flashing and splashing and clashing;
> And so never ending, but always descending,
> Sounds and motions for ever and ever blending,
> All at once and all o'er, with a mighty uproar,
> And this is the way the Water comes down at Lodore.

After a prolonged drought – and the Lake District does have them – waterfalls become mere dribbles. A comic postcard c. 1900 shows a tourist sitting on a rock beneath crags and questioning an apron-clad local woman:

> 'How does the water come down from Lodore?'
> A dry-season Tourist once thought to explore,
> But he failed to discover the famous cascade,
> So enquired in despair of a Cumbrian maid;
> 'Indeed sir,' quoth she, with a toss of her bonnet,
> 'You may well seek Lodore, for ye're sitting upon it.'

The falls are reached from behind the Lodore Hotel, or alternatively by a public footpath through Lodore Wood (NT). A climbing gill-side path takes an energetic person, with a head for heights, to the higher falls.

The poet Thomas Gray was much impressed by his drive past Derwent Water and into Borrowdale in 1769 – with the landlord of the Queen's Head as guide. He made a detailed account of what he saw – much in awe and a little scared.

> ... passing a brook called Barrow beck we entered Borrowdale; the crags named Lowdore-banks begin now to impend terribly over the way, and more terribly when you hear that three years since an immense mass of rock tumbled at once from the brow, barred all access to the dale (for this is the only road), till they could work their way through it. Luckily no one was passing by at the time of this fall; but down the side of the mountain, and far into the lake, lie dispersed the huge fragments of this ruin, all shapes and in all directions.

After describing the falls of 'Lowdore' he goes on:

> Soon after we came under Gowdar-crag, a hill more formidable to the eye, and to the apprehension, than that of Lowdore; the rocks at the top deep-cloven perpendicularly by the rains, hanging loose and nodding forwards, seen just starting from their base in shivers. The whole way down, and the road on both sides is strewed with piles of the fragments, strangely thrown across each other and of a dreadful bulk; the place reminds me of those passes in the Alps, where the guides tell you to move with speed, and say nothing, less the agitation of the air should loosen the snows above, and bring down a mass that would overwhelm a caravan. I took their counsel here and hastened on in silence. Non ragioniam di lor, ma guarda, e passa. [Let us not discuss them, but take a look and pass by – Dante's *Inferno*: Canto 3]

The way up the lakeside, usually by carriage, to Lodore was a major attraction to the first flush of tourists, although a regular coach service up Borrowdale in 1824 did not get off to a good start – one of the vehicles overturned at Grange. At the Lodore Hotel there were two cannons, and for a fee one or both could be hired to discharge and produce satisfactory bangs, with up to nine echoes. Offshore here was the puzzle of the floating island, already discussed, but another enigma was just as baffling. This is the lake's 'bottom wind'. On a perfectly calm day, it is said, the lake's surface becomes agitated and a swell moves from west to east, the effect lasting as long as a day. Some say that it forecasts bad weather.

The crag face on the western bank of the falls of Lodore is Shepherd's Crag, one of the Lake District's most popular rock-climbing spots, offering climbs varying in grades from 'difficult' upwards. The best place from which to watch the climbers is the public footpath that leaves the crags for Great Bay at the head of the lake.

The road runs under Grange Fell (NT), which is on the left, a superb little fell well worth exploration. Brund Fell (415 m) is the highest point and has a surprisingly wide view of the central fells, Derwent Water and part of Bassenthwaite. A second peak, King's How to the north-west of Brund, gives a grand view over Borrowdale.

One reaches GRANGE-IN-BORROWDALE by a stone-arch bridge over the river. The small settlement is on the site of a grain store owned by the monks of Furness Abbey. The abbey once owned the whole of Borrowdale, though unchristianlike disputes occasionally flared up. Distant Fountains Abbey in Yorkshire owned Derwent Island, Watendlath and land at Keswick, which did not seem right.

Grange bridge

Over to the west are the slopes of Maiden moor (575 m), which was mined in places. Looking up-valley from the bridge the scene is overshadowed by woodland-clad Castle Crag, another fine viewpoint, whose summit is reached by crumbling quarry tracks. No Norman tower stands on this crag, for the 'castle' was Romano-British, built of wood long since vanished, behind a system of banks and ditches that can still be traced.

Further up-valley comes Quay Foot, once a profitable quarry known as 'Rainspot' because its volcanic slate contained splash marks. The waste heaps of the quarry have been colonized by a birch wood, later encouraged and planted by the National Trust, and ablaze in the glow of autumn. A hidden car park up in the wood is a popular point for Borrowdale walks. The focal point hereabouts is the famous Bowder Stone, reached by a track to the east of the road, and also high on the Victorians' itinerary. This is a high, isolated rock, perched, apparently precariously, on a narrow base. How it got there has long been a subject for debate. The popular view is that it must have fallen from the fells above. Another view among Victorians was that it had always been there, since the creation. The most likely explanation is that it was plucked off the fell side and left here by glacial ice. Southey criticized its owner for building:

> an ugly house for an old woman to live in who is to show the rock, for fear travellers should pass under it without seeing it, cleared away all the fragments round it, and as it rests upon a narrow base, like a ship on its keel, dug a hole underneath through which the curious may gratify themselves by shaking hands with the old woman.

Steps were built up it so that one can stand on top.

The valley above widens where Stonethwaite Beck joins the Derwent. After heavy rain flooding occurs here, in fact it is the site of an older lake. ROSTHWAITE hamlet, sitting between the two rivers, has a track rising around the side of Grange Fell to Watendlath, and once busy packhorse routes leading via Stonethwaite over the fells to Langdale and Grasmere.

Gilpin, in 1772, walked to Watendlath from Rosthwaite and his description of it is a classic of exaggeration:

> 'Which way to Watenlath[sic]?' said one of our company to a peasant, as we left the vale of Borrodale[sic]. 'That way,' said he, pointing up a lofty mountain, steeper than the tiling of a house.
>
> To those who are accustomed to mountains, these perpendicular motions may be amusing; but to us, whose ideas were less elevated, they seemed rather peculiar ... To move upwards, keeping a steady eye on the objects before us, was no great exercise to the brain: but it rather gave it a rotation to look back on what was past – and to see our companions below clinging, as it appeared, to the mountain's side; and the rising breasts and bellies of their horses, straining path so steep, that it seemed, as if the least false step would have carried them rolling many hundred yards to the bottom.

The packhorse routes from Stonethwaite are great, and make a good walk if the transport can be worked out at either end. The path and bridleway first follow the

Stonethwaite Beck and then divide at the Y where the two feeding becks join the Langstrath. One track then goes by the Langstrath Beck and over the Stake Pass to Langdale, the other going by Greenup Gill and over Greenup Edge to Grasmere. The Langstrath route is the most impressive as it passes beneath Eagle Crag and Sergeant's Crag, two sheer cliffs on the end of the fell mass of Ullscarf and High Raise. Before the making of the improved turnpike roads, this was the 'main road' between the important towns of Cockermouth and Hawkshead.

A path from Rosthwaite also leads across the Derwent and through Johnny Wood (NT), a site of Special Scientific Interest because of its unusually fine growths of ferns and liverworts, to Seatoller. SEATOLLER was at one time merely a farm, but a settlement developed for the workers at Honister Quarries. The road over Honister Pass leaves westwards at this point. A barn at the foot is a National Park information centre.

Going still further up the valley, the narrow road ends at SEATHWAITE farm, the starting point for the popular walks to the high fells. Across the river and a little way back are Borrowdale's ancient yews, 'those fraternal Four of Borrowdale' mentioned Wordsworth.

> ... those fraternal Four of Borrowdale,
> Joined in one solemn and capacious grove;
> Huge trunks! and each particular trunk a growth
> Of intertwisted fibres serpentine
> Up-coiling, and inveterately convolved;
> ... natural temple scattered o'er
> With altars undisturbed of mossy stone.

Though damaged by a storm in 1883, and others since, and intermittently by browsing and bark-stripping animals, three remain as they have remained for 2,000 years – it takes a lot to kill off yews. The trees are now in the care of the National Trust.

THE WAD MINE

Up on the fell side can be seen waste heaps of the once very profitable plumbago, or 'wad', or 'black lead', or 'black cawke', or graphite mines. This jet-black material feels greasy to the touch, owing to tiny flakelets. It can be cut with a blade, machined and sharpened to a point. It is pure carbon, like diamond, yet the paradox is that graphite is one of the softest minerals and diamond the hardest. How it was formed in the earth is not really known. In Cumbria it was first discovered near the earth surface and used for marking sheep, as a medicine, and as a dye, first by the monks of Furness Abbey, for this was their land. Then when it was mined in earnest it was used in foundries for lining mouldings, particularly for cannon and musket balls, as it was a perfect separating layer between casts and moulds, able to withstand high temperatures. It was indestructible. Lower-grade wad was used for protecting iron and steel from rust, and as a lubricant. Then the graphite from these mines launched the pencil manufacturing factory in Keswick from 1811, though pencils were being made long before that. The factory still exists (but now uses imported materials).

In the eighteenth century the high-quality wad was so rare and valuable worldwide that an armed guard in a minehead guardhouse had to be on duty day and night. It seems incredible, but the wad was considered to be the purest in the world, and in today's terms the mine was making profits into the millions. An Act of 1752 made the punishment for stealing wad a whipping, a year's imprisonment with hard labour, or deportation. But thieving continued and the stolen ore was sold in the back-street alehouses of Keswick, giving rise to the term 'black market'. All miners were strip-searched as they left the pit.

Graphite was considered to be a valuable mineral in the sixteenth century when the Seathwaite lead mines were already well known, and was already being used for drawing. An Elizabethan traveller/historian visited the site and reported:

> Here is found in several places that metallic earth or hard glittering stone, which we call Black Lead, used by painters to draw lines and drawings in black and white. Whether it be Dioscorides' Pnigitis, or Melanteria, or ochre burnt black by the heat of the earth, or totally unknown to the antients, I cannot determine, but shall leave to others.

Two royal commissioners were sent to Borrowdale in August 1555 to scout out the locations and assess the production potential. Following their report the mining area was let on lease, and by the end of the century work was done under a number of lessees. In the next century the Company of Mines Royal, whose main interest lay in copper, lead and silver, took an active interest in the wad, and the work continued with German expertise. To begin with, the mineral was exported to Germany, through the connections of the Hechstetters – the importers were cousins. Then London and Newcastle merchants were supplied. To maintain the high price the merchants, as sole customers, entered into covenants with the mine lessees restricting the amount they mined. In 1655, for instance, they required that the mine was to be closed for seven years, and subsequently a pattern of closure and production became normal. More uses, meanwhile, were discovered for the mineral.

Several levels were driven into the hillside, on upper and lower sites, mostly in hope rather than on good evidence. The mineral did not occur in veins, but in 'sops' of irregular masses, or 'pipes', and there was no way of telling if a venture through the very hard rock was going to be successful or not. Once reached, extraction was not difficult, and on getting out into daylight no elaborate dressing floors were required. But security was a problem. At one time the thieves' lanterns could be seen at night as they searched the mine dumps; only the use of dogs could disperse them. William Hetherington and John Martin, who had a lease to mine for copper nearby, made one audacious attempt in 1739. They drove a level in search of copper, and deviated from its line to try to reach a known and valuable wad sop. Their side tunnel was hidden behind a door fronted with timber work, and so well was it screened that anyone was at liberty to view the copper mine. Their undoing came when nodules of wad were found on the floor.

Thieves became desperate enough to use firearms. The guardhouse fronting the mine was attacked in 1750, and was successful. Following a tip-off that another raid was planned the guardhouse was reinforced. In this attack the thieves broke through the slates in the roof and fired down, wounding one of the men. A gunfight ensued that resulted in the death of one of the raiders, and the assault was abandoned. But other raids followed, and over years armed guards were necessary to secure the mine entrances, and relays of men would sleep with their charges overnight en route to customers.

During the early blossoming of the tourist industry, a visit to the wad mines was one of the interests. Bishop Nicolson was an early visitor, and William Wilberforce came later. In 1772 Gilpin was content to see it from a distance:

> I could not help feeling a friendly attachment to this place, which every lover of the pencil must feel, as deriving from the mineral one of the best instruments of his art; the freest and best expositor of his ideas. We saw the site of the mine at a distance, marked with a dingy yellow stain, from the ochery mixtures thrown from its mouth, which shiver down the sides of the mountain.

The mine at last was considered to be barren in 1875, and closed in 1891. All that remain are the spoil heaps, and ruined the walls of a guardhouse.

THE BORROWDALE FOLK

The poet Gray, having journeyed up Borrowdale with some trepidation, was not inclined to get too near Seathwaite, but he made enquiries and wrote:

> ... all further access is here barred to prying mortals, only there is a little path winding over the fells, and for some weeks in the year passable to the dalesmen; but the mountains know well that these innocent people will not reveal the mysteries of their ancient kingdom, `the reign of Chaos and old Night' only I learned that this dreadful road, dividing again, leads one branch to Ravenglass, and the other to Hawkshead.

It can be assumed, if tradition has any truth, that the 'innocent people' would not reveal the mysteries of their kingdom to Gray, or encourage exploration, because up on the fells were secret whisky distilleries, and they were playing hide and seek with the excise men. Who was this strange man asking the questions?

In the eighteenth and early nineteenth centuries the Borrowdale inhabitants were the butt of Keswick jokes. It was reckoned that they were so cut off from the world that they were all simple-minded. The most common story was that the Borrowdale people wanted to keep the valley in perpetual spring and decided that to do this they would have to keep the cuckoo from leaving. So they built a wall at Grange to prevent it flying away. It did not work, because, they reckoned, they had built the wall just one course too low.

Another story is of the Borrowdale man who was sent by a newcomer, with his horse and a couple of sacks, to collect some lime from the far side of Keswick. Lime was unknown in Borrowdale. On returning, near to Grange, it started to rain hard and the lime started to smoke. In alarm the man tried to douse what he thought was an impending fire by throwing a hat full of water over the sacks. This made matters worse, and he thought that the devil must be involved in a fire that could not be doused by water, so he threw the sacks in the river.

Yet another story was of a man riding into Borrowdale on a mule, then leaving it in local care while he went walking. The mule was an object of curiosity to a gathering of locals, as one had never been seen in the valley before. The local wise man, who practised magic medicine for there was no doctor in the dale, was asked to come and identify it. Drawing a circle in the ground around the animal, he consulted his book of magic, then came to the conclusion – it was a peacock. So Borrowdale had the only man in Cumbria to come riding in to the dale on a peacock.

Needless to say, Borrowdale people were not amused by such tales told to tourists. Harriet Martineau records that in her time (mid nineteenth century) a Borrowdale man walked into an inn, and was greeted by a guest calling 'cuckoo'. This triggered a fight.

THE WAYS TO THE HIGH FELLS AND GREAT GABLE

From Borrowdale one has a choice of three routes up to Sty Head Pass. The usual route is past Seathwaite farm, by the east side of the gill to Stockley bridge, across the bridge and by the old packhorse route over Stockley bridge and around Seathwaite Fell. The second is the superior route for those with a head for heights, crossing the bridge at Seathwaite farm, and following the west side of Styhead Gill. At around 300 m the path turns up the side of a ravine. Down this ravine falls TAYLOR GILL FORCE, considered by many to be the most spectacular waterfall in the Lakes. It is not so much the height of it – over 30 m – nor the volume of water; but rather its wild and savage situation, and the view of it from the high path.

In 1966 there was an unusually heavy and sustained rainfall in the mountains, and record floods caused havoc. The packhorse bridge, Stockley bridge, was badly damaged. Large boulders were bouncing down the silt-laden torrents with a noise like artillery fire. Where they formed a blockage, the waters rushed out on either side, tearing away the banks. Then the vast area of the valley floor became completely covered in rock debris. Paths and tracks, walls and fields vanished and roads were torn away. The scene was horrific. Months of clearing followed, and the scars have taken years to heal. But nature being so resilient one would not know now that anything had happened.

The main packhorse track from Seathwaite over STY HEAD PASS (487 m) to Wasdale, Ravenglass and the west coast was once one of the busy highways taking strings of packhorses, walkers and horse riders. Tales abound of how it was used by smugglers, as well as illegal whisky producers. Nowadays fell walkers use the path not 'some weeks in the year' as the poet Gray was told, but all the year round, for ascents of Scafell Pike or Great Gable, or the walk over to Wast Water. In the early days of mountaineering when the majority of practitioners were British, it was said that if you stayed long enough on the pass, every mountaineer in the world would pass you by. More than once it has been proposed to make a public road over the pass, but mercifully it has remained as it is, open to the winds and the sky. Around the tarn the grass has tempted back-packing campers. But the pass can be a wind tunnel, and many a camp has been swept away. A large mountain rescue stretcher box sits on the summit by the side

Great Gable from Scafell Pike

of Styhead Tarn. There could have been a tragedy at the stretcher box once, for a walker climbed inside to get out of the wild weather and the hasp snapped shut as the lid closed, trapping him. Luckily passing walkers heard the muffled cry for help.

Another bridle path branches off from the south of Sty Head Pass to ascend by Grains Gill past Sprinkling Tarn to ESK HAUSE (759 m), a pass with the main route south into Eskdale, and eastwards to Langdale. It is notorious place for getting lost in mist, and the wayward seem surprised to end up in Eskdale whether they wanted to be there or not.

Although the route to the Scafells from Sty Head is a popular one, the Scafells really belong to Wasdale Head (see pp. 583–5). GREAT GABLE, one can say, belongs to Sty Head. After Helvellyn and Scafell Pike, Gable (899 m) is close in popularity. It instantly seizes the attention of anyone who is excited by mountains. Viewed from Wasdale Head its name is apt for it is like the gable end of a monstrous dale church. The best view of all is probably from Lingmell Crag, its southern neighbour on the Scafell range; from there the full extent of its rough steep side, 777 m to the valley floor of Wasdale, can be appreciated. If it is gable-shaped from Wasdale Head and Lingmell, viewed from the east or the west it is a huge hump, thrusting above the shoulders of its lesser neighbours. From the north it is seen as a great arc of cliff. The mountain is separated by

Walkers on Great Gable summit

suitable gulfs from its neighbours in the Scafells, which sit at a respectable distance to the south.

There are two main approaches to Gable's summit. After an ascent to Styhead one assaults it directly up 410 m of rough path. The softer option is from the car park at the top of Honister Pass, along the quarry road to Drum House, then it is a two-hour walk, 594 m in all, by Gillercomb Head, Green Gable and Windy gap. In bad visibility a descent is tricky and the route south-eastwards to Styhead is the safest.

The fell has a lot of interest. Rock climbers contour westwards around from Styhead beneath the summit, on to the Girdle Traverse. This is not a path for inexperienced walkers, nor a reasonable route to the summit, unless one wishes to scramble up the loose scree chute with the apt name of Great Hell Gate. The traverse does pass some of the most exciting rock climbs in the country, however. The first crag is Kern Knotts, then the rough path crosses Great Hell Gate to Great Napes, a large wall of rock. This is the location of many climbs, often with names given to them by their first climbers: Tophet Bastion, Needle Ridge and Gully, Eagle's Nest Ridge and Gully, Arrowhead Ridge and Gully, Sphinx Ridge. Then low on the crag and near the centre stands the famous Napes Needle, a spire of naked rock first climbed in 1886 by the legendary father of rock climbers Walter Parry Haskett-Smith. He tells how he looked at the Needle and threw a stone the size of a brick up on to its top. If it stayed there, he decided, he would follow it! It did, and having achieved the top he wrote:

> There was no means of recording my visit except a small boss near the north edge of the (summit) stone, round which my handkerchief was tied with my brick on top of it to keep it from being blown away ... In the descent hanging by the hands from the top and feeling with my toes for the protuberance provided an anxious moment, but the rest went easily enough, though it must be confessed that it was an undoubted satisfaction to stand once more on solid ground below and look up at my handkerchief fluttering in the breeze.

He climbed it again fifty years later at the age of seventy-four!

The Needle does not always look impressive from the path, but a scramble up the gully behind brings one on to a ledge called the Dress Circle, which is the usual viewpoint. The top of the Needle is a large, separate block of stone: it has not threatened to slip off its perch in spite of the number of climbers who have crawled over it. Beyond Great Napes is another scree run, Little Hell Gate, just as hellish, followed by White Napes, another rock wall; the girdle then continues to Beck Head.

From Beck Head a path, Moses Trod, contours round under the north-facing crags of Gable to Drum House, above Honister Quarries. Moses was a local folk figure, a Cumbrian rogue who is said to have made illicit whisky hereabouts and sold it in Wasdale, or anywhere else. Doubtless there were a number of hidden 'worms' making the hard stuff in earlier years, but excise men would have found it almost impossible to track them down.

The top of Great Gable is a mass of stone blocks and detritus. On the topmost point is a bronze-tablet war memorial that also records the gift of the fell to the National Trust by the Fell and Rock Climbing Club in 1924. Every Remembrance Sunday many walkers, sometimes over a hundred, and sometimes facing seriously bad weather, congregate here to observe a moment's respectful silence.

As one might expect on a clear day the views are long, as far as the Isle of Man, the Scottish Lowland hills and the Yorkshire Pennines. The dramatic view is over Wasdale, from Westmorland Cairn, south-west of the summit.

OVER HONISTER TO BUTTERMERE

HONISTER PASS (358 m) is a road that links Seatoller, near the head of Borrowdale, with Buttermere. It used to be a struggle for early motor cars, but now it is nowhere difficult, though it is narrow in places, making passing tricky. In winter the Buttermere side is sometimes impassable. Fleetwith Pike (648 m) is to the west of the pass, and Dale Head (754 m) to the north. Slate has been quarried from the pass between these fells since Roman times, and since then has been worked by both open quarrying and by mining, depending upon how the veins of desirable rock, varying in thickness, run. The quarries are notable at the pass head on the left of the road. Roofing slates have been produced in great quantities here and supplied in sizes from large to small – or in quarryman's terms as 'Bests, Seconds, Thirds, Best Peggies and Second Peggies'. The manufacture was in stages from extraction; docking, to reduce the size of 'clogs' (blocks) to a manageable size, or sawing with a rotary saw to do the same; riving, that is, splitting the slate along the grain; and finally dressing, that is, shaping the roofing slate on dressing floors, a very skilled job done by hand, but also done by machine quickly but less well.

Quarrying prospered here in earnest in the seventeenth century, but the roofing slates they produced were large and heavy, and production had to be stopped during the winter months. Demand increased, until the peak of 1793 when 6,000 tons were produced – all manhandled in often atrocious weather and cold temperature conditions. Accidents must have been frequent. In the next century the high-quality slate was getting greater appreciation, and the works were extended. The way the slate was brought down from the heights to the transport below was by 'sledding'. The slates were packed into a box sled that had two long shafts at the front. The quarryman took his place between the shafts in front, took the weight off his feet, and the sled raced down the hillside on the sled run. To brake the speed he had to straighten his arms to lift his weight and bear down on the shafts; to raise the speed he allowed the shafts to lift. To an onlooker the operation looked mad and suicidal, but it was constantly repeated. Harriet Martineau in *A Description of the English Lakes* (1858) remarked how the quarrymen seemed to be 'hanging like summer-spiders quivering from the eaves of a house', and records that one quarryman named Joseph Clark seemed to have the record for sledding slate down to the road. On one day he made seventeen runs to bring down 10,880 lb (499 kg) of slate. On another occasion he brought down three record-breaking loads each weighing 1,280 lb (581 kg). His greatest daily effort was to sled down 11,771 lb (5,340 kg). He declared that all he ever suffered from in the severe work was thirst.

In 1882 the Buttermere Green Slate Company felt that they could not expand their activities so long as the slate had to make a laborious horse-and-cart journey from Honister Pass to Keswick railway station. They proposed the building of a railway line from Braithwaite station, west of Keswick, alongside Catbells and between the fells of High Spy and Lobstone Band. Again the Revd Hardwicke Rawnsley led the opposition, arguing that if it went ahead, 'Keswick as a resort for weary men in search of rest will cease to be.' There was strong hostility to the plan, and the parliamentary Bill was withdrawn.

Over the two centuries following, good times followed bad and bad good as

Buttermere

the slate market fluctuated. In 1986 the rising cost of extraction, and the availability of cheaper Spanish slate, meant a decline; but the quarry is still producing roofing slate and the quarry mine is open as an unusual and fascinating tourist attraction. Visitors are kitted out with helmet and head light, and taken down the corridors into the cathedral-like man-made caverns.

The descent to BUTTERMERE from Honister is between Fleewith Pike and Buttermere Fell. The white cross on the fell side of Fleetwith is a memorial to Fanny Mercer, aged eighteen, who after walking on Honister Crag, fell and died after tripping over her walking pole in 1887. She was a servant of the Revd Bowen Smith, a master at Rugby school. If memorials were erected for every fatal fell casualty there would be so many that they would be regarded as obtrusive litter.

Permission for new ones is not granted. However, some of the old ones are landmarks, and poor Fanny's is one that is preserved.

In tourism's early days it was considered fashionable to rave about Buttermere. Buttermere was considered to be the quintessence of natural beauty, showing a perfect harmony of form, and serving as a remote refuge of peace and tranquillity. The still waters of the lake contrasted with the raging white becks pitching down the high crag walls. The level mere and the soft lines of trees were equally matched by the awesome outlines of the fells behind. Hardly anything has changed, and though it is no longer fashionable to rave about the place, one may still be permitted to gasp a little at this unique gem of the English countryside.

The minor road descends past Gatesgarth to the south-eastern side of the lake

Buttermere from Hassness

head. Although the valley is on Skiddaw slate, on the opposite side of the lake is that wall of high crags of Borrowdale volcanic rocks containing great hollow coves, best seen from the lakeshore footpath below the road at this point. The three peaks running from left to right are High Crag (745 m), High Stile (805 m) and Red Pike (756 m), the latter peak being largely composed of granophyre, a type of granite. Most of the land and the lake itself are owned by the National Trust, though the wooded shore of Hassness, with access to the shore, is owned by the National Park Authority. The house is let to the Ramblers Association as a hostel. It is possible, given good footwear, to stroll all round the lake, most of it close to the water, except on crossing farmland at each end.

The lake is fed by Warnscale Beck, from the fells, and Gatescarthdale Beck, which descends from Honister. But rather than these sources it is the becks falling from the High Stile ridge that contribute to Buttermere's drama. These becks, notably Sour Milk Gill, which pours over the crags from Bleaberry Tarn, look particularly wonderful after heavy rain. The lake is over 28 m deep and contains trout, char, pike and perch. Boats and fishing permits are had from Dalegarth guest house. The water varies in colour from green to blue-grey, depending on the weather, the light and the time of year. In squally weather the lake is whipped up into moving spirals of spray by the turbulent wind currents. The great J.M.W. Turner pictured it in a storm.

Buttermere's small village has two hotels and a tiny church. Wordsworth wrote, 'A man must be very insensible who would not be touched with pleasure at the sight of the chapel of Buttermere.' The church we see now was built in 1841 and is actually larger than the one that Wordsworth applauded, but still good to look at. A road from Bassenthwaite over the steep Newlands Pass, sometimes impassable in winter, joins Buttermere by the church.

In the early nineteenth century the village was linked with a story containing all the melodramatic ingredients so beloved in that age (indeed, the story was reproduced on stage in a few of London's theatres). It began when the early tourist, Captain Budworth, described the great beauty of local girl Mary Robinson at the Fish Inn, in his book *A Fortnight's Ramble in the Lakes*.

> ... her face was a fine oval, with full eyes and lips as red as vermilion; her cheeks had more of the lily than the rose. Ye travellers of the Lakes, if you visit this obscure place, such you will find the fair MARY of BUTTERMERE.

Readers of the popular book could hardly wait to see her and the poor lass became a tourist attraction. In 1802 a man falsely calling himself the Hon. Augustus Hope (an actual person conveniently out of the country) persuaded the girl to marry him. He was John Hatfield, a bigamist and a con man. But he was found out. He was taken to Carlisle where he was tried and sentenced to death, not for bigamy, but forgery. The case caused a national stir and curious visitors to the condemned cell included, incredibly, Coleridge and the Wordsworths on their way to Scotland. He was hanged in 1803. Authentic melodrama might require Mary to have been ruined, or to have died of a broken heart, but in fact she married a farmer, had a large family and was buried in Caldbeck churchyard. The story was the subject of many poems, plays and novels, and indeed Melvyn Bragg used the story in his 1987 novel *The Maid of Buttermere*. Wordsworth mentions the story too in 'The Prelude', and recalls the time when he and Coleridge first saw her.

> Must needs bring back the moment when we first
> Ere the broad world rang with the maiden's name,
> Beheld her serving at the cottage inn;
> Both stricken, as she entered or withdrew,
> With admiration of her modest mien
> And carriage, marked by unexampled grace.

It is hard to believe, but during the nineteenth-century fever to build railways, one was proposed to reach Buttermere. There was fierce opposition, but the proposal was dropped because of high costs.

The ridge walk of the three peaks (definitely not to be done in poor weather) is best achieved from the pass of Scarth Gap (sometimes Scarf Gap), which is reached from the south-west end of the lake. The descent is achieved from Red Pike through the Saddle, and by Bleaberry Tarn steeply down to Buttermere village. The walk is exciting, with the best views being from High Stile. The fells separate Buttermere from Ennerdale, with views down over the forest.

One must not forget Hay Stacks (579 m), east of the three peaks, and also approachable eastwards from Scarf Gap, amongst the cluster of bigger fells – 'like a shaggy terrier in the company of fox hounds,' as Wainwright describes it. This was his favourite fell. The summit area is a surprise of little tarns, little peaks, meandering paths, heather, marsh and great views. It is a place to wander and linger in.

CRUMMOCK WATER AND LOWESWATER

A lush area of farmland, formed from the deposition of sediments and eroded rocks left after the ice ages, separates Buttermere from CRUMMOCK WATER 1 km away. It lacks Buttermere's dramatic craggy background because the whole of the area around the lake is of Skiddaw slates. The lake is twice the size of its modest neighbour, and 44 m deep. Like Buttermere it contains trout, pike and perch, but also char, and after July, salmon and sea trout. Boats can be hired from Woodhouse, but the lake is a wind tunnel in some conditions, which can come on suddenly – life jackets should be worn. Scale Force, one of the Lake District's most impressive waterfalls, particularly after heavy rain, drops from the fell wall at the south-western end, which is reached by a footpath from Buttermere.

The lake's narrowest point is at the upper reach, where the rock is hardest. Hawes Point hugs the east side of the lake, and above this is a hill known as Rannerdale Knotts; it is a scramble on rough ground to reach the summit but it affords an excellent view of the lake. It is possible to walk around the lake, but on the west side the going is rough, not easy for anyone carrying fishing tackle.

In the Notes section of his *Guide to the Lakes,* Wordsworth argued that the best view of the lake was from the lake itself:

> It must be mentioned also, that there is scarcely anything finer than the view from a boat in the centre of Crummock Water. The scene is deep, and solemn and lonely; and in no other spot is the majesty of the Mountains so irresistibly felt as an omnipresence, or so passively submitted to as a spirit incumbent upon the imagination.

One reaches LOWESWATER by a minor road running west from the foot of Crummock, past Loweswater hamlet. The small lake, which holds trout, perch and pike, is delightfully situated in woodlands cared for by the National Trust. Unlike any of the other lakes, the water from it flows inwards towards the central valley system, and into Crummock Water. The stunning view of it is from Mellbreak (511 m), an ascent that is particularly enjoyable when the heather is in bloom.

Going back towards Crummock, the road from Crummock Water to Cockermouth passes through the green valley known as LORTON VALE. There are two hamlets in the vale, High Lorton and Low Lorton. A road from Braithwaite crosses Whinlatter Pass (see p. 436) and descends to the Lortons. This is the popular way to Crummock and Buttermere from Keswick, avoiding the steepness of Newlands Pass.

Near Low Lorton is Lorton Hall, part of which is a pele tower dating from the fifteenth century; most of the rest is also medieval but completed by a neoclassical façade from the seventeenth century. The house contains some fine oak panelling.

The village hall at High Lorton was called Yew Tree Hall – appropriately enough, for nearby stands the incredibly old and celebrated yew tree referred to by Wordsworth in his poem on that subject:

> There is a Yew-tree, pride of Lorton Vale
> Which to this day stands single, in the midst
> Of its own darkness, as it stood of yore.

He thought it should be preserved:

> ... a living thing
> Produced too slowly ever to decay;
> Of form and aspect too magnificent
> To be destroyed.

Actually it has been repeatedly damaged by storm. Now it is lop-sided, having lost half of its trunk. Yews are obstinate survivors, however, and it is likely to make a slow recovery. The people of Lorton are making sure of its survival – cuttings grown from the tree have been planted around the village.

It was under this tree that George Fox preached to Cromwell's soldiers and a great crowd of people; so many of them climbed the tree to see him, that a fear arose for its safety.

ENNERDALE AND ITS FELLS

ENNERDALE is one of the more remote and less accessible dales, vehicle access to it being by narrow roads to Ennerdale bridge, and further narrow ones to the foot of the lake itself. Those who need peace and solitude seek it for that reason. The Forestry Commission is the valley's largest landowner, and there are a number of walking trails in the forest. Some 32 km of private forest roads and tracks are freely available for walkers, with the only traffic being commission vehicles, and there are very many more miles of footpaths. It is possible to walk right around the lake, though granophyre rock breaks into blocks, so the going is rough in places and good footwear essential. A leaflet produced by the commission lists eight routes in the forest, pleasant at any time, but especially good options if the weather is too wet for walks in open country. Essentially, too, Ennerdale is on the main walkers' and climbers' route to the fells.

Ennerdale Water is a beautiful lake and one hardly notices the fact that its level has been raised by a dam to provide water for the west coast areas. A much loved inn, the Anglers' Arms, once stood on the rim of the lake, offering superb views from its windows. The inn was not maintained because of plans to raise the lake level further, necessitating the building's destruction, and finally it had to be

Ennerdale, winter

demolished. As it turned out, the plans were dropped and the inn could have stayed. Its site is now a car park.

The head of the lake sits on a bed of granophyre, a hard volcanic rock, but the lake foot is on the friable Skiddaw slates; so that when the glacier carved out the valley it splayed out on reaching the softer rocks. The water is exceptionally pure, restricting the amount of life in it, but there are brown trout, char and salmon, and otters have been seen.

The Forestry Commission aroused controversy when it acquired large parts of Ennerdale and began planting conifers in the 1920s. Two thousand sheep were excluded from their 'heafs' – traditional grazing land. Public access was restricted, and the view of the dark forest, with its straight boundary lines, from the fell was abhorrent. Now the forest has won acceptance, and the commission's recent policy of breaking up the harsh lines, by felling and restocking, and of encouraging public access, has been applauded.

In 1884 an Ennerdale Railway Bill was mooted, but failed on the ground of costs. Luckily the valley remains inviolate – the only Lake District valley without public vehicle access. It really needs to remain so. The commission, backed by the National Park Authority and conservation groups, has resisted pressures to allow car access on their lakeside road. This preserves the valley's quietness and the feeling of remoteness – as near as possible to a wilderness experience. This makes the valley very special to many who come here repeatedly, be they serious walkers, or lakeside strollers.

Another threat hung over the valley in 1978, when the North West Water Authority wanted to raise the level of the lake and modify an extraction point. This happened at the same time as British Nuclear Fuels proposed raising the level of Wast Water with a new weir so that it could increase the amount of water it was taking by eleven million gallons per day. The two schemes together went to a public inquiry in the face of fierce opposition from the National Park. The alternative of abstracting water from the River Derwent was suggested. After fifty-seven days of arguments the secretary of state decided to disallow the applications. It transpired that the extra water was not needed anyhow, and that ample supplies could be obtained from the river and from underground sources.

From the car park provided by the commission at Bowness on the north side – this is as far as a car can go – a short walk up the opposite eminence on to Bowness point gives a great view of the lake.

From the private forest road (but a public bridleway) the main way up the valley runs alongside the River Liza, the lake's main source. This then is Black Sail Pass, and at the end of the commission's plantings can be found the remotest of the Lake District's Youth Hostels, and for that reason it is quite popular; its only concession to modern convenience is having a turbine in the stream to produce electricity. The pass then curves round the west side of Wasdale's Kirk Fell through one of several 'Mosedales' to Wasdale Head.

Archaeologists have discovered that the valley was well settled in the Dark Ages. The Forestry Commission is conscious of this, and when discovered, the sites have been cleared of trees and preserved. Above and beyond the dull conifer plantations on the east side there is spectacular fell country, for here rise the heads of Steeple (819 m) and Pillar (892 m). Pillar rock, jutting out from Pillar mountain, is a classic venue for rock climbing.

A walk from Gillerthwaite at the head of the lake, and above the forest, brings walkers to the peaks. STEEPLE is a pinnacle protruding from the side of Scoat Fell (841 m). From some viewpoints it appears to have been well named, and from a distance it seems impregnable, but in fact it does have an easy slope up to its summit on a side generally hidden from view. The way to Steeple is a direct ascent along a path marked by cairns. The other way is from Netherbeck bridge in Wasdale, by the wild Scoat Tarn to Scoat Fell. In some directions the views from the Steeple's top are extensive, but perhaps more impressive is the feeling of rugged remoteness experienced among a conference of peaks and crags.

The large, bulky and buttressed hump of PILLAR is something else. The ordinary traveller usually sees Pillar, a fell at the head of Ennerdale, from a distance. Though a formidable mass in itself, it has acquired its name from that detached, gnarled and riven PILLAR ROCK standing 180 m high on the Ennerdale side. It is unnoticeable from Pillar Fell itself, as the view of it is on its shorter side. Approaching from the forest on its northern side, one can drink in its full magnificence. From Wasdale Head the way is via the 'high-level route', and by Robinson Cairn. Pillar Rock is reckoned to be the tallest mass of vertical crag in England, and is enough to make any climber wild with anticipation. From its foot there towers an almost vertical face of 152 m, with another higher section above that, Low Man and High Man. It gained some notoriety from Wordsworth who erroneously made it the scene of an accident in his poem 'The Brothers'. John Atkinson, a local man, climbed it first in July 1826, and a year later three local shepherds also made it. It was in 1848 that Pillar Rock was first climbed by Lieutenant Wilson, RN, and it then began to attract the pioneers of rock climbing. Since that time the interest has grown, and new routes have been pioneered. From then on there have been many thousands of ascents, and in spite of its relative remoteness, it is still a major attraction to climbers, offering scores of routes up the crag from moderate to very severe, with names like Slab and Notch, The Curtain, Pisgah, Shamrock, Harlequin Chimney and Hadrian's Wall.

Robinson Cairn, on the high-level route to Pillar Rock, was erected in memory of one of the great early climbers, John Wilson Robinson, a farmer in Lorton who died in 1907. He was a hugely popular man among the early rock climbers, not only extremely clever and fearless, making several first ascents of Lakeland crags, but a man of charm and wit. He had amazing energy and seemed to be everywhere. He climbed Pillar Rock more than a hundred times. The plaque in the cairn reads:

> We climb the hill, from end to end.
> In all the landscapes underneath
> We find no place that does not breathe,
> Some gracious memory of our friend.

It is unique for a climber to be remembered in this way.

BASSENTHWAITE LAKE AND ITS FORESTS

The correct answer to the hoary old conundrum 'How many lakes are there in the Lake District?' is only one – BASSENTHWAITE LAKE (*BAS-sen-thwit*) – for the rest are 'meres' or 'waters'. The lake is west of Keswick and the most northern, 6.5 km long and 805 m wide, and is a nature reserve owned by the National Park Authority. Because it sits on the soft Skiddaw slates its immediate surroundings lack the stark drama of other lakes, but the huge bulk of Skiddaw looms high in the background. The views of the lake from the mountain are splendid, or from the heights of Dodd Wood in Skiddaw's lap, or from Thornthwaite Forest on the west – they are great too. The view up lake from the lake itself is also striking if one keeps well away from the fast traffic on the A66, a road that should never have been put there.

Road apart, nothing much has changed since 1793, when William Hutchinson described the lake in *The History of Cumberland and Westmorland*:

> Parties of pleasure at Keswick neglect this water, they seldom think it worth while to navigate it; its beauties indeed are very different from those of the lake above [Derwent Water] but that is the very cause from whence they become more pleasing ... This affords many bays, where you may in some parts push under the cover of a lofty overhanging grove, and in others rocky coves, where you find the gentler echo, favourable to music and a song. The painter has tamer landscapes here, but they are warmer and more serene than those of Keswick ...

The main source of water feeding the lake comes from the River Derwent, out of Borrowdale and Derwent Water. The land between the two lakes is alluvial, the two having once been one, and occasionally after heavy prolonged rain, they almost become one again. Both lakes are shallow, Bassenthwaite being generally around 15.5 m deep, and both are inhabited by the rare whitefish, the vendace (*Coregonus albala*), which is not found in any other lakes; and there are also pike, perch and trout. In 2001 there was great excitement in naturalist circles when for the first time ospreys nested near the lake. The birds came again in succeeding years after producing young and it is hoped that they will be regular residents, possibly bringing more with them, as it is reckoned that the lake could support several pairs.

Public access to the lake is sadly minimal. The National Park Authority has two places between the A66 and the lake on the south-western end, and an area at the lake's outlet at Ouse bridge. There are public footpaths on the east side. One leads to the little chapel of St Bega's by Mirehouse. It only seems like a strange place for a church if one forgets that the lake was once a highway used by parishioners. Restored in 1874, but with original Norman features, it is one of Lakeland's treasures, for the setting is absolutely superb. The best section of lakeshore about here, available for hire for a small fee, is just south of St Bega's on land owned by the Speddings at nearby Mirehouse. Here is a stone celebrating the writing of Tennyson's 'Morte d'Arthur'; for it was here on the reedy shore that Tennyson was inspired to write about the last episode of Arthur's life in 'The Idylls of the King', in which he imagined the lake being close to the sea.

Bassenthwaite, Mirehouse shore: Tennyson commemorative stone

St Bega's church is mentioned in the poem. When Tennyson visited, it was then in need of repair, with the head missing from the stone cross.

> Then, because his wound was deep,
> The bold Sir Bedevere uplifted him,
> And bore him to a chapel nigh the field,
> A broken chancel with a broken cross,
> That stood on a dark strait of barren land:
> On one side lay the Ocean, and on one
> Lay a great water, and the moon was full.

It was surely here on the shore that Tennyson imagined Bedevere flinging the sword Excalibur into the lake on his king's orders; but on reaching the shore, he was loath to throw away such a magnificent object. Initially he agreed:

So saying, from the ruin'd shrine he stept,
And in the moon athwart the place of tombs,
Where lay the mighty bones of ancient men,
Old knights, and over them the sea-wind sang,
Shrill, chill, with flakes of foam, He, stepping down
By zig-zag paths, and juts of pointed rock,
Came on the shining levels of the lake.

He could not do it, and hid the sword in the 'water flags that whistled stiff and dry about the marge'. Arthur asks him what he saw.

I heard the ripple washing in the reeds,
And the wild water lapping on the crag.

Arthur is angry, for this was not what he expected to hear, and after other attempts and refusals the knight does what he is ordered, and is able to report that he

... beheld an arm,
Clothed in white samite, mystic, wonderful,
That caught him by the hilt, and brandished him
Three times, and drew him under the mere.

Arthur is satisfied and the knight carries his dying king to the water, and places him in the barge with the three mourning queens, who carry him away across the lake. The knight watched

... Till the hull
Look'd one black dot against the verge of dawn,
And on the mere the wailing died away.

The Georgian MIREHOUSE itself is a great delight. It is not very big, but visitors, on occasions when it is open to the public (it is a family home with no spare wing), discover a warm and friendly place with some treasures, and a library that, in its day, was reckoned to hold the sum of human knowledge. The eighth earl of Derby built the house in 1666 as a lodge for his visits to his Cumbrian estates. He sold it to his agent, Roger Gregg, whose family owned it until it was left to John Spedding of Armathwaite Hall, at the north end of the lake. Georgian Gothic bays were added in 1790. In 1830 the south side was rebuilt.

James Spedding (1808–81), who made his home at Mirehouse, was the indefatigable biographer of Francis Bacon – in fourteen volumes. A brilliant but modest

Mirehouse

man, he turned down the post of permanent under-secretary to the Colonial Office, the Regius professorship of modern history and honorary degrees at Cambridge, only accepting the honorary fellowship of Trinity College, Cambridge.

It was while at Trinity that he made friends with Alfred Tennyson and Arthur Hallam. Tennyson, then suffering from poverty, stayed at Mirehouse as his guest in 1835. The fact that he had to sell his Chancellor's Gold Medal for English Verse for £15 to afford the journey shows how much he valued the friendship. Here he met and became the life-long friend of another guest, Edward Fitzgerald (*Rubaiyyat of Omar Khayyam*), and discussed the first draft of 'Morte d'Arthur'. Tennyson stayed here again in 1851 with his new wife.

The great writer Thomas Carlyle (1795–1881), also a close friend of James Spedding and his older brother Tom in London, stayed as a guest on two occasions en route to his home at Ecclefechan in Dumfrieshire. 'Dear hospitable Spedding ... Mirehouse was beautiful and so were the ways of it.' The house has some of his letters.

The grounds are also beautiful, and contain a very imaginative playground for children – all natural, with no fibreglass monstrosities. The lakeshore is used by the nearby Calvert Trust, which was formed in 1974 to provide adventure holidays for the disabled. The converted farmhouses serve as a base for sailing, canoeing, camping and climbing. Mr and Mrs John Spedding donated

Calvert Trust enjoying lake activity, Mirehouse shore

the building, one of which is nearby and the other is at Old Windebrowe in Keswick.

The Wordsworths stayed in the latter house in 1794 as guests of William Calvert. The forest above Mirehouse is also part of the estate, and is managed by the Forestry Commission. Many walks are possible in the forest from the car parks opposite the house; the impressive groves of Douglas firs make for pleasant scenery. The highest point, the Dodd, gives extensive views. In the new millennium a viewing stage was erected for visitors to see the osprey nest on Bassenthwaite and watch the birds bringing in fish. What used to be the water-powered sawmill is now a café.

On the west side and head of the lake is the main part of THORNTHWAITE FOREST. This was the first planting made by the Forestry Commission, above Braithwaite village, in 1919, shortly after it was established. The species were largely Sitka spruce, with Douglas fir, hemlock, red cedar and European larch. WHINLATTER FOREST PARK is a substantial part of it and was *designated* as a 'park' in 1993, which means that public access to it is encouraged. It has an area of 1,215 ha, 250 ha of it open fell. The main access point is on Whinlatter Pass, with car parks, a visitor centre and a café built from the forest timber. The big attraction in 2003 was the provision of a camera focused on the ospreys' nest, transmitting to a screen in the centre, so that visitors had a close-up view of the chicks (only one in 2003) being fed. A number of walks have been marked, including some to attract children – and their parents – and the disabled. And there are educational programmes, with regular visits from schools. This is a very happy place and should be a role model for other forests.

The A66 trunk road runs so close to the west shore of the lake that enjoyment of that side is impossible. The old road follows it for a distance from Braithwaite, and through Thornthwaite hamlet, with its seventeenth-century chapel. A profitable lead mine was sited here early in the last century. Further on Powter How is reached and the Swan Hotel. High above is the oddly named fell, Barf. On its fiendishly steep slope, covered in loose rocks and scree, one can see a white figure, known as the bishop of Barf. It is a protruding piece of crag that is supposed to look like a bishop, though it needs a stretch of imagination. Each year it is whitewashed. Getting to the rock is obviously difficult, but doing so with whitewash and brush seems daft. No one seems to know when the custom began, but at least one person volunteers each year, with the reward of free beer at the Swan. The bishop's Clerk lies a little below, but remains drab.

From the car park beyond the hotel a footpath goes under the A66 to a stretch of lakeshore (NPA). This was a miserly concession from the road builders. The access is quite pleasant if one blanks out the noise from the road. Near the lake foot the A66 takes a short turn away from the lake before turning west for Cockermouth. On a rise here between the road and the lake is Castle How. There are earthworks here of a British hill fort. At a side road is the Pheasant Hotel. A minor road leaves behind it to Wythop (*WITH-up*) Mill, an interesting old corn mill, now a tea room in a quiet little backwater. An ancient sword found near here, iron in a bronze sheath, is now in the British Museum. Leaving the A66 when it turns for Cockermouth, a minor road follows the lakeshore, passing the Bassenthwaite Sailing Club to Ouse bridge, crossing the point where the River Derwent leaves the lake. There is public access here to the shore (NPA). Pocklington, of Derwent Water fame, organized an entertainment here before launching his regattas. The bizarre game consisted of putting horses on to a barge fitted with a plug. When it was well out on the lake the plug was pulled, the barge sank, and bets were laid on which horse would swim to shore first.

Just before the bridge a minor road goes left and crosses the river to ISEL. Here is a lovely old Norman church in an idyllic setting by the river and bridge. The twelfth-century features include the south doorway and two small north windows. John Betjeman was impressed: 'a perfect English harmony of man and nature … All around stretches a lost landscape of pasture and river. O fortunatus nimium!' Isel Hall is a fifteenth-century pele tower with Elizabethan additions. It is not open to the public but can be viewed from the road.

Returning to Ouse bridge and crossing it, one sees Armathwaite Hall, a Tudor mansion, on the left. Now a hotel, it was once the family home of the Speddings. The Castle Inn stands at the crossroads with the Carlisle road.

NEWLANDS

Let us return to NEWLANDS PASS from either Portinscale or Braithwaite. This is a good valley for walking. Until they join to get to grips with the steep ascent of the pass, there are two minor roads along the valley, one on either side of the Newlands Beck. On the eastern side, just before the roads join, is Littletown. Beatrix Potter readers might recognize this as the place where Mrs Tiggywinkle lived. (The artist/writer was staying at Fawe Park on the side of Derwent Water when she painted the illustrations.) The little chapel here fits so well into the landscape. Wordsworth was taken by the setting:

> How delicate the leafy veil
> Through which yon house of God
> Gleams mid the peace of this deep vale,
> By few but shepherds trod!

However, the present church was built in 1843 and restored in 1885, so it is not quite what the bard would have seen.

To the east of Littletown on the fell side a lead mine operated here until the mid nineteenth century. But looking up the valley from Littletown, one can see the hump of a fell with apparently three low peaks: this is Scope End, actually the end of Hindscarf Fell (727 m) that appears to be detached behind. This is where the mining bonanza started. The beckside spoil heaps of Goldscope Mine show its location. Here a copper ore vein, sometimes 3 m in thickness, was worked. The mine also ran into a lead vein, and in its time it also produced some silver and a few traces of gold. The mine was known before the Germans began work on it. In the 1607 edition of Camden's *Britannia*, the Elizabethan mentions the mines (spelling has been modernized):

> At Newlands and other places some rich veins of copper, not without a mixture of gold and silver, were discovered in our age, A.D. 1607, by Thomas Thurland and Daniel Hechstetter, a German of Augsburg, though known many ages before, as appears from the Close Rolls of Henry III. Nor would Caesar, if he had known of these mines, have told us that the Britons made use of imported

> copper, when these and others afford such plenty, that not only all England is supplied from them, but great quantities are yearly exported.
>
> About these mines there was a memorable trial between Queen Elizabeth and Thomas Percie, Earl of Northumberland, but by virtue of the prerogative royal it was carried in favour of the Queen.
>
> In regard of the Queen's prerogative (there being in these mines more gold and silver than copper or lead) they were by ancient law the property of the Queen; and it was agreed that where the gold and silver extracted out of copper or lead was of greater value than the copper or lead, it was a royal mine.

Earl Percy was not pleased by the verdict falling in the queen's favour, and took part in an armed rebellion in favour of Mary, Queen of Scots. After some success the rebellion collapsed, and the rebels were compelled to flee to Scotland. But the earl was, however, held by the notorious Armstrongs, and the reivers 'sold' him to Lord Hundsdon; eventually, with many other rebels, he was executed.

In the *Natural History of Westmorland and Cumberland* (1709), T. Robinson has this to say about Newlands valley:

> In our survey of the mountains of Newlands we found eleven veins opened and wrought by the Germans; all distinguished by names given to them, as Gowd-Scalp, now Gowd-Scalp, Long-Work, St. Thomas' Work, &c., of all which veins the richest was at Gowd-Scalp. We found the vein wrought three yards wide, and twenty fathoms deep above the grand level, which is driven in a hard rock a hundred fathom, and only with pick-axe, hammer, and wedge, the art of blasting with gunpowder being not then discovered. For securing the rich vein, no cost of the best oak wood was spared; and for the recovering of the soles under the level was placed a water gin, and water was brought to it in troughs of wood upon the tops of high mountains, near half-a-mile from the vein.

Goldscope probably got its name from the German miners' description *Gottesgab* – 'God's gift'. The mine, and others in the Newlands valley, were worked continually for over eighty years, but closed for a time during the Civil War in 1651. It is said that 'most' of the miners were killed by Cromwell's army. Could this be so? Or were they drafted into the army?

Goldscope was reopened in the eighteenth century by the duke of Somerset, and closed some time after. The mine was again reopened in 1847 and suffered mixed fortunes until 1852, when a new lead vein was discovered. A shaft was run from the adit level (the access tunnel) to 82 fathoms (150 m). The 12.2 m high waterwheel eventually could not cope with the task of pumping out water from such great depths, and in 1864 the investors were loath to spend their money on expensive machinery for questionable profits. Newlands had proved itself to be rich in metal ores, as undoubtedly it still is; but it was no longer profitable.

Newlands now is a quiet valley. Apart from the fierce climb at Newlands Hause – the head of the pass – the valley has two more notable features. Above on the fell side at Keskadale is the probable remnant of an ancient oak forest. Here the oak is at the limits of its height in what must be a hostile environment, and the trees are weirdly stunted and contorted. At the hause there is a waterfall, Moss Force, with no great volume of water, but spectacular in its way. Coleridge was most impressed by it and wrote this model of skilful description in 1802:

> It is a great Torrent from the Top of the Mountain to the Bottom; the lower part of it is not the least Interesting, where it is beginning to slope to a level. The mad water rushes thro' its sinuous bed, or rather prison of Rock, with such rapid Curves as if it turned the Corners not from mechanic force but with foreknowledge, like a fierce and skilful Driver: great Masses of Water, one after the other, that in twilight one might have feelingly compared them to a vast crowd of huge white Bears, rushing, one over the other, against the wind – their long white hair scattering abroad in the wind. The remainder of the Torrent is marked out by three great Waterfalls, the lowermost Apron-shaped, and though

Keskadale – a remnant of ancient oak woodland?

> the Rock down which it rushes is an incline Plane, it shoots off in such an independence of the Rock as shews that its direction was given it by the force of the Water from above. The middle which in peaceable times would be two tinkling Falls formed in this furious Rain one great Water-wheel endlessly revolving and double the size and height of the lowest. The third and highest is a mighty one indeed. It is twice the height of both the others added together, nearly as high as Scale Force, but it rushes down an inclined Plane, and does not fall, like Scale Force; however if the Plane had been smooth, it is so near a Perpendicular that it would have appeared to fall, but it is indeed so fearfully savage and black, and jagged, that it tears the flood to pieces. And one great black Outjutment divides the water, and overbrows and keeps uncovered a long slip of jagged black Rock beneath, which gives a marked character to the whole force. What a sight it is to look down on such a Cataract! The wheels, that circumvolve it, the leaping up and plunging forward of that infinity of Pearls and Glass Bulbs, the continual change of the Matter, the perpetual Sameness of the Form – it is an awful Image and Shadow of God and the World.

From Braithwaite a track goes up the next valley to the north-west. This is Coledale (formerly Cowdale) and the track is used by fell walkers heading for Crummock Water or the fells above. At the valley head there stands a wall of crags. Facing north-east this would have been the head of a glacier that would have hung on, away from the sun and warm winds, when other valleys had cleared. High Force, a waterfall, cascades from the top. The presence of a mine becomes evident as the crag is reached. Force Crag Mine has had a long career, and it may be one of the mines worked from Elizabethan times; but it certainly came into its own from about 1840, producing lead and silver. The ore was carted to Maryport to be shipped on to Liverpool. The railway came through Braithwaite in 1865, which should have helped, but by this time the price of lead dropped and the mine closed. The mine reopened two years later to extract barytes, a dense, sometimes white, yellow, light brown or red minerals that were initially regarded as useless during lead mining. In fact, they have numerous applications in the chemical industries, including the manufacture of white paint, as a filler in paper, and as a lubricant in oil-drilling operations.

The demand for barytes brought good profits and the transport of the ore from Force Crag Mine was better organized. It was shot down from High Force in water-filled flumes to a mill, and then by tramway down to Braithwaite. Prices again fell and the mine closed in 1879. It reopened to produce zinc intermittently until the 1930s, when it again began mining barytes. During the Second World War the material was needed in the production of explosives, a new mill was built and the track widened to allow transport by trucks. Subsequently an aerial ropeway brought the ore down from High Force to the mill. Traces of all this activity can still be seen on the site.

Flooding and other problems meant that the mine closed, only to be reopened as an ore mine between 1960 and 1966. After that there were unsuccessful attempts to mine lead, zinc and barytes, but this ground to a halt after a massive collapse led to the workings being flooded with water. The mine closed in 1990. It had passed through many hands, and hundreds of workers had toiled here. It was the last to close of the Lake District mines.

There is a great wealth of fells for walking between the Derwent and Bassenthwaite over to Buttermere and Crummock. Although they are in the Skiddaw slate area, unlike Skiddaw mountain itself the north and east faces are often craggy. Some of the fells are connected with first-rate ridge walks. Cat Bells is the hump by Derwent Water in the east and it runs on to Maiden Moor (574 m), High Spy (653 m) and Dale Head (754 m) overlooking Honister. From Dale Head a path runs on to Hindscarf (727 m), strangely named Robinson (736.7 m), overlooking Buttermere. Causey Pike (620 m) has a distinct sharp-nobbed shape when the western fells are seen from the head of Derwent Water. It is a sublime fell, reached from Stair in the Newlands valley, and a superb viewpoint. A path runs on to Crummock via Sail (771 m), and possibly taking in Eel Crag (838 m), then diverting to the plateau of Grasmoor (850.7 m). Eel Crag is another good away-from-it-all viewpoint and can be more directly reached from Coledale and past the Force Crag mine. From the fell path from Braithwaite along the top of the Coledale steeps is one way to Grisedale Pike (790 m). This is the height seen grandly again from the head of Derwent Water. It is an exposed place and not good for a walk in bad weather. In clear weather a ridge walk is then possible to Hopegill Head (769.7 m), pausing to view the rather awesome Hobcarton Crag, and on to Whiteside (706 m), with views to the Solway and Scotland, and Cumbria's west coast.

BY SKIDDAW AND BEYOND

Returning to Keswick and taking the A66 past Threlkeld, a delightful minor road goes north to Mungrisdale (*mun-GRIZE-d'l*) – 'St Mungo's pig dale' – alongside and under the haunted Souther Fell. Mungrisdale is a small village and the church, of course, is dedicated to St Kentigern – 'Mungo', meaning 'blessed one', is his nickname. The quiet little church – nave and chancel in one – was built in 1756, and has a splendid three-decker pulpit.

Going north we cross the River Caldew and reach the small hamlet of Mosedale (*MOZE-d'l*), which has little to it except a Friends Meeting House

(Quakers), a very simple building hardly distinguishable from the surrounding farm and cottage buildings. The lintel is marked 1702, but that represents the date the earlier building was enlarged. It now serves as a coffee house to passers-by, giving the opportunity to view an interior that has hardly changed from its beginnings, with ancient timber seats, panelled walls and two columns of pink sandstone supporting roof trusses.

A minor road goes west from Mosedale up the Caldew valley to reach Carrock mine. The mine was the only one outside Devon and Cornwall to produce wolfram, the chief ore-mineral of tungsten. At the tin mines of the south-west it was originally considered a nuisance, because of the difficulty of separating it from the tin ore during ore dressing. Tungsten became of value when it was needed for light-bulb filaments, because it has a high melting-point and conducts heat well. But other vital uses for it were discovered. It strengthens steel, for instance, and in the nuclear industry it is used to clad fuel rods containing uranium and plutonium. The mine was opened in 1852 by F.W. Emerson, a Cornish man, who was seeking to exploit veins of lead and copper. After mixed fortunes and several owners, production was boosted in 1906 by a new Cumbrian Mining Company which was financed by two Germans, William Boss and Frederick Boehm, and which employed over a hundred workers. But in five years it had folded. A Carrock Mining Syndicate took the mine in 1913, and with some government finance the site's mill was rebuilt and equipped with the latest equipment, and electricity was supplied by water-powered generators. The price of tungsten dropped after the First World War, and the mine fell into disuse until 1942. It was then again exploited using Canadian Royal Engineers, and when most of them left for other duties, Italian prisoners of war and Spanish Pioneers took their place. After that the mine had mixed fortunes again, with interest surging briefly during the Korean War, as Korea was an important producer. Finally it closed for good in 1981. In the next year mining and milling equipment was removed, together with smaller buildings. Presumably if the price of tungsten rises sufficiently the mine could be reopened.

On the north side of the Caldew valley looms Carrock Fell (660 m). The interest here revolves round the remains of a large British hill fort on the summit. The dimensions of the substantially walled enclosure within earthworks are 244 m east to west, and 113 m north to south. These are the largest hill fort remains in the north-west. At one part the wall seems to have been deliberately demolished, and it has been suggested that this might have been done by the Roman invaders.

The road then heads northwards with Carrock Fell to the east, alongside pleasant moorland. Caldbeck Fells, with its many old mines, lie to the east. Eventually we reach the wide street, village green and market cross of quiet, unspoilt HESKET NEWMARKET. Here are some fine eighteenth-century houses. The

Hesket Newmarket, eighteenth-century market cross

one pub, the Old Crown, was threatened with closure in 2003, and local users, plus others, opened a fund and bought it. A small brewery attached to the pub makes a variety of its own special beers. An eccentric-looking square house at the head of the street is Hesket Hall, with a conical roof. The house was apparently built with twelve angles, to represent the twelve months, and so contrived that the shadows give the hours of the day.

CALDBECK is a little more than a km on. Mining and milling made Caldbeck. The Caldbeck Fells (NPA) to the south are riddled with mines and twenty-two minerals are present. There were prosperous times, particularly in the seventeenth century. An old saying goes: 'Caldbeck and Caldbeck Fells/Are worth all England else.' Roughton Gill mine in the fells 6.5 km south-west of Caldbeck, on the west side of the fell, was the most productive. Veins worked there produced not only lead ore, but copper, zinc, manganese, iron pyrites and others. The oldest workings here were done by hand using 'stope and feather': a hole is worked out, then a chisel inserted between two steel wedges (feathers). The chisel is then hammered to split the surrounding rock. This is a hard slow process yet the old workings went down to a considerable depth. Even with the introduction of gunpowder, blasting was a slow process, but it allowed the mine to be worked more extensively, and three lower levels were driven, producing large amounts of lead ore, copper and zinc ores in the process.

A corner of Caldbeck

Another productive old mine, very profitable in its time, was the Driggeth mine, north-east of High Pike, the highest point of the Caldbeck Fells. The lead raised here produced 25 oz of silver in each ton. The mine also produced copper and barytes. Other notable mines were Dry Gill, and the rich baryte mines south-east of High Pike, plus Potts Gill, due south of Caldbeck, and Sandbeds to the east of Potts Gill, which was producing until 1966. All the mines have closed. The National Park Authority, which manages Caldbeck Fells, has fenced off the dangerous open shafts.

The fell on to High Pike (658 m) greatly rewards an exploration. It is of Skiddaw slate so its character is rounded with agreeable grassy areas, and some bracken, and heather, but the water courses have cut deep ravines, and the mines have left their scars. Skylark populations have decreased in areas of modern agriculture, but they give song here in the season. The fell's fine views are to the north into Scotland, and west to Cumbria's Irish Sea coast. South are the central fells as far south as the Coniston Old Man range, and the view includes Scafell Pike and Great Gable.

Great Sca Fell (651 m), not to be confused with the other one, is east of the head of Roughton Gill. From the minor road at Longlands a bridleway goes easily to the top. The views are similar to those from High Pike. Another peak, the Knott (710 m), can be reached in the south-east.

CALDBECK

It is not possible to appreciate the full character of Cumbria until one visits CALDBECK VILLAGE, one of the county's real treats. Welcoming and congenial, it feels like a place to linger in and the cafés and pubs are first-class. The eighteenth-century Priest's Mill, complete with 4 m diameter water-wheel intact, is a good example. Once owned by the rector of Caldbeck, it ultimately milled corn, then it was a sawmill, now it's a well-patronized café, and complex of shops including a bookshop. There cannot be many cloggers left in England, but one can be found here. Clogs were once commonly worn in the countryside until the invention of the revolutionary wellington boot. But a well-made clog is surprisingly comfortable for knocking about in the garden.

There has never been a shortage of running water in the village, and about a hundred water mills flourished, be they woollen mills, fulling mills, corn mills, flax mills and paper mills. Now fell farming and tourism are the main industries.

A little way to the west of the car park a footpath leads past the village pond – formed when clay was dug to produce bricks – to the ruin of what was once a bobbin mill, powered by a huge water-wheel, supplying bobbins for textile mills in Scotland and the north of England. The substantial remains have been made secure and are in the care of the National Park Authority. Beyond it is a local beauty spot, the HOWK, a waterfall within a water-sculpted limestone gorge. In 1803 the Wordsworths visited here with Coleridge and Dorothy describes it as:

> ... a delicious spot in which to breathe out a summer's day – limestone rocks, hanging trees, pools and waterbreaks – caves and caldrons which have been honoured with fairy names, and no doubt continue in the fancy of the neighbourhood to resound with fairy revels.

Judging by the substantial gravestones in the churchyard, one would guess that not all inhabitants were poverty-stricken in the nineteenth century. The most famous gravestone – painted so it cannot be missed – is the one to John Peel, huntsman with his own pack of hounds for fifty-five years, a sort of patron saint of foxhunting. Had the popular song not materialized he might have drifted into obscurity. The words 'D'ye ken John Peel' were composed in the 1820s by John Woodcock Graves, owner of a mill in Caldbeck, after he and Peel had been sitting by a fireside after a happy winter's day hunt. He wrote it to an old tune, 'Cannie Annie', but later William Metcalf, the organist at Carlisle cathedral, set it to the present tune. His coat, by the way, was not 'gay' but grey – made of the local homespun wool, most probably from herdwick sheep, that most country workers wore at the time. It was tough, practically indestructible, even waterproof, but resistant to dyes. Also in the churchyard south-west of the tower, is the grave of Mary Harrison, the 'maid of Buttermere' (see pp. 425–6), who was wronged by a bigamist but later married a Caldbeck farmer.

The church, another dedicated to St Kentigern, is red sandstone like the rest of the village, and dating back to at least the thirteenth century. Pevsner, the architectural historian, in *Buildings of England*, recognized the Norman features (at once, the beak-carved porch entrance), but confessed to confusion about the chronology. But the pillared nave gives the church a medieval feel. Its dedication suggests that the church was built on a much earlier religious site. On the river bank behind the church is St Mungo's Well.

CHAPTER EIGHTEEN

North-east of the National Park: Ullswater to Haweswater

The landscape of the Ullswater area is one of contrasts. At the head of what many 'Lakers' regard as the most beautiful lake, are the crags and peaks of high fells, with the Helvellyn range the greatest of all and, opposite it, Place Fell. Beyond the lake's head is the north-eastern mass of Fairfield and the western side of the High Street range. But at the northern end of the lake there is the softer, rounded landscape of the Skiddaw slates and limestone. At the north-east side are the wild hills of Moor Divock. South of that, the fierce crags of eastern High Street that offer home to Engand's only golden eagles, frown over Haweswater.

Of the two main routes to Ullswater, the first from the south dives into the mountainous head of the valley from the highest road pass in the Lake District. The other starts at the north from Penrith, and runs through gentle countryside and on into the mountains, seeing them from their feet to their glorious crowns.

KIRKSTONE PASS (451 m) is the high gap in the barrier between Windermere and Ambleside in the south and Brothers Water and Ullswater from the north. Two roads up the pass join near the summit: one from Windermere climbs steadily by Troutbeck; and the way from Ambleside passes the great gash of Kirkstone quarry and is steep for a short stretch near the top, well named 'the Struggle'. In the old horse-coaching days passengers had to alight and climb up it on foot. On the descent the coachmen would scare the passengers by speeding down – the period's equivalent of the modern rollercoaster ride. The writer and critic Thomas De Quincey relates a descent in 1807, which was fast but not entertaining:

> Once, in utter darkness, after midnight, and the darkness irradiated only by continual streams of lightning, I was driven down the whole descent, at a full gallop, by a young woman – the carriage being a light one, the horses frightened, and the descents, at some critical parts of the road, so literally like the

sides of a house, that it was difficult to keep the fore wheels from pressing upon the hind legs of the horses.

The road from Windermere is easier, but the descent this way gives the best view – an airy prospect over the deep valley of Troutbeck Park. The inn at Kirkstone's top was built early in the nineteenth century by the Revd Sewell of Troutbeck. The pass can be a very bleak, gale-torn place, and when he was crossing the pass from Patterdale he found a packwoman half-frozen to death there and carried her down to Troutbeck. He then caused the inn to be built for travellers who might find themselves in the same predicament. It is claimed to be the highest inhabited house in England, but surely it is not. The pass gets its name from a large rock on the west side of the road, which, from some angles, and particularly in mist, looks like the gable end of a chapel. Given a clear day the views are very wide southwards as far as Morecambe Bay.

Did a Roman road cross this pass? There is a well-built terraced track on the west side of the road. It looks Roman, though as we shall see a Roman road goes along the ridge of High Street, the fell well to the east. Keen Roman archaeologists see Roman roads everywhere, but from the Dark Ages through medieval times, and most often beyond, the Roman ways became the main highways. And it has been pointed out that a thirteenth-century charter refers to *magna via Kirkestain* – 'the

Troutbeck Park from Kirkstone Pass

great Kirkstone road'. As well as, or later instead of, the sometimes bleak-fell High Street route? This may have been part of a road linking the Roman fort at Brougham, near Penrith, to the fort at Ambleside. The descent north is spectacular with the crags of Red Screes on the left, and Raven's Edge on Hart Crag to the right, then as the view over Brothers Water opens up, one sees Caudale Moor on the right and the Dodds on the left.

BROTHERS WATER (NT) is a small tranquil lake at the foot of Kirkstone Pass by Hartsop village. It is completely natural, although its straight-lined shores might suggest otherwise. It was almost certainly a larger lake and may have joined with Ullswater; but after the last glaciation, and before the fell slopes were stabilized by vegetation, massive deposits of alluvium were washed down from the heights

Brothers Water

thereby separating the two lakes. The lake contains perch and trout. On old maps it was named 'Broaderwater', but it is supposed to have gained its present name from the drowning of two brothers there, and by coincidence two others, in winter 1785 when they fell through the ice while playing on it. Dorothy Wordsworth writes:

> It was upon a New-years day. Their Mother had set them to thresh some corn, and they (probably thinking it hard to be so tasked when all others were keeping holiday) stole out to slide upon the ice and were both drowned. A neighbour who had seen them fall through the ice, though not near enough to be certain, guessed who they were, & went to the Mother to enquire after her Sons. She replied 'they were threshing in the barn'. 'Nay' said the Man, 'they are not there, nor is it likely today.' The Woman went with him to the Barn and the Boys were gone. He was then convinced of the truth, and told her that they were drowned.

It is possible to reach the shore from Cow Bridge to the north. A round walk on public footpaths takes one by Hartsop Hall (NT), now a farmhouse, and possibly dating back to the sixteenth century. The fell above the hall was mined for lead, the waste heap betraying its presence. To the south of the hall are signs of hut circles from an ancient settlement.

The lake is only around 16 m at its deepest and contains trout, perch and pike, and is popular with trout anglers, but the fish are not of great size.

Just to the east at the foot of the lake is the hamlet of HARTSOP, where unspoilt cottages display the old vernacular architecture of spinning galleries and round chimneys. A bridleway goes up the valley to HAYESWATER, a very pleasant 3.5 km walk to the small lake. It passes another old mine, and a fair way up a branch path to Threshthwaite Mouth is another. There was a smelter at Hartsop and no doubt the region's woodlands were extensively quarried for charcoal. It is hard now to think of this as an industrial area.

The road goes on to Patterdale, but the best way to that village for walkers runs from Hartsop above the east side of Goldrill Beck that runs out of Brothers Water – good views back and forward.

PATTERDALE AND GLENRIDDING

At PATTERDALE we are at the head of Ullswater. There is not a lot to Patterdale village. The name was once doubtless 'St Patrick's Dale', and it is said that the saint visited here. He is said to have baptized converts in St Patrick's Well not far away, now restored. Cumbria claims St Patrick, but Wales will have him as a Welshman.

Striding Edge, Helvellyn

According to his autobiography he was the son of a Roman tax collector at 'Banavem Tabernia'. He was captured by sea raiders as a boy and taken as a slave to Ireland. He eventually escaped, got to Gaul, studied in the priesthood and went back to Ireland as a missionary where he became the patron saint. Banavem Tabernia has not been identified. The Welsh say it was close to the Severn. Cumbrians claim that it was close to the Solway when the area was frequently raided from Ireland after Hadrian's Wall had fallen under attack (doubtless by this time making his father's post redundant). And here he is blessing a well and baptizing converts at St Patrick's Dale? The well is on the left of the road as we approach Glenridding. The church of St Patrick is not ancient. It was built by Salvin in 1853, replacing a fourteenth-century chapel, but it is an uplifting place. Appropriately for a sheep farming area, a large embroidery depicts Jesus as the good shepherd.

Patterdale is the home of Patterdale Mountain Rescue Team, the band of volunteers who cover the fells around the Ullswater valley. They have their work cut out, for they cover a large and popular fell area. Patterdale is a fell walker's village. From here one can make the most dramatic ascent of Helvellyn by Striding Edge, starting at the minor road by the bridge, then crossing Grisedale Beck and going up to the path high above the valley to the Hole in the Wall.

And the way up Grisedale is the old route to Grasmere via Grisedale Tarn. Then Patterdale offers access to the east; across the Goldrill Beck there is a spider-web of paths. One goes north by the shores of Ullswater to Howtown, another by Boardale Hause onto Place Fell, or on into Boardale, or Martindale, or the High Street range.

The Patterdale Hotel is probably the 'Dobsons', where Wordsworth, Scott and Humphrey Davy stayed in 1805. The inn was full and Wordsworth and Davy had to sleep in a room hired for the evening by Elizabeth Smith of Coniston, a remarkable linguist and one of the earliest female fell-walkers, and her friends. Unfortunately the party carried on talking into the night. And where was Wordsworth's sense of humour? Well, he and Davy tried to give the party the message by walking under the windows and calling out the hours loudly, like watchmen.

Wordsworth recalls an awesome and memorable experience when he was staying at Patterdale as a teenager, which he describes in 'The Prelude'. He stole a boat one moonlit evening 'from the cavern of a willow tree' and rowed out into the lake, albeit with a pang of conscience, and looked up at the crags. Then, as he rowed, a cliff appeared to grow.

> ... a huge cliff,
> As if with voluntary power instinct
> Uprear'd its head. I struck and struck again,
> And, growing still in stature, the huge Cliff

Rose up between me and the stars, and still,
With measured motion like a living thing,
Strode after me. With trembling hands I turn'd,
And through the silent water stole my way
Back to the Cavern of the Willow tree.
There, in her mooring-place, I left my Bark
And, through the meadows homeward went, with grave
And serious thoughts; and I had seen
That spectacle, for many days, my brain
Work'd with a dim and undetermined sense
Of unknown modes of being; in my thoughts
There was a darkness, call it solitude,
Or blank desertion, no familiar shapes
Of hourly objects, images of trees,
Of sea or sky, no colours of green fields;
But huge and mighty Forms that do not live
Like living men mov'd slowly through my mind
By day and were the trouble of my dreams.

The location was almost certainly by Stybarrow Crag, which abuts the road less than a km from Glenridding. The peak of Glenridding Dodd sits behind the crag, but would be hidden by an observer close to the crag until he moves away, when the Dodd would appear, and would seem to 'grow' so long as the observer receded.

GLENRIDDING village is a little way onwards and by the lake. As a village it is unremarkable, with shops and pubs, hotels and guesthouses and no notable architecture. Some of the buildings are fair, but there are some ugly insensitive intrusions, like the fibreglass children's play area at the Inn on the Lake (formerly Ullswater Hotel). The one church is a new Roman Catholic. One pleasant feature is the amount of green space for picnics. The village is a good base for holiday explorations of the fells and Ullswater. Its advantage over Patterdale is that is has the pier that is the start point for the steamer service, and where boats can be hired. It has also a large car park and a National Park information centre. Most walkers for Helvellyn start from here with several adventurous routes from which to choose. But there is none with a better approach to Striding Edge than the one from Patterdale.

The steamer pier is at the end of a promontory. Thereby hangs a tale. Above Glenridding village are the remains of a very active lead mine, called Greenside. Above it Glenridding Beck was dammed to secure waterpower for it; but in 1927 a great storm burst the dam, and a wall of water descended on the village, demolishing property and carrying flood damaged walls and fragmenting

Glenridding boat hire

buildings to the lake. Luckily none of the villagers was killed. Much of the promontory is formed from the mass of flood debris. Boats can be hired here; and the two 'steamers', *The Lady of the Lake* and *Raven* (Ullswater Navigation and Transit Company), can be boarded here for a tour round the lake, or for walkers the popular trip to Howtown so that one can enjoy the walk back along the eastern shore. Both boats are no longer real steamers as their engines were replaced by diesel. But both are over a hundred years old, and still going strong. *The Lady of the Lake* (1877) originally carried the mail to the surrounding settlements, and has survived several sinkings and a fire.

Glenridding was a mining town then. Greenside mine closed in 1960 after bringing varying economic benefits for three centuries, though it peaked in the nineteenth century when it was one of the richest mines in the north of England. In its lifetime it produced 2.4 million tons of lead ore, and 2 million oz of silver. The labyrinthine mine ran deep under Helvellyn and the principal ore, produced after smelting, was galena (lead), 80 per cent silver at 12 oz per ton. The site had crushing and dressing mills and a smelter. The chimney for the smelter was sited a mile and a half (2.5 km) up the fell, an advantage of this being that some of the lead, in vapour form from the furnace, would condense on the sides of the duct. Waste not want not: the soot and condensed lead were occasionally swept up and carried back to the furnace. The year 1872 was prosperous. The records show that 1,156 tons of pig lead were produced, valued at £26,588 – a fortune then; and there were 9 cwt, 2 qrs, 20 lbs of silver valued at £4,335.

An 1891 innovation in the mine was the use of a water-powered generator which served to electrify the machinery, lighting system, winding gear, a tramway and electric locomotive for the movement of material. The system would never pass safety inspection nowadays. Former miners say that alarming electrical shocks were commonplace.

When the mine stopped being profitable it closed in dramatic fashion. In 1962 it was packed with explosives and detonated, and thereafter used to test instruments designed to detect underground nuclear explosions. The mine buildings are almost all gone, and the few left include the youth hostel and mountain huts. The

Ullswater from Keldas

high 'tailing dams' of waste material dominate the lower site. The waste was graded and levelled and equipped with drainage for stability. The dams could be a threat if drainage was not maintained. The whole site, however, has been acquired and cared for by the National Park Authority, as has Glenridding Common, extending upwards to include Red Tarn Cove and the east face of Helvellyn. There is an interesting and well-designed display about the mine at the National Park information centre in the car park.

The best view of the lower reaches of Ullswater can be gained from Keldas, a wooded high point soon reached by a public footpath south of the village. Across Ullswater from the Glenridding steamer pier is the tall spreading boss of PLACE FELL (657 m), a hummocky, steep-sided, crag-faced fell, the haunt of foxes and buzzards (even of hunting golden eagles) and scattered groups of the Martindale herd of red deer. The views from its summit are exhilarating. To the south of the peak there is a subsidiary peak, Round How; and to the north are the two peaks of the Knight and Birk Fell.

HELVELLYN'S RUGGED SIDE

HELVELLYN's west side has been described as it overlooks Thirlmere (see pp. 364–73). This eastern side of Helvellyn is quite a contrast – faced with crags and cliffs, and five combs, relics of the affect of lingering glaciation, and shaded from the sun, and away from the mild west winds. It looks tremendous, less from a near view as from the lake, or from the opposite lakeshore. From a rock climber's point of view, however, the area is disappointing. Eagle Crag, at the head of Grisedale, offers the only challenge. But in a favourable winter spell ice climbing in Nethermost Cove is excellent. Snow lingers on in these eastern hollows and skiing is possible in a good season on the northern slopes of Raise, below Sticks Pass. But note that it is pointless for visitors to carry skis to Glenridding in anticipation and without enquiry: for seasons vary greatly and snow cover is too often short-lived.

The deep, steep-sided hollow beneath Helvellyn's summit is a classic glacial comb holding a tarn, Red Tarn, a remnant of meltwater. Like Ullswater it is the habitat of a rare post-glacial fish, the schelly. If we approach Red Tarn from Glenridding, with the peak of Catstye Cam on the right, and the high side of Birkhouse Moor on the left, we find that the cove is like a great amphitheatre. Helvellyn's summit is opposite, faced with a towering cliff, and it is walled on both sides with narrow arêtes – thin mountain ridges cut and crushed from the mountain side by two more close-pressing neighbouring glacial combs, Brown Cove to the north and Nethermost Cove to the south. The ridges are well described by Wordsworth as 'Skeleton arms', '... that from the mountain trunk/Extended, clasp the winds ...'

The cliff face that we see from Red Tarn beneath the summit is an area of Special Scientific Interest (NPA). Helvellyn's volcanic rock is acid and impervious. But where springs break through and leach out the rock's minerals to the soil surface among the crags, there are uncommon alpine plants out of reach of grazing sheep. It can be a hazardous area for botanists, though, particularly when walkers on the summit occasionally accidentally, and sometimes even deliberately, roll stones down.

The southern wall of the cove is Striding Edge (see p. 452), while the north wall curving off the summit is Swirral Edge, before it rises to the oddly named peak, Catstye Cam (889 m), but spelt on old maps as 'Catchedecam'. As this peak is visible at low levels from the east, while Helvellyn's summit is obscured, it was once thought to be the mountain's highest point.

STRIDING EDGE is easily the most common ascent of the mountain, and little wonder. The way from Glenridding is across Glenridding Beck and then by the well-marked path onto Birkhouse Moor and then on to the Hole in the Wall. What is more exciting than walking on the top of a wall with nothing above but the sky? Striding Edge is one of the most exhilarating pathways on the Lakeland fells, even though some walkers regard it as being 'too popular' and scorn it. It is indeed so popular that at busy holiday periods it has long columns of adventurers. Walkers can choose to follow the narrow ridge, or cheat like the majority, and take the cowards' paths on either side a little below it. On the route on the Nethermost Cove side of the ridge is an 1858 iron memorial that may give pause for thought, being to a local man who fell to his death there. Whatever route along the edge is taken one is confronted by the 'bad step', a break in the ridge near the summit approach. This requires a tricky descent, and one can spend an amusing hour sitting nearby and watching the contortions of walkers as they attempt to negotiate it. On busy days they appear to be pouring over the edge like lemmings. This is not the last of the walkers' problems, for they are then faced with the last part of the ascent to the ridge, which is steep, loose, and not at all pleasant.

On reaching the summit plateau from Striding Edge one encounters a substantial memorial, with verses on it composed by Wordsworth and Tennyson. It commemorates a dog. In April 1805 one Charles Gough, who had come to Patterdale for a holiday, fell to his death from Striding Edge. He did not appear to be missed, because his body was found only three months later, and astonishingly it was still attended by his emaciated faithful dog. In August of the same year Wordsworth, Sir Walter Scott and Humphry Davy climbed Helvellyn

Bank Holiday on the Edge's 'bad step'

together in good spirits, and Wordsworth told them the story. It was presumed that the dog had survived on carrion but had always returned to its master's side. Wordsworth afterwards wrote his poem 'Fidelity'; but it is Scott's poem of five verses that deserves the honours, for it's bound to cause a lump in the throat if not a tear, particularly as you read it here, near the place where it happened. It starts well:

> I climbed the dark brow of the mighty Helvellyn
> Lakes and mountains beneath me gleamed misty and wide;
> All was still, save by fits, when the eagle was yelling,
> And starting around me the echoes replied.

And it goes on in verse three:

How long didst thou think that his silence was slumber?
When the wind waved his garment, how oft didst thou start?
How many long days and long weeks didst thou number,
Ere he faded before thee, the friend of thy heart?
And, ho, was it meet, that – no requiem read o'er him,
No mother to weep, and no friend to deplore him,
And thou, little guardian, alone stretched before him –
Unhonour'd the Pilgrim from life should depart?

The memorial was erected in 1890 by Canon Rawnsley, the incumbent at Keswick and founder member of the National Trust.

A few metres from the summit is a cruciform wind shelter, the ruined Victorian original having been rebuilt in 1968 by National Park voluntary wardens and other volunteers. On a clear day the summit views are exceptionally fine. All the Lake District's major fells can be seen, the highest peaks at south-west and west. Morecambe Bay and Solway Firth are visible to the south, and the fells of southern Scotland beyond, to the north-west.

Many walkers who have ascended by Striding Edge use Swirral for the descent, usually bypassing Catstye Cam on its end. One can then reach the shore of Red Tarn (NP) and try to spot the trout. Both Striding and Swirral edges are dangerous in snow and ice and are then only for experienced walkers equipped with ice axes. An iced Swirral is particularly tricky, and it has claimed most of the accidents. As a general rule the majority of misfortunes happen on the descent. Catstye Cam is usually given a miss by walkers, but demands an ascent of any dedicated fell walker. Other fell walks on this side of the lake include Glenridding Dodd (442 m) and Sheffield Pike (675 m) above Glenridding.

The Sticks Pass bridle track starts with a zigzag above the old Greenside mine, passes the occasional ski slopes on Raise Fell, then climbs up to the 750 m gap on the Helvellyn ridge between Raise and Stybarrow Dodd; before descending to Legburthwaite at the foot of Thirlmere.

ULLSWATER AND ITS VALLEY

Ullswater is 12 km long, and 1.6 km wide, with a depth of 62.5 m. It provides a water supply for United Utilities to top up the supply from its reservoirs of Thirlmere, Haweswater and Wet Sleddale; but no one would know, for the works are underground and its effect on water levels unnoticeable. This admirable

Ullswater's head at Glenridding

arrangement came after opposition from the National Park, the Friends of the Lake District and conservationists to unacceptable proposals in 1962. The campaign was led by a Cumbrian, Lord Birkett, who had been a judge at the Nuremberg trials of the Nazis.

The lake was probably named after L'ulf, a Norse settler, and many regard it as the most beautiful of all the lakes. Its rather serpentine shape is the result of ice-age glaciers cutting and scouring away at the varying types of rocks. At the lake's foot is the soft limestone and sandstone, which changes to Skiddaw slate further up-lake, then at the head there are the towering crags of the hard volcanic rocks. Movements of lateral ice, plus the influence of the feeder rivers and becks, also have had their effects. A main river source is from the Goldrill

Beck, fed from Kirkstone, Hayeswater and Deepdale; then the waters from Helvellyn, through Glenridding and Glencoynedale and Aira Beck. While on the eastern side the becks of Bannerdale, Boredale and Fusedale add their quota – a lot of water, and not surprisingly the lake occasionally floods. Its outflow, the River Eaumont, runs north-eastwards to join the River Lowther, before being united with the Eden.

Without doubt the best way to view the lake is from the steamer, starting from the pier at its foot at Pooley Bridge, and letting the drama of the hills and crags gradually unfold.

The lake contains perch and trout, as well as shoals of a rare white fish, the schelly (*Coregonus laveratus*), sometimes described as a 'freshwater herring'. It is

Ullswater foot, Pooley Bridge pier

in fact a relic of the ice age. Sometimes, for no obvious reason, dead schellies are found on the shores.

Continuing on north on the road from Glenridding by the pleasant wooded lakeshore in about 3 km we come to Glencoyne and Glencoyne Park (NT). This lakeshore area is a historic place, and some who have suffered under a bad English teacher might wish that it never existed, for it was here that Wordsworth saw those dreaded daffodils, and sister Dorothy's words were the inspiration for his poem 'I wandered lonely as a cloud.' It was 15 April 1802 and the two were walking south by the lakeshore. I quote Dorothy's journal:

> ... we saw a few daffodils close to the water side. We fancied that the lake had floated the seeds ashore and that the little colony had sprung up. But as we went along there were more and yet more, and at last under the boughs of the trees, we saw that there was a long belt of them along the shore, about the breadth of a country turnpike road. I never saw daffodils so beautiful. They grew among the mossy stones about and about them, some rested their heads upon these stones as on a pillow for weariness and the rest tossed and reeled and danced, and seemed as if they verily laughed with the wind, that blew upon them over the lake, they looked so gay, ever glancing, ever changing.

Two years later, doubtless after reading his sister's journal, William wrote the famous lines, which, compared with his deeply philosophical compositions, is surely little more than poetic confectionery. But sadly when most people think Wordsworth they think of daffodils. The Lakeland tourist industry assumes daffodils are a major attraction, and well-meaning village communities and local authorities go mad in planting them everywhere. Unfortunately they are not planting *Narcissus pseudonarcissus*, the wild daffodil, but large fat garden varieties, and botanists worry that the aliens can cross-pollinate with the wild species, thus putting our small wild beauties under threat. And they are already proving to be scarce in other parts of the British Isles.

A little further on a road from Matterdale joins the lakeside road, and immediately afterwards Aira Beck enters the lake through attractive woodland in the care of the National Trust. There is a public car park here, and to see AIRA FORCE – waterfalls – one must park and follow the path. The falls are, of course, best after prolonged rain, when they can be spectacular, but at any time the walk through the woodland and by the beckside is rewarding. It is a cool place on a hot day. Tree enthusiasts will enjoy the sight of some very fine specimens.

Aira Force, lower fall

Wordsworth writes of the beauty of woodlands in this area round the falls in his poem 'Airey-Force Valley'.

> ... Not a breath of air
> Ruffles the bosom of this leafy glen.
> And yet, even now, a little breeze, perchance
> Escaped from boisterous winds that rage without
> Has entered, by the sturdy oaks unfelt,
> But to its gentle touch how sensitive
> Is the light ash! that pendent from the brow
> Of yon dim cave, in seeming silence makes
> A soft eye-music of slow-waving boughs
> Powerful almost as vocal harmony
> To stay the wanderer's steps and soothe his thoughts.

Eye music indeed, and the falls give music for the ear: Vivaldi, perhaps, if there has been a dry spell; Wagner, after long, heavy rain. Care is needed on the approaches to the two viewpoint bridges, at lower and higher points. In 'The Somnambulist' Wordsworth's awful verses (of the Rupert Bear school?), too painful to quote, he repeats an impossible story of the place, with all the sickening tear-jerking ingredients so loved by many Romantics of his age: noble knight; faithful lady awaiting her lover's return from the Crusades; she sleepwalks alongside the falls just as her knight returns; he touches her, she awakes with a shock, and she falls into the ravine; he pulls her out but she dies in his arms. He dies of a broken heart.

De Quincey, in his *Recollections of the Lakes and the Lake Poets* (1834), tells a true story about the place concerning Elizabeth Smith (the scholarly lady who kept Wordsworth and Davy away from their room at Patterdale) – who (see pp. 453 and 562) told him of her experience. She had wandered up by the falls alone with a sketchbook, and in the course of her wanderings found herself cragfast. She was no idiot – she was a fell walker, but she found herself in a spot among steep walls of broken rock where she could see no escape either upwards or around, and with the torrent at her feet. Every move she tried seemed to place herself in a more difficult position until she was on the brink of panic. Then when hope was in danger of slipping away, she saw a figure of a woman 200 metres away, dressed, as De Quincey writes,

> in a white muslin morning robe such as were then worn by young ladies until dinner-time. The lady beckoned with a gesture and in a manner that, in a moment, gave her confidence to advance – how she could not guess; but, in some way that baffled all power to retrace it, she found instantaneously the outlet which previously had escaped her.

Elizabeth continued to advance towards the lady, who now seemed to be on the other side of the torrent. She indicated by gestures the way that Elizabeth should descend and the latter found herself on a 'platform of rock, from which the further descent was safe and conspicuous'. She could only assume that the lady was her sister, but when she approached the spot where she expected to find her to exchange greetings, she found herself alone. Returning to the house Elizabeth found her sister and family there, and was told that no one had left the house.

The well-engineered footpaths now are quite clear and the chances of getting lost or cragfast are minimal. When one leaves the falls, one footpath leads eastwards to the side of the fell from the approach to the lower bridge. This gives some excellent views of Ullswater, and of the rear side of Lyulph's Tower, which might look medieval but was built by the duke of Norfolk as a hunting lodge in 1780. Lyulph was fancied to be a pre-Norman lord owning the land hereabouts. The path leads on into Gowbarrow Park, once enclosed to contain a herd of fallow deer, now long since gone. Here 'The lover of nature might wish to linger for hours,' wrote Wordsworth.

Another footpath leaves the highest point of the falls and takes one to DOCKRAY in Matterdale, a small settlement. The little seventeenth-century church is further up the dale, but a minor road and path westwards lead into remote Dowthwaite, and a path further back to Glencoyne. Going up the road from Dockray through Matterdale End, one passes a conical hill on the right: GREAT MELL FELL (NT) (537 m). 'Great' is to distinguish it from Little Mell Fell (505 m) to its east. The fells consist of conglomerate rock, debris in the form of pebbles welded together, which was laid down before the encroaching sea produced the limestone. The movement of glacier ice has swept away the Silurian rocks above the limestone, and the limestone beneath too, to expose the conglomerate that has been left in a heap. Because the rock has no variation in density the sweep of ice left the profile comparatively smooth and even. There are prehistoric burial sites on both of the fells.

The road meets the A66 at Troutbeck (not to be confused with the Troutbeck near Windermere), the site of a sheep market. Following the A66 eastwards a minor road runs to the left to PENRUDDOCK. There is nothing much to the hamlet. There is little here, apart from a modern little church and a very old Presbyterian (now United Reform) one, built in 1654, and an enterprising shop, Birds' Bistro, that sells bird food, feeders and bird boxes.

Continuing on past lay-by car parking areas on Ullswater's shore, one reaches Skelly Neb and the home of the Outward Bound school. 'Neb' or 'Nab' is a promontory. On the other side of the lake from this point is Geordie's Crag, and between them is the narrowest breadth of the lake. In old times a net was stretched across the lake at this point to catch schelly, hence the name.

Watermillock is the next settlement. It is said that a lakeside chapel stood here once, but now the parish church of All Saints is 2 km westwards up the minor road. Built in 1884, of red sandstone, it is ample and quite superior to some architecture of that period. At WATERMILLOCK, further along from the neb, at Rampsbeck, rowing boats and motor boats can be hired.

On arriving at the foot of the lake, after a road junction, the road runs by the shore under a wooded hill. This is Dunmallard (or Dunmallet). Its summit is crowned by the ditches and ramparts of an ancient hill fort, which is rather difficult to make out because of the encroaching trees. Not a lot is known about these hill forts, which were almost certainly occupied after Roman times. This would have been a good place, commanding a view over the lake and at the crossing of its feeder: the River Eaumont. There was another hill fort, Maiden Castle, just over 1 km to the west on Soulby Fell.

After passing the landing stages for the steamer service, we arrive at POOLEY BRIDGE, a small village and holiday centre, with boats for hire. Across the bridge is Eusemere House, one-time home of the Quaker Thomas Clarkson (1760–1846), who, with William Wilberforce, successfully campaigned against the slave trade. Catherine Clarkson was Dorothy Wordsworth's close friend, and the Wordsworths frequently stayed at Eusemere.

DACRE AND DALEMAIN

From the car park on the east side of the bridge, a footpath leads to DACRE. The village is found off a by-road between the A592 at the foot of Ullswater and the A66. The church is one of the most interesting in the area. It almost certainly stands on the site of a Saxon monastery mentioned by the Venerable Bede in his history: 'near the River Dacore, from which it took its name'. He records a miracle cure there that was attributed to a relic of St Cuthbert when the monastery was in the care of Abbot Swidbert. It was almost certainly here that the Peace of Dacre was signed by Athelstan of England and Constantine of Scotland in 926 (Dacre being in Scotland then). Actually it was an act of homage by the Scot, when both countries needed joint action to resist attacks from the Danes and Norsemen.

Excavations in the church area have shown the layout of assumed monastic buildings, but all that remains of the Saxon structures in the church are traces of foundations. The church is Norman with many additions and modifications and rebuilding. The round piers are from the mid thirteenth century, and the octagonals show some reconstruction around 1400. The Norman tower was rebuilt in 1810. On the south side of the chancel is a stone with a carving, said to represent the Peace of Dacre. In the churchyard are four mysterious carved stones of unknown origin. They may have come from the four corners of the roof of a keep, possibly nearby Dacre Castle, or from Penrith. They tell the following story (see overleaf: anti-clockwise from the north-west): one – a bear rests with its head on a staff or pillar; two – bear attacked by a cat on its shoulder; three – bear reaches to remove the cat; four – bear eats cat. The story's significance is obscure, but it may record an attack on some lord by his inferior. Is there a connection with Warwick (the King Maker), the Neville who owned and occupied the not-so-faraway Penrith castle, and whose emblem happened to be the bear and ragged staff?

Dacre bears: bear and ragged staff

Bear attacked by cat

Bear reaches back to catch cat

Bear eats cat

The Norman castle at Dacre is approached by a public footpath opposite the small green in the village centre. It is not generally open to the public. The castle was built on the site of an earlier structure, but the present building dates from the fourteenth century. Its fortunes varied with those of the Dacre family. The family was a great force throughout the border wars and raids. It was Leonard Dacre who unwisely led a rebellion against Elizabeth I. His forces were defeated by those of Lord Hunsdon, cousin of the queen, close by the River Gelt in 1569. The castle was restored under the ownership of the earl of Sussex in 1675, and further restoration was undertaken in 1789, but it still looks all that a Norman stronghold should be.

A footpath leads from the castle to DALEMAIN. Alternatively from the foot of the lake west of Pooley Bridge a road goes northwards for Penrith (A592), and where it nears the west bank of the River Eaumont, Dalemain is seen on the left as a magnificent Georgian-fronted house in natural pink limestone. It has been the ancestral home of the Hasells since 1665. Cumbria is fortunate in having some superior country houses open to the public. This one is not large, and only a part is open, but it is well worth a visit. It started, like most in this area, as a defensive pele tower, built by John de Morville, brother of Hugh of the Becket murder. It is said that after the crime Sir Hugh found sanctuary at Dalemain before making off to Yorkshire. The pele tower was added to in the 1740s by Edward Hasell, son of the steward to Lady Anne Clifford. It is a restful place to spend a few hours. One can contrast the elegant eighteenth-century portion of the interior with the dark-oaked Elizabethan behind it. Look out for the Chinese room, with hand-painted wallpaper, and a panelled 'fretwork room' with an impressively plastered ceiling. Children are thought of in the inclusion of a nursery with period toys and dolls' houses. A tea-room in the old hall of the house serves homemade fare; and the large sixteenth-century barn has old farming exhibits. The gardens, ranging from formal to wild, are an absolute delight. Tree enthusiasts will want to see the Grecian silver fir, with a girth of 6 m, though the claim that it is the largest in the UK is incorrect. Lob's Wood is a good woodland walk for families.

EAST OF ULLSWATER VALLEY AND HIGH STREET FELLS

Returning to Pooley Bridge a road leads to the sparsely populated east side of the lake. A narrow minor road follows the shore to HOWTOWN, though town it is not; just a small settlement. On its way it passes the base for the Ullswater Yacht Club, then Sharrow Bay and the famous Sharrow Bay Hotel – famous, for it has been a national award-winner for food and hospitality several times, and is one of the best hotels in England. Sadly the two popular men who founded it have died, but the hotel carries on the tradition. Howtown has a hotel, an Outdoor Education Centre, a steamer pier and nearby HALLIN FELL (388 m) that gives some of the most exciting prospects over the lake. One of the Lake District's best low-level walks leaves Howtown by the lake shore of Hallin Fell, then runs mostly along or above the lake shore to Patterdale with viewpoints all the way. Most walkers doing it take the steamer from Pooley Bridge or Glenridding to Howtown and walk back to Patterdale. Halfway along, the walk gives a grand spectacle up into the glaciated eastern coves of Helvellyn.

After Howtown the road climbs steeply to the Hause, past the new nineteenth-century church of St Peter, its best feature being stained glass by Jane Gray; and

Martindale – the old church

at the fork a road goes left into MARTINDALE. In a short distance is Martindale's old church of St Martin, which the modern church made redundant, and after which the dale was named. This simple little tranquil edifice was built in 1633, but it is obvious that there was a place of worship here earlier, for the magnificent yew tree is almost certainly 700 years old with a trunk circumference of more than 6 m. In fact records show that the church has medieval origins at least. A precious place.

There is no point in driving on to the dale head. This is a walkers' route via Boredale Hause to Patterdale, as is the next valley to the west, Boredale itself. Martindale common spreads southwards and the fells are occupied by red deer of the Martindale deer forest, in the ownership of the Hasells of Dalemain. The fell deer are lighter than those of the southern Lakeland forests and their antlers less impressive. In winter they often drift down the valleys and onto the shores of Ullswater, and in severe weather are almost tame. The farm at the dale head once doubled as a hunting lodge.

At Pooley Bridge again the walkers can take the south-east road to the network of paths and bridleways onto Barton and Askham Fells, at Moor Divock, and onto the old Roman road, HIGH STREET, that runs all along, by High Raise (802 m) and Kidsty Pike (780 m). The 'road', now merely a pathway, eventually reaches the Windermere basin, linking the Roman fort at Brougham to the fort at Waterhead, Ambleside. It offers superb walking. The obvious question is why did the Romans build a mountain summit road when less steep routes through the dales could have been used? But man has transformed the present-day landscape since Roman times. Then the fell sides would have been forested, and the valley bases boggy. The route follows a logical line from the Roman fort and crossroads at Brougham to the fort at Ambleside. It is likely that the road was an improvement of one long used by the Britons, known as 'Brettestrete' – 'The road of the Britons' – in the thirteenth century. The road's route can be traced on a large-scale map. Its beginnings cannot be ascertained, but from Tirril, on the Pooley Bridge to Eaumont Bridge road, it is clear as a dead-straight line running south-westerly to Celleron. After that it becomes less distinct as it climbs past Winder Hill farm, skirts to the west of Heughscar Hill; then it can be seen on Barton Fell, then on by the side of Loadpot Hill (610 m). The road continues to climb to 820 m before it descends for 3 km and drops to the valley at Troutbeck Park by a track known as 'Scots Rake', which can be seen from the road up to Kirkstone. Scots Rake was maybe so called because Scots' raiders used the High Street route for their incursions. Or did the Roman road not descend here but continue on? All that can be assumed is that it linked up, somewhere, with the road that cannot be firmly traced, from the fort at Kendal to the fort at Ambleside.

A high point (820 m) on the High Street range lies directly east of Hartsop, and its eastern face towers craggily, with cliffs of 310 m, over the tarn of Blea Water. As a contrast to the savagery of the eastern flank, the top is grassy and even. Having the advantage of direct though long approaches from the north and south, it was until the nineteenth century an annual summer meeting-point for shepherds from Mardale, Troutbeck, Martindale, Patterdale, Kentmere and Longsleddale. The object of the meeting was to bring together stray animals to be claimed by their rightful owners. But, of course, this was also a great once-a-year social event and an excuse for revelries. A fair was laid on, an ample supply of casks of ale were carried up the fell, and there were horse racing, wrestling and games of skill. The summit plateau is still named 'Race-horse Hill' on large-scale maps.

The peaks along the High Street ridge are from north to south, Loadpot Hill (671 m), Wether Hill (674 m), High Raise (803 m), High Street (829 m), then Thornthwaite Crag (783 m), Froswick (719 m), Ill Bell (755 m) and lastly Yoke (703 m). The southern part of Yoke falls evenly to Garburn Pass – the way between Troutbeck and Kentmere.

From the point where the path from Pooley Bridge joins the High Street, there are paths going east to Askham, Helton and Bampton over MOOR DIVOCK, which is extremely rich in signs of Bronze Age settlement. At the point on High Street near this complex of routes can be found a small ring of stones 36.5 m in diameter, called 'the cockpit', which it never was. It was thought to be a stone circle, but it may be the remains of an ancient enclosure. About here the fells are covered with

'The cockpit' – ancient stone circle on Moor Divock

stones, cairns, tumuli and hut circles. It was on the path from the fell to Askham that Wordsworth wrote 'I was a Traveller then upon the moor', and his evocative lines in 'Resolution and Independence':

> All things that love the sun are out of doors;
> The sky rejoices in the morning's birth;
> The grass is bright with rain-drops; on the moors
> The hare is running races in her mirth;
> And with her feet she from the plashy earth
> Raises a mist; that, glittering in the sun,
> Runs with her all the way, wherever she doth run.

Returning to Pooley Bridge, alongside the road between the village and Penrith, Barton's St Michael's church is along a road to the left. There is something fascinatingly odd about this Norman church. At once the short central tower, which appears to have been swallowed by the rest of the building, strikes one as the unusual feature. The tower is Norman, built about 1150, along with the nave and chancel, after which, a century later, the south and north aisles and arcades were built. Inside one can see the effect the additions had on the tower. A Norman window, once on the outside, is on the inside viewed from the south aisle. Then broader lower strainer arches were added below the chancel and nave arches to strengthen the tower structure when the church was in the care of Augustinian canons of York. The crossing then is a sort of dark cavern. Looking up the inside of the tower there is a transverse tunnel-vault, evidence of some very skilled Norman craftsmanship. Wordsworth's grandfather, Richard Wordsworth (1680–1760), is buried in the chancel. During the 1745 Scottish advance he was receiver general of the county of Westmorland, and with a large sum of money in his charge, he left home with it and hid it in Patterdale until the crisis was over. Memorial tablets to several other Wordsworths are dotted about here. Is this a site of great antiquity – chosen to transplant Christianity onto a pagan base? A circular churchyard wall on a raised area, and a nearby spring, prompt the suggestion. In other parts of Britain archaeologists have proved that churches on such sites were built by Celtic Christians on top of pagan religious structures.

The road continues past Tirril, where there is a Quaker meeting house, built in 1731 and now a private house; and Sockbridge, whose hall has Tudor features. Wordsworth's grandfather Richard lived here, as did his elder brother Richard when he was not in London. Where the road passes over the railway is Yanwath, where Thomas Wilkinson (1751–1836), the Quaker friend of Wordsworth, lived in the Grotto (now a guest house). He was a poet as well as a landscape gardener and a farmer, and apart from the Wordsworths he had visits from Coleridge, the statesman and author George Canning (1770–1827) and the Quaker social worker and prison reformer Elizabeth Fry (1780–1845). He landscaped his gardens and built a hidden 'hovel', a sort of summer house, but it was quite luxurious with fireplace, furniture and a window looking out towards Penrith beacon. On a wall he wrote:

Beneath this moss grown roof, this rustic cell
Truth, Liberty, Content, sequester'd dwell;
Say, you who dare our hermitage disdain,
What drawing room can boast so fair a train?

Wordsworth gave him a hand in his landscaping, and subsequently wrote, 'To the Spade of a Friend', 'Composed while we were labouring together in his pleasure-ground.' Here are the first two verses:

Spade! with which Wilkinson has tilled his lands,
And shaped these pleasant walks by Eumont's side,
Thou art a tool of honour in my hands;
I press thee, through the yielding soil with pride.

Rare master has it been thy lot to know;
Long has Thou served a man to reason true;
Whose life combines the best of high and low,
The labouring many and the resting few;

Yanwath Hall, a fourteenth-century pele tower with later additions, is by the river.

The road south from Yanwath, in a little less than 4 km reaches ASKHAM, an ancient village close to the River Lowther and in view of the Lowther castle ruins. Askham Hall is a large house built upon a pele tower dating from the fourteenth century. Other buildings in the village are from the seventeenth and eighteenth centuries and the separate modern buildings are, it must be said, out of sympathy with the old. As mentioned earlier Askham Fell and Moor Divock, to the west of the village, show many signs of substantial ancient populations, including many burial cairns. The 'Cop Stone' a standing stone 1.5 m high, south-west of the village, may have been part of a circle, traces of which are enclosed in a bank. Some very vague signs of an avenue, or avenues, of stones going north-west and west from the stone link a series of cairns.

The church beside the river was rebuilt in 1835 on the site of an older one, and the fifteenth-century south transept has been retained. The LOWTHER estate lies across the River Lowther, and has been in that family's possession for 700 years.

The 'Cop Stone' – ancient stone on Moor Divock

The first Lowther Hall was built in the early thirteenth century. The family's fortunes grew largely from the ownership of the rich mining areas of west Cumbria. Sir Richard Lowther was a sympathizer of Mary, Queen of Scots' claim to the English throne, but managed to survive the indiscretion. In the late seventeenth century Sir James Lowther fared better, for he was a supporter of William and Mary and, in recognition of his good judgement, was granted the title of first earl of Lonsdale. He was the man who refused to consider repaying the debt of £8,000 to the Wordsworth family that he owed their late father, his agent. Sir James extensively rebuilt the hall, but in the 1720s it was struck by a disastrous fire. A new Lowther Castle was designed for the fifth earl, by a young Robert Smirke, who later designed the British Museum.

The building of the hall started in 1806 and finished in 1811. In its heyday its distinguished visitors included Kaiser Wilhelm II and the Prince of Wales, later Edward VII. Unfortunately the castle's proportions proved too extravagant for the twentieth century and it was pulled down, and its contents sold off in 1947, leaving a shell. The unique and spectacular façade, not approachable by the public, is 128 m long.

Even ruins, or especially ruins, are difficult to maintain. The central tower was in danger of collapse in 2003 and English Heritage helped to save it by giving a grant to the Lowther Estate Trust. The trust has plans for the castle ruin, including using the internal spaces for concerts and exhibitions, and intends to rehabilitate the old gardens.

The church of St Michael, across the park to the north, offers an intriguing dichotomy between the restored seventeenth-century exterior and the essentially medieval interior. The capitals in the north arcade have some interesting decorative tooling, although some of this has been reworked. The curious Lowther mausoleum (1857) in the churchyard houses a seated earl.

Of the two Lowther villages, Lowther New Town lies south-east of the church and was designed to replace a settlement originally nearer the church. The

The remaining façade of Lowther Castle

other Lowther village is to the east. Again, it was specially designed, and has been attributed to Robert Adam (1728–1792) or James Adam, his younger brother, and was built between 1765 and 1775.

HAWESWATER

HAWESWATER is in the north-east of the National Park. In the middle of the twentieth century the green valley that contained Haweswater sent 3,000 lb of butter by railway to Manchester market every week. At the valley head was the hamlet of Mardale. Harriet Martineau in her *Guide to the English Lakes* (1855) wrote: 'The inn at Mardale Green is full a mile from the water; and sweet is the passage to it ... The path winds through the levels, round the bases of the knolls, past the ruins of the old church, and among snug little farms.' But Manchester could take or leave the picturesque, and it needed something more vital than butter; it needed water, and the village of Mardale and the dairy farms had to go, for Thirlmere alone could not supply her needs. The Haweswater reservoir scheme was approved and launched, and the construction of the dam began in 1929. At the same time two new roads had to be made: one to the head of the valley above what would be the new water level; and a second to Shap and the railway. A tunnel had to be cut from the valve house halfway down the lake, through to Longsleddale, and from then on by 'cut and cover' pipeline down the valley to connect with the Thirlmere water at Watchgate by the A6. The dam workers were housed in a temporary village built at Burn Banks, below the dam wall. Their work had to be suspended during the economic problems of 1931 and was restarted from 1934; and all was finished and water began at last to flow in 1941. The water level was eventually raised by 29 m.

Haweswater is 6.5 km long, 8 km wide and 60 m deep, and is 240 m above sea level. This makes it a somewhat superior water source in all respects than Thirlmere. It is fed by many becks. From the head, in hanging valleys high on High Street Fells, waters cascade from two mountain tarns: Blea Water, which is 63 m deep, and the beautiful lonely Small Water. Other becks flow in from the heights on the western side. Haweswater is also fed through underground pipes by water pumped from Ullswater. No one would know: Manchester Corporation, following strong opposition by conservationists, learned to be more sensitive. During times of droughts the walls and ruins of the drowned village of Mardale can sometimes be seen.

The scheme was not as controversial as the one at Thirlmere, probably because the valley was not so popular with visitors. The seventeenth-century church was lost, as were its school and four farms. The loss of the inn, the Dun Bull, the base for the annual shepherds' meet, was particularly mourned; and to make amends the corporation built another one, the Haweswater Hotel, halfway down the lake on the side of their newly-made road. Some architect in the corporation's offices was probably proud of the design, which would have looked fine in a Manchester suburb. But, hospitable as it now is, this building does not belong to Cumbria.

The modern Haweswater has its critics who see it as too artificial. As Norman Nicholson put it: '... what we see is not a dale with a lake in it, but a group of fells plunged up to the waist in cold water'. But now, even with some inevitable conifer planting, the bleached shoreline caused by level fluctuations and the concrete dam itself, it is not without its attractions. It is off the beaten track, and the stupendous towering wild crags at the dale head, and the High Street range at its side, loud with falling water, give the upper reaches a wonderful wilderness effect matched only by Wasdale Head. In fact golden eagles nest here, the only nest site in England, and the birds can sometimes be seen coursing the valleys. The nest sites are under the protection of the RSPB with full co-operation by the water authority. In 2003 no young were produced and ornithologists are concerned that the female may be getting beyond the age of breeding.

The lake contains trout, perch and pike. Permits for angling are obtained from the water authority. Since Mardale was wiped out, the two passes that leave the head of the valley have lost their original importance and are now used by walkers. At least there is a road along the lakeside, leading to the start of some great fell walks. A southern way goes over Gatescarth Pass (580 m) and by the River Sprint into Long Sleddale; the other route goes by Small Water Tarn and over Nan Bield pass (610 m) and by the River Kent into Kentmere. They pass either side of Harter Fell (774 m); but a diversion to the summit offers great views, particularly southwards and westwards, with all the high fells of central Lakeland in sight. A very satisfying round walk can be made from Haweswater's head, from Nan Bield pass, and over Harter to Gatescarth; but not in mist.

North-west of Haweswater's dam, by the River Lowther, are the villages of BAMPTON and BAMPTON GRANGE. The church of St Patrick here is built on the site of an earlier one under the wing of Shap Abbey, and is eighteenth century with 1885 restorations. Its make is unusual timber arcades. Bampton Grange was once noted for its grammar school, founded in 1623. A noted son of the parish was Edmund Gibson (1669–1748), who left the school for Queen's College, Oxford, in 1686, and excelled in scholarship. Thereafter he took holy orders, and in 1729 was appointed bishop of London.

Seven kilometres from the head of Haweswater one comes to Wet Sleddale, a 1 km-long reservoir intended to supplement Thirlmere and Haweswater. Its landscape is in stark contrast to that seen around Ullswater. It is brutally austere, a place for those who appreciate utter remoteness.

CHAPTER NINETEEN

The Popular South-eastern Quarter of the National Park

Four roadways lead from Kendal into the National Park's south-eastern area. All of them leave the grey limestone town and surrounding country, for a different landscape of woodland and farmland on Silurian slates. The main A590 runs through Levens, entering the park across the River Gilpin, and by Foulshaw and Meathop Mosses, bypassing Lindale to climb through High Newton to Newby Bridge at the outflow of Windermere, then beyond into Furness. Secondly, the more rural A570 leaves the A590 as it crosses the National Park's boundary at Gilpin Bridge, and goes north-westwards along the foot of the scenic Lyth valley and on by the hamlet of Winster to Bowness. A road leads west from Plumgarths, the roundabout on the Kendal bypass, through Crook to the Hawkshead ferry. And fourthly, the main tourist route – the A591 – which runs from the Kendal bypass northwards and westwards, entering the park by Staveley to Windermere town.

However, before the A590 had been engineered across the boggy mosses, west of the River Kent's flow over the Milnthorpe Sand, the old route for centuries from Kendal to Newby Bridge and on to Ulverston market and Furness, went directly across the fells. It was originally a packhorse track; and coaches and carts had a hard time of it later. This route left from the front of Kendal town hall, up Allhallows Lane, westwards into the park over Scout Scar, and then dropped steeply down to Underbarrow, through the farmland to Crossthwaite. It then went south-westwards through the small settlement of Bowland Bridge, and over the incredibly steep hairpins of Strawberry Bank, over the hill by Gummers How and very steeply down to Newby Bridge. This was tough on the horses, and carriage passengers would undoubtedly have had to get out and walk the steeps, and on descents probably had to close their eyes at the hairpins.

But this latter route takes one into the delectable rural countryside between the Lyth valley and the lake. If one is to follow it, it is absolutely necessary to stop at SCOUT SCAR, just out of Kendal, leave the road at the car park and walk the few metres up the hill opposite and on to the plateau atop the limestone cliffs. The prospect is a grand surprise, and the best reason of all for Kendal to be described as 'the gateway to the Lakes', for here is the portal, and it overlooks great stretches of it, with mouthwatering prospects for exploration. First of all below is the area of field patterns and woods, farmsteads, cottages and streams, almost too rural to be true. Southwards beyond the hump of Whitbarrow Scar lies Morecambe Bay. Then to the west, astonishingly, one can see the fells of Lakeland from Coniston Old Man range, Scafell Pike and Bowfell, Gable and Langdale Pikes, round to Fairfield and the High Street range. Turn around and you are looking eastwards beyond the Howgills and into the Yorkshire Dales National Park, with Ingleborough prominent. The viewpoint 'mushroom' on the summit reveals the details. This place is not to be missed, and it is so near Kendal.

Directly below is the Lyth valley, famous in the spring for its damson blossom. There are flowers on the ridge that like limestone, and some of the trees growing out of the crag below the ridge are the uncommon Swedish whitebeam (*Sorbus intermedia*), and in season the edge has a show of equally scarce hoary rockrose. In the woodlands below, accessed from the southern end of the ridge, can be found flowers typical of woodland on limestone, including orchids.

The road is steep in its descent from Scout Scar into a delightful area that is not for anyone in a hurry. It has its low limestone fell of Whitbarrow, and the rest is criss-crossed by narrow minor roads with humps and bends and hills. The Lyth valley itself, south of our road, is beautiful – it is a valley of damson trees, not so many as in former decades, but still a glory of blossom in spring; and no finer damsons than these can be had anywhere in the autumn. The road drops down to the village of Underbarrow, then the busy little village of Crosthwaite, and crosses the A5074 to Bowland Bridge with its one shop and a pub.

To explore WHITBARROW one must divert from here south-eastwards past the delightfully named Cowmire Hall (but pronounced locally *COM-mer*), which dates from the seventeenth century, built onto its defensive pele tower of the fifteenth. Then a narrow road goes south through woodland to Witherslack Hall. Leaving the road here a steep path ascends Whitbarrow's limestone fell, a Site of Scientific Interest, and a nature reserve managed by Cumbria Wildlife Trust. Whitbarrow is a hump of carboniferous limestone dipping gently to the east but with abrupt cliffs to the west and south. The flora is typically limestone woodland, but one may find surprises. The hoary rockrose again grows on the edges of the limestone cliffs. But the whole area is a complicated pattern of limestone pavement, grassland and trees. Roe deer are often seen on the reserve, sometimes red, and there are badgers and foxes, stoats, weasels and rabbits. On its summit, Lord's Seat, is a memorial cairn to Canon Hervey, founder of what is now the Cumbria Wildlife Trust.

WITHERSLACK VILLAGE is small and tranquil. The church of St Paul dates from around 1669 and was built through a bequest of John Barwick, dean of the rather larger St Paul's in London, with his brother Peter, physician to Charles II – both of whom were natives of the parish. It is built in Gothic style, and placed in a beautiful situation. John Barwick was a Royalist in the Civil War. He made a perilous journey from Cambridge to Nottingham carrying money to Charles I. The tracts that he wrote in support of the king probably cost him his fellowship at Cambridge University, and he had to go into hiding. He was caught and put in the Tower of London, but was considered harmless and allowed his freedom. With the Restoration he was back in favour. Having refused several bishoprics, he became, first, dean of Durham, and then of St Pauls. He died in 1664. Peter, meanwhile, had been practising as a physician among the London population during the plague – attending to the poor at his own cost, before his appointment to the crown.

Returning to Bowland Bridge one must cross the bridge over the River Winster, and divert to take the narrow road south for 1.5 km to one of the very best of Lakeland's little churches. St Anthony's of CARTMEL FELL sits remotely and silently among trees and rocks. There can be no finer haven for a place of worship, which looks as if it has grown out of the ground. Lacking any flamboyant Norman influence, the church, which dates from 1505, is built like a barn, and has escaped the desecrations of Victorian 'improvers'. Inside there are pews of sixteenth and

St Anthony's secluded chapel on Cartmel Fell

seventeenth century, and a three-decker pulpit. The east window has stained glass that originated from Cartmel priory. St Anthony is there, with an attendant pig. An extraordinarily skilful wood carving, 76 cm long, of the torso of the crucified Christ, possibly thirteeenth century, was found here. It is said to have been used to poke a fire! Where on earth did it come from? It has received loving care since, and is now on display at Kendal Museum.

Back to Bowland Bridge and the road goes westwards by Strawberry Bank and the Masons Arms pub, up steep hairpins on to Cartmel Fell itself, and by the forest at GUMMERS HOW. A short walk from the forest picnic area takes one on to the How and a view over the southern reaches of Windermere with the steamer pier below at Lakeside. A steep descent takes one to the foot of the lake.

THE FURNESS ROAD

The main A590 route to Windermere from Kendal turns north-west at the Lindale bypass then goes through farm buildings – though it is still a busy main road to the Furness industries! It then passes through High Newton, which has little to offer except a good inn. Limestone country and a scattering of settlements stretch out to the west. The field walls and houses are built of limestone. FIELD BROUGHTON church, dating from 1893, has a limestone spire. But the road runs on by the Silurian hills of Cartmel Fell on the right to Newby bridge – though there is a sneaky narrow minor road just before it that runs through the idyllic hamlet of STAVELEY-IN-CARTMEL, with its little seventeenth-century church dedicated to St Mary; to join the A591 from Newby Bridge to Bowness near the National Trust's country park of Fell Foot.

NEWBY BRIDGE crosses the River Leven, which flows out of Windermere; this may confuse as the bridge south of Kendal is called Levens Bridge, although it crosses the River Kent. This bridge has five arches, and bays for pedestrians threatened by traffic. Though built in the late seventeenth century, it is bearing strains of traffic now for which it was never intended, but it survives well. On its north side is the famous Swan hotel. Up above the hotel is Waterside Knott (NPA), on which is a tower, marking a viewpoint at 185 m, built by James King of Finsthwaite House in 1797.

From Newby Bridge south the road bisects the hamlet of BACKBARROW. Two industries thrived here: an iron works and a factory producing industrial blue that was initially owned by Lancashire Ultramarine Company and later by Reckitt and Coleman. The blue was used to produce the 'dolly blue' bag, the little bag once deemed essential for adding to the wash to make whites really gleam white. The ingredients were indigo and lime. When the mill worked, everything in the immediate environs was dyed blue, including the workers, and blue can still be found in disturbed soil in its area. In earlier times it was a cotton mill that became infamous for employing children from city poorhouses that were only too glad to be rid of them. They worked six days a week and fifteen hours a day; but in times of drought when the mill wheel would not work they were abandoned and had to subsist by begging. Now the mill is the Whitewater hotel, connecting with the new 'Lakeland Village', a timeshare complex.

Downstream from the blue mill the blast furnace of the iron works was established in 1711 and used large water-powered bellows. John Wilkinson, the iron man himself, was the ironmaster here. The ore came from the mines of Furness, and the charcoal from the surrounding woodlands. The furnace was still using charcoal when others were using coke. It closed down in the 1960s. Some of the buildings have been preserved by the National Park, and the site will likely be developed.

HAVERTHWAITE is the next hamlet south. The old railway line from Furness to Lakeside was not only chopped by Beeching, it was chopped short by road improvements. However, the remaining line from here to Lakeside was acquired by railway enthusiasts and the HAVERTHWAITE AND LAKESIDE RAILWAY runs steam trains for the 3 km or so to the lake, to link with the lake steamers. It makes for a very popular attraction – a wonder for the children and the mechanically inclined, a touch of nostalgia for the elderly. The engine shed also contains some fascinating rolling-stock and artefacts.

Across the road, which cuts the village in two and makes for a dangerous crossing, especially for schoolchildren going to and from the Levens valley school at upper Haverthwaite, we find the site of Low Wood mill. The mill was first an iron works, established in 1746, and thirty-three years later was converted to a gunpowder works, which consisted of a series of water wheels spaced out to power the various meticulous processes of milling and mixing. Saltpetre was imported from India and Chile, sulphur from Italy, and they were both brought inland from the port at Ulverston. The third ingredient – charcoal – came from the coppice woodlands of the area. Alder trees grew in profusion in the wet areas here and that wood provided the best charcoal for gunpowder, inferior only to juniper (locally called 'savins') that was not as abundant. The clock tower and administrative building of the mid nineteenth century are all that remain, as it was very necessary by law that on closure, everything had to be totally cleared to prevent possible accidents caused by hidden pockets of powder. Originally the gunpowder was transported down river to a wharf at Greenodd, but the coming of the railway was a great boost, just as it was to the Backbarrow industries. The barrels and boxes were then carried by a narrow-gauge track to the Haverthwaite sidings over an iron bridge. A pile of remaining stencils for marking the various grades and types of products shows that exports went to twenty-four ports of west Africa for the mines; to copper mines in Spain and Brazil; to dams in Portugal and Peru; to collieries in Scotland, Lancashire and the Midlands; and to local slate quarries as well as some in Scotland and Wales; and iron mines in west Cumbria. Like all the gunpowder works in Cumbria, production ceased between the wars. The site is now occupied by a variety of workshops including a glass engraver's, and artists' studios.

Above the site is BIGLAND TARN that provided a head of water for the works and is now part of the Bigland Hall Country Sports centre. The tarn is well known by anglers for it has some of the best coarse fishing in Cumbria, and pike fishing is renowned. Night angling is also allowed and opportunities are available for the disabled. There is also a trout fishery at the centre.

Downstream from Haverthwaite is ROUDSEA WOOD National Nature Reserve (EN). Its varied interest comes from its location on two ridges of differing rock – Silurian bannisdale slate, which is at its limit here, and the carboniferous limestone that succeeds it. They form an island of diverse habitats for plants and animals: there is salt marsh, a raised bog and peat. Sessile oak grows on the acid soil; yew, ash and hazel on the alkaline; and birch and pine colonize the peat. Adders are common and grass snakes (less so), and one can see slow worms and lizards. Roe deer and red deer frequent the site. The flora includes seventeen species of fern, and uncommon flowers such as the fly orchid; and butterflies abound. Access is by permit only.

THE WINSTER AND THE CROOK ROADS

To return to the routes into the Windermere basin: the A574 begins at the National Park boundary on the A590 west of Kendal, crosses the River Gilpin and goes north through the woods and fields and orchards of the Lyth valley, and on to small, fair WINSTER. The village, which once had two corn mills and a tannery, seems an unlikely place to find a craftsman clockmaker. But Jonas Barber here made grandfather clocks in the eighteenth century – or rather he made the clock movements; a local coffin-maker in Windermere made the cases. There was a Jonas Barber, master clockmaker, in London, but Jonas Barber of Winster, born in 1688, was his nephew and son of Thomas Barber, also a clockmaker of Skipton. He appears first as a clockmaker at Bowland Bridge, but he married into the Garnett family of Winster, and bought the farm complex Bryan Houses, down a minor road to the south. Here with the help of family and apprentices, he produced clock movements that were comparable to the best in the country. His son, also a Jonas Barber, and his grandson, continued the work until the end of the eighteenth century with two workers who had served their apprenticeships. The clocks were supplied to houses both great and humble, and to farms from Kendal to Ulverston. Jonas Barber clocks are now much sought-after by those who admire great craftsmanship.

South of Winster to Cartmel Fell is some of the most delectable country of scattered woodlands and pastures in England – a labyrinth of narrow roads and footpaths. It is hardly ideal for motor tours but fine for any walker – so long as he or she is very good at map reading.

The road for Hawkshead ferry from the end of the Kendal bypass is a winding road that cannot be taken in a hurry. The only village it passes is around midway. CROOK spreads a little alongside the road. Its church was built in 1887, but the tower of the abandoned seventeenth-century church still stands to the south. It is a farming parish, but up to a century ago a score or more of mills were arranged around the watercourses, fulling mills and later bobbin mills. The road passes Windermere golf course before descending the hill directly to the ferry road end, with Bowness a stone's throw away.

THE MAIN HIGHWAY FROM KENDAL

The busiest main tourist route for Windermere leaves the Kendal bypass roundabout and follows the National Park boundary until it enters near STAVELEY. The village is bypassed, and one needs to divert if only to see the Burne-Jones stained glass in the east lancets of St James's church, superb in delicate blue; and the memorable crucifixion (a beardless Christ) and ascension, surrounded by six angelic musicians. The church is only from 1865, though the tower of the old church of St Margaret – fourteenth or fifteenth century? – still stands. Dorothy Wordsworth wrote:

> I am always glad to see Staveley. It is a place I dearly love to think of – the first mountain village that I came to with Wm when we first began our pilgrimage together. Here we drank a bason of milk at a publick house, and here I washed my feet in the brook and put on a pair of silk stockings by Wm's advice.

William echoes the feeling:

> May the writer ... be permitted to say that his heart has never failed to be moved with pleasure, on returning from the southern parts of the Island, at the sight of

> the fair meadows, the pellucid and swift brook and the rugged rocks, which this Village and its Church-tower are environed? For here it is that he has first recognized the appropriate features of this beautiful Country, and felt himself once more within the precincts of the home of his fancy and affections. As a Matter of general interest, it may be added that this Village has a claim, little known, upon the regards of the Patriot, on account of a struggle that was made by a Band of fearless and resolute Peasants, who 200 years ago here pledged themselves to defend the rights which they had inherited from their Forefathers.

The struggle that the bard refers to was the organized protest by tenants of the estates who in the early seventeenth century were threatened to have the rights to pass on their tenures to their descendants revoked. It was a right given to them, for generations, on condition that they would be ready with horse and arms to rise in defence of the Scottish border at the summons of alarm. When King James I acceded he argued that, since the Act of Union of the crowns, the border wars came to an end and thus the right need no longer exist. Tenants of the area assembled at Staveley on the pretext of inspecting a bridge. There they chose their leaders and drew up and published a protest. The lords responded by exhibiting a Bill against them at star chamber, charging them with 'assembling riotously at Stavely chapel'. At last, however, the star chamber came down in the tenants' favour, although King James succeeded in winning monetary recompense for surrendering some of his assumed privileges. The confirmation of the rights of tenure meant that the 'yeomen' farmers or 'statesmen' were a sort of rural middle class, neither gentry nor hired farm labourers. They were virtually land and property owners, though they still paid rent to the lord of the manor.

Staveley was another busy mill village – with eight working at any one time: corn, wool, bobbin and smelting mills for the lead mines. It is still a busy little place and seems to be self-sufficient. A skilled furniture maker attracts those who like fine craftsmanship.

Continuing westwards, one reaches the village of INGS (or Hugill). St Anne's church has one of those stories beloved at a time when hard work was deemed the greatest virtue. Sympathetic churchgoers organized a collection for Robert Bateman, a poor 'parish' lad, to set him up as a pedlar. Wordsworth tells the story that is set in brass in the church nave:

> There's Robert Bateman,
> He was a parish boy – at the church door
> They made a gathering for him, shillings, pence,
> And halfpennies, wherewith the neighbours bought
> A basket which they filled with pedlar's wares;

> And with this basket on his arm the lad
> Went up to London, found a master there,
> Who, out of many, chose the trusty boy
> To go and overlook his merchandise
> Beyond the seas; where he grew wondrous rich
> And left estates and monies to the poor,
> And at his birthplace built a chapel floored
> With marble which he sent from foreign lands.

Bateman, whose portrait is in the nave, caused the church to be rebuilt, in 1743, together with almshouses, and his charity spread beyond the parish. Unfortunately he never saw the church paved with his marble, as he was killed while sailing home on one of his ships. There is some fine stained glass.

North of this main route into Kendal to Windermere one finds in the National Park a great expanse of prime countryside – farmland, fell and crags. From east to west one first encounters BORROWDALE (not to be confused with its northern namesake), which is reached from the A6 road to Shap at Huck's bridge. Up to the dale head remote country leads up to pathless farmland and fell. A bridleway goes down the valley to the Tebay gorge and under the M6 motorway to link up with routes to Tebay north, and Kendal or Sedbergh south.

BANNISDALE is also reached from the A6, and offers more to the walker who needs to get away from everything – for the valley offers just slightly more rugged scenery than Borrowdale. At least it offers a fine viewpoint – from Whiteside Pike (397 m) to the west of the lower side of the valley – but this as easily gained from the next valley to its west. Bannisdale was obviously more congenial to the region's earliest inhabitants as there are signs of their settlements are here. Manchester Corporation has looked at Bannisdale as another prime source of water, undertaking borings for a dam, and a rain gauge. A firm proposal to dam the valley was successfully opposed in the 1960s; but one can never be sure that dust might be blown off the old files and the whole business raised again by the corporation's successors.

The 10 km-long LONGSLEDDALE, further to the west, is something else. It might have been called Sprintdale, for the valley contains the River Sprint. With all the attributes of a typical Lake District dale except a lake, it is completely without modern intrusions. This makes it a very special valley. It remains at least as it was in 1851 when the *History, Topography, and Directory of Westmorland* was published by Mannex & Co. The tone is straightforwardly factual:

> [it is] a wild and picturesque district, about three miles in breadth, and extending from five to eleven miles N. of Kendal. It is intersected by the Sprint

> rivulet, which runs through a deep vale parallel with the road, till it unites with the Kent, about half a mile below Burneside Hall. Verdant fields rise from each side of the rivulet in irregular swells, till the rocky declivities of the mountains preclude all cultivation, except brushwood and coppices, which climb up the steep banks, and in some places find support even in the craggy precipices, which here present their lofty and rugged fronts with much grandeur, having in many places beautiful cascades spouting and tumbling from their summits, and in wild and rainy weather, often broken by gusts of wind into clouds of spangled moisture.

The way up the valley is through the mellow landscape of the Silurian slates, then at the head a dramatic change occurs. Firstly comes a hardly discernible band of Coniston limestone, then the wild chaotic crags of the Borrowdale volcanic rear their heads. There were quarries here during the war, employing Italian prisoners.

The valley is so unspoilt that it is hard to believe that Manchester Corporation took its pipeline down the valley from their Haweswater reservoir (see p. 478). To do this in 1930, they excavated a tunnel from their valve tower, halfway along the lake, to Stockdale, south-east of Sadgill near the Longsleddale's road end, where the main camp of workers was installed. This was an incredible achievement involving more than 8 km of tunnelling. Tackled from both ends, the work took 2½ years, and when the two tunnels met it was estimated that the errors in alignment were less than half an inch in the horizontal plane, and less than one inch in the vertical. After that it took almost two more years to cement the tunnel's sides to ensure the water's smooth run. From there on a pipe was concealed underground in a 'cut and cover' operation to Garnett bridge, to join with their main junction at Watchgate on the east side of the A6.

The long valley is entered from the A6 via Garnett bridge, but the narrow minor road from there to the head at Sadgill cannot be classed as a tourist route for motorists. No through road is available and car parking is informal and restricted. Sadgill, though, is an excellent starting point for walks onto the remoter fells. From Sadgill a track continues over Gatescarth Pass to Haweswater, and by the pass summit a path leads to the splendid Harter Fell summit (see Haweswater, p. 479).

Several old drove roads converged on Sadgill, on the way that cattle were driven from the west of Cumbria to the markets east at Appleby or Yorkshire, and south into Lancashire. The routes may seem somewhat wild and tortuous when looking at a modern map with its web of highways, but the cattle had to be driven freely, between side walls, on roads above the enclosed farms of the lower valleys. One main drove road came over the fell from the next valley of Kentmere. Then from Sadgill the roads divided, one going south for Appleby. An alternative route north for Appleby climbed up Gatescarth Pass, but afterwards could follow routes south into Lancashire and Yorkshire.

The importance of the drove road from the west through Ambleside and then through Longsleddale is shown by a petition written in 1717:

> The inhabitants of Long Sleddale, Langdale, Grasmere, Rydal and Loughrigg, Ambleside, Troutbeck, Kentmere and several other townships in the Barony of Kendall, show that the great road and public highway between Hawksyde, Ambleside, Shap, Penrith and Appleby, very much used by travellers, drovers and others having occasion frequently to pass and repass to and from the said markets with cattle and other goods, in which public highway there is a water or rivulet called Sadgill which by the violent and sudden rain there is often raised and overflows its banks so that no passenger dare venture to cross the same and many times travellers are forced to stay two or three days before they dare venture to cross and are often in danger with their cattle of being lost in crossing the said water to the great prejudice of trade, and pray that a bridge may be erected over the same.

They got their bridge. The little church lies south of the other bridge at Wad's How, and is a nineteenth-century structure. Just south of this is the valley's oldest building. Yewbarrow Hall has the remains of a fifteenth-century pele tower with a house added. The tower was once in the ownership of Robert de Laybourne and his descendants. A John de 'Leyburne' supported the 1715 Jacobite rising, and the family estates were forfeit to the crown.

The next dale to the west is KENTMERE, which contains the source of the Kent, a river that gave its name to Kendal (Kentdale). Like Longsleddale the valley begins at the foot on softer Silurian landscape, but changes to the Borrowdale volcanic crags and heights at the valley head. The river powered many mills. The narrow road up valley from the Kendal road is only 'public' as far as the church. Its use by an increasing number of visitors wishing to drive up the valley to enjoy the superb fell walks has been causing problems. The National Park has designated the valley a Quieter Area, and is trying to persuade walkers seeking the fells at the dale head to use a local 'rambler' bus service.

Kentmere – where is the mere? This dale no longer has the mere that once occupied the flat fields south of the church and the road head. In the nineteenth century it was a small shallow lake and an area of reeds; though referred to as a tarn, it was technically a lake; then the outflow was cleaned out and land drained, with the aim of planting it but it created instead a swamp. All that remains is a swelling of the river where they have been dredging for diatomous earth to supply a processing plant at Waterfoot, the old lake foot. Diatomous or diatomaceous earth, is a sediment containing skeletal remains of microscopic plants. It is used in filters and as a fine abrasive. In 1955 a wooden boat believed to be of tenth-century construction was uncovered during dredging and presented to the National Maritime Museum.

Although the mere has disappeared, a stretch of water can be found at the high valley head: Kentmere Reservoir, dammed to ensure a head of water for valley mills. It no longer serves that purpose, but it is a satisfying feature of the landscape. Round the reservoir the fells are wonderfully impressive, faced on the west with the steep crags of the High Street range, Froswick and Ill Bell. To the north is Mardale Ill Bell (762 m), Harter Fell (774 m) and Kentmere Pike (730 m), a rounded summit to the south-east. The pass of Nan Bield, 640 m east of Harter Fell, links Kentmere with Mardale and Haweswater. Above disused quarries south of the reservoir is Rainsbarrow Crag, an imposing rock-climbing spot.

Below this is Kentmere village, a scattering of farms and houses. The grey church of St Cuthbert has existed for at least 400 years, but little remains of the old structure apart from the roof beams that were reused when restoration was done in 1866. Just beyond the church a track runs westwards over GARBURN PASS (447 m), for Troutbeck, while another goes south, then north-west into Longsleddale by Skeggles Water: both were old drove roads bringing cattle from the west to the markets at Appleby and Lancashire.

Kentmere Hall (not open to the public) is west of the church and the oldest remaining building in the valley. Its defensive pele tower stems from the fourteenth century; the attached sixteenth-century farm buildings replace earlier ones. It is said that the great 9 m-long beam of the house was lifted into position by legendary strong man Hugh Hird, 'the Troutbeck Giant', after ten men failed to move it. Tales surrounding the man were told and retold. It is said that he was born of a nun who relinquished her lodgings, and her vows, on the dissolution of the monasteries. Unbeatable as a wrestler, he was able, so it is said, to pull up trees by their roots. He served Edward VI at the Scottish border wars and was admired by the king, who asked him what he liked to eat. His reply was, 'Thick poddidge [porridge] that a mouse might walk on dry-shod, to my breakfast; the sunny side of a wedder [a whole sheep] to my dinner when I can get it.'

The defensive measures at Kentmere Hall were, as ever, intended to thwart Scots raiders and were built by the Gilpin family. Bernard de Gilpin, who was born here in 1517, became archdeacon of Durham, and as a champion of the Reformation and a charismatic preacher became known as the 'Apostle of the North'. Another resident was Richard Gilpin, one of the claimants to have killed the last boar in England. Another notable member of the family, William Gilpin, was born at Scaleby castle near Carlisle and educated at St Bees school, in 1724;

his book written on his northern tour in 1772 did much to cultivate the appreciation of natural scenery.

Going west again, a minor road from Ings reaches the next valley of TROUTBECK. It is the hamlet nearest to Windermere (and not to be confused with Troutbeck by the Keswick to Penrith road). The road from Windermere to Kirkstone Pass mercifully just passes by it in the lower part of the hamlet. Largely unspoilt, with a scattering of mainly seventeenth- and eighteenth-century houses and farms, it is protected as a Special Conservation Area. A student of vernacular architecture could enjoy many hours of browsing here. Several features recur, such as round chimneys, corbie-stepped gable ends, stone mullions, spinning galleries and date stones showing the initials of the builder and spouse. The main part of the settlement is perched on a hillside among an interesting and purposeful network of roads, tracks and paths, with the buildings set in groups like small conversation pieces. These clusters are named: Town End, Town Head, High Green, Cragg and High Fold. The arrangement stems from the practicalities of sharing communal water supplies: each group is centred on a well, obviously made in more pious times as each one is dedicated to a different saint. They are now disused but can be seen at the roadside.

There are two old but restored inns, the Mortal Man being well known for the doggerel on its amusing sign: 'Oh mortal man that lives by bread, what is it that makes thy face so red? Oh silly ass that looks so pale, 'tis from drinking Sally Birkett's Ale.' Sally Birkett and the famous ale have alas long since gone, and the little inn is now a prime hotel. Long may it preserve the sign.

Several of the farms in the area were at one time owned by 'statesmen' – farmers working a small amount of land who were technically tenants, but farming the land by right. Many would have struggled to make a living. Fortunately one of the more prosperous farms, TOWNEND, with its typical cylindrical chimneys, allows us some insight into the lifestyle of the old statesmen. Townend (NT), opened to the public, was owned by a local family, the Brownes, for many generations. The core, the original seventeenth-century house, is divided into two sections: the 'down house', where the work of the farm was done, and the 'fire house', or living quarters. Further wings and a dairy were added. The interior is typical of its day, complete with carved oak furnishings, including carved 'built-in' furniture in the kitchen and all the tools, utensils and necessaries. It is all authentic and absolutely fascinating.

Troutbeck's Jesus Chapel is ancient, but the structure is from a rebuilding of sixteenth and seventeenth centuries; lying below the village, its apparent detachment is because it served a parish much bigger than the hamlet. The east window is its pride and joy, containing stained glass by the Pre-Raphaelites: Burne-Jones, William Morris and Ford Madox Brown. The figures are typical of the school, and the predominantly green effect of the light is unusual and moving. A window in the north wall is also by Burne-Jones.

The Revd Sewell (see p. 449) is buried in the churchyard. He it was who had the inn built on Kirkstone Pass to shelter travellers stranded in that bleak spot. He was a realist. Once asked by his clerk to pray for rain, as the parish farmers were troubled by weeks of drought, he replied, 'Where's the wind?' his clerk said, 'Comin' from Black Beck' (the north-east). His reply was 'Nay use praying for rain with the wind in that quarter.'

A notable inhabitant of Troutbeck for a time rejoiced in the name of Julius Caesar Ibbetson (1759–1817). He was a well-known landscape artist of his time, nicknamed *The Berghem of England* for his rendering of British scenery in the Dutch idiom. It is rumoured that he painted the first sign for the Mortal Man inn.

For the purpose of farming the grazing area above the village was divided into three divisions called hundreds. These were fenced and made secure by a gate. The cattle had to be kept there during the spring, summer and autumn, and only brought down to where hay and crops had been cultivated in the winter. To make sure that the gate to each hundred was kept closed, and no stock strayed, a constable was appointed among the farmers each year to supervise. Each hundred had a common bull and this gave rise to the boast that 'Troutbeck has three hundred bulls, three hundred gates, and three hundred constables' – which was quite correct.

South of the church a track climbs the fellside north-eastwards past the old quarries to climb through Garbourn Pass to Kentmere – the drove road, and a very pleasant walk. Another bridleway goes northwards above the camp and caravan site and runs on to High Street. Was this part of the Roman road? As the road from Windermere climbs towards Kirkstone Pass, part of the parish of Troutbeck lies east of the road. This is best seen on the descent towards Windermere, from a layby, for the view to the valley far below is spectacular, and the farm, owned by Beatrix Potter, looks like a toy in the dizzy distance. Some of her work was done there. This valley is Troutbeck Park, once a 810 ha park owned by the lord of the manor, but taken away from the landowner's exclusive use long ago. On the piece of land north of the farm, Troutbeck Tongue, there are signs of an ancient settlement.

ENGLAND'S LARGEST LAKE

And so to the lake: WINDERMERE. Just because something is visited by legions of tourists does not necessarily make it vulgar. Some people might feel that the lake loses too much from its popularity; and undeniably Windermere *is* the sum total of the Lake District in the minds of some of its many visitors – especially the day visitors. It is special because it is different – there is no other place anywhere like it in England. Windermere differs from the other lakes in that it has no near commanding heights that shout for attention. Here the lake rests within a landscape of wooded hills and shores, green pastures and parks on both of its sides; and it keeps its fine mountain scenery at an unobtrusive distance beyond its head. Compared with the others Windermere has a rare sort of gentility.

Of course the lake holds many ingredients for the gregarious pleasure-seeker: boats, steamers, nearby villages with many hotels, pubs and guest houses, public parkland and pleasure gardens. Visitors flock in great numbers to Windermere at the height of the holiday season, and those who feel the need to get away from people, go elsewhere in the Lake District. But in a still dawn before most are out of bed, or in the evening when the last are leaving and the water is at rest, then Windermere is very very special.

Windermere is not only the largest lake in England (nearly 17 km long, and 2 km across at its widest point), it is also one of the most beautiful. The colours of the wooded shores of the southern half are glorious in the many greens of spring, and fine in the fires of autumn. Wooded islands straddle the middle reaches with the wooded heights of Claife (NT) on the western shore, and across the lake are high-pasture viewpoints. At the head of Windermere the views change as they reveal that imposing ring of craggy volcanic mountains – the central Lake District.

The lake is a relic of the ice age. The ice-age glaciers, ploughing southwards from the central fells, scooped out the lake basin. The upper reaches were ground down to below sea-level by the weight of ice (the lake is 67 m deep at this end), but the glacier's movement, spent of initial energy, made less impression on the middle reaches, so that the lake is shallower, and there are islands, the largest being Belle Isle. Below the islands of mid lake, glaciers added from the sides accelerated the main glacier's progress and the ice bit deeper into the rock, to depths of 45 m.

The lake is famed for its char – a deepwater trout. Potted Windermere char was a great delicacy on the tables of the middle and upper classes in the seventeenth and eighteenth centuries. Sir Daniel Fleming, a local estate owner, wrote that he made the potted char 'an instrument of social diplomacy', with which he 'sweetened intercourse with politicians and friends at Court'. Char fishing requires special skills acquired only from local knowledge and experience. They are fished from a rowing boat in March through September. Two rods are used, each one being 5 m long and extending at 45 degrees from each side of the boat; the line is 27.5 m long and weighted. The fish are caught on metal 'spinners' with three hooks. The metal can be anything shiny – even gold and silver from old watches have been used. To avoid line tangles the boat has to be kept on the move.

Pike also give fine sport, and there are also perch and trout. Windermere has supplied a harvest of fish since the beginning of recorded time. The monks of Furness Abbey, who owned the east side of the lake, prospered from it. They did not own the lake but had a licence from William de Lancaster to keep one boat on it to carry *maeremium* (timber and building material) and another small boat (*batellum*) for fishing with twenty nets; and similarly on Coniston Water. Up until the nineteenth century netting sites were dotted round the lake shores, 113 of them designated.

Windermere has a resident nesting population of mute swans, mallard, coots, moorhens and mergansers; and the lake feeders are cormorants, great crested grebe and little grebe, pochard and tufted duck. The lake is a haven for wintering ducks and geese. Goldeneye and teal appear, several species of gulls, goosanders, and Canada and greylag geese. And as the lake is on the north–south route of migration, birdwatchers can get an occasional surprise.

The great volume of the water of the lake, and a relatively mild climate, means that it only rarely freezes completely. But it has done so several times within living memory. A big freeze occurred in 1895, and special excursions run by the railways brought large crowds of visitors who enjoyed skating and a general fairground atmosphere on the ice. It froze again in 1929 and 1946 – and in 1963 so hard that some foolhardy motorists drove their cars onto the ice. The cross-lake car ferry from Bowness then was kept running nightly as well as daily, to prevent its passage freezing, and ironically the crossing became impossible at the thaw, when it became obstructed by the masses of moving ice floes. Residents around the lake were surprised at the strange noises made by ice. Loud reports like cannon fire travel across it, and as Wordsworth remarked about frozen Esthwaite Water: it howls like wolves.

From the time of the earliest human settlers Windermere has served as a highway. When the Romans were building their fort at the head of the lake they brought their quarried stone up-lake to the fort's jetty. From medieval times iron ore was similarly transported for smelting at primitive 'bloomeries' in the charcoal-providing woods. Clinker from the old hearths can be seen on the lake shores, and even on the island of Rampsholme. In 1711 a blast furnace stood on the lake shore, the bellows worked by a water wheel where Cunsey Beck joins the lake. A little further up the beck there was a water-powered forge where pig iron from the furnace was hammered to refine the iron and produce bars. Wordsworth remembered by Esthwaite Water hearing 'The distant forge's swinging thud profound' in his early poem 'An Evening Walk'.

Over the centuries the lake remained as a main highway. However, as the Lake District grew more popular the lake was also seen to have a tourist potential. Boat hire at Bowness and Ambleside flourished. Then in the middle of the nineteenth century two competing 'steamer' companies, in one of the first affronts to the lake's calm dignity, fought for the growing tourist custom with cut-rate fares and on-board brass bands. The first steamers were named *Lord of the Isles* and *Lady of the Lake*, and the boat of a rival firm was the faster *Dragon Fly*. When *Dragon Fly* overtook *Lady of the Lake* its band would strike up 'The Girl I Left Behind Me'. The rivalry got quite bitter and when *Lady of the Lake* was destroyed by fire at Bowness pier, arson was almost certainly the cause.

Then the Furness Railway company, already profiting from their Coniston steamers, saw the potential. In 1866 the company began work on a branch line from their main line to Ulverston, through Greenodd and Backbarrow. This would have the dual advantage of benefiting the industries there, carrying saltpetre and sulphur for the gunpowder works at Low Wood and Black Beck, and ore for the ironworks at Backbarrow - but also of exploiting the tourist potential at the foot of Windermere. So the lake was reached at 'Lakeside' and a terminal station was built that soon became a popular focal point, and no wonder. An upper storey to the station housed a refreshment room 20 m long, with fantastic views of the lake over the new steamer wharf. It was so popular that it soon had to be extended to almost twice the size. The branch line was officially opened in June 1869 and immediately the Steam Yacht Company, which had been providing a passenger service with two paddle-boats, *Dragonfly* and *Rothay*, from shallower water downriver near Newby bridge, launched a new 45 m-long, screw-driven steamer built at Rutherglen, and named the *Swan*. It could carry 450 passengers. The vessel had been brought in sections down the new railway line. In 1871 the railway company launched the *Raven*, a steam lighter, to deliver goods along the shores of Windermere – an important service much appreciated.

In 1872 the railway company bought out the Steam Yacht Company, and as the rail and boat service had become so popular they decided to replace the two paddle-steamers with new boats built by the Barrow Shipbuilding Company. They were 30 m long and could carry 360 passengers, with well decks fore and aft and a midships saloon. The *Cygnet* and the *Teal* were launched in 1879. In 1891 the *Tern* augmented the fleet. The ship built at Wyvenhoe, Essex, was 45 m long and capable of carrying 633 passengers. In shape it was little different to the sister boats, but it had a distinctive canoe-shaped bow. In July 1900 came the launch of the *Swift*, built on the same lines as the *Tern*, but 47 m long (bigger, 'to accommodate bicycles') with a carrying capacity of 780.

The Furness Railway was absorbed by the London, Midland and Scottish Railway in 1923. The new company decided to scrap *Teal*, and it was not replaced by the new diesel-powered *Teal* until 1936. The *Swan* was scrapped in 1938 and replaced by a new diesel-powered boat of the same name. Both boats still ply the lake. *Tern* was still in service in 2003.

The 'Raven', said to be the oldest registered steamer afloat

Raven, the old delivery steam lighter, is still on the lake after restoration, and can be seen at the Windermere Steamboat Museum. It is reputedly the oldest registered steam vessel afloat. The lake service is now run by the Bowness Bay Boating Company. Apart from steamers they have modern 'water buses' and smaller vessels, and they sail all year round. The service is among the top tourist attractions in the United Kingdom, carrying over a million passengers a year.

Alas the Victorian Lakeside railway station that brought so many visitors from the towns right to the edge of the water, with its superb refreshment room, has gone, as have the holiday carriages in nearby sidings that offered accommodation. The line was axed in 1965, but luckily a very short stretch of it has been acquired by steam enthusiasts, and the Haverthwaite and Lakeside Railway thrives (see p. 484). On part of the old station site stands the award-winning Aquarium of the Lakes, which reveals some of the natural history of the lakes and Morecambe Bay.

As well as the steamer service, at mid-lake, just south of Belle Isle, the car ferry service connects Bowness to the road to Hawkshead, a way well used by Wordsworth in his youth. There are few signs of human habitation on the western shore of the entire lake's length. From the ferry landing a public footpath on this shoreline runs southwards, and there is a short road, and a bridleway running northwards under the wooded heights of Claife to the grounds of the Victorian extravagance of Wray Castle (NT).

To see and appreciate the lake it is really necessary to take a steamer from LAKESIDE at the foot to Waterhead at the head. Lakeside is a small village that only started life at the coming of the railway. Leaving the Lakeside steamer quay, opposite one can see Fell Foot Country Park (NT), 7 ha of pleasant field, lakeshore and woodland, with picnic areas, boat hire and launch, and a café; on a warm day this is a good place to laze away an hour or two. What was once the pleasure ground of a few inhabitants of an imposing Georgian house (demolished in the nineteenth century and not replaced) has become the pleasure ground of many.

Moving up the lake one can see that, after the YMCA's National Centre, almost all signs of human presence are on the east shore, where the land is divided into private ownerships, though many of the houses are screened by woodland. This means that unlike the west shore, public access is restricted. The first access there, with a fine viewpoint overlooking the lake, is at Beech Hill (NPA).

Up-lake from the Beech Hill, is Storrs Hall, now a hotel. It was originally built at the end of the eighteenth century for the businessman John Bolton, who made his fortune from the Liverpool slave trade. So one would perhaps not expect morally correct Wordsworth to associate with such a man. Well – he was very rich and generous with hospitality. In 1825 he organized a grand regatta on the lake, and Wordsworth, Sir Walter Scott, Robert Southey and George Canning, statesman and author, were among his guests staying at the hall. It was a gay and romantic affair with 'brilliant cavalcades through the woods', music, and flashes of colour from pretty dresses reflected up from the lake as the flotilla meandered its way. The guests also had romantic boat trips in the moonlight.

On a promontory at Storrs the strange small building is a garden house (NT). The temple, or viewing station, was built by Bolton in 1804 to honour the admirals Nelson, Howe, Duncan and St Vincent.

After Storrs the steamers must veer towards the centre of the lake to avoid reefs, and then one reaches the ferry crossing. Inshore from the west shore's ferry landing, on a high rocky platform, is the ruin of a 'station'. Not a railway this time, but a spot recommended by the early guidebooks, where tourists should 'station' themselves to take in the views. On what is now the site of Ferry House, a field two centuries ago used to hold a great annual sporting event that featured wrestling, racing, pole climbing and pig chasing, and it was also the base for a grand regatta.

The Windermere ferry linking Bowness with Hawkshead has been running as long ago as the twelfth century, when the whole area west of the lake was owned by Furness Abbey, and Hawkshead was the base of one of its main markets. Though it was not the only ferry crossing in the early days, it was the busiest. When taking horses and carriages, and farm animals and goods, the ferry was rowed with long oars, or 'sweeps'. One of these old ferries is preserved at the Windermere Steamboat Museum. There was one serious accident in 1635, when a wedding party was returning from Hawkshead to Kendal. The boat was almost certainly grossly overloaded for it sank and forty-eight passengers and seven horses were drowned. In 1870 the introduction of a steam ferry, hauling itself across on cables, was considered a wonderful innovation. It could carry a coach and four with its passengers, and two coaches if the lead horses were detached. In 1960 the steam engine was replaced by diesel, and the modern vessel can now take eighteen cars at a crossing, and regularly serves tourists as well as morning and evening commuters.

Up above the station and beyond the ferry are the woodlands and forest of Claife Heights (NT), criss-crossed by footpaths enjoyed by many walkers, but the home, it is said, of a terrible ghost: 'The Crier of Claife'. Several versions of the story are maintained mostly in local pubs. All refer to a ferryman in the seventeenth century who heard a loud cry on the Claife shore when he was at the Bowness end, and thinking that it was a call for his services, rowed across and vanished entirely. When at last he was discovered he was dumb, completely mad, and died soon afterwards. Terrible cries were heard in subsequent years until the ghost was laid to rest by a priest with bell, book and candle, in Crier of Claife Quarry – marked on Ordnance Survey maps – 2.5 km to the north of the ferry. Tales of hauntings still circulate, and the locals reckon it would take a brave person to walk in the forest at night.

North of the ferry crossing is Belle Isle (formerly Longholme), with its stunning cylindrical house built by a Mr English in 1774. That was a time when the middle classes traditionally took the Grand Tour of Europe and came back home resolved to introduce the classic picturesque building styles of Italy and Greece into England's pleasant land. This building caused a stir. Some were enchanted by it, others were horrified at what they called this 'pepper pot', or 'tea caddy', located

The round house on Belle Isle

at a key point in the lake; and it was in full view too, for the owner had removed a former ruin, felled trees and planted a formal garden to show it off. Seven years later, perhaps hurt by the criticism, Mr English sold the house and island for 1,640 guineas to John Christian Curwen, of Workington Hall, who bought the property for his wife Isabella (hence 'Belle Isle'). Actually he was a Christian (of the family of Fletcher, that included the famous Bligh mutineer) and changed his name to Curwen on marrying Isabella, so gaining admission to the wealthy mine-owning Curwen family. John Christian was a remarkable man, an innovative agriculturist who did much to improve Cumberland farming. On Belle Isle he planted trees and peace was gradually restored. In fact he was a keen tree planter and covered the whole of Claife Heights with forest.

The island was occupied long before that. Roman artefacts have been found there, leading to speculation that it once held a Roman villa. During the Civil War there was a fortified house on the island occupied by the Royalist Philipsons. Parliamentarians under the command of Colonel Briggs besieged it for eight months, when the assault was abandoned through lack of firepower to finish the job. At the time the younger brother of the owner, the impetuous 'Robin the Devil', was campaigning elsewhere. When told of the unsuccessful siege on his return home, Robin rode off in a fury to Kendal with a band of followers to seek out Colonel Briggs for revenge. He it was who rode into Kendal church in search of his enemy, and left his helmet behind when it was knocked off while he tried to exit by a low door (see pp. 340–1).

It is not known how much was demolished by Mr English before the round house was built. Agnes Strickland described the island house at the end of the Civil War:

> In the centre of the island was an antique Gothic house flanked with four strong towers; from several apertures in these projected small pieces of artillery called chamber pieces; turf ramparts have recently been thrown around the mansion on which were cannon of different sizes.

BOWNESS AND WINDERMERE TOWN

BOWNESS (*BOW-ness* or *BOW-nus*) is the big tourist honeypot of the Lake District. The promenade area smacks of kiss-me-quick seaside resorts, with catch-penny attractions, buggy rides, chips and ice cream; it even has – horrors! – an 'amusement arcade', but it just about stops short of an excess of vulgarity. The steamer pier and the boat-hire centres are the main focus, but many in the holiday crowds

Bowness promenade

are just content to enjoy the bustle and the company. The village of Bowness is almost exclusively given over to tourist and souvenir shops, pubs, cafés and take-aways. It is probably criticized more than it deserves, for it is not an ugly village, and it obviously fulfils a need, for it has its followers who return annually. It has a long history, but there is no sign of it apart from the church of St Martin, for the old buildings were swept away, to Wordsworth's disgust, to make way for its new role as tourist draw:

> It has always appeared to me that a person of feeling mind beginning the excursion with Windermere and descending directly upon Bowness would not only be disappointed but perhaps in no small degree disgusted with the bustle, the parade, and drest-out appearance of so many of the objects immediately around it ...
>
> The appearance of the neighbourhood of Bowness, within the last five and thirty years has undergone many changes, and most of these for the worse, for want of due attention to those principles of taste ...

The village has seen more changes since the last war, and has lost some of its quaintness. A large chestnut tree towered over Crag Brow, the main street, but it was considered an encumbrance to traffic, and naturally it was felled with the excuse that it was 'unsafe'. Some of the traditional shops – butchers, baker, grocer – have gone together with the banks. The tourist trade is all.

The church of St Martin was consecrated in 1483 on a previously occupied chapel site, but it has been much interfered with since. Its finest feature is the east window, with some stained glass of the late fifteenth century, thought to have come from Cartmel priory or Furness Abbey after the dissolution. There is an excellent wooden sculpture of St Martin, dividing his cloak in two to give half of it to a beggar. Some very strange texts on the walls, some Victorian, others seventeenth century, are worth reading. In the churchyard at the east end is the tombstone of Rasselas Belfield, 'A native of Abyssinia', who died in 1822.

> A slave by birth I left my native land
> And found my Freedom on Britain's Strand:
> Blest Isle! Thou Glory of the Wise and Free!
> Thy Touch alone unbinds the Chains of Slavery!

Assuming that he was a servant of the Belfield family in Georgian times, one wonders how much freedom he actually enjoyed.

What is now the Belfield Hotel was once a large house, built in 1845. The oldest part of Bowness is behind the church. One of the pubs is the Hole in t' Wall, in which Dickens stayed in 1857.

Before the middle of the nineteenth century a farmstead known as 'Birthwaite', with a few scattered cottages nearby, stood 2 km to the north-west of Bowness. But in 1847 it was transformed. Three years before, capital was raised for a Kendal and Windermere Railway to bring tourists to Bowness, already enjoying a tourist boom, and on towards Ambleside, So popular was the venture that it became over-subscribed. But it faced opposition too. Wordsworth was a key opponent, particularly when he observed railway surveyors near his home in Rydal. He begins one sonnet with the despairing line:

> Is then no nook of English Ground secure
> From rash assault?

However, the main opposition came from landowners along the proposed route beyond Birthwaite. So when the line was built it stopped short there, and the company proposed to go no further. Birthwaite station would not do for marketing reasons, so the company changed the settlement's name to Windermere and WINDERMERE (pop. with Bowness 8,290) town was born, and not surprisingly visitors still arrive there and ask 'Where is the lake?' Very soon the town grew very rapidly, merging eventually with Bowness. In 1858 at the height of feverish building activity the railway station was destroyed by a fire, and in acknowledgement of the place's popularity a splendid new station was built. Windermere had direct links with the Midlands, Bradford and Leeds, Liverpool, Manchester, Blackpool; four daily trains, including 'the Lakes Express', went to London. Between the wars seventeen special trains would arrive in Windermere on a summer Sunday. Now the busy station has gone, along with its four platforms, carriage sidings, goods shed and coal yard, and we must mourn its passing, along with the thirty-four uniformed station staff and twenty-six others it employed. What we see now is a token portion of the station building remaining in the walls of – what else? – a supermarket. The old goods yard is occupied by car parks and a large retail store. An emaciated station still serves as the terminus of the line from Oxenholme, on the main line. All attempts to close this branch line must be resisted absolutely, and there have been threats.

One cannot think of Windermere town without its fabulous viewpoint of ORREST HEAD (NT). It is reached in a half-hour's walk up a signposted lane opposite the station. The view from this rounded happy little summit is a wonderful surprise. The upper half of the lake is backed by a long panorama of the central fells including Scafell Pike, Bowfell and Langdale Pikes. If it is necessary to name them all the view indicator helps. In the nineteenth century at Elleray, below

Windermere from Orrest Head

Orrest Head, lived a man whom one might have found easy to hate, for he was clever, good-looking, healthy, energetic and a great athlete, a writer and poet, a sports promoter (founder of the famous Grasmere Sports) and rich to boot. John Wilson was a famous personality, well known in both literary and sporting circles. He was a regular contributor to the *Edinburgh Review*, using his pseudonym Christopher North. As a poet he was not fêted, and as a writer he could be unscrupulous – for example criticizing Wordsworth under an assumed name, and then defending him in his own.

When the railway came it encouraged a growing number of summer residents, and villas began to be built within reach of the railway, around the lake shores and hillsides. The burgeoning tourist industry was also adapting. Where previously the hotels catered for the well-to-do who stayed for long periods, now they had to serve a less affluent clientele from a lower middle class, who stayed for short periods. Guest houses and boarding houses had to be built. The tourists were largely confined to the Bowness and Windermere town area; but the need to see more of the lakes was fulfilled by an expanding coach and carriage-hire business. At Windermere's new Riggs Hotel (now Windermere Hotel) opposite the station, conveyances could be hired for the day.

The coming of the railway to Windermere also meant that the line could feasibly be used by commuters going to Manchester, Leeds, Bradford and

Liverpool, so permanent residences for stockbrokers and company directors were built. The executives could leave the Manchester Stock Exchange and catch an express train from Manchester Exchange Station at five o'clock. The train had a special open and very comfortable saloon car, reserved for these gentlemen, and further members of the club from Yorkshire were gathered up at Preston and Lancaster. No doubt the developments on 'change were discussed over cigars; and mutally beneficial deals could be brokered. The train would reach Windermere at twelve minutes past seven, where personal transport would whisk them off to their dinners in a paradise far away from the dirt, smoke and turmoil they'd left behind.

Windermere has a clock-tower monument to commemorate one of the Lake District's early guidebook authors: Thomas Bradley.

THE LAKE NORTH OF BOWNESS

The lake had been enjoyed recreationally for two centuries, but it became ever more popular with the growing number of wealthy 'offcomers' to Windermere. Yacht races were held in the first half of the nineteenth century – John Wilson of Elleray was one of the promoters and participants. In 1824 he organized a grand regatta, a race of fishermen's boats, innkeepers' boats and a gentleman's race – which Wilson won. At the end there was a grand aquatic procession, in which almost every boat on the lake took part. This was the beginning of regular meets. Formal boat-race meetings became popular, but some dissatisfaction was expressed with the time-allowance handicap system required when several sizes of boats were taking part. So in 1860 the Windermere Sailing Club was formed with its base on Ferry Nab, the ferry landing from Bowness on the promontory on the west side of the lake. Its main aim was to establish some basic rules.

The first rule was that boats should not exceed a length of 20 ft (6 m). There were eventually two approved classes of fore-and-aft boats. The 22-ft-long (7 m) class that carried 700 square feet (65 sq m) of sail, and a second class of seventeen-footers (5 m). Both boats were built locally to fine specifications. Nathanial Shepherd had five sons, all in the boat-building trade at Bowness, and they were active in producing the Windermere yachts. Borwick's yard on Bowness Bay produced the yachts too, and every other conceivable craft. The twenty-two footers are no more, but the seventeens are still made locally and are objects of beauty. The design of the seventeen-footers was precisely laid down, and included 'Length of yacht onload waterline shall not exceed seventeen feet – the beam shall not be less than 5ft 10in – length of mast not to exceed 19ft 3in – the boom not to exceed 18ft

– hoist or mainsail not to exceed 12ft – luff of jib not exceed 17ft 10in. All yachts to be constructed with natural frames, spaced not more than 1ft 9in apart, with steamed timbers between, with single pine, larch, oak, pitchpine, elm, baywood or teak, planking and decks.' There were rules on amounts of ballast.

Later, the custom of allowing professional sailors from Morecambe to compete in the races was dropped. They were to become exclusively for amateurs. It was a club for the affluent, for the boats they owned were very expensive. In 1887, Queen Victoria's jubilee year, the club received the royal warrant, becoming the Royal Windermere Yacht Club.

Just up the lake from Bowness is the excellent Steamboat Museum, which holds an extraordinary collection of old steam-driven pleasure boats, some of them showing a wealth of Victorian elegance and ingenious machinery. One of the steam launches, *Esperence*, built by Seath and Co. of Glasgow (which also built the *Swift*, one of the Windermere steamers), belonged to Henry W. Schneider (d. 1887), one of the founding fathers of Barrow's 'Iron Age' prosperity. He lived overlooking the lake at Belsfield (now a hotel), having bought it from Baroness de Sternberg in 1845. He employed around twenty domestic staff, and twenty-two gardeners and estate workers. In the morning he would stroll down his lawn to *Esperence*, a servant would serve him breakfast aboard, and he would alight at Lakeside and board his own saloon on the waiting train to Barrow. On return, the boat would meet the train and be ready to serve him tea as it took him home. His boat, by the way, was the model for Captain Flint's houseboat in the children's book *Swallows and Amazons*. Schneider was much involved in the public affairs of Bowness, and very popular.

On occasions at the museum the clock is turned back, and the steamboat owners and friends gather, don Victorian dress and enjoy a lake regatta. No noisy boats these; they are extraordinarily quiet. One boat at least shows an advantage over the combustion engine: the teapot can be filled from the boiler.

Continuing north from the Steamboat Museum one encounters Rayrigg Hall, the summer home, from 1780 to 1787, of William Wilberforce (1759–1833), the politician who successfully campaigned against the slave trade. He was astonished at the growing popularity of the area at that time and wrote 'The banks of the Thames are scarcely more populated than the banks of Windermere.'

Just beyond there is a lake access area at Rayrigg Meadow and adjoining Miller Ground, with an excellent viewpoint above on ADELAIDE HILL (NT), once called Miller Brow, or Rayrigg Bank, until visited by Queen Adelaide (wife of William IV) in July 1840. The viewpoint over the lake was a must-visit 'station' enjoyed by the earliest tourists, and has lost nothing since then. A ferry used to run from Miller Ground to link with the road, now a mere track, from Belle Grange to Hawkshead. The ferryman's house is there with the little bell tower. Presumably the bell was used to summon the boat from the west shore.

Windermere at Miller Ground

Past the hill, across the main Windermere to Ambleside road, and up the road opposite for Kirkstone Pass, garden enthusiasts must visit HOLEHIRD. The house was built in 1854 and gets its name from the farmhouse that it replaced – the holding of Hugh Hird, the strong man of Kentmere. The house is now a Cheshire Home, caring for the sick and disabled, and is not open to the public. But the garden, open in season, is the fine work of the Lakeland Horticultural Society, and made and cared for by bands of volunteers under expert guidance.

Back on the lake, and moving up from Bowness, the shore takes a westerly turn and beyond the landing stages is the old Calgarth Hall. This was a home of the aforementioned Robin the Devil Philipson, he who rode his horse into Kendal church to seek his enemy (see pp. 340–1). A good story, no matter how daft, was always a help to the early tourist industry. The one connected to the hall refers to the finding of two skulls there, belonging to two victims of the notorious Philipson. One was taken to London, but mysteriously disappeared – it had somehow returned to Calgarth Hall, and if at any time one or the other of the skulls was taken away, it always returned of its own accord.

Calgarth Park is a little beyond and not prominent from the lake. This was the house of Richard Watson, the bishop of Llandaff (1713–1816). Surely Llandaff was in Wales? Just so, but he only visited his diocese once every three years. Meanwhile he was a force to be reckoned with in the Lake District. He was a very prolific pamphleteer, criticizing the writers and philosophers of his day. His sermon on 'The Wisdom and Goodness of God in having made both Rich and Poor' might just hint at his political alignment. Wordsworth answered it with a long published letter supporting the French republicans and attacking the British constitution. The bishop was an 'improver' of his extensive estates and properties, but he was hardly a conservationist: one of his schemes was to drain part of the lake and take the resulting hundred acres of land into agriculture. One of his acquisitions was the Cock Inn at Ambleside. To honour the owner the pub landlord changed its name to The Bishop and the inn sign bore the picture of a mitred bishop. A rival innkeeper sought to boost the custom to his inn by renaming his The Cock. The landlord of The Bishop was furious, and had a legend placed below the inn sign of the bishop, which read 'This is the original old Cock'.

Just beyond Calgarth a bay opens up. This was of old called Craams Bay but is now known as White Cross Bay. It is named after the cross on the headland in memory of two young men, Ralph Thicknesse, twenty, and Thomas Woodcock, nineteen, from Wigan, who were drowned when their boat overturned in 1853. An inscription gives a stern warning to all who sail on Windermere: 'Watch, therefore, for ye know neither the day nor the hour.'

Inland here there is a holiday park, suitably screened. It is hard to believe now, but on this site, now enjoyed by holidaymakers, were located important factory units during the last war, producing the Short Brothers' Sunderland flying boats – aircraft that eventually took off from the lake. By and large the aircraft were successfully deployed carrying depth charges on anti-U-boat operations. It was not the first time that seaplanes had used the lake. One of the first experimental flights by a 'waterbird' before the First World War took off from the southern part of the lake and did a short circuit before returning. In July 1990, to commemorate the making of the flying boats on Windermere, one of the surviving crafts made a return trip, landing and taking off on the lake.

At mid lake, roughly opposite this point, Sir Henry Segrave was killed on 13 June 1930 in a bid to break the world speed record on water. Segrave? We know all about Donald Campbell's attempt at the water-speed record, and of the details of his death. He has been called a hero, and at Coniston he has a memorial; even a museum is in prospect. But Sir Henry Segrave was most certainly a hero, and moreover an immensely friendly and popular man, in Britain and abroad. During the First World War he was a pilot in the RAF, and was shot down in 1917. At a time when speed records were more relevant he had already broken a world land speed record, in the 1000 hp super-car *Golden Arrow* at Daytona Beach, Florida, at a measured speed of 231.36 m.p.h. He raced too, and had won the French Grand Prix in 1923 and the Spanish in 1924. He was knighted for his achievements.

In 1930 he staked his life on a bid for the world speed record on water and chose Windermere for the attempt. His boat, *Miss England II*, was designed by Lord Wakefield of Hythe, and was powered by a 4000 hp Rolls-Royce superma-rine engine. It was so powerful that in test runs three screws (propellers) were destroyed by the speed of rotation. As well as Segrave the boat carried the engi-neer, M. Wilcocks, and Mr Halliwell, the Rolls-Royce mechanic. On the third run on the measured mile between Ambleside and Bowness the boat reached 101.11 m.p.h. when it pitched over – just as Campbell's boat was to do thirty-seven years later. Segrave died in hospital later of multiple injuries, and his last words were to ask about his crew: 'How are the two lads?' and 'Did we do it?' They did do it, and Wilcocks the engineer survived, but Halliwell the mechanic was killed. The tragedy was almost certainly caused by hitting a half-submerged log. But why no memorial?

At the north end of the bay is Ecclerigg Crag on land owned by a manage-ment-training centre. One cannot see it from the lake, but the crag face is covered with engravings made in the first half of the nineteenth century by an eccentric, John Longmire. The texts of a few include, 'A slave landing on the British Strand, becomes free', 'The Liberty of the Press. Magna Charta' and 'William IV. President Jackson. Britannia rules the waves', and there is a poignant one: 'National Debt, £800,000,000. O save my country, Heaven!' Longmire carved a list of the poets of the age, pre-Wordsworth, and one large stone has letters a metre long with just one word: 'Steam'.

Immediately beyond this is the jetty of Brockhole, the Lake District National Park Authority's visitor centre. John Gaddum, a Manchester silk merchant, built the house above, and laid out the grounds and garden in 1897. His wife was a cousin of Beatrix Potter, and the Potters were visitors. The property later became a convalescent home for Merseyside women. It was not popular with many of them – 'too far from the shops' – and there was not even a Woolworths at Windermere. The National Park bought the valuable lakeshore asset in 1969 to fulfil its requirement to provide a centre in which the public can learn about the geology, history, natural history and conservation of the Lake District's country-side. The house was adapted to contain displays, exhibitions, lectures and films. Special events are held regularly. Outside, the garden has gradually been returned as near as possible to its original design, with the plants popular at the time. The grounds and the views are delightful.

On the opposite shore is Wray Castle (NT). It appears to be medieval, but in fact is a Victorian extravaganza built between 1840 and 1847 by James Dawson, a Liverpool surgeon. He built it as a surprise for his wife. Rumour has it that she took one look at it and returned to Liverpool. The surgeon even erected romantic ruins in the grounds. (Sadly the National Trust was not so romantically inclined

Wray Castle

after it acquired the property, having to demolish them in the interests of visitor safety.) The owner also built a chapel nearby, and for a time this was served by Hardwick Rawnsley, later Canon Rawnsley of Crosthwaite, Keswick. Beatrix Potter and her parents spent a summer holiday at Wray in 1882 when Rawnsley recognized the young girl's artistic gifts and gave her encouragement. They shared conservation interests, and in later years she was instrumental in gaining many important properties for the National Trust. The castle is now occupied by a training school for radio operators, but the extensive grounds to the lake shore are open to the public. The churchyard is a blissfully quiet place.

Further up the lake on the east side is the Lowwood Hotel, behind a lakeside water sports centre. This hotel replaced an early coaching inn in 1850, and has been added to repeatedly ever since. In its early coaching days it had a long list of notable and distinguished guests, for a stop here at the 'fashionable station or watering place' was absolutely necessary. Father West, author of the first guide to the Lakes in 1788, wrote: 'No other inn has so fine a view of the lake' and he mentioned that a small cannon was kept there to demonstrate the interesting echo effects. No doubt about the view: it is a classic.

The lake widens as we approach its head and we leave the softer landscape of the slates to enter the ring of volcanic heights. Wansfell Pike (482 m) is on the right. Further away to the north is the mass of the Fairfield range of fells, rising to 873 m.

It takes many years to explore Windermere thoroughly, because it has so many 'nebs' and 'neuks' (promontories and bays). Even those familiar with the lake can get lost in mist. It is full of surprises, and although its peace might be disurbed by the sound of boat engines, it is still possible to savour peace and privacy at times among the wooded shores.

AMBLESIDE

The steamer reaches the pier at the head of the lake, WATERHEAD, a km from Ambleside town. A controversy arose about a pier here in 1900. The small boat-hire folk thought that the Furness Railway Company resented their competition, and their suspicions were confirmed when the company decided that the pier here was not adequate for their vessels. They intended constructing a new pier across the mouth of the bay. The boatmen protested, arguing that it was a restriction to lawful navigation on the lake, and took their complaints to the courts. The decision went in the company's favour, but an appeal reversed it, and the present straight-outwards pier is the result.

Steamer 'Swan' leaving Waterhead

The blatant commercialism of Bowness promenade is abandoned here. The Waterhead promenade is too short and the main activity is boat hire and duck feeding. The crowds, if there are any, are round the end of the Wateredge Hotel, in Borrans Park ('borrans': Norse – heap of stones), a popular picnic and strolling area. Further along the shore a public bathing beach became popular after the First World War. The then Ambleside Urban District Council built a bathing pavilion, and provided an attendant and boats. Men bathed in the lake in the morning, women in the afternoon; and mixed bathing took place in the evening. In one season 4,000 people used the place. They were stoics in those days. What has happened to us? Nowadays apparently, no matter how beautiful the setting, water, cold and fresh from the fells, is only for the fish.

Further still is Borrans Field (NT), immediately beyond which the lake is fed by the Rivers Rothay from Grasmere and Brathay from the Langdales. A jetty once stood here – a Roman jetty, for the stones of Borrans Field are what is left of a Roman fort, its substantial buildings long since 'quarried' to build Ambleside. The lake was a Roman highway. What is intriguing is that there have been no substantial signs of Roman occupation in the Furness area – yet undoubtedly some of the sandstone in the fort buildings came from far along that peninsula, before being ferried up the length of the lake. The fort's name has been assumed to be 'Galava', and was built to command the road junctions that were fed by the barely traceable Roman road that came from the Brougham junction south of Penrith, over the fells to this point; and a second untraceable road from the fort at Watercrook, Kendal. A single road then went westwards from the fort to Little Langdale by some route not identified, and then by the clearly seen Roman engineered road, zigzagging over the steep passes of Wrynose and Hardknott, and by Hardknott Fort, through Eskdale to the port and fort at Ravenglass.

Excavations made between 1913 and 1920 by the historian R.G. Collingwood revealed that there had been two forts. The first, possibly from about AD 79, was built of turf and timber; some time later it was covered by a platform above flood levels and a stone fort was constructed on it around 100. The design was of the standard pattern with a large granary, the Principia (or headquarters) and the commandant's house in the centre with the main gate on the east. The barrack blocks that housed the 500 personnel cannot be traced and may have been built of timber. The fort was attacked without doubt. There are signs of burning, and a tombstone that reads:

> To the Good Gods of the Underworld
> Flavius Romanus, Record Clerk
> Lived for 35 years
> Killed in the fort by the enemy

Peace reigned for long periods – as can be seen by the signs of a fairly large civilian settlement north-east of the fort, now buried under modern housing. Evidence from coins and pottery show that the fort was occupied at least until the second half of the fourth century, when the Romans began to withdraw from Britain.

For walkers AMBLESIDE (written 'Ammelsat' in the thirteenth century and still pronounced *AM-el-sit* in local dialect) is a more favourable tourist destination than Windermere for the town nestled in among the fells. LOUGHRIGG FELL (*LUFF-rigg*) is deservedly popular as a local walk, but it is tricky, particularly in mist, as it has a network of paths and several 'summits', the highest of which (335 m) is at the north-west end, with a great view overlooking Grasmere. And close to the east is WANSFELL PIKE, a stiff climb but worth the effort. Fairfield is within walking distance and Helvellyn available in a short car or bus journey. Then there are the scenic low-level walks around Rydal and Grasmere. Langdale Fells are not far away, and there is a quick road to Keswick. Walkers are perhaps too well cared for in the town; one wonders how so many outdoor clothing shops can survive in such a small place.

A small and interesting museum is attached to the purpose-built Armitt Library, just inside the entrance to the St Martin's College campus. The library was founded in 1912 under the will of local historian Mary Armitt, and its new building is a treasure house of books about the area, some antiquarian, covering history, geology, guides and manuscripts by eminent Lakeland authors, academics and poets, and there are some local artefacts. It also houses pictures and drawings, and the exceptional illustrations of fungi, lichens and mosses by Beatrix Potter; and works by Kurt Schwitters. Schwitters (1888–1948) was one of the greatest modern artists of the twentieth century, creating sculptures and first collage. Hitler called him 'degenerate' and in 1938 he fled for his life from his German home, first to Norway, then to England. During the war he was interred, and he finally came to Ambleside, where he lived for three productive years before his sad death in 1948. Buried first at Ambleside, his body was later laid to rest in Hanover. As he sometimes paid his bills in the town with his artworks it is thought that there may be one or two of his now extremely valuable pictures in local attics.

The oldest part of the town is on the north side, Ambleside above Stock – 'Stock' being Stock Ghyll, the watercourse that divides the town; otherwise few visible details of historical interest still exist. Apart from the eccentric tiny Bridge House near the town centre, the town's buildings are largely nineteenth-century products of the redevelopment fever to satisfy the booming tourist industry, particularly when the railway reached Windermere in 1847. The old timber-framed buildings were already being swept away before that, to the distress of Wordsworth:

> Many of the ancient buildings with their porches, projections, round chimneys and galleries have been displaced to make way for the docked, featureless, and memberless edifices of modern architecture, which looks as if fresh brought upon wheels from the foundry where they had been cast.

Ambleside began as a small market town, which boasted several watermills, employed in the fulling of wool. Then when economic circumstances changed they varied their function, becoming bark mills, or paper mills. During the rapid growth of the cotton and woollen industries in Lancashire and Yorkshire, mills were adapted: some became spinning and weaving sheds; others flourished to meet the demand for the production of bobbins, wood being readily available from the coppices of south Lakeland. To augment the local workforce, children from town poorhouses were brought into the village.

Ambleside's oldest building, the Bridge House

The tiny surviving seventeenth-century Bridge House (NT), built upon a bridge over the River Rothay, is the town's feature that has long attracted artists (including J.M.W. Turner) and latterly photographers. It was almost certainly a summerhouse belonging to old Ambleside Hall, now gone, though one less credible alternative story is that it was built by a Scotsman to avoid paying land tax. It has been a shop, and was certainly used as a permanent residence in the nineteenth century when a Mr and Mrs Rigg actually brought up six children in it! It was secured for the National Trust by public subscription.

One other building of note is the Old Stamp House on the corner of Church Street. To supplement his finances Wordsworth became a tax collector – he gained the appointment of distributor of stamps for Westmorland from 1813 to 1843. This was his office, though he did most of his work at home.

The church of St Mary has been widely criticized, notably by Harriet Martineau in 1858, for not being of traditional Lakeland style. It has a steeple, which is a necessary point of reference in lowlands, but alien in hill country where all churches have towers. Martineau wrote in *A Description of the English Lakes*: 'There have been various reductions of the beauty of the valley within twenty years or so and this … is the worst, because the most conspicuous.' Pevsner calls it 'a prosperous and townish-looking church'. Built in the insensitive 1850s it replaces an earlier one, and still retains a custom that has now become a colourful ceremony. Rush-bearing processions of this church and others (notably Grasmere's) date from the times when church floors were earthen, often with burials beneath, and covered with rushes. Once each year the old rushes were removed and replaced with fresh. Flowers might also be brought in to smother the disturbing smells that might arise from shallow burials. In Ambleside the ceremony takes place on the last Saturday in July. It is a procession of children, predominantly girls, carrying rushes and flowers in various arrangements, and preceded by a band. In old times the band was provided by one of the lake steamers.

A local attraction to earlier tourists, less so now unaccountably, was the impressive waterfalls of Stock Ghyll, easily reached by a track behind the market hall. Though hard to imagine, it was the scene of a near riot in the last quarter of the nineteenth century when the land was acquired by a Mr Mackareth, who secured the area with fences and declared that in future there would be a charge for admission to the falls. The loss of a popular area was greeted by outrage, and the iron gates were torn down. In a court case the claim of a public right of way was unproven, so the solution to the controversy was the formation of a committee to raise funds for the land's purchase. Mackareth forced the town and its supporters to pay him the extortionate £4,100, but it was thought that having visitors pay threepence for entry could redeem part of the outlay. In 1880, 23,000 visitors passed through the turnstile. Access to the wooded gorge is now free, and the falls are really worth a visit, particularly after a spell of heavy rain.

Harriet Martineau, famous writer, campaigner, atheist and radical, was the most distinguished resident in the latter half of the nineteenth century. After early struggles to make a living from her pen she wrote *Illustrations of Political Economy*, a series of moral tales illustrating the principles of Adam Smith, David Ricardo and Thomas Malthus. It was a great success. She came to Ambleside at the age of forty-three after suffering from ill-health. She designed her house, 'The Knoll', by the side of the Grasmere road (down a drive by 'Fairfield Hall'), and in the garden she would bathe in cold water, in an open-air tub, every morning. She had a cow house and a pigsty and employed a farmer and domestic staff. Her literary output was tremendous, bristling with intelligent and far-seeing opinions on all the social and political questions of the day, and she received many distinguished visitors of the time, including, of course, William Wordsworth and Ralph Waldo Emerson; and Charlotte Brontë, who stayed for a week in 1850. Wordsworth applauded her for building there – the house would only increase in value. He gave her some advice: she would get many visitors during the summer, and she should deal with them as he did: tell them if they wanted a cup of tea they were welcome, but if they wanted anything to eat they must pay for it!

She involved herself in both local and national issues, and welcomed book borrowers; the folk of Ambleside regarded her with warm respect, perhaps sometimes with awe. She was persuaded to write her *Complete Guide to the Lakes* and the *Description of the English Lakes*, which she did without indulging in the romantic view of former writers, who thought of local inhabitants enjoying a life of innocent rural happiness. This was the age of burgeoning urban industry and it had a negative impact on many people in the countryside: home manufacture was finished, cottages were falling down, fields were untilled and common agricultural workers unemployed. Martineau writes candidly about what she saw in the Lake District valleys:

> The unhealthiness of many settlements is no less a shame than a curse, for the fault is in Man, not in Nature. Nature has fully done her part in providing rock for foundations, the purest air, and the amplest supply of running water; yet the people live – as we are apt to pity the poor of the metropolis for living – in stench, huddled together in cabins, and almost without water. The wilfulness of this makes the fact almost incredible; but the fact is so.

The solution? She suggested the new railways would provide railways to bring in new trades, new markets and new ideas. Maybe she was right. The tourist industry would expand beyond her dreams. But better communications bring negative effects too. They drain young people of talent and aspiration away from the restrictive local sphere. And the problem remains, for like other Lakeland towns, Ambleside has an ageing population.

The road to Hawkshead from Ambleside crosses the River Rothay, turns left to cross the River Brathay, passes the woodland that hides conservation award-winning Skelwith Fold caravan site, then winds through Outgate to the village. A second, minor road, leaves this and takes a higher level to pass the Drunken Duck inn.

THE ANCIENT VILLAGE OF HAWKSHEAD

Returning to Bowness – the ferry serves the road to Hawkshead. On the far shore, Ferry House is the headquarters of the Freshwater Biological Association; although a proposal is on the table to move it to Lancaster University, which has no freshwater at all. The building was once the Ferry Inn, but from 1879 it became a hotel, with modern amenities including its own gasworks. In a little way a path leads up to the Station (NT) – not a railway station, but a viewpoint where you 'stationed' yourself to see the view described by the guidebook. It was customary not to take a full-frontal prospect, but to stand back to it and view it in the 'Claude Glass', a mirror in a pretty frame. This particular station was built as an octagonal tower with tinted windows facing the classic views. It was one of the attractions of the old hotel.

Wordsworth, advising Henry Crabbe Robinson in 1816 on routes for a Lakeland tour, wrote:

> From Hawkshead proceed to the Ferry House upon Windermere, and less than a quarter of a mile before you reach it, stop and put yourself under the guidance of an old woman who will come out to meet you, if you sing or call for her, at a fantastic sort of gateway, and appurtenance to a pleasure house of that celebrated patriot, Mr. Curwen, called the Station.

Southey had no love for it, however: '... a castellated building in a style so foolish, that, if any thing could mar the beauty of so beautiful a scene, it would be this ridiculous edifice.' The viewpoint is now a ruin, and the view is obscured by trees.

The road begins with a steep hill to the hamlet of FAR SAWREY, which pedestrians can avoid by a parallel footpath through the woods on the right. Pevsner thinks St Peter's church of 1866–72 'a decent and honest piece of work'. But the way of Beatrix Potter pilgrims passes by on footpaths to NEAR SAWREY. Those who, as children, remember the stories of Peter Rabbit and friends may find some parts of

Beatrix Potter's hamlet, near Sawrey

this village familiar; for Beatrix Potter lived here at times at HILL TOP (NT), near the inn, and her illustrations were taken from life. Hill Top's interior also figured in her illustrations and has been faithfully preserved by the National Trust according to Potter's instructions. The small cottage receives thousands of Potter devotees every year from home and overseas, and to avoid disappointment would-be visitors are advised to enquire if the cottage is open, at an information centre, or at the Beatrix Potter Gallery (NT) in Hawkshead. Hill Top was not her permanent home, though she stayed there often. The pub next door, the Tower Bank Arms, is illustrated in *The Tale of Jemima Puddle-Duck*, and is also owned by the National Trust. A walk around the hamlet will reveal some of the locations of her illustrations. She bought Castle Cottage, further on from Hill Top, in 1909 and married William Heelis, the local solicitor, four years later, and they lived here until her death in 1943. During this time she was involved in farming and had little time to write. Apart from a legacy she enjoyed a fair income from her book royalties, and was able to acquire property in southern Lakeland, which she handed over to the care of the National Trust.

From both Sawreys one can take a very rewarding easy walk by bridleways to Moss Eccles Tarn and Wise Een Tarn, both in beautiful settings with views to the fells; and beyond are the footpaths in Claife Heights.

One meets ESTHWAITE WATER beyond Far Sawrey. It was much loved by Wordsworth, and he knew it well from his schooldays at Hawkshead – 'that

Wise Een Tarn, near Sawrey

beloved Vale to which, ere long, I was transplanted.' The lake is mentioned in 'The Prelude' as he remembers his schooldays at Hawkshead:

> ... My morning walks
> Were early; – oft before the hours of school
> I travell'd round our little lake, five miles
> Of pleasant wandering. Happy time!

On his first week at school, though, he had an unforgettable experience. Walking by the head of the lake in the evening he saw a pile of clothes by the shore.

> Twilight was coming on; yet through the gloom,
> I saw distinctly on the opposite Shore
> A heap of garments, left, as I suppos'd,
> By one who there was bathing; long I watch'd,
> But no one owned them; meanwhile the calm Lake
> Grew dark, with all the shadows on its breast,
> And, now and then, a fish up-leaping, snapp'd
> The breathless stillness. The succeeding day,
> (Those unclaimed garments telling a plain Tale)

Went there a Company, and, in their Boat
Sounded with grappling irons, and long poles.
At length, the dead Man, 'mid that beauteous scene
Of trees, and hills and water, bolt upright
Rose with his ghastly face; a spectre shape
Of terror even! and yet no vulgar fear,
Young as I was, a Child not nine years old,
Possess'd me; for my inner eye had seen
Such sights before, among the shining streams
Of Fairy Land, the Forests of Romance ...

Esthwaite Water is set among green fields and bounded by woods and reeds. On the approach from the ferry there is a classic view over the lake to distant Langdale Pikes. The area has all the charm of Grasmere or Rydal, but the setting is mellower, set as it is among fields and woods. Alas one cannot walk, as young William did, around the lake except on tarmac, and some of the lake frontages have since become privately owned. The lake is fed by a number of streams that join Black Beck, which flows through Hawkshead, and its outlet feeds through Cunsey Beck into Windermere. The lake is 2.5 km long by 600 m wide and is 24 m deep. Being small, low-lying, relatively shallow and in an area that is intensively

Esthwaite Water

farmed, the water is eutrophic (nutrient-rich) and supports a rich flora and fauna. There are trout, pike, perch, rudd and roach. Permits to fish are obtainable from the trout farm at the southern end of the lake, and the prospects of a good catch are as fine as anywhere in Cumbria. The great crested grebe frequents the lake, and sometimes a wandering osprey pays a visit.

Ecologists from the University of Hertfordshire researched plant life in the lake and compared it with similar research in the 1920s. They showed that the submerged Esthwaite waterweed (*Elodea nutallii*) that grew in Britain only at Esthwaite (and in some other lakes in the world) could no longer be found. The same fate befell the slender naiad (*Najas flexilis*), which owes its extinction to over-enrichment of the water. Other evidence of increased enrichment was the decline of quillwort. The change in the lake's ecology is due to drainage run-off from farmland, and from a poor sewerage system, which is being improved.

Above the lake head is a detached portion of the lake known as Priest Pot – a national nature reserve – which is surrounded by typical fen conditions on a base of accumulated silt. This has been studied over a very long period to record how fen is slowly taking over the shallows and progressing through phases to become woodland. The road passes along the east shore of the lake and when it turns sharp left to round the lake head, on the right is the settlement of Colthouse, where Wordsworth lodged at Green End Cottage, when he was attending Hawkshead grammar school. Green End Cottage is not open to the public.

The seventeenth-century Colthouse Quaker meeting house, where Wordsworth with his fellow pupils were taken by their landlady to worship 'on very hot or very wet Sundays', when it was too inclement to go to Hawkshead church, remains unchanged and is still attended.

Beatrix Potter also came here on occasions. In September 1896 she recorded:

> I liked it very much. It is a pretty little place, peaceful and sunny, very old-fashioned inside, with a gigantic old key to the door. I thought it so pleasant in the stillness to listen to a robin singing in the copperbeach outside the porch. I doubt if his sentiments were religious.

HAWKSHEAD became an important wool town in Norman times, and as a measure of its success, it once had seven inns. Its market was established by the monks of Furness Abbey, who held the manor of Hawkshead for three centuries. The manor house has gone, but on the north side of the village is its oldest building, belonging to the abbey: a gatehouse, now called the Old Courthouse (NT), dating in part from the thirteenth century, but mainly fifteenth century. Hawkshead lost its market status at the dissolution, and lost even more ground when Ulverston, with its advantage as a port, stole the important roles. It became just a small village, somewhat off the beaten track; now it is on almost every Lakeland visitor's itinerary. An exploration of the attractive squares and alleys, passageways and narrow cobbled streets overhung by seventeenth-century timber-framed buildings, is the main attraction, but is soon done. The Beatrix Potter Gallery (NT) is a must for enthusiasts. The ground floor, the office of Beatrix's solicitor husband, William Heelis, is kept as it was. On the upper floor are many of the watercolours left by Beatrix to the National Trust.

Wordsworth described Hawkshead's 'snow-white' church upon its hill as a throned lady, 'sending out a gracious look all over her domain'. The setting is perfect, and the view from the top of the churchyard quite beautiful. Dedicated, like so many hilltop churches, to St Michael and All Angels, the present building dates from the fifteenth century, with Elizabethan improvements. But there are signs of an earlier structure on which the present tower is built. The first record of a chapel here dates from the early thirteenth century, when its revenues were assigned to the abbot of Furness. The building is of undressed stone plastered smooth – but no longer whitewashed. Unusually the nave and chancel are separated from the aisles by arcades. There are some decorations and painted texts dating from 1680. It is occasionally the venue for concerts and recitals.

Next to the church is the 'Free Grammar School of Edwyn Sandys, Archbishop of York' that was founded in 1585 and is little altered. The statutes

Hawskhead church

Hawkshead from the churchyard

declared that the school was to teach grammar (Latin) and the principles of the Greek tongue, with other sciences as necessary. Edwyn Sandys was born at Esthwaite Hall, 2 km south of the village, and the Sandys family of Graythwaite Hall, 7 km south of Hawkshead, has an unbroken connection with the school for over four centuries. The school had a very high reputation, and gathered some pupils from far afield. It is hard to believe that a hundred pupils and four teachers were accommodated in the small classrooms.

William Wordsworth attended the school with brother Richard from 1779 to 1787. Two of the schoolmasters had a vital influence on his future life as a poet: William Taylor, who, said William, 'loved the poets'; and Thomas Bowman, who also loved literature and encouraged William by lending him books, and spurring him on to write. The school is open to the public and one can see some of the original desks and benches. William's name is carved on his desk, but he made a poor job of it. There is also a library containing some of the school books.

The small Methodist chapel is in the village centre in a former private residence dating from the early sixteenth century, and claims to be the oldest building used for Methodist worship in the world.

In Wordsworth's school days no roads led to Hawkshead, the main wagon access being by a track from the Windermere ferry. Otherwise the village was reached by a number of packhorse paths, and packhorses brought their wool into the Monday market. There is an old cottage in Vicarage Lane known as 'Anne Tyson's Cottage' (NT). William lodged with Anne Tyson through his school days, but if he did stay here it was only for a short period, for the Tysons moved from the village centre to Green End Cottage, at Colthouse. William loved the village, the valley and the lake, and he enjoyed fishing, boating and, in winter, skating. And he was fond of the 'kind and motherly dame' who took great care of him and his fellow lodgers. After he had left the school to attend Cambridge he returned here for holidays, and he has much to say about his feelings in 'The Prelude':

> Thence with speed
> Up the familiar hill I took my way
> Towards the sweet valley where I had been reared

The 'familiar hill' was the hill from Windermere ferry.

He recalls his kind landlady:

> Glad greetings had I, and some tears, perhaps,
> From my old Dame, so motherly and good;
> While she perus'd me with a Parent's pride.
> The thoughts of gratitude shall fall like dew
> Upon thy grave, good Creature! While my heart
> Can beat I never will forget thy name.
> Heaven's blessing be upon thee where thou liest,

Old stories are linked to many villages. One true tale of Hawkshead raises curious and unanswered questions. Why were the vicar of Urswick, William Sawrey, and his chaplain so hated in 1548? Why were they in Hawkshead? The vicar was lodging in what is now called the Old Courthouse, and it is recorded that he was besieged for two days by 'a tumult of insurrection', when men assembled armed with 'swords, bucklers, staves, bills, clubs, daggers and other weapons'. Being unable to get at the vicar, they demanded that he should come out 'for they would have one of his arms or legs before going away'. Neighbours eventually dispersed them.

Hawkshead village itself remains unspoilt, and thrives. It has its market hall, a post office and a chemist's, though it lost its courthouse in 2000, and the police station has gone together with its sergeant and constable. Any policing must come by car, through the holiday traffic, from 20 or more km away. There is a National Park information centre giving advice on walks in the area. The beauty spot of Tarn Hows is within reach, and the ascent of Latterbarrow (NT) north-east of the village offers a spectacular viewpoint over Windermere, and a wander round Claife Heights forest. Grizedale forest is also nearby.

Hawkshead village fair

RYDAL VALE

RYDAL WATER (NT) is the first lake one sees after leaving Ambleside northwards on the A591, and this is very much Wordsworth country. The modest little lake, thronged by reeds, was much loved by William's family and sister. They made their home near it in the small settlement of RYDAL from 1813 to 1850. Now, alas, the busy A591 runs too close to the lake shore, and Rydal Water's peace that the poet loved is elusive. Wordsworth's Seat, said to be the bard's favourite viewpoint of the lake, is on a rocky knoll with stone steps by the roadside at the eastern end. The lake is only 17 m deep and is the first to freeze after hard frosts, sometimes hard enough to attract crowds of skaters.

A deservedly very popular and easy lakeside path, along most of the southern shore, is reached by a footbridge from the hamlet, and a short walk through a wood. The path climbs slightly at the western end, rounds Loughrigg Fell and joins Loughrigg Terrace overlooking Grasmere. The path is scorned by some that come to walk in Lakeland to get away from crowds; but the easy walk by the two lakes, with its many very elegant and unique viewpoints, is absolutely imperative if one is to experience the essence of Wordsworthian Lakeland.

Rydal itself consists of a church, two hotels, two fine houses and a few cottages and guest houses. One of the fine houses is RYDAL MOUNT, where the Wordsworths lived as tenants between 1813 and 1850. Although William had already written his greatest works, many of them at his Grasmere home, he was at the peak of his fame, and received many visitors to the house, sometimes a hundred in a day. He designed the garden, and would walk about in it if he were not trudging along the surrounding tracks, composing his poetry. He was, like some of his friends, a great walker – but rarely on the fells. The local people were quite used to seeing him muttering lines to himself as he wandered around, and sometimes scared them at night. De Quincey, who knew the poet and his unusual method of composition more than most, wrote in his *Recollections of the Lakes and the Lake Poets*:

> Wordsworth was, upon the whole, not a well made man. His legs were pointedly condemned by all the female connoisseurs in legs ... not that they were bad in any way which would force itself upon your notice – there was no absolute deformity about them; and undoubtedly they had been serviceable legs beyond the average standard of human requisition; for I calculate, upon good data, that with these identical legs Wordsworth must have traversed a distance of 175 to 180,000 English miles – a mode of exertion which to him,

The Wordsworths' home, Rydal Mount

> stood in the stead of wine, spirits, and all other stimulants whatsoever to the animal spirits; to which he has been indebted for a life of unclouded happiness, and we for much of what is most excellent in his writings.

Nowadays the house, and the re-created garden that Wordsworth planned, attracts as many visitors, if not more, than he welcomed – particularly students and literary enthusiasts. The house is maintained by a trust and furnished in the style of the period. It includes some of the poet's pieces and some of the family possessions. William's room has a view over the lake, while his daughter Dora's has an austere simplicity.

Canon Rawnsley interviewed some of the local people who knew the Wordsworths and recorded their comments in his *Reminiscences of Wordsworth among the Peasantry of Westmoreland*. He interviewed an old lady who had been in service to the Wordsworths at Rydal Mount. The old lady describes how William composed poetry as he moved around the garden:

> Well you kna, Mr. Wordsworth went bumming and booing about, and she, Miss Dorothy, kept close behint him, and she picked up the bits as he let 'em fall, and tak 'em down, and put 'em on paper for him. And you med be very well sure as how she didn't understand nor make sense out of 'em, and I doubt that he didn't kna much aboot them either himself, but, howivver, there's a gay lock o' fowk [great many folk] as wad, I dar say.

The Wordsworths rented Rydal Mount from Lady Fleming of Rydal Hall, which is across the lane. The Le Flemings were important landowners, originally from Coniston Hall. Rydal Hall is mainly seventeenth century with an early Victorian south front. The waterfalls in Rydal Beck in the hall grounds were once high on Lakeland visitors' itineraries; but they are attractive rather than impressive. Nowadays the hall is in the care of the Carlisle diocese of the Church of England and has a busy life as a conference and study centre. Public paths cross the grounds.

Lady Fleming faced complaints from her tenant about much needed repairs to the Mount. In 1826 she proposed getting rid of the problem by eviction and offering the house to an aunt, Mrs Huddleston of Temple Sowerby. William's reaction was to purchase a field known as the Rash, below the Mount, and to tell Lady Fleming that he proposed building a house there if he lost the tenancy. Luckily Mrs Huddleston preferred to stay where she was, and the Wordsworths were allowed to continue their occupation. William then later gave the field that he'd bought to his daughter Dora, and planted it with daffodils. So it remains, in the care of the

National Trust, and Dora's Field, below the church, is visited by thousands yearly at daffodil time.

Rydal church's site design were approved by Wordsworth when it was built in 1823/4. However, he caused further irritation to Lady Fleming by saying that he was less than pleased with the cramped and uncomfortable interior, with hardly room to kneel.

Long ago, when the A591 was but a farm track, the old road from Ambleside to Grasmere came through what is now Rydal Park, past the hall, and past the side of Rydal Mount. It still exists from the Mount, but now as only a pleasant pathway contouring around the fellside below Nab Scar. This became known as 'the coffin road' from the time when there was no consecrated ground at Ambleside, and its dead from 'Above Stock' had to be carried along it to Grasmere for burial. (The dead of Ambleside Below Stock had to go to Bowness.)

Further along the A591 by the lakeside is the old farmhouse (1702) known as Nab Cottage, now a guest house. De Quincey, talented writer and critic, and friend (for a time) of the Wordsworths, stayed at Nab Cottage, and while there he courted the daughter of the house, Margaret Simpson, who subsequently, in 1816, gave birth to a son. De Quincey married her four months later to Dorothy Wordsworth's disgust. She was shocked by the immorality (conveniently forgetting her own dear

Nab Cottage, Rydal

brother's lapse in France) and thought Margaret 'a stupid heavy girl' who would ruin him. William, too, was shocked that De Quincey was marrying below his station, and it led to a hurtful estrangement. In fact the marriage worked very well, lasting the couple's lifetime.

Hartley Coleridge, son of the poet, lodged at Nab Cottage from 1838 to 1849. He was quite talented, and a great favourite of the Wordsworths, though they were distressed by his addiction, not to opium like his father, but to alcohol. Wordsworth remarked:

> If he could only exercise a little self-control, and a little steadiness of purpose and application, he might yet do great things, he has far more learning than I am confident to judge of, and in poetry his ear, like his father's, is faultless, perfect.

His kindly nature also made him popular with villagers.

At the western end of Rydal Water is Whitemoss Common, with car parks on both sides of the road (NT). It is a starting point for the many walks in the area. The River Rothay, linking Rydal Water to Grasmere, flows through the site, which was, before the 1960s, a huge quarry, and a waste dump. Years of accumulated rubbish, much from tourists, contributed to a depressing landscape. A joint effort by the National Trust and National Park had the site levelled, large quantities of soil covered the spoils, then the area was seeded and planted with trees. The result is a pleasing amenity. From here the shore of Grasmere is gained by paths on both sides of the River Rothay, the path on its northern side leading to the lakeside beech woodland of Penny Rock (NPA).

A narrow minor road rises from Whitemoss to give a good view over Rydal Water. This was the original road, passing Dove Cottage, to Grasmere before the section of the A591 below was engineered in 1831. This old road passes through woodland (NPA), the pinewood on the right being a favourite place of William's brother John, the sea captain, on his visits to Dove Cottage. Somewhere hereabouts was the Wishing Gate celebrated by a Wordsworth poem, one verse of which goes:

> The worldling, pining to be freed
> From turmoil, who would turn or speed
> The current of his fate,
> Might stop before this favoured scene,
> At Nature's call, nor blush to lean
> Upon the Wishing Gate.

It was blocked off and he had to write another poem about its loss.

The 'humble cot' – Dove Cottage, Grasmere

DOVE COTTAGE

And so to the Dove Cottage itself, occupied by the Wordsworths. What can be said? It receives legions of visitors, many from overseas, for it was here that Wordsworth wrote many of his greatest works. The cottage with its little garden, on what is now a byroad, has been reconstructed largely as it was; the property is owned by the imaginative Wordsworth Trust, staffed by guides and open to all. The attendant museum and library contain many treasures and occasionally special exhibitions are laid on. Perhaps the majority, but not all the visitors, are Wordsworth enthusiasts. The cottage and museum have become just one of Lakeland's tourist attractions, and the best that could be hoped for is that the casual visitor goes away better informed about a life in the early nineteenth century, and may even read some poetry.

The cottage was originally a small roadside inn, the Dove and Olive Bough. William took the cottage with his sister, at a rent of eight pounds per annum, in December 1799: 'The loveliest spot that man has ever found.' Brother and sister, as orphans, were always very close, thinking alike, Dorothy so often feeding ideas. William had hoped since boyhood to live in the Grasmere vale. He wrote of the dream becoming a reality in 'The Recluse', a long poem that he never finished:

On Nature's invitation do I come,
By reason sanctioned. Can the voice mislead,
That made the calmest fairest spot on earth
With all its unappropriated good
My own; and not mine only, for with me
Entrenched, say rather peacefully embowered,
Upon yon orchard, in yon humble cot,
A younger orphan of a home extinct,
The only daughter of my parents dwells.

And of the place:

'Tis, but I cannot name it, 'tis the sense
Of majesty, and beauty, and repose,
A blended holiness of earth and sky,
Something that makes this individual spot,
This small abiding-place of many men,
A termination and a last retreat,
A centre, come from whereso'er you will,
A whole, without dependence or defect,
Made for itself, and happy in itself,
Perfect contentment, Unity entire.

He owed his freedom to write to a bequest from a student friend whom he had attended during his illness. However, William's existence at Dove Cottage – shared with Dorothy – was frugal, eked out with produce from the small vegetable garden. The compensations to him were obviously great – an uninterrupted view of the lake, some wonderful walking country and no shortage of visiting friends. During his seven and a half years there he wrote: 'The Prelude'; 'Intimations of Immortality'; *Miscellaneous Sonnets*; some lyrical ballads; and a number of other poems, including some of the 'Lucy' poems, the 'Ode to Duty', 'Michael', 'The Brothers', 'To the Cuckoo', 'The Rainbow' and 'The Solitary Reaper'. Dorothy was a brilliant observer and writer, and her journals give a detailed account of their life at the cottage.

Among the visitors to Dove Cottage was the brilliant Samuel Taylor Coleridge, close friend of William and collaborator in *The Lyrical Ballads*; most frequently when he became a resident at Greta Hall in Keswick. The 18 km walk from Keswick was nothing to Coleridge, and once he made the visit via the summit of Helvellyn, arriving in the small hours. Sir Walter Scott was another visitor. As his hosts were abstaining water-drinkers, Sir Walter would sneak off to the Swan Inn for a noggin. The cat was out of the bag when he arrived at the inn with William and the landlord queried 'The usual?'

William's and Dorothy's fortunes changed for the better in 1802 when the very wealthy Sir James Lowther died. He had a long-standing debt to their late father, who was law-agent to the Lowther estate. Sir James's cousin, Sir William Lonsdale, was determined to pay off all long-standing debts, and to the delight of William and Dorothy, the repaid debt meant that they would be free of further financial worries. This came at a good time, for William was planning to marry Mary Hutchinson, a life-long friend of them both. Firstly though, he and Dorothy had to go to France for William to make a settlement with his mistress Annette, and their love child Caroline. William and Mary were married in 1802.

It was in 1805 that William and Dorothy were devastated to learn of the death of their younger brother John, captain of the East India Company's ship, *The Earl of Abergavenny*, sunk in a storm on Shambles Shoal in Weymouth Bay with a loss of 260 lives. They both loved John dearly and were inconsolable. John was an admirer of William's work, and 'I never wrote a line', William said, 'without a thought of it giving him pleasure.' Friends rallied round. Southey was a friend of the Wordsworths, but not close. To his credit he offered at once to come to Dove Cottage and stayed there for two days, sharing their grief, and offered to return. Dorothy stated: 'He was so tender and kind that I loved him all at once – he wept with us in our sorrow, and for that cause I feel that I must always love him.' Coleridge was in Malta, and was laid low by the news. The Wordsworths mourned for weeks, and were distressed by press reports that put the blame for what was a national disaster on the captain. In fact it was the error of an inexperienced pilot that caused the drift onto the shoal. There were many false rumours: that the captain was drunk, though John, like his brothers and sister, was abstemious, that he had lost control and was cowardly, though this was not at all in character. There were reports of his last words – though who could hear, or who would listen to them, in a howling gale on a floundering ship when it was everyone for himself? Charles Lamb, a constant friend, although a sick man, made many enquiries in London, and wrote to Grasmere with as near correct accounts as could be got, which were of great comfort.

Mary subsequently bore three children, John, Dorothy (Dora) and Thomas. Mary's sister Sarah also came to live at the cottage, and when Mary was expecting her fourth child the Wordsworths were forced to look for larger accommodation. Dorothy wrote: 'We are crammed in our little nest edge-full'. In May 1808 they then left to live in the village.

After Dove Cottage became vacant Thomas De Quincey took the tenancy. He was to hold it for twenty-eight years, and lived there for twenty-two, so the cottage has more of him than the Wordsworths. During that time he wrote, among much else, the two works for which he is most familiar: *Confessions of an English Opium Eater* and the *Recollections of the Lakes and the Lake Poets*. The cottage became so crammed with books that his wife must have been driven to despair. That he loved the cottage is not in doubt, for in his *Confessions* he supplies this 'analysis of happiness':

> Paint me, then, a room seventeen feet by twelve, and not more than seven and a half feet high. This, reader, is somewhat ambitiously styled, in my family, the drawing room; but being contrived 'a double debt to pay', it is also, and more justly, termed the library; for it happens that books are the only article of property in which I am richer than my neighbours. Of these I have about five thousand, collected gradually since my eighteenth year. Therefore, painter, put as many as you can into this room. Make it populous with books; and, furthermore, paint me a good fire; and furniture plain and modest, befitting the unpretending cottage of a scholar. And near the fire paint me a tea table; and place only two cups and saucers on the tea tray; ... paint me an eternal teapot – for I usually drink tea from eight o'clock at night to four in the morning.

GRASMERE

GRASMERE is a beautiful lake, surrounded by woodland. The best view of it is from the footpath on the side of Loughrigg – Loughrigg Terrace. It is a mere 1.6 km long with a width half that, and a depth of 23 m. Wordsworths and friends would sometimes visit the lake's sole island.

The public has free access to the lake on foot, thanks to the National Trust, which manages it and most of the land around. The only vehicles in sight and sound are those going by on the A591, which comes regrettably close to the eastern bank. GRASMERE VILLAGE buildings are mainly nineteenth and early twentieth century, but the aspect remains unspoilt thanks to the National Park's planning policy and some restraint from the inhabitants. The village was 'discovered' by the poet Thomas Gray in 1769, and he wrote one of those pieces that helped to bring painters and sketchers flocking to the Lakeland scenery. Coming from Keswick and over Dunmail Raise, he spotted the village and lake below:

> Just beyond it opens one of the sweetest landscapes that art ever attempted to imitate. The bosom of the mountains spreading here in a broad bason

Grasmere

> discovers in the midst Grasmere-water; its margin is hollowed into small bays with bold eminences: some of them rocks, some of soft turf that half conceal and vary the figure of the little lake they command.
>
> From the shore a low promontory pushes itself far into the water, and on it stands a white village with the parish church in the midst of it ...
>
> Not a single red tile, no flaming gentlemanís house, or garden walls break in upon the repose of this little unsuspected paradise, but all is peace, rusticity, and happy poverty in its neatest, most becoming attire.

'Happy poverty'? This was a time when the middle classes thought the local peasants were content in their 'innocent' and simple lifestyles. Happy poverty has now given way to some serious commercialism. Grasmere still attracts artists, however. Prints of the late Heaton Cooper watercolours grace many a wall throughout the country; and his studio still sells work, even after his death. The sports field is famed for its annual Grasmere Sports, in which traditional Cumberland- and Westmorland-style wrestling takes place (in tights and embroidered pants if correct). Another event is the guides' race, which demands of runners a tremendous stamina for the muscle-straining, lung bursting ascent of a horrendously steep part of Lord Crag on the east, and requires an unnatural agility for the breakneck descent. And there are hound trails, where hounds run

The quarry cave on Loughrigg Terrace above Grasmere Lake

on a 'drag' of some miles laid down with rags soaked in aniseed and paraffin. The sport may have originated from the border troubles, when 'sleuth hounds' were used to track down raiders. Now even the Grasmere Sports is becoming commercialized with sideshows, traders and entertainers, and its traditional Thursday date has been switched to a Sunday. At other times the sports field stages, quite lawfully, occasional caravan and camping rallies in full blatant view.

The church of St Oswald dates from the thirteenth century, but some of the alterations since make it something of an architectural curiosity. Wordsworth and his family worshipped here and it has remained unchanged since the poet wrote in 'The Excursion',

> With pillars crowded, and the roof upheld
> By naked rafters intricately crossed,
> Like leafless underboughs, in some thick wood,
> All withered by the depth of shade above.

Until the nineteenth century the floor of the church was earthen, and at intervals the rushes strewn on the floor were cleared out and replaced. This gave rise, as at Ambleside, to the traditional rush-bearing ceremony that is still practised on the Saturday nearest St Oswald's Day. Village children, dressed in their best, carry rushes and flowers to the church, in a procession preceded by a band.

The simple Wordsworth graves are in the north-east section of the churchyard. There is a memorial stone to brother John, drowned at sea; and Catharine and Thomas, their children's graves, are here; as are those of Dora Quillinan the daughter, and her husband, Edward Quillinan, and Coleridge's son Hartley.

By the lychgate is what used to be the school where the Wordsworths' children attended. After it was closed in 1855 Sarah Nelson, a cook, occupied it. Her secret recipe for gingerbread became very well known, and delicious gingerbread is still made here to the same recipe.

The dominant fell directly to the north of the village is often known by the rock formation on its summit. It is, from some viewpoints, 'the lion and the lamb', for it appears roughly like a lion couchant with a lamb between its paws. However, from another viewpoint from the sides of the fell it is 'the old lady playing the organ', for (with a bit of imagination) it looks like a person sitting before a tall console, though why it should be an 'old lady' is a mystery. Wordsworth in 'Johanna' refers to 'That ancient woman seated on Helm Crag', a popular, easy, but steep walk from the village. It was climbed by the intrepid Captain Budworth and a companion in 1792. Before he made the daring ascent he decided that

'The lion and the lamb', Helm Crag summit

refreshment was called for. In the north-west of the village stood an inn, now the National Trust's information centre, where the pair obtained nourishment:

> Roast pike, stuffed, a boiled fowl, Veal-cutlets and ham, Beans and Bacon, Cabbage, Pease and potatoes, Anchovy Sauce, Parsley and butter, Plain butter, Butter and cheese, Wheat bread and oat cake, Three cups of preserved gooseberries, with a bowl of rich cream in the centre; For two people at ten-pence a head.

Surprisingly, after lunch the good captain found the ascent of the modest fell 'formidable'.

The Wordsworths moved from Dove Cottage to the village on 5 June 1808. William rented Allan Bank, a pink-washed house on the village's western side, now seen from a footpath signed for Silver How. Earlier he was horrified when he saw this house being built for a Liverpool merchant – in full view from the cottage – calling it 'a temple of abomination'. But needs must. He had to swallow his pride and take a lease on it. Mary was pregnant and on 6 September daughter Catharine was born. Two years later son William was born. Allan Bank had its fair share of problems. The chimneys would not draw and the house was occasionally full of smoke. To raise the chimney height workmen came and went amid a constant stream of visitors. In June 1811 the Wordsworths moved to the Parsonage, but their new home did not satisfy them either. It didn't get enough sun, it was exposed to public view, and it stood in a wet field, unsuitable for the children to play in. The workmen were in there too to make alterations. A year later Catharine died, as did son Thomas shortly afterwards from measles.

From the village two ways are available for walkers to the north-east, one on the left of the stream to Easedale and the scenic Easedale Tarn, and on the right to Far Easedale. Easedale to the Wordsworths was the 'black quarter', for it was shadowed early at the end of the day – and the bad weather seemed to stem from it. But the Easedale paths were often walked by William and Dorothy, and the poet composed many lines of his poetry in this delightful landscape.

North from Grasmere the road goes through the geological fault and the gap of Dunmail Raise, Steel Fell to the west, and Seat Sandal to the east. It has always been a main highway, but in the late eighteenth century, when William Gilpin (1724–1804) wrote *Observations Relatively Chiefly to Picturesque Beauty*, the climb must have been wild.

> The whole view is of the horrid kind. Not a tree appeared to add the least cheerfulness of it. With the adorning of such a landscape with figures, nothing could suit if better than a group of banditti. Of all the scenes I ever saw, this

> was the most adapted to the perpetration of some dreadful deed. The imagination can hardly avoid conceiving a band of robbers lurking under the shelter of some projecting rock; and expecting the traveller, as he approaches along the valley below.

This is hardly the impression that one gets now. Between the twin carriageways is a large cairn that once marked the boundary between Westmorland and Cumberland. It also marks the spot of – hardly 'a dreadful deed' – a battle between the Norse king Dunmail (Duvenald) of Cumbria, and Edmund of Northumbria in 945. Edmund's victory meant that the land north of Dunmail would go to the Scots, on condition that the Scots king lend support against invaders from the sea when needed.

Several old stories concern the cairn. One old tradition suggests that it marks the grave of Dunmail; but the man was in Rome some time later and died there. Another is that Dunmail fled the battle eastwards up by Raise Beck and flung his crown jewels in Grisedale Tarn to lighten his load and speed his escape. Divers have so far failed to find them! Another theory is that the cairn was raised by Edmund to celebrate the victory. It is also possible that it was built by King Malcolm of Scotland to make a permanent mark of the then southern boundary of Scotland. More appealing, though much less probable, is the theory that it was a battle 'scoreboard'. Before joining battle, it is suggested, each man in one of the armies picked up a stone and dropped it in one spot to make a pile. At the end of the battle each survivor picked up a stone and threw it away: the remaining cairn recorded the fallen and became their memorial. If the latter theory is true the battle must either have been a bloodbath, or the entire army fled the field.

WEST OF WINDERMERE

To come down the west side of the Windermere basin, starting from Ambleside, a road goes west to Clappersgate, and here it forks and we must go left on the Hawkshead road and cross the bridge over the Brathay, where we immediately see Low Brathay Hall. This was the home of Charles Lloyd, a writer of novels and poems, and a translator, who was known to Wordsworth and Coleridge, and was a friend of De Quincey. Regrettably, he was an unstable character who could cause upset. He was eventually committed to an asylum. One day, having escaped, he came weeping to Dove Cottage and asked De Quincey for help, telling him of the brutal treatment that he was receiving at the asylum. De Quincey was appalled at what he said, but could only be sympathetic, and walk back with him in the direction of Brathay, before Lloyd broke away and ran. He was retaken, and was later removed to France, where he died. De Quincey wrote a sad piece about his return visits to Brathay bridge with its sad memories of his friend. He listens to the river and philosophizes:

> I have heard in that same chanting of the little mountain river – a requiem over departed happiness, and a protestation against the thought that so many excellent creatures, but a little lower than the angels, whom I have seen only to love life – so many of the good, the brave, the beautiful, the wise – can have appeared for no higher purpose or prospect than simply to point a moral, to cause a little joy and many tears, a few perishing moons of happiness and years of vain regret! No! that the destiny of man is more in correspondence with the grandeur of his endowments, and that our mysterious tendencies are written hieroglyphically in the vicissitudes of day and night, of winter and summer, and throughout the great alphabet of Nature!

Beyond the Low Brathay Hall a drive runs up to the Georgian Brathay Hall, now a management training centre. Landscape painter John Harden lived here from 1804 to 1833, and sometimes John Constable stayed as his guest. In Brathay Hall grounds is the headquarters of the Brathay Exploration Group that organizes expeditions abroad for young people.

Holy Trinity church was built in 1836 by Giles Redmayne, a London businessman, who was living at the time at Brathay Hall. The churchyard is a tranquil retreat, a good place, early and late in the day, to observe deer.

As we continue on towards Hawkshead a minor road goes left for Wray and Wray Castle (see p. 510), and its little church at which the Revd H.D. Rawnsley (later Canon Rawnsley) was vicar. To the west of Wray is Blelham Tarn (NT), with footpaths around but not to the water. The tarn is a nature reserve, though angling is allowed and licensed by the Windermere Ambleside Angling Association on behalf of the National Trust. Roach and pike are the attractions, along with the idyllic surroundings.

Further on at High Wray access can be gained to the network of paths in the forest of Claife Heights; and further still to the heights of LATTERBARROW (244 m), with a grand viewpoint over Windermere, and west to the high fells.

The road finishes at Hawkshead. Going south the road runs past the popular youth hostel, Esthwaite Lodge, where the novelist Francis Bett Young (1884–1954) lived between 1928 and 1932, and where he wrote *Jim Redlake, Mr and Mrs Pennington*, and *The House Under the Water*. His visitors included Hugh Walpole, who worked on *Judith Paris* during his stay.

Further south on the left is the old Esthwaite Hall, now a private residence.

Archbishop Edwin Sandys (1516–88), founder of Hawkshead grammar school, was born here. And a little further one can access Esthwaite Water at the trout farm, where boats can be hired, and fishing permits are available.

Graythwaite Hall, seat of the Sandys family, is further south. The house is not open to the public, but the lovely gardens are, when in season. Seventeenth-century Graythwaite Old Hall is further south, with a row of yew topiary along the roadside. Then one passed the YMCA national centre, and the old Stott Park Bobbin Mill (EH). This began production during the Industrial Revolution, to answer the huge demand for bobbins in the textile industries of Lancashire and Yorkshire. It ceased production as late as 1971, but of course latterly its machinery was turning other products from the coppice woodlands, such as tool handles. It

Stott Park Bobbin Mill

Bobbin samples

is now preserved as an excellent working museum. It is no longer driven as it once was with a water wheel, though the head of water is maintained from High Dam reservoirs (NPA), prettily contained in woodland. A steam engine replaced the old mechanism and still provides power for the production that can be watched (although the once highly dangerous belt drives have been encased).

The main road to Furness from Hawkshead did not go directly south to Lakeside and Newby Bridge, but branched off onto what is now a minor road just south of Esthwaite Hall; and this goes down the sylvan valley of Dale Park, between woodlands, with Grizedale Forest on the right.

THE GRIZEDALE AREA

The main way to Grizedale Forest, however, is via Hawkshead by a by-road branching south-west just south of the village. The forest's reception area is past the 'restaurant in the forest' on the site once occupied by the hall. The day when the Forestry Commission was unhappy at allowing public access to their forests is history. The problem they feared was fire. But pioneering work at Grizedale proved that the fear was unfounded. The public could act as observers, reporting the beginning of a fire before the foresters could detect it. Thanks to Grizedale the public are now welcome in all the commission-owned forests. Grizedale covers a huge block of forest on Silurian land between Dale Park and Coniston. There has always been woodland here. For 700 years it has sustained the area's main industries. The herds of wild red deer, and the roe deer, have descended from stocks that were here prior to human settlement.

In 1937 the commission took over the Grizedale Hall estate for reafforestation. The large gaps in the existing tree cover were planted with conifers. During the war the hall itself became a German officers' prison camp. Two notable incidents occurred. A U-boat commander who had surrendered his boat was condemned for cowardice by the officers' court and sentenced to be shot – while attempting to escape. The commander obeyed the order to ignore the demands of the guard to halt. He was shot – and though the intention was only to wound, the man died. The other incident was a well-planned escape by Franz von Werra, a Luftwaffe pilot. He was on exercise outside the wire with a group of officers that stopped for rest at a bridge. He stretched out on the bridge parapet and while his colleagues made a diversion, dropped over the side and hid below the wall. Land girls on a farm overlooking the place waved and shouted to attract the guards – to fox the guards the Germans waved back! Von Werra tried to make for the coast but was eventually caught on moorland a considerable distance away short of his target. He escaped again from another camp, and made it to Canada and back to Germany. This very remarkable and resourceful man was eventually killed in action.

After the war, to the dismay of locals, the decision was taken to demolish the hall. It had been built only fifty years before by the Brocklebanks, Liverpool industrialists. The stables and other outbuildings were preserved, however, and they now house commission offices, an information centre and museum, a shop, a café and a theatre. The ground nearby offers accommodation for artists, and there is a very imaginative children's play area, made locally of wood, naturally, with animal and bird shapes.

The forest is crisscrossed by trails for pedestrians, and for cyclists; and one can spend many days of exploration in all seasons. One attraction is the use of the forest by environmental artists who have laid out their various creations, made of natural materials: dry stone walls, coppice wood, running water, fallen trees. Some make you smile, and some make you wonder at the artist's ingenuity and imagination. The wonderful thing about the forest is that it can absorb thousands of visitors while still offering a feeling of remoteness. It is a place to return to time after time.

Beyond Grizedale and heading south is the small village of SATTERTHWAITE, whose church covered a wide parish with a thin and scattered population. Force Mills, just past what must be one of the prettiest schools in the country, was where the locals found work. Here and at Force Forge below were a corn mill and a forge, then later two bobbin mills. The forge – a 'bloomsmithy' – began production around 1640, and consisted of a hearth blown by bellows, worked by water power, and mechanical hammers. In 1711 it became part of the Backbarrow Company until its closure. The large dam that served the mill was filled in in the nineteenth century and is now the lawn of the White Lodge. There was another forge at Stoney Hazel, to the south.

Down past Forge Farm is Rookhow, a Quaker meeting house built in 1725 – not for weekly worship, but as a centre where Quakers from a wide area could meet monthly to organize business. A stable block has been converted to provide accommodation for socially deprived groups, religious retreats, conferences, courses and holidays, and good use is made of Quaker Wood, the woodland surrounding.

We are now in the beautiful wooded area of RUSLAND, and among a net of minor roads in which it is easy to get lost. Turning left at the meeting house, we find Rusland's church of St Pauls, remarkable only for its lovely setting. Arthur Ransome, author of the famous children's books, was much taken by it, and at his request he was buried here (d. 1967), in the south-east corner of the churchyard, together with his wife Evgenia, whom he met in Russia when he was a journalist reporting on the Revolution. She was Trotsky's secretary.

Opposite Rusland church a road goes south and a little way on the right is an old tannery, owned by the National Park Authority. It has been excavated and is well worth a visit. One vital ingredient for tanneries was obtained from the Rusland coppice woodlands – oak bark. The woods also produced charcoal for the furnaces. The charcoal burns were made on man-made platforms – 'pitsteads' – and these can be found throughout the woodlands. The wood was made into tight piles and covered with turf and the burn depended upon the exclusion of air to ensure a very slow combustion. The charcoal burners, and the barkers, lived on the site in temporary huts constructed from local materials. Some of the Rusland woods are owned by the National Park Authority and are open to the public.

There are several small villages in the valley. BOUTH, a pleasant little place with a green, was once of greater importance than its modest appearance now suggests. On the main road from Kendal to Dalton in Furness, it had a market and two fairs annually. The local sport was wrestling, and Bouth wrestlers were famous. And it had an important industry nearby – the Black Beck gunpowder works established in 1860, now a camping and caravan site. It closed in 1929. Hay Bridge nature reserve is up a lane to the north, past the White Hart pub.

Due west from Bouth is COLTON and OXEN PARK. Colton parish covered a large area, and Holy Trinity church sits on a hill looking out over what it can. It dates from at least 1578, and was made larger in 1721 and 1762. Some buildings in Oxen Park date from the eighteenth century.

AMBLESIDE TO THE LANGDALES

South-west from Ambleside lie the wonderful valleys of Great and Little Langdale, to climbers and fell walkers the land of Shangri-La. Cross the River Rothay and in a short distance Clappersgate and on to Skelwith bridge. Just by the bridge the Kirkstone green slate quarries have a showroom, shop and café. The slate takes a high polish and its beauty is recognized by architects who use it to face prestigious buildings, and to pave important floors. It can also be used in domestic settings.

A riverside footpath followed upstream reveals SKELWITH FORCE, not a high waterfall, but its sheer volume of water can make an impression; it can be spectacular, for the river is fed by a large water catchment area in the fells. The footpath continues to the side of the small lake of ELTERWATER (NT). 'Elter Water' is a derivative from old Norse meaning 'swan lake'. It is a strange, irregularly shaped lake with a length of 800 m, half-hidden by reeds, and it is well named, for in winter the shy whooper swans, natives of Scandinavia, sometimes pay a visit.

Elterwater

The pretty lake is at the confluence of Langdale Beck from Great Langdale, and the Brathay, flowing from Wrynose Pass through Little Langdale. The lakeside path gives a view up-valley to the Langdale Pikes. The lake, a wildlife conservation area, is only 50 m deep, but there can be a fair flow of water through it.

ELTERWATER VILLAGE is at the head of the lake and the centre for walks, the finest being onto heather-covered Lingmoor (467 m), the long fell that separates the two Langdales. The village industry is now quarrying, and some of that beautifully marked fine slate can be obtained here; but a former industry was the manufacture of gunpowder. Critically the powder had to be very finely ground and mixed – the more thorough this process the more effective the result. So the materials had to pass through a series of millstones along the Langdale Beck, each kept apart from its neighbour in case of accidents. Accidents there were, including fatalities. The gunpowder was in demand for the mining and quarrying industries, and in the First World War, for armaments. Now the site of the works is a timeshare holiday complex with luxury accommodation and heated swimming pool – which apparently is just what this beautiful valley needed. It is, however, well screened. What does the ghost of the killed gunpowder worker, who is rumoured to appear there, think of it?

It was in a barn at Elterwater, loaned to him in 1945 by a friend, Harry Pierce, that the famous German artist Kurt Schwitters (see p. 513) produced a masterpiece, a large three-dimensional collage on the barn wall. He intended it, he said, 'to stand close to nature, in the midst of a National Park, and afford a wonderful view in all directions'. And so it did for a while, until, after his death, it was moved for safe-keeping to the Hatton Gallery at Newcastle.

A second route to Elterwater leaves the road from Ambleside at a bend near Brunt How and goes by LOUGHRIGG TARN (NT). The tarn is approachable only on foot, but from the path photographers enjoy a classic view across the water with the Langdale Pikes in the background. Another route comes from Grasmere up the fearsome steepness of Red Bank on a minor road, and over the viewpoint hill under Hunting Stile.

A little way up-valley from Elterwater is the village of CHAPEL STILE. Holy Trinity church is nineteenth century and on the site of the old chapel. Harriet Martineau recounts the time when the chapel clergyman, a Mr Frazer, had just begun his sermon in the rickety pulpit with the text 'Behold I come quickly', when it collapsed and he fell on an elderly lady in a front pew. He apologized and hoped she wasn't hurt and got the reply, 'If I'd been kilt, I'd be reet sarrat [rightly served] for you threatened ye'd be comin doon sune.'

Beyond Chapel Stile one enters Great Langdale. The glaciated valley once had a lake – and sometimes after prolonged rain it has the makings of one. But at some point in the distant past the water broke through a gap at Chapel Stile, and only

Loughrigg Tarn

the remnant is visible as meandering Great Langdale Beck in the valley bottom. On the right is the flat ridge that separates Langdale from Easedale and the Grasmere fells, an area for the wanderer rather than the peak bagger, though the highest point, among the rocky knolls, is Blea Rigg (542 m).

Turn the corner and there they are in full glory: the Langdale Pikes, the most prominent feature of the Lake District, a magnet for fell walkers and the rock climbers. That first rock-climbing area is on the fellside to the right. Scout Crag is where would-be climbers receive their schooling; though increasingly nowadays training seems to be done on the artificial crag of soulless gymnasium climbing walls. A sterner challenge lies above, on the crags in the deep gash of White Gill.

The car park (NT) by the Dungeon Ghyll New Hotel is the popular place to begin the great fell walks. Thousands tread the path to Stickle Tarn every year. The path follows the Stickle Ghyll to the tarn's outflow, and it is steep. An easier route is by the old packhorse zigzags on the right of the gill that eventually comes at the tarn at its east side. STICKLE TARN is the limit of the walk for many, and it is a classic. Actually it is dammed, originally to keep a head of water for a mill below. The tarn was quite small in an area of bog when the dam was breached in the 1950s, and one of the first tasks of the brand new National Park was to repair the dam and bring up the water level to reveal the tarn in its old beauty.

At the back of the tarn is the huge craggy hump of PAVEY ARK (698 m). It is

Langdale Pikes from Lingmoor Fell

possible to see a line in the crag running from the bottom on the right, to near the top on the left. At a distance the line looks impossible as an ascent route for anyone except a rock climber. But it is a walker's path, almost a natural stairway in a groove, though flexible limbs and a head for heights are needed. It is not recommended as a descent route. As Wainwright says:

> Care should be taken to avoid falling down the precipice or sending stones over the edge. Falling bodies, human or mineral, may constitute a danger to unseen climbers on the rocks or the scree below, or to grazing sheep.

The summit can be reached without facing the crag head on; it can be circumvented on its right and approached from its back. The view from its top is extensive. The face of the crag has several interesting rock-climbing routes on it.

From Stickle Tarn a path goes north-east to a junction. The path on the right from here goes by way of Easedale Tarn to Grasmere, the leftwards leads on to the prominent point of Sergeant Man (736 m – a 'man' being a summit cairn). The sense of achievement gives rather more satisfaction than the view which is wholly of mountain tops. Beyond the man is the rather featureless higher point of HIGH RAISE (762 m). This is as near to the centre of the Lake District's fells as one can get. Here is an open area of rough grassland, and in season one might hear that uncommon sound of the countryside nowadays – the song of skylarks. In the winter it is uncomfortably exposed. The views are of course extensive, as far as Yorkshire to the south-east, Morecambe Bay in the south, the Irish Sea to the west, Solway Firth and a glimpse of Scotland to the north.

THE PIKES

Now to the two pikes. The one to the east is Harrison Stickle, and on the west Pike o' Stickle (or Stickle Pike). They can be reached from Stickle Tarn, but are best taken by the regular route. The first recorded ascent of the pikes by a fell walker, in November 1797, was that of Captain Budworth, a one-armed veteran of the siege of Gibraltar. He employed a guide from the village – actually a young farm boy. He ascended, but was very scared of the descent. He found himself on a path with a horrendously steep drop to his right, and states that he could not proceed until that view was obscured by his guides tying a scarf round his right eye. He held out his staff to the boy and was led safely down across the slope. It has been suggested that the path was Jack's Rake, but not so. The description fits the often used shepherds' path on the north side of Dungeon Ghyll.

Harrison Stickle from the Pike Ridge

The chasm of Dungeon Ghyll, to the left of Stickle Ghyll, was a big attraction when viewing waterfalls was imperative in the days of Victorian tourism. Harriet Martineau:

> Strangers who arrive untired [at Millbeck farmhouse for a meal] generally go to the Ghyll while their ham and eggs are preparing. The green path on the hill-side will be pointed out from the farm: and the traveller must take care not to make for the water-fall he sees in front. The path he wants tends to the left, till it reaches a fence and a gate, when it turns sharp to the right; after which there is no possibility of losing the way. It presently joins the stream from the force, which leads up into a dark fissure, – 'Dungeon' and 'Ghyll' both meaning a fissure. There is a well secured ladder, by which ladies easily descend to the mouth of the chasm; and when they have caught sight of the fall, they can please themselves about scrambling any further. There is the fall in its cleft, tumbling and splashing, while the light ash, and all the vegetation besides, is everlastingly in motion from the stir of the air. Above, a bridge is made, high aloft, by the lodgement of a block in the chasm. The finest season for visiting this force is in a summer afternoon. Then the sun streams in obliquely, - a narrow, radiant, translucent screen; itself lighting up the gorge, but half concealing the projections and waving ferns behind it. The way in which it converts the spray into sparks and many-coloured gems can be believed only by those who have seen it.

No ladder, well secured or otherwise, is there now. But the scramble to gain the view is worthwhile. The block of rock which bridges the gill is mentioned in Wordsworth's poem 'The Idle Shepherd Boys':

> Into a chasm a mighty block
> Hath fallen, and made a bridge of rock;
> The gulf is deep below,
> And in a basin black and small,
> Receives a lofty waterfall.

There are several ways to HARRISON STICKLE. The commonly used way goes left of Dungeon Ghyll and above Raven Crag, a grand rock-climbing spot, and passes well to the right of Gimmer Crag – another climbing crag, so popular that there is sometimes a queue to use it. The Harrison Stickle path then branches to the right. As can be expected the airy views from the top are thrilling.

The round boss of PIKE O' STICKLE can clearly be seen from Harrison and is easily reached, despite there being a bit of a scramble to the top. Here, again, the view meets expectations. Just below the summit in the loose rock on its east side is one of the sites of Cumbria's earliest industry: the making of stone axes from around 3,000 BC. The rock outcrop below the pike, discovered by Langdale's Neolithic settlers, is a particular form of volcanic tuff, a very hard volcanic rock that fractures when struck, like flint, into shell-like edges. At this place, and in other parts of the fells where the rock juts out, the axes were roughed out, then it is assumed, taken to the sandstone on the coast for sharpening and polishing. A 'Langdale stone axe', seen in many museums, is an impressive piece of craftsmanship and was very efficient. How did those early inhabitants find the outcrops?

THE HEAD OF THE LANGDALES

Back in the valley, many ways lead up to the fells. From the head of the valley the old packhorse route to Langstrath and Borrowdale climbs northwards over Stake Pass (480 m), in a series of zigzags, shown on old maps as a road. From the foot of that pass a bridleway climbs by Rossett Gill to Angle Tarn, though strangely throughout the years of fell walking it has been neglected in favour of a desperately uncomfortable direct ascent up the gill. Angle Tarn is a wild raw remnant of the ice age, a pool in a classic comb carved from the pressure of ice from the high crags around. It is one of those high places where people linger, and is often depressingly littered. Some walkers camp here, but it is a surprisingly windy hollow. A bridleway leads on to the great high crossroads of the fell paths on ESK HAUSE (760 m), and a path runs from there to Scafell Pike; another by Sprinkling Tarn to Sty Head and Wasdale; another by Grains Gill to Borrowdale; and another southwards down the wilderness of upper Eskdale and by the River Esk to Ravenglass. With all those options it is little wonder that it is a great place in which to get lost in a mist.

It is possible to reach one of the finest mountains of all from the north side of Angle Tarn, by Ore Gap, to BOWFELL (903 m) (*BOE-f'l*). But the fell really is the top wall of Langdale and the more usual ascent from the valley is from Stool End via a spur of rock known as the Band, and by Three Tarns (actually there are five). Its cone is one of the most frequent features of the fell landscape from many angles. It is the huge pyramid above Eskdale, and on the approach by Langstrath from Borrowdale it is impressively dominant. It is a profile of a mountain drawn by a child. Below the summit are the rock-climbing areas of Flat Crag, Cambridge Crag and the Slab. The summit is a mass of shattered rock, very rugged, with some places unstable underfoot, and the whole of the eastern and northern faces are extremely craggy. The summit view on a clear day – what can one say? – is stupendous, stretching to the Pennines as well as most of the main peaks. To dispel a myth – many guidebooks warn walkers that iron in the mountain deflects compass needles. It is nonsense – true only in one or two places if the compass is laid on the ground.

A path south from Three Tarns runs along one of the finest wild ridge walks in Cumbria. CRINKLE CRAGS is well named, for its skyline is indeed crinkly – serrated. This is the top end, the highest crinkle being at the south end (859 m). It is easily within the ability of the ordinary fell walker, but it should not be attempted in mist, when it is easy to go wrong – it does not go in a straight line. The descent to Langdale (or ascent if done the other way) is by Red Tarn, and the clear path to (or from) Stool End.

We are mentioning here only the popular fells that can be reached from Great Langdale. LITTLE LANGDALE is approached by a narrow steep road almost opposite the Dungeon Ghyll Old Hotel. This passes Blea Tarn, a scene described in Wordsworth's 'Excursion': Book II – 'A liquid pool that glittered in the sun/ And one bare dwelling; one abode, no more!' The one abode was the lone farmhouse Bleatarn House, enlarged since the bard saw it. The classic views of Langdale Pikes – 'those lusty twins' – are from the tarn. There is not much to Little Langdale apart from a tarn, pub and some easy low-level walks. However, the River Brathay, which flows through the valley, makes a sudden descent at COLWITH FORCE (*COL-ith*) that can only be seen from the road to the valley from Elterwater.

Blea Tarn

West of Little Langdale the road follows the route taken by the Roman road over Wrynose Pass, past the THREE SHIRES STONE, where the boundaries of Lancashire, Westmorland and Cumberland once met. This road has very steep sections indeed, and it is so narrow that in most places two cars cannot pass each other. The rule is that descending traffic should drive into a passing place to give way to ascending; but because some don't follow the rule, chaos can prevail. Beyond Wrynose the problem is not over, because the next pass of Hardknott is similar if not worse.

TARN HOWS

From Hawkshead a road fringes Grizedale Forest and runs to Coniston. However, a road from it gives access to TARN HOWS (NT), a famous beauty spot on high ground accessible by car, and on footpaths from Hawkshead. Its picture has appeared on innumerable calendars, chocolate boxes, greetings cards and murals. Its beauty is not marred by its popularity. While not typical Lake District, being surrounded by alien conifers rather than Scots pines, the total effect of water and trees, against a background of mountains, is stunning (see p. 562).

Tarn Hows is the name of a farm below the tarn to the west. Until recent years the signs pointed to 'The Tarns', for there were once two tarns, later joined into one by a dam. The walk around the tarn is easy, and with good pushers, accessible by wheelchair. The best view of the central fells is up above the tarn on Tom Heights to the north-west. Walking to the beauty spot is recommended for car parking space is limited there, and in an area of outstanding landscape, Tarn Hows is the eminent classic.

CHAPTER TWENTY

Coniston to Wasdale

Mountains, crags and hills dominate the National Park's south-west quarter, and in between them, magnificent unspoilt river valleys, including the exquisite major ones, the Esk and the Duddon. Coniston lake is one of the Lakeland's four largest, superbly framed with the forest on its eastern side, and to the west the great sprawl of the Coniston Old Man range. Then over towards the sea is magnificent Wasdale, with England's highest mountain and its deepest lake. The view across the foot of Wast Water to the mountains is world-class. We begin at Coniston.

Coniston is soon reached from the road from Hawkshead, and also by the A693 from Ambleside. CONISTON village was formerly called 'Church Coniston' to distinguish it from the nearby 'Monk Coniston' at the far side of the lake head, which was owned by Furness Abbey. It has almost as dramatic a setting as the town of Keswick, but the wild and craggy summits characteristic of Borrowdale volcanic do not keep a respectful distance. The village sits on a floor of Silurian slates and shales looking across the expanse of Coniston Water to the heavily wooded, rounded Silurian hills of the eastern shores. Coniston's geology was the reason for its growth. Although minerals may have been mined here on Coniston Old Man since Roman times, Coniston really became a mining village from the eighteenth century and extracted great wealth from the fellsides. Later, quarrying become more important to the local economy.

A proposal for a railway line to the village from the Furness line at Broughton was received with enthusiasm by the Coniston Mining Company and the lady of the manor of Coniston, and the capital was duly raised. The line would carry ore and slate, which at the time was transported by barge down the lake and the River Crake, or by horse and cart to Ulverston canal. It was opened in 1859. The great John Ruskin, who lived across the lake at his home at Brantwood, was not a railway enthusiast and wrote:

> 'A Coniston peasant' who used to walk the twelve miles to Ulverstone would now walk three miles in a contrary direction to the railway station, and travel twenty-four miles by train. Not only did this make him `idle, dusty, stupid; and either more hot or more cold than is pleasant to him', but cost two shillings plus the price of beer consumed, so that he arrives at Ulverstone, jaded, half drunk, and otherwise demoralised, and three shilling, at least, poorer than in the morning.

The great man did use the railway line, however. It later became an important tourist link, and the picturesque line from Broughton-in-Furness was included in the Furness Railway excursion tours. But the railway with its spectacular fellside station, with some of the finest views of any, was axed by Beeching in the 1960s and the tracks removed. It is a matter of regret that the then National Park Planning Board did not take up the offer for the acquisition of the land. It would have made a superb public bridleway.

Since the loss of the railway the popularity of Coniston as a holiday destination has declined in comparison with others, even though it has much going for it. No one could call the village picturesque, but it is a friendly place and an excellent base for exploration. Coniston Hall (NT) is the oldest building there and is by the lake shore south of the village. 'Hall' conjures up something grand, but it is not so. Many of the old farmhouses, remnants of days when their owners were independent property-owning 'statesmen', are called halls. This, though, was the home of the Le Flemings, the largest landowners in the sixteenth century, eventually becoming wealthy enough from the mines to move to a grander house in Rydal. With its tall round chimneys, typical of the time, Coniston Hall looks rather like a steamer ready to launch itself into the lake. It is cruck-framed formed over large, naturally curved, sections of tree trunks joined together at the top to form an arch. It also has some unusual architectural features for its age, notably the large windows.

The church of Church Coniston dates from Elizabethan times, and the grave of John Ruskin is in its churchyard. Ruskin lived at Brantwood on the east side of Coniston Water for twenty-nine years, and died in 1900. During his quarter of residence he was the object of local awe and respect that has lasted to today. A monument of local stone, cut from a quarry at Tilberthaite, marks his grave. It was designed by local artist and aid to Ruskin, W. Collingwood, and consists of a large decorated Anglo-Saxon cruciform design.

The idea of a museum was encouraged by Ruskin, who in 1884 donated 124 mineral specimens. After Ruskin's death in 1900, Collingwood encouraged supporters and admirers of Ruskin to contribute to the building of a special museum. Work started at once and the Ruskin Museum was opened in 1901. It has seen changes since, and the present museum was opened in 2000. A Ruskin gallery contains some of his brilliant architectural studies, along with pictures, letters, manuscripts, meticulous notebooks and photographs. Examples of the small-scale rural industries that he encouraged include wood-carving and lace-making. Ruskin was a keen geologist, so the region's rocks are explained, and there are minerals on display. Fascinating items on the Coniston mines, quarrying and farming can also be found.

A second notable visitor to the area was, of course, Donald Campbell, who was killed on Coniston Water in 1967 while attempting to take the world speed record on water. The lake has less traffic than Windermere and for this reason has been used on several occasions for world speed attempts. Campbell was killed when his boat somersaulted at an estimated speed of 515 km.p.h. Campbell's body was not found and recovered until 2001 as his boat *Bluebird* sank to great depths. His memorial is in the form of a slate seat on a green in the village centre. He is buried in the village's cemetery, near to a wall on the far left after one enters through the lychgate. The Ruskin museum has a display of photographs of Campbell and his team, and there is a slide presentation. Mercifully this is in a room separate from Ruskin's; previously they were cheek by jowl. The old philosopher would have been horrified to be associated with a noisy world speed attempt on his beloved lake. It is hoped to build a separate Donald Campbell wing.

CONISTON WATER is a superb lake. It was once a main highway and remains a highway in law. Like Windermere the lake lies above Silurian slates, but its west

Coniston Water, lake head

Coniston Water, lake foot

side encroaches upon the Borrowdale volcanic of the Old Man range. The drama, then, is on the west side, while the east is rounded and heavily forested (Grizedale). The lake drops to 56 m at its deepest point, and is approximately 8.5 km long and 804 m wide. Its three small islands include Peel Island (NT) and, in the southern reaches, Wild Cat Island, mentioned in the popular children's book *Swallows and Amazons*. The lake is fed from several sources at the lake head, but the main flow is from the Coniston Old Man range.

One can reach the lake shore by foot at several points on the east side, but the main access is at the head, at 'Monk Coniston'; and along the west side south of the village, a splendid footpath runs 4 km along the wooded shoreline of Torver Back Common. The road on the west side is some distance from the lake to Torver village, then a road left takes one close to the lake for 1 km to a car park and picnic area at Old Brown How. On the east side of the lake the minor road is very narrow and needs to be taken carefully. The Forestry Commission and the National Trust mainly own the land, and both have provided parking areas. The boat services on the lake follows a timetable. One of them stops at the pier of Brantwood, the most important feature of this side of the lake.

Brantwood, John Ruskin's home, overlooks the lake from the east side. The house receives visitors from all over the world, such has been the impact of his philosophy and his love of art. He lived here for the last twenty-nine years of his life. The house was a century old when Ruskin bought it in 1871 for £1,500, but his extensions and modifications transformed the original. At the height of his fame, as artist, author, critic, and first Slade professor of fine art at Oxford, Brantwood was his much loved retreat, and he became an ardent advocate of the preservation of the Lake District. The house contains many of his drawings, paintings and personal possessions, and is open to the public. His philosophy inspired many: socialism owes much to his writings, and his humanity and advocacy of non-violence made a lasting impression on such political activists as Mahatma Gandhi.

When the railway reached Coniston it became one of the three most visited lakes and the Furness Railway Company saw the potential of operating a passenger steamer service. There was already a privately owned pleasure steamer,

Coniston Water and Coniston Old Man from Brantwood shore

Queen of the Lake, operating from 1855, but it was sold before the railway company invested in a new 42-ton steamer, *Gondola*, launched in 1860. It is said to have been designed by James Ramsden, the Barrow engineer-industrialist, but it was built at Liverpool at a cost of £1,200. The *Illustrated London News* reckoned it to be 'the most elegant little steam vessel yet designed'. So it was, from her distinctive bow, carrying the figurehead of a gilded serpent, to her clipper stern, with a luxuriously appointed cabin, and a capacity of 200 passengers. Its engine gave a beautifully smooth and quiet run. Her highest recorded success was in 1897 when she carried 22,445 passengers.

In 1908 the company planned to replace her with another twin-screw steamer, *Lady of the Lake*, built as Southampton. She was two-decked and capable of carrying 400 passengers, and had a spacious cabin. But the *Gondola* stayed in service and both boats ran on the lake until 1939. After the war the *Gondola* was sold as a houseboat, and the *Lady of the Lake* was scrapped.

The *Gondola* had run on the lake for nearly eighty years, with only a four-year break during the First World War. Then after the Second World War it lay neglected and swamped at Nibthwaite, at the south end of the lake, only to be rescued and wonderfully restored by the National Trust, with much work from the Barrow Vickers shipyard, and once again it plies for trade. To sail on her is a rare experience.

The steamboat 'Gondola'

Human settlements have clustered in the land around Coniston Water since the Bronze Age, and there was considerable Norse settlement. The lake was once called Thurston's Mere, Thurston being a local lord. After the Norman Conquest the whole of the land at the lake head, and the whole of the land to the east to the shore of Windermere, was owned by Furness Abbey, and they exploited the minerals and the extensive woodlands.

One of the most important industries of southern Lakeland, and particularly round the lower reaches of Windermere and Coniston Water, was the production of charcoal. This made huge demands on the woodlands. The charcoal was vital to the smelting of metals and it was sometimes more economical to bring the ore to the charcoal-producing woodlands. In the Middle Ages iron ore from the mines in Furness would be brought up the lake and smelted in small 'bloomeries'. Traces of these sites can be found in many places on the lake shore, where masses of clinker are mixed with the lakeshore pebbles. It is not known how long these bloomeries were in action, but they were certainly active between the fourteenth and seventeenth centuries, and there are doubtless more ancient ones. At times the forests of the southern Lakes were clear-felled to produce charcoal, and have recovered remarkably since. But there is no completely natural forest left; the hardwoods on the lakeshores have, for the most part, been planted from the nineteenth century onwards. The huge block of alien conifers on the eastern side of the lake is part of the Forestry Commission's Grizedale Forest, but quite a proportion of the oak woodlands are also in its care.

Coniston Water holds char, trout, pike and perch. Boating activity is concentrated at the lake head, where the yacht club has their base at Coniston Hall, and boat hire is available from the village landings (NPA). There is a 10 m.p.h. speed limit on the lake.

THE OLD MAN

High above the village is the Coniston Old Man range, the southernmost of the central fells of the Lake District, a huge sprawl of high humps and peaks of Borrowdale volcanic rock between Coniston Water and Dunnerdale. It can be seen from many distant viewpoints. Wetherlam (763 m), at the range's north-eastern end, dominates the western view from Windermere, but the highest point is the Old Man itself (or himself?) at 803 m. Old Man? 'Man' in Cumbria is a stone cairn, and no doubt the cairn on the summit is old. However, the range has been extensively mined. For some reason, in times past a miner who spent most of his

Coniston Old Man summit, winter

time underground was an 'old man'. A Coniston miner would thus be an 'old man of Coniston'. Confusing.

The mountain is well used by fell walkers, and the summit of Old Man is easily achieved from a variety of routes. The view from the highest point is extensive: southwards and westwards across Morecambe Bay and the Duddon Sands, and out to the Isle of Man. All the main summits of the Lakeland fells are also in view. Five tarns sit among the hollows of the mountain. Above Coniston village Levers Water, once enlarged by a dam to serve the mines, now provides water for many of the villages of south Lakeland. Above old quarries on the most popular route to the summit is Low Water, which very often appears as a brilliant blue when viewed from above, and photographers who capture it on film are accused of using filters. Goats Water sits under the impressive 180 m cliffs of Dow Crag (*doe*) (779 m) at the range's south-western arm, and holds char and trout. The soaring face of Dow Crag has always been one of the great rock-climbing crags of Lakeland, and indeed the sport was pioneered there. On the southern shoulder of Dow is Blind Tarn ('Blind' to rhyme with 'tinned'), a small tarn without a visible flow exit. On the fell's western flank Seathwaite Tarn has been enlarged as a reservoir for the Furness area.

Other summits on the range include Swirl How (802 m), Great Carrs (785 m) and Grey Friar (773 m). From Coniston village, Walna Scar, an ancient road, now a rough track, skirts the southern flank of the fell to Seathwaite in Dunnerdale. It passes the remains of a prehistoric settlement.

The range has been mined since Roman times, although that is not apparent from a distance. But (to quote an old ex-miner) 'the mountain is so full of holes it's like a maggoty old cheese'. Holes can be found all over the fells, and the most dangerous have been fenced. The main workings were above the village at the head of Church Beck in Coppermines Valley, higher up in Red Dell; and at Tilberthwaite on the east side of Wetherlam. All the mines were very profitable in their time and employed hundreds of workers. In the sixteenth century German miners, who had settled in Keswick, were employed here. The ore was carried laboriously by packhorses to the Keswick smelters. A report of the number of mines on the Old Man in 1684 listed nine mines, and went on:

> When the Ore which was gotten at Coniston came to be smelted at Keswick, they found it so much to exceed the Copper Ore of either Caudbeck or Newlands, that they let fall the Works of both these places, and sent the Workmen from thence to Coniston-fells, and little or none of the other Ore was made use of: So that there was above Sevenscore Workmen kept constantly at the Works in Coniston-fells. The Ore which they got there did sufficiently furnish and supply the Smelt-houses at Keswick.

At one time 600 workers were employed at the mines, which no doubt included women and children working at the surface. The mines in Coppermines Valley were more efficiently exploited in the early twentieth century and were profitable until the end of the First World War. Some of the mines are being explored by skilled researchers, so it is important to note that stones should not be thrown down holes – there may be someone down there!

As mining declined slate quarrying developed to compensate. Bursting Stone quarry below the Old Man is one of the county's largest. Like the other Lakeland quarries in the volcanics, the slate is very hard, grey or grey-green, and takes a high polish; it is widely exported for decorative facing on modern buildings world-wide.

The range is very popular because it is so rich with interesting features for the climber, walker, geologist, mineralogist, archaeologist, naturalist and industrial archaeologist.

THE CONISTON AREA

At the southern stretch of Coniston Water, beyond Torver on its west side, is an area of low fell land popular with walkers: Blawith Common and Torver High Common (NPA). There is a fine walk to Beacon Tarn and onto the Beacon itself (225 m).

From a bend in the road to Ambleside before High Yewdale, a side road runs up the valley of Tilberthwaite. Near the head of the valley a car park can be found on old quarry waste, and a steep path leads to another of those early tourist attractions – a waterfall in Tilberthwaite Gill (NPA). In those early days, several bridges were built, the better for viewers to get a close look at the falls, but during the last war the ravine was used as a military training area and the bridges were destroyed. Now one new bridge serves, and a full view is not quite revealed.

Further along the road to Ambleside one can see an old farmhouse on the left with a surviving 'spinning gallery', a place where domestic tasks could be done in a better light than indoors. Then a little further is Yew Tree Tarn (NT), which is kept stocked with trout by the Coniston Anglers' Association. From here a path leads up the woods on the right to the beauty spot of Tarn Hows (see p. 552).

On the opposite shore of Coniston Water from the village, in 'Monk Coniston', is Tent Lodge. The house stands on the site where Elizabeth Smith lived in a tent at the end of her days suffering from tuberculosis. She was one of Cumbria's intellectuals in the eighteenth century and well known to Wordsworth and his circle. She was a brilliant linguist, and could speak and read Italian, French, German and Spanish, and had some knowledge of Arabic, Persian, Latin and Greek. She translated works from German and translated the book of Job from Hebrew. She also wrote poetry. She died at the age of twenty-nine in 1806 and was buried at Hawkshead. There is a memorial tablet in the church.

Tarn Hows

Tent Lodge was later let as a holiday home and Tennyson and his new wife stayed here on their honeymoon in 1850, and their visitors included Thomas Carlyle, Matthew Arnold and Edward Lear. They stayed again in 1857 and their guests included Charles Dodgson – before he became Lewis Carroll, author of the Alice books.

Moving south from Coniston one reaches the hamlet of TORVER (once 'Torvergh'), with footpaths leading onto the Old Man and Dow Crag, and the lake shore. It once had a corn mill and fulling mill in one. It had a station and when the railway came to it in 1859, a goods yard where quarry stone was loaded and a group of railway cottages. The nineteenth-century church replaces an old chapel. There are many signs of Neolithic/Bronze Age settlements on the fells above.

One road from Torver runs to Broughton-in-Furness, and the other branch makes for the lake shore in its southern reaches. There is public access at Old Brown How (NPA). Water Yeat (Yeat = gate) is south of the lake, and once had a corn mill and a smithy. It is part of BLAWITH (*blaith*) further south, which is little more than a few houses. A chapel stood here in Elizabethan times, and it is now a ruin. A church, built in 1883, is now closed, as is the old school, now a residence.

Across the River Crake that flows out of Coniston Water a water-powered iron furnace was built in 1735 at NIBTHWAITE. It is hard to believe that in this quiet spot cannons were being manufactured in its casting house in 1745. Its products were barged to Greenodd for shipping from a quay in the river. A century later the works had been converted into a bobbin mill, which was built on top of the old building after its stack was removed. Another building, which stored the charcoal, has been converted into a residence.

Below Nibthwaite the river flows through Lowick bridge at LOWICK. A corn mill was working near the bridge from as far back as 1250. The village school is threatened with closure (as of 2003) and the community is fighting strongly to keep it. The nineteenth-century church, on a very attractive site, replaces a chapel built in Elizabethan times. Lowick Green to the south was a rural industrial site that included two tanneries, a swill (basket) maker's, a smithy and a spade and shovel forge. However, the village can boast the most unusual cottage industry that lasted into the twentieth century – the making of whale-bone corsets.

Downriver still, before it leaves the National Park at Greenodd, is SPARK BRIDGE. Here again there was an iron furnace in production from 1715 to 1848, after which it was demolished, and like its neighbour upriver, rebuilt as a bobbin mill. The mill continued to work until 1983, latterly producing other turned products. Upriver a little way there was a cotton mill until 1867, which started life as a woollen mill.

Downriver, fringing the National Park boundary, is PENNY BRIDGE, named after the Penny family, which was responsible for building another iron furnace in 1748 that was in production until 1780.

BROUGHTON-IN-FURNESS

A road from Torver also connects the valley to the foot of the next one at Broughton. The railway line once followed the same course. A narrow road follows it in parallel after a steep ascent, and above it is a quarry, and a forest. This runs down to the hamlet of Broughton Mills around the River Lickle. Mills here ground corn, and later produced bobbins. A mill also processed wool that was woven in cottages in 'Shuttle Street'. Here, also, on the edge of limestone, there were lime kilns. Coppice woodlands were also productive. The Blacksmith's Arms is a pub that has resisted changes since the eighteenth century. Its oak beams are genuine, and the open fire welcomes walkers who have had a wetting on the fells; but it is loved by 'locals' from a wide area.

Broughton-in-Furness (*BRAW-ton*) was mentioned in the Domesday Book, and was once a market town of importance until it lost out to Ulverston when that town was linked to the sea by canal and became a port. It is another Cumbrian gem – a great little town with a unique character, with its old houses gathered round a market square under trees facing a market hall. A plaque here records that the square was given by John Gilpin and was designed in 1766 by 'a London architect' – no less this when London was considered almost a foreign country.

Broughton-in-Furness square

The town hall clock dates from then too, and still hammers out the hours. An obelisk in the square commemorates the Golden Jubilee of George III. The stone slabs of market stalls are still there. Broughton is still a place to stop at and shop; it is quite unspoilt, and is a small friendly community with rare old traditions of hospitality. Discerning tourists who prefer to be away from the crowded central towns and villages use it as a base. The town hall serves as an information centre.

The church of St Mary Magdalene is Norman, but much altered and added to over the centuries. It boasts a ring of ten bells, unusual for such a small community. In its heyday the town was busy and self-sufficient. It was once the centre for the manufacture of the very durable 'swill' baskets, made from strips of boiled oak, that were used extensively in mills, mines and ports throughout the country. Many Cumbrian farms still use them. But among the streets and yards there were tanners, saddlers, shoemakers, blacksmiths, hatters and dressmakers. There is still a livestock market.

Nearby Broughton Tower, not open to the public, was, from the Norman Conquest, the seat of the Broughton family, and is built around a defensive tower. Sir Thomas Broughton lost the estate when he unwisely allied himself to the cause of Lambert Simnel, claimant of the crown of England, who landed from Ireland into Furness in 1487 with 2,000 mercenaries. After Simnel's defeat at Newark, Henry VII had Sir Thomas's possessions seized and Broughton Tower was given to the Stanleys, who later sold it to the Sawreys.

The market charter was granted by Elizabeth I, with permission to hold a fair on 1 August. Each year the ceremony of reading the charter is carried out at noon at the obelisk, preceded by a procession. New pennies are thrown out to the children and the local burghers refresh themselves at the expense of the lord of the manor (now Cumbria County Council).

THE VALLEY OF THE DUDDON

The old railway line to Coniston came through Broughton, linked to the line from Barrow to Millom and the west coast at Foxfield, 2 km south of the town. This latter line is still running, but the link has been lost. Foxfield is on the edge of the Duddon Sands, across which roams the River Duddon.

Several tracks available at low tide cross Duddon Sands, but are dangerous without a guide. Cockles from the Duddon Sands were once said to be the finest to be gathered, and were available in large quantities. Salmon were also caught and salted down by local people. It is now a lonely sea-swept stretch of mud and sand with the distant signs of Millom's old industry at the end. It is a place for birdwatchers. In the autumn greylags stop off here, but this is mainly a place for ducks and several thousand waders, as well as mallard, teal, widgeon, shelduck and pintails.

The wonderful DUNNERDALE – the valley of the River Duddon, so loved by Wordsworth – is best seen moving from the mouth to near the source. West of Broughton-in-Furness the road climbs over High Cross, over the crossroads and down to Duddon Bridge. The banks of the river are a wonderful sight in spring – covered in wild daffodils. Cross the bridge, turn right up the road immediately afterwards, and here in the woods to the left was an eighteenth-century blast furnace. The choice of this rather remote site might seem odd, but the materials were all to hand: woodlands vital to supply the large amounts of charcoal needed; water power for the bellows; iron ore brought by boat from various mines in the area; and even limestone from the band of Coniston limestone in the area, or from Furness over Duddon Sands. The furnace site is in an unusually excellent state of preservation and can be entered, as it is owned by the National Park Authority. Anyone interested

Duddon furnace, eighteenth and early nineteenth century

In Dunnerdale

in industrial archaeology would be fascinated by a visit, the whole process being explained on information panels. One notable feature, apart from the exceptional building skills shown in the furnace, is the large size of the charcoal storage buildings – huge amounts were needed to feed the blast furnace. One wall has been turned into glass by the heat where charcoal has been accidentally ignited.

Turning back over the bridge and turning left up the minor road, after a steep climb, one sees Duddon Hall across the other side of the river. The Georgian hall is not open to the public. The hall replaces a building known as Wha House, or Whoyes, that was in possession of the Cowper family, whose presence in the area was recorded as early as the thirteenth century. A Cowper of the eighteenth century, by which time the family were known as Cooper, became famous. Myles Cooper was born in 1736, educated at Carlisle and Oxford, and later became president of Columbia University. In that role he expanded the college, inaugurated the medical school and promoted New York Hospital. George Washington met Dr Cooper several times, corresponded with him, and invited him to Mount Vernon. Duddon Hall has changed hands several times, and is now divided into flats. It is said to be haunted.

Two km on, a ruin might be seen on a hilltop across the river. This is Frith Hall, once a hunting lodge of the Huddleston family in the seventeenth century, and later an inn catering largely for travellers on the pack-pony trail that passed this way. There are stories of dark doings. Smugglers used it. Marriages of the Gretna Green type were performed here. Then there were stories of murder. Later, more prosaically, it became a farm. To the north-east are the Dunnerdale fells, which are largely unvisited, being fairly low-level, but they reward the explorer.

The road reaches the river at last, and crosses it. Down the road on the left there was a mill and a forge, and it is another very narrow and winding road to Duddon Bridge. But immediately on the right is ULPHA, an interesting Norse name. Two theories attempt to explain its meaning: one suggests that it was the 'hay' or park of local lord Ulf; the other that it means 'wolf hill', from the Norse *ulf-hauga*. The hamlet contains a row of almshouses, a pub and a school with a good reputation but an unfortunate design. The small St John's church is of no great antiquity but built four-square on high ground in a delectable setting. Its interior walls have interesting wall paintings. From Ulpha, the house near the foot of a steep road on the left was once the Traveller's Rest inn. Wordsworth and Coleridge stayed there in 1802 and Coleridge noted 'The public house at Ulpha a very nice one, & the landlord, a very intelligent man.' In fact he was well educated, like many who were, and still are, content to sacrifice ambition to settle in the Lakes; and there is a story that a group of arrogant students, refreshing themselves at the inn, wrote a note in Latin to the landlord asking for the bill. They got one – written in Greek.

The road crosses the river at Hall Dunnerdale. A road on the right here goes over the fell to Broughton Mills. It is narrow and hardly used, but up it on the left is a drystone wall to make one wonder at the strength of the man who lifted and fitted these enormous stones into place. Going on up the Duddon, above the river's north bank is the cliff of Wallowbarrow Crag, a rock-climbing area.

Soon one arrives at the tiny hamlet of Seathwaite. Its pub, the Newfield Inn, is famous for its 'shepherds' meets', and its small chapel once had one of the Lake District's most famous parsons. The original chapel, in spite of John Ruskin's protests, fell prey to those terrible vandals, the nineteenth-century 'improvers', in this case H.W. Schneider of Barrow fame, but it is still fairly primitive. Schneider would have approved of Wonderful Walker, the parson made famous by Wordsworth's reference in 'The Excursion'. He was the sort of hard-working character much loved by the Victorians. Born in the dale in 1709, the twelfth son of Nicholas Walker, he was considered too unfit to be a farmer, and was encouraged to study instead. After studying at Ulpha down the dale, he became a teacher at Gosforth, and later at Buttermere. He then took holy orders, went back to his birthplace and was appointed to the living of Seathwaite with a stipend of five pounds per annum; he was then twenty-seven and married. He remained curate in charge of this little chapel for no less than sixty-six years and died at the age of ninety-two, in the same year as his wife. Although he was poor, he was the soul of thrift and even had enough put by for charitable work in the valley. He worked every day in the fields as a farm labourer, spun his own wool and his wife made their clothes. He taught the local children in his church for eight hours every day, wrote letters for his illiterate parishioners and ministered to the sick. The couple raised and educated a family, and when 'Wonderful Walker' died he left in his will the tidy sum of £2,000. Seathwaite is a good base for a walk along the river. Opposite the church is a very graceful packhorse bridge.

The road then follows Tarn Beck, which flows from Seathwaite Tarn, way over to the north-west in the western arms of the Coniston Old Man range. The tarn is a reservoir serving the Furness area, an enlargement of a natural tarn and not in the least artificial in appearance, but wild and remote. Footpaths lead to it, but a walk around it is not recommended. The road crosses Tarn Beck, and just beyond this crossing, the ancient road of Walna Scar comes over from Coniston after contouring round the flanks of the Old Man.

Continuing up the Duddon, we see Dunnerdale Forest rising on the far side. When this land was acquired for planting in 1935 the Forestry Commission met

The Duddon

some very heated opposition from a long list of lords, bishops and leading academics. Some 13,000 people signed a petition. One arrogant reply stated: 'there are always a certain number of people who prefer that a land should produce nothing rather than trees'. It had been raising sheep for centuries. The planting still went ahead, but at least it led to a compromise – the commission agreed that there should be no further planting in the heart of the Lake District; but this was only a 'gentlemen's agreement', and there have been a few rumours of new proposals since. But surely now all is safe. Public access is allowed, even encouraged, in the forest, and routes can be taken up to the intriguingly knobbly summit of Harter Fell (649 m) (not to be confused with a fell of the same name in the eastern fells). A walk down from the car park and bridge is recommended, in order to view Birks Bridge. The stone footbridge itself is handsome but the gorge below, carved into smooth shapes by pounding and grinding pebbles, and swept by blue or blue-green water, is stunning. Many try to photograph it, but none can do it justice. This is Wordsworth's 'Faery Chasm' in his Duddon Sonnet XI.

Further now and the road meets the Wrynose – Hardknott road from Little Langdale into Eskdale. This is Cockley Beck and one of the most remote of the Lakeland farms. The Roman road across the passes did not follow the modern road at this point. It came straight, south-west to Black Hall farm, before turning right towards Hardknott's summit.

One can enjoy the whole valley again in the other direction, with a close encounter with the river on foot. It is music to the ear and the eye. Wordsworth praised the valley in his sonnets, while imagining himself looking back:

> I thought of Thee, my partner and my guide,
> As being past away. Vain sympathies!
> For, backward, Duddon! as I cast my eyes,
> I see what was, and is, and will abide;
> Still glides the Stream, and shall for ever glide;
> The Form remains, the Function never dies;
> While we, the brave, the mighty, and the wise,
> We men, who in our morn of youth defied
> The elements, must vanish; be it so!
> Enough, if something from our hands have power
> To live, and act, and serve the future hour;
> And if, toward the silent tomb we go,
> Through love, through hope, and faith's transcendent dower,
> We feel that we are greater than we know.

WEST TO BLACK COMBE

Taking the Millom road from Duddon Bridge, one leaves a narrow road about 2km to the right. A footpath from it leads to SWINSIDE STONE CIRCLE. Well off the beaten tourist track, it is in some ways more impressive than the popular circle at Castlerigg near Keswick. The size is similar, but the more regular circle is tighter, with fifty-five stones. It is difficult to decide why the circle was sited on this spot; being hidden by the hills, it is far from prominent. The circle can be seen only from a public footpath, as it is in a private farm field. Permission from the nearby farm is needed for a closer approach.

Swinside stone circle

Back on the Millom road the huge bulk of BLACK COMBE (*coom*) (600 m) is on the right. Being separated from the Lake District's central fells by a large area of comparatively uninteresting moorland, it is neglected by walkers. Yet its views, westwards over the sea towards the Isle of Man and Ireland, and towards the hills of Scotland and Wales, are magnificent. In 1813 Wordsworth wrote a poem in its praise – 'View from the Top of Black Combe' – and in the same year he wrote a poem in slate pencil on the side of a stone up there, praise of Colonel Mudge, a distinguished surveyor whom he met on the fell.

Geologically, the fell belongs to the Skiddaw slate series and has a typical round and heavy structure of friable shale. It makes for easy walking if generally lacking in excitement. The path from Whicham, at its south-west nose, is the most pleasant, with sea views.

To reach the next valley west – the equally inviting Eskdale – the steep road from Ulpha must be taken across the wild Birker moor. In a lay-by a high point of about 28 m offers a fine view way over to the Scafells. A little further on the road is crossed by a track, and following it left – on foot – takes one to DEVOKE WATER. When is a lake not a lake, but a tarn? Devoke Water is as large as Rydal Water, or Elterwater, so why is it not included among the sixteen lakes? A walk to Devoke Water will furnish the answer. Its setting is austere – in wild, high-level, windswept moorland – and the visual contrast between this and Rydal Water is extreme. Dr T.T. Macan of the Freshwater Biological Association has suggested that a tarn can be biologically distinguished from a lake by its emergent vegetation. In a lake, to take one example, the characteristic plant is the common reed, whereas in tarns the common emergent plant is bottle sedge (*Carex rostrata*). Evidence from peat samples indicates that Devoke Water was once a 'lake' in quite a different landscape, that is, when it was surrounded by forest. The clearance of the forest happened around 1000 BC at a time when the area was populated by Bronze Age settlements: very many burial cairns and hut circles of that age are scattered around the area. A decline was probably accelerated by a change in climate, and the land became heather moorland.

Devoke Water, beautiful in a rough and ready way, is 14 m deep. It is too bleak for some, but ideal for those who have a monkish wish to abandon the world. It holds trout and Millom and District Anglers control the fishing.

ESKDALE AND THE ROMAN FORT

ESKDALE (dialect: *ESH-d'l*), with its head amongst England's highest land, and its foot in the sea, is one of the most interesting and beautiful dales in Cumbria. Esk Hause (759 m), at the dale top, is the highest pass (by footpath only) in the Lake District. It is one of the 'crossroads' of the fells and is well trodden by walkers on the way to the Scafells, Langdale, Borrowdale and Wasdale. It is notoriously easy to lose one's way there in thick mist.

The path from the hause falls steeply and roughly, along with the beginnings of the River Esk, to Great Moss. There is nothing like this place anywhere else in Cumbria. This dale head is awesome and dwarfing, and the most remote. It is a wet, high and wild valley, walled by a complete horseshoe of high fells. On one side are the great eastern crags of the Scafells; at the head is the Hause and Esk Pike (885 m); and Bow Fell (902 m) and Crinkle Crags lie to the east. The floor is littered by detached rock fragments, some of them huge, and a group is aptly named Samson's Stones. A beck from the summit of the Scafells above pours to the floor down a steep wall. This is Cam Spout, and it is hard to believe that the intrepid Coleridge made his lone descent alongside it in August 1802 during an expedition to Scafell.

Descending lower down, the valley is crossed by a dyke – now frequently used as a footpath above boggy ground. This is what remains of a substantial wall put there by the monks of Furness Abbey, under licence from the Lord of Millom, to enclose an extensive grazing area for sheep, and possibly cattle. The monks were required to keep the wall low enough to allow deer and fawns to cross it. Deer have long left this wet desert, once a well-wooded area. All upper Eskdale was once managed by Furness Abbey.

Following the growing river the dale drops down a step to a lower valley, the water falling steeply and beautifully at Throstle Garth; and it is then joined by Lingcove Beck, which had its source under Bowfell. The contours soften and one descends to another green floor under the eye of Hardknott Roman fort. Just by the farm of Brotherilkeld (a farm once owned by the brothers of Furness Abbey) the track joins the road from Hard Knott Pass, and it is only from here, and down the valley via a public road, that Eskdale is known to the greater number of tourists, though it is little more than half its total length of 21 km.

Hardknott Roman fort is up the road to the left. Hard Knott itself is a crag-peaked fell. Hard Knott Pass lies above and roughly follows the Roman road from Ambleside Roman fort, through Little Langdale and over Wrynose Pass. Wrynose and Hard Knott are two of the most awkward roads in England, HARD KNOTT PASS being the more severe. The narrow road has hairpin bends and gradients of up to one in three. Although the surface has been improved (to the regret of some) the road is still testing to vehicles and drivers: despite this, or perhaps because of this, the road is sometimes heavily used, particularly at weekends. As there are stretches, on both passes, where it is impossible for two vehicles to pass each other, jams are frequent and can last for hours. The unwritten rule is that descending vehicles should give way to ascending but not all drivers conform. At times a pervading smell of burning clutches and brake linings fills the air. Unprecedented handbrake starts on one-in-threes are too much for some, and being forced to stop can cause chaos. In such conditions on these passes holding a heavy motorcycle can be disastrous.

The substantial remains of HARDKNOTT ROMAN FORT are passed by motorists keen only on negotiating the pass, and many, if not most, are blissfully unaware of its existence. The fort has been thought to be 'Mediobogdum' but the title is

The remains of Hardknott Roman fort high above Eskdale

now seriously open to question. Dramatically sited on a high shelf overlooking Eskdale, with the highest fells in England to the west, this is one of the most exciting of Britain's Roman fort sites. Standing in the fort's centre one is surrounded by high fells. It was built to command the road from Ambleside to the fort and port at Ravenglass. Traces of the road can be seen zigzagging over both passes. At one point it is even cut through solid rock. Although at the time of building, the fort was probably surrounded by tree-covered land, the occupying garrisons must still have felt a sense of wild desolation. No outside village nestled close to the fort. With typical Roman thoroughness – or maybe to occupy the troops to prevent boredom – a level parade-ground of over 3 ha was cut into the fellside. Considering the nature of the rocky and boggy terrain this must have been quite a feat. A tribunal, or review platform, approached by a ramp, was built into the north side. It is thought that the fort was occupied by a *cohors quingenaria equitata*, a mixed unit of foot and horse. The ground must have been prepared for the use of drilling cavalry as well as infantry, for to prevent injury to horses when practising speedy manoeuvres it was crucial that the ground was level.

An inscription on good Lakeland slate, which must have been carried from Langdale, confirms that the fort was built at the time of Hadrian. Translated it reads: '... for the Emperor Caesar Trajan Hadrian Augustus, son of the divine

Trajan, conqueror of Parthia – by the fourth Cohort of Delmations.' The 'Delmations' or Dalmatians, came from the country east of the Adriatic Sea. This puts the building (or rebuilding or repairing?) at some time prior to AD 139. Pottery fragments have been found that suggest that the fort was not occupied later than the third century. Why not later than that, for the forts at Ravenglass and Ambleside were occupied for another hundred years? One theory is that the fort gradually dwindled to the status of staging-post, with only nominal caretaker personnel.

The walls, 1.5 m thick, still stand to some height in spite of the fact that the fort became a free 'quarry', its stones carted away for later building. They are backed by an embankment and form a square 114 m across. A tower stood at each corner.

Hardknott Roman fort granary foundations

The fort follows the regulation pattern of all forts, but is square; the main gate is on the south-east, and other gateways are in each wall, in spite of the fact that the one in the northern wall leads nowhere except to a cliff edge! Was this where they tipped their rubbish? The foundations of the headquarters building are in the centre; and to the side are the granaries, where 300 tons of grain would be stored – enough to feed the garrison's 500 men for two years. The men's quarters would have been built of wood. The bath house is below the fort to the south-east, and one can see that it was divided into three compartments: caldarium, the very hot; tepidarium, less hot; and frigidarium, freezing with a cold plunge bath. A separate round building was the laconicum, the hot dry room that would have been welcome on this site.

Hardknott Roman fort, view of the Scafells from the west gateway

Walkers continuing on down Eskdale need not worry about dodging traffic on the road, for delightful footpaths flank the river. The Roman road from Hardknott fort came this way, and traces of it can be found. The tourists' Eskdale, then, is much less dramatic than the head of the valley, but it is extremely beautiful. The drystone walls and the old buildings are made from the warm pink Eskdale granite. The fellsides, capped with rocks and broken by cliffs, are bright green in spring and russet brown in autumn. The River Esk, falling down steps of pink and grey stone, curls around the banks of broadleaved trees. The changing scene is idyllic.

After the well-known Woolpack Inn, one encounters the hamlet of BOOT. A walk past the pub leads to an old stone bridge over Whillan Beck and an old water mill with an 'overshot' wheel which the county council has restored. The loft above the mill had a tiled floor where grain was dried before grinding. In 2003, the council put it up for sale, hoping that a buyer would preserve it as a working mill and allow public access.

Several iron mines were cut into the granite of this area. Above Boot was the profitable Nab Gill mine, and across the other side of the river lay the South Cumberland mine. Traces now are difficult to see. Some waste from the mines has been used to surface paths and tracks, and the red of iron oxide and pieces of hematite can be picked up. The mines became uneconomic in the 1840s.

Just below the village of Boot is Dalegarth, a focal point for Eskdale's unique attraction: a narrow-gauge railway. This is the terminus for the 10 km run from Ravenglass (see pp. 135–7). The railway used to serve the Eskdale mines, and later the quarry, taking ore and rock to the mainline railway. This railway company is now the Ravenglass and Eskdale Railway, but everyone knows it as 'L'aal Ratty', and it runs a regular service for visitors and locals. The steam engines are scale models of railway engines of the past. The run, through fields and woodlands, is a happy experience.

A lane from Boot leads down to the river and the small hidden church of St Catherine. It would be hard to find another church with a more blissful situation, the murmuring of the river sounding like a congregation in perpetual prayer. There was a chapel here, maintained by Cistercians. The present church, while not old, fits perfectly into the scene. It is thought that St Catherine's became a parish church with a burial ground in the fifteenth century, but what we see is something from the Restoration period (late seventeenth century). Wasdale residents, without a burial ground, had to carry their dead 7 km from Wasdale Head chapel directly north of Boot, over the rough track of wild Burnmoor to be buried here. The walk between the two valleys, under the south face of Scafell and by Burnmoor Tarn, is a great adventure, in fine weather. The funeral party would need to pray for such. A sad story concerns a pony carrying the coffin of Thomas Porter; the animal took fright and vanished in the mist. One version of the tale has

'The Ratty', Ravenglass and Eskdale Railway

it that pony and body were never found. Among the headstones in the churchyard is one to Tommy Dobson, the huntsman who was as famous to Cumbrians as John Peel. The stone is skilfully carved with fox and hound.

Below Dalegarth a track goes riverwards from opposite the old school. This leads over the deep-pooled river on a stone bridge and past Dalegarth Hall, home of the Stanleys, not open to the public. The hall has the cylindrical chimneys common to old Cumbrian houses. A path beyond leads to STANLEY GILL (NPA), a ravine in a geological fault, through which a waterfall descends in three drops. The approach to the falls is by a granite path through the green ravine, overhung with trees and covered with mosses, ferns and liverworts. The gill in spate, falling and swirling through rock pools, is captivating. The lower falls are visible from a bridge, but to view the higher drop one needs to be well shod and have a head for heights; it is definitely not the place for small children or loose dogs.

The road forks at an inn below Dalegarth. The road on the right passes Ratty's Eskdale Green station. ESKDALE GREEN itself is nothing more than a few houses, and some old buildings. The Outward Bound has a school here. The railway loops to the far end of the village by Irton Road Station, just short of Bower House, a small country hotel. It then leaves Eskdale to run down the valley of the River Mite. To follow the Esk one must take the southward road east of Eskdale Green, turning right again before the kennels of the Eskdale foxhounds. This route leads down a narrow road, meandering as wildly as the river, to a junction with the A595. The road turns north to Muncaster Castle (see pp. 134–5), and the little that is left of Eskdale can then be followed by footpaths to Ravenglass. One good walk from Eskdale Green to Ravenglass follows the south side of Muncaster Fell on a bridleway. However, recommended is one very fine walk over the top of the tongue of Muncaster Fell (231 m), with views over the Esk and out to the Isle of Man on a clear day, as well as back to that glorious mass of fell at the head of Eskdale.

From Eskdale the road climbs over and down into the next valley of the River Irt at Santon Bridge. Down on the east side of the Irt by the roadside is Irton Hall, now converted to private homes. A footpath leaves this to cross the fields to St Paul's church. Alternatively one can take the ruler-straight road, and a track goes up to the church on the right. The church began life in King John's reign but was rebuilt and rededicated in 1857, and includes some fine stained glass by Burne-Jones. The view from the churchyard seizes the attention – looking grandly up to Wasdale Head – but it's the stone cross, over 3 m high, that is its great treasure. It is over 1,200 years old, and its vines, interlacing and rosettes suggests Irish-Celtic. Irish missionaries would have been reaching the north around this time. The Irt was once said to have freshwater mussels containing pearls. It has trout, and salmon in season, and angling permits are obtainable from the hotel at Holmrook at the end of the road.

MITERDALE

The valley next to Eskdale is MITERDALE. It is not surprising that tourists pass it by without knowing of its existence, for its access road from Eskdale is very narrow and peters out after a short distance. It is really a walkers' valley. The River Mite rises in a hollow below Burnmoor Tarn and disappears underground for a short length before making a descent through Eskdale Green to flow by the side of the Ravenglass and Eskdale railway.

Once the valley had an inn, but now there are only a couple of ruins, a few farm buildings and the story of a violent death, told so well by Dudley Hoys in *English Lake Country*. A farmer's wife at the lonely farm at Miterdale Head was alone while her husband had gone on an overnight journey to Whitehaven market. A strange-looking woman called by at twilight, saying she had been lost on the moor, and asked for shelter. It was readily given and the woman, overcome by the hot fire, fell asleep in a chair; her head dropped, her jaw sagged and the headscarf slipped off to reveal that this was not a woman but a man. Being sure that he was a robber in disguise to gain access, and having no hope of fleeing in the night with her small child, the farmer's wife, on impulse, took a ladle of scalding fat out of the fireside pan (from which she was making candles) and poured the stuff down the man's open mouth. When the farmer returned in the morning he found a distraught wife and a choked corpse. The farmer buried the body and did not tell the story until long after the family had left the farm. One theory is that the victim was an escaped convict.

One path leaves north-westwards through the plantations to Nether Wasdale, but more adventurously a path leaves this on the ridge of Whin Rigg for one of the district's most exciting walks – along the top of Wast Water Screes to Illgill Head (609 m), with fantastic airy views.

WASDALE

Most travellers first see WASDALE (*WAS-d'l*) from the road that leads into mid-dale from Gosforth, or they join the end of that road coming from Eskdale Green. The view comes suddenly, and is stark and startling: in front and below is a wide, dark, rock-girt lake and directly behind is a huge wall of loose crumbling rock, the famous 600 m-high Wast Water Screes, looking near vertical from this angle and about to fall bodily into the water. For some people the atmosphere is too austere, even strangely hostile; but at the same time it has an irresistible haunting quality.

Visitors sometimes have confused memories of the dales, but they never ever forget Wast Water and the Screes.

Yet if one were to approach the lake from the south by the public footpath around Low Wood, by the lake's outlet, a completely different impression would be gained. The foreground is framed by handsome trees, the Screes are seen edge-on, showing a lesser angle, and way across Wast Water, softened by distance, are the great banks of mountains, shoulder to shoulder: Yebarrow, Kirk Fell, Great Gable and Lingmell. If one captures that rare moment when the reflections are right, and if there is snow on the summits touched by the sun, probably no finer view exists in the world.

WAST WATER is the deepest lake in England. The Screes continue their angle of slope down to the lake bottom, a depth of about 80 m. And the Screes do occasionally slide into the water. In the spring, especially, rock avalanches sometimes occur continuing a process that has gone on since the last ice age. (The glacier, then thrusting down from the high fells, combined to scoop out the lake bed and undermine a fellside.)

The only village, really a scattered hamlet, is STRANDS, in Nether Wasdale, on the River Irt, west of the lake foot. It looks like a typical English village, with two pubs and a church, facing a green with a maypole erected in 1897 to celebrate Queen Victoria's sixtieth year of reign. The maypole is classed as a grade II listed

Wasdale Head in mild mood

Wastwater Screes

building! May celebrations still take place here on the first Saturday in May, with a brass band procession of children in fancy dress, and dancing. The typical dales' church is built like a barn and is full of atmosphere. There are texts on its ornate ceiling, and the carving of pulpit, panelling and lectern are seventeenth century and come from York Minster. The royal arms are those of George III.

The road from the village to the lake passes Wasdale Hall (NT), now a youth hostel. It was once reputed to be haunted by a previous owner's wife whose child was drowned in the lake in the 1820s. The ghostly figure has been seen, it is said, walking around the lake edge. Up-lake, beyond the Gosforth turning, two becks, Nether Beck and Over Beck, flow down waterfalls into the lake, but the falls have to be sought out by walking up the banks.

Much of the head of the dale is owned by the National Trust, and the trust has made a campsite within a tree screen, which has effectively done away with unsightly camping that used to be scattered along the lake shore. West of the site, by Lingmell Gill, is the commonly used way of ascent for Scafell Pikes or Scafell Crag. The narrow road beyond the lake finishes at WASDALE HEAD near the smallest church in Cumbria ('in the country', locals say), a tiny dales' church beloved by many. There is a memorial window to Queen Victoria and in one window is a little panel with the words, 'I will lift up mine eyes unto hills.' It is sometimes claimed that the church's rafters were made from ships' timbers. This

Wast Water and Wasdale Head

could be true: Cumbrians are thrifty, and pieces from a ship breaker's yard would not have come amiss. But the tradition that such rafters came from a Viking ship probably gained some credibility from the Viking habit of building roofs like ship's hulls, or even of using upturned boats. Appropriately the church is dedicated to Olaf, a Viking saint.

In the churchyard are buried some early climbers who died on the local mountains.

Nearby is the Wasdale Head Hotel, famous for its popularity with climbers since the birth of the sport. Names revered in early climbing history are honoured here. W.P. Haskett-Smith, Owen Gllynn Jones and the photographer brothers George and Ashley Abraham. In the last century it began life as the farmhouse home of Will Ritson, who sold liquor from here – illegally – and he was fined for it. He then got a licence and called the farm Huntsman Inn. It was said of Wasdale that it had the highest mountain, the deepest lake, the smallest church and the biggest liar in England. Will Ritson was the king of liars, famed for his tall stories. During a lie-telling competition at a local sports day he listened to many tall stories and when it came to his turn he asked to withdraw. He was asked why and replied, presumably with a straight face, 'Because I can't tell a lie'. He won the competition. He extended his inn in 1857, and after he retired it was taken by Dan Tyson who called it the Wastwater Victoria Hotel. Then it became known as the

Wastwater Hotel. Behind the hotel is a fine example of an arched packhorse bridge. Cross this and follow the left bank of Mosedale Beck, to reach the attractive Ritson Force; to get a good view of this waterfall some scrambling is required.

The old track up Mosedale to Black Sale Pass is on the other side of Mosedale Beck. This is the route to Ennerdale and is a fell walkers' route to Pillar. Beyond the church the track joins the Sty Head path, the route to Borrowdale. The present path is a recent one, made in the 1920s, the older one winding its way on the south side of Lingmell Beck. A plan to make a road highway over the Sty Head route mercifully never materialized. Great Gable towers over the head of the Sty Head track to its north; to the south are Lingmell and Scafell Pikes.

The little school at Wasdale Head is now, alas, disused. Nearby there was once a farm named Down-in-the-dale ('downydale'). This was demolished at the beginning of the Second World War, and the stone was used to build a pumping station at the foot of the lake; its function was to supply water to ammunition factories at Drigg and Windscale, and now supplies BNFL at Sellafield.

In its amphitheatre of great fells, Wasdale Head is a memorable stretch of landscape. The view down-lake provides a contrast in scenery accounted for by the change in geology: the high fells, including Illgill Head, the fell to which the Screes belong, are all of the Borrowdale volcanic, while the lake foot is mainly Eskdale granite. The granites, though very hard, break down in a different way to

Row Bridge, Wasdale Head

the other volcanic rocks and have yielded to the accumulated pressure of an ice age glacier. The dry-stone walls, built of material close to hand, make an interesting study. At Wasdale Head they are all rounded, river-bottom boulders, often of massive thickness. In the lower, Nether Wasdale area the walls are largely of granite blocks and shapeless granite boulders.

The high fells around Wasdale are popular, while the lower fells north-west of Wast Water (Copeland Forest) are hardly walked, but offer some reward to seekers of solitude. The fells include Yewbarrow (627 m), the great hump west of Wasdale Head, High Fell (615 m) and Seatallan (690 m). Among these fells are three tarns: behind High Fell, and the source of Nether Beck, is Scoat Tarn; further south, and feeding Over Beck is Low Tarn; in an eastern hollow of Seatallan Fell is Greendale Tarn, which is reached by a pleasant path alongside Greendale Gill.

Wast Water is a clear pure lake (oligotrophic) – so much so that it holds little natural food to support freshwater life. It does, though, contain char and brown trout.

THE SCAFELLS AND THE HIGHEST LAND IN ENGLAND

The route to the Scafells starts alongside Lingmell Gill and rock climbers turn off it to get to the great crags of Scafell. SCAFELL (*SCAW-f'l*) (964 m) is a completely separate mountain to its close neighbour north of it, Scafell Pike, which is superior in height by 13 m. But Scafell is a huge impressive monster – one of the greatest sights in the Lakes – with the north face of the mountain towering above the path. This is savage, near-vertical rock architecture, 300 m high, the Lake District's most awesome wall and the largest in England. The wrinkled and fissured face has challenged rock climbers since the pioneers of the sport claimed it at the beginning of last century. Some of them paid the price and are buried in Wasdale's churchyard. Even the better-equipped modern-day climbers treat the climbs with great respect. The great cliff is split by the three main chasms of Deep Gill, Steep Gill and Moss Gill. To their left is the Central Buttress. The whole rock face is covered with climbing routes, but the big challenge is Central Buttress – 143 m of exposed steep walls, and tricky traverses, followed by an ascent of 20 m, up an almost vertical groove: the flake crack, with a slight overhang at the top. It was first climbed in April 1914, after a number of unsuccessful attempts. The most difficult point – the crux – was achieved by the climb leader standing on the shoulders of his second who was hung in loops of rope below the overhang. The leader was Siegfried Herford

View from Scafell Pike towards Scafell, with the notorious Broad Stand seperating them

(killed afterwards in the war), with two other climbers, G.S. Sansom and C.F. Holland. It has been climbed almost every year since and does not get any easier.

The only direct route to the summit for walkers is by a diagonal east-to-west scree gully known as Lord's Rake, crossing the foot of Deep Gill. But this is a rough and undignified scramble; and falling stones are an ever-present danger. In 2003, after a rock fall, it became hazardous and warnings were given. It is a no-go for walkers when filled with snow and ice. By comparison there is an easier, longer route away from the crag via the slopes of the west side.

The mountain is separated from its neighbour, the Pike, by a short, steep ridge known as Mickledore. This has to be negotiated if a walker wants to take in both peaks directly, but it has a short but treacherous overhang, called Broad Stand, that has claimed many casualties. An ascent from the Pike to Scafell requires a blind grope for hand hold, a little faith, and some contortions. Going down from Scafell is worse, and walkers, in an attempt to bypass the hazard, can find themselves in even greater difficulties. Needless to say, the direct approach for walkers between the two mountains cannot be recommended. It is better to take the longer route on the south side by Foxes Tarn.

Of the several fine viewpoints on Scafell's heights, some require steel nerves. The best views from the actual summit are very long and mostly west to the sea, as the Pike obscures the eastern side.

One early ascent of Scafell was recorded by the poet S.T. Coleridge in August 1802. He climbed it from Wasdale Head via Broad Tongue to the south, an easy, relatively crag-free route until near the top, but a long slog. He wrote of the summit:

> O my God! What enormous mountains these are close by me ... But O! what a look down under my feet! The frightfullest Cove that might ever be seen. Huge perpendicular precipices ... two huge pillars of lead-coloured stone – I am no measurer but their height and depth is terrible.

The map he carried, by Hutchinson, was rudimentary to say the least. It suggested to him that Scafell Pike was Bowfell. However, he was determined to reach it and dropped down the dreaded Broad Stand! And then he dropped down rocky steps in the descent to Eskdale.

> [I] went on for a while with tolerable ease – but now I come ... to a smooth perpendicular rock about seven feet high – this was nothing ... I put my hands on the Ledge, and dropped down. In a few yards came just such another. I dropped that too, and yet another ... but the stretching of my hands and arms, and the jolt of the fall on my feet, put my whole limbs in a tremble.

He continued down yet more drops in the same way to two final ones:

> ... of these two the first was tremendous. It was twice my own height, and the ledge at the bottom was exceedingly narrow, that if I dropt down upon it I must of necessity have fallen backwards and of course killed myself. My limbs were all in a tremble. I lay upon my back to rest myself, & was beginning according to my custom to laugh at myself for a Madman, when the sight of the crags above me on each side, & the impetuous clouds just over them, posting so luridly and rapidly northward, overawed me. O God, I exclaimed aloud – how calm, how blessed I am now. I know not how to proceed, how to return, but I am calm and fearless and confident.

He then noticed a 'rent' in the rock. He got into it and 'slipped down as between two walls'.

SCAFELL PIKE (*SCAW-f'l*) is one of a number of 'pikes' on the Scafell range. At 978 m, one of them is England's highest point and this is popularly known as the Scafell Pike. An inscription on the summit cairn records that the peak was taken into the care of the National Trust as a memorial to those who died in the First

World War. The rest of the range, down to the 610 m contour, was presented to the trust by three donors, including the Fell and Rock Climbing Club in the 1920s.

After Helvellyn, Scafell Pike attracts more walkers than any other high fell in England. It must be said, however, that some don't make it, overcome by the long uphill walk from Borrowdale. Although many lesser peaks offer more attractive walking, the highest of all has the glamour. Alas over the years its accident rate has been high. It is not a more dangerous mountain than any other: it is an easy excursion on a fine day. But a proportion of the very high number of walkers is bound to include the unwise, the unprepared, the ill-equipped, the unfit, the late starters, the foolhardy and the plain unlucky. Changeable weather is the enemy. It is often extreme on the heights when the valleys are mild. Snow cover can surprise walkers in early summer. Mist can clamp down suddenly and the summit area is an easy spot on which to lose bearings. The prudent seek a weather forecast before planning.

The highest point is often busy with visitors, but the other pikes are interesting too: Broad Crag (931 m) to the north-east, Ill Crag (927 m) to the east, Lingmell (808 m) to the north-west; and at the northern end, the magnificent mass of Great End (909 m), which holds snow in its northern gullies longer than any other fell, and which in the winter is much used by ice climbers.

All the summit routes are well known and beaten out – so much so that badly eroded sections have been restored by National Trust workers. The shortest route is 6 km from Wasdale Head via Lingmell to the north of the pike, and Lingmell Coll. The most exciting option, however, is to take an early start and go by the longer route of 10 km from Seathwaite in Borrowdale, via Styhead Tarn, then by an exhilaratingly airy ascent along the west side of the mountain on the path known as the Corridor. The route crosses the top of the great gash of the deep gully of Piers Gill. In 1921 a fell walker fell into the gill and broke both his ankles. He lay there for eighteen days before being found. Unusually warm weather and a supply of water nearby kept him alive. The incident is well remembered by mountain rescue teams, on the rare long searches for missing walkers, as a reminder that initial failure does not necessarily mean that all hope for a casualty's survival is lost.

The summit ridge is a bleak mass of bare rock scree and detritus, grim and uninspiring in grey weather, but on a clear day the views are magnificent, taking in nearly all the district's fell tops. The summit is seldom without refreshing (or aggressive!) winds. But Wordsworth in his *Guide to the Lakes* quotes a letter, written by his sister Dorothy, about a magic moment on her ascent with a friend and a guide in 1818:

The rough summit of England's highest land, Scafell Pike

On the summit of the Pike, which we gained after much toil, though without difficulty, there was not a breath of air to stir even the papers containing our refreshment, as they lay spread out upon a rock. The stillness seemed to be not of this world; we paused, and kept silence to listen; and no sound could be heard: the Scawfell Cataracts were voiceless to us; and there was not an insect to hum in the air ... the majesty of the mountains below and close to us, is not to be conceived. We now beheld the whole mass of Great Gavel [Gable] from its base, – the den of Wastdale at our feet – a gulf immeasurable, Grasmere [Grasmoor] and the other mountains of Crummock; Ennerdale and its mountains; and the sea beyond!

Epilogue

Hills and dales; mountains and lakes and tarns; forest and pastures and farms; sea shores, sea cliffs and sea ports; salt marshes and sands; lush woodlands and wild moorland; rivers, streams and waterfalls; ancient stone circles, castles and towers; ruined abbeys and priories; old churches and chapels; villages and country towns; urban towns and city; and a rich blend of native communities and cultures, they are all there in this superb county of fascinating contrasts.

Only a fool could claim that he knows this large area extremely well. It offers a lavish banquet of visual and eventful experiences, and the best that a researcher can do is pick up and taste as many morsels as he can. The guide book author cannot be absolutely satisfied that he has done the county justice, but writes in hope that errors are few and nothing of great importance has been omitted.

Bibliography

Bailey, Bill, *The Vikings, Wasdale Head & Their Church* (W. Bailey, 2002)
Banks, A.G., *H.W. Schneider* (Banks, 1999)
Barker, Juliet (ed.), *Wordsworth: A Life* (Penguin, 2000)
——, *Wordsworth: A Life in Letters* (Penguin, 2002)
Bingham, Roger, *Kendal: a Social History* (Cicerone Press, 1995)
Blake, Brian, *The Solway Firth* (Hale, 1959)
Bott, George, *Keswick: The Story of a Lake District Town* (Cumbria County Library, 1994)
Bowden, Mark (ed.), *Furness Iron* (English Heritage, 2000)
Bragg, Melvyn, *Land of the Lakes* (Secker & Warburg, 1983)
Brooke, Christopher J., *Safe Sanctuaries* (John Donald, 2000)
Broughton, John, and Nigel Harris, *British Railways Past and Present, No.1* (Cumbria Silver Link, 1985)
Brunskill, R.W., *Vernacular Architecture of the Lake Counties* (Faber & Faber, 1974)
Budworth, Captain, *A Fortnight's Ramble to the Lakes in 1792*, reprint (Preston Publishing, 1990)
Byatt, A.S., *Unruly Times* (Vintage, 1997)
Byers, Richard L.M., *The History of Workington* (Byers, 1998)
Clare, T., *Archaeological Sites of the Lake District* (Moorland Publishing, 1981)
Collingwood, W.G., *The Lake Counties* (Frederick Warne, 1932)
Cumbrian Amenity Trust Mining History Soc., *Beneath the Lakeland Fells* (Red Earth Publications, 1992)
—— *The Mine Explorer* (Red Earth Publications, 2002)
Cumbrian Federation of Women's Institutes, *The Cumbrian Village Book* (Countryside Books, 1991)
Davies, Ken, *Lakeland Pleasure Craft* (Regional Publications, 2001)
Davis, R.V., *Geology of Cumbria* (Dalesman Books, 1977)
Falkus, Hugh, *Master of Cape Horn* (Gollancz, 1982)
Fraser, George MacDonald, *The Steel Bonnets* (Barrie & Jenkins, 1971)
Gambles, Robert, *Lakeland Valleys* (Elliot Publications, 1978)
Gilpin, Leslie R., *Grange over Sands: A Resort and Railway* (Cumbria Railways Association, 1998)
Hardy, Eric, *The Naturalist in Lakeland* (David & Charles, 1973)
Hay, Daniel, *Whitehaven: A Short History* (Whitehaven Borough Council, 1968)
Hayter, Alethea, *The Wreck of the Abergavenny* (Macmillan, 2002)
Hebron, Stephen, *William Wordsworth*, British Library Writers' Lives series (OUP, 2000)
Hindle, Paul, *Roads and Tracks of the Lake District* (Chatto & Windus, 1994)
Jones, Kathleen, *A Passionate Sisterhood: The Sisters, Wives and Daughters of the Lake Poets* (Virago, 1998)

Maclean, Fitzroy, *Bonnie Prince Charles* (Guild Publishing, 1988)
Mannex & Co., *History, Topography of Westmorland with Lonsdale, 1851*, reprint (Moon, 1978)
Marshall, J.D., *Old Lakeland* (David & Charles, 1971)
Marshall, J.D. and Davies-Shiel, Michael, *Industrial Archaeology of the Lake Counties* (Moon, 1977)
Martineau, Harriet, *A Description of the English Lakes, 1858*, reprint (E.P. Publishing, 1974)
Mee, Arthur, *The Lake Counties* (Hodder & Stoughton, 1943)
Mitchell, W.R., *Around Morecambe Bay* (Dalesman Books, 1966)
Moorman, Mary, *William Wordsworth: The Early Years* (OUP, 1968)
——, *William Wordsworth: The Later Years* (OUP, 1968)
Nicholson, Norman, *Cumberland and Westmorland* (Hale, 1949)
——, *The Lakers* (Hale, 1955)
——, *Greater Lakeland* (Hale, 1996)
——, *Portrait of the Lakes* (Hale, 1972)
Norman, K.J., *The Furness Railway* (Silver Link, 1994)
Parker, John, *Cumbria* (John Bartholomew & Son, 1977)
Pearsall, W.H., and Pennington, W., *The Lake District* (Collins New Naturalist, 1973)
Perry, Seamus (ed.), *Coleridge's Notebooks* (OUP, 2002)
Pevsner, Nikolaus, *Cumberland and Westmorland* (Penguin, 1973)
——, *North Lancashire* (Penguin, 1969)
Postlethwaite, John, *Mines and Mining in the English Lake District*, 1913, reprint (Moon, 1975)
Rawnsley, H.D., *Reminiscences of Wordsworth among the Peasantry of Westmoreland*, reprint (Dillons University Bookshop, 1903)
Robinson, Peter, *Cumbria's Lost Railways* (Senlake, 2002)
Rollinson, William (ed.), *The Lake District Landscape Heritage* (David & Charles, 1989)
——, *A History of Cumberland and Westmorland* (Phillimore, 1978)
——, *A History of Man in the Lake District* (Dent & Sons, 1975)
——, *Life and Traditions in the Lake District* (Dent & Sons, 1974)
Selincourt, Ernest de (ed.), *Wordsworth: The Prelude* (OUP, 1970)
Shelbourn, Colin, *Lakeland Towns and Villages* (Hunter Davies, 1988)
Tetley, Laurence, *The Lake District Angler's Guide* (Cicerone Press, 1999)
Trescatheric, Bryn, *Barrow 2000: A Millennium Souvenir* (Trinity Press, 1999)
——, *The Last Place God Made* (Trescatheric, 1998)
Tyler, Ian, *Cumbrian Mining* (Blue Rock Publications, 2001)
——, *Seathwaite Wad* (Blue Rock Publications, 1995)
Welsh, Frank, *The Companion Guide to the Lake District* (Collins, 1989)
Westall, Oliver M., *Windermere in the Nineteenth Century* (University of Lancaster, 1976)
White, Dick, *The Windermere Ferry* (Helm Press, 2002)
Whyte, Ian and Kathleen, *On the Trail of the Jacobites* (Routledge, 1990)
Woof, Pamela (ed.), *Grasmere Journals by Dorothy Wordsworth* (Oxford, 1993)
Wordsworth, William, *Guide to the Lakes* (1835)
——, *The Poems (2 vols)* ed. John O. Hayden
——, *The Prose Works (3 vols)* ed. W.J.B. Owen & Jane Worthington Smyser, 1974
Yee, Chiang, *The Silent Traveller* (Country Life, 1942)

Index